ADR PRINCIPLES AND PRACTICE

AUSTRALIA
LBC Information Services Sydney
Sydney

CANADA and USA
Carswell
Toronto—Ontario

NEW ZEALAND
Brookers
Auckland

SINGAPORE and MALAYSIA
Sweet & Maxwell Asia
Singapore and Kuala Lumpur

ADR PRINCIPLES AND PRACTICE

SECOND EDITION

HENRY J. BROWN
Solicitor of the Supreme Court of England and Wales
Consultant, Penningtons

ARTHUR L. MARRIOTT Q.C.
Solicitor of the Supreme Court of England and Wales
Solicitor of the Supreme Court of Hong Kong
Partner, Debevoise & Plimpton

 Sweet & Maxwell
A THOMSON COMPANY

First published in 1999 by
Sweet & Maxwell Limited of
100 Avenue Road London NW3 3PF.
http://www/smlawpub.co.uk
Typeset by Tradespools Ltd
Printed in England by MPG Books Ltd, Bodmin, Cornwall
Reprinted in 2002

A CIP catalogue record for this book is available from the British Library.

ISBN 0421 579 609

No natural forests were destroyed to make this product, only farmed timber
was used and re-planted.

ISBN 0-421-57960-9

9 780421 579606

©
H J. Brown & A. L. Marriott
1999

FOREWORD TO THE SECOND EDITION

Six years have passed since the first edition of this book was published. That is not, by historical or legal standards, a long period. But the last six years have brought changes which are extraordinary both in their number and their scope: enactment of a new and innovative Arbitration Act; radical reform of the procedure of the civil courts; introduction of new bases for the funding of civil litigation; first steps towards establishment of a community legal service; governmental recognition that ADR offers an economical and socially desirable way of resolving some civil disputes and, in some cases, responding to crime; evidence of increased resort to ADR, with (very often) startlingly successful results.

These and other changes are reviewed in this second edition, to which the authors again bring their deep comparative knowledge of the subject, their gift for clear and comprehensive exposition, their probing critical judgment and their great practical expertise.

This book contains an invaluable description of where we now stand in the hugely important field of ADR. But the authors have given much informed thought to the opportunities, challenges and pitfalls which lie ahead. The greater the readership and influence of the book, the better our chances of exploiting the opportunities, rising to the challenges and avoiding at least the worst of the pitfalls. The authors are entitled to our gratitude, and to our close attention.

Lord Bingham of Cornhill
Lord Chief Justice of England and Wales

PREFACE

The debate to which we referred in the first edition as to how we should resolve conflicts and disputes in an increasingly pluralist and complex society, has proceeded apace in the last six years. It has been prompted by a growing realisation that the civil justice system in England and Wales is in a state of crisis. The overwhelming majority of citizens and small businesses are cut off from access to justice. Those concerned with the consequences of marriage breakdown have realised that existing processes for dealing with this are no longer appropriate. They are looking for alternatives, including in particular mediation.

In the first edition we argued strongly that ADR has a crucial role to play in providing access to justice and in facilitating the resolution of civil and commercial disputes, family issues and community disputes. The case for that seems stronger then ever. There are also encouraging signs that ADR has a significant role to play in dealing with environmental and social issues, and that it can have a beneficial effect in the easing of tensions between the victims and perpetrators of crime. Its longstanding role in relation to employment disputes has been reviewed and developed in recent years.

The spirit of reform is in the air. Certain pragmatic steps have been taken in recent years to change the procedures by which we resolve disputes in the courts and in the parallel and vitally important system of arbitration. A major change has come about as a consequence of Lord Woolf's reforms. Now, since April 26, 1999 a common procedure exists in the High Court and the County Courts with cases divided into three tracks each with its own procedural and cost characteristics. The reforms embrace fully the doctrine of case management now adopted in many common law jurisdictions as the core measure of reform. Lord Woolf has encouraged the use of ADR as part of his reforms. Judges now have the power to enquire what steps the parties have taken or intend to take towards negotiating a settlement; and judges can make orders of various kinds, including adjournment, to enable negotiations to take place whether direct or involving a third party. Case management, evaluation and mediation are also at the root of family law reform, designed to alleviate one of the most important social issues in recent decades, as more and more marriages end in divorce and families have to adapt to changed circumstances.

The commercial community should benefit from the new Arbitration Act of 1996, which, after a slow and tortuous process, ultimately reached the statute book in an acceptable and welcome form. Arbitration remains very significant and provides a parallel system of justice for the resolution of civil and commercial disputes, particularly in certain industries of great economic importance, such as commercial real estate and construction. The 1996 Act embraces the same objectives as Woolf, but with a greater emphasis, as befits the arbitral process, upon party autonomy. There is now no reason why the old complaints about arbitration, namely that it was a poor relation of litigation and more expensive, need be heard. Arbitrators have the power and the obligation to conduct cases expeditiously, economically and fairly. By so doing they can provide a vital service to the commercial community.

Probably the most significant reform of all is the firm attempt by the Government to change the funding and provision of legal services to the greater part of the population. Changing the way in which civil litigation was funded began in the mid-1990s when the then Government indicated that the public purse was not bottomless. It was said that change was necessary because the lawyers failed to put their house in order. It is clear that the impetus for serious procedural reform has come principally from Government and from the senior judiciary rather than from practitioners.

The steps taken by the Conservative Government have been accelerated by its successor. The objectives have been broadened in that the Lord Chancellor is a committed advocate of a Community Legal Service. The Government has also indicated that legal aid in its present form will be abolished and replaced by a Community Legal Fund with greater control over the allocation of resources between types of litigation and the encouragement of a wider range of funding by conditional fees and insurance. The Government also wishes to encourage alternatives to litigation such as mediation and the use of Ombudsmen. These changes are in their very early stages, but it is clear that if implemented fully, they will change significantly the ways in which the legal profession and the provision of dispute resolution services in this country are organised. It is more doubtful whether the reforms will improve access to justice in that a large part of the community will continue to be barred from the courts.

The reforms in court procedures have provoked an increasing interest in the use of ADR, regarded hitherto by English lawyers with very considerable scepticism and initially seen as an American device to cope with the severe and supposedly unique problems of the US litigation system. But there is now, we believe, an awareness that the problems which face our civil justice system are not unique to this country; and, that there is much we can learn from what happens elsewhere, particularly in common law countries with which we share a legal tradition and heritage. Lord Woolf was clearly influenced in deciding to adopt case management as the measure at the heart of his reforms, by what he saw and learnt about procedural reform in the United States, Canada and Australia. In those countries, as we discuss in Chapter 5, case management is practised in conjunction with mandatory ADR systems, which are regarded as essential to an effective system of civil justice.

Out experience in this country with civil court attached ADR is very limited. For all practical purposes we have had only two pilot schemes of significance. The first, and by far the more important, was at the Central

London County Court and the second is in the Court of Appeal. One of the authors has been intimately involved with both schemes. It is too early to say what effect the pilot scheme in the Court of Appeal is having upon the work of that Court, but important conclusions can be and have been drawn from the scheme at the Central London County Court. We discuss this in Chapter 3 and draw particularly upon the outstanding work of Professor Hazel Genn, whose report published in July 1998 by the Lord Chancellor's Department, is in our view the single most significant contribution to the understanding of ADR and the courts, published in this country.

Various organisations are now considering with some degree of urgency how ADR practitioners can work, both integrated with the courts and separately in the private sector. Thus, the Law Society for example, has developed new rules of conduct for solicitor mediators; and, organisations such as the Centre for Dispute Resolution (CEDR) and the ADR Group have done sterling work in the education and training of those who would mediate in civil and commercial disputes. Parallel developments have taken place in the family field, with no less than seven family mediation bodies being approved for training and practice by the United Kingdom College of Family Mediators. These include for example the Family Mediators Association, National Family Mediation, the Solicitors Family Law Association and Family Mediation Scotland. The debate has now begun in earnest as to the regulation, training and accreditation of mediators, particularly important if there is going to be a court-attached system whether voluntary or mandatory.

The Lord Chancellor's Department has been roundly criticised in the past for being reluctant to consider and effectively support innovative methods of dispute resolution within the court system. Any such criticism no longer has validity. The LCD has encouraged those who wished to introduce pilot schemes and has supported the Central London scheme in particularly helpful ways by making court officials available as well as the facilities of the court, and by financing the work of Professor Genn and publishing her report. The LCD also accepted that the pilot scheme at Central London should become a permanent feature of the work at that court.

It was the far sighted initiative of His Hon. Judge Sir Frank White and His Hon. Judge Neil Butter Q.C. which led to the introduction of the pilot scheme at Central London County Court. There is little doubt that the introduction of ADR in the Central London pilot schemes has aroused the interest of many members of the judiciary. The Judicial Studies Board has made sure that circuit judges have been made aware of the experience at Central London and has informed the judiciary generally about the uses of ADR. The encouragement of ADR by the Commercial Court and by the Technology and Construction Court has also been important in making judges and practitioners aware of the role of ADR in promoting settlements.

Both statistical and anecdotal evidence indicate that private sector ADR is on the increase both in domestic United Kingdom disputes and in international disputes where the venue of the mediation is London. Both authors have been increasingly involved in the mediation of civil and commercial disputes, ranging from individuals, professional partnerships and small businesses to substantial corporations, domestic and international. It is now clear that there are a number of practitioners who are frequently involved in ADR in commercial matters.

Similarly, the use of mediation for family issues is slowly and steadily increasing, and there are now estimated to be well over 1,500 family mediators in the United Kingdom. There were some expectations that the ill-fated Family Law Act and the Legal Aid Board's requirements for mediation would dramatically increase the demand for family mediation. To some extent, an increase has occurred, but overall the take-up of mediation has been much less than expected. Arguably, any greater expectations were not realistic. Our perspective on this is that family mediation has been growing gradually over the last two decades, and will continue to do so. The proposed legislation and the LAB's stipulations have slightly increased awareness and take-up, but the growth of mediation will continue with or without these factors. The Lord Chancellor is said to be committed to incorporating mediation into any reforms of family law, and clearly that would provide a further impetus.

This second edition appears as the United Kingdom has embarked on radical change in the civil justice system. Many other countries are facing similar issues. We seek to contribute to reform by drawing attention to the principles and practice of ADR with much the same emphasis as we did in the first edition. The procedural changes in the courts have led us to re-write substantially the previous Chapter 3 on litigation and to introduce a new Chapter 5 on court attached ADR in various jurisdictions. We have also substantially re-written Chapter 4 to reflect the changes in arbitration law and in arbitration practice made possible by the Arbitration Act 1996.

We have extensively amplified the chapters dealing with all aspects of mediation, including civil and commercial, community, environmental and social issues and criminal reparation, which now has a separate chapter. We have widened the chapter dealing with family issues to examine all the different ways in which these can be addressed, including counselling, mediation, the legal process and evaluation. We have updated the provisions relating to other ADR processes. And we have looked at the embryonic but increasing relevance of information technology and cyberspace communications for dispute resolution.

We have reviewed evaluative processes in a new Chapter 16. It seems to us that ADR processes can be divided into those that are purely facilitative and those in which some attempt at evaluation is made, to assist the parties in reaching their own decisions in an informed way.

There have been many developments and discussions concerning the administration, regulation and funding of mediation and other ADR processes. We have mentioned these and related aspects. We have developed a section dealing specifically with drafting and containing a schedule of relevant precedents and documents.

We refer where appropriate to certain developments in the law as it affects mediation such as good faith in negotiation and privacy and confidentiality of the mediation process. There has been a continuing affirmation by the courts of certain basic principles, that the settlement of disputes is to be encouraged as a matter of public policy; that the mechanisms for settlement agreed upon by the parties are to be recognised and enforced; and, that the procedures will be conducted with the privacy and confidentiality necessary to ensure their efficacy. However, Lord Ackner's comments in *Walford v. Miles* on good faith being repugnant to the conduct of adversarial negotiation, continue to cast a long shadow.

As we made clear in the first edition, it is the principal purpose of ADR to encourage parties to reach fair and timely resolution and there is a range of methods by which this can be achieved. We have discussed them in the light of our experience in the last six years and we have diluted some of the distinctions which we sought to make in the first edition between facilitative and evaluative mediation. Such distinctions are increasingly sterile and if too rigidly adhered to, can inhibit the resolution process. But it remains the case that mediators must exercise care in establishing the points of difference and in expressing any views of their own. They must be flexible and constructive in trying to find ways of bringing the parties together. Where they have agreed to do so, they must respect the confidentially of communications to them in order to encourage parties to be open and constructive in finding solutions to their disputes. Most importantly, they must maintain ethical propriety and guard against abuse of the process. We have, as in the first edition, drawn attention to differences of approach which may be required in different kinds of disputes.

Our thanks are due again to Lord Bingham of Cornhill, both for the encouragement which he has given to the use of ADR to resolve disputes and for the admirably succinct and persuasive Foreword to this edition. Our thanks are due also to other members of the judiciary who have helped us to achieve a better understanding of the problems of court attached ADR in the English system. We thank in particular Mr Justice Laddie, His Hon. Judge Ford and His Hon. Judge John Toulmin CMG Q.C. We were greatly assisted in our comparative survey of court attached ADR in Chapter 5 by Master Tomas Kennedy Grant of the High Court of New Zealand and by Donna Stienstra of the Federal Judicial Centre in the United States, a particular source of great experience and wisdom. We are indebted to Doug Jones and his colleagues at Clayton Utz in Australia and to Ed Chaisson Q.C. of Lardner Downs in Vancouver for their help in discussing court attached ADR in Australia and Canada.

We are grateful also to many others who have helped us in various ways: to Professor Hazel Genn for allowing us to draw heavily upon her excellent report on the Central London County Court scheme; to Alan Sharland of Hillingdon Mediation Service for his contributions to Chapter 12 on the mediation of community and neighbour disputes; to Martin Edwards of Mace & Jones for helping with information about developments in employment mediation; to Inspector Judith Johnson of Thames Valley Police for information about restorative justice schemes; to Toby Starr, Layla Bunni, Michael Ostrove and Wolfgang Hohensee of the London and Paris offices of Debevoise & Plimpton for their work; and to Roger Tabakin, Emma Harte and Peter Webster for their help with research. We are grateful to Caroline Morris of the Court of Appeal for her help with our description of the work of that court and her assistance with research.

Thanks are also due to all the organisations that have provided information for this edition and precedents for inclusion in the appendix, particularly the

Law Society, the Centre for Dispute Resolution (CEDR), the City Disputes Panel, which has pioneered evaluative processes for disputes in the financial services sector, the UK College of Family Mediators, Mediation UK, the Solicitors Family Law Association and the Family Mediators Association. To Elsa Brown and Jan Hammond special thanks are due for their painstaking work on the manuscripts and preparation of the work generally and their great patience. Thanks for patience and support must also go to our publishers, Sweet & Maxwell. The errors are ours alone. The law is as stated at June 30, 1999.

Henry Brown
Arthur Marriott
July 1999

CONTENTS

Contents

CHAPTER 20: JURISDICTION, FORUM AND LAW

CHAPTER 21: ETHICS AND VALUES, FAIRNESS AND POWER BALANCE

Contents

CHAPTER 22: CONFIDENTIALITY AND PRIVILEGE

CHAPTER 23: ENFORCEMENT OF ADR OUTCOMES

CHAPTER 24: REGULATION, FUNDING AND INSURANCE

Contents

TABLE OF CASES

All references are to paragraph numbers

TABLE OF STATUTES

United Kingdom

All references are to paragraph numbers

OTHER JURISDICTIONS

Australia (New South Wales)

Belgium

Germany

Hong Kong

Ireland

Netherlands

New Zealand

South Africa

TREATIES AND CONVENTIONS

ARBITRATION AND PRACTICE RULES

RULES OF COURT

CODES OF PROCEDURE

CHAPTER 1

CONFLICT AND DISPUTE

1. THE NATURE OF CONFLICT

What is conflict?

The concept that many people have of conflict is of something negative and destructive. It is defined as "a state of opposition or hostilities", "a fight or struggle" or "the clashing of opposed principles".[1] Uncontained conflict may manifest itself in verbal and behavioural disagreements and ultimately in some cases in violence; and in the case of international conflict, war. Because of the potential violence in uncontained conflict, it is often condemned. Conflict is, however, an integral part of human behaviour, and there could be no movement or change without it.[2]   **1–001**

Decision-making necessarily contains an element of conflict; exchanges of ideas involve conflict; the democratic process is built on the basis of the normalcy of a conflict of ideas and interests.   **1–002**

John Crawley[3] defines conflict as "a manifestation of differences working against one another" which have "ingredients" (the differences that inherently exist between the people in conflict such as cultural and value differences, interests, beliefs and patterns of behaviour), "combinations and conditions" (their contact with one another and the structures in which they operate) and "the spark" (what happens when their differences clash). These can either lead to a smouldering fuse with an explosion, or if constructively managed, a cooling of the heat, leading to a readjustment and a settling.   **1–003**

Edward de Bono[4] does not limit himself to the concept merely of conflict, which he defines as the existence of a clash of interests, values, actions or directions. He invents some new words to help identify and work with the   **1–004**

---

[1] Concise Oxford Dictionary.

[2] Andrew Floyer Acland in *A Sudden Outbreak of Common Sense: Managing Conflict through Mediation* (1990), p. 69, suggests that "the purpose of conflict is related to change...all conflict is about the attempt to achieve or resist change". In *The Magic of Conflict* (1987), Thomas F. Crum says that conflict is "the interference patterns of energies caused by differences, that provide the motivation and opportunity for change". Conflict, he says, is not a contest, and resolving conflict is rarely about who is right, but about the acknowledgment and appreciation of differences.

[3] In *Constructive Conflict Management: Managing to Make a Difference* (1992, 1995) at pp. 10 and 11.

[4] The originator of the concept of "lateral thinking", in *Conflicts: A Better Way to Resolve Them* (1985).

process of conflict resolution, namely "confliction", which is what he calls "the process of setting up, promoting, encouraging or designing conflict" and "de-confliction", which is the opposite, namely the effort required to evaporate or demolish a conflict. He believes that our methods for resolving both conflicts and disputes are crude, primitive, inadequate and destructive, and in his work he seeks better ways to approach the resolution of conflicts.

1–005 Various management writers point out that conflict is a fact of life in organisations, though destructive handling of it does not need to be.[5] Other writers make similar points on a more general basis.[6]

1–006 Clearly, conflict has a healthy and positive function. It is when it becomes dysfunctional that problems arise. When it becomes irreconcilable and the natural mechanisms for managing and resolving it, for example by discussion and negotiation, are inadequate or go awry, then the conflict may become potentially damaging and other processes may be needed.

2. THE NATURE OF DISPUTES

What is a dispute?

1–007 A dispute may be viewed as a class or kind of conflict which manifests itself in distinct, justiciable issues. It involves disagreement over issues capable of resolution by negotiation, mediation or third party adjudication. The differences inherent in a dispute can usually be examined objectively, and a third party can take a view on the issues to assess the correctness of one side or the other.

1–008 D. Foskett Q.C. in *The Law and Practice of Compromise* says that "an 'actual' dispute will not exist until a claim is asserted by one party which is 'disputed' by the other,[7] and that where no such dispute about an issue can be discerned, no subsequent agreement between the parties will be found to have compromised that issue."[8] He points out, however, that "potential" issues between parties, even if not yet having the status of an "actual" dispute, can be compromised in appropriate circumstances.[9]

1–009 The question as to whether or not a "dispute" exists can be highly relevant, for example where an arbitration or other dispute resolution provision in a contract provides that "disputes" are to be referred to arbitration or any other stipulated process. If no dispute exists, then a party wishing to enforce any aspect of the contract may do so through the courts; but if a dispute does exist then the specified process must be followed. Section 9 of the Arbitration Act 1996 provides that if a party to an

---

[5] *e.g.* Lax and Sebenius in *The Manager as Negotiator* (1986) and Kolb & Bartunek, *Hidden Conflict in Organisations* (1992) at pp. 1 *et seq.* And Whetten, Cameron & Woods in their *Effective Conflict Management* (1996) say that "conflict is the life-blood of vibrant, progressive, stimulating organisations. It sparks creativity, stimulates innovation and encourages personal improvement."

[6] Susan Stewart says that "the evidence of history suggests that conflict is more characteristic of human behaviour than is harmony." *Conflict Resolution: A Foundation Guide* (1998) at p. 9.

[7] p. 5 (4th ed., Sweet & Maxwell, 1996).

[8] *ibid.*, p. 5.

[9] *ibid.*, p. 9. See also *Kitchen Design & Advice Ltd v. Lea Valley Water Co.* [1989] 2 Lloyd's Rep. 221 and *Tudor Grange Holdings Ltd v. Citibank* [1992] Ch. 53.

arbitration agreement commences legal proceedings through the court against any other party to that agreement in respect of any matter agreed to be referred to arbitration, the latter may apply to the court for a stay of the court proceedings. In that event, the court is required to stay the proceedings unless satisfied that the arbitration agreement is null and void, inoperative or incapable of being performed.

The courts have on a number of occasions considered the meaning and implications of the reference to a "dispute" in relation to this provision of the Arbitration Act. In *Ellerine Brothers (Pty) Limited and Another v. Klinger,*[10] there was a provision for disputes to be referred to arbitration. The defendant failed to account as required under the agreement, but did not assert that a dispute existed until after a writ had been issued seeking an accounting and payment. The Court of Appeal held that "silence does not mean consent" and that:

    1–010

> "the fact that the plaintiffs make certain claims which, if disputed, would be referable to arbitration and the fact that the defendant then does nothing—he does not admit the claim, he merely continues a policy of masterly inactivity—does not mean that there is no dispute. There is a dispute until the defendant admits that a sum is due and payable."[11]

This question was addressed in the case of *Hayter v. Nelson*[12] where the court expressed the view that the ordinary meaning of the words "disputes" or "differences" should be given to those words in arbitration clauses. The fact that a dispute could be easily and immediately resolved by demonstrating beyond doubt that one was right and the other wrong did not mean that a dispute did not validly exist. That dispute should be referred to the private tribunal that the parties had bargained for in their contract. The reference in the Act to disputes should be taken to mean that "there is not in fact anything disputable", that is, no "real dispute".[13]

    1–011

The Court of Appeal expressed the view in *Mayer Newman & Co. Ltd v. Al Ferro Commodities Corp. SA*[14] that an arbitral "difference" to permit the appointment of an arbitrator should involve a "genuinely disputable issue", and not merely the assertion of the existence of a claim or the bare denial of liability.

    1–012

Kinds of disputes

There are many variations in relation to disputes: the range of subject matters is very wide; within any category, a multitude of issues can arise; various factors can influence parties who disagree; and there are some conflicts which are not readily amenable to dispute resolution processes.

    1–013

A proper understanding of the dispute and its implications will assist a

    1–014

---

[10] [1982] W.L.R. 1375.

[11] *per* Templeman L.J., at 1383.

[12] *The Times*, March 29, 1990; [1990] 2 Lloyd's Rep. 265.

[13] *per* Saville J., *ibid.*, at 270. Saville J.'s view was accepted by the Departmental Advisory Committee on Arbitration Law whose work led to the Arbitration Act 1996. The provisions for a stay of proceedings are found in section 9: the distinction between domestic and non-domestic cases has now been abolished.

[14] *The Times* April 9, 1990.

practitioner in a number of ways. First, it will enable the practitioner to select, and if necessary to design, a process most suitable for the particular issues. Secondly, the practitioner will have a better insight into the parties' motivations, aspirations, concerns and interests. Thirdly, parties will invariably have greater confidence in a practitioner who clearly understands their dispute, and the underlying issues, which in turn is bound to help the practitioner to work more effectively.

1–015 Disputes are not readily capable of neat categorisation. Attempts at classification illustrate the range and variety of disputes and the inadequacy of taxonomy. Nevertheless, some analysis and broad classification may provide a better understanding of what a dispute may involve, and where it fits in the range of disputes, conflicts and possible resolution processes.

Subject-matter

1–016 The following is a basic classification of some of the possible subject-matters of disputes (although many disputes are complex and boundaries may overlap and blur). Different rules and cultures generally apply to different fields within which disputes occur; and different knowledge bases may be needed to work within these different areas.

- International—including matters of public law.

- Constitutional, administrative and fiscal—including issues relating to citizenship and status rights; local authorities, governmental and quasi-governmental bodies; planning permission; taxation; and social security.

- Organisational—including issues arising within organisations involving management, structures and procedures, and intra-organisational disputes.

- Employment—including pay claims and industrial disputes.

- Corporate—including disputes between shareholders, and issues arising on liquidation and receivership.

- Commercial—this is very wide and includes contractual disputes, issues arising in commercial relationships such as partnerships, joint ventures and others. Issues can arise in different fields of commercial activity, such as banking, shipping, commodities, intellectual property, the construction industry and many others.

- Consumer disputes—between supplier and consumer.

- Property disputes—including those between landlord and tenant, or joint tenants, rent reviews, boundary disputes and the like.

- Issues arising in tort—including negligence and failure of duties, and including also insurance claims relating to these.

- Issues arising on separation and divorce—including those relating to children, property and all financial matters.

- Other family issues—including Inheritance Act claims, family businesses and disputes within families.

- Trust issues—including issues between trustees and beneficiaries.

- Disputes giving rise to consequences in criminal law.

- Neighbourhood, community, gender, race and ethnic issues.

- Interpersonal disputes arising between individuals.

Nature of issues

Disputes may relate to money and be quantifiable, involving amounts ranging **1–017** from a few pounds to vast sums. Or they may relate to rights, status, lifestyle, reputation or indeed any other aspect of commercial or personal behaviour. They may relate to a single issue, or may be complex and involve various kinds of issues including:

- Issues of fact, which may arise from the credibility of the parties themselves, or from data supplied by third parties, including interpretations placed on such data.

- Issues of law, which will generally arise from opinions given by respective legal representatives.

- Technical differences, including different opinions from professional and technical experts on each side.

- Differences of understanding arising, for example, from ambiguous use of words or from differing assumptions.

- Differences of perception of fairness, concepts of justice and morality, culture, values and attitudes.

While in any dispute one party may be right and the other wrong, it is also **1–018** possible for there to be some element of right on each side. For example, one party could be right on some issues and the other party on other issues; or both a claim and counterclaim may be meritorious. There could be an apportionment of responsibility between the parties; or one party may be morally right and another legally right; or genuine differences of perception or concepts may allow each to be right from different vantage points.

Submerged issues

There are often wider ramifications to a dispute than may immediately be **1–019** apparent on presentation.

There is sometimes an "iceberg" factor in disputes, in which only part is **1–020** initially apparent, but where much lurks below the surface. This may particularly be the case with regard to disagreements involving parties who have or had some form of relationship with one another, which may have degenerated over a period of time. So, for example, in a partnership dispute the issue that has surfaced may not necessarily be the whole or the real problem, which may be more complex, involving underlying differences. There may be hidden agendas in other business or personal relationships, of which the parties themselves may not necessarily be fully conscious. This is by no means limited to personal disputes. Hidden agendas can exist in all kinds of disagreements.

1–021   There may be other factors affecting the attitudes that a party to a dispute may have, and the manner of resolution, including for example:

- Financial and economic implications: these will obviously affect the attitudes of the parties, including the relationship of the amount in dispute to the overall financial position of each party and the effect which the outcome of the dispute will have on the party.

- Issues of principle may be contested even if the financial implications are slight, although sometimes matters which appear superficially to be questions of principle may not prove to be so, or it may not be possible to separate the principle from the actual dispute.

- Perceptions of fairness and justice as well as parties' understandings and prejudices may well differ and will affect their approaches to the issues.

- Cultural differences between parties may well affect the way in which each views and approaches the dispute.

- Claims and defences may be strategically made, for example, to persuade someone to enter into negotiations or to delay payment of a debt which is properly payable.

- Where an issue affects the liberty or status of an individual, or where a binding precedent needs to be established, it may be essential to obtain a ruling from a court. Similarly, in some cases it may be vital to obtain the protection of a court order or injunction, initially in any event.

- Sometimes the subject of a dispute may have a symbolic value, for example indicating the limits of a party's tolerance or defining a power relationship.

- Publicity may be a relevant factor, either because of a party's vulnerability to adverse attention, or because of a positive wish to attract media coverage.

- Emotional factors may affect attitudes, for example where a party is motivated by anger, distress, indignation, humiliation or other strong feelings, or where action is taken to vindicate a personal position, or to punish actual or perceived grievances. If it were possible to construct a rational/emotional continuum, the further a party genuinely was towards the "rational" end, the more likely that objective standards might apply to its resolution. The further a party was towards the "emotional" end, the more difficult it might be for objective standards to prevail.[15]

---

[15]This is an important topic that will be addressed in this book. It is not an argument for rational responses rather than emotional, nor vice versa. It is merely a recognition of the power of

- Personality factors will influence a party's approach to contention, for example some people may find the prospect of litigation stressful and oppressive, whereas others may face it with equanimity, or may indeed have to satisfy a personal "need to win".

- Practical considerations are of course relevant, including the cost factor, the proportion this bears to the issue in dispute, each party's ability and willingness to meet legal costs, whether or not legal aid is available, what delay and other time constraints are applicable, and the level of risk, always inherent in litigation, which each party is willing to run.

It is thus clear that there can be disputes about different kinds of subject-matters, and the kinds of issues that may arise can be very different from one case to another. More significantly, the presenting issue is by no means necessarily the whole story. Submerged issues may have a profound effect on the way that each party views the dispute. Yet by their nature, submerged issues will not necessarily be known to those charged with resolving the dispute (and indeed, not always to the disputants themselves). **1–022**

3. Behavioural Conflict Or Justiciable Dispute

There are some conceptual differences between "conflict" and "dispute" although these are sometimes blurred.[16] **1–023**

Conflict management or resolution is usually approached through processes providing an understanding of the conflict and seeking to deal with it by consensual means. In personal or family terms this may, for example, involve counselling or therapy; in organisational terms, management consultancy or task forces; in international terms, diplomacy and rapprochement. Some conflicts can be regulated by procedures such as litigation, arbitration or mediation; but conflicts are not necessarily amenable to resolution by dispute resolution processes. **1–024**

In the organisational rather than judicial context, Calvin Morrill[17] describes the disputing process as distinguishing between "grievance expressions" which arise when people define and respond to deviance by their fellows. "Conflicts" arise when principals express grievances privately or publicly "Disputes" occur when third parties become involved as supporters or settlement agents and the conflict becomes public. **1–025**

So if a person frequently plays his music loudly and his neighbour gets **1–026**

---

underlying emotional issues, even where a party might deny the existence of any emotional aspect, and might indeed be unaware of its existence and power.

[16] The *Glossary of Terms* issued by Mediation U.K. says that: "A conflict exists, in the mind of an individual, when he/she perceives a situation of incompatibility among objectives. . ." which may be internal, interpersonal or social; whereas a dispute is "a conflict of which both parties are conscious and which is the subject of altercation between them." In a family context—but the principle may be extended to other fields—Marian Roberts describes disputes as "specific, identifiable issues which divide parties", distinguishable from the "wider conflict" associated with family breakdown: see the second edition of her book, *Mediation in Family Disputes* (1997) at p. 77.

[17] In Kolb & Bartunek, *op. cit.*, at p. 94.

upset and recriminates, leading to indignation and defiance, that incompatibility of interests will constitute a behavioural conflict, and negotiation or a form of third party intervention may be necessary to find a way to resolve it. To the extent that there is a difference of opinion as to a legal right either to play the music, or to be protected from noise nuisance, then that will be a justiciable dispute, and legal rights can be established and enforced. The problem may be approached at either level, or indeed both.

1–027   John Haynes distinguishes succinctly between conflicts between couples over issues, normally about resources, access to resources or values, and conflicts of behaviour, which relate to the dynamics of a couple's relationship. He says that "conflict over issues is resolvable in mediation; conflict over behaviour is resolvable in therapy."[18]

1–028   In an article on the roles of those who intervene in the fields of conflict and dispute resolution, Daniel P. Joyce suggests that "dispute settlement refers to an altering of perceptions that often results in parties settling for less, whereas conflict resolution seeks to address underlying causes of conflict."[19]

1–029   The distinction between behavioural conflict and justiciable dispute, although this may not always be clear, is relevant to Alternative Dispute Resolution ("ADR"). Different approaches may have to be adopted towards each; and practitioners need to be aware of the limitations of dispute resolution procedures when faced with those kinds of conflicts that are not readily justiciable.

4. DEALING WITH CONFLICTS AND DISPUTES

1–030   There are a number of different approaches to conflict management and resolution. A group called "The Centre for the Analysis of Conflict" (CAC) has for example, undertaken extensive academic research and practical intervention into conflict. This group has observed common patterns within and between interpersonal, community and inter-state conflict. It developed an analytical, problem-solving approach to conflict, identifying the most effective stage for dealing with conflict (early in its development, rather than after the commencement of hostilities) and addressing criticism about its approach. There are views that neutral intervention might be a force against change, or that it might just constitute appeasement of aggression. The group has continued its work on collaborative, analytical problem-solving as an alternative to traditional mediation.[20]

1–031   A comparative study of conflict management approaches divides these into five categories. These are "forcing" (the facilitator asserts his or her authority); "avoiding" (the facilitator side-steps dealing with the issues);

---

[18] John M. Haynes and Gretchen L. Haynes, *Mediating Divorce* (1989) at p. 2.

[19] "The Roles of the Intervenor: A Client-Centred Approach" in (1995) M.Q. 12(4), in turn crediting J.W. Burton "Conflict Resolution as a Political System", Working Paper No. 1–33. Fairfax, Va.: Institute for Conflict Analysis and Resolution, George Mason University, 1988.

[20] The work and practices of the CAC are outlined in the *Handbook of conflict resolution: the analytical problem-solving approach* by Christopher Mitchell and Michael Banks (1996), which provides a theoretical base and exercises for practical skills' development.

"compromising" (the facilitator seeks an expedient solution irrespective of effectiveness); "accommodating" (the facilitator treats harmonious relations as top priority); and "collaborating" (joint problem-solving). The collaborative approach, while not appropriate for all situations, is described as the one that, when used appropriately, has the most beneficial effect on the parties involved.[21]

Where conflicts have assumed the quality of disputes, with specific issues   **1–032** that need to be addressed, a number of further approaches can be taken. Some disputes may have to be resolved by adjudication. In such event, the main questions may be whether litigation, arbitration or some other form of adjudication is the appropriate procedure and whether the issues for adjudication can be clarified or narrowed in any useful way. Other disputes may be able to be resolved by negotiation, without any need for third party assistance. For others, the assistance and dynamic of an impartial third party may well facilitate and expedite resolution. That third party can introduce carefully devised procedures for examining and, where appropriate, perhaps helping with the evaluation of the issues, for exploring interests, concerns and options, for dealing effectively with emotional and hidden factors, and for generally assisting the parties towards resolution of the issues.

The range of processes for dealing with disputes is set out in Chapter 2   **1–033** and is developed throughout this work. Mediation is the main alternative dispute resolution process, but other ways of dealing with disputes may be used. It is essential that procedures be selected or designed appropriate to the requirements of the individual dispute. These may range from relatively informal processes suitable for personal disputes to very sophisticated professionally designed procedures that can be used for major, complex and often highly technical issues.

One final point needs to be considered in relation to conflict and dispute   **1–034** resolution. This is the question as to whether it is sufficient to help parties to deal with their presenting issues or whether effective intervention demands that any underlying conflict also needs to be resolved. This question raises some important differences of approach to this whole area of activity. It also highlights the distinction between "conflict" and "dispute" resolution.

Those primarily involved with conflict management and resolution tend to   **1–035** see the resolution of the conflict as their objective. One conflict writer, for example, says that "*Conflict transformation* and *healing* are [terms] used to describe the ideal outcomes of the process whereby the attitudes, feelings and behaviour of the disputants are so changed that lasting peace is assured."[22] Conflict resolution is similarly described as "an outcome, in which the issues in an existing conflict are satisfactorily dealt with through a solution that is mutually acceptable to the parties, self sustaining in the long run and

---

[21] See *Effective Conflict Management* by David A. Whetten, Kim Cameron and Mike Woods (1996). The authors state (p. 24) that "while the collaborative approach produces the fewest negative side effects, all the approaches have their place. The appropriateness of a management strategy depends on its congruence with both personal style and situational demands."

[22] Susan Stewart *op. cit.* at p. 23.

productive of a new, positive relationship between parties that were previously hostile adversaries...."[23]

1–036   Those primarily concerned with dispute resolution tend to see the resolution of the dispute itself as their objective. Obviously, where underlying conflict can be resolved in the context of the dispute resolution process, that is welcomed; but it is not necessarily seen as the primary objective of the process. ADR processes are "widely used.... alongside arbitration or litigation proceedings to complement and improve settlement negotiations. Most civil litigation ends in out of court settlement, but usually late in the day 'at the courthouse door', 'on the steps of the court' or 'in the hall'. ADR can bring forward such settlements to save the parties some time and costs, and possibly to lead to a more satisfactory process for the parties and better, or at least different outcomes than they might otherwise have achieved."[24]

1–037   In civil and commercial disputes, arriving at a settlement of the presenting issues is the primary goal. If a party makes a claim, whether or not it is formalised through the court, then the settlement of that claim settles the dispute. It may not settle all conflicts between the parties. So, for example, one of the authors of this work has dealt with a number of High Court disputes involving family businesses, where one family member has made claims against others in the business. In each case, the priority for everyone has been to find settlement terms that all could accept. The process could not necessarily repair the damaged family relationships. In the event, the collaborative nature of the process and the success of the outcome have generally tended to create conditions in which the damaged relationships could start to heal, but these processes would be seen as settlement geared and not necessarily "conflict" resolution. Similarly, the approach of the judiciary is more likely to be settlement orientated rather than conflict resolution geared.

1–038   In dealing with marriage and cohabitation breakdown, the position is more complicated. The authors of this work do not see issues arising on separation and divorce as necessarily being "disputes", and accordingly do not view "dispute resolution" processes as being exclusively applicable to family issues.[25] Insofar as disputes exist, "....the mediator helps the people in dispute to define the problem. This is done in a way which does not benefit any one person over the others and so achieves a mutual problem definition."[26]

1–039   Once the problem has been mutually defined, approaches to family mediation vary. For some, the problem-solving approach continues to predominate. For others, a bargaining approach is used and "positions are modified, options traded, and the give-and-take of bargaining occurs".[27]

---

[23]Mitchell and Banks *op. cit.* at p. xvii.

[24]Karl Mackie, David Miles and William Marsh *Commercial Dispute Resolution: An ADR Practice Guide* (1995) at p. 7.

[25]See Chap. 10.

[26]John Haynes *Alternative Dispute Resolution: The Fundamentals of Family Mediation* (1993) at p. 3. Haynes regards working with the mutual problem definition as being equivalent to defining the legal issues in an adjudication.

[27]Haynes *op. cit.* at p.4. He recognises that there are "complex emotional issues as well as mundane practical matters" to be addressed (p.15). Ultimately, though, he is clear that "the mediator provides mediation which is, after all, what the clients come for: to negotiate an

Another approach that has attracted interest is the "transformative" **1–040**
approach to conflict resolution. This is the view that "mediation's
fundamental objective must be to bring about the resolution of conflict."[28]
The main thesis is that conflict affords opportunities for moral development,
and that "mediation's greatest value lies in its potential not only to find
solutions to people's problems but to change people themselves for the
better, in the very midst of conflict."[29] This "transformative" potential is
achieved by a reassessment of "what conflict is and what a constructive
response to conflict must entail." Empowerment and recognition are
described as the central goals of transformative practice. The underlying
problem-solving approach to conflict is seen as being too limited.

The transformative approach to conflict resolution has attracted many **1–041**
supporters. Most practitioners are likely to find aspects of it that are
attractive. It does, however, raise some fundamental questions about what the
parties themselves want from the process, and whether they have chosen
"transformation" or merely dispute resolution. Perhaps these are not mutually
exclusive outcomes; but they commonly may be, and the practitioner needs
to have a clear idea of what he or she is providing to the parties. What, after
all, is the contract with the parties?[30]

Opinions may continue to differ about the relative values of problem- **1–042**
solving, settlement bargaining and transformation. Perhaps elements of each
have their own value, and some accommodation may have to be found
between them. Meanwhile, practitioners should be aware of these continuing
issues.

---

agreement on practical issues." (p. 16).

[28]Foreword by Jeffrey Z. Rubin to *The Promise of Mediation: Responding to Conflict through Empowerment and Recognition* (1994) by Robert A. Baruch Bush and Joseph P. Folger.

[29]Bush & Folger *op. cit.,* Preface at p. xv.

[30]See the article by Michael Williams *"Can't I Get No Satisfaction? Thoughts on Promise of Mediation"* in (1997) M.Q. 15(2), at 150 raising ethical questions about the nature of the mediator's contract with the clients. "The clients tell us what they want, and we agree with them about the terms on which we will try to help them to get it."

CHAPTER 2

DISPUTE RESOLUTION OUTLINE

1. ADR DEFINED

2–001   Alternative Dispute Resolution or "ADR" may be defined as a range of procedures that serve as alternatives to litigation through the courts for the resolution of disputes, generally involving the intercession and assistance of a neutral and impartial third party.[1] In some definitions, and more commonly, it excludes not only litigation, but all forms of adjudication.[2]

2–002   Arbitration is mentioned in this book because of its history as part of ADR and because its practices and procedures have influenced some hybrid ADR processes. An understanding of its operation is essential to an appreciation of dispute resolution generally. This book will not, however, try to cover the detailed practice of arbitration, expert determination or informal adjudication. The focus will instead be on non-adjudicatory forms of dispute resolution.

2–003   Negotiation is not on its own an ADR process. It is the most fundamental way of trying to resolve differences, and when it fails, ADR processes may become employed. While negotiation is invariably one of the main components of ADR processes, it is only when it is accompanied by neutral intercession and a more structured process framework that it becomes ADR.

2. THE PHILOSOPHY OF ADR

2–004   As ADR has developed, it has become increasingly clear that there is no single philosophy underpinning it, but rather a number of different strands, sometimes but not always overlapping.

2–005   All ADR practitioners accept the proposition that it is more beneficial for parties to resolve their differences by negotiated agreement rather than through contentious proceedings.[3] This proposition is hardly novel. It was a

---

[1] For the usage of "neutrality" and "impartiality" see paras 21–040–041.

[2] The Academy of Experts published a glossary on "The Language of ADR" (1992) which defines ADR as "any method of resolving an issue susceptible to normal legal process by agreement rather than an imposed binding decision". However, that would include as ADR, inter-party negotiations with or without lawyers, which would be too wide a definition.

[3] Some academics such as Prof. Owen Fiss have expressed reservations about parties being encouraged to settle their disputes rather than having them adjudicated. The consensus view among practitioners and writers, however, is that agreed settlements are preferable to litigation.

fundamental precept of Roman Law that it was in the interest of the state to see an end to litigation. The common experience is that ADR processes preserve or enhance personal and business relationships that might otherwise be damaged by the adversarial process. However, ADR is not limited to disputes involving relationships. It is widely used for issues where there is no relationship between the parties.

Most practitioners share the experience that parties using ADR processes tend to arrive at settlements that are more creative, satisfactory and lasting than those imposed by the court. However, ADR can be used simply to establish a deal that eludes the parties in bilateral negotiations, either personally or through their lawyers. **2–006**

Differences of philosophy and approach are difficult to identify because models of practice and individual beliefs and approaches are very diverse. Any attempt to categorise these into coherent ideologies or schools of thought will inevitably result in refutable generalisations. **2–007**

It is possible to distinguish some broad approaches to ADR. One is settlement-geared and cost-saving. This may go hand in hand with supporting a bargaining style of negotiation, seeking to trade issues in a search of a deal. For some practitioners, this does not reflect the spirit of ADR. There is another view of ADR, as a forum in which parties are helped to adopt a problem-solving approach in order to find a "win–win" outcome, with the neutral exploring underlying issues in order to understand those that have been presented. Most practitioners support this, but for some it is an aspirational ideal that cannot always be implemented in practice. **2–008**

There is yet another view that considers the problem-solving approach to be inadequate, in that it neglects a critical element of the process. That critical element is seen as the transformative potential by which people in dispute can change by the mediator adopting policies that help to empower them and give them a greater sense of their own efficacy.[4] **2–009**

Another school of thought sees mediation and other ADR processes through the lens of a communications perspective, urging greater attention to be given to this. They see conflict as a "socially created and communicatively managed reality occurring within a socio-historical context that both affects meaning and behaviour and is affected by it".[5] **2–010**

There are different models of working. The model they follow affects mediators' intervention strategies.[6] The position is complicated by the fact that models and philosophical approaches do not follow predictable patterns. With the development of practice in the United Kingdom and elsewhere, such distinctions have become blurred, as models have learned and borrowed from **2–011**

This is also the policy which underlies the Woolf reforms. Indeed, the "without prejudice" rule rests on the public policy that parties should be encouraged so far as is possible to settle their disputes without resort to litigation. See Chap. 18 for further consideration of the reservations about ADR processes.

[4] See paras 1–040 and 21–132–134. See also paras 6–044–048, 7–016–018 and 21–116 *et seq.* regarding issues of power and empowerment.

[5] *New Directions in Mediation: Communication Research and Perspectives* edited by Joseph P. Folger and Tricia S. Jones (1994) at p. ix.

[6] In the family field, see "Divorce Mediation: Four Models and Their Assumptions about Change in Parties' Positions" by Andrew I. Schwebel, David W. Gately, Maureena A. Renner and Thomas W. Milburn in (1994) M.Q. 11(3).

one another, bridging the differences and developing ways of working that draw the best from different models and approaches.

2–012   The different fields of mediation each tend to have their own culture of practice, which differ from one another; and within each field there are differences, sometimes significant.

2–013   ADR forms can stand in their own right as alternatives to adjudication; or they can complement the court's procedures for example by court-annexed arbitration or court-annexed mediation, private judging or other adjunct to litigation and arbitration procedures which supplement and assist them and which facilitate settlements within these systems. In practice, ADR variously serves all of these functions, all of which are legitimate, proper and useful. Lawyers and other practitioners need to be aware of the occasions when litigation, arbitration, mediation or any other ADR process has its appropriate value and to advise accordingly.

2–014   ADR is also widely motivated by the fact that it is said to reduce the costs and delays of litigation. Certainly, in the United States where litigation costs are very high and not recoverable and trial delays very long, the search for more expeditious and cheaper alternatives is understandable. The question is sometimes asked whether ADR is as relevant in the United Kingdom where those conditions are said not to apply. There are a number of answers. First, litigation in the United Kingdom is in fact expensive and generally also involves delays of varying degrees. Secondly, there has been an increasing consumer resistance to the costs, delays and risk of litigation which, together also with adverse media comment and professional recognition of the shortcomings of the present system, has fuelled the search for alternatives in Britain. We discuss in Chapter 3 the scope and possible effects of the Woolf reforms and the role of ADR within them. Thirdly, the benefits of ADR are perceived as going beyond the mere savings of costs and time, although these are significant factors.

2–015   The cost-savings element of ADR is based on the assumption that it will be effective. The costs of running a mediation or even a mini-trial will invariably be much lower than a full scale trial; and the costs savings can be considerable. If, however, the ADR process does not resolve the issues and the parties have to proceed to adjudication, then the cost of the ADR will have to be aggregated with the costs of trial. Nevertheless, there is often some value added by virtue of the ADR process, such as helping to gather information and clarify or narrow issues; and ADR discussions which do not produce an immediate resolution sometimes provide the basis for a later settlement.

2–016   The issue of the appropriateness of dispute resolution forms is central to any philosophy of ADR. Diverse kinds of disputes involving varying circumstances and parties with a range of differing possible concerns and interests may well require different kinds of procedures and approaches. Simply being able to offer adjudication, frequently including explicit or implicit elements of contest and threat, is increasingly felt by many practitioners to be inadequate. Other ways to assist parties to arrive at consensus can be provided through ADR.

2–017   Robert Coulson, as President of the American Arbitration Association wrote:

"Lawyers are in a bind when it comes to managing their clients' disputes if they are locked into the courts. Litigation has not kept up with modern, fast-moving society...there have been revolutionary changes in business practices since the basic court structure was adopted from English common law...Compared to modern business, civil courts have changed very little...Alternative dispute resolution gives lawyers an opportunity to use new processes, encourages a problem-solving attitude (and) an openness to compromise. . ."[7]

Complaints about the delays, costs and risks of litigation may not always   **2–018**
be as sharp in other jurisdictions as they are in the United States, but they are nonetheless familiar elsewhere, and processes that address these are universally welcome. Furthermore, processes that offer greater flexibility in dealing with disputes, that tend to sustain working or personal relationships and that offer greater possibilities for achieving mutually satisfactory outcomes are bound to attract interest in any litigation system. This will be the case although there may also be a corresponding awareness that they have their own shortcomings, and cannot remedy all the imperfections of existing systems.

While acknowledging the difficulty in achieving any one agreed ADR   **2–019**
philosophy, the following might perhaps embody much of the essence of ADR:

ADR complements litigation and other adjudicatory forms, providing processes which can either stand in their own right or be used as an adjunct to adjudication. This enables practitioners to select procedures (adjudicatory or consensual) appropriate to individual disputes. ADR gives parties more power and greater control over resolving the issues between them, encourages problem-solving approaches, and provides for more effective settlements covering substance and nuance. It also tends to enhance co-operation and to be conducive to the preservation of relationships. Effective impartial third party intercession can help to over come blocks to settlement, and by expediting and facilitating resolution it can save costs and avoid the delays and risks of litigation. Sometimes, but not necessarily, it can help to heal or provide the conditions for healing underlying conflicts between parties. ADR processes, like adjudicatory procedures, have advantages and disadvantages which make them suitable for some cases but not for others.

3. OVERVIEW OF DISPUTE RESOLUTION PROCEDURES

Some ADR writers divide all dispute resolution processes (traditional and   **2–020**
alternative) into three primary categories[8]:

---

[7]See article entitled "The Lawyer's Role in Dispute Management" in *Dispute Resolution* published by the American Bar Association Standing Committee on Dispute Resolution, Issue 25 Spring/Summer 1989.

[8]See, *e.g. Dispute Resolution* by Goldberg, Green & Sander (Little Brown & Co. 1985), p. 7.

- negotiation

- mediation

- adjudication.

2–021   Others extend them to up to six primary categories: negotiation, mediation, the judicial process, arbitration, and the administrative and legislative processes.[9] This effectively amounts to a sub-division of adjudication into its constituent parts.

2–022   While the division into three primary categories is valid and useful (and was followed in the first edition of this work) it may also be helpful to view dispute resolution processes as a continuum. At the one end is negotiation. This is the process in which a party has the most personal power and decision-making authority with regard to the terms on which the dispute is resolved. At the other end is litigation. This is the process in which a party has the least personal power and decision-making authority with regard to the terms on which the dispute is resolved, inasmuch as the determination of the dispute is placed in the hands of a third party, who makes a binding decision. All dispute resolution process, both traditional and ADR, fall somewhere within this continuum.

2–023   Each of the three primary processes (negotiation, mediation and adjudication) can be used in its own right without adaptation. In addition, by drawing elements from any combination of the primary processes and "tailoring" them, an ADR practitioner can design a permutation of procedures and approaches that fits all the nuances of the parties' needs and circumstances without being constrained by prescribed rules. For example, it may be appropriate for the practitioner to have informal discussions with the parties, arrange for certain facts or technical questions to be investigated, and then allow each of them to present their respective cases informally to one another before resuming further attempts at settlement through facilitative (or evaluative) mediation. Any permutation of requirements can be met by devising a sequence of procedures specifically designed for that dispute and those parties.

2–024   Certain common combinations of usage of the primary processes have developed in this way, and have become known as hybrid processes. These include the mini-trial, med–arb, the neutral fact-finding expert, early neutral evaluation, and court-annexed arbitration, all of which are considered further below.

2–025   The three primary processes and their "hybrid" combinations can probably most usefully be divided into two main categories. The one comprises **adjudicatory** processes (where the third party neutral makes a binding determination of the issues). The other comprises **consensual** processes (where the parties retain the power to control the outcome and any terms of resolution). Within the consensual category, parties may be assisted in arriving at an agreed resolution in various ways. Some may be purely

---

[9]See *Processes of Dispute Resolution: The Role of Lawyers* by Murray, Rau & Sherman (Foundation Press, 1989), p. 69.

facilitative, others may involve the neutral in helping the parties to evaluate the issues or the proposed terms of settlement.

The authors of this work now view these dispute resolution processes, **2–026** adjudicatory and consensual, as ranging along a continuum based on the parties' control over deciding the outcome and the extent to which a third party neutral influences them. On this basis, the main dispute resolution processes (both traditional and ADR) would broadly fall as follows, starting with the processes offering least control to the parties and moving to those which offer greatest control:

Litigation

The neutral is a judge, district judge, master or other official appointed by the court to make a binding determination.

Parties have least control. Third party neutral has most power. Procedural rules are prescribed.

Private judging

Where this procedure has been adopted, the court refers the case to a referee chosen by the parties to decide some or all of the issues, or to establish any facts.

Similar to litigation, but parties can choose the neutral and can agree to simplify procedures.

Arbitration

The neutral, privately chosen and paid by the disputants, makes a binding determination. Procedural rules may be statutory or imposed by an arbitral organisation.

Similar to litigation, but parties have more say in agreeing choice of third party neutral and procedural rules.

Contractual adjudication

In some industries such as construction, a neutral adjudicator is required by contract or by statute to make summary binding decisions on contractual disputes without following litigation or arbitration procedures.

Similar to arbitration, but procedure and neutral's decision may be more summary.

Administrative or statutory tribunals

Binding adjudication based on statutory requirements, such as establishing rent levels, compensation awards or social security benefits through tribunals and appeal tribunals.

As for litigation, but procedures are supposed to be more informal.

Expert determination

Parties appoint expert to consider issues and make a binding decision or appraisal without necessarily having to conduct an enquiry following adjudicatory rules.

As for arbitration, but procedure accords with contractual instructions given by parties to the expert.

Med–Arb

Neutral acts as mediator, and if parties cannot agree, becomes an arbitrator to make a binding determination. There are variations giving parties rights to opt out of this process in some versions.

As for mediation during the first stage; but if parties are bound to the arbitration phase then the next stage may be viewed as for arbitration. In some versions a different person may arbitrate in the second stage

Court-annexed arbitration

In some jurisdictions, the arbitration is initially non-binding, but may become binding if neither party appeals. In other jurisdictions, arbitration through the court is immediately binding.

Where the award is not initially binding but may become so, this is almost a half-way house between binding and non-binding processes. Where it is binding right away, it is the same as arbitration.

Neutral fact-finding expert

Neutral expert is appointed by the parties to investigate issues of fact, technicality or law, produces a report, helps towards settlement, and if agreed, the report may be used in adjudication.

If the neutral's role is to produce a report that all parties accept, this gives the neutral great power. If, more commonly, the report is non-binding, then it still has authority. The neutral may also be given a mediatory role.

Ombudsman

Independent neutral deals with public complaints against maladministration. Also used in certain sectors such as legal and financial services. Can investigate, criticise and publicise, and sometimes can award compensation.

Degree of party control depends on terms of reference of individual ombudsman. Usually power is in the hands of the neutral. Sometimes compensation award allows one party freedom to choose acceptance or not.

Evaluation

Independent neutral makes an evaluation of the case, usually its merits or some aspect, which is not binding on the parties but helps them in their decision-making.

This falls into the category of non-binding evaluative processes. Power remains with the parties, but neutral can influence them by evaluating.

Early neutral evaluation (ENE)

A form of evaluation in which neutral evaluator makes an early assessment of the merits to help parties narrow and define issues; also helps promote efforts to settle.

As for evaluation

Mini-trial (Executive Tribunal)

Lawyers for the parties present their cases to a panel comprising the parties and a neutral. The neutral helps clarify the issues and evaluate the merits, and may also have a mediatory role. No binding determination is made, but the process helps the parties evaluate realistically.

As for ENE, but here the parties form part of the evaluating panel and have slightly more control.

Summary jury trial

U.S. adaptation of mini-trial. Instead of a single neutral, the case is presented to a mock jury, which makes a mock (and non-binding) determination.

As for ENE, but here there is no single expert to influence the parties, rather a mock jury panel to give them guidance how a real jury might decide the case.

Negotiation (through representatives)

No neutral involved. Representatives of each party negotiate with one another. Parties retain power to agree terms.

Parties retain control over outcome but little control over process, which is in hands of representatives.

Mediation (with evaluation)

Neutral has no authority to make any decisions, uses skills to assist parties to negotiate settlement terms and arrive at their own resolution. Evaluative element means neutral may express some view on merits of issues.

As for evaluation, but neutral's primary role as facilitator means that any evaluation is less likely to diminish parties' control.

Mediation (facilitative only)

As for evaluative mediation save that neutral does not evaluate.

Parties retain power, not directly influenced by neutral in decision-making.

Negotiation (by parties personally)

No neutral involved. Parties negotiate directly with one another.

Parties have control over process and outcome. Maximum power.

Each of these processes is considered in greater detail in this book.[10]

4. TERMINOLOGY

2–027 Some of the terminology used in ADR will be familiar to lawyers and others engaged in dispute resolution. Other terms are less familiar, and not necessarily consistently employed. Unfortunately, the field is not free from jargon.

2–028 Glossaries of ADR terms have been prepared, and a committee of practitioners has written a report on "the language of ADR" which may be of some assistance in following the terminology.[11] A glossary of common terms in ADR and general dispute resolution usage appears on page 649 of this book.

2–029 The term "alternative" in ADR has generally been understood to refer to the alternatives to litigation. Arbitration was originally widely included as part of ADR. However, as arbitration has entered the mainstream of dispute resolution processes, and in the light of its adjudicatory nature, the current tendency has shifted away from regarding arbitration strictly as ADR and has tended to limit this term to consensual processes. Practice, however, varies quite extensively in this regard and many still see arbitration as ADR (including, for example, the Legal Aid Board).

2–030 In everyday usage the term "alternative" may suggest a non-conformist approach to dispute resolution, but that is not the usage employed in this book or by most dispute resolution professionals. Most ADR practitioners view it as requiring a high level of professional skill and responsibility.

2–031 Karl Mackie points out the paradox in the fact that most proponents of ADR now agree that the term "alternative" is inappropriate.[12] Much of ADR's value lies in the notion of a spectrum of dispute resolution mechanisms, with alternatives adding to, rather than replacing the litigation option. Mackie notes a growing tendency to omit the word "alternative" from works on dispute resolution, but nevertheless observes that the term "Alternative Dispute Resolution" and its acronym ADR remain the most widely recognised terms of art to describe the range of processes, other than litigation, to settle disputes.[13]

2–032 In this book the term "Alternative Dispute Resolution" is similarly used to describe processes which add to and enhance the range of resources and mechanisms to settle disputes.

---

[10]For litigation, see Chap. 3. For arbitration, expert determination and contractual adjudication, see Chap. 4. For non-binding evaluative processes, see Chap. 16. For mediation, see Chaps. 7 and 8 generally, and further chapters for individual fields of activity. For negotiation, see Chap. 6.

[11]See the Report (February 1992) of the Committee into the Language of ADR, convened under the auspices of the Academy of Experts. See also the glossary prepared by Mediation U.K. with its related *Directory of Mediation Projects and Conflict Resolution Services*. A glossary has also been published by the CPR Institute for Dispute Resolution on the Internet: *The ABCs of ADR: A Dispute Resolution Glossary* at http://www.cpradr.org/glossary.htm (November 1995).

[12]See *A Handbook of Dispute Resolution: ADR in Action* (1991) ed. by Karl Mackie, at pp. 3–5.

[13]In Karl Mackie's later book, written jointly with David Miles and William Marsh, *Commercial Dispute Resolution: An ADR Practice Guide* (1995) the authors talk of "Appropriate, Additional or Complementary dispute resolution" (p. 7) but retain the acronym "ADR".

CHAPTER 3

LITIGATION AND COURT REFORM

1. THE NEW RULES

On Monday April 26, 1999, the new Civil Procedure Rules[1] came into force **3–001**
in England and Wales. The new Rules apply both to proceedings in the High
Court and the County Court and are regarded by most commentators as the
most radical reform of civil procedure since the great reforms of 1872 to
1875.

As is well known to United Kingdom practitioners, the new Civil **3–002**
Procedure Rules flow from the recommendations for reform of the civil
justice system which Lord Woolf made in the Interim and Final reports of his
Working Party.[2] Those recommendations were very largely accepted by the
Major Government and following a rapid review by Sir Peter Middleton
published in September 1997,[3] were accepted by the Blair Government. A
remarkable feature of the widespread consultation which Lord Woolf
undertook and the public debate which he encouraged, was the high degree
of almost uncritical acceptance by Government, judges, practitioners,
administrators and the public of the need for reform of the civil justice
system and especially of the proposals for case management which he was
advocating.

Some voices of dissent were raised. Prominent amongst them was **3–003**
Professor Michael Zander Q.C., who, in a series of speeches and articles, cast
doubt on the wisdom of introducing extensive case management by judges,
the measure which is at the heart of Lord Woolf's reform. The Association
of Personal Injury Lawyers and others concerned with clinical negligence
issues also expressed reservations. The Law Society and some of Lord
Woolf's judicial colleagues, notably Sir Richard Scott, V.-C. and Head of
Civil Justice (the latter position created upon Lord Woolf's recommendation),
thought that the introduction of the new Civil Procedure Rules should be
delayed. But the Lord Chancellor, Lord Irvine, would have none of it and the
new Rules came into force as planned. All opposition and reservations about
the reforms were swept aside.

---

[1] The Civil Procedure Rules, Lord Chancellor's Department (Brown Book).
[2] Interim Report to the Lord Chancellor on the Civil Justice System in England and Wales, June
1995; and Access to Justice, July 1996.
[3] Review of Civil Justice and Legal Aid, Sir Peter Middleton, September 1997.

2. FINANCING CIVIL JUSTICE

3–004   The procedural reform recommended by Lord Woolf and expressed in the new Civil Procedure Rules is but one of a number of measures initiated by the Lord Chancellor to reform the civil justice system radically and quickly.

Unfortunately, but entirely predictably, Lord Woolf's mandate did not include considering what changes were necessary in the funding of the civil justice system, not only of the court system itself, but also with regard to legal aid to litigants.

3–005   The Government came to the conclusion (rightly) that expenditure on civil legal aid cannot be controlled effectively under the system which was established after the last War. The Government pointed to the fact that in 1992–1993 the amount spent on all forms of civil and family legal aid was £586 million. By 1997–1998 this figure had reached £793 million, a growth three times the rate of inflation for the period, which the Government considered "cannot be sustained in future". Furthermore, despite increased expenditure fewer cases were dealt with.

3–006   Procedural reform based on case management is unlikely to produce overall cost savings of any great significance, whether in the administration of the courts or in fees incurred by litigants; and there are those who argue, almost certainly correctly, that the new case management techniques will increase the overall burden of cost falling upon litigants.

3–007   Funding of the civil justice system is a highly complex topic involving as it does such matters as the structure and remuneration of the legal profession, rights of audience, constitutional rights of access to the courts, and the allocation of scarce public resources between competing needs. Should, for example, priority be given to the speedy and effective resolution by the courts of disputes arising from marital breakdown rather than to the victims of personal injury or clinical negligence or, by way of further example, to aggrieved consumers? These and like questions are inherently bound up in any radical reform of the civil justice system.

3–008   The Government has taken steps to change fundamentally the way in which civil litigation in England and Wales is funded. It has done so as part of achieving the Lord Chancellor's ultimate goal of a Community Legal Service. Thus, legal aid has been withdrawn from certain categories of litigation namely trust law, partnership law, boundary disputes, making of wills and matters to do with businesses. Lawyers may tender for block contracts to provide legal services of various kinds for which the State is prepared to pay. Moreover, clients may enter into conditional fee arrangements with lawyers and a greater use of insurance schemes will be encouraged to finance litigation and to guard against the heavy cost consequences which can flow from an unsuccessful result.

3–009   The Government's objectives can be clearly seen from Lord Irvine's Foreword to the Lord Chancellor's Department paper entitled Modernising Justice.[4]

"A fair and efficient system of justice, operating in the interests of people

---

[4]Modernising Justice—the Government's plans for reforming Legal Services and the Courts, December 2, 1998.

who use it and the wider public, is a vital part of a civilised, modern, inclusive society. People should have ready access to information about their legal rights. And they should be able, if necessary, to resolve disputes and enforce those rights through the civil courts, at a cost that is predictable and proportionate to the issue at stake.

The justice system should serve everyone, regardless of their means. People should be able to find effective solutions to their legal problems. Justice must not be restricted to the very wealthy, who can well afford high legal fees, or the very poor, who may qualify for legal aid. At the same time, taxpayers deserve value for the money they contribute to legal aid and the courts."

and:

"A Community Legal Service will revolutionise ordinary people's access to information about their rights, and new avenues to good quality legal services.

As part of the Community Legal Service, legal aid spending will be refocused on the people and cases where it is most needed and can do most good. More money will reach both the not-for-profit sector (which has particular expertise at dealing with the types of problems faced by poor people), and better ways of resolving disputes, like mediation.

Modern ways of funding litigation, like 'no win, no fee' agreements, and a new 'fast-track' system in the courts, leading to fixed-cost hearings, will open up access to civil justice to people on modest income who do not qualify for legal aid, and dare not risk going to court at their own expense because of the impracticable cost."

In order to achieve these laudable objectives the Lord Chancellor signalled **3–010** his intention to encourage increased competition between those providing legal services by, for example, increasing rights of audience and by setting up a Legal Services Commission which will develop local regional and national plans:

"to match the delivery of legal services to identified needs and priorities, and replacing legal aid with a community legal service fund managed by the Legal Services Commission".

As paragraphs 3.6 and 3.7 of Modernising Justice put it:

" ... any system for funding legal services in civil and family cases should ... :

- direct the available resources to where they are most needed, to reflect clearly defined priorities
- ensure, so far as possible, that disputes are resolved in a manner which is fair to both sides

- provide high quality services that achieve the best possible value for money
- have a budget which is affordable to the tax payer, and can be kept under control

... the following areas should have greatest priority:

- social welfare cases
- other cases of fundamental importance to the people affected. This covers cases involving major issues in children's lives (like care and adoption proceedings); and cases concerned with protecting people from violence
- cases involving a wider public interest. This category includes two types of case: those likely to produce real benefits for a significant number of other people, or which raise an important new legal issue; and those challenging the actions, or failure to act, of public bodies (including cases under the Human Rights Act), or alleging that public servants have abused their position or power".

3–011   As can be seen, the Government seeks a fundamental reform in the provision of funding for civil litigation. It describes the Community Legal Service Fund as resting on three pillars which it regards as complementary and flexible. Those pillars are defined in paragraph 3.10 of Modernising Justice as a planning system, contracting and a new funding assessment, all designed to allocate resources where most needed.

3–012   The Government expects the Legal Services Commission to take an innovative approach to funding of civil dispute resolution on a wider basis than that provided by the existing Legal Aid Board. Thus, the existing Legal Aid Board has been asked to take the first steps by developing a larger role for services provided by non-lawyers, developing new ways of delivering information, advice and assistance harnessing modern technology, funding some "second tier" agencies, offering specialist advice, support and training to front-line service providers; and funding mediation in appropriate civil cases, as well as family cases.[5]

3–013   No sensible person would dissent from the objective, as the Lord Chancellor put it in *Modernising Justice*, of seeking to:

"create a justice system that is no longer so daunting, so uncertain and so expensive that ordinary people have no real access to justice".

The question is: will the reform work?

3. DENIAL OF ACCESS TO JUSTICE

3–014   At the time of the first edition of this book, it had long been clear that the civil justice system in England and Wales was in crisis. Civil litigation was excessively expensive and protracted. Legal aid was available only to the

---

[5]Modernising Justice.

most disadvantaged in society and only those with the deepest private purse could afford to pay for litigation themselves. It was obvious that the cost of civil litigation in England and Wales was out of hand. This led to a denial of access to the courts affecting the majority of citizens and to severe injustice.

Even for those who could afford it, civil litigation was an extremely **3–015** expensive and hazardous undertaking. Only if very considerable sums of money or fundamental principles were at stake, was it worth contemplating. It was also clear that in certain kinds of dispute the cost of delay in resolution was wholly disproportionate to the amount in issue and that was particularly true in complicated cases where extensive factual investigation was required. As the authors pointed out in the first edition of this work, construction cases were a particular example of abuse and under the pre-Woolf procedures even substantial claims could be uneconomic to pursue or defend. The cost of such litigation was beyond the resources of small and medium-sized companies and even the largest corporations were concerned by and sought ways of reducing substantially the cost of litigation to which they were subject.

4. THE ADVERSARIAL SYSTEM

At the heart of the common law system of civil justice as practised in the **3–016** United States and England is the adversarial system. The adversarial process starts from the issue of proceedings, if not before. Every procedural step to trial is a potential battleground. Traditionally, this system has cast judges in a passive role. A civil trial is not a search for truth. It is a process by which the parties place before the judge evidence of the facts which are relevant. The judge is obliged to apply the law and the parties are under a duty to bring to the judge's attention all relevant authorities and principles. Of course, judges are not completely passive and a socratic dialogue between Bench and Bar is commonplace. Yet adversarial processes, rules of evidence and attitudes derived from the jury system remain at the heart of the English procedural system.

The role and approach of lawyers

Criticism has been made in the United States of declining professional **3–017** standards in the conduct of litigation. There are grounds for believing that the conduct of civil litigation in England has become more abrasive and aggressive. This is perhaps a reflection of a legal profession which has expanded rapidly in recent years, the sense that the practice of law has become more of a business than a profession, and a sign of the continuing decline in the standards of tolerance and courtesy in society generally. Perhaps the duty to collaborate imposed by the new Rules will improve matters.

All litigation, whether under adversarial or inquisitorial systems, common **3–018** law or civil law, is labour intensive. The principal cause of the high cost of litigation is the unavoidable fact that lawyers in all jurisdictions enjoy a privileged economic position. The legal profession is protected by rules and regulations—usually but not invariably—in the public interest, which require professional qualifications, minimum levels of professional skills and competence; ensure protection, by compulsory insurance and disciplinary action in the interest of the public to whom legal services are offered; and grant a monopoly of certain kinds of legal work, principally litigation.

3–019   It is the general level of lawyers' charges and the labour intensive nature of the procedures which drives the cost of litigation to current levels. Although the pressures of the market place may well force reductions in lawyers' fees, the impact on the overall cost of litigation is marginal. It is idle to expect that this will change or that the State will be prepared, through taxation, to increase significantly the financial resources available for the administration of civil justice: successive Governments have made it plain that they will not. This has led to the attempt to reform the system by organisational and procedural changes inherent in case management.

The overriding objective

3–020   The overriding objective of the new Civil Procedure Rules is expressed by Rule 1.1 to be "enabling the Court to deal with cases justly". By Rule 1.1(2) dealing with a case justly:

"includes so far as is practicable—

(a) ensuring that the parties are on an equal footing;

(b) saving expense;

(c) dealing with the case in ways which are proportionate—

(i) to the amount of money involved;

(ii) to the importance of the case;

(iii) to the complexity of the issues; and

(iv) to the financial position of each party;

(d) ensuring that it is dealt with expeditiously and fairly;

(e) allotting to it an appropriate share of the Court's resources while taking into account to allot resources to other cases".

3–021   By Rule 1.4 the court is obliged to further the overriding objective by actively managing cases. Under 1.4(2):

"Active case management includes—

(a) encouraging the parties to co-operate with each other in the conduct of the proceedings;

(b) identifying the issues at an early stage;

(c) deciding promptly which issues need full investigation and trial and accordingly disposing summarily of the others;

(d) deciding the order in which issues are to be resolved;

(e) encouraging the parties to use an alternative dispute resolution procedure if the court considers that appropriate and facilitating the use of such procedure;

(f) helping the parties to settle the whole or part of the case;

(g) fixing timetables or otherwise controlling the progress of the case;

(h) considering whether the likely benefits of taking a particular step justify the cost of taking it;

(i) dealing with as many aspects of the case as it can on the same occasion;

(j) dealing with the case without the parties needing to attend at court;

(k) making use of technology; and

(l) giving directions to ensure that the trial of a case proceeds quickly and efficiently."

Encouraging settlement

The new rules make provision for the division of cases into three tracks each with specific procedural characteristics, designed to achieve speed, economy and fairness. A major change from the old procedural regime is that litigation must be preceded by compliance with pre-action protocols (of which only two existed as at the April 26 1999 namely, for clinical negligence and personal injury claims). The objective of pre-action protocols is full disclosure of relevant evidence to facilitate case management and to see whether compromise can be reached and proceedings avoided.   **3–022**

Other pre-action protocols will come into force, but pending their introduction it is the duty of the parties in accordance with the overriding objective   **3–023**

"to act reasonably in exchanging information and documents relevant to the claim and generally in trying to avoid the necessity for the start of proceedings."[6]

The conduct of the parties before the litigation commences, and in particular the efforts made to settle before starting proceedings, are now relevant matters for the court to take into consideration when considering costs. Failure by the lawyers to comply with the overriding objective may well result in cost orders against them.

Rule 1.4(2)(e) and (f) reflect the importance given to settlement. It was a primary and express theme of Lord Woolf's reports to encourage and promote the settlement of disputes before litigation starts; and, if that is unsuccessful, to streamline procedures so as to facilitate the negotiation of settlements before the trial of the action. Most cases settled under the old system: the object now is to encourage earlier settlement on fairer terms.   **3–024**

Lord Woolf's Interim Report assumed the conceptual justification for encouraging settlement before and during litigation. But the assumption that settlements are preferable to adjudication is not universally shared. Some American academics, notably Professor Owen Fiss[7], have suggested that disputants should be encouraged to use the adjudicatory approach rather than be deterred from it; and that they should not have their rights to obtain the decision of the court eroded by alternative means of dispute resolution. This is a minority view which nowadays has no influence. No modern practitioner would seriously deny the advantage of promoting settlement. The primary case rests on the broad principle that the resolution of disputes by consensus and by compromise contributes to the well-being of society as a whole. It was a maxim of Roman law that *interest republicae ut sit finis litium;* the   **3–025**

---

[6]*Unilever plc v. The Procter & Gamble Company* [1999] 2 All E.R. 691.

[7]Against Settlement, (1984) 93 Yale L.J. 1073, Prof. Owen Fiss.

interest of the State should be an end to litigation. That maxim has been followed in the English civil justice system. The courts as a matter of public policy encourage and enforce settlement. Paradoxically, however, the role of the courts hitherto has been confined to creating an over-elaborate system of without prejudice and confidential communication in order to keep settlement discussions from going before the court at all.

3–026   English judges, whilst sometimes prepared by a nod and a wink to encourage settlement, have shied away from actively participating in the process. Thus, if case management is to work, English judges will have to be much more interventionist[8] than hitherto in controlling procedures, curbing delay, capping costs and encouraging settlement. Under the new Civil Procedure Rules they have the power to do so. This runs somewhat contrary to the English tradition, for despite the clear and emphatic direction of Lord Templeman and Lord Roskill in *Ashmore v. Lloyd's*[9], most English judges at first instance have not intervened and have not exercised their powers of control.

Court-annexed ADR

3–027   In his Interim Report Lord Woolf, whilst recognising the value of ADR, made it plain that he did not favour a system of court-annexed ADR. He suggested merely that ADR be considered at case management conferences and pretrial reviews. But in his Final Report Lord Woolf was more emphatic. Thus, he recommended that information on sources of ADR should be provided at all civil courts and that legal aid funding should be available for pre-litigation resolution and ADR. He suggested that the court should encourage the use of ADR at case management conferences and pre-trial reviews and should take into account whether the parties have unreasonably refused to try ADR or behaved unreasonably in the course of ADR.

3–028   In the Final Report Lord Woolf emphasised that it was a significant aim of his recommendations to encourage the resolution of disputes before they came to litigation:

"for example by the greater use of pre-litigation disclosure and of ADR, and that of encouraging settlement, for example by introducing plaintiffs' offers to settle and by disposing of issues so as to narrow the dispute".

He regarded it as an essential element of his proposals for case management that the parties should be encouraged and assisted to settle cases or at least to agree on particular issues and that the use of ADR should be encouraged. He recommended that, by various means and at an early stage the court should explore the scope for ADR or settlement and see whether there is any way in which the court could assist the parties to resolve their dispute without the need for a trial or a full trial. This needs to be developed by the judges who have now a duty to ensure resolution by appropriate and proportionate means.

---

[8] Some courts were interventionist under the old system, notably some judges in the Technology and Construction Court and in the Commercial Court.
[9] *Ashmore v. Corp. of Lloyd's (No. 1)* [1992] 2 Lloyd's Rep. 1.

This will involve real consideration not only of procedural measures to reduce time and cost, but of ADR to promote settlement.

The significant shift in Lord Woolf's views between his Interim and Final   **3–029**
Report was reflected in his consideration of the issue of whether ADR should be made mandatory or should be a purely voluntary process. He indicated in his Final Report that he remained:

> "of the view, though with less certainty than before, that it would not be right for the Court to compel parties to use ADR and to take away or postpone their rights to seek a remedy from the Courts, although this approach has been successfully adopted in a number of other jurisdictions. Nevertheless, where a party has unreasonably refused a proposal by the Court that ADR should be attempted, or has acted unco-operatively in the course of ADR, the Court should be able to take that into account in deciding what order to make as to costs".

Lord Woolf saw clear scope for the use of ADR in specific classes of case.   **3–030**
Thus, he recommended that ADR mechanisms should be encouraged in clinical negligence, especially for smaller claims and he considered that ADR mechanisms had a role to play in housing litigation. But he rejected compulsion, considering in the case of medical negligence and also generally:

> "As a matter of principle I think it is preferable to encourage rather than compel its use".

Lord Woolf's recommendation on cost sanctions as reflected in the new   **3–031**
rules raises real and difficult problems. How can a court properly assess who was "unco-operative" in an ADR process? Are parties who stand firm in a principled way and do not change their position significantly, to be so regarded? Who is to tell the judge? Do costs sanctions, whether imposed by the mediator or by the court following a mediator's report, damage the integrity of the process? If may be that there is a difference in practice between civil and commercial mediations and family mediations and that these and other questions are more easily answered in the former case. However, the authors believe that mediators whether civil and commercial or family in England are unlikely to agree to pass judgment on a party's behaviour.

5. ADR in the Civil Justice Rules

The new Civil Justice Rules reflect Lord Woolf's ideas on the use of ADR.   **3–032**
In Part 3 of the Civil Procedure Rules, under the general heading of The Case Management Powers of the Court, the court has by Rule 3.1(2)(b) and (f), the power to adjourn or bring forward a hearing or to stay the whole or part of any proceedings or judgment either generally, or until a specified date or event.

By Rule 26.4 the court may, at a preliminary stage, stay proceedings to   **3–033**
allow for settlement of the case. Rule 26.4 provides as follows:

"(1) A party may, when filing the completed allocation questionnaire. make a written request for the proceedings to be stayed while the parties try to settle the case by alternative dispute resolution or other means.

(2) Where—

    (a) all parties request a stay under paragraph (1); or

    (b) the court, of its own initiative, considers that such a stay[10] would be appropriate,

the court will direct that the proceedings be stayed for one month.

(3) The court may extend the stay until such date or for such specified period as it considers appropriate.

(4) Where the court stays the proceedings under this rule, the claimant must tell the court if a settlement is reached.

(5) If the claimant does not tell the court by the end of the period of the stay that a settlement has been reached, the court will give such directions as to the management of the case as it considers appropriate."

3–034   It is curious that there is no specific provision to encourage mediation at a later stage as well. There are indications from experience in the U.S. that mediation later may be more successful. Experience in the Technology and Construction Court in England suggests that parties are seeking a stay for mediation at a later stage in the procedure. It is also noteworthy that Rule 26.4 seems to equate ADR with mediation. Other forms of ADR, *i.e.* Early Neutral Evaluation or mini-trial are also valuable particularly at later stages. Rule 26.4, if it is to be used as successfully as it might be, should be regarded as a mechanism to enable the judge to investigate with the parties what kind of settlement procedure would most assist them and thereby enable the judge to make appropriate orders.

3–035   Lord Woolf's views on sanctions find expression in Rule 44.5 where in assessing whether costs were proportionately and reasonably incurred, the court must now have regard to the conduct of all the parties including in particular (44.5(3)(a)(ii)):

"the efforts made, if any, before and during the proceedings in order to try to resolve the dispute".

As indicated above, this Rule is fraught with difficulty both conceptual and procedural. No satisfactory guidelines have yet emerged for the exercise of this power.

Sir Peter Middleton

3–036   Sir Peter Middleton in his report[11] to the Lord Chancellor, the first attempt to reconcile the proposed procedural and financing changes, concluded that Lord Woolf's reforms should succeed. However, Sir Peter made the point that:

---

[10]*i.e.* at the beginning.

[11]Review of Civil Justice and Legal Aid, Sir Peter Middleton, September 1997.

"the legal system is capable of destroying any changes, however desirable".

But he expressed the view that if the senior judiciary shared Lord Woolf's vision and his determination, there was no reason why with a supportive approach and a rigorous attitude, the new regime should not succeed. On the issue of costs and delay savings, Sir Peter concluded that the reforms:

"are capable of delivering real overall benefits".

He expected delay in the average case to be reduced and therefore considered that there would be an increase in efficiency and a decrease in cost.[12]But significantly (and correctly) Sir Peter concluded that:

"because more cases are likely to pass through the system as a result, I would not necessarily expect total expenditure to fall"

The hope must be that case management involving the use of ADR will lead to a more efficient use of resources, thereby enabling disputes to be resolved more speedily and creating the opportunity to redirect limited resources to resolve other disputes which are of more importance to society. **3–037**

As Sir Peter recognises, the more readily accessible we make the courts, the more they are used, as the expansion of small claims arbitration in the county court more than amply demonstrates. One effect of this will be an increasing number of litigants in person and hopefully Lord Woolf's procedural reforms will make it easier for them. **3–038**

The Government is clearly right in its decision that reform of the civil justice system cannot be confined to changes in court procedure, however desirable these may be. It is the cost of lawyers and the amount and funding of their charges which is a central cause of delay and cost in the civil justice system. It is the level of fees which lawyers are able to command which, combined with the inefficiencies of the civil justice system, have been the major contributors to the financial crisis and to the breakdown of the system. Even if the new procedural changes and market forces reduce cost—a questionable assumption—the overheads of law firms are substantial and have to be paid for whether by hourly rates or some other fee structure. The scope for radical cost savings in lawyers' fees is limited despite the competition in the marketplace and the increasing realisation by law firms that they must improve their efficiency and control costs. **3–039**

In achieving procedural reform, it is essential, in the authors' opinion, that ADR play a full and constructive role, for otherwise the effect of case management will be diminished. But we must be careful in estimating with too great confidence the overall effect of procedural reform itself. As Judge William Schwartzer, sometime director of the Federal Judicial Centre in the United States has pointed out: **3–040**

---

[12]Since March 1, 1999 the higher judiciary have been required to assess costs in interlocutory hearings up to one day in length. It will be interesting to see what control they are able to exercise.

"There is still a surprising dearth of information about the process of resolving disputes, either by traditional means or by the procedure we call alternatives. We know little, for example, about the comparative cost and time effects of different forms of ADR and the traditional litigation process. We also know little about what litigants are seeking when they come to court; what prompts some litigants and not others to consent to ADR; what litigants value and what satisfies them. Much remains to be learned about assessing the effects of ADR.[13]"

This remains so as the debate provoked by the Rand Report and other research reports in the United States shows.[14]

3–041   The difficulty with case management is that it is itself expensive and time-consuming if it is to be done pro-actively. It requires substantial pre-reading by judges and significant additional time before case management conferences and pre-trial reviews for the lawyers to prepare. Without a considerable increase in the number of judges or the introduction of some form of civil magistracy, the existing system may well not be able to cope with any significant increase in the work of the judges, especially of the district judges. The Government appears reluctant to pay for the introduction of case management; rather, it seeks to reallocate resources in the provision of funding for limited classes of litigation leaving the market to determine the provision of funding for other cases.

3–042   The authors believe that many judges will use their powers to control litigation to achieve the "overriding objective" and there will be a development of the work already begun in certain courts such as the Commercial Court and the Technology and Construction Court. However, without extensive use of ADR the Government's measures will produce little significant change in access to justice, though undoubtedly there will be savings to the public purse in that the recent rate of increase in expenditure on civil legal aid will be capped. Regrettably, limitations on legal aid funding will deny access to the courts to persons who previously enjoyed it. This will be a perverse result of reform. There may well be others.

6. COURT-ATTACHED ADR IN ENGLAND AND WALES

3–043   There is certain limited experience in England and Wales with the use of ADR in conjunction with litigation. In recent years the courts have drawn attention to the value of ADR in the resolution of disputes and it has been the subject of certain practice directions[15].

---

[13]William Schwarzer, ADR and the Federal Courts: Questions and Decisions for the Future, 1994 7 F.J.C. Directions 2.

[14]An Evaluation of Mediation and Early Neutral Evaluation Under the Civil Justice Reform Act, The Institute for Civil Justice, 1996.

[15]Practice Directions of Mr. Justice Waller dated June 7, 1996: Practice Statement: Alternative Dispute resolution: December 10, 1993, Cresswell J. See also Appendix III.

The Commercial Court and the Technology and Construction Court

Use of ADR in the courts has been limited. In the Commercial Court judges   **3–044**
have been prepared to adjourn cases to permit ADR to take place. Some
commercial judges have been more robust than others in exercising the
power of adjournment. The results are interesting. One notable example of
ADR was the adjournment of the claim between H.M.G. and Arthur
Anderson arising from the ill-fated De Lorean investment in Northern
Ireland. This complicated and long-running litigation was settled by
mediation. According to Mr. Justice Colman in an interview in the Law
Society's Gazette of January 8, 1998 over 100 adjournment orders for ADR
had been made and in the overwhelming majority of cases settlement appears
to have been reached. This power has also been used quite frequently in the
Technology and Construction Court. Also in a few cases in the Commercial
Court and in the Technology and Construction Court, judges have given non-
binding advisory opinions (Early Neutral Evaluation) as to the merits of a
case which have resulted in settlement.

Rule 26.4 is a somewhat blunt instrument in promoting settlement. The   **3–045**
control which judges have over proceedings and the obligation to consider
ADR and the promotion of settlement gives judges the opportunity to use
their powers first, to encourage settlement by direct negotiation between the
parties and secondly, if necessary by the intervention of a third party. Judges
in some courts are already doing this in a variety of ways and these
initiatives can be followed. Thus, for example, judges can make procedural
orders which may enable parties to focus more clearly on the points which
divide them. They can compel early disclosure of relevant documents or
order experts to exchange views and to meet to record their points of
agreement or disagreement. Other possibilities include establishing a
timetable for settlement talks. Judges must be innovative and robust in
exercising their powers.

It is only if judges are robust and innovative not only in encouraging   **3–046**
settlement, but also in streamlining the procedural conduct of the case if it
proceeds to trial, that the necessary changes in old attitudes will be achieved.
The new Rules are intended to encourage and require effective collaboration
between the parties at all stages of the litigation. A change in the attitude of
practitioners is therefore essential if the new Rules are to work. By
temperament and experience some judges will be more interventionist than
others in requiring collaboration by the parties' lawyers; but if judges remain
passive and do not intervene then the Woolf reforms will fail.

Regrettably, welcome though the shift in emphasis between Lord Woolf's   **3–047**
Interim and Final Reports is, the wording of the new rules does not create the
impression that settlement, whether by direct negotiation or with the aid of a
third party, is as vital an objective of case management as the efficient
organisation of the case for trial. It might have been better if the "overriding
objective" of Rule 1.1 had contained a reference to the promotion of just,
fair and timely settlement, rather than leaving settlement to be treated as one
example of proper case management under Rule 1.4.

As experience in the U.S. and Australia makes clear[16], effective case   **3–048**

---

[16]See Chap. 5.

management allied to a well-administered ADR scheme can achieve very considerable results of benefit both to the court and to the parties.

Family law disputes

3–049   There is a scheme in operation with respect to family law disputes, the Ancillary Relief Pilot Scheme (Family Courts).

3–050   In 1996 some 28 courts in England and Wales embarked on the Ancillary Relief Pilot Scheme, which was designed to explore new and improved ways of dealing with the resolution of financial and property issues arising in family cases.[17] The aim of the scheme was to provide stricter court control and improved procedures to reduce delay, limit costs and facilitate settlements.

3–051   The scheme has a number of interesting features. The court has taken greater control over the procedural timetable. Whereas previously parties could more easily proceed at their own pace, now there is a specified and strict time frame within which procedural steps must be taken. A form has been created, Form E, which parties must use to disclose their respective financial circumstances. This replaces the looser and more varied way in which disclosure used to take place. Within a specified time of either party applying for ancillary relief from the other, the court now fixes a First Appointment. By the time of that appointment, parties are required to have exchanged information including the Form E, questionnaires, schedules of documents sought, and statements of issues as perceived by each party. Parties and their lawyers are expected to prepare properly for the First Appointment. At that appointment, the district judge gives directions on questionnaires, valuations, expert and other evidence and on the further conduct of the matter. Interim orders or costs orders may be made. The district judge is required to refer the case to a Financial Dispute Resolution (FDR) appointment, unless he decides, exceptionally, that such a referral is not appropriate.

3–052   The FDR meeting is held with a district judge on an evidentially privileged basis to explore possibilities of settlement. That district judge cannot hear the case if it is not settled: a different judge will have to be appointed. At the FDR meeting, the judge will establish what proposals have been exchanged and may comment on these. The judge may indicate what ruling or judgment he or she would make on any aspect if he or she had been hearing the case. Armed with these indications and with the benefit of the judge's comments, the parties and their lawyers will withdraw and be afforded a private opportunity to discuss settlement. The FDR appointment may be adjourned for a short time to allow discussions to take place outside it, or for a longer time if that would be helpful. The court may make a consent order if appropriate, or may give directions for the course of the matter and its hearing.

3–053   In the past, parties were not obliged to indicate what orders they sought, but could leave this undisclosed. Now, if the matter proceeds to a final hearing, each party must make open statements of the orders they seek or

---

[17] Rules 2.71 to 2.77 of the Family Proceedings Rules 1991 contain the procedure for the Pilot Scheme.

propose. Parties must keep costs in mind throughout the proceedings, and must produce estimates at each hearing.

Accountants KPMG were commissioned to report on the Scheme and did so following a quantitative and qualitative approach. Form E was regarded as a significant improvement. FDR had a more mixed response, with discrepancies between different district judges. Settlement rates had improved. Costs data were inadequate, but the indications were that costs savings were not significant. KPMG recommended the introduction of the Scheme nationally, with strict adherence to timetable, sanctions for failure to comply without good cause and some further comments on making the scheme and its implementation more effective. These matters and information from the Principal Registry of the Family Division and from practitioners were all discussed at a seminar on the Pilot Scheme organised by the Solicitors Family Law Association towards the end of 1998.[18]   **3–054**

Reports at the seminar from the Principal Registry and practitioners indicated support for the Scheme, although some aspects required further attention. For example, some improvements were suggested to Form E and attention was drawn to inconsistencies that existed between district judges in the amount of control they exerted and in the way they conducted the FDR appointments. There was almost unanimous support for district judges expressing a view of a case if they held one.   **3–055**

The Pilot Scheme is to be extended to become the national norm with effect from June 2000.   **3–056**

The Court of Appeal

A voluntary scheme has been introduced in the Court of Appeal for appellate mediation. This is an entirely private initiative enjoying the full support of Lord Woolf as Master of the Rolls and also of the Lord Chancellor's Department. A panel of mediators drawn from the ranks of experienced silks and solicitors in various parts of the country has been established, able to mediate cases of various kinds both in London and elsewhere. There are members of the panel with great experience for example, of clinical negligence, personal injury and of commerical cases. The informal and *pro bono* private scheme began with the mediation of a number of appeals pending from decisions at the Central London County Court in cases of awards against the police for false imprisonment and assault. The mediation of these cases followed the clear indication by Lord Woolf in the *Thompson* case[19] that disputes of this nature were clearly suitable for mediation. Of the initial seven cases so mediated, four resulted in immediate settlement, one in a settlement at a later stage and two failed to settle and proceeded to appeal.   **3–057**

But the Court of Appeal scheme is broader in scope than mediation in police assault and false imprisonment cases and has been extended to a number of other appeals such as commercial matters, personal injury damages and clinical negligence.   **3–058**

---

[18] A report on the seminar is contained in an article by Christine Gentry, Eleanor Ingham and Louise Spitz "Ancillary Relief Pilot Scheme seminar" in the SFLA Review, Issue 76, December 1998.

[19] *Thompson v. Comissioner of Police of the Metropolis (and Hsu v. Commissioner of Police of the Metropolis)* [1997] 2 All E.R. 762.

3–059   The scheme is overseen by a multi-disciplinary steering group which meets twice a year and considers both progress and possible improvements to the operation of the scheme. The scheme was most recently refined in November 1998. Now, as soon as an appeal is lodged with the Civil Appeals Office, a letter of invitation to consider ADR, signed by the Master of the Rolls, is sent to the parties' solicitors. The letter encloses an explanatory leaflet and a response form Invitations to consider ADR are sent out in all appeals save for immigration, judicial review, employment, and family cases. A member of staff is available to answer queries, provide general information and help with specific cases. As of May 31, 1999 experience was that about five per cent of appeals had opted for ADR.

Central London County Court

3–060   The main experience with court-annexed mediation in civil cases in England and Wales has been in a pilot mediation scheme at the Central London County Court which is the principal trial centre for county court cases in the south-east of England.

3–061   The mediation scheme was a direct result of the far-sighted initiative of His Hon. Judge Sir Frank White who was the Presiding Judge at the Central London County Court and of his successor His Hon. Judge Neil Butter Q.C. The scheme was established in 1996 and has now become permanent. The scheme was designed to provide a mediation service in non-family civil disputes with a value over £3,000, the then limit of the county court arbitration scheme. The pilot scheme was the subject of a comprehensive report by Professor Hazel Genn of the Faculty of Laws, University College London. Her report is published as No. 5/98 in the Research Series of the Lord Chancellor's Department.[20]

3–062   The scheme was entirely voluntary and operated after court sitting hours by a team of mediators, all volunteers, drawn from various mediation organisations.

Professor Genn's report

3–063   Professor Genn's report shows that:

> "The rate of which both parties accepted mediation offers remained at about *five percent* throughout the life of the scheme and despite vigorous attempts to stimulate demand. Demand was virtually non-existent among personal injury cases, although these comprised almost half of the cases offered mediation. Contract, goods/services disputes and debt cases had the highest levels of demand although the joint acceptance rate was less than ten percent. The joint demand for mediation was *lowest* when both parties had legal representation.
>
> Acceptance of mediation was highest amongst disputes between businesses. Interviews with solicitors rejecting mediation revealed:

---

[20]Research Papers 1997, No. 5/98 the Central London County Court Pilot Mediation Scheme— Evaluation Report, Professor Hazel Genn.

- lack of experience and widespread ignorance of mediation among the legal profession;
- apprehension about showing weakness through accepting mediation within the context of traditional adversarial litigation:
- evidence of litigant resistance to the idea of compromise, particularly in the early stages of litigation." (emphasis added in original)

Although the take-up on an entirely voluntary basis was disappointingly   **3–064** small and reflected widespread ignorance and opposition, particularly on the part of those engaged in personal injury litigation, the outcome of cases mediated was encouraging. As Professor Genn reports:

"The majority (62%) of mediated cases settled at the mediation appointment and this settlement rate remained constant between case types, indicating that mediation can be used across a wide spectrum of cases. Other findings on outcome were that:

- where the plaintiff had legal aid the settlement rate was lower than average;
- the settlement rate at mediation was highest (72%) when neither party had legal representation at the mediation;
- mediated cases had a much higher settlement rate overall than non-mediated cases, whether or not settlement occurred at the mediation appointment, supporting the contention that mediation promotes settlement even after an unsettled mediation.

Plaintiffs settling at mediation appointments appear to be prepared to discount their claims heavily in order to achieve settlement, with average levels of settlement in mediated claims being about £2,000 lower than in non-mediated settlements."

Professor Genn's report found:

"Even on a very conservative estimate, mediated settlements occurred several months earlier than among non-mediated cases. Most parties whose cases settled at mediation believed that the mediation had saved time, although those whose cases did not settle often felt that the mediation had involved them in extra time. Solicitors felt strongly that mediation saved time. There was much more equivocation on the question of cost savings. Only half the plaintiffs settling at mediation believed they had saved costs. Solicitors tended to be more likely to think that costs had been saved. There was a common view that failure to settle at mediation appointment led to increased costs."

Those who mediated, both litigants and advisers, were in favour of the process and Professor Genn concluded that:

"• Mediation is capable of promoting settlement in a wide range of civil cases when parties have volunteered to accept mediation.

- Personal injury cases are amenable to mediation even when both liability and quantum are in issue.
- Mediation offers a process that parties to civil disputes on the whole find satisfying.
- Conflict can be reduced and settlement reached that parties find acceptable.
- Mediation can promote and speed-up settlement.
- It is unclear to what extent mediation saves costs and unsuccessful mediation can increase costs.
- Mediation can magnify power imbalances and works best in civil disputes when there is some rough equality between the parties or in representation.
- Mediators require special personal qualities, good training and experience.
- Demand for mediation is very weak and the legal profession has a crucial role in influencing demand."

Interestingly for those concerned with the debate about the use of evaluation in mediation, Professor Genn found that some of the most successful mediators were barristers, many of whom were prepared to be explicitly evaluative during the course of mediation.[21]

3–065   The very low rate of take-up of the offer to mediate was a matter of particular concern to the proponents of the scheme. Professor Genn investigated the reasons for rejecting offers of mediation, which was done by means of a mediation reply form attached to the mediation offer letter and a number of telephone interviews. She reported that two of the most common reasons given for refusing the offer of mediation were simply that mediation was considered "inappropriate" to the particular case, or that "the case involved complex matters of evidence that would require oral evidence to be given in Court, cross-examination of witnesses etc." Professor Genn records that 17 per cent of plaintiffs and 18 per cent of defendants gave this reason. Other common reasons for rejecting mediation were that there was a dispute over fact, law or both and that this was cited more often by plaintiffs than defendants, and that the case would settle in any case so that mediation was unnecessary (11 per cent of plaintiffs and 10 per cent of defendants).

3–066   With respect to personal injury cases Professor Genn concluded that:

"Agreeing to early settlement discussions does not fit in with defence strategy of making plaintiffs wait before offers of settlement or payments into court are made".

---

[21]Executive Summary, Mediators.

Professor Genn tabulated the reasons for rejecting mediation as follows: **3–067**

Reasons given to the Court by plaintiffs and defendants for rejecting mediation

Reason for rejecting mediation given on mediation reply form sent to court	Plaintiffs (n = 207)	Defendants (n = 197)
Mediation "inappropriate" (no explanation)	17%	10%
No common ground/case won't settle	14%	12%
Complex evidence/expert evidence	17%	18%
Dispute over fact/law/both	11%	4%
Case will settle in any case	11%	9%
Need a court ruling/want to go to trial	9%	8%
No merit in claim/defence	6%	8%
Offer of mediation too early in litigation	3%	15%
Not appropriate for personal injury cases	6%	7%
Too expensive to mediate	4%	1%
Want case transferred to arbitration	0%	4%
Just don't want to do it	1%	5%

Professor Genn concluded from her telephone interviews with solicitors   **3–068**
that there was a considerable lack of knowledge about mediation. She stated
that:

> "If mediation and other forms of ADR are to become more widely
> accepted and used in appropriate cases, there is a genuine challenge in the
> need rapidly to educate the grass roots of the legal profession. The fact
> that the litigation departments of commercial megafirms are beginning to
> speak the language of 'dispute resolution' will not have any immediate
> effect on the approach to litigation in the High Street."

Professor Genn concluded with respect to the attitude of the profession   **3–069**
that:

> "The evidence of the research indicates that, at the grass roots, the
> profession lacks knowledge and experience of mediation. As a result,
> solicitors are generally unenthusiastic, frequently apprehensive and
> occasionally positively hostile to a dispute resolution technique that is not
> well understood and does not fit well with conventional adversarial
> litigation strategy. These are facts rather than criticisms and are matters
> that can be partly addressed through education. However, the enormity of
> the culture change that would be necessary to achieve even a modest shift
> from traditional litigation strategy to mediation, especially among personal
> injury litigators and their clients, should not be underestimated."

3–070   With respect to savings of time and cost, Professor Genn noted that the difficulties of reliably establishing this kind of assessment are profound even when objective measurements are available. She attempted to assess savings with respect to case lengths. Her general conclusion was:

> "that even where settlement is not achieved with mediation, the overall length of the case to settlement is shorter than might be expected."

and that:

> "mediation when successful, is capable of bringing cases to a more rapid conclusion than if cases were settled during the course of normal litigation procedures."

3–071   Interestingly, some 60 per cent of those who responded to Professor Genn's enquiries thought that the mediation had reduced the amount of time spent on the dispute:

> "Amongst those that settled at mediation, however, over three quarters (77%) believe that the mediation had saved time whilst amongst those whose cases had not settled at mediation, only one third (32%) felt that the mediation had saved time and the same proportion (36%) thought that the mediation had increased the amount of time spent on resolving the dispute."

3–072   It had been thought by those monitoring the scheme that the absence of legal aid was a positive hindrance to those who would otherwise be interested in mediating their disputes. That reason was given on a number of occasions for the failure to accept the offer to mediate. After some negotiation and discussion with the Legal Aid Board, legal aid was made available subject to certain limits for the provision of assistance and representation at the mediation. It was only used in one case, which tends rather to suggest that the absence of legal aid may have been used as an excuse by those unwilling for other reasons to participate in the mediation scheme. Though there is no doubt that were mediation to become a regular feature of the civil justice system and particularly if reference to court-annexed mediation was to become mandatory, the provision of financial assistance would be essential. The Government recognises this in its proposals for the Community Legal Service and for the operation by the Legal Services Commission of the Community Legal Fund.

3–073   Professor Genn's conclusions on the different styles of mediating are interesting. Professor Genn concluded that the "counselling/therapeutic" approach was not generally welcomed by those concerned with the resolution of commercial disputes. Far more effective was the bargaining approach particularly with mediators as Professor Genn put it prepared to,

> "cross the line between probing strengths and weaknesses of the parties cases, to communicating subtly or even directly their own view of the parties' chances of succeeding at trial."

A "bullying" approach to a settlement on the part of mediators was on the whole not well received. It was a cause of complaint and: **3–074**

"led parties sometimes to reflect that they had been pushed into a compromise to which they might not otherwise have agreed."

Professor Genn concluded that: **3–075**

"In civil disputes mediation clearly has the potential for achieving acceptable outcomes and for facilitating reconciliation where the parties have, or would like, a continuing relationship. There are, however, important questions to be addressed about procedures, training, ethics and accountability."

Professor Genn pointed out that:

"whatever the future holds in terms of formal policy in relation to compulsory mediation, the growing emphasis on the value of mediation and the development of grass roots ADR initiatives in courts, suggests that discussion about the training of mediators and mediator quality control would be timely. There is also a need for ADR to be planted firmly within the law curriculum."

The Patents County Court

Another pilot scheme was established at the Patents County Court, part of the **3–076** Central London County Court. The Patents County Court was established to offer litigants a faster and cheaper specialist court for the resolution of patent and registered design disputes. This reflected growing concern that these cases were much more expensive to litigate in the High Court than in equivalent jurisdictions in continental Europe such as Holland and Germany.

His Hon. Judge Peter Ford, the presiding judge, took the initiative in **3–077** setting up an arbitration and mediation scheme with the support (given entirely *pro bono*) of some retired judges, practitioners and others. Unfortunately, the Patents County Court has achieved only modest success. Apparently, practitioners find it difficult to abandon adversarial procedures and old habits die hard. The arbitration scheme has not been used and while practitioners have enquired about the mediation scheme it also has not been used, though indications are that some cases may have been mediated privately. Hitherto, Judge Ford has not had the power to compel mediation or arbitration, but since April 26, 1999, he may (like any other judge) exercise his powers under section 26.4. It will be interesting to see if these powers enable the Patents County Court to realise the hopes of Judge Ford and others involved in its establishment.

It is understood that there are no plans to introduce in the High Court **3–078** mediation schemes in patent and registered design cases. There is no lack of willingness to do so, on the contrary. The difficulty is simply that it has long been a feature of this branch of the law (currently to be found in section 70 of the Patents Act 1977 and other legislation[22]) that it is actionable to threaten to take proceedings in respect of alleged infringement.

3–079   Thus, if a party has what he considers to be a good claim of infringement and would like to negotiate a settlement, he cannot threaten proceedings and then negotiate, as would for example be perfectly permissible if the case was one of personal injury or clinical negligence, for the mere threat of proceedings is enough to found an action by his opponent. It also makes the application of the cost sanctions rule somewhat problematic. It is clear that some revision of section 70 of the Patents Act 1977 and the other legislation may be required to facilitate settlement of disputes which have not reached litigation. In an interesting and persuasive judgment on the extent of without prejudice protection for negotiations between disputants in patent cases, Mr. Justice Laddie held that:

> "In absence of binding authority, it seems to me that, at least, a threat which consists of no more than a statement of the patentee's rights and his intention to sue on them and which is made in the course of without prejudice negotiations with the source of allegedly infringing goods is protected from being used as the basis of subsequent proceedings. Were it otherwise, the owners of patents (and registered designs and registered trade marks) could never take part in preemptive discussions to prevent litigation and the threats provision in s. 70 of the Act (and its equivalent in the Registered Designs Act 1949 and the Trade Marks Act 1994) would have had the effect of making litigation more likely. In this type of case the public interest in suppressing threats is weaker than the public interest in encouraging compromise. But different considerations might apply where the threats are made in a deliberately damaging way and beyond what is fair and appropriate. For example there is a stronger public interest in discouraging patentees from writing virulent threatening letters to their competitor's customers. It may be—it is not necessary to decide the issue in this application—that if one trader were to send threatening letters to his competitor's customers each bearing a without prejudice label, he would be prevented from taking advantage of the privilege. The court might not accept that the claim to privilege was made bona fide or it may say that such an exercise was primarily designed to inflict damage on the competitor and for that reason is to be treated as sufficiently improper to justify lifting the veil."[23]

7. THE CIVIL JUSTICE COUNCIL: ADR SUB-COMMITTEE

3–080   The Civil Justice Council set up as a consequence of Lord Woolf's reforms has an ADR sub-committee under the chairmanship of Professor Martin Partington of Bristol University. Both the Committee and the Lord Chancellor's Department are considering the future of ADR schemes attached to the courts as part of the civil justice system. The Lord Chancellor's

---

[22]See also Registered Designs Act 1949 s. 26; Copyright Designs and Patents Act 1988, s. 253 and Trade Marks Act 1994 s. 71.

[23]*Unilever v. Procter & Gamble*, see n. 6.

Department has yet formulate its policy, but the indications are that ADR is increasingly regarded by those responsible for the administration of the civil justice system as a very important aspect of access to justice.

It remains to be seen whether the Lord Chancellor's Department will take   **3–081** the initiative in establishing a national scheme of court-annexed mediation or whether it will leave it to local initiative to establish schemes along the lines of the one at the Central London County Court. But it is clear, whether national or local schemes are implemented, that the support and participation of the private sector is essential if court-annexed mediation is to work. This in turn emphasises the importance of such issues as training, accreditation, responsibility and ethics. However, at the root of the debate is the question whether references to mediation should be mandatory. In both the Central London County Court and Court of Appeal pilot schemes which are entirely voluntary, the acceptance rate was approximately five per cent of those interested.

Although there is a high rate of settlement in cases which do proceed to   **3–082** voluntary mediation, the impact of the voluntary schemes in, for example, relieving the pressure on judicial resources, is marginal. Only if court-annexed ADR schemes are made compulsory is there any real prospect of substantial benefits both to the courts and to litigants.

The authors believe that the case for court-annexed mediation being made   **3–083** mandatory in most civil and commercial cases is becoming compelling and it is only a matter of time before the economic and commercial pressures to achieve wider and more cost efficient access to justice will lead to the introduction of mandatory schemes. This is what has happened in the United States.[24] But if mandatory schemes are to be introduced very careful consideration must be given to ensuring that the fundamental constitutional right of access to the courts is safeguarded and that the courts are vigilant in excluding cases which ought not to be referred, and equally vigilant in preventing abuse of those cases which are referred.

If judges are to exercise their powers to promote settlement they will need   **3–084** to have confidence in those who undertake mediations and this in turn places a high responsibility on the Court Service and professional bodies such as the Bar Council and The Law Society to ensure high standards of competence and integrity of those who offer ADR. It also means that judges will require some training in ADR and there will need to be some system of accreditation and monitoring of those who mediate.

8. CONCLUSIONS

3–085

Something had to be done about the crisis in the civil justice system. No democracy can tolerate such a massive denial of access to justice. Lord Woolf's attempt to remedy serious procedural abuse and injustice merits recognition and full support. The Lord Chancellor's objectives of improving access to justice not only by supporting Lord Woolf's proposals, but by

---

[24] See Chap. 5.

changing radically the financing and structure of the provision of legal
services are more controversial. The question is: will all these radical and

3–086 comprehensive proposals work?

Sir Peter Middleton's warning that the lawyers can wreck the Woolf
reforms and that the judges have a high responsibility to make them work, is
clearly true. Too many well-meaning and apparently sensible attempts to
introduce procedural change have ended in procedural failure, frustrated by
incompetence and narrow self-interest. One example in recent years is the
exchange of witness statements pre-trial. This has been seriously abused and
there has been a significant increase in the cost of preparing for trial with no
commensurate reduction in the lengths of hearings. Another example is the
abuse of the role of expert witnesses in litigation. Despite Lord Wilberforce's
characteristically principled definition of the purpose of expert testimony[25]
and Cresswell J.'s clear guidelines in the *Ikarian Reefer*,[26] all too frequently
unnecessary evidence is given by little more than partisan advocates
masquerading as independent experts. A whole industry of expensive
litigation support services has developed in the last 20 years, largely on the
back of the legal aid fund and uncontrolled by the judges who bear

3–087 considerable responsibility for the resulting abuse.

The Woolf reforms give judges the obligation and power to eradicate
procedural abuses such as these. It remains to be seen if they will use their
power, but there is no alternative to robust and determined judicial
intervention if case management is to work. There is a clear need for
effective monitoring of the effect of the Woolf reforms, perhaps by an
official body which in conjunction with the Lord Chief Justice and the
Division Heads would have the power to issue Procedural Directions to assist
the proper implementation of the Woolf reforms. There is also a clear need
for effective monitoring of ADR schemes. It would be difficult, perhaps
impossible, and clearly very expensive to monitor every scheme as
thoroughly as Professor Genn did at Central London County Court, but some
system of monitoring and reporting needs to be established to understand

3–088 what is happening and to be able to make informed decisions for change.

Case management means that judges must be far more interventionist than
hitherto in directing and controlling the timetable and speed of litigation. If
judges exercise their powers properly they will ensure a far greater control
than hitherto over the presentation of evidence both documentary and oral

3–089 which the parties wish to bring before the court.

Case management, robustly implemented, will improve the quality of
decision-making and ought to result in more efficient and economic
proceedings and earlier and fairer settlement. But it will not save money in
the overall administration of the civil justice system. Some individual
litigants may benefit from cost savings, though litigation is labour intensive
and will remain so even under Woolf. Lawyers' fees are high and beyond the
reach of most citizens. The scope for introducing fixed fees for certain
classes of work is limited. If such fees, for a high volume case load, fail to

---

[25]*Whitehouse v. Jordan* [1981] W.L.R. 246.
[26]*The Ikarian Reefer* [1995] 1 Lloyd's Rep. 455.

produce a satisfactory financial return for lawyers, then the work will not be **3–090** done, or it will be done very badly.

The experience of the County Court Small Claims arbitration system in the last 15 years illustrates well the complexities of improving access to justice. The county court scheme clearly meets a real public need for fast and very low cost claims recovery with a negligible risk of liability for costs if an adverse result is obtained. There are signs that the county court system is not used by the most disadvantaged members of society, but the answer to that **3–091** problem does not lie wholly in procedural reform.

Under Woolf the financial limits of the arbitration scheme have been raised again. This is welcome and the level might well have been raised yet higher, perhaps to £10,000 to the extent of subsuming the Fast Track. But increases in the limits merely serve to increase the burden on the district judges who are grossly overloaded with work and will have even greater responsibilities **3–092** for efficient case management under Woolf.

There may be scope for improving the speed and efficiency of the county court arbitration scheme by further procedural changes. Practice amongst the district judges varies considerably. Some are interventionist and blunt the edges of the adversarial system. Others go further and act more like mediators trying to coax the parties towards settlement. Some are formal and **3–093** traditional in their approach.

Such differences are unavoidable and no system of procedural change will remove them. If the small claims system is to develop it will require either a very substantial increase in the number of district judges or the use of private sector arbitrators and mediators operating a form of court-annexed mediation on a fast and very low cost basis.

Funding

As Lord Woolf clearly recognised, proper funding is essential to the success **3–094** of his reforms. Unfortunately, the funding of his reforms was beyond his remit. The Government has proposed radical changes in funding. There is reason to believe that the funding of personal injury and clinical negligence litigation will be largely provided by the private sector in a myriad of ways. Thus, for example, trades unions and professional organisations can provide more litigation support than they do at present. The insurance market is already responding to the requirements of the market place by offering various kinds of insurance to enable proceedings to be brought and to give some protection against the cost impact of an adverse result. Conditional and contingent fees have a role to play and enterprising lawyers, both solicitors and barristers, will use such arrangements increasingly and find ways of implementing them efficiently and properly.

The Government has made it plain that legal aid will continue to be **3–095** available for actions involving the citizen and the State, so that abuse of executive power will still be curbed by the courts. However, there is little doubt that because of limited funding for litigants, the financial and procedural reforms now in place will not improve access to justice for the vast majority of citizens. On the contrary, the funding changes will prevent access to justice for many of those who were hitherto eligible for legal aid. More people will be disenfranchised.

Settlement

3–096 A central theme of Lord Woolf's reforms is the promotion of settlement. At present the overwhelming majority of cases before the courts settle. The acid test of Lord Woolf's reforms is whether cases will settle earlier without the pressure of costs and therefore whether those settlements are fairer, driven more by the merits of the case than the cost hazards of losing it.

3–097 It is here that judges will need to be particularly watchful and robust. Pre-action protocols and case management with its emphasis on earlier and fuller disclosure of the strengths and weaknesses of a litigant's position, involve a greater expenditure before and in the early stages of litigation than traditional methods.

3–098 But the information which such expenditure produces under the new Rules must be used not only to organise the proceedings more efficiently, but as a basis for settlement negotiations. This is essential if Woolf is to work.

3–099 It may be that the need for third party intervention in all cases will be reduced, particularly if judges are interventionist in encouraging the parties to settle early through direct negotiation. To do this the judges will need to make it clear that they expect as a matter of course and of obligation to the court, that parties and their advisors will have tried to settle before the commencement of litigation. Also judges will sometimes need to indicate in a preliminary and non-binding way what they think of the parties' respective positions.

3–100 There is nothing novel or daring about this: in many civil law jurisdictions there is a procedural obligation upon a judge to indicate how a case could be settled as, for example, the practice of the German and Swiss judges makes clear. This principle is already found in the Ancillary Relief Pilot Scheme in use in many courts in England and Wales.

3–101 Judges now have the power under Rule 26.4 of the Civil Procedure Rules to adjourn cases for ADR to take place; and they have the additional power, by denying or giving cost awards, to punish unreasonable behaviour on the part of the litigants either in refusing to go to ADR or in abusing the system. The courts will need to establish how best to exercise these powers, particularly in making cost sanctions. As indicated earlier this is not free from difficulty. An enquiry by the judge into the conduct of the mediation will simply provoke time-consuming and expensive satellite litigation and will also breach a fundamental precept of mediation, namely confidentiality.

3–102 A solution which has been discussed is that in very exceptional circumstances—where, for example, the judge had himself adjourned a case for mediation and no principled explanation for the failure to settle had been given—the judge without extensive enquiry might reflect that in his cost orders. No hard and fast guidelines can be laid down in the abstract. If the power to adjourn is exercised frequently and judges appear to be willing to impose cost sanctions where mediations fail, then pragmatic and principled guidelines will need to be established taking fully into account the entirely proper concerns which experienced mediators have about the integrity of the process. These considerations carry even more weight if a system of automatic mandatory referral is introduced in certain cases. Perhaps there may be scope for considering compulsory disclosure of the results of negotiation prior to any automatic references, and the judge may be informed of this at the end of the case. This may help the judge to decide whether or not either or both parties genuinely tried to reach a settlement.

Alternatively, perhaps there may be scope for either party at the end of an **3–103** inconclusive mediation, to summarise their proposals on the basis of a *"Calderbank"* letter, and to submit these to the other party to put them at risk as to costs.[27]

The reforms have fudged the issue whether or not court-annexed mediation should be voluntary or mandatory. In robust hands the powers given to the judges may well acquire a mandatory flavour. But whether mandatory or not, practitioners will realise that they will be asked whether attempts have been made to settle and that they will have to advise their clients about settlement. Hopefully, the principal barrier to commencing negotiation, namely the desire not to appear weak, will be removed, and once parties know they are expected to talk about settlement, they may well then reach agreement.

It should not be forgotten that, although negotiation and mediation are at **3–104** the heart of the process, ADR involves many different techniques of bringing parties together. Particularly relevant to the resolution of disputes in court is neutral evaluation of the strengths and weaknesses of the parties' case. Many parties want this, as experience in the United States and as Professor Genn's report on the Central London County Court Pilot Mediation Scheme clearly show. Probably there is scope for expanding the provision of early neutral evaluation.[28] However, the judiciary has not the resources to provide neutral evaluation on any large scale. Only the private sector can do so.

It would be unrealistic and grossly unfair to judge the Woolf reforms and **3–105** the Lord Chancellor's ambitions in the short term. The authors believe that there will be an improvement in the efficiency of litigation and the increasing and alarming drain on the public purse of civil legal aid will now be capped. The market place will provide for those able to pay or able to effect insurance, and enter into conditional and contingent fee arrangements with enterprising and efficient lawyers. We will, however, need to develop safeguards to ensure that citizens are protected against injustice. The Lord Chancellor's "75 per cent" test (the notion that legal aid should only be granted where there is a 75 per cent or more chance of success) is too blunt an instrument to be applied in all cases. And litigants may not want to bring claims, but they may be forced to defend them.

It may well be that with the decline in legal aid for individuals, special **3–106** interest groups turn to the courts and finance litigation in such areas as environment, health and consumer law. It may be that other forms of group action develop so that the gap caused by the removal of legal aid for the individual is partially filled by spreading cost and risk amongst many. Thus, cases of public importance may continue to reach the courts, though the certainty of severe injustice to individuals in certain cases now that legal aid has been removed, remains.

It is also very speculative to assess the possible effects upon the conduct **3–107**

---

[27] A *"Calderbank"* letter is one that is without prejudice and evidentially privileged during the case, but which may be shown to the judge after judgment has been given, to see its effects on costs. If a party has not achieved more in the trial than was offered in the *Calderbank* letter, that party may be ordered to pay the costs incurred after the *Calderbank* letter.

[28] See Chap. 16 for a more detailed consideration of the different forms of neutral evaluation.

of civil litigation of the European Convention on Human Rights, now part of our statute law. It is thought by many that the effect of the Convention (particularly Article 6) will be most felt in the criminal courts as an antidote to procedural abuse by the prosecution and failure to fulfil the obligations, clearly established and all too often disregarded, to prosecute fairly. But the Convention has a very definite role in the civil courts in preventing abuse due to inequality of arms and safeguarding the right to a fair and properly conducted trial. Case management and court-annexed ADR systems properly administered can produce access to justice and ensure compliance with the Convention. Oppressive case management and badly administered court-annexed ADR will erode access to justice and breach human rights.

3–108   There are grounds for cautious optimism in thinking that judges will be more interventionist than they have been hitherto in encouraging settlement. But only ADR services of various kinds attached to the courts and provided by the private sector have any real prospect of achieving Lord Woolf's objectives of earlier and fairer settlement. Also the Lord Chancellor's ambitions of improving access to justice by providing a range of measures for dispute resolution through a Community Legal Service will only work if ADR is allowed to realise its full potential. That will require policy decisions by the Government and the provision of resources both financial and administrative. We may well end up in Professor Sander's multi-door court-house.[29]

---

[29] See Chap. 5.

CHAPTER 4

ARBITRATION AND OTHER ADJUDICATION

1. ARBITRATION

Arbitration has a long history. For many centuries it has been widely used for **4–001** the settlement of a variety of disputes between states, state entities and private parties and between private parties. This chapter is concerned principally with arbitration as a means of dispute resolution in commercial contracts. Statistical evidence of the use of arbitration is scant, but such as exists combined with the evidence of experience, suggests that in some jurisdictions the role of arbitration is at least as important in commercial dispute resolution, if not more so, as the role of the courts. In England the use of arbitration in certain specialist fields such as construction, maritime, commodity, and commercial and agricultural property leases, is clearly greater than resort to the courts. It is also clear that since the New York Convention of 1958 there has been an unprecedented growth in the use of arbitration for the settlement of disputes in international trade.

Rastell, *Termes de la Ley* (1624) contains an excellent definition of the **4–002** arbitrator, who is "a disinterested person, to whose judgment and decision matters in dispute are referred".

But defining arbitration is not so easy. No statutory definition is available **4–003** in English law. Textbook writers do set out necessary requirements for a means of dispute resolution to be treated as arbitration,[1] but there is an apparent acceptance of the lack of a general definition, perhaps typical of the common law approach. The foreign reader of Mustill & Boyd should therefore not be surprised to find reference to the celebrated observation of Scrutton L.J. on the definition of an elephant (as being incapable of definition but not of recognition) before finding a discussion of the requirements of arbitration.[2]

Arbitration in English law may be defined as a private mechanism for the **4–004** resolution of disputes which takes place in private pursuant to an agreement between two or more parties, under which the parties agree to be bound by the decision to be given by the arbitrator according to law after a fair hearing, such decision being enforceable at law.[3]

---

[1] *e.g.* Mustill & Boyd, *The Law and Practice of Commercial Arbitration in England*, (2nd ed., 1989), pp. 41 *et seq.*
[2] *ibid.* pp. 38–52.
[3] See also P. M. B. Rowland, *Arbitration Law and Practice*, (1988), p. 1: " ... [A]rbitration is a

49

4–005   One leading French commentator has defined arbitration as follows:

> *"L'arbitrage est l'institution par laquelle les parties confient à des arbitres, librement désignés par elles, la mission de trancher leurs litiges"*;[4]

and Schwab has defined arbitration as follows:

> *"Schiedsgerichte . . . sind Privatgerichte aus einem oder mehreren Schiedsrichtern, denen die Entscheidung bürgerlicher Rechtsstreitigkeiten an Stelle staatlicher Gerichte durch private Willenserklärung übertragen ist".*[5]

Arbitration of commercial disputes

4–006   Since the Second World War and particularly since the New York Convention of 1958,[6] the growth of domestic arbitration in certain countries (for example, in the United Kingdom and the United States), and of international commercial arbitration has been quite dramatic.

4–007   The sources of the law of arbitration in international commercial disputes are international conventions such as New York 1958 and the European Convention of 1961, international model laws and model rules, institutional rules such as those of the International Chamber of Commerce (ICC) and the London Court of International Arbitration (LCIA) and municipal legislation, with some jurisdictions such as France, having separate statutes for international and domestic disputes. To those formal sources must be added an increasing body of academic writing including reports of awards to which practitioners look for guidance though not for precedent.

4–008   In England, the Departmental Advisory Committee (DAC), appointed to advise the Secretary of State for Trade and Industry, in its report published in September 1989[7] on the UNCITRAL Model Law[8] ("the Model Law"), advised that a new arbitration statute should be enacted which would consolidate existing legislation, codify the more important and uncontroversial principles of English arbitration law and do so following the structure and logic of the Model Law and where appropriate use the actual language of the Model Law. The object was to produce a statute in straightforward language, comprehensible to the layman. This is particularly important given that a striking feature of English domestic arbitration (not one shared by civil law jurisdictions) is that most arbitrations in England are conducted by lay arbitrators sitting alone and are not subject to the supervision of an institution beyond the initial appointment of the arbitrator.

---

consensual system of judicature directed to the resolution of commercial disputes in private".

[4] "Arbitration is the institution by which the parties entrust to Arbitrators, freely chosen by them, the task of resolving their disputes." de Boisséson, *Le droit français de l'arbitrage* (2nd ed., 1990), p. 5.

[5] "Arbitration Tribunals are private courts of one or more arbitrators to whom is transferred by agreement the power of decision in relation to civil legal disputes in place of state courts." Schwab, *Schiedsgerichtsbarkeit* (3rd ed., 1979), p. 1.

[6] 330 U.N.T.S. (1959) 38.

[7] Commonly known as the Mustill Report after the then Chairman of the Committee.

[8] Subtitled "A New Arbitration Act?".

As paragraph 109 of the report shows, the DAC was particularly conscious of the need to preserve London in the van of preferred venues for international commercial arbitration.

The Arbitration Act 1996

After a long and difficult gestation the Arbitration Act 1996 came into force **4–009** on January 31, 1997. The Act represents a radical development in English Arbitration Law.

The main policy is expressed in a trilogy of sections, namely 1, 33 and 40. **4–010** This expresses a quite new and radical policy. What the Act seeks to do is to recognise and reinforce the principle of party autonomy which has been the dominant principle of international commercial arbitration since the New York Convention. The Act recognises party autonomy, but it imposes upon arbitrators and the parties certain duties in order to achieve the objectives expressly set out as general principles in section 1 of Part 1 of the statute.

"1. The provisions of this Part are founded on the following principles, and shall be construed accordingly:

(a) the object of arbitration is to obtain the fair resolution of disputes by an impartial tribunal without unnecessary delay or expense;

(b) the parties should be free to agree how their disputes are resolved, subject only to such safeguards as are necessary in the public interest;

(c) in matters governed by this Part the court should not intervene except as provided by this Part."

By section 33 the arbitral tribunal must, and the provision is mandatory,[9] **4–011** apply these principles in acting (a) fairly and impartially as between the parties giving each party a reasonable opportunity of putting its case and dealing with that of its opponent, and in (b) adopting procedures suitable to the circumstances of the particular case, avoiding unnecessary delay or expense so as to provide a fair means for the resolution of the matters falling to be determined. The tribunal by subsection 2 is expressly enjoined to comply.

"with that general duty in conducting the arbitral proceedings, in its decisions on matters of procedure and evidence and in the exercise of all other powers conferred on it".

By section 40 the corresponding general duty is imposed upon the parties **4–012** who are by subsection 1 of section 40 obliged to:

"do all things necessary for the proper and expeditious conduct of the proceedings".

This obligation by subsection 2:

---

[9] See Sched. 1 to the Act of 1996.

"includes—(a) complying without delay with any determination of the tribunal as to procedural or evidential matters, or with any order or directions of the tribunal, and (b) where appropriate, taking without delay any necessary steps to obtain a decision of the Court on a preliminary question of jurisdiction or law (see Sections 32 and 45)".

4–013   The powers of the tribunal under section 33 are reinforced by a number of provisions of the statute particularly those to be found in section 34 which cover procedural and evidentiary matters. These provisions in effect enable the arbitrators to control the procedure which is to be adopted. This is of particular importance given the English tradition in arbitration of general commercial disputes (rather than the specialist ones) of requiring considerable disclosure of documents and the presentation of evidence orally, buttressed by extensive oral argument from the advocates. The combination of sections 33 and 34 enables the arbitrators when confronted with a procedural dispute to find the procedural solution which is most economic, most expeditious and fair. What the tribunal cannot do, and this was a matter of some debate within the DAC and elsewhere, is to impose its will as to procedure and evidence in contradiction to any agreement of the parties.

The essential features of arbitration

4–014   The arbitral process is consensual in nature, for it rests on agreement between the parties. There can be no arbitration proper without an arbitration agreement, and there can be no arbitration initiated by, or conducted against, a person who is not a party to the arbitration agreement. Developed arbitration law admits the validity of arbitration agreements and enforces them, which means that the ordinary courts may not (in principle) hear a dispute which is to be referred to arbitration and will stay proceedings to enable the arbitral process to function.

4–015   As a general rule, the courts have limited jurisdiction, when the parties have entered into a valid arbitration agreement.[10] First, the courts have jurisdiction to grant interim relief of various kinds, for example, to preserve the subject matter of the dispute[11]; secondly, they have jurisdiction in order to support the arbitral process where it breaks down, such as in the appointment of arbitrators (supportive function); thirdly, they have jurisdiction in order to ensure that basic standards of justice are upheld (the supervisory function); and fourthly, they have jurisdiction to enforce the award.

---

[10] This idea is reflected in Art. 5 UNCITRAL Model Law 1985: "In matters governed by this Law, no court shall intervene except where so provided in this Law". For a discussion of the relationship between courts and the arbitral tribunal when parties have entered into a valid arbitration agreement see Goldman, "The Complementary Roles of Judges and Arbitrators in Ensuring that International Commercial Arbitration is Effective", in *60 Years of ICC Arbitration—A Look at the Future* 257 (1984); M. Rubino-Sammartano, *International Arbitration Law* (1990) at pp. 229–250.

[11] See, *e.g.* Art. 9 UNCITRAL Model Law 1985: "It is not incompatible with an arbitration agreement for a party to request, before or during arbitral proceedings, from a court an interim measure of protection and for a court to grant such measure." See also Art. 8.5 ICC Rules of Conciliation 1988.

Procedural freedom

The policy expressed in the 1996 Act of recognising party autonomy by 4–016
allowing arbirators and parties freedom is in accord with international
practice in the developed arbitral jurisdictions. The second main feature of
modern commercial arbitration practice in developed systems is that the
parties may organise their proceedings as they like and, for example, may
choose an adversarial or inquisitorial procedure, or a mixture of the two.[12]
The tribunal itself can be appointed by the parties either directly, or by some
appointing authority agreed upon by them. The courts in their supportive role
will assist in this process,[13] or alternatively, if the arbitration is institutional
such as under the aegis of the LCIA or the ICC, the institution will do so.[14]

Although the parties appoint the arbitrators, the tribunal has a duty to be 4–017
impartial and to act judicially.[15] A breach of that duty may result in the
arbitrator being challenged and eventually removed by the court or, by the
arbitral institution concerned.[16] It may also lead to an annulment of the
award.[17] There is an increasing trend internationally to define what is meant
by independence and impartiality of arbitrators and to establish codes of
ethics and conduct.[18] Some consider this trend may have gone too far.

The freedom of the parties to organise their procedure is constrained by 4–018
basic principles of fairness referred to in different legal systems by different
terms of art, but very similar in intention, *e.g.* natural justice, due process,
principe du contradictoire, rechtliches Gehör, and *droit dêtre entendu.* In the
continental European systems as well as in the United States legal system,
such fundamental rules apply to arbitration because the arbitrators are
perceived to be performing a judicial function.[19]

It is sometimes not realised that the freedom of the parties to organise the 4–019
arbitration procedure as they like (even in domestic cases) has been a striking
feature of the English law of arbitration.[20] Although it was the orthodox view
in this country before the 1996 Act that arbitrators were bound by the law of
England, even as to admissibility in the taking of evidence, and should
conduct the proceedings in adversarial fashion, the importance of these
principles was greatly reduced in practice as the parties were free to agree on
other rules and methods. Such an agreement did not need to be express and
was readily implied.[21]

---

[12]This is a far more significant feature of arbitration than the freedom which the parties have to
choose the proper law, for parties have this equally, whether in arbitration or before the court.

[13]*e.g.* 1034, German Code of Civil Procedure 1998.

[14]Art. 2 ICC Rules of Conciliation 1988; Art. 5 London Court of International Arbitration Rules
1998.

[15]This requirement is expressed in international arbitration conventions (see, *e.g.* Art. 14
Washington Convention), arbitration rules (see, *e.g.* Art. 2 of the ICC Rules of Arbitration
1998 or Art. 5.2 Rules of the London Court of International Arbitration 1998) and national
legal systems (see, *e.g.* 51 Italian Code of Civil Procedure). See also Art. 12 of the
UNCITRAL Model Law 1985.

[16]815–831 Italian Code of Civil Procedure (removal by court).

[17]See, *e.g.* 1484, para. 6 French *Nouveau Code de Procédure Civile.*

[18]See, *e.g.* Canon II of the AAA–ABA Code of Ethics for Arbitrators in Commercial Disputes
(1977), reprinted in ABA, *Commercial Arbitration for the 1990s,* pp. 349 *et seq.*

[19]de Boisséson, *Le droit francçais de l'arbitrage,* p. 180: "*l'arbitre est un véritable juge...*";
Burshell v. March, 58 U.S. 344, 349 (1955): "arbitrators are judges chosen by the parties."

[20]*ibid.* pp. 48–49 and 279–280, Mustill & Boyd.

[21]*ibid.* pp. 59 *et seq.* Mustill & Boyd.

4–020   Now, by the new statute, any residual doubts as to arbitrators' powers to control the procedure have been swept away. Sections 33 and 34 make it clear that the yardsticks of economy, expedition and fairness must be observed and the specific powers under section 34 of the Act give the arbitrators a full panoply of power.

4–021   There is strong anecdotal evidence to suggest that the standards in domestic arbitration in England, particularly with respect to the construction industry, declined during the 1980s. Despite decisions to the contrary by very distinguished judges such as Lord Goff in *Carlisle Place v. Wimpey*[22] (a construction case) and frequent public pronouncements to the same effect by leading judicial figures, arbitrators continued to conduct proceedings slavishly following High Court procedures. Part of the problem was undoubtedly due to the fact that unlike many other jurisdictions, domestic arbitration in England is largely conducted by sole arbitrators who are not legally qualified. They are drawn from other professional disciplines, principally civil engineering, architecture, building surveying and accountancy. Matters reached the stage where it became commonplace when negotiating construction contracts for the parties expressly to consent to a right of appeal to the court on a point of law. There is also evidence to suggest that commercial parties were avoiding arbitration altogether by providing that their disputes should be resolved in the courts. It is to be hoped that statutory application of party autonomy will encourage arbitrators to be bold and innovative in finding procedural solutions which give effect to the objectives of section 1 and that arbitrators will observe the requirements of section 33.

A binding award

4–022   It is a principal feature of commercial arbitration that the award should be binding.[23] It may or may not be final. In some jurisdictions it is possible to challenge an award, if there are defects in it. In other jurisdictions, such as Switzerland,[24] the parties are generally at liberty to agree to exclude the control of the courts over an award made in the country. But there is no trend to such exclusion agreements. The Dutch, for example, felt it unnecessary to have such a provision in their 1986 statute preferring to limit the grounds for review of awards in domestic or international cases to essentially those set out in Article V of the New York Convention 1958.

---

[22] *Carlisle Place Investments v. Wimpey Construction (U.K.) Ltd,* (1980) 15 Build. L.R. 109, QBD

[23] Usually, arbitration is a one-tier procedure. Some national legal systems and rules of international arbitration institutions (GAFTA), however, allow the parties to provide contractually for a full appeal to a second arbitral instance. (See, *e.g.* 594(1) of the Austrian Code of Civil Procedure or Art. 1050(1) of the 1986 Netherlands Arbitration Act.).

[24] S. 192 of the Federal Private International Law Act 1987. Art. 192 of the Swiss Act permits the parties to exclude proceedings to set aside an award, provided both parties are domiciled, or have their habitual residence, registered office or branch office in Switzerland. The Federal Supreme Court has decided in *S. v. K. Ltd,* an ICC Arbitration Tribunal in Zürich, ATF/BGE 116 II 639, that an exclusion agreement must be evidenced by and made in express terms and that words to the effect that the award shall be binding and subject to no appeal are insufficient; a reference to the ICC Rules of Arbitration will therefore not operate as an exclusion agreement under Swiss law. For further discussion see Schneider & Patocchi, "The New Swiss Law on International Arbitration", (1989) 55 *Arbitration* 268, 279; Lalive, "The New Swiss Law on International Arbitration", (1988) 4 *Arbitration International* 2, 18–22.

2. ARBITRATION DISTINGUISHED

Arbitration distinguished: expert determination

There are certain methods of private dispute resolution which are not **4–023**
recognised as arbitration. Perhaps the best known is a decision by an expert
appointed pursuant to some contractual provision. The use of expert
determination seems to be increasing. Apart from the commercial real estate
industry in which its use has long been recognised, it is used in the oil and
gas industry for the determination and re-determination of interests in oil and
gas fields. Accountants are often used as experts in the implementation of
contractual provisions for the valuation of assets or shares in limited
companies and joint ventures.[25] As Professor John Uff Q.C. stated in his
Foreword to the admirably concise and informative book on the subject by
John Kendall[26]:

> "Expert determination has existed in the shadows for well over two
> centuries, rubbing shoulders uneasily with the law of arbitration and
> certification. Like some forms of commodity arbitration it seems to owe
> its survival to the simple fact that it works and is found commercially
> useful—A and B agree to abide by the decision of C. The system is
> infinitely flexible: there need not be a dispute, no writing is necessary and
> any form of procedure can be adopted".

In English law, there are now several leading cases, of recent origin.[27] The **4–024**
report of the expert is contractual and binding, for he gives a report or
decision as part of the performance of the contract by the parties. Absent
agreement, only fraud or an excess of jurisdiction will cause the expert's
decision to be set aside. As the House of Lords said in the *Mercury* case[28]:

> "if [the expert] ... makes a determination on the basis of an incorrect
> interpretation, he does not do what he was asked to do".

But mere error will probably not suffice.[29]

Other jurisdictions recognise this distinction between arbitrator and expert, **4–025**
for example, Switzerland, France[30] and Germany.[31] In Switzerland, the test is
a twofold one. First, a court will have to determine the real intention of the
parties as evidenced by the express and implied terms of their agreement as a
whole, taking into account the language of the contract, without being bound
by the legal words used or the classifications chosen by the parties. That

---

[25]See the web site of the Academy of Experts: http://www.academy-experts.org.
[26]John G Kendall, *Expert Determination,* (2nd ed., 1996).
[27]*Jones and Others v. Sherwood Computer Services plc* [1992] 1 W.L.R. 277, CA; *Nikko Hotels
(U.K.) Ltd v. MEPC plc,* [1991] 2 E.G.L.R. 103; *Mercury Communications Ltd v. Director
General of Telecommunications and Another,* [1996] 1 All E.R. 575, HL; *Brown and Others v.
GIO Insurance Ltd,* [1998] Lloyd's Rep. I.R. 201, CA.
[28]*Mercury Communications Ltd v. Director General of Telecommunications and Another* [1996] 1
All E.R. 575, HL.
[29]John G. Kendall *Expert Determination* (2nd ed., 1996) Chapter 15.
[30]de Boisséson, pp. 181 *et seq.*
[31]See, *e.g.* Schlosser, *Das Recht der internationalen privaten Schiedsgerichtsbarkeit* Rz 20 (2nd
ed., 1989); Schwab, *Schiedsgerichtsbarkeit,* pp. 6 *et seq.* (3rd ed., 1979).

intention must be to obtain a decision of a judicial nature which puts an end to a dispute. Secondly, a court will also look at the way in which the third party understood and carried out the instructions received. The fact that the third party does not decide any and all disputes, but only a limited point, was held to raise an inference in favour of the existence of a report and not an award. Although this factor is not in itself conclusive, the kind of proceedings which took place before the third party, if at all, are also relevant: the more they differ from arbitration proceedings, the more the "report" classification will be favoured. The same is true of the form of the report itself. This criterion has to be viewed against the background of a practice of arbitration in which formal arbitration represents the rule. French courts favour a twofold test as well: first, whether the dispute exists, then secondly, and subjectively, the parties' intention to regard the appointed party as invested with a judicial function.[32] The same is true for Germany.[33]

4–026   The distinction between arbitrators and experts is also recognised in international arbitration rules[34] and rules of arbitration institutions.[35]

Arbitration distinguished from contractual adjudication

4–027   Contractual adjudication, a form of expert determination, (sometimes called "interim" or "fast-track" adjudication) is now frequently used to resolve certain types of commercial dispute. It is of increasing relevance in construction and has been the subject of statutory enactment governing the construction industry in England. Hitherto, the engineer or architect under the standard contract forms has been authorised to decide matters of dispute, such as the amount of interim payments, extensions of time for performance, faulty work and the scope of works as specified. The administration of such contracts has long rested upon the fiction that the engineer or architect could exercise certain of his functions as a certifier and valuer, quite independently of the employer. Predictably, public authorities responsible for public expenditure have been increasingly reluctant to delegate power to a neutral and independent engineer when as a consequence they may lose control of the total cost of the project. So too, and for the same motive, have employers in the private sector. It is in the commercial interest of the parties (perhaps principally of the employer) to have a disputes' resolution procedure which can be applied during the currency of the contract to resolve, albeit on an interim basis, disputes which may otherwise impede or threaten timeous completion. As dissatisfaction with the role of the engineer has grown, so parties have turned to other methods such as reference to an impartial adjudicator.

4–028   Where an adjudicator is engaged on this basis, his terms of reference and authority will be contained in the relevant contract. There is no standard basis, but there are a number of common threads that usually exist. First, the adjudicator will usually be a third party neutral who, unlike the engineer or architect, will not have any personal involvement in the contract. Secondly, the adjudication takes place as soon as possible after the dispute has arisen

---

[32] de Boisséson, above n. 30.
[33] See above n. 31.
[34] See, *e.g.* Art. 27 UNCITRAL Arbitration Rules.
[35] Compare the ICC International Centre for Expertise Rules (effective January 1, 1993).

rather than waiting until completion of the works. Thirdly, the procedure is likely to be more summary and informal than arbitration, with the adjudicator making such enquiries and accepting such submissions as he may consider appropriate. Fourthly, the adjudication has a binding quality, insofar as the parties are bound by it unless and until there is a subsequent arbitration award, court judgment or agreement between the parties varying the adjudication. Fifthly, the right is commonly reserved for either party to refer the matter to arbitration (or to litigation if this is envisaged under the contract) notwithstanding that an adjudication has been made; consequently the adjudicator's decision has the interim quality to it noted above. It should incidentally be the overall aim of any construction dispute scheme to achieve resolution of disputes by or very shortly after the end of a contract.

There is now a considerable degree of experience with adjudication in the construction industry. The system was introduced into Hong Kong Government construction contracts as part of a three-tier process of dispute resolution existing together with mediation and arbitration. **4–029**

In Hong Kong in the mid-1980s, prompted by increasing concern that major infrastructure works contracted for by the Government were subject to cost overruns, delay and disputes, attempts were made to reform governmental administrative guidelines and to streamline dispute resolution by a number of means including faster and less complicated arbitration and the introduction of mediation. **4–030**

For various reasons it proved virtually impossible to reform radically the arbitral processes. Old habits were too ingrained and died hard. The biggest obstacle to reform was the attitude of lawyers. **4–031**

The introduction of mediation was successful and its use spread to the private sector in Hong Kong. Mediation was made compulsory in the Airport projects and some major disputes like the *Kwai Chung Viaduct* case were resolved. Mediation is now almost certainly the primary means of dispute resolution in the Hong Kong construction industry. Adjudication was introduced in Hong Kong in the early nineties and has been used in some major infrastructure contracts to resolve major contractual difficulties and not merely disputes about routine payments due under the contracts. **4–032**

Adjudication in the construction industry found statutory expression in England, rather clumsily and ineptly, in the Housing Grants, Construction and Regulation Act 1996. This Act sought to give effect to many of the recommendations of the reports by Sir Michael Latham published in 1993 and 1994 into practices in the United Kingdom construction industry. The Act makes it mandatory to include adjudication in construction contracts entered into after May 1, 1998. The object is to resolve quickly disputes as to payment of sums allegedly due under construction contracts. This problem is particularly acute given Lord Denning's graphic reference[36] to interim payments being the life blood of the construction industry and that most contracts provide for arbitration to take place only at the end of the work. **4–033**

The provisions of the Act were considered for the first time by Mr Justice Dyson, a very experienced construction judge in *Macob Civil Engineering* **4–034**

---

[36] *F.G. Minter Ltd v. Welsh Health Technical Services Organisation,* (1980) 13 Build. L.R. 1, CA.

Limited v. Morrison Construction Limited, a case decided in the Technology and Construction Court in February 1999.[37]

The proceedings raised, as the judge put it:

"questions as to the enforceability in the courts of an adjudicator's decision in circumstances where the contract contains a clause by which the parties agree to refer to arbitration disputes about a decision".

4–035   In *Macob* it was common ground that the parties' contractual provisions for adjudication did not comply with the 1996 Act. Accordingly, by section 108(5) of the Act, the statutory scheme for adjudication applied and, by section 114(4) the statutory scheme is deemed to have effect as an implied term of the contract.

4–036   The statutory scheme is cross-related to the Arbitration Act 1996 in that if an adjudicator has made a decision, a party can apply to the court under section 42 of the Arbitration Act 1996 for a court order to enforce it.

4–037   Mr Justice Dyson in *Macob* indicated that "the adjudicator is given a fair and free hand" in deciding how to conduct the adjudication. He must act impartially, but can choose his own procedure whether adversarial or inquisitorial. Mr Justice Dyson recognised the intentions of Parliament to provide a rapid mechanism for the resolution of these disputes and to do so on a mandatory basis.

4–038   It is highly regrettable that the adjudication scheme of the Act was rushed into effect without proper consideration of the practical difficulties and also that there was no proper liaison between the two Departments of State concerned, the Department of the Environment with the Housing Act and the Department of Trade and Industry with the Arbitration Act. The result is a muddle which as John Riches and Christopher Dancaster, the very experienced authors of *Construction Adjudication,*[38] remark, has given rise to a number of clauses being introduced providing for adjudication which have caused controversy "and in some quarters outrage". It is quite clear that many parties are trying to find a way around adjudication clauses in order to avoid or postpone payment due under contracts.

4–039   The problems of dispute resolution in the construction industry derive largely as a consequence of unclear or badly drafted specifications, physical conditions which one party says were unforeseeable and have caused economic dislocation to the contract and changes in economic conditions which effect the equilibrium of the contract.

4–040   It is also regrettable that the opportunity was not taken in this country to develop a comprehensive and fair regime for the resolution of construction contract disputes. This is a highly complex subject. It is beyond the scope of this book. But it is worth remembering as was once said that to every complicated question, there is a simple answer and it is usually wrong.

4–041   The adversarial approach to contract management in an increasingly competitive industry, has led in recent decades to an undoubted increase in

---

[37](1999) 96 (10) L.S.G. 28.
[38]John L. Richards and Christopher Dancaster, *Practical Construction Guides, Construction Adjudication,* (1999).

the number of disputes, often acrimoniously conducted. Traditional adversarial methods of arbitration and litigation have compounded the difficulties and expense of dispute resolution. Under the traditional English system it is simply uneconomic to litigate or arbitrate all but the largest or least complicated disputes. Great injustice is caused often to sub-contractors and to suppliers. The cost and delay in the resolution of disputes in the construction industry in the United Kingdom is a public scandal.

There are signs of encouraging change. More enlightened public and **4–042** private authorities and their contractors are trying to find methods of contract management which enable disputes to be resolved at management level quickly and efficiently. A collaborative approach has been favoured and parties are experimenting with different forms of collaboration.

However, the complexity of civil engineering work in particular means that **4–043** disputes are inevitable and ways must be found to settle them expeditiously, economically and fairly.

There is no doubt that adjudication has a role to play in construction cases. **4–044** However, it is vital that the parties understand that adjudication is really no more than a form of summary judgment obtained rapidly and to be complied with unless clearly given in breach of natural justice. In that sense adjudication does resemble a form of fast-track arbitration or litigation. It is best used as part of a comprehensive process that provides for the parties to try to resolve their problems by direct negotiation between those on all sides charged with the management of the contract. Failing that, there should be some form of mediation and then adjudication, subject to the ultimate safeguard that the adjudicator's decision can be reviewed by an arbitrator in due course.

There is little doubt that adjudication provisions properly drafted and **4–045** implemented can work. The experience in Hong Kong demonstrates that and the signs are that in England the system may be working quite well. But it is early days.

The interim nature of the adjudication, its contractual basis, the informality **4–046** of the procedure including the adjudicator's ability to make a decision without hearing the parties, and the provision for an arbitration award or court judgment to supersede the decision combine to distinguish the process from arbitration and remove it from the statutory regime applicable to arbitration.

Arbitration distinguished: mediation/conciliation

Arbitration is quite different from conciliation or mediation.[39] There are five **4–047** main points of comparison.

First, both systems are consensual and rest on agreement, but agreements **4–048** to enter into arbitration will be enforced by the courts whereas the common wisdom is that agreements to enter into an ADR process will not be: though there is now authority in several jurisdictions to indicate that agreements to mediate (often the first stage in comprehensive dispute resolution provisions) will be enforced.[40]

---

[39]For the principles of mediation, see Chap. 7.
[40]See Chap. 20 regarding the enforceability of agreements to use ADR.

4–049   The second difference is that arbitration has, as its object, the rendering of a final and binding award. Although the intention in mediation and conciliation is to bring the parties to the point of making a binding agreement to resolve either in whole or in part the matter in dispute between them, it is by no means an automatic consequence of the process. The arbitrator has the authority to make a binding decision, but the mediator or the conciliator does not.

4–050   A third and very important difference is that mediation and conciliation are subject to no statutory regime in England, whereas arbitration is subject to the extensive statutory regime already described. To some extent, there is a statutory regime elsewhere for mediation and conciliation as expressed in Hong Kong, for example, in section 2B of the 1989 Arbitration Ordinance. Some jurisdictions such as Bermuda, India and Singapore have made specific provision for ADR when reforming their arbitration laws.

4–051   A fourth point of comparison lies in procedures adopted in arbitration and in mediation and conciliation. Arbitral procedures are often said to have the advantage over the courts of informality, but nonetheless they are constrained by the rules of natural justice. Yet, the rules of natural justice would not help a mediator or conciliator who must be free to see the parties together or separately, with the utmost flexibility as to what is disclosed from one party to the other.

4–052   The fifth and final point of comparison between arbitration, mediation, and conciliation, is the basis upon which decisions are reached. A striking feature of arbitration in many systems, both domestic and international, is the power of arbitrators to act as *amiables compositeurs*; and at first blush this appears to blur the difference between arbitration and mediation and conciliation.

3. AMIABLE COMPOSITION

4–053   The concept of *"amiable composition"* is originally French. Nowadays, it is foremost a civil law concept, unknown in common law systems.[41] Most international arbitration rules[42] and rules of arbitration institutions[43] provide for *amiable composition*.[44] Likewise, Article 28 of the UNCITRAL Model Law expressly acknowledges the concept of *amiable composition*, if the parties expressly authorize the tribunal so to act, unlike for example Swiss law and other systems.[45]

4–054   *"Amiable composition"* is often used in conjunction with the power to

---

[41] Note, however, that common law arbitrators base their decisions with great frequency on equitable considerations.

[42] See Art. 33(2) of the UNCITRAL Arbitration Rules: "The arbitral tribunal shall decide as *amiable compositeur* or *ex aequo et bono* only if the parties have expressly authorised the arbitral tribunal to do so and if the law applicable to the arbitral procedure permits such arbitration".

[43] Art. 17(3) ICC Arbitration Rules 1998.

[44] M. Loquin, *L'amiable composition en droit comparé et international* (1980).

[45] Art. 28(3): "The arbitral tribunal shall decide *ex aequo et bono* or as *amiable compositeur* only if the parties have expressly authorized it to do so". Art. 28(4): "In all cases, the arbitral tribunal shall decide in accordance with the terms of the contract and shall take into account the usages of the trade applicable to the transaction."

decide *ex aequo et bono*.[46] While some legal systems use both terms interchangeably, others distinguish between them.[47]

Legal basis for amiable composition

Most legal systems require that the parties confer the power to act as *amiable* **4–055** *compositeur* by express agreement, or that the power must be inferred unequivocally from the parties' submission. Absent such agreement, the parties are presumed to have agreed to regular arbitration.[48] Commentators justify this presumption on the basis of parties' hypothetical intent and the quasi-judicial function of the arbitrator.[49] In contrast, some legal systems like the Argentinean, Bolivian or Ecuadorian systems establish a presumption for *amiable composition* when the parties' agreement is silent on the question of arbitration or *amiable composition*.[50] One commentator believes that the authority of *amiable compositeur* is included in the appointment of international arbitrators.[51]

Legal nature and scope

By submitting to *amiable composition,* the parties accept that their disputes **4–056** are not exclusively resolved on the basis of the rules of the applicable substantive law, but also equity. The arbitrator in turn is bound to act as *amiable compositeur.*

For the arbitrator, *amiable composition* is not only a power, but also a duty **4–057** the nonadherence to which may result in the vacating of his decision.[52] One commentator argues that in various jurisdictions the *amiable compositeur* has a duty to settle the dispute.[53]

The power of *amiable composition* has been defined in a variety of ways **4–058** arbitrators "are not bound by legal formalities"[54]; "shall settle the dispute according to their knowledge and understanding"[55], shall render an award

---

[46]In fair dealing and good faith.

[47]Rubino-Sammartano, (1990) *International Arbitration Law* 273.

[48]See, *e.g.* Art. 1054(3) of the 1986 Netherlands Arbitration Act or Art. 1474 of the new French Code of Civil Procedure (*Nouveau Code de Procédure* (Dalloz 1992)) which states: "*L'arbitre tranche le litige conformément aux règles de droit,* à *moins que, dans la convention d'arbitrage, les parties ne lui aient conféré mission de statuer comme amiable compositeur*". ("The arbitrator decides the dispute in accordance with rules of law save where in the arbitration agreement, the parties have conferred upon him the mandate of deciding as *amiable compositeur*".)

[49]de Boisséson, *Le droit français de l'arbitrage interne et international no. 344* (1990).

[50]See Art. 766 Argentine National Code of Civil and Commercial Procedure, reprinted in Smit & Pechota, 2 *World Arbitration Reporter*, at 631, 637: "If the submission is silent as to whether the arbitration is by arbitrators who decide *de jure* or by *amiable compositeur,* or if the arbitrators are authorized to decide *ex aequo et bono*, it shall be deemed to be arbitration by *amiable compositeur*"; see also Art. 739 of the Bolivian Code of Civil Procedure (1975), reprinted in Smit & Pechota, 2 *World Arbitration Reporter*, at 968, 971 and Art. 1016 Organic Law of the Judiciary of Ecuador, reprinted in Smit & Pechota, 2 *World Arbitration Reporter* at 1527, 1529.

[51]Goldman, *La lex mercatoria dans le contrat et l'arbitrage internationaux, réalité et perspective* (Clunet 1979), at 461, 481.

[52]de Boisséson, above n. 34, at 371.

[53]Rubino-Sammartano, (1990) *International Arbitration Law* 273.

[54]See Art. 769 of the Argentine National Code of Civil Procedure, above n. 66, at 637 or Art. 735 of the Code of Judicial Organization of Paraguay (1981), reprinted in Smit & Pechota, 2A *World Arbitration Reporter* at 2298, 2301.

[55]See Art. 289 of the Code of Civil and Commercial Procedure of Guatemala, reprinted in Smit

"according to what they believe just and fair".[56] *Amiable composition* does not mean that the arbitrator can refuse to apply municipal law at all. Rather, it means that the arbitrator is not strictly bound by the applicable substantive law, and he can introduce principles of equity. Conversely, a clause purporting to bind the arbitrator not to apply any municipal law does not necessarily amount to a clause providing for *amiable composition*. The power of *amiable composition* broadens the arbitrator's mandate amounting to a diversification of the sources of law that may be applied.[57] However, cases where a clause providing for *amiable composition* is coupled with an express choice of law clause are not infrequent in practice.

4–059   There are certain limitations imposed by domestic laws on tribunals acting as *amiable compositeur*. Under French law, for example, the *amiable compositeur* is permitted to apply equity with respect to the applicable rules of law and the contract, but cannot alter the subject-matter of the dispute or modify the parties' agreement.[58] Several legal systems require that the *amiable compositeur* respect *ordre public*[59] and apply any applicable trade usages.[60] Other systems compel him to give the parties adequate opportunity to be heard and to submit any evidence deemed necessary, yet some systems direct that he follow any rules of procedure stipulated by the parties.[61] The limitations imposed on the arbitrators vary to such a degree that it was impossible for the drafters of the UNCITRAL Model Law to agree on specific limitations other than those expressed in Article 28(4).[62]

Amiable composition in practice

4–060   According to some commentators, *amiable composition* is chosen in instances where parties feel that the international or technical character of the contractual relationship is too complicated for domestic substantive laws to resolve.[63] However, parties may also be reluctant to agree to *amiable composition* for fear of arbitrariness and subjectivity.[64]

4–061   According to one commentator, the choice of *amiable composition* will depend upon the nature of the parties' contractual relationship. Thus, *amiable composition* is not recommended in short-term contracts but strongly recommended in long-term contracts, such as turn-key contracts or licensing agreements, where a lack of uniformity and repetition may make it difficult to apply general and abstract rules of law and where it is often impossible to foresee and provide for all the events which may influence the performance

---

& Pechota, 2A *World Arbitration Reporter* at 1807, 1811; Art. 890 Honduran Code of Civil Procedure (1906), reprinted in Smit & Pechota, 2A *World Arbitration Reporter* at 1823, 1827.

[56]Art. 1756 Panamanian Judicial Code of 1917, reprinted in Smit & Pechota, 2A *World Arbitration Reporter* at 2285, 2287.

[57]de Boisséson, above n. 34, at p. 345.

[58]*ibid.* at 357.

[59]*ibid.* at 354.

[60]See, *e.g.* Art. 1054(4) of the Netherlands Arbitration Act or Art. 28(3) of the UNCITRAL Model Law 1985.

[61]Art. 289 Code of Civil and Commercial Procedure of Guatemala, reprinted in Smit & Pechota, 2A *World Arbitration Reporter* at 1807, 1811.

[62]See Holtzmann & Neuhaus, *A Guide to the UNCITRAL Model Law on International Commercial Arbitration* 771 (1989).

[63]*ibid.* at 347.

[64]*ibid.*

of the contract.[65] According to another commentator, *amiable composition* was especially popular in East–West trade.[66]

In most legal systems, *amiable composition* has the same binding effect as   **4–062** ordinary arbitration; it ends in an award and is enforceable as such.[67] This is said to correspond to the parties' intent: when parties agree to *amiable composition,* they do not want conciliation, they want equitable arbitration.[68] However, this is not the case in England. Under English law, an arbitrator must decide according to law. If he acts as *amiable compositeur,* the decision is not an award and not enforceable as such.

The basis of the appointment of mediators and conciliators in relation to   **4–063** the resolution of a contractual dispute is quite different from the principles applicable to arbitrators, even when acting as *amiables compositeurs.* In the mediation or conciliation of a contractual dispute the inediator has no authority to make any decisions which bind the parties, but merely acts as a facilitator to assist them in reaching their own resolution. The criteria applied in mediation are those which the parties themselves consider to be the most relevant: this may involve an analysis of what might be termed the commercial reality taking into account the relationship between the parties, what has happened between them and what has gone wrong. It may necessitate an examination of the contractual and legal implications of the dispute but could, if the parties prefer, be dealt with on the basis of commercial or equitable principles, or even disregarding the contract entirely or rewriting it, if so agreed.

4. DIFFERENT KINDS OF ARBITRATION

One of the characteristic features and strengths of English arbitration is the   **4–064** diversity of arbitration procedures tailor-made to the requirements of different trades and industries. Thus, for example, there are specialist institutions and rules for commodity and maritime disputes, construction and commercial real property disputes, electricity supply and consumer disputes.

Final offer arbitration (or pendulum arbitration)

There are types of dispute resolution (primarily American) which though the   **4–065** word arbitration is used, such as final offer arbitration, may be, strictly speaking, not arbitration at all. (Final offer arbitration is known in the United Kingdom industrial field as "pendulum arbitration", and in the United States is called "baseball arbitration" because of its use in relation to the resolution of disagreements concerning the salaries of baseball players). Under this process, in the absence of agreement, each party makes a final settlement

---

[65] de Boisséson, at p. 349.

[66] de Boisséson, at p. 349.

[67] An exception is Art. 2.025 Columbian Code of Commerce of 1971, reprinted in Smit & Pechota, 2A *World Arbitration Reporter* at 1358, 1364: "Decisions of *amiable compositeurs* have a contractual binding effect between parties, but shall not have the force of an arbitral award."

[68] de Boisséson, at p. 346; Goldman, *Rev. Arb.* 1970, 214.

offer indicating what the award should be and the arbitrator is required to chocse the one considered more reasonable.

4–066   The idea in this kind of arbitration is to discourage extravagant claims (since each party needs to maintain a reasonable position if the arbitrator is to be expected to choose its proposals), and to reach a rapid decision. In continental jurisdictions, where the idea of the judicial function of the arbitrator is deeply rooted, such arbitration clauses might be regarded as clauses which will ultimately result not in the making of an award, but an expert report *sui generis*. It may be doubted whether such "arbitrations" amount to arbitration in English law.

"Documents only" arbitration

4–067   Where appropriate a dispute may be resolved by a "documents only" arbitration. This procedure is particularly used in the context of commodities and maritime claims and, when properly used, provides a cost- and time-effective means of resolving the dispute. Section 34 of the Act of 1996 has provided arbitrators with the power to decide on documents only unless the parties have agreed otherwise.

4–068   There are also some institutional provisions referring disputes to this type of arbitration, such as the Joint Contracts Tribunal (JCT) and the Institution of Civil Engineers (ICE) contract forms.

4–069   Although in many cases it is possible for the arbitrator to conduct the arbitration by means of documents alone, there are some circumstances in which the personal involvement of the parties may continue after submission of the documentation.

4–070   Where an arbitrator considers that further documentation or submissions are required or indeed that a meeting with the parties may be helpful, he can ask for these to be arranged, and they may serve to supplement the documents initially placed before him. Where appropriate, the arbitrator may then either give directions, or, if he is in a position to do so, make an award.

What may be arbitrated

4–071   Mustill and Boyd consider that in English law "any dispute or claim concerning legal rights which can be the subject of an enforceable award, is capable of being settled by arbitration."[69] That view, expressed before the 1996 Act remains the case but it is subject to the essential qualification of Mustill and Boyd, that an arbitrator is limited by considerations of public policy and by the fact that he is appointed by private parties, not by the state.[70] He cannot exercise certain judicial remedies and powers such as the imposition of fines or penalties, and an arbitrator's decision is binding only on the parties who appointed him and not upon third parties. Thus, for example, an arbitrator cannot grant a divorce decree, a winding-up order, or exempt an agreement from the provisions of Articles 85 and 86 of the Treaty of Rome.[71]

4–072   There is now a recognised trend in England and in developed jurisdictions

---

[69]Mustill & Boyd, *op. cit.*, p. 149.
[70]*ibid.*
[71]*ibid.*

elsewhere, to broaden the range of disputes which may be submitted to arbitration and to interpret the scope and meaning of arbitration clauses and agreements widely and favourably. There are also indications that the powers given to arbitrators particularly with respect to interim orders including injunctive relief, are being clarified and expressly provided for.[72] Examples are found in section 39 of the 1996 Act and in certain institutional rules such as the World Intellectual Property Organisation (WIPO) Rules and the latest edition of the ICC Rules in force since January 1, 1998.

This reflects the change manifest in England and elsewhere in the relationship (fundamental to a proper understanding of arbitration) between the courts and the arbitral process, to permit in the public interest the wider development of arbitration as a private and independent system of resolving disputes which otherwise would fall to be adjudicated in the courts.[73]   **4–073**

The courts are also increasingly prepared to see issues arbitrated which touch and concern vital public and political interests. In the United States, for example, the Supreme Court has permitted an affirmative claim to be arbitrated in an international arbitration based on breach of an antitrust statute,[74] and subsequently has extended the jurisdiction of arbitrators to domestic cases involving antitrust infringement.[75] There appears to be no objection in English law to similar developments, and disputes which may involve breach of Articles 85 and 86 of the Treaty of Rome are capable of being arbitrated, though the power of the competition authorities to take action cannot be excluded or usurped.[76]   **4–074**

There are also examples in Australia and New Zealand of arbitrators who have decided cases which have involved economic issues of fundamental national importance. The *Mobil Oil* case in New Zealand is perhaps the high-water mark of the tide of arbitrability,[77] but as Mr Andrew Rogers Q.C. formerly the Presiding Judge of the Commercial Court of New South Wales has argued, arbitrability, particularly in cases of national economic importance should have its limits.[78]   **4–075**

In seeking to construe arbitration clauses there has been an increasingly favourable approach by the courts and a readiness to find an intention of the parties to arbitrate all disputes connected with the relationship. Thus, the often sterile and academic arguments of the early cases seeking to define and distinguish what was meant by such terms providing for the arbitration of disputes or differences "arising from", "under", "in connection with", "arising out of", "in respect of" and "with regard to", have been largely swept away by this modern approach as exemplified by the Court of Appeal   **4–076**

---

[72]See, *e.g.* R. von Mehren, "From Vynior's Case to Mitsubishi: The Future of Arbitration and Public Law", 12 *Brooklyn J. Int'l L.* 583 (1986), reprinted in 2 *International Commercial Arbitration: Recent Developments* 179 (Gaillard & von Mehren (eds.) 1988) for discussion of such a trend in the United States.

[73]See, *e.g.* Haight, "How Judges View Arbitration", (1988) 20 *The Arbitrator* 1: "Judges and arbitrators work together as laborers in the same vineyard of Justice. The procedural differences are less important than the substantive common purpose".

[74]*Mitsubishi Motors Corp. v. Soler Chrysler-Plymouth Inc.*, 473 U.S. 614 (1985).

[75]See R. von Mehren, above n. 91.

[76]Mustill & Boyd, at p. 150; Schlosser, above n. 50, at *Rz. 320.*

[77]*A.-G. v. Mobil Oil N.Z. Ltd* [1989] 2 N.Z.L.R. 649.

[78]Second Goff Lecture delivered in Hong Kong on September 26, 1991.

decision in England in *Elmer v. Ashville*.[79] There have been corresponding developments in other jurisdictions.[80]

5. SEPARABILITY: KOMPETENZ–KOMPETENZ

4–077 Ultimately, the independence and autonomy of the arbitral process rests upon a legal fiction of the doctrine of separability and the related concept of *Kompetenz–Kompetenz*. By separability, is meant whether the arbitration clause within a contract may be regarded as an agreement separate from the other contractual provisions, so that the disputes between the parties may be arbitrated pursuant to the clause, notwithstanding that the existence of the contract itself may be null and void *ab initio*. By *Kompetenz–Kompetenz*, is meant the extent of the arbitrator's power to decide upon his own jurisdiction.

4–078 Separability can have different meanings and effects. One possible meaning is related to the substantive law and gives rise to the question whether the validity of the arbitration clause is affected by the invalidity of the main contract. The converse question also arises, (but that is not a question of arbitration law): is the validity of the main contract affected by the invalidity of the arbitration clause? Another possible meaning relates to the conflict of laws and gives rise to the question whether the arbitration agreement is necessarily governed by the law by which the main contract is governed. A further possible meaning of separability goes to the law of procedure and gives rise to the question of *Kompetenz–Kompetenz*, namely whether the arbitrators are entitled to rule themselves on the validity of the arbitration clause, the very basis of their jurisdiction, or are they to surrender the examination of this question to courts of law?

4–079 Although these concepts have been of critical importance to the development of international commercial arbitration, particularly in France, they have not been so regarded in this country. Indeed, to Mustill and Boyd, the issue of *Kompetenz–Kompetenz* in the English context is "of quite modest practical importance"[81]: and, the doctrine of separability is considered to be confined to exceptional cases.

4–080 Judge Schwebel considers that separability is necessary for the proper functioning of international commercial arbitration, and with Oliver Wendell Holmes he concludes that, if the life of the law is not logic, but experience, then experience has entrenched the doctrine of separability.[82] The justification for separability in international commercial arbitration is pragmatic and rooted in common sense. The practical consequences of denying separability would be virtually unfettered scope for frustrating the arbitral process, first by procedural devices causing delay, and secondly, in many cases leading the courts, under the guise of deciding jurisdictional questions, to decide the substantive disputes arising from a contractual relationship. It is clear that the

---

[79] [1988] 3 W.L.R. 867; [1988] 2 All E.R. 577.
[80] Schlosser, *Das Recht der internationalen privaten Schiedsgerichtsbarkeit Rz. 421 et seq.*
[81] Mustill & Boyd, at p. 109.
[82] Schwebel, "The Severability of the Arbitration Agreement", in *International Arbitration: Three Salient Problems, Hersch Lauterpacht Memorial Lectures* (Cambridge, 1987).

doctrine applied both internationally and domestically is here to stay. It is embodied in various international rules and in various municipal laws.[83]

In *Harbour Assurance and Kansa,*[84] a strong Court of Appeal clarified the **4–081** doctrine of separability in English law holding that a dispute as to initial illegality of the primary contract was arbitrable.

Now, by section 7 of the Arbitration Act 1996 the doctrine of severability **4–082** is enacted. As to Kompetenz–Kompetenz, the position in English law has been well-settled since the decision of Mr Justice Devlin in *Brown v. Genossenschaft Österreichischer Waldbesitzer.*[85] An arbitrator faced with a challenge to his jurisdiction is neither obliged to stop the arbitration nor to continue it. He can do what he thinks convenient and right. But his decision is provisional and bind the parties. The arbitrator cannot rule definitively on his own jurisdiction. Only the court can do so. By section 30 of the statute, the doctrine of *Kompetenz–Kompetenz* (or a version of the doctrine *Kompetenz–Kompetenz*) has been enacted. Thus, the arbitral tribunal may rule on its own substantive jurisdiction which as the Act says goes "to (a) whether there is a valid arbitration agreement (b) whether the tribunal is properly constituted and (c) what matters have been submitted to arbitration in accordance with the arbitration agreement". It should be borne in mind that the decision of the tribunal is not final. It may be challenged and there are specific provisions in the statute, namely sections 31, 32, 45, 67, 70 and 73 which go to the procedure and timing of challenge to jurisdiction.

The difference between this country and elsewhere on the effect of the **4–083** doctrine of *Kompetenz–Kompetenz* is probably more a question of timing than of substance. *Kompetenz–Kompetenz* as understood abroad is distinct from the English position in that, first, it is assumed that the challenges to the arbitrator's jurisdiction are best dealt with by the arbitrator, and secondly, that the courts are not necessarily in a better position to deal with issues of law such as are involved in deciding upon an arbitrator's jurisdiction, than is the arbitrator himself.

6. Increasing Use of International Commercial Arbitration

The use of arbitration in international trade and business has expanded **4–084** substantially and has become the norm for the resolution of commercial disputes. There are a number of reasons for this growth. The first is the enormous increase in world trade since the Second World War and the increasingly global activities of major multi-national companies. The ICC International Court of Arbitration has been in the forefront of international commercial disputes for over 70 years. As at December 31, 1998 the number of parties involved in ICC international arbitrations was 1,151. These parties were from 104 different countries.

---

[83]See, *e.g.* Art. V of the European Convention on International Commercial Arbitration of April 21, 1961; Art. 17.2 of the ICC Rules of Arbitration 1998; Art. 14 of the London Court of International Arbitration. See also Art. 178(3) of the Swiss Private International Law Act.
[84][1993] Q.B. 701, CA.
[85][1954] 1 Q.B. 8, 12 and 13.

4–085   The second reason is the desire of the international business community to have neutral and competent tribunals to decide their commercial disputes. This factor, which has inspired the growth of domestic arbitration in many jurisdictions as well, stems from the difficulties in many parts of the world in finding courts which are competent to resolve commercial disputes and untainted by such problems as corruption and delay.

4–086   Arbitration of commercial disputes is perceived by the business community both domestic and international, as having certain substantial advantages over litigation.[86] First, the parties can select their own tribunal according to the nature of the dispute. Thus, for example, a highly technical dispute involving the transfer of technology can be decided by an arbitrator experienced in that field to whom the jargon and techniques are very familiar. A second advantage is that of privacy. Arbitration proceedings are private and in many countries, such as England, protected by laws of privilege and confidentiality. This may be of great importance in commercially sensitive disputes involving, for example, know-how, lists of clients, the development of business strategy, and other commercially confidential matters.[87]

4–087   A third advantage is ease of enforcement. Many domestic regimes permit the registration and enforcement of awards as court judgments, and internationally, because of conventions and the principle of comity, it is often easier to enforce an arbitral award given in one country in the courts of another than it is, for example, to enforce court decisions across national boundaries. There are two principal conventions, the Geneva Convention of 1927 and the New York Convention of 1958 (by far the more important). The main and important difference between the two is that in the case of Geneva, a party seeking enforcement has to demonstrate that his award was a proper and valid one for enforcement, whereas under the New York Convention it is the party resisting the enforcement of the award who has to show that the award is in some way objectionable.

4–088   A fourth advantage claimed for arbitration, both domestically and internationally, is that of cost and speed. While that is still true in relation to specialist arbitration such as trade, commodity, and maritime disputes, it is not true where there is, as in some countries such as England, a greatly experienced commercial court capable of resolving commercial disputes speedily and effectively. It must be borne in mind that the parties have to pay the arbitrators, but do not have to pay judges, except indirectly through taxes, and the parties must pay for the physical facilities of the arbitration, such as hotel conference rooms and transcripts.

4–089   Finally, an advantage of using arbitration in the international context is thought to be the avoidance of uncertainties of foreign litigation. Such uncertainties include whether a foreign court will assume jurisdiction to hear the case; the necessity for advice and representation by lawyers of that jurisdiction; the necessity for translation of documents and interpretation of evidence; exposure to technical and formal rules of procedure and evidence;

---

[86]See, *e.g.* M. Domke, *The Law and Practice of Commercial Arbitration* (Rev. Ed., Wilner, 1984), 2–01; S. Goldberg, E. Green & F. Sander, *Alternative Methods of Dispute Resolution* (1985), pp. 189–190; Born & Westin, *International Civil Litigation in United States Courts* (1989), p. 606.

[87]See *International Commercial Arbitration in the United States* (1994), Gary B. Born.

and the risk of having a major international commercial dispute resolved by inexperienced and incompetent judges.

7. HARMONISATION: THE UNCITRAL MODEL LAW AND RULES

The growth in international commercial arbitration has provoked rapid **4–090** development towards the harmonisation of the law and particularly the practice of international arbitration. The prime example is the New York Convention of 1958, which was a major achievement in the process of harmonisation. Two later examples are the UNCITRAL Model Law and the UNCITRAL Rules. The Model Law has been adopted in a number of countries, usually, however, where there is no long tradition or experience of international commercial arbitration; and where domestic experience is recent.[88] There are however, certain exceptions such as Germany, which has enacted the Model Law by incorporating it in a reform of Book 10 of the *Zivilprozessordnung* (ZPO).[89]

In countries such as England, the Netherlands, France and Switzerland, **4–091** which have a long tradition of commercial arbitration, the Model Law has not been adopted but serves rather as a useful yardstick against which to draft new legislation on international commercial arbitration. Thus, as noted earlier, in England the Mustill Report recommended in paragraph 108 that any new arbitration statute in this country should follow the structure and form and, where appropriate, the actual language of the Model Law, but that it was neither necessary nor desirable to enact the Model Law itself.[90] However, the Model Law has greatly influenced the new statute. It has been respected in spirit and, to some extent, in the letter. But all provisions of the Model Law find an echo in the new Act.

The trend towards harmonisation is also reflected in the many new **4–092** arbitration statutes enacted in recent years in a number of countries. To some extent, the process may be said to have begun in England with the Arbitration Act 1979 (as subsequently interpreted by the House of Lords) which represented a milestone in arbitral law concerning the relationship between the English courts and arbitration, by limiting appeal of arbitrators' awards. Many countries of the Commonwealth, such as for example, Hong Kong, India, Singapore and Australia have enacted new arbitral statutes influenced by the Model Law. There have been new laws in France, one in 1980 on domestic arbitration and the other in 1981 on international arbitration, the latter clearly enacted with reference to Paris as the seat of the International Chamber of Commerce and the leading venue for ICC arbitration. A new and radical law in Belgium in 1985 provided that the Belgian courts in an international arbitration have no jurisdiction to review an arbitrator's award. Yet this radical legislation was thought by many international practitioners to discourage the choice of Belgium as a venue.

---

[88]Those countries include Canada (see Chiasson & Lalonde, "Recent Canadian Legislation on Arbitration", 2 *Arbitration International* 370 (1986)), Cyprus and New Zealand. See also Ireland with the Arbitration (International Commercial) Act 1998. See also Hong Kong.
[89]*Zehntes Buch der Zivilprozessordnung. Schiedsrichter liches Verpalsen* ss. 1025–1066.
[90]See para. 4–008.

The Act was amended in 1998.[91] There have been new arbitration acts in the Netherlands in 1986 and in Switzerland in 1987.

4–093   There is little doubt that these new statutes are prompted by a desire to attract international commercial arbitration to the jurisdictions in question. A measure of harmonisation has been achieved by resort to comparative law and by the consideration of the merits of the different jurisdictions which compete for international arbitration business. Thus, the new Swiss rules on international arbitration are based to a significant extent on the French philosophy of international arbitration, if not directly on the basis of French statutory example. Like France, Switzerland has enacted a law for international arbitration which is not exhaustive, but creates a framework. The Dutch statute, detailed and comprehensive, is based on the Model Law, despite the fact that the Netherlands did not want to adopt the Model Law. The English Act of 1979 drew upon an international trend in favour of the finality of awards, while trying as a matter of policy to continue the development of English commercial law by permitting review by the courts in certain limited circumstances. The Act of 1996 largely follows the same policy though there are now important differences such as the abolition of the distinction between domestic and international cases. This was done to respect fully the anti-discrimination provisions (Article 6) of the Rome Treaty.

4–094   All these new arbitration statutes, while reflecting the tradition and experience of their respective jurisdictions, seek to encourage and strengthen the use of arbitration, both domestically and internationally. Thus, many of these new statutes expressly recognise the concept of separability of the arbitration clause and permit procedural flexibility, allowing arbitrators and the parties freedom to run the proceedings in the way they choose, provided that certain basic safeguards of procedural fairness are observed. There are express limitations upon judicial review and restraints imposed upon the courts from interfering, both in the conduct of the reference and in the review of the award. The statutes also provide for support and assistance to the parties during the course of the reference, such as, for example, in England by the granting of "freezing" injunctions or obtaining *subpoenas* requiring the attendance of witnesses. As a consequence, parties may arbitrate with confidence in the traditional arbitration centres, whether under institutional or ad hoc rules.

4–095   Of particular importance has been the increasing use of the UNCITRAL Rules in ad hoc arbitrations. There is now wide experience with the UNCITRAL Rules, particularly as, with slight modification, they have been used to resolve the disputes before the Iran/U.S. Tribunal in The Hague. Many arbitral institutions will also act as the appointing authority under the UNCITRAL Rules.

8. A VARIETY OF COMMERCIAL DISPUTES

4–096   The principal commercial disputes in which arbitration is used involve a

---

[91] Belgian Judicial Code, Sixth Part: Arbitration, May 19 1998.

variety of transactions and relationships. Of very great importance in England is the role of arbitration for resolving disputes involving the use and occupation of commercial property. Thus, matters of rent review and dilapidations are resolved predominantly by arbitrators and by experts.

The domestic construction industry in England (and in other common law jurisdictions) at all levels of building and civil engineering, looks to arbitration as the primary means of dispute resolution. Arbitration clauses are incorporated in the standard forms of building and civil engineering contracts, such as the Institution of Civil Engineers (ICE) and the Joint Contracts Tribunal (JCT) forms. Partnership and other long-term agreements usually provide for dispute resolution by arbitration, and such clauses have been standard in the bread and butter commercial relationships of distribution, agency and licensing agreements.   **4–097**

Recent years have seen a growth in consumer arbitration in England prompted perhaps by small claims procedures attached to the county courts and by the growth of special trade schemes, such as those promoted by the Association of British Travel Agents for resolving the complaints of travellers and holiday markers, and by the Royal Institute of Chartered Surveyors (RICS) for resolving disputes between surveyors and their clients. The arbitration of consumer disputes found statutory expression in the Consumer Arbitration Agreements Act of 1988, but the Act of 1988 was repealed by the 1996 Act and provisions for Consumer Arbitration are now found in sections 89 to 91. The fact that legal aid is not available in arbitration may well operate as a very real restraint to its wider use in consumer disputes.   **4–098**

Hitherto, contracts of insurance have not usually provided for dispute resolution by arbitration though various devices have been employed to avoid litigation, such as obtaining an opinion from a Queen's Counsel in professional indemnity cases. Prompted, no doubt, by difficulties in the market, Lloyd's of London introduced a scheme for arbitration which is still in operation but there are very few ongoing arbitrations as at July 1999. This is due to the Settlement Offer that took place in 1995. The Lloyd's Arbitration Scheme will remain operative, however, as an alternative dispute resolution method for Lloyd's members.   **4–099**

In the United States, which, predictably, has the largest domestic arbitration practice in the world, the use of arbitration in commercial disputes has expanded into fields of activity as yet unknown in England. Recent years have seen an extraordinary increase in the use of arbitration in the securities industry in the United States, a process sanctioned as constitutional by the Supreme Court. It is likely that there has been more resolution of disputes in contracts concerned with high technology in the United States than in England and elsewhere.   **4–100**

Arbitration is widespread in maritime and commodity contracts. London and New York are the leading locations for maritime and commodity arbitrations. There are specialist trade organisations such as the Grain and Feed Trade Association (GAFTA) pursuant to whose rules arbitrations are conducted by a specialist body of arbitrators and practitioners. Such arbitrations reflect the considerable importance of London as a centre of maritime and commodity trading and the use of English commercial law by   **4–101** foreign parties to govern their transactions, often with no other commercial or physical connection with England.

4–102   The City Disputes Panel (CDP) was set up in 1994 to provide a specialist dispute resolution system for the financial services industry. The original intention was to provide an alternative to litigation by providing specialist arbitration panels. Each panel was to be presided over by a highly experienced commercial lawyer, drawn either from the ranks of the retired senior judiciary or from the practising bar. Other members of the panel were to be drawn from experts in the particular area of dispute, for example reinsurance, capital markets or derivatives. In this way, it was hoped that a specialist tribunal of great authority and expertise would be available. CDP also offered mediation services, though the original expectation was that arbitration would be a primary means of dispute resolution preferred by the parties.

4–103   CDP is sponsored by such institutions as the Bank of England, the Corporation of London, the Financial Services Authority and Lloyd's. It enjoys the support of leading financial institutions, law firms and accountants. Interestingly, demands for the arbitration services have been limited. Of greater interest has been the demand for mediation and evaluation; and CDP has achieved some notable successes such as in the reconstruction of Lloyd's insurance market after the scandals which threatened to destroy it.

4–104   An essential element in the reconstruction and renewal plan for Lloyd's was the process by which the reserves required to meet the syndicates' liabilities to be reinsured into Equitas were estimated. As part of this process, the reinsurance cover held by syndicates which was disputed had to be valued, and where the dispute was years from judgment, the strength of the syndicates' claim against the reinsurer had to be determined. For this purpose, CDP developed a special evaluation process headed by Lord Ackner and Lord Templeman, which was fast and flexible.

4–105   A further area in which CDP has used the breadth of its expertise is in international capital markets where, once again, market experience is of paramount importance. A notable concillation carried out in this sector required not only expertise and experience, but undoubted authority.

4–106   CDP lays great emphasis on evaluation as being required by those concerned to resolve financial sector disputes. It uses a combination of legal and financial expertise in mediation and evaluation. The chairmen of CDP arbitration and evaluation tribunals are appointed because of their judicial expertise, but they are always complemented by financial practitioners who usually form part of the tribunal. In smaller cases, a sole arbitrator is occasionally assisted by an expert in a particular field. Similarly, a mediation team having expertise appropriate to the case is, in CDP's experience, always more successful than a sole mediator who will inevitably have only some of the required skills.

4–107   Internationally, arbitration is widely used in the construction industry and, for example, a provision for arbitration is included in the standard form *Federation Internationale des Ingenieurs Conseils* (FIDIC) contract which is extensively used for major civil and engineering works. The international oil and gas industry is a major source of arbitrations, as concession agreements, exploration and production agreements and contracts for the supply of technical and other services almost invariably contain arbitration clauses. So too do contracts between host governments and multinational companies for the development of other natural resources.

A central theme of many international arbitrations in recent years and one **4–108** of increasing importance, is the filling of gaps in contracts on the one hand, and the adaptation of contracts in cases of hardship, or changing circumstances, on the other.[92] This is of vital importance, because many contracts which contain international arbitration clauses are of long duration. Long-term investment contracts, often 20, 30 or sometimes 40 years in duration, are commonplace and usually govern the investment by a multinational or a joint venture in a host country to develop a plant or a mine, or some other natural resource. The parties are quite incapable, at the beginning of such a contract, of taking into account all events which may occur in the course of its life and which may affect their initial bargain. International arbitrators have increasingly been asked to fill the gaps in contracts and to adapt them in changing circumstances particularly of economic dislocation.

English law adopts a rather pragmatic approach. It asks what the parties **4–109** have intended. Have the parties given the arbitrators by use of wide enough language in the arbitration clause, the right to determine a dispute as to how the gap in a contract should be filled or, how a contract should be adapted? If they have, then arbitrators will give effect to that and the courts will support them.[93] Two common law cases, one in the Court of Appeal in England[94] and the other in the Privy Council,[95] illustrate this approach towards gap-filling and adaptation. The same approach is taken by courts in the United States[96] and in civil law jurisdictions.[97]

An interesting footnote to the development of international arbitration **4–110** regarding its capacity to fill gaps and to adapt contracts, is that in 1978 the ICC produced a special procedure for the adaptation of contracts outside the arbitral process[98] which has, however, not been well received and never been used.[99] It is thought that in reality the parties prefer to rely upon the arbitration process itself and (where appropriate) by giving arbitrators power to decide *ex aequo et bono.*

---

[92]For further discussion of this topic see, *e.g.* Horn (ed.), "Adaptation and Renegotiation of Contracts" in *International Trade and Finance* (1985): Bartels, *Contractual Adaptation and Conflict Resolution* (1985); Bernini & Holtzmann, *"Les techniques permettant de résoudre les problèmes qui surgissent lors de la formulation et de l'exécution des contrats à long terme",* *Revue de l'arbitrage 18* (1975); Jarvin, "The Sources and Limits of the Arbitrator's Powers," *Arb. Int'l* 1986, 140; Rubino-Sammartano, above n. 86, at pp. 10–11.

[93]Steyn, National Report for England, VIII Y.B. Comm. Arb. 10–11 (1983).

[94]*F. & G. Sykes (Wessex) Ltd v. Fine Fare Ltd,* [1967] 1 Lloyd's Rep. 53.

[95]*Queensland Electricity Generating Board v. New Hope Colleries Pty. Ltd* [1989] 1 Lloyd's Rep. 205, PC.

[96]See, *e.g. Georgia Power Co. v. Cimarron Coal Corp.,* 526 F.2d 101 (6th Cir. 1975), cert. denied, 425 U.S. 952 (1976) or *Management Technical Consultants S.A. v. Parsons-Jurden International Corp.,* 820 F.2d 1531 (9th Cir. 1987).

[97]For Germany see Schlosser, "Right and Remedy in Common Law Arbitration and in German Arbitration Law," *J. Int'l Arb.* 27 (1987); See also Schlosser, n. 50 at *Rz. 29 et seq.* with references to similar situation in France, Switzerland and Italy.

[98]*"Adaptation des contrats,"* ICC Publication No. 326 (1978), reprinted in Craig, Park & Paulsson, *International Chamber of Commerce Arbitration* App. III. (2nd ed., 1990).

[99]For a critical assessment of the rules, see Craig, Park & Paulsson at pp. 693–696.

9. INSTITUTIONAL AND AD HOC ARBITRATION

4–111   Institutional arbitration is arbitration conducted according to the rules of a specified institution which may, to a greater or lesser extent, exercise a supervisory and supportive role over an arbitration conducted pursuant to its rules. The best-known international arbitration institutions are the International Chamber of Commerce, the American Arbitration Association, the London Court of International Arbitration, the Hong Kong International Arbitration Centre and the International Centre for Settlement of Investment Disputes. An ad hoc arbitration is an arbitration without an arbitral institute. Ad hoc arbitration is preferable on grounds of expense and speed to institutional arbitration where the arbitration takes place in a country such as England with a developed arbitral system and where the courts of that country support the arbitral process.[1]

4–112   One of the important matters with which the DAC was concerned and on which it acted in response to the very clear comments made by the international commercial arbitration community generally, was the position of arbitral institutions. The framers of the new statute were concerned to ensure that where parties agreed to arbitrate according to the rules of a given institution, those rules, being part of the parties' agreement, should be enforced as any other provision of the parties' agreement to arbitrate. Therefore in many places in the statute there are references to the fact that before the court will intervene, if indeed it will intervene at all, the procedures of the institution must have been gone through.[2]

4–113   Arbitral institutions are given a corresponding immunity to that given to the individual arbitrator and this is found in section 74 of the Arbitration Act 1996. This was a pure act of policy, as indeed was the grant of immunity to individual arbitrators. It is a sad fact of life that as the opportunity to challenge arbitral awards in the courts of various jurisdictions is more and more hedged around by restriction, so parties and their lawyers attack the arbitrators or for example the arbitral institution for appointing a particular arbitrator. Challenges for conflict are now increasingly made. There is a considerable difference of opinion between Western European practitioners and their counterparts in the United States, influenced unduly as the latter are by conflict rules in domestic U.S. litigation, particularly in California. It is a matter of regret, as some distinguished Swiss arbitrators said publicly some years ago, that the ICC would appear in its requirements for independence declarations to be going a little too far down the American road.

4–114   But be that as it may, the provisions for immunity are there as a matter of policy, to protect arbitrators and arbitral institutions against unmerited attack, though they will not be immune if they have acted in bad faith. It must be borne in mind that many arbitral institutions have little or no financial

---

[1]For further discussion of the strengths and weaknesses of institutional versus ad hoc arbitration see Golsong, "A Guide to Procedural Issues in International Arbitration," 18 *Int'l Law,* 633, 636 (1984); Higgins, Brown & Roach, "Pitfalls in International Commercial Arbitration," 35 *Bus. Law,* 1035, 1036–38 (1980).

[2]There is a case currently before the English courts in which a party having been unsuccessful before the ICC in a challenge to the appointment of an arbitrator, is asking the English court under the 1996 Act to remove the arbitrator.

resources and simply could not afford to defend themselves, particularly in expensive court proceedings in either England or the United States. It was hoped that a provision of this kind in an English statute would bar such proceedings in England and would make them perhaps more difficult than they otherwise would be in the United States.

The advantages of arbitral institutions are most apparent when dealing with State enterprises. More and more disputes involve States and State enterprises. The advantage of the institution to private parties confronted with such disputes, is that the institution can provide considerable assistance in the conduct of the reference, particularly if the state, or the state enterprise concerned, defaults or delays the conduct of the arbitration. An important role of the institution is the supervision of the award with particular reference to enforceability. It is a striking feature, for example, of ICC awards that the majority are honoured without difficulty. There is a very strong moral and practical pressure upon a state, or a state enterprise, to honour an award adverse to it. **4–115**

Of increasing importance is arbitration in the context of bilateral investment treaties, of which there are now over 700. Important also is arbitration in agreements for the furtherance of trade and investment by groups of nations, of which the most important example is NAFTA, the association between Mexico, Canada and the United States. As developments such as the Energy Charter make clear, there is every reason to believe that arbitration of disputes arising from international investment and trade agreements will assume increasing importance. **4–116**

The distinction has evolved between those arbitral institutions which seek to play a global role by providing a service for the resolution of disputes on a global basis, and those which do so only as regional institutions. The principal international arbitral institution is the International Chamber of Commerce, which was founded in 1919 and has its headquarters in Paris. The International Court of Arbitration at the ICC had 926 pending cases at the end of 1998. The venue for 76.9 per cent of these arbitrations is divided between Paris and Geneva, with London as the third principal venue. **4–117**

The International Chamber of Commerce has made a major contribution to international arbitration and has taken the initiative in relation to such matters as the Geneva and New York Conventions. However, it has been heavily criticised on grounds of delay and excessive expense said to derive from its centralised organisation, its concern to monitor the progress of arbitrations conducted according to its rules, and the effect of certain specific procedural requirements such as Terms of Reference under Article 13 of the Rules. The most recent revisions to the Rules have done something to allay these concerns.[3] **4–118**

Neither London nor New York (the principal international arbitration centres) have institutions to rival the International Chamber of Commerce. The American Arbitration Association has a vast domestic caseload, but as yet a relatively small number of international arbitration cases. However, this is changing as the AAA is now increasingly involved in international **4–119**

---

[3] See Commentary by Derains and Schwarz.

arbitration, reflecting the internationalisation of American business.[4] The United States is the leading exporting nation and many American companies are trading more and more in international markets and are perhaps becoming less reliant on their domestic market. The AAA has seen its international case load increase and has concluded many agreements of co-operation and collaboration with arbitral institutions elsewhere. It is becoming a very powerful force in international arbitration.

4–120 In London, international arbitration is the prerogative of the commodity and maritime institutions as far as those specialist disputes are concerned, and of the London Court of International Arbitration (LCIA) for other commercial disputes. Although the LCIA was founded in 1892 and is the oldest arbitral institution in the world, in its modern form (new rules were promulgated in 1998) it is comparatively new. It has a very much smaller caseload than the ICC and AAA,[5] but has endeavoured through establishing user councils in Europe, North America and the Far East, to expand its influence and to exploit the long and respected tradition of London as a major international arbitration centre. It is particularly open to international influence for it actively seeks the participation and advice of practitioners from other jurisdictions and has an extremely flexible and well-drafted set of arbitration rules specifically for international use. The LCIA still requires (and deserves) much more support, particularly from the English arbitral community, to become a major force in international arbitration, particularly in Europe.

4–121 A recognised global institution is ICSID, the International Centre for Settlement of Investment Disputes, based in Washington, D.C. ICSID was established under the auspices of the World Bank in 1965, in order to provide a forum for the arbitration of disputes between States and companies investing in those States. The caseload of ICSID is very small though many of the disputes have been of considerable economic importance to the companies and countries concerned. ICSID has been subject to some criticism, because of its appellate process,[6] not something normally associated with an international arbitral institution, though not unknown in some specialist commodity institutions such as GAFTA.

4–122 Of very great interest and importance for the future of commercial arbitration, both domestic and international, is the growth of regional centres. There have been various arbitral institutions established by the Chamber of Commerce such as in Stockholm, Vienna and Zürich; and, some national institutions such as the Netherlands Arbitration Institute have been active in promoting international arbitration. Some cities, because of their particular geographical and political situation, have gained a reputation for resolving disputes of a particular kind, such as Stockholm, which has long been a preferred venue for disputes in East–West trade.

4–123 Recent years have seen the creation of many new centres. Examples in

---

[4] See International Arbitration Rules of the American Arbitration Association (effective April 1, 1997).

[5] The London Court of International Arbitration had approximately 100 pending international arbitration cases at the end of July 1999.

[6] See, *e.g.* Redfern & Hunter, *Law and Practice of International Commercial Arbitration* (3rd ed., 1999).

Europe, include Lyon, Lille and Milan; and, in the Middle East and Asia, Cairo, Kuala Lumpur, Sydney, Singapore and Hong Kong.

Until the dramatic events in Central and Eastern Europe in 1989 and 1990, **4–124** the arbitral institutions of the trading agencies and ministries of former Comecon countries were extremely important for regulating trade and commercial disputes within Comecon and (to a lesser extent) with Comecon. There was a very sophisticated and effective mandatory international arbitration system and collaboration between states, based on general and uniform conditions of delivery and supply, uniform rules for arbitration and the Moscow Convention of 1972. All that has now gone. The State arbitral institutions are being replaced by private agencies as has happened in Poland, Hungary, and in what were formerly East Germany and Czechoslovakia. These private arbitral institutions are caught up in the modernisation of their respective economies and in the political change from dictatorship to democracy.

Approaches to procedure

As a general rule the procedures of the main institutions such as the AAA, **4–125** the ICC and the LCIA are very flexible and are regularly revised. The ICC, the LCIA and the AAA did so recently in an attempt to streamline their existing procedures. The LCIA was responding to the 1996 Act and sought to make its rules compatible with the new statute. The institutional rules tend to leave to the parties and the arbitrators very considerable latitude as to the conduct of the case. The rules are so framed as to permit the conduct of an arbitration according to civil or common law concepts. However, in both institutional and ad hoc arbitration, (particularly where the ad hoc arbitration is being conducted according to UNCITRAL Rules), an interesting trend has been that the more effective elements of the civil law procedures and of the common law procedures are being combined in order to promote the faster and more economic conduct of the reference. All three institutions have revised their rules recently.

Thus, for example, the civil law procedures, which place considerable **4–126** emphasis upon the written word, tend to prevail when it comes to pleading a case in writing. Matters of fact, evidence and law in issue are set out in full in writing, whereas the common law system with its emphasis on orality, tends to be brought into play in relation to such important matters as the cross-examination of material witnesses and in the debate (which is a characteristic of the Anglo-Saxon system) between the tribunal and the advocates, conducted to seek clarification of the points in issue and to test the force of conflicting arguments. A major difference between the two systems has been the approach to the disclosure and production of documents in the possession of the parties. English arbitration law and section 34 of the Act of 1996 give the arbitrator control over the process. It has long been a cardinal feature of the AAA rules in the United States, particularly for construction industry disputes, that the requirements of pre-trial discovery in the United States, both as to documents and to witnesses, do not have to be followed.

Differences of approach to procedure and, in particular, to disclosure of **4–127** documents, are becoming of less importance in international arbitration as procedures are harmonised and blended. This process has to some extent been institutionalised in the International Bar Association (IBA) Rules of Evidence published in 1983 and currently under revision.[7] These arose as a consequence of the IBA Conference in Berlin in 1980 when considerable concern was expressed by both civil and common lawyers, at the diversity and disparity between the common and civil law systems and the need to harmonise them if at all possible was clearly recognised.

4–128   The significance for international commercial arbitration is that intelligent and flexible use of different procedures can enable arbitrators and parties to proceed as they wish, subject only to following any mandatory rules which may exist in the given venue and being certain that they observe generally accepted rules of procedural fairness.

4–129   There has been one development in relation to procedure, however, which is disturbing to English lawyers. That is the attempt to delocalise the procedure, *i.e.* to say that it is possible to have an international arbitration which floats and is not rooted in a municipal system.[8] Both English lawyers and the English courts have set then face firmly against this notion. Section 2 of the 1996 Act introduces into the statute the concept of juridical seat so as to define the scope of application of its provisions.

Applicable law

4–130   Two points need to be distinguished. They are linked but nevertheless to a considerable extent independent of each other. They are, first, how is the applicable law determined (by national rules for the conflict of laws, or by other methods? (See Article 17 of the ICC Rules.)). Secondly, what are the rules capable of constituting the proper law of the contract (such as the law in force in a given country, general principles, *lex mercatoria,* the principles common to a number of jurisdictions on a given question, international standards in a given commercial area such as the international oil or gas trade)? There has been a trend away from municipal standards in recent international practice and this trend goes both to the way in which the proper law is determined and to the concept of the proper law itself.

4–131   Attempts have been made not only to delocalise procedure, but also to delocalise rules of conflict to ascertain the applicable law in cases where the parties have not stipulated in their contract the law which is to govern it. This is given expression, for example, in the ICC Rules under Article 17(3) where absent indication as to the applicable law intended by the parties, the arbitrators may determine the law which they are going to apply to the dispute without reference to any given system of conflict of law. This provision is dictated by a practical need and is generally welcomed.

4–132   Yet, to some extent, conflict of law arguments in international arbitration are, or ought to be, academic, for commercial men of whatever nationality expect much the same result from the performance of their contracts, regardless of the system of law that is being applied. But it is the case that in circumstances where arbitrators have a freedom to apply a system of law, some of them are not applying a given municipal system because the results

---

[7]See Redfern & Hunter at App. 13.
[8]Rubino-Sammartano, above n. 69, at p. 287 *et seq.* with further references.

may be unduly harsh or uncertain, but have turned to what are known as general principles. Indeed, in many oil and gas contracts there is provision for disputes to be decided by reference to general principles, usually in conjunction with a given system or systems of law, when the general principles will prevail over the given system of law in the event of conflict.

The move away from municipal systems has also produced the *lex mercatoria,* largely it must be said, the creation of certain civil lawyers. To English lawyers, the *lex mercatoria* suffers from the drawback devastatingly illustrated by Lord Mustill in his *Festschrift* paper for Lord Wilberforce, that it is difficult to explain to a commercial man exactly what it is.[9] A somewhat different view is taken abroad.[10]   **4–133**

The view of English lawyers on *lex mercatoria* is generally that far from helping the commercial man, its use may militate against what ought to be a central objective of commercial arbitration, particularly international, namely, certainty as to the law. Businessmen are entitled to expect from the arbitral process certainty that their arbitration agreement will be recognised and enforced, certainty that a particular system of law will apply; certainty as to the procedures that are going to be followed; and, certainty that the result will be reached by a fair and appropriate procedure.   **4–134**

Section 46 of the Act of 1996 makes provision for the arbitrator to assent agreement between the parties to apply the law determined by the conflict of laws rules which it considered applicable. The DAC expressly rejected the French approach of the *voie directe.*[11]   **4–135**

Hostility to arbitration

Despite the growth in international commercial arbitration, there are many parts of the world where international commercial arbitration is not accepted at all. In some cases, this is because it has been seen traditionally as a tool or device of Western multinational commercial concerns to further and to protect their own commercial interests at the expense of developing countries.   **4–136**

Almost certainly that perception was right, but there have been significant changes in the attitude of arbitrators in recent years. International arbitrators (no longer drawn exclusively from the ranks of European and American lawyers), have been much more prepared, for example, to find that contracts are governed by the law of the host government and, indeed, absent an express choice of law, an advocate in an international arbitration who seeks, for example, to argue that the contract for the building of a factory is governed by some law other than the country in which it is built, has an uphill struggle. Yet, such developments notwithstanding, many countries in the Middle East and particularly in the Gulf, resent international arbitration and have become hostile to it, particularly to arbitration conducted under the auspices of the ICC. As a consequence, many countries refuse to have any   **4–137**

---

[9] (1988) 4 (2) *Arbitration International.*
[10] Schlosser, above n. 99, *Rz. 193 et seq.*
[11] A system by which arbitrators go straight to the law they think should be applied without the conflict rules of any given system of law.

international arbitration provisions in their contracts and if they accept arbitration at all, prefer it to be under their own domestic system.[12]

4–138   The perception of international lawyers and businessmen is of universal and profound hostility within South America to international arbitration (the Calvo doctrine). There are constitutional provisions in certain South American countries, notably Ecuador and Peru, which prohibit arbitration of international disputes involving their citizens taking place in those countries. Attempts to enforce international arbitration agreements with Brazilian states or nationals are frequently met by the *compromisso* argument to deny jurisdiction to the arbitrators. Homologation of an international award given outside Brazil may be met inside Brazil by a series of highly technical procedural defences.

4–139   Yet the paradox is that over 100 years ago there were movements within South America towards a harmonisation of trade law including arbitration. It is also said that more and more contracts with South American countries have international arbitration clauses and it appears that international arbitrators have become less and less patient with defences to jurisdiction being raised by South American parties to international arbitration. There is certainly a growing interest in arbitration amongst South American lawyers and the old hostility may be waning.

4–140   In some parts of the world, commercial arbitration is rejected on cultural grounds. In China and Japan it is contrary to the culture of those countries and the practices of the business community, to resolve disputes in an adversarial or confrontational manner. Disputes are normally resolved by negotiation. Failing negotiation, they are resolved by conciliation, or by mediation.[13] They are not usually resolved by arbitration, or by litigation. This has given rise, for example, in the People's Republic of China, to developing systems in use before the Cultural Revolution, which combine both arbitration and conciliation within the same proceedings, sometimes without being able to recognise one stage from another; a kind of rolling procedure. To some extent, this is being imitated in Hong Kong where, in view of the particular importance of Hong Kong as the conduit for much of China's foreign trade, and given the return of sovereignty to the People's Republic in 1997, attempts are being made to devise hybrid procedures of arbitration and conciliation based on the statutory authority of section 2B of the Arbitration Ordinance.[14]

4–141   There have been some attempts to see whether mediation and arbitration could be combined in a Western context. Thus, for example, the AAA introduced med–arb, or mediation-arbitration in construction disputes.[15] But there is considerable suspicion of such procedures, on the well-founded belief that parties will be reluctant to disclose everything to a mediator, if the same person then arbitrates the dispute.[16]

---

[12]This attitude was expressed, *e.g.* in a 1967 OPEC resolution, reprinted in 19 I.L.M. 773 (1980) which provided that "disputes arising between a government and operator shall fall exclusively within the jurisdiction of competent national courts".

[13]See, *e.g.* Lee, *Commercial Disputes Settlement in China,* pp. 15–17 (1985).

[14]*ibid.*

[15]Construction Industry Dispute Resolution Procedures (Including Mediation and Arbitration Rules), January 1999.

[16]See Chap. 16 for further discussion about med–arb. See also the seminal paper by Michael

A significant omission in the Act of 1996 is any reference to alternative **4–142** dispute resolution. That is why the statute is an Arbitration Act and not, for example as in India, an Arbitration and Conciliation Act. In recent years, alternative dispute resolution has been used increasingly by the commercial community for a resolution of its disputes. There are many reasons for this which reflect concern at the formality, expense and delay of the arbitral process. Most arbitrations settle. Best modern practice recognises that arbitrators have an obligation to enquire of parties whether there is anything the arbitrators can do by consent to assist the parties to achieve settlement. Some arbitration statutes and rules expressly so provide, see for example Hong Kong. But in England there was no prospect of incorporating ADR provisions in an arbitration statute. Such provisions may well have to form part of a general regime for ADR if it becomes a very important aspect of the civil justice system.

A major criticism of the arbitral process is cost, particularly of institutional **4–143** arbitrations where substantial deposits on account of administrative fees and expenses are often required, sometimes well in advance of the substantive hearings.

In reforming English law, the DAC attached great importance to questions **4–144** of costs. There has been a long-running debate in England as to whether access to the courts is much too expensive. Similar concerns were felt about arbitration. Indeed, anecdotal evidence suggests that the level of fees of English and U.S. law firms in international commercial arbitration is higher than that of their civil law counterparts. This is not because hourly rates are markedly different, but more because of a difference of approach to the preparation and presentation of evidence and argument. The English and American adversarial tradition and procedures have led to very labour-intensive dispute resolution.

Sections 59 to 65 provide a comprehensive regime for assessment and **4–145** recovery of costs. Probably the only power of any interest is the wholly novel one in section 65 which gives the arbitrators the power on their own motion to limit recoverable costs of the arbitration or any part of it, to a specified limit. This power was regarded by the DAC as perhaps going some way to redress the inequality of arms which can occur when one side possesses greater financial resources than the other.

A criticism of arbitration is the failure of many systems to provide for **4–146** multi-party or multi-contract disputes. Despite the pressures brought to bear by the construction and maritime industries in particular, there is no provision in the new statute for consolidation of arbitration. Instead, in section 35 there is a general encouragement to agree that arbitral proceedings should be consolidated or concurrent hearings should be held, but without such express power the tribunal is powerless to order such measures on its own motion.

The reasons given by the majority on the DAC for this decision were a **4–147** mixture of practice and principle. It was pointed out, not without some justification, that the arbitration community in many developed jurisdictions

---

Schneider at the 1996 Conference of the International Council for Commercial Arbitration in Seoul reported in ICCA Congress Series No. 8 published by Kluwer Law International (1996).

has found it very difficult to formulate consolidation measures and some of the institutions, notably the ICC, are perceived to be against it. The point of principle was that arbitration is essentially consensual and it would be wrong to compel parties who had not agreed to arbitrate with each other, to involve themselves in arbitration on a consolidated basis. But these arguments ignore the reality that it is not beyond the wit or imagination of arbitral institutions and practitioners to devise sensible procedures for consolidation and the organisation of concurrent hearings. Most developed civil litigation systems, certainly the system in England, have long had effective procedures for consolidation and the organisation of concurrent hearings. Secondly, there are many industries and spheres of economic activity in which business is conducted by a network of contracts. Thus, for example, large infrastructure projects have a network of contracts and persons entering into them know that. It is not unreasonable therefore for them to expect that a dispute in one case may be the same as a dispute in another and that common sense and cost may dictate a consolidated or concurrent hearing.

4–148   But perhaps more importantly the debate illustrates a fundamental misconception which has certainly bedevilled the development of English arbitration in recent years as, for example, the problem over the power of arbitrators to strike out the arbitration for excessive delay demonstrates. Incidentally, this problem is now solved by the Act of 1996, which conveys such an express power.[17] It is wrong to over-emphasise the consensual nature of arbitration. Arbitration is a derogation of the sovereignty of the State. What the State is saying is that it will agree to lend its power to the recognition and enforcement of arbitration agreements and arbitration awards, rather than compelling such disputes to be resolved within the State courts. There is therefore a vital public interest in the proper operation of the arbitral system. That public interest should be paramount, which to some extent is now the case in England because it underlies the very important sections 1, 33 and 40.

4–149   A further question mark over the arbitral process is confidentiality. Nowhere in the Act is there reference to privacy and confidentiality. This has become a highly controversial topic. It has long been the accepted wisdom in England that arbitral proceedings are both private and confidential, though it is recognised that there are limits on confidentiality such as the obvious one that awards on enforcement through the courts become public documents. The debate has largely been prompted by the decision of the High Court of Australia in the *Esso* case[18] and the realisation that public interest widely defined may dictate that certain arbitration proceedings should not be confidential. But it was decided that the law of confidentiality was such a difficult topic in itself that it was best left to development in the courts through individual cases.

The future

4–150   The commercial pressures which have promoted international commercial

---

[17]S. 41(3) Arbitration Act 1996.
[18]*Esso Australia Resources Limited & Others v. Plowman* (Minister for Energy and Minerals) & Others (1995) 128 A.L.R. 391.

arbitration are as powerful now as at any time since the New York Convention in 1958; indeed, perhaps more so. The growth of trade in a single unified market of the European Community already outstrips the capacity of the court systems within the Community to cope with commercial disputes, both domestic and international, and serves to emphasise the weakness of those jurisdictions which lack efficient and experienced commercial court arbitration systems.

The extraordinary developments in Eastern Europe as countries seek to **4–151** transfer from planned economies to market economies, also increases the need for efficient resolution of domestic and international commercial disputes. Although it should not be forgotten that under the Comecon arrangements the "Socialist" countries succeeded (admittedly by a mandatory system) in achieving a measure of uniformity, comity and efficiency in resolving trade disputes which has so far eluded others. The increasingly global role of American multinational companies will continue to stimulate U.S. interest in international commercial arbitration, but American influence will be resisted if American practitioners seek only to export American litigation procedures and drive up the cost.[19]

While it is clear that commercial arbitration—both international and **4–152** domestic—will grow, there is an increasingly widespread belief that practitioners will have to be prepared to embrace new ideas of procedure and practice if the proper objectives of the commercial community, both domestically and internationally, are to be satisfied. Arbitration, particularly institutional, is becoming too formal, too rigid, too drawn out and too expensive. Although ADR methods are increasingly considered not only as an alternative to litigation, but also as an alternative to arbitration itself, it is more likely that such methods will be used to complement and expedite arbitration than wholly to replace it.

---

[19]See the concluding remarks by Mustill and Aksen at 75 ICC Conference, Geneva, September 1998, "Outcome of discussions and reflections of the Future".

CHAPTER 5

COURT ANNEXED ADR

5–001   In preparing his proposals, Lord Woolf considered the experience of other jurisdictions in attempting procedural reform, particularly by using case management techniques. The problems of expense and delay which afflict the civil justice system in England and Wales are by no means unique. They exist elsewhere, and not only in the common law world. Lord Woolf looked in particular at the United States, Canada and Australia but was also influenced by experience in Germany where, it was suggested, litigation was perhaps more efficiently conducted at a more acceptable level of cost to the litigant.

5–002   Although the problems of access to civil justice are common to many developed jurisdictions, comparisons even between jurisdictions with a common legal heritage and tradition should be approached with caution. Social and economic conditions differ, the structure and size of the legal professions may differ and the training, experience and numbers of the judiciary may well be different. Thus, for example, Germany has a system of career judges who enter the judiciary at an early age. Germany also has a far higher ratio of judges to population than does the United Kingdom. Various factors and particularly the impact of crime, marital breakdown and other major social problems may have great influence on how a civil justice system works. Nonetheless there is much that we can learn from informed comparisons.

5–003   One significant feature of some civil law systems has already been noted, namely the expectation that judges will express a view to the parties on how the case might be settled. In some courts such as in Stockholm, cases can be referred to a judge (other than the trial judge) who will attempt to reach compromise with the parties. In the Chinese legal tradition there are methods of combining mediation with litigation in a type of rolling procedure. Such experience as we have of other jurisdictions suggests that judicial intervention directed to settlement can be helpful.[1]

5–004   Under Woolf, it is unlikely that English judges will intervene to the point of indicating terms upon which a case might be settled. Rather, the general

---

[1] Thus, the German statistics show that: in the period 1981 to 1991 the percentage settlement rate as a consequence of judicial intervention was approximately 9% in the Amtsgericht; approximately 16% at first instance in the Landgericht; approximately 13% in the second instance of the Landgericht; and approximately 17% in the Oberlandesgericht: Federal Ministry of Justice, Bonn.

expectation is that English judges will exercise the powers given under Rule 26(4) of the new Civil Procedure Rules. The rule permits the adjournment of cases for ADR to be attempted. CEDR (The Centre for Dispute Resolution), one of the leading civil commercial mediation organisations in the United Kingdom, believes that this new power to adjourn for ADR will lead to an "explosion"[2] in its case load and has increased its casework staff in anticipation.

There is scope (as was indicated in Chapter 4) for expanding the role of the small claims arbitration scheme in the county court and changing the procedures so that district judges could be encouraged to be more interventionist and flexible to the point of acting as mediator in such disputes. But without extra resources from Government being applied to the existing small claims scheme, it is clear that any expansion will require substantial assistance from the private sector in providing facilities and personnel to make an expanded court-annexed system of small claims arbitration or mediation work.

5–005

1. COURT-ANNEXED ADR IN THE U.S.

Any examination of court-annexed schemes must start with the United States. The Americans have by far the greatest experience with court-annexed systems of arbitration and various forms of ADR and there is much we can learn from them.

5–006

The principal objective of court-annexed ADR in the United States has been to achieve settlements or, failing that, to streamline litigation at both first instance and on appeal. ADR is widely used in the state and federal courts. Statutory approval of ADR in the federal district (trial) courts is given under the 1990 Civil Justice Reform Act, but use of ADR in the courts goes back to the mid-1970s when the first arbitration pilot project began and to the 1980s when experiments such as the summary jury trial and early neutral evaluation were introduced. The Civil Justice Reform Act of 1990 required district courts to develop, with the help of an advisory group of local lawyers, scholars and other citizens, a district-specific plan to reduce costs and delay in civil litigation. ADR was one of six case management processes recommended by the statute which led to greater use of ADR in the federal district courts. The most recent legislative step was taken on October 30, 1998 when President Clinton signed the Alternative Disputes Resolution Act of 1998.[3]

5–007

This Act requires each federal district court to authorise the use of ADR in all civil cases and to establish its own ADR programme. The Act also requires the district courts to establish procedures for making neutrals available, to adopt local rules regarding confidentiality, compensation, and conflict of interest and to appoint a judge or staff person to administer the programme. The courts must also adopt rules requiring litigants to consider

5–008

---

[2]See the observations of Anthony Monaghan, ADR Services Senior Case Manager at CEDR reported in the Law Society's Gazette 96/18 6 May 1999.
[3]Public Law 105–315 codified at 28 U.S.C., ss. 651 *et seq.*

ADR and they are given authority to compel parties to use mediation and early neutral evaluation. The courts are also given authority to exempt cases or categories of cases from using ADR.

5–009   The Act is the culmination of years of experience and research, which led Congress to adopt the policy of extending ADR to all federal district courts. The policy appears to be supported by bench and bar. A 1992 survey of federal judges in the US found that a considerable majority favoured the use of ADR in the federal courts. Some 86 per cent thought that the role of the federal court should be to assist parties in resolving their dispute through whatever procedure is best suited to the case.

5–010   By 1994 at least two-thirds of the courts were authorising one or more forms of ADR. In some courts this is no more than a statement of encouragement, but in others there are detailed rules and administrative structures to promote ADR and under the 1998 Act this will now become mandatory. The most common form of ADR authorised by the courts is mediation. Some courts move cases into ADR through automatic referral by case type or other criteria, while others rely on judge or party identification of cases appropriate for ADR. Ten courts are authorised by statute to compel certain types of cases to use arbitration,[4] but court-annexed arbitration appears to have fallen from favour, four of the ten courts no longer maintain their arbitration programmes.

5–011   In 1996 the Federal Judicial Centre and the CPR Institute for Dispute Resolution, a leading private U.S. ADR body, published a report entitled "ADR and settlement in the Federal District courts".[5] The report concluded that there was insufficient information and statistical knowledge of the operation of ADR schemes in the district courts to draw any conclusions about the effectiveness of ADR. However, the report noted that there was increasing recognition that ADR can be used earlier in the case than had previously been considered desirable. Many observers had thought that, compared to early court ADR programmes, ADR was appropriate only for cases ready for trial, but the report found that ADR is:

"more often integrated into a court or judge's overall case management practices and is considered much earlier in the case".

5–012   The report also found that:

"across all courts, it is not uncommon today for discovery planning to be linked to the mediation process and for the mediation session to take place before discovery has been completed".

5–013   The report made some interesting observations on fees for ADR. Initially, the ADR schemes in the U.S. courts were largely implemented on a *pro bono* basis. But by 1996 of the "41 courts offering attorney based mediation, only

---

[4] 28 U.S.C., ss. 65 *et seq.*
[5] *ADR and Settlement in the Federal District Courts: A Sourcebook for Judges and Lawyers,* Elizabeth Plapinger and Donna Stienstra, 1996.

9 provide that service *pro bono*". Three others generally offer mediation without fees:

> "although in some circumstances the parties may be required to pay the mediator".

The remaining courts—that is two-thirds of the courts with mediation programmes—require that parties pay a fee. The report discovered that the market rate fee found in 10 courts is the most common, with a number of courts reserving the right to review the reasonableness of the fee. The report also revealed that many courts had special provisions in their rules regarding low income or indigent parties, generally waiving the fee altogether and that:

5–014

> "interestingly there appears to be little relationship between where the fees are assessed and whether the referral to ADR is mandatory or made only with party consent".

Thus, by 1996 ADR in the federal courts was well-established, but as the joint Federal Judicial Centre and CPR Institute Report[6] recognised, more information was required. The report looked forward to publication of two reports required by the Civil Justice Reform Act, one a comparison of ten pilot and ten comparison districts then being conducted by the RAND Corporation, and the other a study of five demonstration districts then being conducted by the Federal Judicial Centre.

5–015

The RAND report[7] of late 1996 was entitled "An Evaluation of Mediation and Early Neutral Evaluation under the Civil Justice Reform Act". It provoked a very considerable debate, as did the report[8] submitted in January 1997 by the Federal Judicial Centre on the five demonstration programmes. Opponents and proponents of ADR in the court found much to justify their respective points of view from the evidence and analysis made in these two seminal reports, though it is clear from the passing of the 1998 Act that Congress recognised the value of ADR in the federal court system to the point of requiring all district courts to authorise use of ADR in all civil cases, subject to limited exceptions.

5–016

The RAND report was part of a series of reports produced by RAND on the workings of the Civil Justice Reform Act of 1990, the other reports being largely concerned with evaluating judicial case management under that Act. As regards ADR, the RAND report was essentially neutral in its findings. In the Introduction, RAND made clear that it regarded prior research on various ADR mechanisms as "quite thin". The report indicated that:

5–017

> "previous empirical research on court annexed arbitration suggests that

---

[6] *ADR and Settlement in the Federal District Courts: A Sourcebook for Judges and Lawyers*, Elizabeth Plapinger and Donna Stienstra, 1996.
[7] Evaluation of Mediation and Early Neutral Evaluation under the Civil Reform Act, the Institute for Civil Justice, 1996.
[8] Report to the Judicial Conference Committee on Court Administration and Case Management. A study of the five demonstration programmes established under the Civil Justice Reform Act of 1990, January 24, 1997.

these programs have at best modest contributions to make to managing civil litigation more expeditiously and more economically. However, they offer litigants a more satisfying form of justice than is accorded through the combination of bilateral negotiation and judicially faciliative settlement that is the practical alternative in today's trial courts''.

The report continued:

"previous empirical research on other forms of court annexed ADR such as mediation and neutral evaluation is much more limited in volume than research on arbitration; the available findings could not provide an adequate basis upon which to make definitive policy recommendations''.

5–018   In that sense therefore the jury according to RAND is still out on the efficacy of ADR in court-annexed systems in the United States, but, as a result of the analysis, RAND drew certain summary conclusions which merit close study. With respect to time to disposition RAND concluded that there was:

"no strong statistical evidence that time to disposition is significantly affected by mediation or neutral evaluation''.

5–019   As to costs of the litigation, interestingly for those advocates of case management (which is the centrepiece of the Woolf reforms), RAND's main Civil Justice Reform Act evaluation concluded that:

"early management was associated with significantly increased lawyer work hours''

and:

"because of these other potential influences on the time that lawyers spend, we do not believe that [there is] any clear evidence that neutral evaluation, by itself, will necessarily lead to increased lawyer work hours''.

5–020   RAND studied the administrative costs to the court by taking the total expenditure in most of the six districts under study and translating it into a cost per case. These costs were in a range from U.S. $130 to U.S. $490 per case. The width of the range was explained by the fact that some districts had a low number of referrals combined with a high administrative cost whereas in others the opposite was true. Predictably, the greater the number of referrals the lower the cost to the court service.

5–021   RAND's findings on settlement as a result of mediation or early neutral evaluation showed a connection between settlement and when the ADR session is held, in that settlement is more likely to occur just before or after the ADR session where the session is held later in the life of the case. RAND indicated that the percentage likelihood of settlement ranged from 31 per cent early on to 72 per cent later on:

"Discovery may be completed and cases may be more ready to settle by the time of the later session; thus, the fact that the lawyers and parties must meet for mediation or neutral evaluation may be the precipitating event required to finalise agreement".

RAND also considered and reported on perceptions of fairness and found **5–022** that lawyers in about nine out of 10 cases in all programmes felt that mediation or early neutral evaluation was fair, though a slightly lower percentage of litigants agreed. But RAND was unable to make any statistical inferences with confidence regarding litigant views due to the inadequacy of the litigant data. As to the ADR session itself, only a minority of the respondents were dissatisfied with ADR: a majority were either neutral or satisfied.

RAND's overall assessment in summary was that: **5–023**

"mediation and neutral evaluation programs implemented in the 6 districts are not a panacea for perceived problems of cost and delay, but neither do they appear to be detrimental. We have no justification for a strong policy recommendation because we found no major program effects either positive or negative. This lack of a demonstrated major effect on litigation costs and delay is generally consistent with the outcomes of empirical research on court related ADR".

RAND's conclusions were surprising to some of those who advocated **5–024** ADR and who had expected that research would show decisively that ADR offered real benefits both in cost and time savings. The RAND report was generally neutral in its findings, though the report by the Federal Judicial Centre, whilst drawing attention to the difficulties of statistical analysis, reported certain findings favourable to court-annexed ADR systems.

In discussing whether court-annexed ADR saved time, the authors of the **5–025** report warned against too ready an interpretation of statistics because:

"given the many fluctuating conditions in a court at any given time, it is often very difficult to discern the effects of a particular court program on litigation time".

But in their analysis of results from one district it is clear that over a four-and-a-half year period and with a case load of some 3,000 cases:

"the median age at termination for cases required to participate in the program . . . was more than two months shorter than that for cases not allowed to participate in the program."

Interestingly, the belief of a high proportion of attorneys was that ADR **5–026** reduced time to disposition in their case. More than half the attorneys in certain districts thought that their cases had settled in whole or in part as a result of ADR and the conclusion drawn was that the programmes

"appeared to be achieving the goal of effecting settlements".

5–027   The Federal Judicial Centre study reported other benefits of ADR such as reports by attorneys that ADR was helpful in encouraging the parties to be more realistic about their respective positions. It also became clear that the timing of the ADR session was important, but that depended in part on the culture of the court and in part on the lawyer's expectation of what the ADR session would accomplish. Most striking, because it is different from conventional wisdom and the RAND report, is the finding in one district of high settlement rates and high participant satisfaction even though cases were referred to ADR within 30 days of defences being filed. It was clear that client attendance, which was a requirement in the three ADR demonstration districts, was highly desirable and probably necessary. So too was having a neutral of high quality. The findings of the report for California Northern show:

"the quality of the neutral is directly related to a number of measures of ADR effectiveness, including whether ADR reduced disposition time, lowered litigation costs, prompted settlement and provided a satisfactory outcome and fair process".

5–028   Another interesting finding was that in the Northern District of California where parties are all expected to use ADR but permitted to choose which ADR process to use:

"the benefits of ADR are greater when the attorneys may select the particular process in which they would participate".

5–029   In the Northern District of California it was also notable that most attorneys selected early neutral evaluation, which suggests that lawyers there want an expert evaluation when they use ADR.

5–030   The report makes it plain that in order to make court-annexed ADR programmes work, it is essential to have the full commitment of the bar[9] and the judiciary as well as reliance on professional ADR staff. That approach is expensive, and it is interesting to note that the cost per case referred to ADR during the demonstration was roughly U.S. $480 in California Northern and U.S. $700 in the district of Missouri Western. The Federal Judicial Centre found that:

"while the judges believe that they have experienced a reduction in their work loads as a result of these expenditures, greater savings have probably been realised by the parties, whose savings, as estimated by their attorneys, were $15,000 per party in Missouri Western and $25,000 per party in California Northern. On the other hand, attorneys in West Virginia Northern also reported substantial savings, $10,000 per party, and considerably less cost to the court—about $7,000 per year or $45 per case referred to settlement week during the demonstration period".

---

[9] There are indications in the U.K. that professional bodies recognise that a commitment must be made. The Law Society of England and Wales for example has resolved to give a full commitment to ADR.

On the whole attorneys thought the programmes were fair, with a very 5–031
small minority, some 11 per cent to 15 per cent, thinking otherwise. They
considered that the various types of ADR used in these programmes met the
requirement of basic procedural fairness.

Predictably, these two reports, and particularly that of RAND, stimulated 5–032
very considerable debate in the United States. To some extent that debate
found an echo in England and supporters and opponents of Woolf, of case
management and of ADR, each drew comfort from the findings. It is
however important to note that in the United States the Congress has
reinforced the policy of court-annexed ADR by enacting the Alternative
Dispute Resolution Act of 1998. While the debate may not be over, the
essential decision has been taken.

2. MULTI-DOOR COURTHOUSE

One of the most significant developments arising out of the relationship 5–033
between ADR procedures and the court system has been the creation in the
United States of multi-door courthouses.

The author of the concept of multi-door courthouses was Professor Frank 5–034
E. A. Sander, Professor of Law at Harvard University, who delivered a paper
in 1976 to the National Conference on the Causes of Popular Dissatisfaction
with Administration of Justice, jointly sponsored by the Judicial Conference
of the United States, the Conference of Chief Justices and the American Bar
Association.

Certain criteria were considered by Professor Sander to be important for 5–035
determining the effectiveness of a dispute resolution system, namely: "cost,
speed, accuracy, credibility (to the public and the parties), and workability. In
some cases, but not in all, predictability may also be important."[10]

Professor Sander identified two questions as important: 5–036

"(1) What are the significant characteristics of various alternative dispute
resolution mechanisms (such as adjudication by courts, arbitration,
mediation, negotiation, and various blends of these and other devices)?

(2) How can these characteristics be utilised so that, given the variety of
disputes that presently arise, we can begin to develop some rational
criteria for allocating various types of disputes to different dispute
resolution processes?"[11]

In setting out the range of ADR systems, Professor Sander regarded the 5–037
factor of decreasing external involvement by a neutral in the process as
critical. He outlined a spectrum of processes, on a decreasing scale of
external involvement. At the maximum end of the involvement scale he
placed adjudication (through the court, by arbitration, and through
administrative processes). Next, half-way between adjudication and mediation
he placed the ombudsman and fact-finding enquiry. Mediation came next,

---

[10]See the Pound Conference report, cited as 70 Federal Rules Decisions (FRD) 79 at p. 113, n.7.
[11]*ibid.* p. 133.

followed by negotiation; and at the minimum involvement end he put "avoidance" (an approach he described as "clearly undesirable").

5–038   Professor Sander pointed out that while these different systems were distinct in theory, there was in practice often considerable interplay and overlapping between them. Thus, the process of fact-finding might very closely resemble the process of adjudication, and concillation could also be part of the adjudication process.

5–039   Professor Sander's analysis led him to recommend:

> " . . . a flexible and diverse panoply of dispute resolution processes, with particular types of cases being assigned to differing processes (or combinations of processes), according to some of the criteria previously mentioned. Conceivably such allocation might be accomplished for a particular class of cases at the outset by the legislature, that in effect is what was done by the Massachusetts legislature for malpractice cases. Alternatively, one might envision by the year 2000 not simply a court house but a Dispute Resolution Centre, where the grievant would first be channelled through a screening clerk who would then direct him to the process (or sequence of processes) most appropriate to his type of case."[12]

5–040   Professor Sander's theories have been tested in practice in several states and most notably in the District of Columbia. The experience has been favourable and encouraging albeit gradual.[13] In the District of Columbia, Chief Judge Moultrie initiated a multi-door courthouse programme organised and controlled by the Superior Court and with the active support of the D.C. Bar and community groups.

5–041   In the District of Columbia ADR programmes have been introduced for such cases as small claims (mediation); domestic relations (mediation); accelerated review of civil disputes, particularly for use in complex multi-party cases; mandatory non-binding arbitration in cases where the amount in question was less than U.S. $50,000; settlement weeks drawing on the experience in Ohio and California; and summary jury trials.

5–042   The multi-door concept has been tested in experiments in various other parts of the United States such as New Jersey, Houston and Philadelphia, and a number of states now offer multi-door programmes. Several federal district courts, such as California Northern also provide litigants with an array of ADR options.

5–043   The state court programmes enable a member of the public to contact the court in person or by telephone, with a complaint or dispute. A preliminary analysis will then be made of the case in order to be able to recommend which dispute resolution process is most suitable to resolve it. Various criteria will be applied, including, for example, the kind of issues involved, what kind of compensation is likely to be awarded if successful, whether witnesses or other evidence will be needed, whether rights need to be protected and what services are available. The inquiring party is then advised

---

[12]*ibid.* p. 130.
[13]See "Maine Route: Multi-Door proposal reflects growing role of ADR" by James Podgers, 79 A.B.A.J. (September 1993).

about the processes that might be most appropriate to the case and is given relevant referral details, which may be to departments within the court, or may perhaps be to outside agencies.

5–044

This initial preliminary analysis or "intake screening" is the "key feature of the multi-door courthouse".[14] Working with a network of courts, government agencies and ADR centres, it aims to give an individual and specialised answer to each inquirer. This may also involve referring any non-legal problems brought in by parties to the appropriate social services agency.

5–045

The case analysis is done by an intake officer, whose role requires quite a high level of skill; and the question has been raised as to whether that degree of attention can reliably be expected from intake officers. Other questions have also been raised, for example, as to whether the choice of process remains with the inquirer, as presumably it must; whether represented parties need to go through this process, or whether it can be assumed that lawyers can help their clients to make these choices; and, indeed, whether lawyers themselves are adequately trained in advising clients on dispute resolution choices.[15]

5–046

In an analysis of the benchmarks of a successful multi-door courthouse, in the context of a 1988 District of Columbia survey, the following factors were considered relevant: first, to have a viable plan for permanent funding in place from the outset; secondly, to employ programme staff including experienced administrators with knowledge of the court system as well as professionals with proven ADR expertise; thirdly, to have competent and enthusiastic volunteers to undertake training and operate the service (though for complex civil cases the report indicated that there would need to be provision for properly compensating skilled mediators); fourthly, to have support from the judiciary and from legal practitioners; and finally, to have a range of ADR techniques and resources but to select them for use with caution and judgment.[16] The multi-door courthouse concept has been described by the American Bar Association as "an exciting and innovative idea". At the 1989 Annual Meeting of the ABA the National Conference of State Court Judges and the Judicial Administration Division arranged a programme entitled "The Multi-door Courthouse Experience: the Judicial Perspective" which it was said "will serve to stimulate judges and other attenders to explore new concepts for their court systems and provide better service to the citizens of their communities".[17]

3. COURT-ANNEXED ADR IN CANADA

An omission from the first edition of this book was any discussion of court-annexed ADR in Canada, an omission for which the authors were gently chided by their Canadian friends. In this edition the authors refer to

5–047

---

[14]See the section "Note on the Multi-door Courthouse" in Dispute Resolution by Goldberg, Green & Sander (1985) at pp. 514–516.

[15]See Murray, Rau & Sherman, *Processes of Dispute Resolution: The Role of Lawyers* (1989) at p. 279.

[16]See Kessler and Finkelstein, *op. cit.*

[17]ABA's Dispute Resolution Issue No. 25, Spring/Summer 1989 at p. 1.

experience in Canada which Lord Woolf also considered when preparing his proposals for litigation reform.

5–048 In 1996 a Task Force of the Canadian Bar Association reported on systems of civil justice within Canada, which like the United States and Australia has a dual court system. The report of the Task Force took almost exactly the same approach as Lord Woolf by recommending measures for the promotion of settlement, the streamlining of procedures and the harnessing of new technology, all seeking to achieve lower cost and improving access to justice. Thus, the Task Force recommended that the civil justice system should contain:

"opportunities for litigants to use non-binding dispute resolution processes as early as possible in the litigation and at a minimum at or shortly after the close of pleadings and again following completion of examinations for discovery".

5–049 Another recommendation was that there should be:

"a requirement that litigants certify that they have availed themselves of the opportunity to participate in a non-binding dispute resolution process or that the circumstances of the case are such that participation is not warranted or has been considered and rejected for sound reasons, before being entitled to proceed to trial".

5–050 A further recommendation was that:

"rules of procedure should impose upon all litigants the continuing obligation to canvass settlement possibilities and to consider opportunities available to them to participate in non-binding dispute resolution processes".

5–051 A very important element of the Task Force proposals was the introduction of case flow management systems to provide for early court intervention and the definition of issues and for the supervision of the progress of cases. Court intervention for the purposes of facilitating settlement was proposed as an integral part of the case flow management system.

5–052 Two chapters of the Task Force's report were specifically concerned with settlement in the civil justice system. Chapters 3 and 4 of the report are thus of particular interest in considering the efficacy of court-annexed schemes. Both Lord Woolf and the Task Force appear to share the same vision of a civil justice system for the modern age. Both contemplate a civil justice system that provides many options to litigants for dispute resolution and in the words of the Task Force report which:

"provide an incentive structure that rewards early settlement and results in trials being a mechanism of value but a last resort for determining disputes".

5–053 The Task Force however went much further than Lord Woolf in defining how what it called a "multi-option civil justice system" could work ensuring that disputes rest within the court system in order to preserve the basic right of access to the courts and respecting basic principles of fairness. The multi-option civil justice system envisioned by the Task Force involves a mandatory role for the parties at various stages of the dispute resolution process. Hence the proposed obligation upon parties to explore settlement possibilities and the duty which it was proposed the court should have to ensure that that obligation was met.

The Task Force proposals (like those of Lord Woolf) placed great **5–054** emphasis on costs and contained a number of specific proposals for imposing costs sanctions upon a failure to observe procedural requirements or unreasonable behaviour in the conduct of the litigation.

The Task Force drew on the experience of pilot schemes in Canada. **5–055** Certain provinces have been using ADR systems. In Saskatchewan, mediation was made mandatory in civil cases and mediation orientation mandatory in family cases. In British Columbia, mediation has been used extensively in insurance cases. In British Columbia in 1991 a new small claims process was introduced. The monetary limit was Can. $10,000 and a mandatory settlement conference conducted informally by a judge was a feature of the reform. In their excellent dispute resolution handbook entitled *Bypass Court*,[18] Genevieve Chornenki and Christine Hart describe how the judge:

"spent 20 to 30 minutes with the parties assisting them to address their needs and interests in a mediative way, and possibly expressing an opinion on the strengths and weaknesses of each side's case. The judge was empowered to make orders to facilitate a speedy trial if no settlement was reached."

The authors reported that an external evaluation of the project determined: **5–056**

"that the settlement conferences settled 60% of the cases reaching that stage. It was found that cases in which lawyers attended without their clients were unmediable since all of the interests were not available to participate and they rarely settled. Consequently, the rules were changed to require party attendance. Other changes enabled the settlement conference judge to make a determination whether there is any cause of action or defence".

duced to 8 per cent of the claims filed. Many courts such as Alberta have **5–058** used judicial mini-trials with the judge rendering an advisory opinion at the conclusion of the exchange of information.

A major ADR project was started in Ontario, integrated with the court and involving random referral of 40 per cent of the non-family civil cases in the **5–058** Toronto region to the ADR Centre for Mediation. The mediation projects in Ontario and Saskatchewan took civil cases prior to discovery, whereas in Alberta mini-trials were convened after discovery, and mediations in Quebec

---

[18] *Bypass Court: A Dispute Resolution Handbook* by Genevieve A. Chomenki and Christine E. Hart (Butterworths, 1996).

also take place after discovery. The Toronto project is generally regarded to have been successful. Speaking at a conference on civil justice reform in February 1996, the Chief Justice of the Ontario Court of Justice when describing the projects, stated that they:

"have been generally very successful and demonstrate that a case managed civil action will reduce by 50% the average time of resolution. After some initial concern, the concept has earned wide support from the Bar".

5–059 The Task Force report has clearly influenced the use of court-annexed ADR in Canada. Since January 4, 1999 all new civil non-family case-managed actions must first submit to mediation before litigation may commence in Toronto and Ottawa Carletons General Division Courts unless a judge can be convinced that the file merits exclusion.

5–060 The Government of Ontario has plans to introduce mediation systems outside the court. It has in place and is developing dispute resolution programmes for a wide range of state agencies such as the Ontario Securities Commission, the Human Rights Commission and the Financial Services Commission.

5–061 In Saskatchewan the pilot project in mandatory mediation is being extended over time throughout the whole province. Alberta is considering the introduction of mandatory mediation pre-trial conferences in the Court of Queen's Bench. In Quebec mediation is already used in family matters and the provincial Government is considering the application of mandatory mediation to other High Court cases.

4. COURT-ANNEXED ADR IN AUSTRALIA

5–062 Lord Woolf was also impressed by work in Australia. Australia has statutory mediation in many important areas of economic and social activity and court-annexed systems of ADR. Professor John Wade considers that mandatory mediation clauses are now routine in new legislation and describes the result as a "legislative avalanche".[19]

5–063 Thus, for example, there is legislation in New South Wales providing for statutory mediation under the Legal Profession Reform Act 1993, Rules of the Industrial Court, Native Title (NSW) Act 1994; Courts Legislation (Mediation and Evaluation Amendment) Act 1994. The Commercial Arbitration Act of 1994 provides by section 27(1) that parties to an arbitration agreement:

"(a) may seek settlement of a dispute between them by mediation, conciliation or similar means; or (b) may authorise an arbitrator or umpire to act as a mediator, conciliator or other non arbitral intermediary between them".

---

[19] "Current Trends and Models in Dispute Resolution" by Prof. John Wade, *Australian Dispute Resolution Journal*, February 1998.

Similar provisions apply in other Arbitration Acts of other parts of the **5–064** Commonwealth. Model legislation and court rules for court-annexed mediation have been formulated. It is clear that court-annexed mediation combined with case management is regarded as being effective, though there are dissenting voices.[20]

Since 1987 there has been a court-annexed programme of assisted dispute **5–065** resolution in the Federal Court of Australia. The scheme has been described by the Hon. M. E. J. Black, Chief Justice of the Court in a paper delivered on November 12, 1995. Statutory powers were conferred on the court in 1991.[21] The mediation scheme is an integral part of the court's procedures. The majority of the mediations are conducted by the registrars of the court who have been specially trained, as have some of the judges. By statute, the process is utterly confidential and the mediators have been given the same immunity as judges.

There is a system of early identification of cases suitable for mediation and **5–066** at the date of the Chief Justice's paper directions to mediate could only be made by consent. Mediation has been used in the Federal Court scheme not only for the settlement of substantive issues arising in the cases referred, but also to resolve disputes on taxation of costs which the Chief Justice stated "has proved quite popular"; and for the resolution of procedural disputes as well, thereby streamlining the conduct of the proceedings.

The role of ADR in the Federal Court was increased in 1996 and there is **5–067** now a power to direct parties to mediate. The decision of the court to expand the ADR system was based on conclusions drawn from the results of the scheme in the years 1987 to 1995. As the Chief Justice put it:

"Of the 1,109 matters referred for mediation, 938 (85%) have been completed and 171 (15% are still current. Of the matters completed, 736 (66%) of all matters referred settled at mediation conferences, 168 (15%) proceeded to trial, mediation having been unsuccessful in producing a settlement, and 34 (3%) were transferred to State courts. Of the matters referred to mediation to date, only 27 have been mediated by judges. Of those, 17 (63%) settled, 7 (26%) proceeded to trial and 3 (11%) are still current. Needless to say, if a judge endeavours to mediate in a matter which does not settle, another judge takes the subsequent trial".[22]

The Chief Justice also made clear his opinion that: **5–068**

"The Court's system of case management has always been well suited to a programme of court annexed ADR because the process of directions hearings brings cases before judges at an early stage and so enables cases suitable for ADR to be identified. The policy of identifying cases suitable

---

[20]See, *e.g.* "Compulsory Mediation" by Jane Hider in A.C.L.N. Issue 62 commenting adversely on the mediation process for construction cases in the Victorian Supreme Court and the Domestic Building Tribunal. See also "Standards for Victorian Mediators" by Michael Redfern in *Australian Dispute Resolution Journal*, May 1997.

[21]The Courts, Tribunals and ADR *Australian Dispute Resolution Journal*, May 1996.

[22]The Courts, Tribunals and ADR, the Hon. M.E.J. Black Chief Justice of the Federal Court of Australia, *Australian Dispute Resolution Journal* May (1996) 138.

for referral to ADR as early as possible enhances the likelihood of resolving disputes that might otherwise proceed to a trial as a result of the investment of legal costs".

5–069 In explaining why the ADR scheme had been successful and merited expansion, the Chief Justice concluded:

"The evaluation of the mediation scheme has reinforced the view that the process is beneficial and worthy of expansion. The ADR programme has assisted both the parties and the court. A substantial number of the matters have in fact settled and those that have proceeded to trial have often done so with the issues better defined. Whilst many of the, matters may have settled without the intervention of mediation, the results of the evaluation suggests that in many cases a settlement was achieved sooner as a result of mediation. This results in savings to the resources of the court and the parties, as well as achieving the desirable results of having parties in dispute for shorter periods. In response to the evaluation questionnaire, although 42% of responding parties whose case has settled indicated that the matter would probably have settled in any event, 54% advised that the mediation brought the settlement date forward. Only 12% indicated that mediation was irrelevant to the ultimate settlement of the matter".

5–070 There are a number of ADR initiatives in various parts of the Commonwealth. In the Northern Territory there are settlement conferences. In the New South Wales Land and Environment Court there are mediation programmes as well as mediation and early neutral evaluation programmes in the New South Wales Supreme Courts. The Supreme Court of South Australia has ADR programmes including mediation and the Tasmanian Supreme Court has a trial mediation settlement conference programme. The Victoria County Court has powers to refer without consent the whole or any part of civil proceedings to mediation or arbitration and similar powers exist in the Supreme Court of Western Australia. In Queensland the Rules of the Supreme, District and Magistrates Courts enable references to be made with or without the parties' consent.

5–071 The experience in Australia with court-annexed schemes is encouraging and the conclusions of Chief Justice Black for example are very broadly consistent with experience for example in the U.S. and in Canada. The Chief Justice's conclusions serve as a timely reminder that it is important to harness well-thought out and administered systems of ADR to effective case management. In this way obvious and legitimate concerns about fairness and the prevention of abuse ought to be allayed. And it emphasises yet again the necessity of effective action by the judiciary both to initiate and supervise the process.

5. COURT-ANNEXED ADR IN NEW ZEALAND

5–072 New Zealand provides a particularly interesting comparison with England. In January 1997, the Courts Consultative Committee published a report on Court

Referral to Alternative Dispute Resolution. The report is cautiously, conservatively and well-written. It explored and invited discussion upon a whole range of matters relevant to court-annexed ADR systems in the context of a proposal by the High Court Review Committee that the court should have legislative authority to enable judges to refer cases to mediation or arbitration, probably shortly after the defence has been filed. The Courts Consultative Committee is of the view that any scheme should cover the district courts as well.

Parties would have the right to elect arbitration or mediation. If parties   5–073
chose to go to arbitration they would leave the court process altogether or alternatively one of the parties could apply for an order that their case is not referred if special reasons apply such as previous bona fide attempts at ADR. Parties would have a right to choose a mediator but this would be subject to ratification by the court which could also appoint mediators or terminate appointments in defined circumstances.

The Report drew heavily upon experience elsewhere and was clearly   5–074
influenced strongly by the need to protect the fundamental right of New Zealand citizens to access to the courts. The report was clearly also influenced by the arguments deployed by Lord Woolf in both his Interim and Final Reports.

Appendix 3 to the report describes existing ADR options in New Zealand   5–075
legislation and describes the work done in the Disputes Tribunal established under the Disputes Tribunal Act 1988 requiring referees to settle small claims without formal process and strict application of the law. It refers also to the obligation of the referees to "assess whether in all the circumstances it is appropriate—to assist parties to negotiate an agreed settlement" (section 18(1)), and only if this is not possible:

> "to determine the dispute according to the substantial merits and justice of the case, and in doing so shall have regard to the law but shall not be bound to give effect to strict legal rights or obligations or to legal forms or technicalities, 18(6)".

In the Employment Tribunal the report recorded that: 5–076

> "mediation has a long tradition in industrial disputes which has continued under the Employment Contracts 1991 under which mediation services are provided free of charge as part of the process prior to a tribunal or court hearing. It appears that around 80% of cases go to mediation and 90% of these cases settle."

However participation in mediation is voluntary.

The Residential Tenancy Act of 1986 provides funded mediation services   5–077
as part of the process prior to court hearing. The report stated that mediation is consensual but strongly encouraged by the administrative process. Sixty per cent of cases which go to mediation apparently settle. With respect to family matters the Family Proceedings Act of 1980 provides that parties must attend counselling which is arranged by the registrar prior to the court appearance. Similar arrangements can be made under the Guardianship Act

1968. There are judicial mediation conferences in the Family Court. Apparently, research shows that parties tend to receive an indication of the way a judicial finding could go on some issues. The research also indicates that the presence of a judge rather than a mediator tends to expedite settlement of issues.

5–078   There is a compulsory and funded conciliation procedure under the Human Rights Act of 1993 which may be instigated under the discretion of the Commissioners prior to referral to the Complaints Review Tribunal. The Resource Management Act of 1991 has a provision, section 268(1), enabling the Planning Tribunal with consent of the parties to ask one of its own members or another person to conduct mediation, conciliation or other procedures designed to facilitate resolution. Apparently this provision has not been used extensively and there is some controversy as to whether mediation is in fact appropriate in many environmental cases.

5–079   As of May 1999 the position with respect to the High Court Review Committee's proposal and to the Courts Consultative Committee's work was that there had been no progress by the authorities in the introduction of an ADR scheme.

6. CONCLUSIONS

5–080   There are certain conclusions which, however tentatively, can be drawn from this comparison of some of the main common law jurisdictions where court-annexed ADR has been practised or has been contemplated.

5–081   What is clear is that to establish proper court-annexed ADR programmes requires a substantial degree of innovative administration. The programmes cannot work satisfactorily without the wholehearted commitment of judges and of practitioners. Indeed, in the United States many of these schemes were started on an experimental basis by local practitioners who gave their services *pro bono*. There is a strong *pro bono* tradition and indeed an ethical obligation upon American lawyers to provide *pro bono* services. Without that tradition it is likely that ADR schemes attached to the courts in the United States would not have been as widespread or successful as they are. It is also clear that litigants and lawyers expect in court-annexed schemes a measure of evaluation. Alternative dispute resolution is taking place not simply in the shadow of the law, but in the shadow of the courts. Parties are aware that if ADR fails the case will go back to the judge. There is a very direct and pressing need to form some opinion as to the likely outcome of the adjudicatory process.

5–082   It is also clear (unsurprisingly) that the quality of the ADR process is closely related to the quality of the mediator. It is essential to have mediators who are well-trained and of high quality. This in turn raises questions as to training, accreditation and control. If court-annexed ADR schemes are to work then the allocation of resources by both Government and the private sector is required. Government must be prepared to devote part of the expenditure on the court system to providing for the administration of court-annexed ADR. Initially there must be a considerable contribution from the private sector which must take the initiative in establishing pilot schemes. At the beginning mediators in such schemes should be prepared to work *pro bono* even in commercial and civil cases in order that the system will be used and confidence can develop. Thereafter, it is essential that, as in the United States and also in Australia, a fee structure should be established. This offers considerable opportunities particularly, but not solely, to the legal profession to develop new skills and new competence in dispute resolution.

It is striking that common law jurisdictions as important and as diverse as   **5–083**
England, the United States, Canada, Australia and New Zealand, have all opted for rigorous case management of civil litigation and that all consider ADR has a role a play. It is true that the United States has gone much further down the mandatory road than the others, though Australia and Canada are following fast.

As most informed commentators recognise, introducing ADR in the court   **5–084**
system raises difficult constitutional and ethical questions. The constitutional right of access to the courts is central to the workings of a democratic and pluralist society. It is therefore essential that if ADR schemes are to be mandatory as part of the court system, safeguards exist against abuse. This means that the court has a role to play in developing systems which, though mandatory, fit easily within adjudicatory processes. It also means that courts must insist on high standards of training, ethics and competence on the part of mediators to whom cases are going to be referred.

Ways and means of ensuring that high standards are established and   **5–085**
maintained, will vary from jurisdiction to jurisdiction and even from court to court. The authors consider that the reliance put upon cost orders as an effective sanction to achieve high standards and rates of settlement may well be misplaced. Other means may be necessary.

It is in our view false to judge the efficacy of court-annexed ADR only by   **5–086**
applying economic yardsticks familiar to management consultants, to test speed of settlement and establish savings in time and cost, both to litigants and to the court system. Such yardsticks do have a place, for example, in evaluating changes which may become necessary in existing systems or in deciding to which of a range of ADR methods resources should be applied. But the relationship between case management and ADR within the court system and establishing the cost, and possible savings in time and money, of combining ADR with case-managed systems is rather complex and difficult to measure. Both the RAND and the Federal Judicial Centre Report indicate the difficulties of determining ADR's effects on litigation cost and time.

Judgment on the value
The issue of court-annexed ADR transcends statistical analysis. All   **5–087**
democratic and pluralist societies, such as England, must be vitally concerned to ensure access to civil justice, by which is meant that citizens are able to take their legitimate complaints and grievances to the courts for fair, skilled and impartial resolution. It is clear that the existing systems have failed as for example the damning indictment of the English civil justice system by Lord Woolf makes clear. We have therefore no choice but to seek new ways of resolving civil disputes, but to do so respecting traditional and essential values of justice, fairness and equality before the law. The objectives must be to settle cases and, failing settlement, to ensure that cases are properly

prepared for trial in a manner appropriate and proportionate to the issues and amounts at stake.

5–088   Despite the imperfections of statistical analysis, we have enough evidence to decide as the Americans have done that ADR has a vital role to play in ensuring access to justice, indeed some may say an essential role. It was considerations of that kind and a realisation of the importance of doing all that can be done to ensure access to justice, which prompted the U.S. Congress to enact the 1998 Legislation.

5–089   There is no need for England to follow slavishly the course adopted in the U.S. and other common law jurisdictions. Learning from U.S. experience and that of other common law jurisdictions, we can devise our own solutions. But it would be arrogant and short-sighted for us to ignore what is happening elsewhere, or to dismiss the experience of others as irrelevant to the English Civil Justice system. Too often in this country we have been content to rest upon the laureis of past achievement. We should not forget Professor Roy Goode's timely warning [about the importance of English law in commercial transactions]:

> " ... We cannot take it for granted that this will continue. We may feel that our laws and procedures are superior to those of other States but if we cut ourselves off from outside influence we may discover sooner than we think that our ideas have become outmoded, that they are no longer seen to be responsive to the needs of the international business community ... So while others might look to us for leadership we are all too often followers rather than leaders ... ".[23].

---

[23]Freshfields lecture, 1991.

CHAPTER 6

NEGOTIATION

Everyone engaged in dispute resolution will find that they need to have a   **6–001**
sound theoretical and practical knowledge of negotiation. This is the
fundamental key to all consensual ADR activity. This Chapter will outline
the principles applicable to bilateral negotiations. It will be highly relevant to
ADR practice, both from the point of view of the individual representatives
of each party and from the viewpoint of the ADR practitioner who helps
parties with their negotiations.

Negotiation: the primary tool
Negotiation has been defined as "the process we use to satisfy our needs   **6–002**
when someone else controls what we want."[1]

Everyone learns to negotiate from the earliest age. As time passes, our   **6–003**
negotiation, becomes more refined. We learn to use it as the way to get what
we need or want. Usually, we must give up something in order to get
something else in return. By adulthood we will probably have negotiated
many different kinds of agreements, personal and financial, and we will have
developed our own individual styles for trying to persuade others to give us
what we want—which is what negotiation involves. We may bargain with
ease or be uncomfortable with haggling; we may explicitly or implicitly
adopt a pleading manner or a browbeating style; we may hector, cajole or
threaten; we may avoid or withdraw from situations which involve
confronting others in resolving differences; or we may use the threat of
withdrawal as a strategy. These and many other ways of negotiating will to
some extent become part of our individual personalities, although obviously
learned negotiation skills will enhance and augment natural inclinations.

Negotiation as a learned skill
Negotiation has not in the past been widely offered as an integral part of   **6–004**
professional training although this is now slowly changing. Many people who
are required to negotiate as part of their work may well have had to learn
these skills informally from colleagues, employers and opponents, as well as
from observation and immersion in the hurly-burly of live situations. As a

---

[1] *Successful Negotiation* by Robert Maddux (2nd ed., 1999) at p. 5. According to Maddux,
negotiation normally occurs "because one has something the other wants and is willing to
bargain to get it."

result, and given the differences between individual personalities, skills and approaches vary considerably. Some people may adopt a reasonable and principled approach, some negotiate by bargaining, others by browbeating; sometimes negotiation involves a combination of all of these.

6–005   The practical instruction of trainee solicitors, involving as it does working alongside experienced solicitors, is likely to be influenced by the style of the principal and the other members of the firm. This may be by way of emulation of the styles observed, or in some cases avoidance; and where necessary reconciling the differing approaches observed.

6–006   The learning of negotiation is often pragmatic, achieved by experience, rather than theoretically based. It is, however, important to have some awareness of the different theories of negotiation in order to be able to employ these effectively and appropriately or to help others to do so.

1. THEORIES OF NEGOTIATION

6–007   There are various theories of negotiation, which may be classified in different ways. One important distinction lies between the problem-solving and the competitive approaches. Where the problem-solving approach is used to increase the joint gains for both or all parties, it is also sometimes called "integrative" bargaining. This often involves a more principled approach, even though the ultimate aim may also be to achieve the best outcome for each party. The competitive approach is sometimes called "positional", "distributive" or "distributional" bargaining, in that there are seen to be limited resources for distribution and the more that one party achieves, the less there will be for the other.

6–008   There are many proponents of each approach. A representative sample will be taken of each and of overlapping areas between these. Other theories will be mentioned briefly.

A problem-solving approach

6–009   The problem-solving approach to negotiation is very helpful to ADR practice, which seeks effective consensual approaches.

6–010   Roger Fisher and William Ury developed their particular form of principled, problem-solving negotiation in their now almost classic book, *Getting to Yes: Negotiating Agreement Without Giving In,*[2] which proposes certain negotiation principles:

- Avoiding taking and defending positions but rather concentrating on parties' respective interests.

- Adopting a problem-solving approach and not allowing personality differences to side-track this.

- Before making decisions, generating as many options as possible, particularly those creating mutual benefit.

---

[2]First published in 1981 by Houghton Mifflin and subsequently by Penguin Books. Fisher and Ury were respectively Director and Associate Director of the Harvard Negotiation Project.

- Establishing objective and fair criteria for a resolution, rather than the judgment of either party.

Getting to Yes describes in greater detail the ways in which these **6–011** principles can be achieved in practice. It introduces a concept that it calls BATNA, or the Best Alternative to a Negotiated Agreement, which informs each party as to what the best outcome would be if the issues were not settled by negotiation.

John Haynes has developed a concept which he calls WATNA, or Worst **6–012** Alternative to a Negotiated Agreement, which is the worst outcome if the issues are not settled by negotiation.[3] Negotiators need to be aware of their own and the other side's best and worst alternatives to a negotiated settlement, and by focusing on these they are better able to make decisions whether or not to settle and on what terms to do so.

The following may serve as an illustration[4]: a plaintiff consultant claimed **6–013** £60,000 damages for breach of contract from a company which alleged that it had been forced to terminate the consultancy because of poor performance. In settlement discussions, the plaintiff required at least £50,000 and costs. The defendant's maximum was £25,000; so discussions stalled. The plaintiff's best alternative to a negotiated settlement was to go to trial and win the full £60,000 plus £40,000 costs; but he would be liable for irrecoverable costs of £20,000 so his net receipt would be £40,000. Even if he succeeded, some publicity would be adverse. His worst alternative to settlement was to lose the case, receive no payment, and pay his own costs of £60,000 and the defendant's costs of about £40,000, totalling £100,000; with very damaging publicity. With this information, and an estimate of success prospects, the plaintiff could assess his prospects and risks and formulate a sensible settlement strategy. This resulted in a settlement of over £35,000 plus interest and costs in full, and positive publicity in an agreed form. Both parties considered this settlement to be fair and satisfactory.

Professor Marc Galanter points out[5] that as "transaction barriers" such as **6–014** legal costs increase, so there is a greater range of possible settlements within which the parties may be better off settling rather than proceeding to adjudication.

Roger Fisher and Scott Brown have written a sequel to *Getting to Yes* **6–015** called *Getting Together: Building a Relationship that Gets to Yes*[6] developing further the ideas in the original work, and dealing in particular, though not exclusively, with disagreements within relationships, and the ways to nurture and maintain relationships. William Ury has also written a follow-up, *Getting Past No: Negotiating with Difficult People,* which, as its title indicates, deals with the subject of negotiating with people who do not use a principled, interest-based approach.[7] *Getting to Yes* has been criticised for being too

---

[3] *Mediating Divorce* by John Haynes & Gretchen Haynes (1989), p. 11.
[4] This illustration is based on a case that took place before England's new Civil Procedure Rules came into effect, when costs could escalate out of proportion to the sum in issue. Although the new Rules should maintain proportionality of costs, the principles of the illustration continue to serve as a valid example.
[5] See "The Quality of Settlements" *Journal of Dispute Resolution,* Vol. 1988, p. 82.
[6] Business Books (1989).
[7] Published by Bantam Books (1991).

naive in the face of tough and unprincipled negotiators.[8] Roger Fisher has rebutted this criticism.[9] It would seem that many negotiators find the *Getting to Yes* principles helpful and important, as part of a negotiating armoury rather than providing an exclusive way of working.

6–016 Another of the most important works on negotiation is Howard Raiffa's *The Art & Science of Negotiation*.[10] Raiffa distinguishes between the two types of bargaining mentioned above, distributive (the more one party gets, the less the other gets) and integrative (where there are a number of issues to be resolved, these can be integrated to arrive at the best result creating joint gains for both or all parties). Distributive bargaining particularly applies in relation to single issue disputes but integrative can only be applied where there are a number of issues.

6–017 One area in particular which Raiffa develops is that of undertaking detailed assessments of the risks of litigating, of analysing the parties' positions and prospects of success, and of examining the criteria for settlement on each side. He deals with the concept of "zones of agreement" which are the parameters of the range of possible terms of settlement within which a particular dispute may be resolved, given the aspirations of each party and any other factors relevant to settlement.[11] He also raises questions and outlines perspectives for negotiators. These cover preparation (understanding needs, wants, aspirations, alternatives and opponents' perceptions, analysing options, and considering negotiating conventions); opening gambits (who should open the bargaining, how to respond, and how to protect integrity); "the negotiation dance" (understanding the pattern of concessions and reassessing perceptions and aspirations during negotiations); and "end play" (signalling limits, changing position and helping opponents to do so. He deals with third party intervention including introducing a neutral mediator or arbitrator.

6–018 A recurring theme of problem-solving negotiation is looking beyond stated aspirations and trying to assess underlying needs or preferences. This is suggested by Menkel-Meadow,[12] and by an example given by Lax and Sebenius.[13] The latter relates to a conflict between an electric utility company's wish to build a dam, the needs of farmers and the concerns of environmentalists—met after years of expensive litigation by examining the underlying interests of all the parties concerned and resolving these through agreeing on the size of the dam, guarantees about water usage and flow and the protection of the natural habitat of certain birds affected by the construction.

---

[8] *e.g.* see James J. White, Essay Review: "The Pros and Cons of Getting to Yes" (1984) 34 J.L.E. 115–117.

[9] *e.g.* in his article "Negotiating Power" in (1983) 27 *American Behavioural Science;* and in *The Processes of Dispute Resolution: The Role of Lawyers* by Murray, Rau & Sherman, (Foundation Press 1989), pp. 99–100.

[10] Cambridge: Harvard University Press.

[11] Where a zone of agreement exists, it will be found in the overlap between the bottom end of what a claimant will ultimately accept and the top end of what a respondent will ultimately offer.

[12] "Toward Another View of Legal Negotiation: The Structure of Problem Solving" (1983) 31 U.C.L.A. L.Rev. 754.

[13] *The Manager as Negotiator: Bargaining for Co-operation and Competitive Gain* (The Free Press, Macmillan Inc., 1986).

The following anecdote, in distinguishing between needs and wants, is **6–019** inspired by a talk given by John Haynes:

"When a student who has to undertake certain practical educational training involving attending at institutions at irregular hours tells his father that he 'needs a motor car', one may discern that what he wants is a motor car, what he needs is a way to travel at awkward hours. His underlying need could be met by having a motor car; it could alternatively be met by having a motor-cycle or a bicycle, or by taking public transport when available and taxis when public transport was not available, or by arranging to get lifts with others on some paying basis, or perhaps by some other solution."

An examination of the underlying need, rather than the form in which an **6–020** aspiration is expressed, can allow many opportunities for arriving at creative solutions in all fields of activity.[14]

Another theme, which recurs among negotiation writers and practitioners, **6–021** is that it is possible to create value by using the problem-solving approach, and indeed even by taking advantage of the differences which exist between the parties. The existence of differences, for example in relation to aspirations and priorities, allows more scope for constructing a settlement that accommodates those differences.

The notion of creating joint gains is that a co-operative, problem-solving **6–022** mode, with pooled information, a flexible and creative approach and an appreciation of one another's interests and concerns, will enable parties to arrive at an outcome which enhances the position of all parties, rather than having one party as a "winner" and another as a "loser".

Another proponent of a problem-solving approach is Edward de Bono, the **6–023** originator of the term "lateral thinking".[15] de Bono believes that the traditional methods of resolving conflicts and disputes are primitive, inadequate and destructive and that a fundamental shift of approach is needed. He believes that this is to be found by changing to a new way of thinking about conflicts, and adopting techniques that facilitate the creative designing of solutions to problems. In his work *Conflicts: A Better Way to Resolve Them*[16] he analyses modes of thinking and the way the mind works and considers why people disagree. He suggests why the disputants themselves are worst placed to resolve their own issues (parties are caught up in a "tension of hostility" and in taking positions which do not allow them to communicate with or to trust one another easily, nor, therefore, to design creative solutions). By using lateral thinking and adopting a problem-solving, creative approach to the designing of solutions, de Bono encourages and assists with finding ways to generate alternative solutions to issues, large or small.

The following example may illustrate the problem-solving approach. The **6–024**

---

[14]Andrew Floyer Acland in *A Sudden Outbreak of Common Sense* (1990) deals well with the relationship between positions, interests and needs: he recommends mediators to discover the interests behind the positions, and the needs behind the interests.
[15]Lateral Thinking: A Textbook of Creativity (Penguin Books Limited, 1970).
[16]Penguin Books Limited (1985).

four shareholders in a fast-food company with a number of branches find it impossible to continue working together. They split into two groups, each of which wants to buy out the other and take over the company. Neither will sell to the other, and each threatens court action. Their impasse leaves them at loggerheads. In this example, problem-solving negotiation helps them to create joint gains. They examine ways of dividing the company and arrive at a division, with each group taking over the branches in an agreed area, with an appropriate cash adjustment. They will operate independently, but will liaise on activities that can benefit all branches, such as some joint publicity and occasional bulk purchasing to achieve advantageous buying prices.

6–025 This example demonstrates how the negotiators could have used differences between parties to achieve a deal. It might be found that Group A were more willing to put cash into the business than Group B who had less liquid resources and were concerned about over-extending themselves. This might have lent itself to a deal in which Group A acquired more branches and paid a cash adjustment to Group B. Group A might have wanted to expand to a wider geographical area, whereas Group B shareholders might have preferred to consolidate locally. This might have helped with the way in which the different branches were allocated. Personal preferences might have led to parties placing different values on individual branches and aspects of the business. Other differences of need and perception might have allowed the deal to be structured to give each group as much of what they wanted as possible. Of course, following the point made by Lax and Sebenius, there would ultimately be a tension between the creation of joint gains and the division of the resources. There would no doubt also be hard bargaining about the allocation and valuation of the branches and the size of a cash adjustment. Nevertheless, the problem-solving approach would allow greater opportunities for positive and mutually beneficial outcomes than a purely "value claiming" approach.

Partnering

6–026 The concept of adopting a problem-solving approach is fundamental to the concept of partnering, which has developed in some areas, notably the construction industry. "Partnering" is a voluntary, non-binding collaborative process that focuses on solving common problems between different groups working on the same project or sharing a common purpose. This is done in various ways, such as by developing teams with common goals, establishing and implementing project action plans and establishing conflict resolution machinery.[17] It is primarily a means of dispute prevention rather than dispute resolution.

6–027 The American Arbitration Association's Dispute Avoidance and Resolution Task Force has published a set of partnering guidelines entitled *Building Success for the 21st Century: A Guide to Partnering in the Construction Industry.* The guidelines indicate that to be successful, partnering must be initiated in a disciplined manner at the outset of the project, and senior management must develop relationship-building among the participants by

---

[17]See, *e.g.* Abrams & Imperati "Successful Skills & Strategies for Partnering in a Diverse and Demanding Work Environment" SPIDR November, 23 1997.

demonstrating personal commitment to the partnering goals. The construction industry in the U.S. is said to be accepting partnering rapidly, with a survey showing that 25 out of 30 partnered projects were completed on or before schedule.[18]

Competitive theory

This approach to negotiation is summed up by its name. Negotiation is a form of contest in which there will be a winner and a loser, and that in order to be the winner, the negotiator needs to be tough, powerful and skilful in maximising his, or his principal's, self-interest. Competitive negotiation is "distributive" of the limited resources considered to be available for distribution. It is therefore geared to achieving the best individual outcome for the negotiator or his or her principals, irrespective of the overall effect on others.[19]

6–028

Competitive negotiators may consider any gesture of goodwill as a mistake because there is no certainty that such a gesture will be reciprocated and because it may be construed as a display of weakness, and may produce an even tougher response from the opposing negotiator. Toughness involves opening high, making few concessions and being untroubled by the prospect of an impasse.[20]

6–029

Murray, Rau and Sherman[21] analyse the risks of adopting strategies favoured by competitive theory. These strategies tend towards a hostile and confrontational approach and response, focusing on manipulation and threat rather than on trying to understand the issues sufficiently to find a mutually acceptable solution. This means that joint gains cannot be identified, communications are distorted and tension, mistrust, anger and frustration may result. It is not uncommon that the brinkmanship inherent in the competitive approach results in deadlock and a breakdown of negotiations, with consequent delays, stress and additional costs of all kinds. Yet many negotiators, concerned not to be outdone by their opponents in the adversarial system, continue to use this model of negotiation.

6–030

The question that inevitably arises is how a negotiator who adopts a problem-solving approach can cope with one who adopts the competitive approach. Will the latter not easily outmanocuvre the former, accepting all concessions and giving little or nothing in return, to achieve a much better result through sheer toughness and unwillingness to compromise? This question is addressed by William Ury in *Getting past No: Negotiating with difficult people*,[22] which shows how to use a problem-solving approach in order to "disarm tough bargainers, dismantle stone walls, deflect attacks and dodge dirty tricks". Various practical techniques are explained, such as recognising and responding appropriately to tactics used by the other side,

6–031

---

[18] See "DART Task Force adopts Guidelines for Partnering" in *Punch List* Vol. 20, No. 1, Spring 1997.
[19] See Murray, "Understanding Competing Theories of Negotiation" (1986) 2 *Negot. J.* 179.
[20] See *Everything is Negotiable: How to Negotiate and Win* by Gavin Kennedy, (Arrow Books Limited, 1982), including, *e.g.* Chap. 5 "The Myth of Goodwill-conceding".
[21] In *Processes of Dispute Resolution: The Role of Lawyers* (Foundation Press Inc., 1989), pp. 78–80.
[22] Business Books Limited (1991).

making acknowledgments without conceding, using questions skilfully, reframing tactics, exposing tricks and helping the other side to save face.

6–032   Should the tactics suggested by Ury, or any other strategies of a problem-solving nature, not be fruitful in dealing with a tough negotiator, at least if the different theories and strategies are understood, an appropriate response can be chosen. This may involve examining the best and worst alternatives, maintaining a principled position, trying to seek mutual gains through a problem-solving approach and resisting all attempts to bully, threaten and cajole, even if this may lead to an impasse. A problem-solving negotiator does not have to be weak, but can maintain a strong, principled approach in the face of the toughest negotiator.

Other theories and models

6–033   In addition to competitive and problem-solving theories, there are other negotiation theories, models and approaches, which may contain elements of each.

6–034   Balancing between the competitive and problem-solving approaches are Lax and Sebenius[23] who view these two perceptions of the bargaining process as being a distinction between "value creators" and "value claimers". Value creators are those who consider that the negotiators should be sufficiently co-operative and resourceful to ensure that their agreement produces more positive results for each party than if they had not reached an agreement. Value claimers believe that negotiation involves hard bargaining to ensure that they, or the people they represent, obtain the most favourable terms, thereby "winning" as against the other party who thus necessarily "loses". Lax and Sebenius consider that both kinds of process are present in negotiation, and that there is an "essential tension" between the creation of value and the division of it. Their understanding and synthesis of problem-solving and competitive approaches results in one of the most useful models of negotiation available.

6–035   Another model of negotiation, with a socio-anthropological base, is described by Gulliver, comprising various phases covering the search for an appropriate arena for the resolution of the dispute, defining the issues and asserting differences, then narrowing these through the bargaining process, eventually "ritualising" the outcome.[24]

6–036   Murray, Rau and Sherman[25] refer to another methodology: the "Game Theory" which is in fact a method of analysis used to establish the optimum settlement strategy to be adopted in any particular case. In essence, it involves a "tit for tat" approach allowing for parties to negotiate co-operatively as long as both of all do so, but changing to a competitive and retaliatory approach as soon as anyone defects from a co-operative mode.

6–037   Steven J. Brams and Alan D. Taylor have devised some rather complex processes for creating fair divisions, whether of goods or preferred positions on a set of issues in negotiations.[26] Their approach involves three elements. The first is to set forth explicit criteria, or properties, that characterise

---

[23]In *The Manager as Negotiator,* The Free Press, a division of Macmillan Inc.
[24]See *Disputes and Negotiations: a cross-cultural perspective* (Academic Press, 1979).
[25]*ibid.* pp. 89 *et seq.* See also Axelrod, *The Evolution of Co-operation* (1984).
[26]*Fair Division: From cake-cutting to dispute resolution* (1996).

different notions of fairness. The second is to provide systematic procedures, or algorithms, for obtaining a fair division. The third is to illustrate these algorithms with applications to real-life situations. This approach brings together work drawn from different disciplines. They include philosophical questions of fairness and justice, economists' issues of the requirements of a fair scheme, and mathematical concepts. An empirical approach and regard for psychological elements of perceptions of fairness have also been taken into account. Brams and Taylor seek to establish what they call "envy-free" divisions by the use of their suggested approaches.

This is not an exhaustive or comprehensive chronicle of negotiation **6–038** theories and methodologies, but serves to indicate their range and approach. There are many excellent specialist works on negotiation which are well worth further examination.

2. SKILLS, STRATEGIES AND STYLE

Whereas theories of negotiation describe the objective principles inherent in **6–039** any particular way of negotiation, skills, strategies and style are subjective matters relating to the individual negotiator.

Negotiation skills refer to the adeptness of the negotiator and include **6–040** techniques and methods for dealing with situations as they arise; these may be learned or intuitive. Strategies refer more specifically to the actual approaches and tactics that a negotiator may employ in order to achieve the required end. These will relate to the facts and circumstances of each individual matter under negotiation. Style refers to the way in which a negotiator presents himself or herself, and generally depends upon individual personality and attributes such as personal authority, humour, flair and demeanour.

As pointed out by Murray, Rau and Sherman,[27] the terms strategy, theory **6–041** and style are often confused and used interchangeably, whereas their differences are important; and there is not necessarily a relationship between them. A negotiator may well use an informal, relaxed style, while following an approach which falls, in theory, squarely into the competitive camp, and having a strategy which may be to make slight concessions in order to gain far more substantial winning advantages.

Individual strategy will be affected by a number of factors, including the **6–042** following:

- The negotiating theory followed by the negotiator: a competitive approach will give rise to a different strategy from a problem-solving approach.

- The negotiating approach adopted by the other negotiator: if both (or all) adopt a co-operative approach, then the strategy is likely to be relatively open and creative, seeking joint gains and the most effective outcome for all. If the approach is competitive, the strategy is likely

---

[27] *ibid.* at p. 75.

to be withholding of information and co-operation, manipulating and manoeuvring, scoring points, seeking ways to achieve a better result than the opponent. If, however, one negotiator starts by adopting a competitive and aggressive approach while the other is co-operative, then the strategy on each side will need to be carefully considered. The competitive negotiator will try to gain as much advantage as possible from what may be perceived as the soft opponent; and the co-operative negotiator will need to adapt his or her negotiating strategy to accommodate the reality of the situation. This may require changing to a competitive mode or declining to negotiate but pursuing the alternatives such as litigation or confrontation, though neither of these strategies alone is usually effective. Better responses tend to involve maintaining a strong, principled approach which does not allow the aggressive negotiator to score any points, can be as tough as the other on substance while keeping the possibilities for co-operation open, and continues to seek outcomes which work for both parties.[28]

- The relative power bases of the parties: this is dealt with in greater detail below.[29]

- The culture within which the negotiator is operating and the values of the negotiators and their principals, also by hierarchical, gender, race and ethnic perceptions.

- The aims, aspirations and underlying needs of the principals.

- The psychological make-up of the negotiators, the extent of their mandate and authority, their own private agendas, the skills which each uses, and the perceptions which each has of the personalities and aspirations of the other side. It may also be affected by whether the negotiators are representing themselves or principals, and in the latter event, whether those principals are observing the process (perhaps causing the negotiators to feel that they must "put on a show" for them).

- The emotional factors underlying the issues may affect the strategy adopted, or indeed the extent to which a party may be able to devise or implement any strategy.

6–043   Actual strategies, involving the more detailed techniques of negotiation, are contained in various of the works on negotiation.[30]

---

[28]See the discussion above, and see also Chap. 18 of Wilkinson, *ADR Practice Book* (1990) entitled "Effective Negotiation" by Gerald R. Williams.
[29]See p. paras 6–044 *et seq.* and Chap. 21.
[30]For example, Fisher & Ury, *Getting to Yes* and Ury, *Getting Past No* within the problem-solving mode; or Kennedy, *Everything is Negotiable: How to Negotiate and Win* using the competitive mode.

3. POWER, CULTURE AND GENDER

Power[31]

Power may exist in various different forms including for example the   **6–044**
relationship between the parties, their hierarchical structure and patterns of
behaviour; their relative economic and financial circumstances; status and
authority; relative prospects of successfully litigating the issues; greater
access to relevant information; or the power to harm the other side or
damage the other side's interests Power may, however, be less obvious, and
could for example reside in a morally strong (even if perhaps legally
doubtful) position; the ability to withhold co-operation; the ability to inflict
damage on another through damaging oneself (as where a debtor goes into
bankruptcy leaving the creditor suffering a loss). There is even the power of
irrationality—that someone will act unpredictably and irrationally with
uncertain effects and consequences if a particular result is not achieved.[32]

Although power may be real, it may also be blurred by the perceptions   **6–045**
which parties have of their own power and the power of the other side,
neither of which may necessarily be accurate.[33] Power is not a static concept
and may change, as for example where relationships change, or where one
side's vulnerability to adverse publicity may lessen, which in turn may
weaken the other side's power base.

In negotiation, parties may use their power directly in the form of an   **6–046**
actual or implied threat, or indirectly merely by allowing the reality of the
respective power bases to be understood. Where power vests wholly or
substantially in one party, others may capitulate, or may just decide to
withdraw from the negotiations. Some may try to work out the best outcome
achievable, recognising the other's power.

However, it is unusual for all the power to be on one side and none on the   **6–047**
other. More commonly, even if the one side may appear to be more powerful
than the other, there may be balancing forces and consequences flowing from
the exercise of power which make it necessary for power to be used with
some circumspection.

A negotiator will need to understand the realities of his or her own power,   **6–048**
strengths and weaknesses as well as those of the other side, and will be
guided by these in formulating a strategy for the conduct of the negotiations.

---

[31] See also Chap. 21 on power balance in mediation. An appreciation of power issues is crucial to
effective negotiation and all processes involving negotiation. It has been addressed by works
such as Galbraith, *The Anatomy of Power* (1963), Fisher's article in *American Behavioral
Scientist* Nov.–Dec. 1983, "Negotiating Power: Getting and Using Influence" and Chornenki's
chapter "Mediating Commercial Disputes: Exchanging 'Power over' for 'Power with'" in
Macfarlane, *Rethinking Disputes; the Mediation Alternative* (1997). Most writers on
negotiation and ADR deal with it. See for example Murray, Rau & Sherman, *Processes of
Dispute Resolution*, pp. 212–220; Goldberg Green & Sander, *Dispute Resolution*, pp. 24–33; de
Bono, *Conflicts: A Better Way to Resolve Them*, pp. 148–152; Karrass, *The Negotiating Game*,
pp. 56–72; Haynes Chap. 14, "Power Balancing" in *Divorce Mediation: Theory & Practice*
(Folberg & Milne) pp. 277–296; Parkinson, *Family Mediation*, Chap. 8.
[32] As to irrationality in bargaining, see Murray, Rau & Sherman, *Processes of Dispute Resolution*,
pp. 215–216.
[33] As to perceptions, see p. paras 6–054–056.

Culture gender and values

6–049   These factors may affect negotiation:

Culture may relate to a number of different aspects:

- There is the culture of the country in which the parties are operating. This may affect the way in which negotiations are conducted: for example, the culture of negotiation would be different in, say, the United States from that in Japan or Nigeria. Such differences may be of substance or of nuance.

- There is the culture of the community or group in which the dispute arises and to which it relates. The culture of negotiation within a community in the Hebrides might perhaps vary from that of a community in Surrey, or one in the East End of London, or in an orthodox Jewish community, a devout Muslim community, or any other particular group or community.

- There is the culture of the industry or field of work in which the dispute arises. If, for example, the issue is a commercial one relating to commodities, say metal trading, there is likely to be a sub-culture within the metal trading industry which may have an influence on negotiating practices, and what is and is not acceptable. Similarly, there may be sub-cultures operating within many other areas of commercial, professional and social activity.

6–050   In an increasingly complex and diverse world, an effective negotiator will first need to appreciate the influence of cultural diversity on the course and outcome of any negotiations in which such differences exist. Secondly, he or she will need to understand with some sensitivity the culture or cultures in which the negotiations are taking place, which may involve a learning process. Thirdly, even where these cultural differences are discerned and understood, it remains necessary to translate such understanding into a practical strategy.

6–051   Much has been written about the topic of cultural diversity in negotiation and mediation, which will help negotiators and mediators to a better understanding of the subject.[34] Certainly, flexibility and a non-judgmental approach are required, and an ability to obtain the acceptance of the parties in the process; the negotiator needs to be alive to the assumptions being made by the parties and their respective perceptions of fairness; and an avoidance of stereotypical responses is essential.

6–052   *Gender* in relation both to the parties in dispute and to their negotiators may influence the position, in which connection the following factors are relevant:

---

[34]See, *e.g.* D.C. Locke, *Increasing Multicultural Understanding: A Comprehensive Model* (1992); R.W. Downing, "The Continuing Power of Cultural Tradition and Socialist Ideology: Cross-Cultural Negotiations Involving Chinese, Korean and American Negotiators" (1992) 1 J.D.R.; and J. Klugman, "Negotiating Agreements and Resolving Disputes Across Cultures" in SPIDR "Beyond Borders" 1991 Proceedings and in (1992) 9(4) M.Q. See also the special issue of *Mediation Quarterly,* "Diversity: Some Implications for Mediation" (1992) 9(4) M.Q.

- There are certain common images and perceptions of men and women as negotiators which reflect the gender stereotypes of society. For example, men are perceived as tougher and more competitive, women as more concerned and co-operative. These stereotypes have been under challenge, and one interpretation of some of the studies on the subject would suggest that these perceptions of gender differences may be a factor of power and status differentials rather than an effect of gender distinctions.[35]

- Similarly, perceptions exist about the gender implications of the parties themselves, which may also be a factor of power and status rather than only gender. Nevertheless, the fact may remain that for whatever sociological, personal or other reasons, parties of different gender may sometimes have real differences of power in the negotiating forum. This can be particularly relevant in family and domestic disputes, where patterns of behaviour between a man and a woman may result in disparities of power and influence.[36] This has led to reservations among some observers and women's groups as to the use of processes which involve women in having to negotiate with their male domestic partners in circumstances where patterns have been abusive and power imbalanced.[37]

- Writing and research on the relationship between gender and negotiation effectiveness and style is as yet inconclusive. One writer analysing the research on this subject concluded in this regard that "whether there are gender differences, how they are manifested, and with what consequences remain open questions."[38] A research programme in Cleveland, Ohio relating to the mediation of misdemeanours as an alternative to adjudicated court trials suggests that mediator style may be reflected in gender, which in turn could have an impact on effectiveness. Findings from this report indicated that male and female mediators were equally effective at reaching settlements in misdemeanour cases, though there were some differences in emotionally charged cases and in the binding quality of the settlements, with female mediators being more effective in those areas. However, the author of an article on that report takes the view

---

[35]See Carol Watson in SPIDR "Beyond Borders" 1991 Proceedings, 19th Annual Conference, "An Examination of the Impact of Gender and Power on Managers' Negotiation Behavior and Outcomes: Implications for ADR Practitioners".

[36]See Ellis & Stuckless (1996), Chap. 6. They point out that structural inequality favouring males is (correctly in their view) taken for granted in feminist critiques of mediation. They consider whether gender inequality and systemic power differences at societal level necessarily translate into power imbalances affecting individual men and women who are separating or divorcing. Their findings are complex, and include a conclusion that gender differences in marital power vary across issues.

[37]See Neumann, "How Mediation Can Effectively Address the Male–Female Power Imbalance in Divorce" in (1992) 9(3) M.Q. and the authorities cited by her. See also Ellis & Stuckless (1996), Chap. 6. One of their conclusions is that husbands who abuse their wives have greater persuasive strength (marital power) than vice versa.

[38]L. Stamato "Voice, Place, and Process: Research on Gender, Negotiation, and Conflict Resolution" (1992) 9(4) M.Q. 377.

that "conclusions about style based on gender must be considered tentative."[39]

- A study of the methodology of conversation analysis, with mediators from a psychosocial background, concluded that women are neither generically advantaged nor disadvantaged by the *process* of mediation, although certain aspects of it may seem to have a more masculine character. Mediators themselves were treated as gender-neutral, except occasionally in the context of hostile interactional moves.[40]

6–053   *Values* are individual ideals and principles, and the way in which the parties and their negotiation hold these is likely to have some influence upon the negotiations. A party who lives according to deep religious or ethical convictions may well take a different approach from a party who takes a robust competitive view of life and negotiations. Strongly-held views and convictions about the subject of the dispute may actually make a party less likely to bargain than would a give and take approach. Sometimes it may be necessary to examine whether the issues are intractably bound up with principles, in which event negotiation might be very difficult; or whether they can be separated from the principles so as to leave the principles intact but the issues negotiable.

Perceptions and psychology

6–054   *Perceptions* about the negotiators may influence the dynamic of the negotiations. These perceptions may or may not have any basis in reality, but their mere existence as notions has its own effect. Individual negotiators may be seen as weak or strong and this itself may affect the approach.

6–055   Perceptions may arise from preconceptions and prejudices about the negotiators. Hierarchical factors may influence thinking: the more senior and experienced a negotiator appears to be, the more respect may be accorded to him or her, at least initially (although there could be an opposite effect where the senior person is perceived to be ineffectual). A junior and inexperienced negotiator may be considered easy to overcome (although an alert and well-prepared junior may be handled with some circumspection).

6–056   There may also be perceptions arising from gender or ethnic background, notwithstanding that these are generally without foundation. Murray, Rau and Sherman point out that stereotypes persist despite the fact that men and women have been shown to behave similarly in most negotiation settings; and that although people from different ethnic backgrounds and cultures may think and behave differently they are still "equally logical and rational".[41]

6–057   *Psychological and emotional factors* will of course influence negotiations. They cover both the inherent psychological make-up of the negotiators and

---

[39] D. Maxwell "Gender Differences in Mediation Style and Their Impact on Mediator Effectiveness" (1992) 9(4) M.Q., reporting on the Cleveland Prosecutor Mediation Program.

[40] See Dingwall, Greatbatch & Ruggerone "Gender and Interaction in Divorce Mediation" 1998 M.Q. 15(4) 277.

[41] *ibid.* 230–235, dealing more fully with gender issues; and with various further references of their own including to P. Casse and S. Deol, *Managing Intercultural Negotiations* (1985) in respect of the quoted words.

their principals, and the emotions and undercurrents affecting the particular issues.

Negotiators should be aware of the extent to which individual personality   **6–058**
traits affect negotiations. This is outlined by Murray, Rau and Sherman[42] as involving combinations of variables such as self-esteem, personal drive, risk-taking propensities, aggressiveness, tolerance for ambiguity and confrontation, and ethical flexibility. The opposing negotiator will have his or her own set of variable traits, which could result in the same dispute negotiated by one set of negotiators producing a different outcome from that negotiated by another set.

In addition to the influence of the psychological make-up of the parties and   **6–059**
their negotiators on the process, parties may also use psychological factors and ploys in the way they proceed. Strategies are to some extent based on a judgment as to how the other side will react to a given offer, response or movement. This necessitates sensitivity by negotiators and some ability to understand the other side and their own motivations and aspirations, and to have some insights into their psychology. This ability to appreciate the interests of the other side necessitates "probing psyches".[43] Emotional considerations about the issues or about the parties themselves are different from psychological factors, being more transitory in nature. People may have strong feelings about those with whom they are in dispute, as may be obvious for example in relation to a divorce or partnership dispute, with overt or veiled emotions (perhaps not even perceived or acknowledged by the parties) such as anger, hurt, sadness or humiliation. They may also have strong feelings about the particular matters in contention, wishing to achieve the redress of some grievance or the righting of some wrong, whether real or perceived. Negotiators cannot ignore such strengths of feeling, and may need to seek ways in which they can be expressed without damaging the negotiating process so that negotiations can continue, or in which they are addressed within the solutions sought.

Good faith in negotiation

In considering the concept of good faith in relation to the process of   **6–060**
negotiation, the question arises as to what duty of good faith is owed by one negotiating party to another.

It is here that a fundamental difference of approach, though not necessarily   **6–061**
of result, appears between the common law systems, including for example, those of the United Kingdom, the United States and most Commonwealth countries, and the civil law systems, such as France, Germany, Switzerland and various other European countries. Civil law systems are traditionally more ready than common law systems to impose pre-contractual liability upon parties for a failure to negotiate and transact in good faith. Indeed, in

---

[42]*ibid.* p. 221. Murray, Rau & Sherman also offer some valuable insights into the negotiating and litigation styles of lawyers, and the way in which some may tend to make assumptions and unwittingly practise self-deception. This may be partly because of background personality factors and to bolster self-confidence and partly because of a genuine commitment to the client's cause. This may sometimes result in lawyers tending to predict their clients' prospects of success more favourably than an objective lawyer might do.

[43]Lax & Sebenius, *The Manager as Negotiator,* p. 86.

civil law systems there is an overriding principle of good faith in the formation and performance of contracts. Common law systems, on the other hand, have traditionally been reluctant to impose a duty of good faith on negotiating parties, save where a specific fiduciary relationship exists.

6–062   In the United States, courts have traditionally accorded parties the freedom to negotiate without risk of pre-contractual liability. Similarly in England good faith and fair dealing have so far played a limited role in English contract law. In fact, the House of Lords has gone so far as to say that "the concept of a duty to carry on negotiations in good faith is inherently repugnant to the adversarial position of the parties when involved in negotiations. Each party to the negotiations is entitled to pursue his (or her) own interest, so long as he avoids making misrepresentations. To advance that interest he must be entitled, if he thinks it appropriate, to threaten to withdraw from further negotiations or to withdraw in fact, in the hope that the opposite party may seek to reopen the negotiations by offering him improved terms."[44] This decision was, however, made in the adversarial context, and it may not apply where the parties choose to negotiate within an ADR context. To some extent, this may necessitate examining to what extent ADR processes can be said to be "non-adversarial". On the one hand, the parties seek consensual resolution and the framework is geared towards principled, good faith negotiations. On the other hand, they remain adversaries with separate interests, and each still aims to negotiate the outcome most favourable to himself, even if it may be arrived at through a principled and problem-solving approach.

6–063   The issue of enforceability of agreements to negotiate in good faith was considered in *Halifax Financial Services Limited v. Intuitive Systems Limited*.[45] In that case, a contract for software design included a provision that, in the event of any dispute arising, the parties would "meet in good faith and attempt to resolve the dispute without recourse to legal proceedings". The clause also provided for structured negotiations with the assistance of a neutral advisor or mediator. McKinnon J. considered that the clause was not "nearly an immediately effective agreement to arbitrate, albeit not quite" as in *Channel Tunnel Group Limited v. Balfour Beatty Construction Limited*.[46] The court had a discretionary power to stay proceedings where there was a dispute resolution clause of the appropriate type. In the present case, however, McKinnon J. accepted submissions that the courts had consistently declined to compel parties to engage in co-operative processes, particularly "good faith" negotiations, because of the practical and legal impossibility of monitoring and enforcing the process. He followed *Walford v. Miles*.

6–064   It is suggested that the approach applied by McKinnon J. is unduly conservative and not in accordance with the accepted approach of the courts both in England and in other jurisdictions such as Australia or the U.S., of giving effect to the dispute resolution mechanisms agreed by the parties. It would be unfortunate if this approach were to be generally adopted.

---

[44] Lord Ackner in *Walford and Others v. Miles and Others* [1992] 2 W.L.R. 174 at 181.
[45] [1999] 1 All E.R. 303.
[46] [1993] 1 All E.R. 664 at 678 *per* Lord Mustill.

The position with regard to good faith and pre-contractual liability was **6–065** summarised by Bingham L.J. in *Interfoto Library Ltd v. Stiletto Ltd:*

> "English law has, characteristically, committed itself to no such overriding principle but has developed solutions in response to demonstrated problems of unfairness."[47]

Bingham L.J.'s approach in *Interfoto* was expressly relied upon by Brooke **6–066** L.J. in *Laceys Footwear (Wholesale) Limited v. Bowler International Freight Limited & Another.*[48] Brooke L.J. also mentioned examples of the requirement of good faith given by Lord Steyn in his 1991 lecture.[49] Finally Brooke L.J.[50] noted the effect of "25 years' involvement in the European Union". He said:

> "As the world gets smaller, and communications between lawyers and judges from different legal systems becomes easier, there is everything to be said for a common approach to the solution of problems like this unless principle or precedent stand irremovably in the path of progress. In my judgment it is infinitely better for common law to be able to fashion a fair result in a case like this by adopting the approach which was identified by Bingham L.J. in *Interfoto* and which is well founded on authority than to have to resort to interpretative devices of almost Byzantine sophistication to arrive at a result that the words of a contract do not mean what, on the face of it, they clearly do mean."

There is a tendency both in the American and the English legal systems to **6–067** recognise the concept of pre-contractual liability. Thus Professor Farnsworth remarks with respect to the United States:

> "In recent decades, courts have shown increasing willingness to impose precontractual liability".[51]

And Lord Steyn added with respect to England:

> "... there are signs that the English legal culture may become (or may have to become) more receptive to such notions".

He has also pointed out:

> "The aim of any mature system of contract law must be to promote the observance of good faith and fair dealing in the conclusion and performance of contracts. The first imperative of good faith and fair

---

[47][1989] Q.B. 433; (1988) 7 Tr.L.R. 187, CA.
[48][1997] 2 Lloyd's Rep. 369.
[49]"The Role of Good Faith and Fair Dealing in Contract Law. A Hair-Shirt Philosophy", the 1991 Royal Bank of Scotland Law Lecture—The Hon. Mr. Justice Steyn.
[50][1997] 2 Lloyd's Rep. 369 at 385.
[51]E.A. Farnsworth, "Precontractual Liability and Preliminary Agreements: Fair Dealing and Failed Negotiations" Colum. L. Rev. 87(2), 217.

dealing is that contracts ought to be upheld. But there is another theme of good faith and fair dealing: the reasonable expectations of honest men must be protected."[52]

6–068   Overall, the concept of liability for a failure to negotiate in good faith is still relatively undeveloped in both countries. There are, however, instances in which common law courts and academic commentators have acknowledged the possibility of pre-contractual liability.

- *Duty not to negotiate with third parties.* English courts acknowledge that a party involved in negotiations with one party has a duty not to negotiate with any other party if there is a valid lock-out agreement in force. That is an agreement under which a party agrees, for good consideration and for a specific period, not to negotiate with third parties.[53] American courts seem to agree. In the absence of a valid lock-out agreement or exclusive-negotiation clause, a party would seem to be free to negotiate concurrently with a third party. It has, however, been argued by at least one commentator that the parties are required by the duty of fair dealing to keep each other informed of relevant proposals from third parties in order to allow for an opportunity to respond to any offer made.[54]

- *Duty to disclose.* Under American law, non-disclosure of a material fact amounts to a breach of fair dealing if it amounts to a misrepresentation. However, the same requirement of disclosure, if it does not amount to a misrepresentation, is thought to be inappropriate in ordinary contract negotiations, unless there is a fiduciary negotiating relationship, when disclosure is required.

  A similar approach is taken in England, where negotiations are governed by the principle of caveat emptor (buyer beware). In *The Law and Practice of Compromise,* Foskett points out that under English law "ordinarily, the non-disclosure of a material fact will not constitute a misrepresentation unless it makes that which is represented false."[55] However, he adds that contracts *uberrimae fidei* (requiring the utmost good faith) require a full disclosure of all material facts; but he takes the view that ordinary compromises of disputes do not automatically require *uberrima fides* and may be enforceable notwithstanding the suppression of material facts.[56] He examines some examples and concludes that each case would need to be individually considered to see whether a full disclosure was being insisted upon by the parties, which in most cases, except perhaps

---

[52](1992) 58(1) *Arbitration* 51.

[53]This principle was confirmed in *Walford v. Miles* at 182 (see n. 44). Lord Ackner said that "there is clearly no reason in the English contract law why A, for good consideration, should not achieve an enforceable agreement whereby B, agrees for a specified period of time, not to negotiate with anyone except A in relation to the sale of his property."

[54]Farnsworth, *op. cit.*

[55]Referring to the case of *Dimmock v. Hallett* (1866) L.R. 2 Ch. App. 21.

[56]In reviewing this he refers to various cases, notably *Turner v. Green* [1895] 2 Ch. 205 and *Wales v. Wadham* [1977] 1 W.L.R. 199.

disputes in relation to partnerships or title to land, is unlikely. Matrimonial settlements can probably be added to this list: a material non-disclosure could result in such a settlement being set aside or varied.

- *Duty not to break off negotiations.* American courts have recognised that parties must make a reasonable effort at good faith bargaining to reach an agreement. The more common situation in which U.S. courts may impose liability occurs where parties have signed a letter of intent in which they agree to bargain in good faith. Even such an agreement is of dubious enforceability, as it is but an agreement to agree. Nevertheless, and leaving aside the difficulty of a court's determining whether the good faith obligation has been met, the trend appears to be in favour of finding these obligations to be valid.[57]

In the absence of such an agreement to negotiate in good faith, **6–069** courts leave parties wide berth to break off negotiations as they see fit. In *Racine & Laramie Ltd v. Dept. of Parks & Recreation,*[58] the parties had been bargaining for several years regarding the amendment of a concession agreement before the state broke off the negotiations. A jury found the state liable for a breach of a covenant of good faith and fair dealing. The appellate court reversed the decision, holding that (absent an agreement to act in good faith or statutory obligation) the "fact that parties commence negotiations . . . does not by itself impose any duty on either party not to be unreasonable or not to break off negotiations, for any reason or for no reason".

As stated in *Racine,* there are situations in the U.S. where a statute **6–070** will impose a duty of good faith negotiations. This seems most likely in the labour arena.[59]

In England the position is that parties can in the ordinary course of **6–071** events, and in the absence of fraud, terminate negotiations at any time without liability.

- *Duty to perform in good faith.* No such duty has been imported into English law, but the remarks of Sir Thomas Bingham M.R. (as he then was, now Lord Chief Justice Bingham) in the case of *Philips v. BSkyB* are significant. He said: "For the avoidance of doubt, we would add that we would were it material, imply a term that BSkyB should act with good faith in the performance of this contract. But it is not material".[60] This may be viewed as a preliminary shot across the bows of the traditionalists who assert freedom of contract over good faith obligations.

In civil law systems there are express statutory requirements of good faith **6–072**

---

[57]See, *e.g. Venture Assocs. Corp v. Zenith Data Sys Corp.,* 96 F.3d 275, 277–78 (7th Cir. 1996) (basing decision on Illinois law); but see *Prenger v. Baumhoer,* 939 S.W.2d 23, 27 (Mo. Ct. App. 1997) (agreement to negotiate unenforceable under Missouri law).
[58]See 11 Cal. App. 4th 1026, 1034–35, 14 Cal. Rptr. 2d 335, 340–41 (Cal. Ct. App. 1992).
[59]See, *e.g.* Cal. Lab. Code S 1153(e) (labour negotiations must be conducted in good faith).
[60][1995] E.M.L.R. 472, CA.

and fair dealing such as are found in the Swiss and German codes and there is also the concept of *culpa in contrahendo* which does not have a statutory foundation.

6–073   *Culpa in contrahendo* has been developed by courts and commentators by way of analogy to individual statutory provisions. According to this doctrine, the mere initiation of negotiations creates a pre-contractual relationship as a matter of law which imposes on the negotiating parties a reciprocal duty of care. Negligence must be present to found an action for breach of the duty and the duty is quite comprehensive and includes the following obligations:

- Under German law, *the duty not to harm the other party.* In some cases, this duty can actually lead to a duty to do something (such as the duty of a supermarket to remove a banana skin from the floor).

- Under both German and French law, *the duty to disclose* unusual information known to one party arises when that party knows that the other party's decision to contract would be influenced by the knowledge of that information (*"Aufklärungspflicht"*, *"obligation de renseignement"*). The scope of the duty to disclose varies according to the relative intellectual and economic positions of the parties, a party's need for information, and the possibilities for informing the other party.

6–074   One example is the case,[61] in which the German Supreme Court had to decide the liability of the owner of a property which was used for a specific purpose, who received an administrative order prior to the conclusion of a sale agreement, declaring the then use of the property illegal. The property owner sold the property without informing the purchaser of the administrative order. The Supreme Court held the seller liable for the purchaser's damages.

6–075   Two other cases[62] in which the German courts granted *culpa in contrahendo* claims illustrate the doctrine. In negotiations regarding the sale of a piece of property, the prospective seller showed the prospective purchaser a sample agreement and told him if they agreed upon the sale such an agreement would be executed. In addition, the owner permitted the prospective purchaser to start construction on the site and the prospective purchaser did so. Eventually, the parties agreed, in principle, upon the sale and the purchase price. However, the seller presented an entirely different agreement without specific reason and no agreement was executed. The court held that the owner was liable on the ground of the *culpa in contrahendo* doctrine and had to compensate the prospective purchaser for its wasted expense in connection with the start of the construction work on the property.

6–076   In the second case, the owner of an apartment and prospective tenant were negotiating a lease agreement. The owner gave the tenant the impression that the agreement would definitely be executed. On the strength of that, the prospective tenant terminated his current lease. Later, the owner refused without reasonable cause to rent the apartment. The court held the owner was liable for the prospective tenant's damages.

---

[61] German Supreme Court, NJW, 1998, 1290.
[62] German Supreme Court, in MDR 1961, 49.

English law would have no difficulty in fashioning remedies in both these cases applying doctrines of misrepresentation or promissory estoppel. **6–077**

- Under both German and French law, there is a *duty not to break off negotiations* without reasonable cause if one party has led the other party to expect that the contract will be concluded in any event and if there is no reason to withdraw.

The civil law concept of good faith could become increasingly integrated **6–078** into the English legal system as the United Kingdom moves increasingly into the sphere of influence of European systems. An article on this subject refers to the complaints of English traditionalists that the concept of good faith may be introduced into English law, and who wonder whether English law is "in the process of being stealthily 'Europeanised'".[63]

Good faith for lawyer negotiators
The issue of good faith in negotiation may require specific consideration in **6–079** relation to lawyer negotiators. The United States Bar has enacted ethical norms creating explicit rules of behaviour for lawyers in the process of negotiation, including, for example, a requirement to be fair and truthful.

The ABA Model Rule (4.1)[64] provides that: **6–080**

"Rule 4.1 Truthfulness in Statements to Others

In the course of representing a client a lawyer shall not *knowingly:*
  (a) make a false statement of material fact or law to a third person; or
  (b) fail to disclose a material fact to a third person when disclosure is necessary to avoid assisting a criminal or fraudulent act by a client, unless disclosure is prohibited by Rule 1.6".

The ABA Model Rules first included, but later rejected, explicit rules **6–081** requiring lawyers to be truthful in negotiations. ("The fact that neither the Model Rules nor Model Code deals directly with the problems of an attorney as a negotiator is not the result of mere oversight or ignorance on the part of the American Bar Association (ABA). When the Model Rules were drafted, the ABA specifically rejected rules requiring absolute truth and fairness in negotiations."[65]) The rejected rule would have provided:

"**4.2(a)** In conducting negotiations a lawyer shall be fair in dealing with other participants."

The rules as adopted do not address negotiations in particular. Even in the **6–082** absence of such a rule, fraud and deceit are not permitted. Within such limits, however, not stating a true fact and puffery are permitted. The normal

---

[63]Richard B. Mawrey Q.C., "Good faith" *The Commercial Lawyer* July/August 1995.
[64]The American Bar Association Model Rule.
[65]See, *e.g.* Paul Rosenberger, "Laissez-'Fair'; An Argument for the Status Quo Ethical Constraints on Lawyers as Negotiators", 13 Ohio St. J. Resol. 611, 676–17 (1998). See also an article by J. White "Machiavelli and the Bar: Ethical Limitations on Lying in Negotiation" in *Dispute Resolution* (1985) by Goldberg, Green and Sander at pp. 67–77.

rules applicable to lawyers and laypersons alike regarding fraud in the inducement would appear to cover these situations.

6–083   In England, solicitors are required to follow a principle of practice[66] (17.01) which states:

> "Solicitors must not act, whether in their professional capacity or otherwise, towards anyone in a way which is fraudulent, deceitful or otherwise contrary to their position as solicitors. Nor must solicitors use their position as solicitors to take unfair advantage either for themselves or another person."

6–084   This is understood to mean that while a solicitor may not always be in a position to volunteer the true facts, he should not lie or mislead if asked a question. This may mean that a solicitor is not automatically under a duty to correct a misconception; though there could be a risk that an agreement entered into as a result of an uncorrected mistake could in some circumstances be vulnerable to be set aside under the general law. If a lawyer puts forward a proposition that is false, that may be "inevitable if it forms part of the instructions received in good faith."[67] However, a deliberate infringement of this practice rule could result in disciplinary action against the solicitor.

Good faith in the ADR context

6–085   The decision of *Walford v. Miles,* in which the concept of good faith was described as "inherently repugnant" to the adversarial position of parties in negotiation, was made in the adversarial context.[68] However, the concept of a contract negotiation as "a battle of wits where each tries to manoeuvre the other into an unfavourable position, alone found in common law countries, seems deeply unattractive in the late twentieth century."[69] This is a view shared not only by civil lawyers and by those common lawyers who have moved towards acceptance of at least some of the principles of good faith in contracts, but also by many practitioners concerned with the development of alternative forms of dispute resolution.

6–086   ADR processes are designed to function within an adversarial context. Consequently, they may be used whether parties are negotiating in a hostile adversarial mode or a co-operative problem-solving mode. However, most consensual ADR processes would be enhanced by an obligation on participants to negotiate in good faith. This could not imply a duty on parties to act against their best interests, but rather a duty to conduct negotiations in a proper and constructive manner. There would also seem to be a distinction between two different good faith aspects. The one concept imports good faith principles into the process, by attempting in good faith to arrive at a settlement agreement, even if the negotiations are conducted with individual self-interest. This at least would be required. The other concept would import principles of good faith into the substance of the negotiations.

---

[66] *The Guide to the Professional Conduct of Solicitors* (7th ed., 1996).
[67] Foskett, *The Law and Practice of Compromise* (4th ed., 1996).
[68] See n. 44.
[69] Mawrey, see n. 63.

Whatever the future of the good faith concept in English law may be, a **6–087** question remains as to whether *Walford v. Miles* would have been decided in the same way if it had arisen in the context of a consensual ADR process. The distinction would be that parties would have chosen a non-adversarial context for their negotiations. In such event, it would be arguable that any good faith provision in their contract should be respected and enforced, reflecting the established policy of the courts to give effect to the dispute resolution mechanisms to which the parties have agreed. Of course, even in a non-adversarial, consensual process, parties in dispute remain adversaries with separate interests. Each still aims to negotiate the outcome most favourable to himself, even if it may be arrived at through a principled and problem-solving approach. So there could well be a counter-argument that, paradoxically, parties remain engaged in an adversarial process even where they have chosen a non-adversarial forum to try to resolve the dispute.

Any changes to the principles so vigorously enunciated by Lord Ackner **6–088** would probably have to be introduced and implemented as part of a legislative programme, though judicial decisions may well lead the way for this.

There are some who consider that Lord Ackner went too far. It is not inconsistent with adversarial negotiations for parties to act in good faith, particularly where they have agreed to negotiate their differences. For the moment, parties who enter into obligations to negotiate with or without the assistance of a neutral third party would be well advised to incorporate express good faith or best endeavour requirements.

4. The Neutral Negotiation Role

The principles of negotiation outlined in this chapter apply in relation to **6–089** bilateral or multilateral negotiations. They are not specifically geared to implementation through a neutral role. They are, however, also relevant to a neutral for a number of reasons:

- An ADR neutral facilitates negotiation between the parties and needs to understand and work with the different ways of negotiating likely to be used by them.

- An ADR neutral needs to be able to adopt a problem-solving role in order to be able to help the parties to do the same. This necessitates an appreciation of the theories, practice, benefits and shortcomings of problem-solving negotiation.

- An ADR neutral will need to draw on his or her own negotiating experience and skills to assist the parties with their negotiations. This will be done in a neutral and ethical way, being tilted towards neither party, nor unduly influencing the parties in any way not expressly or implicitly envisaged and agreed by the ground-rules for the process.

Some ADR practitioners may initially be uncertain how to convert their **6–090** negotiating experience and skills into a neutral role. When conducting separate meetings, do they negotiate with each side as if representing the other? Or do they hold back because they are in a privileged position and have some idea where the respective strengths and weaknesses lie? This uncertainty may have a paralysing effect and it is vital for an ADR practitioner to be comfortable in the neutral role of facilitating the parties' negotiations without becoming the champion of either.

6–091   An ADR neutral has various roles and functions, which include managing the process as well as facilitating the negotiations which may involve using various strategies and skills.[70] The practitioner can help the parties to move away from conflict and into a creative and constructive frame of mind. He or she can help to implement the agenda, help the parties to generate and explore options and help them with reality testing by asking appropriate questions. In these and many other ways, the practitioner helps them to engage in constructive dialogue and negotiations.

6–092   Where the parties to an ADR process remain in joint session throughout the whole process, the practitioner will obviously need to be able to work in an open way, with both or all parties constantly aware of the steps being taken to move them towards resolution. This offers opportunities to get the parties to communicate with and hear one another, and to help them to do their own negotiating. However, where the process is conducted through separate private meetings with each party and shuttle diplomacy, the practitioner uses his or her overview to facilitate a settlement. The practitioner may carry authorised communications and proposals from the one to the other, and use his or her neutral vantage point to help each side to think creatively, to develop and consider options and to narrow and close gaps. This must be done with proper regard to confidentiality and with absolute integrity and consistency.

---

[70]See Chap. 15.

CHAPTER 7

MEDIATION: THE FUNDAMENTALS

1. MEDIATION AND CONCILIATION DEFINED

Mediation is a facilitative process in which disputing parties engage the **7–001**
assistance of an impartial third party, the mediator, who helps them to try to
arrive at an agreed resolution of their dispute. The mediator has no authority
to make any decisions that are binding on them, but uses certain procedures,
techniques and skills to help them to negotiate an agreed resolution of their
dispute without adjudication.[1]

The term "mediation" has tended to be used interchangeably with **7–002**
"conciliation", though "mediation" has become the preferred term.
Sometimes mediation is understood to involve a process in which the
mediator is more pro-active and evaluative than in conciliation[2]; but
sometimes the reverse usage is employed.[3] There is no national or
international consistency of usage of these terms.[4] In this book, the term
"mediation" is used, and treated as synonymous with "conciliation". Where
a mediator introduces any element of evaluation, that is described as
evaluative mediation.

Mediation differs from arbitration in that the role of the neutral third party **7–003**
in arbitration is to consider the issues and then to make a decision which
determines the issues and is binding on the parties. The neutral third party in
mediation does not have any authority to make any decision for the parties,
nor is that the mediator's role or function.

Even where the mediator expresses a view about the merits of the dispute, **7–004**
which may happen in some but not other models of mediation, this would
only be a non-binding opinion, and in no circumstances would a mediator
have the power to impose this view on the parties. Indeed, any such power
would be contrary to the spirit of mediation, which is inherently consensual.

---

[1] See also the definitions of family mediation and civil and commercial mediation adopted by the
Law Society of England and Wales in their Codes of Practice, (see the Appendix II).
[2] *e.g.* in the labour field. See Chap. 11.
[3] The City Disputes Panel (which offers a range of dispute resolution processes, facilitative,
evaluative and adjudicatory) describes conciliation as "a process in which the conciliator plays
a proactive role to bring about a settlement" and mediation as "a more passive process than
mediation". (*1997 Handbook.*)
[4] Attempts to achieve consistency, *e.g.* by the Academy of Experts through their Committee on
the Language of ADR, have not been as effective as general public and professional usage,
which has gradually favoured "mediation".

7–005   The use of the term "mediation" may suggest a consistent uniform procedure; but in fact mediation comes in different models and covers different fields of activity, each with its own traditions, ethos and culture. Consequently, a mediator practising in the commercial arena may adopt different procedures and have different views and approaches from a mediator working with neighbourhood and community disputes, and both may differ from labour mediation or divorce mediation. Nevertheless, certain fundamental principles and core skills run through all the diverse forms of mediation.

2. THE PRINCIPLES OF MEDIATION

7–006   The following common threads run through all different forms of mediation:

The use of a mediator
It may be trite, but mediation cannot take place without a mediator.[5] Mediation brings a neutral third party into the dispute whose presence creates a new dynamic that does not exist when only the parties themselves or their representatives undertake direct negotiation. This element of third party intercession can be very helpful to the resolution process, but some traditional litigators find it difficult to accept.[6] Edward de Bono in the introduction to his work *Conflicts: A Better Way to Resolve Them*[7] says that "In any dispute the two opposing parties are logically incapable of designing a way out. There is a fundamental need for a third party role."

The impartiality of the mediator
7–007   Mediator impartiality is fundamental to the mediation process. The mediator must have no interest in the outcome nor be associated or connected with any of the disputing parties in a way that would inhibit effective, even-handed intervention.[8]

7–008   A distinction is sometimes drawn between "impartiality" and "neutrality". There is a view that mediator neutrality implies that the mediator will not bring his or her personal values into the process.[9] As this may be difficult if not impossible to achieve, some consider that "neutrality" should not be

---

[5] Some lawyers say that they "already practise as conciliators". What they mean is that they handle their adversarial cases in a conciliatory way, seeking settlements where possible. However, they do not "mediate" or "conciliate" because the presence of a neutral third party in the process is essential to it.

[6] For example, in an article in the *Law Society's Gazette* of March 11, 1992, "What's alternative about ADR?" Peter McGarrick says that "... lawyers should not need help to settle." And in the "*Obiter*" column of *Law Society's Gazette* of 5 March, 1997, another solicitor is reported as having issued a press notice under the headline "Mediation is for wimps". He says that in his experience, clients interpret suggesting mediation as an admission of weakness. Much of the scepticism about ADR arises from the belief that litigation lawyers do not need help in reaching settlement. Yet a common experience of mediators is that many of the cases that settle in mediation failed to settle in earlier inter-lawyer negotiations.

[7] (1985) Penguin Books.

[8] But parties can agree to engage a mediator whose past connection with either or both parties is known or disclosed provided that this is not precluded by the mediator's Code of Practice. For further comments on conflicts of interest and other ethical considerations, see Chap. 21.

[9] See Lisa Parkinson's *Family Mediation* (1997) at p. 491.

offered unless the word "neutral" is used specifically in relation to outcome rather than process.[10] Generally, the concept of neutrality is given its everyday usage, which is defined in the Oxford dictionary as "not helping or supporting either of two opposing sides, especially states at war or in dispute". It is in this sense that neutrality is usually mentioned in an ADR context.

No authority to make a determination
If a mediator has authority to make any binding determination of the issues, that would be inconsistent with the notion of mediation.[11] Mediators may though make decisions in the exercise of their management functions, which would not transgress this provision.

7–009

Authority derived from the parties
The mediator has no power or authority other than that given by the parties expressly or implicitly.[12] If any party decides to withdraw power and authority from the mediator, that ends the mediation. If mediation is part of a court-annexed procedure, and the parties are compelled by the court to enter into it, they should nevertheless have the freedom to decide to end it with or without a resolution.

7–010

Any sanctions that may be imposed on parties for failing to settle in the course of mediation, such as the refusal of state funding for litigation, are likely to be geared to government budgetary considerations or the wish to reduce court lists rather than to the requirements of the mediation process.

7–011

Consensual resolution
The only binding outcome of mediation is one on which all the parties agree. If the parties are unable to reach agreement on the resolution of their dispute, they will be free to have their issues dealt with in some other forum.

7–012

Resolution objective
Mediation has as its primary objective the resolution of differences between the disputants by negotiated agreement.[13] Because of the need to reach

7–013

---

[10]See Principles III (i) and (ii) of the Council of Europe's Recommendation No. R (98) 1 on Family Mediation (1998) which provide that the mediator is "impartial between the parties" and "neutral as to the outcome".

[11]If the mediator has authority to make a binding decision following an unsuccessful attempt to mediate, that would be "med-arb": see p. paras 7–106 *et seq.* The binding decision would be made in the arbitration phase.

[12]See the article by Bernard Mayer (1987) 16 M.Q. 75 on "The Dynamics of Power in Mediation and Negotiation" dealing with the sources of a mediator's power. These sources include the structure and credibility of the process, the mediator's personal authority and qualities, substantive and process expertise, procedural control, and the value of his or her neutrality and independence in helping to achieve a resolution.

[13]In the first edition of this work, this was said to be a "settlement objective". That remains substantially true. Indeed in Prof. Hazel Genn's Evaluation Report of the Central London County Court (CLCC) Pilot Mediation Scheme (July 1998) at Para. 7.7.3 parties and their solicitors indicated that "the primary motivation for agreeing to mediate was the desire to end the litigation as quickly and cheaply as possible". However, some mediators do not see "settlement" as the objective, but rather addressing and resolving the conflict causing the dispute. "Resolution" with its wider context is accordingly now used, which embraces both concepts.

agreement and because the process allows more ingenuity and nuances than is usually possible in the adversarial process, mediation aims for a resolution which maximises all parties' interests. (This is sometimes referred to as a "win–win" outcome, as distinct from litigation, which is said to produce a "win–lose" outcome.)

Facilitation of negotiation

7–014 The mediator's primary role is to assist the parties with their negotiations. All mediation involves some element of such facilitation, which is enhanced by the mediator's communication, negotiation and other skills. The mediator does not, however, negotiate with the parties, but rather assists them to negotiate with one another.

Providing a secure negotiating environment

7–015 Mediation should create conditions that are conducive to discussion, negotiation and the exploration of settlement options and possibilities. This applies to the physical arrangements, to the ambience that is created by the mediator, and to the ground rules regulating the process. Parties need to be able to negotiate freely, without fear, threat or harassment.[14] It also includes the arrangements for confidentiality and evidential privilege.

Empowerment of the parties

7–016 In traditional adjudicatory processes, dispute resolution is generally in the hands of lawyers, who use procedures and a language and reasoning of their own to resolve the issues for the parties.[15]

7–017 Empowerment means the increase in the parties' ability to make their own decisions and the corresponding reduction of their dependence on third parties including professional advisers. This arises in mediation because the parties are directly involved in the process and retain control over whether they wish to settle and on what terms. In some cases, particularly in family and inter-personal issues, the dynamic of the process, the way in which communications can be improved, and the attention given to power imbalances can all have an empowering effect on an individual party.

7–018 Empowerment is an important part of ADR, and to some, an essential one.[16] This is true in the sense that parties will always have control over the outcome. However, the personal empowerment aspect may sometimes be minimal or virtually non-existent. For example, in commercial cases the

---

[14]Though in mediation as in other processes, the threat of litigation or other lawful action that underlies negotiations may be very powerful.

[15]Linda Singer, a Washington D.C. lawyer, mediator and arbitrator, puts this succinctly in "The Quiet Revolution in Dispute Settlement" in (1989) 7(2) M.Q.: "Court or administrative action displaces litigants' power over their own disputes. The legal process distorts reality; not only are speed and economy affected, but the real issues in dispute and the treatment of disputants by the professional dispute resolvers escape our control as well. Even top corporate managers feel as if their business problems take on a legal life of their own once they are turned over to the lawyers and courts".

[16]See, *e.g.* Paul Wahrhaftig's article on "Nonprofessional Conflict Resolution" in *Mediation Conflicts and Challenges* (1986) (ed. by Palenski & Launer) referring to mediation as the attempt by "everyday people to wrestle back control" over their issues. And see Bush and Folger's book *The Promise of Mediation* (1994), sub-titled *Responding to Conflict Through Empowerment and Recognition*.

parties may choose to be represented by lawyers in the mediation, or in family issues the couple may not seek empowerment but may merely wish to have help in sorting out practical matters.

Confidentiality

Although parties are free to agree that mediation is to be public or that the outcome is to be publicised in some way, one of the principles in all forms of mediation is that it is by nature a private and confidential process. The mediator will invariably offer confidentiality to the parties, who may be asked also to agree to mutual confidentiality.[17]

7–019

No substitute for independent advice

Whatever model of mediation is followed, and whether or not an evaluation is made, a mediator will not ordinarily give advice to the parties, either individually or jointly, though information may well be provided.[18] In mediation, parties are responsible for their own decisions, and where appropriate may need to take independent advice, whether on legal, technical or other issues, but not from the mediator.

7–020

Containment of escalation

Whereas the adversarial system has a tendency towards a competitive approach and confrontational communications, the mediation process tends to encourage a problem-solving approach, to facilitate communications and to allow feelings to be expressed in a controlled and constructive forum. Consequently, mediation generally has the effect of containing escalation of issues and antagonism. This in turn means that parties in disagreement who have a relationship with one another, whether business, family or personal, are generally more likely to sustain that relationship, or to vary or end it in a more co-operative way, by using mediation than through the adversarial process.

7–021

3. MEDIATION: FIELDS OF ACTIVITY

Mediation practice tends to vary in different fields of activity, each of which may have its own traditions, culture and ways of dealing with conflicts and disputes.

7–022

Commercial and civil disputes including claims for breach of duty[19]

These tend to be factual, legal and/or technical disputes, which can range from simple single-issue disagreements to substantial and complex multiple-issue and multi-party disputes. They may arise in relation to virtually any kind of civil matter.

7–023

---

[17]There are necessarily limitations on confidentiality. See generally paras 22–020 *et seq.*

[18]The term "advise" may have different meanings. It may for example mean offering counsel, as lawyers acting for parties might. In this sense, mediators should not advise parties. However, another usage of this word may simply be providing information, and in this sense mediators can "advise".

[19]See Chap. 9.

7–024   Solutions commonly have to be arrived at on a businesslike basis, but not uncommonly there may be other issues or feelings involved, which may require sensitive handling. For example, partnership, shareholder or negligence disputes may contain high levels of emotional content; and even simple contractual disputes can sometimes arouse strong feelings in the disputants.

7–025   Mediation is generally available for these kinds of issues from mediators from a range of different backgrounds and disciplines, offering general process skills and/or specialist knowledge of particular fields.

7–026   Many organisations now offer this kind of mediation, including, in the United Kingdom, the Centre for Dispute Resolution (CEDR), the ADR Group, the Academy of Experts, the City Disputes Panel, The London Court of International Arbitration and various specialist and regional associations, companies, consortia and individuals.[20]

Family disputes including issues arising on separation and divorce[21]

7–027   Mediation may be used to help couples with issues relating to their children, or it may cover all issues arising on their separation and divorce, including children, property and finance ("all-issues mediation").

7–028   Organisations which specifically offer both child-related and all-issues mediation include the Family Mediators Association (FMA), National Family Mediation (NFM), the Solicitors' Family Law Association (SFLA), the British Association of Lawyer Mediators (BALM) and a number of other private companies and groups such as Professional Development and Training (PDT). Court welfare officers may undertake child-related mediation in the course of carrying out their functions.

7–029   A national umbrella family mediation organisation, the U.K. College of Family Mediators, was established in 1996 to advance public education about mediation, to develop and maintain professional standards in family mediation practice, and to maintain a register of member mediators. The Law Society of England and Wales regulates solicitors who undertake family mediation as part of their practice. It is establishing a specialist panel of family solicitors and Fellows of the Institute of Legal Executives who work as family mediators.

7–030   Mediation is also used for other kinds of family disputes such as inheritance and trust disputes, disagreements about family businesses, parent/adolescent disagreements, and issues between siblings or other family members.

Employment and labour disputes[22]

7–031   There is a well-established record of mediation and conciliation being used to settle employment disputes in the United Kingdom. ACAS (the Advisory, Conciliation and Arbitration Service) uses its conciliation officers to help negotiate the settlement of disputes, and will also engage the help of mediators where the neutral role is required to be more pro-active. This is

---

[20] See Appendix I containing a list of ADR organisations in the U.K. and elsewhere.
[21] See Chap. 10.
[22] See Chap. 11.

one of the areas in which "conciliation" is understood to relate to a less interventionist process, whereas "mediation" allows a greater level of neutral intervention. Some management consultants now use mediation for employment and organisational issues.

Community and neighbourhood issues[23]

Local mediation groups offer mediation in relation to a variety of local issues, such as problems between neighbours, schools disputes and community issues. They commonly use non-professional mediators, often drawn from the local community, although some professional practitioners work in this field on a voluntary basis.

7–032

Many of these groups and individuals in the United Kingdom are members of the umbrella organisation, Mediation U.K. This body publishes a quarterly magazine and newsletter, sponsors training events and workshops, operates an accreditation scheme, maintains a directory of mediation projects in the British Isles, including Ireland and generally seeks to promote mediation and the maintenance of high standards of practice.

7–033

As at 1996, Mediation U.K. reported that despite the shortage of financial resources,[24] the number of mediation services in the United Kingdom had grown to about 100, which included some 65 community mediation services, as well as victim/offender mediation services and conflict resolution programmes in schools.

7–034

Victim/offender mediation and reparation[25]

This involves the principled and informed practice of conducting mediation between the victim and the perpetrator of a crime. The objectives (sometimes but not exclusively) are to arrange a form of reparation, whether financial or by way of services to be performed, to establish offender accountability and to seek some kind of reconciliation between the parties. These schemes may be court-based, or may precede any court action.

7–035

In the United Kingdom this practice developed from experimental schemes established by the Home Office during 1985 to 1987. Similar projects were developing in other parts of the world, including the United States and various European and British Commonwealth countries.

7–036

In 1997 a Restorative Justice Consortium was created in the United Kingdom consisting of independent organisations seeking to promote aspects of restorative justice. The aim is to improve collective resolution of issues relating to the aftermath of crime, complementary to the civil justice system.

7–037

Victim/offender mediation, arising as it does from the criminal justice system, may not readily be seen as an ADR process. Indeed, the existence of a dispute to resolve is not at all apparent, and the application of mediation procedures may be questioned in these circumstances. In the United States, however, this process has been viewed as essentially consistent with the

7–038

---

[23]See Chap. 12.
[24]Funding has become a major issue for Mediation U.K. itself.
[25]See Chap. 13.

definition and criteria for mediation provided by a major dispute resolution organisation, the National Institute for Dispute Resolution[26]

Environmental and public policy issues and social conflict[27]

7–039 Inter-group mediation can be used to help resolve differences between groups of people on matters of public policy at local and national levels. These may relate to land use or environmental issues, housing allocation and management, and various kinds of social or community conflict, such as ethnic conflict and police–community problems. Much mediation of this kind has been done in the United States.

International issues: public and private

7–040 In private law, disputes are mediated between individuals and corporations based in different countries, and some organisations are specifically geared to cover such situations. Collaborative agreements between ADR organisations in different countries have been entered into in order to facilitate this.[28]

7–041 In public law, mediation has frequently been used to help resolve disputes between countries, and much has been written about these activities,[29] although this book will not deal further with this aspect.

Other mediation usages

7–042 Mediation has extended into many other fields in various countries. These include, for example, mediation in academia, in the Church, in hospitals and health care systems, for consumer disputes, for gender, race and ethnic issues, to assess claims for asbestos injuries, and to deal with farmer/lender debt issues. It has also dealt with prison grievances and been used for many other disparate purposes, even the mediation of gang warfare.

7–043 In the United Kingdom, mediation has been used for various issues and purposes. For example, it has been used to deal with complaints by patients about doctors. A Multifaith and Multicultural Mediation Service has been established. Mediation facilities exist to help families involved in adoption make contact arrangements for the children. A dispute resolution service deals with disputes within voluntary organisations; and projects have been established for "elder mediation", by which older persons are helped to resolve conflicts arising in relation to their families, and to community and residential care.

7–044 ADR has also extended into information technology, the Internet and Cyberspace. With the rapid growth of this technology, experimental dispute resolution schemes have been set up, and established organisations have

---

[26]See an article by Mark S. Umbreit, "Mediation of Victim Offender Conflict" in (1988) *J.D.R.*, 85–105.

[27]See Chap. 14.

[28]*e.g.* the International Chamber of Commerce; and the Centre for Dispute Resolution has an agreement with the London Court of International Arbitration for the resolution of transnational disputes by ADR processes.

[29]See, for example, Fisher & Ury, *International Mediation: A Working Guide* (1978); "US Mediation in Revolutionary Conflicts 1944–1986" by John D. Orme (1989) 7(1) M.Q. 59; "International Mediation" (1991) by J. Bercovitch (ed.); "Conflict Resolution Perspectives on civil wars in the Horn of Africa" by Hizkias Assefa, (1990) 6 *Negot. J.* 173; *Keeping Faith: Memoirs of a President* by Jimmy Carter (1982).

adapted their processes into these fields. The dissemination of information and the promotion of activities through web sites are now common, and the use of e-mail has become the norm.[30]

4. MEDIATION MODELS AND APPROACHES

Mediation practice varies depending on a number of factors including the **7–045** model and approach used by the mediator. The factors outlined below will indicate some key aspects that distinguish different forms of mediation. There are, however, two important points to note. First, there can be and often is a range of permutations of the different models and approaches; and secondly, within each aspect, there can be shades of grey. So, for example, a substantially facilitative approach might have scope for an evaluative element at some stage, or a settlement-seeking model might also have therapeutic or transformative elements.

Voluntary or mandatory mediation
Although parties generally enter into mediation voluntarily, in some situations **7–046** they may find themselves compelled to enter into it.

First, in some fields there are court rules that provide for mediation to take **7–047** place or at least to be considered as an integral part of the court proceedings. This is the case in relation to certain family disputes, where the court rules provide for an attempt to be made to deal with the issues by conciliation before the matter is brought before the court formally.[31] Also, some civil courts in England and Wales require ADR to be explored before a case will be set down for trial.[32] The Woolf reforms may well result in more use of ADR in litigation. However, the issue of whether court-annexed ADR should be mandatory is highly controversial and there are powerful voices such as that of Sir Richard Scott, the Vice Chancellor and Head of Civil Justice, raised against it. But there are many who feel that some form of mandatory mediation is inevitable if the Woolf reforms are to work.

Secondly, some commercial contracts stipulate that the parties are initially **7–048** to try to resolve any dispute by mediation before arbitration or litigation is undertaken.[33] Mandatory arbitration is a feature of many construction contracts. For example, in Hong Kong Government contracts for the construction of the new airport and the access roads and railway, mediation was compulsory as part of a three-tier dispute resolution system with mediation, then adjudication and finally arbitration. So far, though there is no obstacle of policy in United Kingdom Government contracts for construction, procurement and supply, there is no evidence of use.

In the United States, more than 4,000 operating companies, including some **7–049** major corporations such as Microsoft Corporation, Ford Motor Company, General Motors, American Express, Eastman Kodak and Mobil Corporation,

---

[30]For more information on this subject, see Chap. 17.
[31]See p. paras 10–040–046.
[32]See Chap. 3. Various states in the U.S. have a form of mandatory mediation for certain kinds of cases: see Chap. 5.
[33]See Appendix II for examples of such clauses in contracts.

have committed themselves to the CPR Corporate Pledge. This is a pledge organised by the Center for Public Resources, obliging subscribers to explore negotiation, mediation or other ADR techniques in any disputes they may have with one another. Although this falls short of a binding legal commitment to use ADR in all cases (as parties are freed from it if they believe that any particular dispute is not suitable for ADR), it is a powerful moral commitment.

7–050   All that mandatory stipulation for mediation or ADR can achieve, whether in the family or commercial arena, is to get the parties to a negotiating table, but of course, it cannot compel them to negotiate.[34]

7–051   Whether the mediation is mandatory or voluntary, the parties will reserve their right to have the matter resolved by adjudication if it is not settled by agreement.

Differences of culture and practice

7–052   Distinctions of culture and practice between fields of activity in mediation are likely to mirror the differences that exist in traditional practice.

7–053   So, for example, the way in which family issues would be dealt with in the traditional context may well influence a family mediator in the mediation context. In the United Kingdom, full and frank disclosure of all financial circumstances is required before a couple can be expected to decide what kind of settlement terms might be appropriate. There is also a culture of affording parties the opportunity to obtain independent legal advice before expecting them to bind themselves to any terms. A family mediator would be likely to mirror these requirements in mediation practice. A civil or commercial mediator, on the other hand, would not expect parties to give full disclosure of all relevant facts (and indeed might be surprised if this was volunteered). If parties to a civil or commercial dispute chose to agree settlement terms without legal advice, a formal and binding agreement would be likely to be prepared and executed without delay.

7–054   A conciliator or mediator in the employment field would probably have to bear in mind that disputants were going to have to work together after the dispute had ended, and would take care not to upset the balance of power between the parties. The concept of empowerment would not be likely to be relevant. Family mediators, however, who would similarly have to bear in mind that couples with children are going to have to co-parent after their settlement, might take a different view. They might consider in specific cases that power imbalances between parents need to be addressed if future co-parenting is to be effective. A commercial mediator, seeking a solution, may use the future relationship between parties as a basis for finding acceptable commercial terms; but where parties have no continuing relationship the mediator may simply help them to strike a bargain. Attitudes to empowerment, as to so many other aspects, may therefore vary in different areas of activity.

---

[34] The Legal Aid Board may though impose sanctions if mediation is not used effectively in family issues, by refusing a legal aid certificate to litigate. The Legal Aid Board has made legal aid available for voluntary mediation in the Central London County Court and Court of Appeal pilot mediation schemes, but there have been no sanctions if a legally-aided party either refuses to mediate or abuses the process. However, as court-annexed schemes develop, legal aid sanctions as well as cost sanctions generally may well be applied.

Cultural differences may arise from regional divergences, ethnic, social or **7-055** religious background, business or professional variations or other kinds of distinctions. Consequently, a civil mediation undertaken in relation, say, to a construction dispute may take a different shape from one relating to a medical negligence issue: each will introduce their own expectations, attitudes, cultures and approaches. Similarly, a family mediation with an elderly orthodox religious couple may involve different criteria and attitudes from one conducted with a young, free-thinking couple: procedures may be similar, but the sense and approach of the process may be quite different.[35]

Pure facilitation or an evaluative component

The distinction between facilitative and evaluative mediation has reflected **7-056** quite a substantial divide between the different models of mediation, though the differences on careful examination are not as great as they may superficially seem.[36] Regrettably, some mediation practitioners have divided the two approaches almost to articles of differing faith. The objective of facilitating the resolution of the issues is the same; but there is commonly a difference of perception as to what each kind of practice covers.

All mediation is facilitative in that the parties are assisted with their **7-057** communications and negotiations generally and are helped to explore options and enhance their mutual interests. In a purely facilitative model, the mediator does not evaluate in any way or express any view on the merits of the dispute. Historically, this approach has been known as "interest-based".

Mediation may have an evaluative (rights-based) component in which the **7-058** mediator works in a facilitative mode, but may in some cases express a view on the respective merits of any of the issues between the parties, or on any matter under discussion. The evaluation is not binding but may influence the parties to reassess their respective strengths and weaknesses. This may in turn help them towards a resolution broadly in line with what they perceive as reflecting their respective rights and prospects.

Some ADR practitioners take the view that a mediator's only proper role is **7-059** purely facilitative and that a mediator has no business undertaking evaluation. Others find that too limiting.[37]

Settlement-geared or therapeutic

For some mediators, mediation stands alongside negotiation and adjudication **7-060** as one of the processes to help disputants resolve their issues. Its value lies in the way in which it facilitates communication, negotiation and settlement. This view broadly sees settlement as an objective and the bargaining process as the route to that.

For other mediators, the mediation process does more than this. It is seen **7-061** as having the capacity to help communication and understanding between parties, and consequently to have some healing function. Further down the

---

[35]See p. paras 6–049–052 for discussion about the implications of culture and gender on the mediation process.

[36]The first edition of this work distinguished between "facilitative" and "evaluative" mediation. That now seems too stark a distinction, since all mediation is facilitative, and there are degrees of evaluation that might be added to some models. See Chap. 16.

[37]For a more substantial review of non-binding evaluative ADR processes, see Chap. 16.

spectrum of this view, there is the transformative approach. This is that mediators may indeed help people to change by achieving greater personal efficacy and empowerment while allowing for respect and recognition of the other party.[38]

7–062   This distinction is reflected in the way mediators approach the process. Those who are settlement-geared are probably more likely to concentrate on trade-offs and bargaining and to seek practical ways of resolving impasse. They might well regard the expression of emotions as an inevitable part of the process, but would bring the parties back to negotiation as quickly as possible. Those who tend towards the therapeutic approach are more likely to favour problem-solving rather than competitive negotiation. They would be more responsive to the expression of emotions; they would examine interests and needs rather than rights; and they are more comfortable with uncertainty and a slower pace in the conviction that the parties have the competence to work things out for themselves eventually, given appropriate help. Each approach has its own merits and disadvantages. For inter-personal issues, elements of a "therapeutic" approach may well be helpful. However, for disputes pending in court, this approach was found unsuitable in the Pilot Mediation Scheme conducted in the Central London County Court (CLCC). At Paragraphs 6.3.1 and 6.3.2 of Professor Hazel Genn's Evaluation Report (July 1998), this approach was said to be "least well suited to the types of disputes, the types of parties and the expectations of parties in the mediations in the CLCC." It led to frustration and dissatisfaction among both business litigants and individual litigants. It was "least successful" in meeting parties' needs and expectations (Paragraph 7.6.3.).

Level of intervention

7–063   Levels of intervention vary between mediators. The following factors influence the extent to which a mediator will take a pro-active, reactive or passive approach to intervention:

- The model, style and mode of intervention according to which they were taught will obviously influence mediators.

- Inevitably, mediators will tend to reflect their individual personalities and styles in their work, as well as being influenced by their background disciplines. While mediators must "be themselves" if they are to be fully effective, they will have to learn to shape instinctive reactions to the needs of the process and the parties.

- Different situations may require different responses from the mediator. For example, parties who are very stuck or emotionally entangled are likely to need a higher level of mediator pro-activity.[39] However,

---

[38] The transformative approach is embodied in an important and challenging work *The Promise of Mediation: Responding to Conflict through Empowerment and Recognition* by Robert A. Baruch Bush and Joseph P. Folger (1994).

[39] Prof. Genn's Evaluation Report of the CLCC Pilot Mediation Scheme considers "a more directive, interventionist approach emphasising the value of settlement" to be better suited to non-family civil disputes. (p. vii). And in family issues, Richard D. Mathis, in an excellent review and analysis of the authorities, suggests in his article "Couples from Hell: Undifferentiated Spouses in Divorce Mediation" (1998) 16(1) M.Q. 37, that with such couples,

where parties need to be able to communicate with one another, a high level of mediator intervention would be less appropriate. Mediators cannot be ideologically hidebound on this issue. Flexibility is essential.

- There are some different views about levels of intervention. The minimalist view is, broadly speaking, that a mediator has a limited role which covers facilitating communications between the parties, providing a forum and ground rules for discussion and acting as a conduit between them, leaving them in control of their bilateral negotiations.[40] At the other end of the spectrum, the mediator adopts a pro-active role with aggressive intervention, putting pressure on the parties to reach a settlement, whether one suggested by the mediator or the parties.[41]

Reservations about a high level of mediator intervention arise for a number of reasons. First, whereas mediation is seen as empowering, giving parties greater control over their issues, substantial mediator intervention may seem more like the traditional method of professionals telling clients what they ought to do.   **7–064**

Secondly, the mere existence of a mediator brings a new dynamic into the relationship between the disputants, which could transform their perceptions of their situation and the issues. While that could be helpful, it also carries a risk of abuse, even if inadvertent; and the greater the intervention, the greater the risk.   **7–065**

Thirdly, there is a concern that whereas litigation provides some objective standards and safeguards for the actions of the neutral, mediation could allow individual mediators to impose their own undisclosed and unregulated standards and prejudices on the parties. The risk of this is even greater if the mediator is seen as someone with status and authority; hence the less interventionist the mediator, the less the risk of this occurring.[42]   **7–066**

Against this, parties who enter mediation are entitled to expect effective mediator intercession and the test of effectiveness is whether the intercession of the mediator helps bring the parties closer to resolution. Parties accept such intercession because they are unable to resolve their issues themselves and seek competent and productive professional help to do so. Many mediators find that "minimalist" intervention (if it means merely providing the forum and facilitating communication) is not generally effective and that something more than this is needed. The concept of "minimalist" intervention should not be confused with "facilitative" mediation, which might go well beyond this minimal level of intervention.   **7–067**

---

mediators "must be more active . . . and . . . should take firm control immediately . . . ." (p. 47).

[40] See, *e.g.* the articles by Simon Roberts "Mediation in Family Disputes" (1983) 46(5) M.L.R. 537 and "Toward a Minimal Form of Alternative Intervention" (1986) 11 M.Q. 25.

[41] See, *e.g.* the paper *A Procedure for the Voluntary Mediation of Disputes* presented in September/October 1991 at the 10th Biennial Conference of the Section on Business Law of the International Bar Association in Hong Kong by Kenneth Feinberg (1988). Feinberg recommends a procedure whereby he indicates early on in the mediation the settlement which he considers appropriate, and uses that as a basis for subsequent discussion and negotiation.

[42] For reservations and cautions about ADR generally, see Chap. 18 at paras 18–097 *et seq.*

7–068   Some writers and practitioners equate minimalist intervention with facilitative mediation and aggressive intervention with evaluative mediation. But this is to confuse different approaches to seeking resolution. All mediation is of necessity interventionist. The degree of intervention is a matter of judgment and experience in each case. If there is a spectrum between minimalism and aggressive intervention, most mediators probably fall somewhere between these two, perhaps on the minimal side of a notional mid-point. They will generally help parties effectively with their negotiations, establish relevant information as necessary, examine and consider options, explore possible settlement terms, test reality and use impasse strategies to help break deadlocks. However, most mediators will not tell the parties what they think the parties ought to do, nor directly or indirectly coerce the parties into settlement. Mediators who have had effective training and follow a code of practice should be fully alive to the question of limits and propriety of mediator intervention.

7–069   The issue of intervention is different from that of evaluation, although this distinction is sometimes misunderstood. A facilitative mediator may be highly interventionist without being evaluative; or an evaluative mediator may generally work in a minimally interventionist way. It could be said, though, that evaluating a dispute and expressing an opinion on the issues or the settlement terms is itself a high level of intervention. This could help to explain the confusion that sometimes exists between the two concepts.

Formality of process and "professionalisation"

7–070   Mediation is sometimes said to offer the opportunity to avoid the rigidities imposed by professionals (or "professionalisation").[43] The "core of mediation" in the family context has been graphically described as "reconnecting people to their own inner wisdom or common sense".[44]

7–071   This view however also accepts that mediation involves a professional discipline.[45] Even those uneasy about professionalisation acknowledge that it is "an ambiguous concept". It can refer either to elements of professional activity perceived as dubious, such as elitism, detachment and client disempowerment, or to those more positive and inherent features of professions, such as independence, training, responsibility, expertise and a commitment to appropriate values.[46]

7–072   In the U.S. and elsewhere, mediators generally co-exist satisfactorily

---

[43] See, *e.g.* Goldberg, Green & Sander, *Dispute Resolution* (1985) p. 4, referring to the "growing mood of antiprofessionalism" in the U.S. which followed the increase in adversarial litigation; and *Partisans and Mediators* by Gwynn Davis (1988) at pp. 4 and 5 referring to the general move towards "informalism" in the resolution of disputes.

[44] In an article by John M. Haynes: "Mediation and Therapy: An Alternative View" (1992) 10 (1) M.Q. 26.

[45] The U.S. organisation S.P.I.D.R. (the Society of Professionals in Dispute Resolution) includes as its purposes "to enhance professional skills of mediators . . . " and other neutrals and more specifically "to promote professionalism of neutrals . . . ". In doing so, it accepts that neutrals do not need to have specific qualifications as professionals in other disciplines or degrees to be excellent neutrals.

[46] Tony Marshall, for example, writing on behalf of Mediation U.K. in the *Victim & Offender Mediation Handbook* (1993), refers to the developing "professionalism" of mediation "in the best sense of professionalism—concern with efficient procedure, good quality service and developing practice, not bureaucracy and exclusiveness".

whether or not they view mediation as an autonomous professional discipline. Lawyer mediators follow the principles of mediation rather than traditional adversarial processes.[47] In England, those who view mediation as a profession in its own right have similarly been co-existing with lawyers who mediate within their legal practices. That co-existence, however, may be under threat as pressure increases in some circles for the recognition and regulation of a separate and autonomous profession of mediation that would exclude lawyers mediating as part of their practices.[48]

It may be illustrative to consider the position of arbitration. The conduct of arbitration is regulated by statute: it requires knowledge, skills and ethical awareness. The professional standing of arbitrators, and of the Chartered Institute of Arbitrators, is not in doubt. An arbitrator has every right to be considered as a professional in the field of dispute resolution. Some arbitrators may work as professional arbitrators independently of the professions from which they come. Others may arbitrate as part of their professional practices, including law. A barrister or solicitor appointed as an arbitrator will function in arbitral mode, and will comply with the requirements of being an arbitrator; but that will not mean that he or she is not also a barrister or solicitor. Similarly, a solicitor who is engaged as a mediator does not have to cease being a solicitor to work effectively and in an ethically proper manner as a mediator. **7–073**

Lawyer mediators will undoubtedly share the view with all other mediators that mediation should be conducted in a professional way, and that mediation, like arbitration, can be seen as a legitimate profession within dispute resolution. There seems no reason, however, why there cannot be freedom to choose either to mediate as an autonomous profession or as part of a legal practice. **7–074**

On the issue of expertise, while inter-personal and neighbourhood issues may be effectively dealt with by lay people, technical and commercial disputes and complicated family or other relationship issues generally require some level of experience and expertise from the mediator. Some knowledge of the law and of legal concepts may well also be helpful, particularly when trying to settle cases in the context of pending litigation. **7–075**

An argument against expertise is that the greater the perceived expertise and authority, the more the parties may be influenced into accepting the mediator's authority and moved away from their own control of the **7–076**

---

[47] A Commission on Ethics and Standards in ADR, sponsored by the Center for Public Resources Institute for Dispute Resolution and Georgetown University Law Center, with support from the William and Flora Hewlett Foundation, has drafted a proposed Model Rule of Professional Conduct for lawyers acting as third party neutrals (April 1999). The proposed rule is designed to be incorporated in lawyers' ethical codes and wholly accepts the principle of the lawyer working as a mediator. see paras 21–025 *et seq.*

[48] See Marian Roberts's *Mediation in Family Disputes* (2nd ed., 1997) where she says at p. 66 that the Law Society "seems bent upon determining its own professional mediation standards for solicitors. This could be damaging to the carefully-nurtured development over many years of mediation as a distinct and autonomous professional activity." See also Michael Palmer and Simon Roberts's *Dispute Processes: ADR and the Primary Forms of Decision Making* (1998) at p. 336: "The claim to mediation *as part of legal practice* that is currently evolving may have consequences beyond hampering the development of an autonomous profession of mediators."

resolution.[49] Another argument is that expertise in the substance of the issue does not guarantee satisfactory process skills in dispute resolution. There is little doubt that, given a choice between the mediator having expertise in the subject-matter of the dispute or expertise in the process of mediation, process expertise is far preferable.[50] However, a mediator may have both substance expertise and process skills, which can be an excellent combination, provided that the mediator respects the autonomy and authority of the parties.

7–077   Some mediation organisations require their mediators to have certain professional qualifications. For example, the Family Mediators Association specifies that mediators must be qualified and experienced in family law or in certain specified fields, including psychotherapy, counselling or social work. The Solicitors' Family Law Association only trains and accredits practising solicitors or Fellows of the Institute of Legal Executives with prescribed experience in family law. Some organisations do not require professional qualifications.

Disciplinary background of the mediator

7–078   Mediators come from different backgrounds and cultures. The way in which they mediate is likely to reflect this. Within the commercial field, mediators come from a wide background including law, accountancy, engineering, architecture, surveying and the construction industry, management consultancy, information technology, commerce and industry. In the family field they include solicitors, barristers, psychotherapists, counsellors, social workers, probation officers, court welfare officers, psychologists and psychiatrists. In the community field (and in some family mediation organisations) it is unusual for there to be any professional background requirement for this work.

7–079   A mediator's background can enhance the process, by providing expertise, experience and skills to draw upon which may be relevant to the issues in dispute. However, mediators must be aware of the distinctions between their roles as mediators and their professional or business backgrounds to ensure that these are not confused. So, for example, lawyers bring their legal expertise and experience into the mediation but should not direct or advise the parties as they might in their traditional role. Psychotherapists, counsellors and others in the mental health field bring their skills into the process, but should not provide therapy or counselling in a disguised form. Social workers, probation officers or court welfare officers bring their skills and experience to bear, but should guard against becoming unduly interventionist or acting in a traditional role.

Sole mediation or co-mediation

7–080   It is difficult to establish what proportion of mediators work on a sole basis, and what proportion co-mediate. Differences exist from one country to

---

[49] This might bother less practitioners whose approach is settlement-geared than those who place a high value on empowerment and problem-solving.

[50] An experienced lawyer mediator, David Shapiro, is reported (L.S.G., July 15, 1998) as having been asked by parties considering appointing him as a mediator what he knew about the subject-matter of the dispute, namely pizza crust technology. He is reported to have replied: "What do you want, an expert pizza maker or an expert mediator?"

another, depending on how the process developed. It does seem, however, that a significant majority of mediators work alone, but that there is a substantial minority who work together as co-mediators.

In the family field in the United Kingdom, both sole mediation and co-mediation models are used. Although in commercial and civil disputes sole mediation predominates, co-mediation can be used in appropriate cases, particularly where a combination of different kinds of expertise is required. It is also commonly used in community mediation.   **7–081**

There are advantages and disadvantages in the co-mediation model. Those who co-mediate refer positively to its value.[51] The *advantages* are that there is mutuality of support in a demanding activity. One mediator can reflect and observe while the other is more actively engaged. There is also a different dynamic from sole mediation. Co-mediators may provide a model of communication and management, including conflict management, by working co-operatively together, and even by disagreeing constructively.   **7–082**

Co-mediation can also be advantageous where a multidisciplinary approach is required or where gender balance or ethnic diversity is relevant. This also creates a workable dynamic, reducing the risk of triangulation, though not necessarily avoiding it.[52] In a large commercial dispute, it could be helpful to have a multidisciplinary team, for example, a lawyer and engineer co-mediator team for a construction industry dispute.   **7–083**

Newly-practising mediators can work with experienced practitioners and gain experience, insights and skills in the mediation process.   **7–084**

The *disadvantages* of co-mediation relate first to the cost of funding two mediators. This is a serious inhibition, especially for professionals in private practice, whose usual built-in overhead expenses tend to make co-mediation uneconomic. However, the cost factor needs to be measured against its comparative effectiveness, cost and time scale.[53]   **7–085**

Co-mediators need to work effectively and respectfully with one another. If they cannot do so, their working together may be less efficient and less useful than a sole mediator working competently.   **7–086**

Co-mediation may involve one mediator having to travel to the other, liaising between sessions, duplicating the copying of documents, and twice as much difficulty (with corresponding delay) in fixing appointments.   **7–087**

If a mediator wishes to co-mediate with a mediator of a different discipline or organisation, that will need to be acceptable to the ethics of each discipline, and each organisation. For example, where solicitors co-mediate with non-lawyers, they must ensure that they do so within the Law Society's ethical rules regulating the sharing of fees with non-lawyers.[54]   **7–088**

---

[51] See, *e.g.* the article in the U.S. Academy of Family Mediators' *Mediation News* Vol. 11, No. 3, Fall 1992, "Team Mediation: Are Two Heads Better than One?" by Elizabeth Allen J.D., Robert Kory J.D. and Donald Mohr M.A.

[52] As to triangulation see paras 18–135 *et seq.*

[53] Comparative statistics are unavailable, but there is anecdotal evidence of co-mediation's effectiveness. However, sole mediation seems to provide comparable results, but at a lower cost.

[54] Co-mediation involving a solicitor and a non-solicitor would not automatically constitute a profit-sharing partnership. However, each arrangement needs to be considered on its own facts. Where co-mediators habitually offer joint services and share expenses before dividing fees, they are likely to be construed as being in partnership together, especially if they do so under a joint practice name. This would infringe Law Society rules. A similar outcome might result

Joint or separate meetings

7–089   The distinction between joint meetings and separate meetings (caucuses)[55] is substantially procedural, but it can also indicate a difference of philosophical approach by the mediator towards the mediation process.

7–090   Virtually all mediators in all fields of activity and models of practice are likely to use joint meetings to some greater or lesser extent, though not in every case. Practice varies more widely, however, with regard to separate meetings. In many models especially in relation to commercial and civil disputes, the mediator will also have separate, private meetings with each party as an integral part of the process. These private meetings are used as an opportunity for the mediator to discuss matters more freely with each party, to examine their concerns and to help them to consider and explore settlement options.

7–091   Family mediators, who work primarily through joint meetings, tend to vary in their attitude to separate meetings. Some will meet the parties separately if they think that it would be helpful to do so. Others will do so briefly at the outset, for example as part of a screening process for domestic violence or abuse. Others may do so as an occasional strategy to resolve an impasse, or only in exceptional circumstances. There are mediators who would rarely or never meet parties separately.

7–092   With regard to confidentiality, it may be agreed between the parties and the mediator that any matters discussed separately will be brought back into the joint meeting by way of disclosure. However, more usually confidentiality is the object and a precondition of the separate meetings with the mediator. This creates an obligation on the part of the mediator to maintain the confidences of each party, only disclosing to the other what he or she is authorised to reveal.[56]

7–093   Joint meetings demand a high level of openness between the parties, as the parties say everything within the hearing of one another. This places a considerable responsibility on the mediator to guard against a more calculating party who may withhold concessions, gaining an advantage over a more open party who may be readier to make concessions. It also means that the mediator's power is contained by the fact that everything he or she says or does is heard and observed by both parties together: the mediator holds no secrets and thus gains no additional power.

7–094   Separate meetings, on the other hand, allow the parties to express their thoughts, concerns and negotiating positions to the mediator more freely, particularly where confidentiality is assured. This can make it more difficult for a party to exploit the other party's willingness to be open and make concessions. The corollary of this is that the mediator necessarily assumes greater power, enhanced by the fact that he or she is the repository of secrets from each party. Being the only person who knows what each side is

---

where, even if there is no partnership, the appearance of a partnership is promoted. Where, however, co-mediators make it clear that they are not in partnership and their fee is overtly divided in specified proportions, that would not seem to constitute fee-sharing, and would thus be acceptable.

[55]For further information about separate meetings, see paras 8–094–095. The term "caucusing" is considered by some to be jargon. "Separate meetings" or "private meetings" may be preferred.

[56]For confidentiality in family mediation caucusing, see para. 10–168.

separately saying on a confidential basis, and not sharing this, gives the mediator greater power.

For both ideological and practical reasons, some mediators (especially   **7–095**
interpersonal and family) prefer not to hold separate meetings with the parties. They feel that they should not assume the greater power that caucusing offers them, which correspondingly disempowers the parties. They may also feel that separating the parties, and having them negotiate apart from one another, erodes the spirit of joint problem-solving. From a practical point of view, separate meetings can create concern for the party who is not at that particular time being caucused, especially in family matters. Parties in some non-family disputes may have similar concerns. Such concerns could translate into mistrust of mediator impartiality and lack of confidence in the process, though most parties seem to understand the need for such a procedure, and its value. Joint meetings, however difficult, tend to decrease suspicion and enhance direct communications between the parties. However, joint meetings can be potentially destructive where feelings between the parties are high and they are unable to overcome their animosities.

Caucusing may take place either on an isolated basis, to deal with specific   **7–096**
issues, or more commonly it may form part of a series of meetings that a mediator will have with each party, shuttling to and fro carrying proposals and ideas as differences are narrowed and eventually resolved.

Codes and rules of practice
Models and approaches will also vary according to the distinctions created by   **7–097**
the different Codes of Practice or rules of the various organisations offering mediation. Some organisations, for example, will allow mediators to recommend settlement terms if the parties require this, others would not allow this. Some might require mediators to have regard to the legal rights of the parties in carrying out their functions, others would not regard this as part of the mediator's proper role. Codes and rules are likely to vary notwithstanding that the underlying concepts of mediation may be similar.

Neutral dispute management
The concept of neutral management of the conduct of dispute resolution is   **7–098**
not well formulated in ADR literature. In practice, some element of this may be provided by ADR organisations, as when they set up a mediation at the request of the parties.[57] In the United States, organisations and individual practitioners may do this to some extent; but it is a less familiar notion in the United Kingdom and Europe.[58]

There are two stages in the process of neutral dispute management. The   **7–099**
first and main one arises in setting up the mediation or other process. The second applies to the conduct of the case if the initial process does not resolve the issues.

It is very important for the mediation to be set up effectively.[59] This   **7–100**

---

[57] *e.g.* the City Disputes Panel, has a small Panel Executive, which offers case management functions.
[58] Except in the court process, where U.K. reforms have tended to give judges more power to manage the timing and conduct of a pending case.
[59] See the article "The Importance of Process Design to a Successful Mediation" by Paul M.

involves not only choosing the process best suited to the individual dispute, but also the neutral most appropriate to facilitate it. Ideally, the dispute manager will have some initial knowledge of the issues. This will enable the manager to assist the parties in dealing with these matters, and to assess the timetable for the process. For example, the manager could consider with the parties whether the days set aside for it should be consecutive or whether there should be an interval between the days[60]; and issues such as information exchange could also be dealt with.

7–101   Neutral dispute management can include monitoring the dispute resolution process being used, and guiding the parties to another process if necessary. So, for example, if the parties enter mediation and find that it does not result in the resolution of the issues, the dispute manager may help the parties and their lawyers in moving into arbitration or some other form of adjudication. The role could continue in helping to appoint an arbitrator, keeping the issues narrowed, and watching for and taking up settlement opportunities. This secondary aspect of the neutral management role remains to be further tested and developed.

5. MEDIATION TIMETABLE

7–102   Different kinds of mediation may involve different time frames for the mediation. In civil and commercial mediation, it is usual to set aside a specific period of time for the conduct of proceedings, in the hope that matters may be resolved in that time, subject perhaps to any adjournment that may be needed.[61] So, commonly, a day or two may be allocated. The time set aside for a civil or commercial mediation tends to be based on the parties' judgment of timing, pragmatically reflecting the time that they wish and consider appropriate to spend on it. Timing also needs to be based objectively on the issues, complexity, history of the dispute, intractability and other factors.

7–103   Family mediation is more likely to be conducted on the basis of shorter meetings (commonly one-and-a-half hours each, but occasionally two hours or more) at periodical intervals, for example, fortnightly or irregularly. Agreed action can be taken between meetings, such as getting valuations, checking legal or other questions, formulating or considering proposals or dealing with other aspects.

7–104   There may be permutations of these options. A civil mediation may, for example, run for a day or so, and then be adjourned so that the mediator may shuttle between the parties, visiting each of them at their premises or inviting them to visit him or her, over whatever time span may be agreed. This might

---

Lurie in *Punch List* Vol. 19, No. 4, Winter 1996/97, which reviews an article by D. Henderson, "Mediation Success: An Empirical Analysis" in 11 Ohio S.L.J. No. 1 (1996).

[60]It may be difficult to assess this in advance. It is more likely to be the mediator's function to consider the need for this in the light of developments during the mediation. In some circumstances, however, it may be possible to anticipate the need for an adjournment.

[61]Whenever mediation takes place pursuant to a pre-existing contractual requirement, often as part of a structured system of dispute resolution which may culminate in arbitration or litigation, it is commonplace to find provisions requiring the mediation to take place within a fixed period after reference of the dispute.

then be followed by another session for a fixed period if that was thought to be helpful.

A mediation may enable matters to be resolved within a matter of hours,[62] or may, especially in more complex cases, require a series of meetings which could run to four or five or more days and span a period of months.

    7–105

6. MED–ARB (MEDIATION–ARBITRATION)

Med–arb is a variation of the mediation process in which the mediator changes role if the matter does not settle in mediation, and becomes an arbitrator with the task of making a binding determination.

    7–106

Most disputants will seek adjudication of their dispute if attempts to resolve it by agreement are unsuccessful. A mediator is likely to become familiar with the facts of the case and the respective contentions and concerns of the parties. Some parties may well be willing to entrust that mediator with the duty of making a binding determination, especially if during the mediation the parties have both come to trust the mediator.

    7–107

In the med–arb process, the decision to move to an arbitration mode, if mediation is unsuccessful, is one to which the parties commit themselves in advance, before the process commences. This offers the advantages, real or perceived, that the process will produce a resolution, one way or another. There may be a belief that parties may try harder to be reasonable and to resolve the matter during the mediation phase. It may also be considered that if adjudication is needed, there will be no loss of time or cost in re-acquainting a new neutral with the facts of the case and the issues.

    7–108

What parties may not necessarily realise when choosing the med–arb process, however, is the way in which it must necessarily affect the mediator's ability to function effectively in either mode, as a mediator or as an arbitrator.

    7–109

Parties in mediation must not only trust the impartiality of the mediator. They must also be able to make disclosures to the mediator either in the separate caucus meetings or in the joint meetings, which they know will be maintained confidentially and could not be used in evidence if the dispute went to adjudication. They also know that they can make concessions in an evidentially privileged situation. If the parties know that the mediator is to become the adjudicator if the case does not settle, this may well inhibit effective negotiation and must change the whole dynamic of the mediation process.

    7–110

The position also becomes more complicated in the arbitration mode. Does the neutral ignore information received during the mediation phase that may be prejudicial to a party? Even if the neutral is able to do this, can the process be seen to be fair to the participants once they are faced with the reality of it and with the neutral making a finding against one of them?

    7–111

---

[62] In the Central London County Court Pilot Scheme, three hours were allowed for each mediation. Some found this too short; but most mediators agree that some such limit is essential, especially to maintain proportionality of time and cost to the value of the subject-matter of the dispute. Proportionality between time/cost and subject-matter value is becoming an important concept in dealing with disputes.

7–112   Where the same person serves as mediator and then as arbitrator, serious reservations have been expressed as to whether, in addition to damaging his efficacy as a mediator, he will not have "fatally compromised the integrity of his adjudicative role."[63]

7–113   To meet these concerns, alternative forms of med–arb have been formulated which accept the principle of following an unsuccessful mediation with arbitration, but not automatically using the same person as mediator and arbitrator.

7–114   In one of these, if the mediation does not result in an agreed outcome and the matter needs to proceed to adjudication, the mediator checks at that stage with all the parties whether they are agreeable to his continuing to act, but henceforth in the different role of arbitrator. If any party does not wish him to do so, they have the right to opt out of the process, and the mediator ceases to act in any capacity. That allows the parties the choice of allowing the neutral to proceed to arbitration rather than either automatically accepting or excluding this. If the parties want a neutral to adjudicate who has acquainted himself fully with the issues in the mediation, whom they trust and who, in the event, has not actually been compromised by the mediation, there is a view that they should be allowed to agree to this. This process has been called "med–arb-opt-out."[64]

7–115   Another alternative to automatic arbitration if the mediation does not resolve the dispute was devised by Brett and Goldberg, based on an experiment which they conducted on the American coal industry. Under their model, the neutral would be a "mediator-adviser" as a step in a process that would lead on to arbitration in the absence of agreement. The neutral would conduct a mediation in the ordinary course, trying to shift the parties from a rights emphasis to an examination of their respective interests, and would endeavour to facilitate a settlement. If agreement could not be achieved, the mediator would become an advisory arbitrator, furnishing a non-binding opinion for the guidance of the parties, but not a formal arbitrator making a binding decision: the parties would need to engage someone else to arbitrate formally. This process seemed to produce highly satisfactory outcomes, with costs and time savings, and a high level of party satisfaction.[65]

7–116   Med–arb has largely been used in the United States in relation to employment issues, many in the public sector. Reference has also been made to its use in child custody cases in California. It has also been used in the construction industry. There are both advocates and opponents of the process. However, the structural shortcomings at the basic level make it a very worrying process to recommend or use.

7–117   Med–arb should not be confused with the concept of parties attempting to mediate their differences and agreeing in advance to proceed to arbitration if

---

[63]See the comments of Goldberg, Green & Sander in *Dispute Resolution* (1985) quoting in turn from an article by Prof. Fuller "Collective Bargaining and the Arbitrator" Proceedings, Fifteenth Annual Meeting, National Academy of Arbitrators 8, 29–33, 36–48 (1962).

[64]See the *Dispute Resolution Supplement 1987* by Goldberg, Green & Sander, p. 69.

[65]See the article by Deborah M. Kolb "How existing procedures shape alternatives: the case of grievance mediation" in the *J. D. R.,* Vol. 1989 at 73, referring to two articles by Brett and Goldberg, namely "Grievance Mediation in the Coal Industry: A Field Experiment" 37(1) Indus. & Lab. Rel. Rev. 49 (1983) and "Mediator-Advisers: A New Third Party Role" in *Negotiating in Organisations,* M. Bazerman & R. Lewicki (eds.), (1983).

settlement is not achieved in mediation. In that event, different people have the roles of mediator and arbitrator. That is an increasingly common and entirely acceptable procedure.

7. What is Real Mediation and Who Decides?

This question bears asking. It reflects a debate that has been conducted over the years, and raises a serious question about those who purport to decide on what is or is not "real" mediation.   **7–118**

The question was raised in 1996 by Ericka B. Gray, the Executive Director of the U.S. Academy of Family Mediators.[66] She considered that there seemed to be no consensus among mediators as to the best answer to this question. The issue arose largely between those practising mediation without any evaluation, and those who evaluate as part of the mediation. Her underlying question was whether an evaluative form of mediation could still properly be termed "mediation".   **7–119**

Her concern is: "are we truly in a position to definitively state what constitutes 'real' mediation and what doesn't?" Even if a definition could be agreed, "how do we measure whether something fits that definition?" And if "experts" are to decide, "who will be the experts?"   **7–120**

Further questions arise. Can family mediators impose their definition on mediators practising in other fields? Or vice versa? Or can mediation be "a flexible tool, responsive to the variety of needs" of the people who seek it? She asks whether it would be "better to consider mediation as a continuum from facilitative to evaluative, with a variety of styles of practice, a number of approaches, and a wide assortment of contexts in which it is practised".

Different ADR practitioners are likely to have different answers to these questions, and each may have their own validity. The authors of this book subscribe to the view that all mediation is facilitative, but that some mediators may add elements of evaluation along the continuum to which Ericka Gray refers. But that is not to answer the question posed in the heading of this section. Debate and discussion may be healthy; but those who claim to "own" the right to decide what "real" mediation is, may need to re-examine their attitudes and motives.   **7–121**

8. Multi-party Disputes

A view is sometimes heard that multi-party or multi-contract disputes are not appropriate for ADR. This is understandable, having regard both to the problems of getting all the participants to agree to the process and to the mechanics and logistics of organising the process with various parties having differing positions and interests. There is, however, another view, namely that ADR is particularly appropriate in such disputes precisely because they are complex and expensive to litigate, and impossible to arbitrate without the   **7–122**

---

[66]"What is 'Real' Mediation?" *AFM Mediation News* Vol. 15, No. 2, 1996.

consent of all parties.[67] Also, the processes of ADR can work just as effectively with numerous parties as with two parties.

7–123   There are a number of examples of successful ADR processes involving several parties. Randall W. Wulff, a San Francisco litigation lawyer, writes of having taken part as a mediator or as an advocate in numerous cases, over 90 per cent of which were settled by mediation. Many of these were multi-party disputes, one involving 28 parties and their respective counsels, and another necessitating the hire of a hotel banquet room and suites to accommodate some 60 participating client representatives and witnesses.[68] Another American lawyer, Gerald S. Clay, writes from his personal experience that neither the degree of complexity of a case nor a multiplicity of parties are any hindrance to mediation.[69] Goldberg, Green and Sander write of the mini-trial that although most of these have involved two entities, some have involved multi-party disputes.[70] Public law disputes in the United States generally involve multiple parties, and mediation is used for dealing with many of these.[71] Professor Lawrence Susskind considers that "the mediation of multi-party, multi-issue disputes at the local level, such as battles over the design and location of public facilities, the setting of policy priorities (like how to spend public funds), and the specification of health and safety standards (like acceptable levels of risk) can be particularly effective."[72]

7–124   In the United Kingdom, a number of disputes have been resolved by mediation where large numbers of parties were involved. For example, a dispute was mediated arising from claims of mismanagement of an investment portfolio of a pension scheme. The respondents included the pension trustees, company directors, legal advisers, bankers, investment advisers and insurance underwriters. All were represented in the mediation, in what proved to be a complex negotiation involving seven different parties. Proposals were obtained from all and after these were exchanged and discussed, settlement terms were agreed.

Some practical points for multi-party civil/commercial mediation

7–125   The following practical suggestions are based on the experience of multi-party civil/commercial mediation in the United Kingdom:

- Multi-party mediation requires significantly more planning than two-party mediation. Adequate time should be allowed for this.

- It can be helpful to meet each of the parties or their legal

---

[67]The International Chamber of Commerce has observed the problems relating to multi-party arbitration, see its paper "Multi-party Arbitration", published in 1991, containing views from international arbitration specialists. The Departmental Advisory Committee in its work on the 1996 Arbitration Act (see Chap. 4) refused on grounds of principle to include provisions for the mandatory consolidation of arbitral disputes. S. 35 of the 1996 Act is merely permissive and encouraging.

[68]See "A Mediation Primer" by Randall W. Wulff in Wilkinson, *ADR Practice Book* (1990) at p. 114.

[69]See Chap. 9 "Counseling clients on mediation", *ibid.*

[70]See *Dispute Resolution* (1985) at p. 275.

[71]See, *e.g.* "Public law disputes" in *Processes of Dispute Resolution: the Role of Lawyers* by Murray, Rau and Sherman (1989) at pp. 329–336.

[72]"Multi-Party Public Policy Mediation: A Separate Breed" in *Dispute Resolution Magazine*, Fall 1997 (ABA Section of Dispute Resolution).

representatives separately at the outset, before written statements are furnished. This allows the mediator to obtain information about each party's position, and to start building rapport. It also helps to identify parties whose interests may coincide and who may decide to join one another for the purpose of mediation discussions.

- The simultaneous exchange of written statements by the parties can be difficult to arrange and to implement effectively. It may be advisable to have them all sent (with copies if required) to the mediator, who can dispatch them simultaneously to the parties when all are received.

- Parties can be asked to send draft statements to the mediator on a confidential and interim basis, in advance of their final versions. This can be especially helpful where time constraints exist. This allows the mediator to consider the position and if appropriate to seek clarification or particularisation.

- Co-mediation is commonly indicated for multi-party disputes. If a sole mediator is initially appointed, these preliminary exchanges allow the mediator to assess whether a co-mediator is needed.

- The time between separate meetings is invariably longer in multi-party disputes. If this is explained to parties in advance, they will be more prepared for the delays between separate meetings and less likely to be troubled by them. The mediator may suggest that they bring work files, reading matter or anything else to occupy themselves between meetings.

- To avoid the opening oral presentations taking too long, time limits should be agreed. Five to 10 minutes each might be sufficient for most cases. Focusing on the desired outcome (in general terms) should be encouraged, rather than rehearsing the arguments or reading the written statement.

- Co-mediators must decide whether to conduct their meetings together or separately. If time permits, they may wish to be together for the initial meeting in the mediation with each party, but then separate for subsequent meetings.

- The mediator needs to have a separate room as a base for managing the discussions. This is particularly important for co-mediators, who may also wish to have a flip chart for keeping a record of their meetings. This can also help to tell one where the other is at any time, in case the one completes a meeting and wishes to join the other.

- If long delays between meetings are expected once the process is under way, the mediator may wish to release parties from waiting, by agreeing a time to return or being available on short notice. This can relieve the frustration of waiting perhaps hours between meetings.

- Personal meetings can be supplemented by telephone discussions with parties who are unable to attend in person or who are not immediately available.

7–126   John. H. Wilkinson suggests that the key to using ADR in disputes involving multiple parties is to get the process going with those who are willing to participate, and others may join in later. Even if they do not, those parties participating in the ADR process may be able to arrive at resolutions helpful to their mutual interests.[73] While this view has been shown to be workable in practice, it does call for some note of caution in that a mediation or other ADR process which proceeds without all the essential parties being involved runs the risk of being abortive. If the missing parties are not crucial to the outcome or if the participating parties can identify areas in which limited agreement would be helpful to them, then there is no reason why the process should not proceed without full participation. This is a view shared by Professor Susskind, who says that it may be desirable to convene a meeting of parties who want to meet, leaving it open as to whether the process continues or concludes after that.

7–127   Michael T. Lesnick and John R. Ehrmann suggest a number of strategies for dealing with multi-party disputes.[74] They focus on three main phases: entry into the dispute; designing and initiating the intervention; generating and assessing options, bargaining, and reaching and implementing consensus.

7–128   The initial phase is obviously more complex than a dispute between two parties, and the suggestion is made that in suitable cases an advisory committee can be useful, especially in disputes having legislative or administrative aspects, or in community disputes. In commercial cases, this may not be appropriate.[75] Instead, the neutral or any ADR organisation involved in the matter may need to liaise with the various interested parties in order to achieve agreement as to the use of an ADR process, the appointment of the neutral and the issues to be addressed.

7–129   The second phase involves making the necessary practical arrangements for the process such as designing its structure and establishing an agenda. Special questions arising from the multiplicity of parties, including venue and frequency of meetings, will need thoughtful attention, especially where the parties are located any distance from one another. One of the questions will be whether co-mediation may be a suitable way to work: the advantage of this being the sharing of the workload and the possible introduction of different areas of expertise. The disadvantages, however, are cost and a risk that unless the co-mediators co-ordinate carefully with one another, misunderstandings could arise. Professor Susskind advocates a team approach, especially where there are many parties. This will enable members of the mediation team to maintain contact with all the parties between mediation sessions.

7–130   Lesnick and Ehrmann suggest a useful negotiating model, although it is

---

[73] At pp. 22, 23 of the *ADR Practice Book* (1990).

[74] See their article "Selected Strategies for Managing Multiparty Disputes" (1987) 16 M.Q. 21–29.

[75] Indeed, in commercial cases rather than those with a community or administrative background, some of these strategies may be less relevant, though they can be adapted. All material parties would be required to participate in a civil or commercial mediation.

more geared to political and community issues than to commercial disputes. Based on their ideas, but adapted for more general usage, there would be an initial meeting of all parties in plenary session, at which the ground rules of the process are agreed, the role of the neutral is established, the agenda is discussed and the timetable considered. Arrangements for the furnishing of statements, submissions and documents could also be dealt with at this preliminary meeting. This procedural meeting might be held by the neutral with the lawyers only if that was acceptable to all concerned.

At the substantive meeting of all parties, which would follow the **7–131** procedural meeting according to the agreed timetable, a working agenda would be formulated, based on the preliminary discussion of it. The neutral could propose an agenda for discussion. Presentations by each party would then follow, as in the case of a two-party mediation. The parties would then separate into their different groups, and caucusing would take place in accordance with usual mediation practice or whatever ADR process was being followed. Joint meetings could be held as and when the neutral considered this helpful.

During the third stage facilitation of the negotiations takes place, with **7–132** options being generated and explored, and shuttle mediation continuing. Further adapting the model outlined by Lesnick and Ehrmann, the neutral could use conventional ADR two-party process and strategies, liaising closely with his or her co-mediators where these are also engaged. Notes and records would have to be most carefully maintained, and key points might be written up on flip-charts.

One strategy for complex and prolonged multi-party disputes might be for **7–133** the neutral from time to time to prepare interim summaries of the position as it develops, which clarify the extent of agreement reached and the range of issues still outstanding. This would, of course, need to have careful regard to such duty or confidentiality as may exist in relation to the respective parties. The agenda can be reviewed from time to time in the light of any such interim summaries and reports.

If agreement is reached in multi-party disputes, it is crucial for all parties **7–134** to review and comment on any draft document and to execute it when it is in its final approved form. This needs careful structuring and monitoring. Procedures for obtaining court orders where necessary, for implementing the agreement and for dealing with any residual issues should they arise may also need to be considered.

CHAPTER 8

MEDIATION: STAGES AND FACETS

8–001   Mediation can be divided into a number of stages, though these will not necessarily follow the same sequence or be present in every case. There are different ways in which these stages can be formulated.[1] The framework used in this Chapter does not attempt to be definitive: it merely serves as a useful structure to describe these different phases and facets.

8–002   Ten stages are identified in this book, split into three phases[2]

Before mediation

Stage 1: Engaging the parties in the mediation forum

Stage 2: Obtaining commitment and agreeing mediation rules

Stage 3: Preliminary communications and preparation

During the substantive mediation

Stage 4: Establishing the venue and meeting the parties

Stage 5: Establishing the issues and setting the agenda

Stage 6: Information gathering

Stage 7: Managing and facilitating discussions and negotiations

Stage 8: Employing impasse strategies

---

[1] Folberg and Milne in *Divorce Mediation: Theory and Practice* (1988) say that writers divide or categorise the stages of mediation differently, and they list their own eight stages. Andrew Floyer Acland in *A Sudden Outbreak of Common Sense: Managing Conflict through Mediation* identifies nine stages, from preparation, designing the mediation process and bringing the parties together through to formulating and formalising the proposals. Lisa Parkinson in *Family Mediation* refers to a 12-stage process for family co-mediation. But a staged model has been challenged. See n.3 below.

[2] The 10 stages used in the second edition of this book follow the same stages as adopted in the first edition. The authors are obliged to the members of the Mediation Standards Working Party of the Family Law Committee of the Law Society, particularly Robin ap Cynan, for the discussion leading to the further development of these 10 stages into three clear phases.

The end of mediation and afterwards

Stage 9: Concluding the mediation and recording the outcome

Stage 10: Post-termination

These stages are used in various other chapters, to facilitate consideration **8–003** of the mediation process. It must be emphasised that not every stage exists in every mediation or every kind of mediation. Nor do the stages necessarily manifest themselves in the same sequence, but may well overlap and blur in practice. Reference to stages is merely a device to help provide a useful and coherent framework for the process.[3]

There is a risk that identifying stages and outlining current practice may **8–004** rigidify the mediation process into existing patterns. That would be a great pity. Part of the value of ADR is its capacity to develop new ways of working that are appropriate to the needs of the situation, whether or not they fit into existing frameworks. Practitioners are therefore cautioned against viewing the stages and practices that follow as a rigid norm that has to be observed.

1. Phase One: Before Mediation

Stage 1: Engaging the parties in the mediation forum

There are many ways in which disagreements can be addressed and a number **8–005** of forums for doing so. Parties who may be negotiating between themselves will need to decide at what stage they will engage third party assistance and what kind of help that should be. They can choose whether to appoint representatives (such as respective lawyers) to take up their negotiations. If this fails, or if they prefer to omit this step and go straight to adjudication, they can have their dispute adjudicated (through the courts or by way of arbitration, contractual adjudication or expert determination). As a further option, they can engage a neutral third party to help them resolve the issues through ADR, with mediation being the most common form.

Parties may consult their lawyers to advise them and help them select the **8–006** forum. Increasingly solicitors will need to take a broader view of the issues and be able to explore with their clients the respective merits of the different available procedures rather than automatically moving into adversarial mode as they have tended to do in the past.[4] This is not to suggest that parties will

---

[3] A staged model has been questioned by some mediators, though they acknowledge that this concept has "served the field well". See the article "Is a Stage Model of Mediation Necessary?" in (1999) 16(3) M.Q. by James R. Antes, Donna Turner Hudson, Erling O. Jorgensen and Janet Kelly Moen. The criticism is that the actual practice of mediation is not fully compatible with stage models and that there are several anomalies. The authors of the article support the concept of transformative mediation (see para. 1–040) and prefer a non-sequential model that focuses on whatever emerges for the parties (the "emergent-focus" model).

[4] A survey during 1998 by solicitors Dibb Lupton Allsop and the Centre for Dispute Resolution revealed that 63% of company respondents had not been advised by their solicitors about the possibility of using mediation for their cases (L.S.G. September 30, 1998). This confirms the findings of the mediation pilot scheme conducted in the Central London County Court which

not want and expect their lawyers to champion their cause, but the ways in which this can be achieved are likely to become more extensive.

8–007   Advice agencies are also likely to face increasing enquiries from the public about mediation and other alternative dispute resolution resources available to them. One consequence of this is that the Advice Services Alliance has set up an ADR project to examine what ADR services are available and to give guidance to national advice agencies about the various forms of ADR.[5]

8–008   Mediators, lawyers and parties need to weigh up the considerations as to which forum is the most appropriate to their situation. Using the language of computers, the current "default" programme is adversarial. This means that while the decision to litigate can be made automatically, any other decision (including mediation) currently involves a positive decision to override the default mechanism.

8–009   This in turn requires a clear understanding of processes other than litigation (such as mediation) and an appreciation of their relevance to the needs of the parties.

8–010   Most people are broadly familiar with the traditional adversarial processes and, even if unaccustomed to dealing with lawyers and the courts, will have some idea what to expect from litigation (even if their actual experience may eventually differ from their expectations). When clients consult lawyers, they usually seek advice or representation, which can be immediately provided.

8–011   Although public and professional awareness of mediation has increased and is rapidly continuing to do so, a decision to use the mediation forum may still not be an easy one to make. An initial inquiry about the process needs to be carefully addressed. First, the mediation process may still be relatively unfamiliar, and the inquirer may not have a clear idea what it entails. Secondly, even when the process is understood, the inquirer may be uncertain whether mediation will be appropriate and can be trusted. Thirdly, the inquirer may not know whether the other party to the dispute will agree to enter into mediation and may be unsure whether an approach to the other party to agree to mediation may be perceived as signalling weakness or a lack of confidence.

8–012   It is because of these features and the need to address them carefully and sympathetically that the initial mediation inquiry and the selection of the forum is treated as the first stage of the process. All ADR organisations and practitioners will have experience of one party being interested in mediating, but the consensus to proceed being absent, either because the initial party does not want to test the possibility, fearing a rejection, or because the other party refuses to mediate. This is not merely a marketing issue: consideration must be given to the appropriateness of the mediation forum for the issues and the parties, and if it is appropriate, care and skill may still be needed to help engage both parties in it.

8–013   Most organisations and individual practitioners will have their own methods of dealing with initial enquiries. These may include any or all of the following:

---

reported that solicitors' attitudes inhibited the growth of ADR (See headline article in the L.S.G. of July 29, 1998 and the report of Prof. Hazel Genn, outlined at paras 3–063–064
[5] Members of the Advice Services Alliance include, *e.g.* the Law Centres Federation, the National Association of Citizens' Advice Bureaux and the Federation of Independent Advice Centres.

Providing written material

Furnishing written material gives information about the mediation process **8–014** and can show its relevance to particular kinds of disputes. It can outline the procedure and ground rules, give estimates of time scale and costs, indicate what qualifications, experience and training the mediators have, and generally anticipate and answer standard questions which inquirers have. It can update practitioners and the public about developments in mediation and the extent of its usage. It can, for example, comprise:

- A corporate or individual brochure, ranging from a simple sheet of paper, perhaps folded A4 size, through to a sophisticated booklet with extensive information.

- Packs of data, which may include copies of relevant newspaper or journal articles and other promotional material.

- Newsletters or other periodical publications.

- Biographical notes about individual mediators.

- Ground rules and terms on which the mediation is undertaken.

Providing oral information

Many inquirers will wish to have the process explained to them personally, **8–015** commonly on the telephone, rather than having to glean it from written material, although the latter can be useful to supplement oral information. Personal meetings may be appropriate to discuss the process before deciding whether or not to use it. In the family field, the Family Law Act 1996 had provision for parties intending to divorce to attend an information meeting where they would receive information about mediation, counselling and legal advice and representation. These provisions have been abandoned, but practitioners will devise appropriate alternatives.[6]

It is vital that the person who explains mediation has a clear and accurate **8–016** understanding of the process and how it works. It needs to be properly explained to the inquirers, so that they do not get a wrong impression of the process. The person giving the information should be able to deal efficiently and sympathetically with whatever questions and reservations the inquirer may have.

The proposed mediator may personally deal with these preliminary **8–017** inquiries. The advantages of this are that the mediator can be sure that all information about the process will be accurate, and that he or she will have engaged the parties by the time the mediation commences. It also enables the parties to get some sense of the mediator's handling of process matters, and to begin to establish some working relationship with the mediator. They may be pragmatic considerations, however, such as cost effectiveness and availability, making it impractical for mediators to handle all preliminary enquiries personally.

Some parties may wish to start discussing the merits of the issues with the **8–018** mediator at this stage, which might in some kinds of cases be premature and

---

[6] See also Chap. 10.

inappropriate. A family mediator would generally avoid separate discussions with each party at this stage about the merits of their issues.[7] A commercial mediator, anticipating separate and confidential meetings, might be readier to allow parties to indicate what those issues were, but generally without engaging in them. Mediators might wish to avoid the perception by either party that the mediator has prematurely started such discussions with only one party. For this reason, a mediator may prefer as a general rule to deal at this early stage with matters of process and procedure and not with the merits of the dispute.

8–019   Mediation organisations with panels of mediators generally tend to respond to inquiries through a central system, and not by reference to the individual mediator concerned, who may well only be appointed once the parties have reached a decision to mediate. Ideally, the personnel responding to inquiries should either be mediators themselves or *au fait* with the process.

8–020   Consortia of mediators, who have joined together as a group for mutual support and marketing, will have procedures best suited to their specific needs. Some may have a central inquiry system. In this case, they may either arrange for someone to have central responsibility for dealing with calls, or they may arrange a rota system, perhaps using a "movable" telephone number, with each member having a fixed period of responsibility. Others may list the individual details and telephone numbers of their members in their promotional material so that the public can contact them direct.

Video, internet and e-mail

8–021   Information about mediation and other forms of ADR can be provided in other ways besides written and oral material. One method that some organisations use is showing a video that demonstrates and explains the process. The use of promotional videos is relatively undeveloped in the United Kingdom, perhaps because of the inhibiting cost factor. It is, however, a resource that can clearly help to provide a better understanding of the process.

8–022   The Internet and e-mail have become increasingly significant vehicles for providing information about all kinds of dispute resolution resources including mediation. Many organisations, including law firms and individuals, have established web-sites through which they offer preliminary information and establish contact with interested parties.[8]

Engaging all parties

8–023   In addition to furnishing information about the mediation process, ADR organisations and practitioners will generally assist a party to gain the agreement to mediate of any other party or parties to the dispute. To this end, some may agree to approach the other party or parties for this purpose.

---

[7]However, as part of a screening process for domestic violence, separate discussions about behaviour may be held.

[8]See *e.g.* the following sites:

Center for Public Resources: *www.cpradr.org*

ADR Group: *www.adrgroup.co.uk*

Solicitors' Family Law Association: *www.sfla.co.uk*

Family Mediators Association: *www.familymediators.co.uk*

The Family Law Consortium: *www.tflc.co.uk*

In some cases, this may be unnecessary or a mere formality, and the party **8–024** may be able to discuss the suggestion with the other side and procure agreement to it. Sometimes the same end can be achieved by the suggestion coming through the respective solicitors, if the dispute is already in legal hands. The approach to the other party will generally need some care. This is less likely to raise any problems where the parties have retained trust and respect for one another. There can, however, be a risk that the other party may be sceptical, not least because the proposal comes from the opponent. Also, the party proposing mediation will not wish the suggestion to be perceived as a sign of weakness.

Karl Mackie's ADR Route Map[9] touches briefly on this issue; and Randall **8–025** W. Wulff[10] points out how delicate it is to introduce the subject of mediation to an opponent in order to avoid a stigma of weakness. He suggests, as do other writers and practitioners, that proposing mediation can be presented as an act of confidence rather than weakness. The approach could be that the party proposing mediation is sufficiently confident to agree to a neutral third party coming in to assist in discussions: is the other party similarly confident and willing?

There are a number of different ways in which an ADR organisation or an **8–026** individual practitioner can assist a party to engage the opponent in the mediation process. They may advise the party orally on how to approach the other side; or send the inquiring party written material to send on to the other; or write directly to the other side, explaining their neutral services, enclosing written material and inquiring if the party would be interested in mediation; or contact the other side by telephone; or meet the parties separately or together for a preliminary discussion about the process itself, without entering on the merits.

Not surprisingly, people may be apprehensive about mediation until they **8–027** have had their first experience of it. Commonly they then become supporters of it. The first stage is one of addressing proper and understandable uncertainties and reservations.

Is mediation appropriate?

In the ordinary course of a dispute, parties may go through a number of **8–028** stages. First, they may try to resolve it themselves. Next they may seek professional advice to establish the strength of their position. Their professional adviser, usually a lawyer, may be asked to contact the other side or their representative to try to achieve a resolution either by persuasion or threat. If this does not settle the matter, legal action may follow. During the course of this action, respective lawyers may enter into settlement negotiations. If these do not succeed, there is sometimes machinery for making formal settlement proposals, if only to protect against an award of costs or under new procedural rules. Ultimately adjudication is necessary if none of these procedures result in a settlement.

There are two fundamental questions that need to be asked about **8–029** mediation against this background. First, is mediation appropriate to the

---

[9]Published by CEDR, the Centre for Dispute Resolution, 1991.
[10]Chap. 7, "A Mediation Primer" in Wilkinson, *ADR Practice Book*.

individual dispute at all? Secondly, if it is, at what stage is it most effective to introduce it?

8–030   Mediation is likely to be appropriate in virtually all circumstances in which the parties wish and have the legal capacity to settle their differences, however far apart they may be in their thinking. There are however some circumstances in which mediation would be inappropriate. These are primarily if either party does not have legal capacity to enter into an agreement, or if the issue affects status or constitutional rights, or if it is essential to have a precedent or injunctive relief, or where either party has no genuine intention to settle or is likely to abuse or undermine the process.

8–031   As to the best timing for the use of mediation, this will depend on the individual case. In most cases, it cannot be too early to mediate; but there is a view that the process will be more effective when the issues have crystallised, and perhaps especially where the parties have been unable to resolve the issues themselves and feel readier to avail themselves of the mediator's help.[11] Some litigators consider it preferable to wait for the issues to be identified in pleadings and for documents to be disclosed through the court process. However, there is no reason to believe that these are significant factors in the effective use of mediation.

8–032   The information meeting piloted under the Family Law Act 1996, now abandoned, had a mixed public reception. Part of its failure arose from the inflexible constraints on information allowed to be given. Information provided by a neutral person and geared to each couple's individual circumstances would probably have been more useful and successful.[12] Equivalent procedures in the civil commercial or other fields are not readily available from neutral sources.[13] There are analogous procedures in other jurisdictions, particularly the multi-door courthouse concept in the United States, which uses prescribed criteria for allocating different kinds of disputes to different dispute resolution processes, at least in broad and general terms.[14] This task falls to the individual advisers of the parties. ADR organisations, neutrals and advice agencies may explain ADR, but need to be aware that these processes may not necessarily be appropriate in every case. They should assist parties in establishing the forum most suitable to the effective resolution of their issues.

8–033   Dispute resolution provisions in contracts now increasingly tend to reflect the resolution process in stages. In the first stage, the parties are required to try to settle the issues themselves by negotiation. In the second stage they do so through mediation or other ADR processes, with a time-limit sometimes imposed for achieving an agreed outcome. If these do not succeed, then the third stage is an adjudication, with provision for arbitration if this is what the parties require.

Stage 2: Obtaining commitment and agreeing mediation rules

8–034   Parties who decide to use mediation to deal with their issues opt for a process that inherently involves a more significant personal involvement and

---

[11] As to timing, see Chap. 18.
[12] For further information about the matrimonial context, see Chap. 10.
[13] But see the concept of a neutral dispute manager at paras 7–098 *et seq.*
[14] See paras 5–033 *et seq.*

commitment than representation and litigation through solicitors. While this should be evident from the first stage of the process, it will be crystallised by the contract to mediate.

The contract to mediate has two components: first, the contract between the mediator and the parties; and secondly, the commitment as between the parties themselves to use the mediation process and to enter into negotiations with one another with a view to resolving their issues.[15]

8–035

The agreement to mediate may arise on an ad hoc basis after a dispute has arisen. This may be spontaneous or may have been directed by the court. Alternatively, it may flow from a provision in a contract between the parties that any disagreement between them is to be dealt with by mediation in the first instance before litigation or arbitration is commenced.

8–036

Where the parties agree to mediate without being obliged to do so by any preexisting contractual provision, they may be required to enter into a written agreement with the mediator, or where applicable with the ADR organisation providing the mediator's services. That contract will regulate the relationship between the mediator and the parties.[16] It may explicitly or implicitly provide that the mediation will take place under the rules or provisions of a particular code of practice to which the mediator and/or the organisation subscribes.[17] The rules or code in question may be appended to the contract, summarised or paraphrased, or imported into the contract by reference.

8–037

The mediation contract serves a number of functions:

8–038

- It is a formal contract recording matters such as confidentiality, privilege, payment of fees and other practical aspects that need to be agreed. It can also record that the parties may not call the mediator or have access to the mediator's notes in any subsequent proceedings that may take place. If required it can, for example, include a provision excluding the mediator, and the ADR organisation if applicable, from any liability arising out of any alleged act or omission by the mediator in the mediation.

- The terms of the contract can outline the ground rules of the mediation. To some extent these may be explicitly or implicitly incorporated into the contract. For example, a contract may specify the procedure for furnishing information and documents and set out the time to be spent in different stages of the process, or it may deal with issues of confidentiality applicable to joint sessions and separate meetings by way of caucus.

- It requires each party to give a considered commitment to the mediation process. In some contracts, the parties may be required to agree to negotiate in good faith and to make a confidential disclosure of their strengths and weaknesses to the mediator. Whether such an undertaking would be enforceable even if a breach could be proved, is

---

[15] See paras 6–060 *et seq.* for the effect of an agreement to negotiate in good faith.
[16] For examples of agreements to mediate see Appendix II.
[17] See Chap. 21 dealing more fully with codes of practice and their implications. For specimen codes, see Appendix II.

questionable[18]: but the intention of this is to require the parties to commit themselves fully to the process. This is to some extent achieved by the act of their entering into the mediation contract and may be enhanced by the terms of the contract.

- It informs the parties that although the process may be informal, it will be conducted in a professional and businesslike way.

- It may be the basis on which the ADR organisation or the mediator obtains indemnity insurance cover, since the standard terms of the mediation contract may well affect the terms of any such insurance.[19]

- It may assist a court in deciding on the enforceability of any agreement reached or claimed to have been reached during the mediation, should this become an issue.

8–039   With one exception, all mediation voluntarily entered into involves some form of contract, explicit or implicit. Meeting with a mediator to try to resolve issues in dispute, even if not formally agreed, implicitly requires some form of agreement between the parties and with the mediator. Where, however, court rules specify that mediation must take place, the concept of a contract may be absent. So, for example, parties attending a conciliation appointment required under family court rules may not be "contracting" to do so. They are merely complying with court rules.[20] This should be distinguished from mediation voluntarily entered into by parties where a court has adjourned proceedings so that the parties can explore the possibilities of ADR.[21]

8–040   It follows that the contract to mediate does not have to be in writing. Parties may informally and orally agree with a third party neutral that he or she will act as a mediator, and no further formality than this is needed. The contract to mediate may indeed be implicit. It is, however, good practice to have a written agreement which records the terms and ground rules of the process and avoids any possible misunderstanding later about the basis on which the mediation was undertaken.[22] In some circumstances such terms may be very important, especially if parties do not reach agreement in mediation and seek to refer in later court proceedings to documents or events which arose in relation to the mediation. For example, the terms as to confidentiality or privilege may become relevant. Or it may be relevant that the parties agreed that the mediator could not be called or his notes *subpoenaed*. It may be necessary to be clear whether any agreement in the mediation was or was not to be "subject to contract" or to the parties first

---

[18]See n. 15 above.

[19]As to the question of insurance cover for ADR activities, see Chap. 24.

[20]Arguably, as long as they have the right not to attend a conciliation appointment, attendance might be said to be by agreement. This is, however, probably stretching the point.

[21]Court practice and rules in England and Wales increasingly provide for this. Adjournments for mediation or other ADR processes to be considered have already started to increase significantly under the Woolf reforms and other new procedures See Chap. 3.

[22]Some Codes of Practice may specify this. See for example the Law Society's recommended Code at Para. 4.1, at para. A2–065 below.

obtaining independent professional advice. All these terms could be crucial to any later attempt to involve mediation events in court proceedings.

The contract, where it is recorded in writing, should be signed before the mediation is actually commenced. This may be done before the first meeting, or sometimes the parties may be given the contract in advance to approve, and are asked to sign it at the beginning of the initial mediation meeting. Signing it together at the start of the mediation, having all approved it in advance, has a symbolic significance, committing the parties to the search for a resolution.   **8–041**

Stage 3: Preliminary communications and preparation

Having agreed to enter into mediation, and before the substantive meeting, the parties are likely to have some preliminary communications with the mediator or with the organisation arranging the mediation. This may be by telephone or in writing or in some cases personally.   **8–042**

Pre-meeting communications

Pre-meeting communications are likely to address procedural matters. They may cover arranging the venue and timetable for the mediation, explaining what documents and information are required, and arranging to obtain summaries of the parties' respective cases and contentions. This may include copy pleadings and affidavits if court or arbitration proceedings have already commenced (or selected extracts if the documents are extensive). In some models, the mediator may meet the parties together or separately on a preliminary basis to ensure that both or all parties are ready for mediation and that they appreciate what the process involves.   **8–043**

These early communications can be important for several reasons. First, this may be the parties' first experience of mediation and of the mediator, and it can help to get started on the right foot if their experience of this is positive, and if they are clear that the mediator will act with proper authority and impartiality. Secondly, this is an opportunity for the mediator to begin establishing a working relationship with the parties and their lawyers, which will develop during the mediation. Thirdly, the better the picture of the issues the mediator has, the more effective the substantive mediation can be (though in some models, the mediator does not establish the issues in advance, but does so spontaneously at the first meeting).   **8–044**

In this preparatory stage the mediator should ensure that all necessary parties attend the mediation. The whole process can be frustrated if a party is missing whose agreement to a settlement is essential to make it effective.   **8–045**

Where the parties are legally represented, the mediator may consider it helpful at this stage to have preliminary communications, or a meeting, with their legal representatives. The lawyers can, where appropriate, help to identify the issues as they see them, and the aims and objectives of the mediation can be clarified. The role of the lawyers within the process can be discussed and agreed. If there are any matters of particular concern to the lawyers, these can be aired. Procedure, documentation and timetable can be considered.   **8–046**

Preliminary communications with parties' lawyers should not erode the broad principle of the parties' freedom to identify the issues and their   **8–047** responsibility for the outcome of the mediation. It should be viewed as enhancing and supporting the parties, and not overriding them.

8–048   In this preliminary stage, the mediator will check whether parties will be attending the mediation alone, or with legal or other representatives. If one party is bringing a lawyer, the other should be notified in advance and given the opportunity to do the same.

8–049   Where corporate or institutional parties are involved, their representatives attending the mediation need to have authority to negotiate and reach agreement. It is important to check that everyone attending the mediation has the necessary authority to settle. Where parties are indemnified by their insurers, they should make prior arrangements with the insurers to honour any agreement reached by them, perhaps within specified parameters; or alternatively the insurers might send a representative to the mediation.[23] In a multi-party dispute, the mediator will generally want to ensure that all parties whose agreement is essential for an effective resolution attend.[24]

8–050   Where authority is limited or conditional upon some external event, such as approval by a board of directors or subject to the parties obtaining legal advice before finalising, this needs to be known to the mediator and to all parties before the substantive mediation starts. Any agreement which may be reached will need to reflect this conditional basis appropriately, and, if necessary, reciprocally.

Venue

8–051 As to the choice of venue, if the mediator or the ADR organisation can provide or arrange these facilities, that would help to ensure that the mediation takes place in surroundings which are felt by the parties to be neutral. Holding the mediation at the premises of one or other of the disputing parties may be pragmatically necessary on some occasions, but is "home territory" for one party and may prejudice the process by making the other party feel uncomfortable and perhaps less open. Using the premises of the solicitors for either party may in some cases be acceptable.

8–052   There needs to be a room in which the parties and the mediator can all meet jointly; and in those models which involve the holding of separate meetings, also separate rooms for each party. The rooms should, if possible, be sufficiently far apart or sound-proofed for each party to feel able to talk freely without any risk of being overheard. The joint meeting room can usually double as a room for one party. If only one room is available, the mediator may use this as a base, calling the parties in and out of it for the separate meetings; but this is less than ideal.

Timing

8–053 The time to be set aside for the mediation depends on the model of mediation being used. In civil and commercial mediation, it is usual to fix a single session, which may last anything between a few hours and a number of days. In these cases, part of the process is to seek to resolve matters

---

[23]As to the relationship between insurance interests and compromise, see Foskett, *The Law and Practice of Compromise* (4th ed., 1996).

[24]Sometimes though the mediation can take place on a more limited basis with some parties missing. See "multi-party disputes" in Chap. 7.

within the allotted time. However, it may be necessary and beneficial to have adjournments while different aspects of the dispute are addressed. For example, after a day's mediation it may become apparent that matters cannot be finalised until certain accounting issues have been resolved. The mediation might then be adjourned to enable those to be dealt with. The Central London County Court Pilot Scheme mediation sessions lasted three hours. In the pilot scheme in the Court of Appeal, the evidence suggests that much more time is required, more akin to the time required for private sector civil and commercial cases.

Other models, such as in family mediation, tend to have shorter meetings at periodical intervals. Sessions may typically (though not necessarily) be for one-and-a-half or two hours every two or three weeks or so. Here again, these cannot be fixed in advance, nor can their length or frequency be pre-arranged. This is usually a matter to be decided as the mediation progresses.　**8–054**

2. PHASE TWO: DURING THE SUBSTANTIVE MEDIATION

Stage 4: Establishing the venue and meeting the parties
Reception arrangements
Mediators should bear in mind that parties arriving for mediation might well feel anxious about the prospect of meeting and negotiating with one another. In some cases, where feelings are or have been running high, the tension is likely to be even greater. Consequently, reception arrangements should ideally be planned to provide that the parties, and their lawyers if accompanying them, are not kept waiting together in the same waiting room if there is a high level of animosity or tension between them.　**8–055**

Some practitioners try to arrange separate waiting rooms for each party. In family cases, this is an aspiration recommended by the Legal Aid Board. More usually, there is no practical alternative to having the parties together in the same reception area. In this event, the mediation should commence promptly without the parties having to spend any undue length of time together waiting for the mediator. This will usually necessitate ensuring that receptionists are prepared for the arrival of parties or groups who may evidence hostility to one another while waiting. They should be instructed to inform the mediator immediately each group arrives; and the mediator should ensure immediate availability to meet the parties as they arrive.　**8–056**

It may also be necessary or advisable in such circumstances for one party or group to be asked to wait in the meeting room while the other waits in the reception area. Providing tea or coffee or other refreshment during this waiting period can help a little to defuse tension.　**8–057**

Seating arrangements
Although such details may seem trivial, the seating arrangements for parties meeting together in joint session need care. Some mediators, especially in relation to inter-personal disputes, prefer not to have a working table separating the parties and the mediator, but rather to have an informal arrangement of chairs in a triangle or circle, perhaps with a small coffee table in the middle. The chairs are arranged so that the parties are neither　**8–058**

facing one another directly (which could feel confrontational) nor side by side facing forwards (which could inhibit their turning to address one another directly), but rather at an angle to one another. This makes it easier for them to turn either to face the mediator or one another. The distance between each party, and between the parties and the mediators, should be carefully spaced, to ensure that it is neither too close, which might feel invasive and uncomfortable, nor too distant, which might feel remote and uninvolved.[25]

8–059 The mediator may seat the parties on each side of him or her, around a table. If lawyers attend, some mediators prefer to seat them next to their client, further away from the mediator. This enables the mediator to deal more directly with the parties personally, rather than exclusively through the lawyers as in the more traditional adjudicatory process.[26] The seating arrangements will depend on the number of people in attendance and the shape of the available table. Views about table shape vary: a round or square table is useful for three or four people, an oval or conventional rectangular boardroom table for larger numbers. In practice, most mediators are usually limited by the resources actually available, and manage perfectly well with those.

The mediator's opening address

8–060 The first phase of the initial joint meeting will generally involve the mediator making an opening address to the parties, welcoming them and explaining the principles, procedures and ground rules of the mediation. Depending on the model of mediation being followed, the aspects that may need special mention in this address could include:

- The mediator's neutral role and impartiality.

- The procedure and timetable that will be followed and the ground rules that will apply.

- The rules of confidentiality applicable to the mediation and the privileged nature of the discussions (making clear which aspects will not be privileged or confidential, should this be the case).[27]

- The opportunity that will be given for each to outline their respective positions (in those models where each makes a presentation).

- The procedure for conducting separate meetings (caucuses), and the way in which this will be done in addition to joint meetings, where applicable. The special provisions regarding confidentiality of matters discussed during those private sessions may also be covered, and whether matters discussed in the separate meetings will be disclosed by the mediator to the other party or will be maintained confidentially.

- The right of each party or the mediator to terminate the mediation.

---

[25]See the comments about personal space and about seating arrangements in Chap. 15.

[26]Lawyers representing clients in mediation have a different role from traditional adversarial representation in that, while maintaining their duty to represent their client's best interests, they may need to operate in a more problem-solving mode: see Chap. 19.

[27]See Chap. 22 regarding the issue of confidentiality and privilege in mediation.

- The way in which the parties' respective lawyers can participate and assist in the process.

- Any particular rules or qualifications relating to the particular mediation, for example if the "agreements" reached in the mediation are not to be binding but conditional upon some further event such as seeing respective solicitors or getting board approval, that should be clarified.

The mediator will then answer any questions the parties or their lawyers **8–061** may have about the process before proceeding with the substantive mediation. If the parties have not already signed the Agreement to Mediate, they would ordinarily be asked to do so at this point. This signals the end of the formal stages, and the commencement of dealing with the substantive issues.

Stage 5: Establishing the issues and setting the agenda
Establishing the issues
One of the mediator's first tasks is to establish the issues between the parties. **8–062** This may appear to be straightforward, and often it is. In many cases, however, the issues that are initially presented prove to be "the tip of the iceberg" and other issues, often underlying, emerge.

Different fields of activity and models of mediation vary in the way in **8–063** which the issues are presented to the mediator. In civil and commercial models, each party will usually furnish the mediator and one another with written statements of their position. They will then be given an opportunity to make oral presentations outlining and amplifying their views.

In such cases, the mediator will ask each party, or (usually but not **8–064** necessarily) their respective lawyers if they are legally represented in the mediation, to present an outline of their case to the mediator. A guideline or maximum time may be allotted, appropriate to the complexity of the issues.

Although presented to the mediator, this opening address by each party is **8–065** intended not only to inform the mediator, but to allow the other party or parties to hear each party's views and perception of the position.

How this presentation is made will depend upon many factors, including **8–066** whether it is the party or the lawyer doing so; individual personality, style, skills and strategy; the nature and complexity of the issues; and the emotional factors involved. Ideally, this presentation will be clear and well reasoned, will explain why the party makes a claim or feels aggrieved or will respond to the other's claims and grievances. It will impart any relevant facts and technical issues precisely and will help the mediator and the other party to appreciate the presenter's position and feelings about the issues. While this opening statement may outline the redress sought, it is not helpful for it to take entrenched positions from which it may be difficult to extricate.

The mediator can give prior guidance to the presenters as to what is **8–067** required. For example, where emotions are high and volatile, presenters (if asked to make a statement at all) might be asked to limit their statements to no more than say five or 10 minutes, by way of explanation and clarification rather than contention.

8–068   Following the presentations, the mediator may raise questions in a non-partisan way to help clarify or amplify relevant aspects. Questions and interruptions by other parties are not allowed during a presentation: the mediator should make this clear in advance. If the presenting party makes abrasive comments or references during the presentation, it will be a matter for the mediator's discretion whether to allow this to continue for a short while[28] or to intervene and ask the presenter to avoid using inflammatory language.[29]

8–069   When the parties have made their presentations, the mediator may allow questions, but generally of a clarifying nature rather than in the form of cross-examination. In the mediator's discretion, these may either be direct to the other side, or indirectly through the mediator. This may also be the opportunity for a further exchange of information, views and comments about the subject-matter of the dispute. The mediator will exercise judgment during this phase to ensure that discussions do not degenerate into hostile or unproductive exchanges that might make the following stages more difficult. There is a view that the expression of strong feelings at this juncture might not do any harm, and might be just as well expressed now rather than later.[30]

8–070   Not all models of mediation involve written statements of the issues followed by oral presentations.

8–071   In some fields, for example in many community-based or inter-personal approaches, there is unlikely to be a preliminary written statement. The mediator will instead allow the parties to explain the issues informally.

8–072   In other fields, for example in relation to separation and divorce, there is likely to be some form of preliminary written statement, such as a referral form or preliminary information form, but less frequently (and in some models rarely if ever) separate oral presentations of the issues.

8–073   Many mediators, in the family field for example, prefer to work with parties in what is described as "future-focused" exploration rather than requiring a statement of their views and positions (which in any event may still be unformed at that stage).[31] Some might meet each party separately for a short time to allow each to outline their preliminary thoughts and concerns, before meeting both parties together.

8–074   As the mediation progresses, it sometimes becomes apparent that the issues between the parties are wider or more complex than originally presented. This is especially likely to be the case in inter-personal, family and relationship disputes. It may, however, also be the case in civil and commercial disputes, for example (but not limited to), partnership or

---

[28] Allowing parties some freedom to express feelings is part of the mediation process, but this needs to be balanced against other considerations including the negative effect this may have on other parties. See paras 15–071 *et seq.*

[29] Some mediators initially seek authority from all parties to intervene in certain events, such as to end abusive conduct. They feel that this enhances their authority. Others feel that they have an inherent right and duty to intervene if they see fit as part of their management function without specific authority.

[30] *e.g.* Andrew Floyer Acland in *A Sudden Outbreak of Common Sense* suggests that the more that comes out at this early stage, the fewer the new issues that will emerge later when agreement may be approaching.

[31] "Future focus" diverts parties from a potentially negative exploration of past problems and hurts. Other views, while not necessarily denying the value of a future focus, believe that a proper respect for the past is essential.

shareholder issues or clinical negligence claims, where underlying issues may take time to surface. Mediators should be sensitive to the possibility of further issues emerging, and should watch for them through direct or indirect remarks and body language, and gently probe where appropriate.

Setting the agenda

With the benefit of an understanding of the issues as presented, the mediator will need to construct some kind of agenda for dealing with those issues.　**8–075**

In some cases, the mediator may consult the parties or, where appropriate, their lawyers about the preparation of an explicitly agreed agenda. In others, the agenda may be implicit from the written statements and presentations. The agenda may be formulated by the mediator as a working guideline, having regard to the parties' indications but without any specific reference to or agreement by them.　**8–076**

If the mediator feels that a discussion about the agenda in the joint meeting is likely to be unhelpful, then obviously it should be avoided. The way in which the mediation is structured and the issues are approached is an implicit part of the mediator's management function and authority.　**8–077**

An agenda is not necessarily a rigid construct, but should rather be a flexible tool, guiding the progress of the mediation. Where mediation takes place over a series of meetings, it may be advisable for the mediator to check the agenda at each meeting to ensure that new or other issues do not need to be addressed, or the prioritisation of issues reorganised.　**8–078**

Stage 6: Information gathering

A mediator must have sufficient relevant information about the dispute to be able to mediate effectively. All kinds of mediation involve the mediator in obtaining such information, but the way in which this is done, and the kind of information that is gathered may vary.　**8–079**

Where the mediation is to take place in one block of time such as a civil dispute fixed for a day or two, all necessary information has to be with the mediator before the substantive mediation begins. Where, however, the mediation takes place over a number of sessions, say fortnightly for five or six sessions, information may be received throughout the process, supplemented and amplified as required.　**8–080**

Although information gathering is reflected as a discrete stage of mediation, it may in fact occur over a period throughout the mediation.　**8–081**

Information may be of different kinds and come from different sources:　**8–082**

- Facts about the parties and the issues, and each party's views and submissions, may be obtained from an initial referral form or from written statements furnished by the parties.

- Relevant documents, including copy pleadings or affidavits where adversarial proceedings are under way, may be obtained by the mediator from the parties.

- Oral submissions and comments by each party may be made at the initial joint meeting and/or in separate meetings with the mediator.

- The mediator or any party may raise questions as the mediation progresses, which the other party or parties may be asked to deal with. Supplementary information, oral or written, may be obtained in this way.

- Technical data and other information, which may include expert opinions, legal opinions, valuations, assessments of damages and other specialised data, can be introduced into the mediation through the respective lawyers, experts and other professional advisers of the parties. The parties alternatively might decide to obtain such information and opinions from neutral sources.

- Witnesses of fact are not involved as such in the mediation process, though this has been suggested[32] and is sometimes done in the mini-trial, which may be viewed as a structured form of evaluative mediation.[33]

- The way in which these different aspects of information gathering are dealt with in detailed practice will depend upon the field of activity to which the mediation relates and the model of mediation being used, also on the needs of the individual case and the judgment of the mediator.

- Information of a formal nature will be supplemented by the mediator's observations during the course of the mediation. The dynamic between the parties, their attitudes to one another and to the issues and their underlying concerns all comprise part of the broader picture. These may all be relevant to the resolution of the dispute. The mediator establishes matters such as these by careful and sensitive observation and questioning, and by his or her communication skills.[34] Indirect and sometimes quite subtle clues may help the mediator to gain insights into the motivations, concerns and aspirations of the parties. These may not necessarily be clearly articulated. Tone of voice, a remark out of context, a nod, a smile, a gesture of disapproval or irritation, a shift of the eyes, signs of distress—these are all indications that a mediator will note and pursue right away or perhaps at some appropriate later stage.

Displaying information: the flip-chart[35]

8–083 Some of the data and information gathered during the course of the mediation will be noted and retained by the mediator, and some will need to be shared and perhaps more prominently displayed for the mutual benefit of

---

[32]Peter Lovenheim in *Mediate Don't Litigate* says at p. 94 that a mediator may suggest that witnesses of fact should be called. However, this appears virtually never to be done in mediation.

[33]See Chap. 16 on neutral evaluative processes.

[34]See Chap. 15 and in particular the section on communication skills such as listening, observing non-verbal communications and questioning.

[35]Electronic "flip-charts" now exist which can instantly produce A4 or other size copies of material written on the screen. The principles outlined here apply to any such method of displaying information.

the parties and the mediator. In the latter regard, a flip-chart is an invaluable aid to the displaying of information, and also serves other functions.

- The flip-chart is a practical way to record information where it can be seen by both or all parties, and is especially helpful when the mediator wants to keep that information in focus. It does not necessarily replace note-taking by the mediator, but may supplement it.

- Data may be maintained on the flip-chart and reverted to as matters develop through the course of the process. For example, financial data relating to each party in family mediation may be recorded on a flip-chart, and amended from time to time as supplementary data is received, valuations are obtained, and information becomes clearer.

- The sharing of information, especially where one party has more information than the other, tends to be an empowering process, and writing up data on a flip-chart can enhance this process.

- Some facts are more graphic when they appear on a chart, and can have an impact on the parties without having to be orally articulated.[36]

- Using a flip-chart to record responses received during a brainstorming session, or to record options being developed for the resolution of the issues, helps to create a positive sense of seeking problem-solving approaches to the dispute. It is also useful to maintain visually, and to extend, lists of options.[37]

- The flip-chart can serve as a management tool. When the mediator stands up to write on the chart, that provides a point of focus for the parties' attention and can help to distract them from negative exchanges. However, the mediator needs to bear in mind that standing and writing on a chart can develop into a lecturing posture, and can take the mediator's attention away from the parties.

There can be no standard answer to the question as to how much **8–084** information it is necessary for the mediator to have in order to be able to mediate effectively. Much will invariably depend on the nature of the issues. As a general proposition the mediator needs to know enough to understand the issues properly. If this can be achieved with a minimum of data, there is no need for a proliferation, mimicking the traditional document disclosure process in litigation.

Indeed, it is the experience of most dispute resolvers in ADR, as well as **8–085** lawyers working in the traditional adversarial process, that a well-selected

---

[36] See the examples of using a flip-chart to get messages to a couple, as mentioned by John Haynes in *Mediating Divorce* by John M. Haynes and Gretchen L. Haynes (1989) at p. 23.

[37] There is a corollary to this. The deletion from the flip-chart of an option may inhibit parties from reopening a deleted option if on subsequent reflection it may be less unacceptable than originally expressed. Consequently, in the course of narrowing options, it may be better to focus on preferred options without physically deleting those initially expressed to be unsuitable.

rather than an indiscriminate bundle of papers is likely to be most effective in getting issues resolved, whether by a mediator or an adjudicator. It is not the totality that is generally needed, but the essence.

8–086   The view is sometimes heard that settlement discussions cannot take place effectively before pleadings have been served so that the issues can be identified. This view may extend to particularisation, so that clarification can be obtained (and the other party embarrassed by the questions, if possible). A further extension is to disclosure of documents (in case the other side reveals some document that may change the shape of the case). On this principle, there would be few settlements before the opportunity had been taken to test the credibility of the other side by cross-examination at the trial.

8–087   In fact, most cases that settle do so before all evidence has been obtained and tested, and almost certainly before there has been a complete disclosure of all available information and documentation. Parties take views as to whether any further information is likely to have a material impact on possible terms. They assess what balance is appropriate between on the one hand trying to maximise information and on the other hand deciding that there is enough information available to discuss settlement terms. The position is no different in mediation.

8–088   An interesting principle that may be imported in this connection is the 80–20 Principle, based on the pattern identified towards the end of the nineteenth century by the Italian economist Vilfredo Pareto, and more recently articulated and developed by Richard Koch.[38] In essence, the 80–20 Principle "asserts that a minority of causes, inputs or effort usually lead to a majority of the results, outputs or rewards."[39] Koch cites many examples of this: 20 per cent of criminals account for 80 per cent of the value of all crime; 20 per cent of products or customers usually account for about 80 per cent of an organisation's profits; and 20 per cent of the energy of the internal combustion energy generates virtually all of the engine's output, the other 80 per cent is wasted in combustion. In relation to information technology, Koch considers that the same principles apply, as he believes they do in all fields of activity. He quotes with approval that " ....80 per cent of the benefits will be found in the simplest 20 per cent of the system, and the final 20 per cent of the benefits will come from the most complex 80 per cent of the system."[40]

8–089   It is not essential to accept the 80–20 Principle to realise the truth of the proposition that most of the relevant information, data and documents in relation to a dispute can be obtained within a relatively short time, and that the greater part of the time and resource is spent on obtaining the relatively small residue. Of course, the measurement must be qualitative as well as quantitative; but there is no reason to assume that the principle outlined in this paragraph does not apply equally to the quality as well as the quantity of data. In any event, while not necessarily definitive, this is a factor that needs

---

[38] The authors wish to acknowledge a talk by Prof. Karl Mackie as providing the inspiration for the concept that the 80–20 Principle might apply to the sufficiency of documentary evidence.

[39] See *The 80–20 Principle: The Secret of Achieving More with Less* published by Nicholas Brealey Publishing Limited, 1997, at p. 4.

[40] Koch's quotation is from Chris Vandersluis, (1994) "Poor planning can sabotage implementation" in *Computing Canada* 25 May 1994.

to be weighed in deciding how much information is sufficient to enable a matter to be referred to mediation, or how much information it is productive to pursue.[41]

Stage 7: Managing and facilitating discussions and negotiations

This is the substantive phase of mediation, during which the mediator helps **8–090** the parties to communicate with one another, either directly in joint session, or indirectly by means of separate meetings (known as "caucuses"). The mediator also facilitates the parties' negotiations with one another with a view to narrowing their differences and helping them eventually to resolve their issues.

After the introductory phase and the parties' presentations where these are **8–091** required, the procedures that then follow will depend on the model of mediation concerned. Approaches and strategies relevant to this phase of the mediation include the following:

Managing the process

The mediator is the manager of the process and responsible for: **8–092**

- Making all necessary administrative arrangements for the mediation.

- Supplying all necessary facilities and practice documents and taking steps to ensure that all documentation necessary for the process is received in time.

- Chairing the meeting and maintaining an orderly, secure and constructive working environment.

- Deterring abusive or inappropriate conduct.

- Identifying the agenda and updating, amending and implementing it.

- Setting and following appropriate ground rules and complying with the applicable Code of Practice.

- Helping parties to use their time productively.

- Helping parties to record the mediation outcome appropriately.

New mediators sometimes struggle with the concept of managing the **8–093** process firmly and effectively while asserting that the parties are responsible for the outcome and for substantive decision-making. Similar issues can arise for mediators who believe that management decisions belong to the parties and that all authority must come from the parties. So, for example, if an

---

[41] It is a matter of speculation how judges will exercise their powers of adjournment under the new Rules to enable mediation to take place. Some—but a definite minority—have some training in ADR. It is likely that judges will draw upon this experience both at the Bar and on the Bench of settlement negotiations in particular categories of cases. Thus, to take an obvious example, judges may well be prepared to invite parties to go to mediation in cases such as personal injury or medical negligence where liability is usually conceded and where the real issue in dispute is the amount of damages. Specialist courts such as the Commercial Court or the Information Technology and Construction Court will probably continue much as they do now.

issue arises as to whether one party may make a tape recording of the session, some mediators may seek a consensus from the parties about this. In fact, this is a management decision that the mediator needs to make, mindful of the effect that this would have on the process and on the mediator personally. If the mediator were willing to allow it, but wanted first to check with all parties as to acceptability, that would be fine; but if the mediator felt that it was inappropriate, then that should be final even if all parties agreed that it should be allowed. The mediator does derive authority from the parties and cannot and should not be autocratic, riding roughshod over the parties' views and wishes. This does not, however, mean that the mediator should not, after due consultation where appropriate, make management decisions that he or she considers necessary.

Joint or separate meetings (caucuses)[42]

8–094   A mediator may meet the parties together, or may see them separately. In civil and commercial mediation, it is common to start with a joint meeting and then to move into caucusing, perhaps with a joint meeting at the end or occasionally between caucuses. Most family mediation is conducted by way of joint meetings, with occasional caucusing. (Some family mediators start with a separate meeting with each party before meeting them both jointly.) Practice in neighbourhood and community mediation varies. Usually there will initially be separate meetings to ensure that the parties are willing to meet together jointly.

8–095   The following factors are relevant to the conduct of joint meetings or of caucuses:

- Conducting mediation exclusively through joint meetings demands substantial mediator skill and care. Parties do not have any opportunity to speak privately to the mediator, so the mediator must continually be alert to the parties' stresses, power imbalances and negotiating inequalities. Separate meetings demand different kinds of skill and care. Mediators are subject to competing party pressures and greater risks of triangulation, and need to exercise great judgment and care in carrying proposals and communications between the parties.

- Working throughout in joint session requires a mediator to be permanently open to both or all parties. There are no secrets between parties and the mediator. Separate meetings, on the other hand, inherently involve private communications between each party and the mediator, especially where the mediator promises each party confidentiality. Consequently, this places the mediator in a more powerful position as the keeper of separate secrets. There are mediators who do not favour being placed in this position and who therefore prefer not to undertake separate meetings.

- The issue of confidentiality in separate meetings must be addressed. The mediator needs to make it clear whether discussions in the

---

[42]Caucusing simply means having separate meetings with each party. As to the different meaning of this term in the industrial relations field, see Chap. 11.

separate meetings will be shared with all parties, perhaps by way of paraphrasing and summarising, or whether separate confidences will be maintained.

- It is usual in civil and commercial mediation for the matters discussed in the separate meetings to be strictly confidential to the individual party, and the mediator will make it clear that nothing will be disclosed to any other party without specific authority.[43]

- To assist the mediator and to ensure that the confidentiality of separate meetings is maintained, it is good policy for the mediator to keep notes of the matters discussed, indicating clearly which aspects may be revealed to the other side, and which may not.

- The mediator will ordinarily encourage each party in the separate meetings to disclose their aspirations, interests, needs and concerns and to indicate broadly what nature of settlement terms would be acceptable. The mediator may try to establish any hidden agendas of each party, going behind their stated positions and aspirations to seek information to help them devise options that will meet all underlying needs.

- Separate meetings are commonly conducted on a shuttle mediation basis. The mediator moves between the parties, as part of a strategy to narrow and help resolve the issues between them. Alternatively, the mediator may remain in a room and the parties may move in and out of it, but this is less satisfactory. In some instances, only a single separate meeting with each party is held, to deal with one or a limited number of specific issues, before reverting to the joint meeting.

- Where lawyers are involved in the mediation, the mediator may want to see a party's lawyer alone, or a party without his or her lawyer, if it is thought that this would be helpful. This may need to be carefully explained to avoid unnecessary suspicion and concern arising. If parties are legally represented in the mediation, some mediators will not meet them without their lawyers.

- Although separate meetings can be valuable, and are regarded as essential in some models, they need to be used with care. First, by their nature they reinforce detachment and division, which may not be appropriate in some cases especially where the process is required to try to heal relationship rifts. Secondly, some parties may fantasise about what is being said to the mediator by the other party during the separate meeting, which can lead to anxiety, annoyance and possibly some loss of trust. Thirdly, a party waiting for the return of the mediator can feel isolated (especially if the party is alone: where there is some support, whether of another party, a lawyer or a supporter, that may help to make the separate meetings more viable). Mediators need to be aware of these possible effects of separate meetings.

---

[43]See para. 10–168 for confidentiality in family mediation caucusing. As to the provisions relating to confidentiality generally, see Chap. 22.

- The mediator can arrange for the waiting party to use the waiting time usefully by giving that party a constructive task such as considering particular aspects or undertaking specified enquiries or activities while the mediator is engaged with the other party. Also, if the mediator needs to spend a long time with one party while the other is waiting, it is a good idea to let the other party know of the likely delay, or to maintain occasional interim contact.

- Separate meetings require ample time to be effective. This may mean that at least a half-day or perhaps a day will be required for disputes requiring shuttle mediation, and more where the issues are substantial and complex. The mediator may wish to start by simply hearing each party and trying to understand the underlying issues before any negotiations commence. Parties will usually position themselves for their aspired terms, and are unlikely to reveal their ultimate positions before having had some rounds of negotiations through the mediator. Not uncommonly they will want to explain and justify themselves to the mediator, and time is needed for this. The mediator will usually guard against becoming a pure messenger, and will want to help the parties to be effective in their negotiations.

Facilitation

8–096   One of the primary roles of the mediator is to facilitate and enhance the parties' negotiations with one another. This is a key feature of the process. There are various theories of negotiation, the one most suited for this phase being the problem-solving approach. Mediators may try to help parties to use this approach in conducting their negotiations although that will not always be possible or practicable: parties commonly adopt a competitive approach, and in the mediation process may move to a mixture of this and problem-solving.[44]

8–097   The mediator will also try to facilitate communications between the parties. This may be particularly important where they have a continuing relationship such as parenting or partnership. Usually this can better be achieved through joint rather than separate meetings. Where there is no continuing relationship, the improvement of communication, while it may be marginally helpful to the parties, is less significant.

8–098   Facilitation is achieved by using the various skills and approaches outlined in this section.

Generating and developing options

8–099   When parties are in dispute, they cannot always see their options clearly, often focusing on one specific outcome instead of viewing matters more widely. A significant part of the mediator's role is to help the parties to generate and consider their options, and to develop them into viable courses of action.

8–100   When the mediator starts to explore options with the parties, they will usually suggest options themselves; but the mediator can often add to these.

---

[44]Theories of negotiation are outlined in Chap. 6.

Sometimes the mediator may suggest ways in which other people in disagreement have dealt with similar situations, or may indicate different approaches that courts have taken. There should be no inhibition on the mediator adding ideas, as long as these are expressed in a way that does not cause them to be perceived as "the mediator's recommendations". As parties examine and work through their options, narrowing or eliminating some and widening others, their ability to work together in finding a solution is likely to increase.

The development of options is an intrinsic part of the problem-solving **8–101** approach that characterises mediation.

Brainstorming[45]

One of the ways in which a mediator can help parties to generate options is **8–102** by brainstorming. This involves the mediator encouraging the parties to put forward as many ideas and options as possible as they come to mind without inhibiting their flow by considering them individually at that stage, or rejecting any, even if at first sight, they may seem unworkable.

The mediator may need to manage the brainstorming session firmly and **8–103** creatively, helping parties to build on and develop options as they arise and deterring parties from examining them while they are being generated.

It can be helpful when options are being generated to write them all down, **8–104** on a flip-chart if one is being used, and to prioritise them later, rather than eliminating them as they emerge. Even when subsequently considering options, it is not a good idea to eliminate any of them notwithstanding that the parties may agree that particular options are unacceptable. It is not uncommon that options initially considered to be unacceptable later come back into focus as possibilities, perhaps by way of permutation with other ideas.

Building trust and understanding

People in conflict may find it difficult to trust one another, especially where **8–105** they are or have been in a personal or business relationship that has deteriorated. Also, respective positions may not be properly understood, individual values and perceptions of fairness may differ and communications may be strained. The mediator can try to help to improve the trust and confidence of the parties in one another, where appropriate.

This is not an exhortation to "trust one another", which can easily be **8–106** abused and is likely to be viewed as naïve. It is rather a process of providing the parties with opportunities to demonstrate their sincerity and credibility. This could, for example, take place where possible solutions are tested for short periods before they are applied on a longer-term basis. The mediator can also help the parties to understand one another more clearly by presenting their perceptions in a way that the other can comprehend and by correcting distortions or misunderstandings. Of course, many disputes are resolved pragmatically without trust or understanding; but these factors are

---

[45]See Edward de Bono's *Lateral Thinking* (1970). He suggests that the three principal elements of brainstorming are putting forward ideas to stimulate others; suspending judgment, so that no idea is thought to be too ridiculous to put forward; and a relatively formal setting.

helpful in the process of resolving issues consensually. It is also particularly important where the parties are hoping to re-establish working or personal relationships.

8–107   It can sometimes help to normalise the lack of trust by pointing out that this commonly happens in situations where relationships break down. The parties now have an opportunity to start exploring ways of restoring that trust.

Using communication and other skills[46]

8–108   The mediator uses various skills at all stages of the proceedings, but especially during this negotiating phase. These include listening carefully to each party, observing body language and understanding the issues properly, both those that are presented and, as far as possible, those that may be underlying and hidden. It involves helping parties to hear and understand what others are saying. It includes summarising their positions accurately and appropriately, acknowledging their views and concerns and where appropriate mutualising their concerns and interests. It may where necessary involve reframing what they have said so that it may be better understood in its context. The effective use of questions is also a considerable mediator skill.

8–109   The mediator's skills constitute a critically important ingredient in mediation. While some people may have many of the required attributes and skills to enable them to mediate effectively, mediators invariably need to undertake mediation training. This helps to make the transition from their occupation of origin to mediator, and develops and adapts those skills with a view to ensuring that they are effectively and appropriately used.[47]

Encouraging a problem-solving mode

8–110   Some parties enter into mediation receptive to a problem-solving mode, others tend to be in a competitive mode, because of their strong feelings or because they believe that to be the most effective way to negotiate. One of the mediator's skills is to help the parties to move towards a more creative and problem-solving negotiating approach.

8–111   This is not to suggest that parties will abandon their self-interest when they enter the mediation process: that would be nonsense. It does mean that the mediator helps the parties to realise that although each will continue to maintain their own aspirations in the negotiations, these may be more readily achieved in the context of an approach which seeks imaginative and resourceful solutions for joint benefit.

8–112   Negotiation even in a problem-solving mode will still involve tensions between the needs, wants and aspirations of the parties, and these will not disappear in mediation. Hard bargaining may inevitably continue even in the mediation context. One of the skills of the mediator lies in creating a balance between these different negotiating tensions.

Testing perceptions, positions and proposals

8–113   One of the difficulties about arriving at a settlement in the traditional

---

[46] The skills used by mediators are set out more fully in Chap. 15.
[47] See Chap. 24 for training and accreditation aspects.

adversarial process is that either or both parties may have unrealistic or slightly skewed perceptions as to any of a range of matters. These may include, for example, their views about the issues, their perceptions of the other party's position, their judgment as to respective merits or the acceptability of intended proposals for settlement. The mediator may need to test the parties' realism about these matters by checking that the parties appreciate their implications and consequences. The mediator can test these perceptions by asking appropriate questions ("What if...?") which compel the party to reflect on the position more carefully, or by making appropriate observations which do not damage the mediator's impartiality. This is generally known as "reality-testing".

This exercise can be very important. In the nature of conflict and dispute, **8–114** parties tend to see their own positions, concerns and grievances more clearly than they can see the other side's. They may often develop their own "view of the world" based on their understanding of the facts (not always complete) and issues. Prospects of success are assessed on the basis of those views and understandings.

Lawyers representing parties will usually try to help their clients to **8–115** establish a realistic view of their positions and prospects. Contrary to popular public belief, lawyers do not generally create the escalation and animosity that the adversarial process generates. This is inherent in the system of adversarial proceedings, and is what many clients require when they are feeling aggrieved. Parties usually expect their lawyers to support them by first, giving them a realistic assessment of their rights and prospects, and secondly, by helping them to make the best of the position. This means that if prospects seem reasonably good, the lawyer should help to bring a successful action or to settle on substantial terms. If the prospects are thought to be poor, the lawyer should help to maximise the position and if necessary to achieve an outcome that is better than capitulating.

This process, however, easily becomes distorted. Lawyers, while giving **8–116** realistic assessments, will generally do so within the context of supporting the client. This may result in the client feeling more justified in his or her grievances and strength of feeling, and readier to litigate. Many litigation lawyers believe (correctly) that their clients wish them to be partisan on their behalf, to champion their cause and to act positively for them. This often makes it very difficult to express strong views that contradict the client's views and expectations. The parties themselves often create conditions in which their reactions against adverse comment inhibit those comments from being made forcefully. Even when they are told the true position and risk, they do not always act on that advice.

It is against this background that mediators may be "testing reality". The **8–117** mediator's challenges are unlikely to be welcomed by the party concerned, but this may be an essential exercise if the mediator is to have an effective function in helping the parties to move towards a realistic settlement.

There is, of course, a subjective element that the mediator brings into this **8–118** process of reality-testing. One person's fantasy may be another's reality. What one person considers reasonable and proper another may believe to be unreasonable and improper. Consequently, this exercise must be undertaken with particular sensitivity and judgment. Some mediators believe that by asking questions rather than expressing a view, they can avoid influencing parties. They should be aware, however, that merely by questioning a perception, the mediator may well be experienced by the party to be subtly expressing a negative view about that perception. This may be an intended consequence; but mediators must appreciate the possibility of this happening even when it is not intended.[48]

Sensitivity to the expression of emotions[49]

8–119 People who are in conflict and dispute with one another will often have strong feelings about the position. They may be distressed, angry, frustrated, apprehensive or disappointed, or they may experience other emotions, without even necessarily being consciously aware of them.

8–120 Mediators need to be sensitive to the feelings of the parties. It is not possible or appropriate to work with those emotions. They are not therapists or counsellors, or if they are, they are not working in that capacity. They can, though, recognise and acknowledge them and help a party who is experiencing strong feelings to be able nevertheless to deal with the substantive issues in the mediation.

8–121 This can often be necessary. For example, submerged anger can sabotage attempts to reach an agreed resolution, as the anger manifests itself in a disguised form, such as destructive comments or an unwillingness to co-operate with the other party or the process. Other emotions may block progress towards resolution in the short term, apart from any adverse long-term implications.

8–122 A release of anger or other emotions in a joint meeting can, however, be upsetting to other parties or can provoke a similarly outraged or distressed response, in either event leading to the possibility of either party terminating the mediation. The mediator's usual role is to maintain a balance, providing a safe environment for emotions to surface and accepting the normalcy of that, but ensuring that it does not destabilise the process. The mediator will generally try to bring the parties back to the task of dispute resolution as quickly and gently as practicable. Mediation is not a counselling or therapy process (although it can in some cases, especially inter-personal, have a therapeutic effect).

Evaluation

8–123 In some models of mediation, a mediator may, in addition to the usual facilitative role, also adopt an element of evaluation of the issues, or may be required to assist in the formulation and development of settlement terms. This is dealt with in Chapter 16.

Stage 8: Employing impasse strategies

8–124 An impasse is a deadlock or stalemate from which the parties find that they are unable to extricate themselves. In one sense, parties may be said to be at

---

[48]See para 16–012 at p. 355 for the way in which reality-testing, even by asking questions, might in some circumstances constitute a form of evaluation.

[49]For further consideration of emotional aspects, see n. 9 above and Chap. 9 at paras 9–104 *et seq.* in relation to civil and commercial disputes, and paras 10–139–143 and 10–158–160 at Chap. 10 in relation to family issues.

an impasse at the start of every mediation, because if that were not the case they would not require the intervention of a mediator.

However, mediation procedures usually provide a framework within which **8–125** the parties are able to generate some momentum towards the resolution of their issues. As long as these are having an effect, and negotiations have not ground to a halt, opportunities to settle the issues continue to exist.

When negotiations come to a halt because of a particular point of **8–126** difference that seems irreconcilable or because neither party will shift generally, and the mediation seems set to terminate, that would constitute a mediation impasse. In this event, some strategies may be appropriate to try to help the parties back into negotiation. Although this may occur at any stage of the process and is not a distinct phase, it will be treated here for convenience as a separate stage of mediation.

An impasse strategy is not something which aims to settle all issues but **8–127** rather a course of action that helps to get parties back into negotiation with one another.

Mediators will need to devise strategies specific to the impasse. In this **8–128** regard, the following strategies are relevant to this stage:

Pause and reflect
This applies to every kind of mediation. There may be a temptation in an **8–129** impasse to rush into looking for a strategy to try to overcome it. Sometimes that works, but sometimes it is more beneficial just to stand back from the situation and review it.

The mediator may want to consider cause of the impasse, and how it can **8–130** best be addressed. Some of the questions that the mediator may want to ask himself or herself are:

- Is the blocking issue subjective to either or both of the parties? Does it arise from one party's perceptions or strong feelings?

- Does the issue arise because of particular terminology or because of its symbolic relevance?

- Has the issue arisen because both parties in good faith have received conflicting legal or technical advice?

- Is the issue caused by differing perceptions of fairness?

- Is the impasse a negotiating strategy by either or both parties? Or have they actually reached their respective "bottom lines"?[50]

- Is the mediator perpetuating the problem by perhaps being stuck in one approach or by unwittingly supporting one position? What does the mediator need to do to change the dynamic?

This is the kind of reflection that the mediator is likely to give to the **8–131** impasse in order to try to devise a way past it.

---

[50]Mediators would generally try to avoid using terms like "bottom line" in discussion with the parties, as they tend to limit flexibility.

Blocks caused by terminology or symbolism

8–132 Where the impasse arises because of terminology or a symbol, it can help to bypass the deadlock by removing the focus from the words or symbols in question, and to examine the underlying needs and concerns giving rise to the impasse.[51] So, for example, partners may be stuck on an issue of principle as to whether the senior partner should have a casting vote at partners' meetings. By examining the underlying concerns and the circumstances in which partners envisage that the casting vote would be exercised, and by making appropriate provision to accommodate all concerns, the issue could be defused and negotiations reinstated.

8–133 Similarly, in a divorce context, a couple may be unable to move forward because one insists on a "clean break" (in which neither party has any further maintenance or any other claims against the other) and the other will not agree to that. Here again, the mediator could help the parties to examine their underlying concerns. Wanting a "clean break" is likely to indicate a concern about giving an open-ended commitment to payment. Under what circumstances would continued payment be needed, and at what point, if ever, might it end? What reassurances, if any, can the recipient give about seeking payment? Opposing a "clean break" is likely to indicate a concern about managing in the future and long-term security. How can that person arrange his or her affairs to reduce those concerns? What arrangements can be made to enhance security, for example through pensions or insurance? What adjustments could be built into the current settlement terms to help address these concerns?

Differences of perceptions: fairness and other aspects

8–134 Where there are differences of view about the fairness of the proposals, it can help to explore what this means to each party. What aspect of the proposals is not fair? What does each party consider needs to happen to make it fair? There are different perceptions of fairness and this exploration may not be conclusive, but it may nevertheless be useful to allow each side to obtain a better understanding of the other's sense of fairness, and to confront one notion of fairness with another equally strongly held one.

8–135 Perceptions can also differ in other respects, such as with regard to the motives and aspirations of other parties and their likely patterns of behaviour, and the facts and events giving rise to the disagreement. It may be thought that facts are simply a matter of proof; but facts can be difficult to establish and parties will frequently place their own interpretations on events. Where these perceptions differ substantially from one another, it can be extremely difficult to progress to a resolution. The mediator can help parties by identifying and normalising differences of perception, explaining that they are quite common and refusing to be drawn into accepting either side's views.

---

[51] One of the authors sometimes refers to a "ginger jar factor": in family issues, as a possible resolution approaches, the parties may adopt strong positions about something which does not appear to have any significant economic value, such as a ginger jar (as in one case), causing an impasse. This kind of impasse (which is not limited to family issues) is often symbolic: *e.g.* the item was a gift from someone who would not have approved of the behaviour of the person now claiming it. To overcome impasses based on symbols it may be necessary to identify and discuss the issues underlying the symbolism. Sometimes creative solutions can then be found with the benefit of these insights.

Rather, the mediator can seek ways of clarifying the factual position and reframing the differences.[52]

Emotional blocks

An impasse may arise because of a strong emotional response by the parties or their representatives in the mediation. It is not only individuals involved in family or other inter-personal disputes who may have an emotional response to the issues in the mediation. Contrary to a popular perception that commercial disputes are free from emotionality, there is often a high degree of emotional intensity in civil and commercial disputes. Perhaps an employee was involved in the events leading to the dispute, or developed hostility towards someone on the opposing side. Perhaps the representative has strong feelings about the issues in dispute.

8–136

In such event, the mediator may need to allow the emotional issues to surface, if only to acknowledge the strength of feeling rather than allowing it to fester. It is often better to bring such issues into the open where they can be recognised and acknowledged, even if they cannot be resolved. In family or inter-personal cases, where a continuing relationship such as parenting is required, the mediator may in some circumstances wish to discuss with the parties the possibility of their seeking other professional help such as counselling, especially where the emotional blocks run deep.[53]

8–137

Where the individual representatives of corporate parties are unable to move forward because of their emotional involvement with the issues, the mediator may consider suggesting that different people take over or augment the representation of the parties. This may, however, not always be possible or appropriate; and in any event would need to be handled with tact and discretion.

8–138

Conflicting legal or technical advice

A mediator working in a purely facilitative mode would not express his or her own view when faced with parties who are deadlocked because they have received conflicting advice from their respective lawyers or technical advisers.

8–139

The mediator can, however, help both parties to ease out of their impasse by reality-testing with each. The mediator may also help the parties to formulate questions to take to their respective advisers with a view to helping them each to obtain private clarification about the stuck issues. A mediator working in an evaluative mode might, however, express a view: see Chapter 16.

8–140

Where the deadlocked issue which is capable of some form of third party adjudication, it may help to suggest that the parties refer it to an appropriate third party for a non-binding opinion while the mediation is pending. Where the sticking point is a legal one, the mediator could, for example, assist the parties to formulate an agreed form of instructions to solicitors or counsel, whose opinion would be helpful but not binding. That opinion could then be

8–141

---

[52]For reframing, see paras 15–065 *et seq.*

[53]But only where this is appropriate and necessary. Parties in mediation are seeking assistance in this forum and should not lightly be referred from one professional to another. For further information about counselling, see paras 10–007 *et seq.*

brought into the mediation as a discussion document to help move matters forward.[54]

Deferral or short-term solutions

8–142   It may help for a blocked issue to be deferred while other aspects of the conflict are considered. That could allow the parties time to get the problem issue into a different perspective, especially if meanwhile further progress is made towards an overall resolution. There is a risk, however, that this will merely postpone the deadlock and perhaps make it even more difficult to resolve later, so deferment should only be considered if the mediator considers that there is a reasonable prospect of the delay assisting in the defusing of the issue.

8–143   If parties cannot find a long-term solution to their differences, it can in some situations help for them to formulate short-term agreements, and to review the position after a while. This is more appropriate to mediation conducted over a number of sessions than to mediation that is expected to be finally concluded in one tranche of time (unless it becomes necessary and appropriate to adjourn while the short-term solution is implemented).

Draft summaries as an aid to resolving impasse

8–144   In some cases it may assist the parties if the mediator furnishes them with a draft summary reflecting the aspects so far agreed in the mediation, and those still outstanding. The mediator can use the summary as a vehicle for formulating alternatives for the issues in deadlock, based on ideas already put forward and permutations of these.

8–145   Depending on the model of mediation being used and the wishes of the parties, the mediator may also incorporate into the summary new ideas for resolving the deadlock. This summary can then be used as a basis for continuing discussions.

Considering alternatives to reaching agreement in the mediation

8–146   It can help the parties in their decision-making, as well as serving as an impasse strategy, to examine with each of them, or to guide them in examining, the implications of their not reaching agreement in the mediation. In doing so, the parties can consider the cost, delay and risk factors and other relevant considerations. The examination of their respective best and worst alternatives to a mediated agreement should help to guide them.[55]

8–147   Each might ask their legal advisers what level of assurance can be given that the desired outcome will be achieved, with estimated percentage prospects of success, cost estimates and other relevant information. With the benefit of this information, parties can make a more informed choice about settling in the mediation, and the best and worst alternatives to doing so.

---

[54]See Chap. 16 on non-binding neutral evaluations generally. Such an opinion would have to be sensitively drafted, balancing the need to provide a useful indication of the position with an awareness that it will be used in a negotiating process, hence it should not ordinarily be unduly dogmatic.

[55]See Chap. 6 and the references to BATNA and WATNA: (best and worst alternatives) in the section "A problem-solving approach". The subject is also dealt with in Chap. 9 under Stage 8 at paras 9–122 *et seq.*

Where the impasse cannot be resolved and the parties cannot continue in **8–148** the mediation, it will obviously have to be terminated. Informing the parties that the process will have to be ended may sometimes serve as an impasse strategy itself and a stimulus to their finding a way to resolve the impasse.

Other strategies

The impasse strategies outlined above are by no means comprehensive, but **8–149** are examples of the kinds of strategies that a mediator might wish to consider. Sometimes, a simpler approach might be effective. A mediator might for example simply wish to acknowledge the dilemma of the parties and the difficulty in dealing with the impasse. By reviewing progress made to date and mutualising concerns, parties can sometimes be helped to persevere in their attempts to reach a consensual resolution.

Sometimes there is no easy answer for the parties, and they are faced with **8–150** a stark choice either to settle or to litigate. "Just do it!" may be their watchword but it will need to come from their advisers rather than from the mediator, though the mediator might wish to indicate that this is often what parties have to do.

Where the impasse strategy brings the parties back into negotiation, it will **8–151** have served its purpose. Where the parties remain stuck, adjudication may well be necessary and appropriate. This is the prerogative of the parties, and mediators should not treat the parties as if they have "failed" if they find that they need an adjudicator to decide their issues. The mediation may still be able to serve a residual but useful function in this event, by helping the parties, if they so wish, to examine ways of narrowing the issues to be adjudicated upon, and ways of minimising antagonism notwithstanding the adjudication.

3. PHASE THREE: THE END OF MEDIATION AND AFTERWARDS

Stage 9: Concluding mediation and recording the outcome
Terminating mediation
Mediation may terminate in a number of circumstances, for example: **8–152**

- All the issues may have been totally resolved.

- The parties may have resolved some issues and decide to take the others into a different ADR forum or process, for example to arbitration, as in med–arb.

- The parties may have resolved some issues and are content to resolve the remaining ones themselves or through lawyers.

- In a family or inter-personal context, the parties or an individual may decide to enter into counselling; or in a commercial relationship context, to seek management consultancy advice.

- The parties, or any of them, may decide to terminate the mediation even though some or all of the issues are unresolved, and to have their differences determined by litigation or arbitration.

- The mediator may decide that it is inappropriate to continue with the mediation.

8–153   Where settlement terms have been agreed, the mediator may bring all the parties together into a joint session (if they have been working in separate meetings) and check the terms with everyone. Alternatively, the mediator will assist the parties or their lawyers in preparing a document recording the terms, and will bring the parties together to go through and sign that document as part of a concluding formality. Sometimes the parties may prefer to sign the settlement agreement separately, without the formality of a joint meeting. In some models, especially in the family field, the agreed terms may be conditional on each party obtaining legal advice and the respective lawyers preparing the final form of agreement or court order. In such cases, it is common for the mediator to prepare a summary of the proposals that would be acceptable to both parties.

8–154   Where the mediation ends without settlement terms being agreed, there are no specific formalities. In some commercial models,[56] the mediator may as a concluding act, if so requested by both parties and if he or she agrees, produce a non-binding and off the record written recommendation on appropriate terms of settlement. As this may be perceived as damaging the mediator's neutrality, this would not ordinarily be done except as a last resort when the mediation ends. (In this event, it is sensible to suggest that each party inform the mediator privately whether or not the recommended terms are acceptable. This would mean that if one party agreed to accept the terms and the other did not, the parties would merely be told that the terms could not be agreed. Neither would then know whether the other accepted or not.)

8–155   Where terms have not been agreed, the mediator may sometimes wish to write to the parties as a concluding formality, confirming the ending of the mediation.

8–156   Where the mediator has ended the mediation because it is inappropriate to continue, the mediator may well wish to explain to the parties why he or she is doing so. In some circumstances, however, explaining the reason for terminating may breach confidentiality or may for some other reason be inappropriate. The mediator may in that event be guided by the applicable Code of Practice and by the contractual and personal relationship with the parties as to whether to give reasons.

Agreements and summaries

8–157   At the conclusion of the mediation, the mediator will have to consider whether a written record of the outcome is needed, and if so, in what form and by whom it should be prepared.

8–158   In some cases, particularly in commercial mediation, an agreement binding the parties to the terms of a settlement reached in the mediation will be prepared while they wait. This may be done by the mediator or by the parties' lawyers if in attendance, or jointly between them. The parties would not leave before executing this agreement. In other cases, summaries or

---

[56]See in Appendix II, *e.g.* the Model Mediation Procedure of CEDR, the Centre for Dispute Resolution, at Para. 12.

agreements are not required to be signed right away. These will commonly be prepared by the mediator after the end of the mediation and sent to the parties for consideration; and in the meanwhile they will not be bound. In yet other cases, particularly in relation to neighbour or community disputes, written summaries will either be very informally prepared or will not be required at all, with the parties relying on their oral understandings.

The question of drafting is dealt with in more detail in Appendix II, which   **8–159**
also contains precedent and specimen agreements.

Stage 10: Post-termination

In most cases, the termination of the mediation and the recording of the   **8–160**
settlement terms will signal the end of the mediator's role. However, it is possible for the mediator, or the ADR organisation that arranged the mediation, to have some function in relation to the implementation of the settlement terms, or later.

Post-termination functions may for example include: **8–161**

- *Stakeholder*: The parties may wish the mediator or the ADR organisation to act as a stakeholder in relation to funds to be released on agreed terms, or to hold documents in escrow pending the implementation of the settlement. It is rare in practice for mediators in the United Kingdom to hold funds, as the parties' solicitors are more likely than mediators to carry out this function. However, as a specific example of document-holding, one of the issues in a mediated dispute related to documents that were alleged to show irregular conduct by one of the parties. Although irregularity was not admitted, the destruction of those documents was one of the settlement terms. The party in possession of the documents would not part with them before implementation of the settlement. The party requiring their destruction would not implement the terms unless assured that they would be destroyed. Consequently, as part of the settlement, the documents were placed in safekeeping with the organisation that had arranged the mediation, with joint instructions to destroy them on implementation of the settlement terms.

- *Continuing mediator*: The parties may agree that if any issues should arise in the course of executing their settlement obligations, these will be referred to mediation for further discussion. If this is required, it should be specified in the settlement agreement. Another role as continuing mediator sometimes arises where there is a continuing relationship between the parties (whether working or personal, as in parenting) and the parties agree that if any new problems arise in the future, they will revert to mediation. In this event, the mediator who dealt with their issues in the first instance might commonly be re-appointed to deal with any new issues.

- *Adjudicator*: The parties may appoint the mediator to act as an arbitrator, expert or adjudicator in relation to any issues that may in the future arise in relation to the fulfilment of the settlement terms. This should be distinguished from med–arb, where all the initial issues are dealt with by arbitration if mediation does not resolve them. In this case, the initial issues are indeed resolved in the mediation, but any residual aspects of the agreed terms are dealt with by informal adjudication. Nevertheless, the cautions relating to med–arb may be relevant and need to be noted.[57]

- *Settlement supervisor*: The parties may wish the mediator or the ADR organisation to help supervise the implementation of the settlement terms in other ways. In practice, this is rare; but it is a role that is sometimes used in other jurisdictions, and there is no reason why it might not be used in appropriate situations.

---

[57]See paras 7–109 *et seq.*

CHAPTER 9

CIVIL AND COMMERCIAL MEDIATION

1. CIVIL AND COMMERCIAL ISSUES

With some qualifications, this category of mediation relates to all kinds of **9–001** disputes that might be dealt with in the civil and commercial courts. The qualifications concern areas of overlap with other fields of mediation activity. So, it would be correct to say that this kind of mediation excludes family disputes, but only with reference to couples' issues, particularly on separation and divorce. Other kinds of family disputes would ordinarily fall within the ambit of civil and commercial mediation, including for example, family business disputes, property or other civil disputes between siblings or between parent and child, or contentious issues concerning the administration of trusts involving family members.

Another qualification relates to disputes that might be dealt with in the **9–002** context of community or neighbour mediation. A community mediator will commonly deal with disputes between neighbours; but there are some neighbour disputes that assume mammoth proportions, with parties crippling themselves financially in High Court litigation. Disputes of that sort, where litigation is in progress, may well fall within the civil and commercial ambit rather than the community field.

A very wide range of cases fall into the civil and commercial field. They **9–003** include all kinds of issues arising under contract or tort. It is impossible to list these comprehensively, but they would cover all contractual and general business and property disputes. They would certainly also include claims for negligence and breach of duty and personal injury cases. Business and personal relationships would be covered, such as partnership disagreements, shareholder and other company disputes and claims for maladministration of estates or trusts. Specialist areas such as libel, intellectual property and passing off, disputes in the construction industry, shipping disputes, commodity disputes, banking, insurance and other financial disputes, computer software and other information technology disputes would all be appropriate.

One of the advantages of mediation is that it does not have to be linked to **9–004** any particular jurisdiction or country. It is therefore suitable for both local and cross-border disputes.

2. SOME ISSUES IN CIVIL AND COMMERCIAL MEDIATION PRACTICE IN ENGLAND AND WALES

Court and publicly funded mediation or private sector mediation

9–005   Unlike the family field, where some mediation organisations concentrate on the public sector and others on the private sector (though not exclusively in either case), there are no civil and commercial mediation bodies that focus primarily on publicly funded or low cost services.[1]

9–006   Civil and commercial mediation organisations working in the private sector include the Centre for Dispute Resolution (CEDR), now one of the main ADR organisations in Europe; the Academy of Experts; ADR Net; the British Association of Lawyer Mediators (BALM); the International Chamber of Commerce; and the City Disputes Panel.[2] Some of these, include mediation among a wider range of dispute resolution services. There are also many smaller private dispute resolution services, made up of groups or individual mediators. Some of these are general civil/commercial mediators, others specialise in particular fields, such as the construction industry, medical negligence cases, partnership disputes or computer disputes.

Community and neighbour disputes tend to be undertaken by local
9–007   community mediation services.[3] There are no or few low-cost civil and commercial mediation organisations. Rather, established civil and commercial bodies may offer a low-cost or *pro bono* option for the public sector, though to date this has tended to be by way of local court pilot schemes.[4] These have been serviced by a mixture of committed practitioners and volunteers anxious to develop publicly-funded mediation or keen to gain experience.[5] There are not understood to be any established, long-term programmes currently in existence that will offer free or low-cost civil and commercial mediation to the public.

There are, however, some options for the use of publicly-funded or low-
9–008   cost civil and commercial mediation:

- Pilot schemes have been conducted in certain courts, and some of these may still be in force, or may be extended.[6]

- Legal aid is now available for civil and commercial disputes, following a ruling that this should be provided.[7]

---

[1]Members of the mediation umbrella organisation Mediation U.K., largely geared to the public sector, have undertaken civil and commercial disputes, particularly as part of court pilot schemes.

[2]Contact details are set out in Appendix I.

[3]See Chap. 12.

[4]For further information about court pilot schemes, see Chap. 3.

[5]The Bar and the Law Society have both developed groups of practitioners willing to give time to do work free or at a reduced cost (the Bar's Free Representation Unit and the Solicitors' Pro Bono Group). These *pro bono* groups have supported ADR pilot schemes.

[6]See n. 4 above.

[7]The Legal Aid Board's Costs Appeal Committee decided the case of *Wilkinson* in October 1998. See Chap. 3 for a discussion about ADR and legal aid generally.

- Mediation U.K. has a directory of local services that may be able to assist with any disputes.[8]

- Private sector mediation organisations are keen to be involved in the public sector as well, and are likely to wish to participate in any public developments. Some may also be willing to provide low-cost services by special arrangement.

Specialist sectors

Within the field of civil and commercial mediation, there are a number of specialist sectors. For example, a group of leading mediation organisations around the world has established "The Millennium Accord" to provide help to anyone encountering differences or disputes arising from the anticipated problems in I.T. systems coping with the year 2000 date change. The Accord Procedure is described as "a flexible fast-track negotiation and mediation procedure."[9] The Software Publishers Association has established a Software Industry Mediation Service.[10] There are specialist construction industry sectors and intellectual property groups. Specialist sectors have been established for clinical negligence cases and insurance disputes; and the City of London has established its own specialist financial dispute resolution sector. The voluntary sector has developed a dispute resolution group, co-ordinated by the National Council of Voluntary Organisations with CEDR. The rail industry in the United Kingdom has set up the Railways Industry Dispute Resolution Scheme (RIDR) to create a forum among the 90 or so owners of former British Rail businesses. These are just examples of specialist sectors focusing on dispute resolution within their industries.

9–009

Lawyers and rights in civil and commercial mediation

It is widely accepted that rights significantly influence parties in civil and commercial mediation. This is because they mediate "in the shadow of the law"[11], in the sense that they could rely on their respective rights if they chose to resolve the matter in an adjudicatory forum. Having said this, there are costs and risks in litigating, and many factors apart from rights, such as continuing relationships, may influence the parties in seeking a solution. This is, after all, why they chose the mediation forum. It is probably fair to say that they will have regard to rights, but not necessarily as an exclusive consideration.

9–010

The significance attached to legal rights is at least in part reflected by the extent to which parties tend to be represented by their lawyers in civil and commercial mediation, in the private sector in any event. The experience of CEDR is that by far the majority of mediations take place with legal representatives in attendance.

9–011

Mediators tend to be drawn from a wide range of background disciplines. This reflects the fact that law does not dominate civil and commercial

9–012

---

[8] See details of Mediation UK in Appendix I.

[9] These include the Centre for Dispute Resolution in the U.K., JAMS-Endispute in the United States, LEADR in Australia, the Hong Kong International Arbitration Centre and the Singapore Mediation Centre.

[10] See: *www.spa.org/mediation/* for further details.

[11] See Chap. 10, para. 10–019, n. 10.

mediation. Not surprisingly, solicitors and barristers almost certainly constitute the largest group based on background disciplines. The Law Society has recognised the part that solicitors play in dispute resolution generally and mediation in particular, and has developed a Code of Practice and training standards for solicitors who undertake civil and commercial mediation.[12]

9–013 It is important to distinguish between mediation that is purely facilitative and mediation that may contain an element of evaluation of the respective rights of the parties. Many civil and commercial mediators, in common with their colleagues from other fields, will only mediate on a facilitative basis. They will decline to offer any element of evaluation. Others, however, may be willing, if required by the parties, to introduce some non-binding evaluation if the facilitative approach proves to be insufficient.[13]

3. The Stages of Civil and Commercial Mediation

9–014 The stages outlined below follow, with some inevitable repetition, the outline contained in Chapter 8, to which reference should be made for the general principles applicable to each stage. These stages constitute a notional framework to facilitate consideration of the process.

Phase One: Before Mediation

Stage 1: Engaging the parties in the mediation forum

9–016 Historically, parties have not had much choice of dispute resolution forum for their civil or commercial claims. They would litigate through the courts as soon as they had exhausted communications between solicitors, unless arbitration was provided for in their contract or agreed on an ad hoc basis. It was only with the development of mediation and other ADR options in recent years that people started to become aware that they had a real choice of forum.

9–017 Throughout the world, this early stage of engaging the parties in the mediation forum appears to require most careful attention. There are many misconceptions about the process, which need to be addressed. It is essential that whatever process parties choose, they should be well-informed about it and its implications. Parties and lawyers who participate in mediation often come to appreciate its value. However, getting both sides to the table can be a slow and difficult process especially as parties may be unsure what ADR involves and whether they can adequately trust in its effectiveness.

9–018 The Law Society of England and Wales has accepted its responsibility for ensuring that solicitors are fully aware of all relevant dispute resolution processes, so that clients are offered a genuine choice of process, rather than

---

[12]The Law Society regulates solicitors in all aspects of their practices, including mediation. Solicitor mediators must comply with the Code and regulations of any mediation organisation to which they belong, but this does not avoid the necessity for them also to comply with Law Society requirements.

[13]See Chap. 16 for a discussion about evaluative mediation.

automatically opting for litigation.[14] Where litigation is initially chosen, clients may wish to consider mediation or other processes at some strategic stage.

Commercial ADR organisations have been active in raising public awareness of the availability, practice and potential value of using ADR for civil and commercial disputes. They have published brochures, leaflets, explanatory material and booklets. They have held seminars, workshops, conferences, discussion groups and other meetings of interested parties. They have published articles in the professional and general press, talked to the judiciary, professional firms and businesses, and extended awareness in many other ways such as through the media and by way of individual communications.

9–019

ADR organisations may comprise members from different backgrounds including between them the legal, accounting and other professions, the construction industry, and many other fields of industry and commerce. This means that an understanding of ADR is gradually extending through its practitioners to different fields of commercial activity, enhancing awareness and the prospects of referral. It also means that panels of mediators have been established, from whose ranks the organisations can offer mediators who, in many cases, not only have mediation skills but also expertise in the subject-matter of the dispute.

9–020

ADR organisations will usually offer to send written material to an inquiring party, and will have trained personnel to deal with the inquiries in person or on the telephone and to explain how mediation or other ADR forms work. Where appropriate, and by arrangement with an inquiring party, they will engage the other disputants in order to see whether ADR can be agreed upon.

9–021

In the United States, one of the primary ADR organisations, the Center for Public Resources, on which to some extent CEDR was modelled, requires its corporate members to sign a pledge to consider using ADR before embarking on an adversarial process. No United Kingdom organisation is understood to stipulate this requirement to its members, though CEDR reports that the fact of CEDR membership is often used by other parties as an implicit statement of interest in considering ADR in a dispute, albeit that there is no formal pledge.

9–022

Mediators approached individually rather than through ADR organisations may similarly endeavour to engage the parties, and will usually encounter the same problem of getting both sides to agree to the process. They may encounter the additional difficulty that, if one party suggests them, the other may question their neutrality by reason merely of their nomination by the first. In this respect, ADR organisations or mediation consortia have an advantage over individual practitioners, because their neutrality cannot easily be called into question. An individual mediator suggested by a party or lawyer directly may be more acceptable to the other if known by reputation or recommendation.

9–023

---

[14] It has taken steps to inform its members about ADR options. These include arranging the publication of an ADR handbook and other informative material, arranging a series of seminars nationally, establishing a family mediation panel, and generally raising awareness among members.

9–024   One way to enable parties to decide whether or not to engage in mediation is for them or their lawyers to arrange a preliminary meeting with the mediator, at an agreed cost, at which the process can be discussed, the ground rules explained, and any queries dealt with. If they decide to proceed with mediation, the opportunity can be used to agree a timetable and agenda (if required), to arrange for the submission of statements and documents and generally to deal with any other practical matters that may be necessary.

Stage 2: Obtaining commitment and agreeing mediation rules

9–025   There is currently no statutory or other mandatory provision in England and Wales for commercial or civil disputes or claims relating to the breach of legal duties to be dealt with by mediation. This differs from family issues, where legal aid requirements or prescribed court procedures may require parties to consider mediation in certain circumstances. Civil or commercial disputes or claims can only be dealt with by way of mediation if the parties agree to use this process, either in general terms at the time that the original contract was entered into or in specific terms after a dispute has arisen.[15]

9–026   Judges may adjourn civil/commercial proceedings and require parties to consider using ADR processes including mediation to resolve their dispute.[16]

9–027   Parties may commit to the mediation process either by entering into an agreement to mediate on an ad hoc basis or as a consequence of a dispute resolution clause in an earlier substantive contract. In the latter case, a further agreement, between the parties and the mediator or organisation, may still be necessary, unless the original contract rendered it unnecessary, for example by incorporating its essential terms in full or by reference.

9–028   Parties may contract to try mediation at the outset, and if this fails to resolve the dispute, to refer it to arbitration, either retaining as arbitrator the same person who acted as mediator, or appointing someone else. In any event, the right to proceed to adjudication if the mediation is unsuccessful will invariably be reserved, implicitly or explicitly.[17]

9–029   The parties should agree to the procedural rules that will apply to the mediation, at least in broad outline. This would cover matters such as legal privilege (ensuring that discussions are off the record), confidentiality, whether a written agreement is needed to create binding obligations, and other such matters. Mediation organisations and individual mediators are likely to have standard terms of agreement embodying these matters. It is good practice for that agreement to be based on the Code of Practice to which the mediator or organisation works, and to incorporate the Code by reference or by attaching it.[18]

9–030   Almost invariably, the mediator will be a party to the agreement to mediate or will be identified in it.

9–031   There are no particular rules as to how or when the agreement should be executed. A common practice is to send a draft to the parties when they are

---

[15]See Chap. 20 "Jurisdiction, Forum and Law" regarding the contract to mediate and Appendix II for specimen forms of contract terms.

[16]See Chap. 3.

[17]For a discussion about med–arb, see Chap. 7.

[18]See, *e.g.* CEDR'S model mediation procedure, s. 3 at para. A2–104.

considering mediation, and to inform them that the document will need to be signed before the substantive mediation starts. They may be invited to raise any queries or to propose any amendments in advance of the meeting, so that these can be considered and dealt with. Any proposed amendments would have to be acceptable to the mediator and the other party. Once the terms are agreed in advance, the document can be signed at the start of the mediation meeting. This can be a positive symbolic act to launch the process.

Stage 3: Preliminary communications and preparation

Having engaged the parties in the mediation forum and agreed on the contract to mediate and the ground rules, a number of preliminary communications may then be necessary before the substantive mediation commences.   9–032

If the dispute is particularly complex or substantial, the mediator may wish to have a preliminary meeting with the parties, or more with likely their legal representatives, to discuss a framework for the process and the furnishing of information.[19] At that preliminary meeting, the contract to mediate can be finalised if this has not already been done, a timetable can be agreed for the furnishing of documents and information, and in effect, "directions" for the mediation can be agreed. These may for example cover what the bundle of documents will include, who will attend the mediation, the nature of authority they will have, and whether each party will address the mediator and, if so, for how long and on what basis. This is a good opportunity to discuss and clarify the ground rules, including principles of confidentiality and privilege. The parties may wish to discuss whether the mediator is required to give an evaluation on any aspects at any time, or (if so requested by the parties) to recommend terms of settlement that he or she considers appropriate if the parties cannot arrive at an agreement.   9–033

If these matters are not discussed at a meeting, it is in any event often helpful for them to be discussed on the telephone in advance of the substantive meeting.   9–034

Lawyers for the parties ordinarily appreciate having some such preliminary discussion with the mediator, and it enhances the process. The mediator can indicate what expectations he or she has about the preliminary presentation, and can give guidance on this, especially as to timing.   9–035

The mediator is likely to need certain preliminary information and documents in advance of the meeting. Commonly the following will be required: 9–036

- A written statement from each party, copied to the other, of the relevant facts, submissions and claims or responses. Such a statement is intended partly to inform the mediator of the issues and what the disputant seeks to achieve in the mediation, and partly to enable the disputant to formulate his position and aims in a manner and in language understandable to the other party. It will usually be less

---

[19]Philip Naughton Q.C., in his article "Mega mediation—a case history" [1996] A.D.R.L.J. 215, considers that (in a substantial and complex mediation in any event) "a pre-mediation meeting is invaluable".

formal or structured than statements of case in litigation, and may combine a summary of the relevant facts with legal, technical and/or factual submissions, and a summary of the party's claims, defences or contentions. The strict rules of evidence are not applicable, and the form of these statements is quite variable. The mediator might stipulate a maximum length for these written submissions.[20]

- A bundle of copy documents and correspondence relevant to the issues, if possible agreed between the parties, but otherwise furnished separately by each party. These do not have to be complete, as they might be in litigation. Rather, they are a selection of documents that either party thinks would be helpful to explain and support the case.

- A set of copy statements of case filed in the proceedings, affidavits, orders and other formal documents if the case has already been commenced in the courts or by way of arbitration. If the pleadings and other formal documents are very extensive, the parties may agree to select relevant extracts.

9–037   Having considered the statements and documents, the mediator can meet the parties with an understanding of the issues. If the statements, documents or information appear to be incomplete, or if supplementary information is needed, the mediator can ask for amplification prior to the meeting. The mediator may prefer to do this during the mediation, but in such event, the required documents may not be readily available, and delay or frustration could result.

9–038   If there are technical issues in the case, and if experts have been engaged on both sides, the mediator may wish to see the experts' reports. In some cases, valuation reports, accounts, illustrations, photographs or any other existing data may need to be produced in relation to specific issues.

9–039   Practical arrangements for the meeting will be made. Usually a period will be allotted, appropriate to the issues. This may vary between a few hours and a number of days.[21] A balance needs to be struck between on the one hand not allotting more time than is necessary and economic, and on the other hand allowing sufficient time to mediate effectively. The aim is usually to conclude the mediation within the allotted time; but in some cases, an adjournment may be necessary and beneficial. This may for example be necessary where further information is essential to the outcome, or some interim action is needed, or ideas or proposals need to be developed.

---

[20]Parties seem to find ways of extending the limits to cover what they need to say. Given a page limit, some parties have used tiny print fonts, others have removed all margins, some have done both. Others just ignore the limitation and say what they have to; and it is then difficult to reject the summary. Rather than make rigid rules that are not observed (or are observed by only one party) some flexibility on this instruction may be preferable.

[21]In the Central London County Court pilot scheme conducted during 1997/98 three hours were allowed for each mediation. That focused the parties, and many mediators approved of this limit. Others found it too short. It is more usual to set aside a day for the mediation, sometimes two days, and occasionally (but rarely) up to about a week. Philip Naughton Q.C., in his article "Mega mediation—a case history" [1996] A.D.R.L.J. 215, suggests that "no matter how complex the dispute, two days should be the longest period available for the mediation". Sometimes, however, more time is needed.

Phase Two: During the substantive mediation

Stage 4: Establishing the venue and meeting the parties

This stage deals with the substantive mediation meeting with the parties. It **9–040** covers the setting up of the venue and the initial formalities of the meeting.

Venue and seating

The venue of the mediation will usually be neutral, such as the mediator's **9–041** premises. Where this is not practicable, other premises such as those of one of the solicitors acting for a party may sometimes be used. A minimum of two separate rooms will be needed. One should be large enough to accommodate all the parties and their representatives as well as the mediator for joint sessions. The other room should be sufficient for one party including lawyers and allowing space for the mediator to joint them for private meetings. Ideally, a third room should be available, which the mediator may use between shuttling and which may also be used for special meetings, for example if the mediator wants to meet the lawyers or anyone else separately while the parties remain in their rooms. In practice, it is not always easy to obtain three rooms, and two will suffice.

The seating arrangements will be for the mediator to decide.[22] To facilitate **9–042** direct communication, the mediator may sometimes choose to have the parties, rather than their lawyers, seated nearest to him or her. If, however, the legal representatives are likely to have a substantial role, then the conventional procedure of having them seated nearest to the neutral may remain appropriate. Conventional wisdom dictates that hostile parties should not sit facing one another during the joint session. That creates unnecessary tensions. Seating arrangements will depend on the logistics of the situation, numbers of participants and available resources. Possibilities include having the mediator on one side of the table, and the parties and lawyers on the other side (though this is a bit formal). Another option may be to have each opposing group on either side of the table, but to have parties sitting diagonally opposite one another rather than directly opposite.

Legal representation

It is up to the parties whether they choose to be represented by their legal **9–043** advisers in mediation. That will usually depend on the nature, substance and complexity of the issues, the availability of funding and the preferences of the parties. In most commercial disputes, it is likely that parties will be legally represented. In smaller disputes or cases of a personal nature, such as partnership disagreements or family business disputes, legal representatives might not necessarily attend. They might though advise their clients, and if required attend at a later stage of the process, for example at an adjourned meeting.[23]

Where they participate in the mediation, lawyers can have different kinds **9–044** of roles. They might be actively involved, including making the presentation

---

[22]See Chap. 8 at paras 8–058–059.
[23]See Chap. 19 for the role of the parties' lawyers in representing their clients in ADR procedures.

and leading the negotiations. Alternatively, they might attend in support of their clients, who would in such event deal primarily with the case. Much will depend on the individual client, the lawyer and their relationship. Many solicitors find it difficult to take a subsidiary role, but that may well be what is required in some cases. That is a matter for the party, but the mediator can help to influence this where appropriate, for example, by where he or she seats the solicitor in the joint session and by directing questions to the party rather than necessarily through the lawyer. An exercise of judgment by the mediator is required.

Opening the mediation session

9–045 There is no set way to open a mediation session. The following is simply an example of how this might be conducted:

- The mediator would welcome the parties to the mediation, trying to put them at ease. It can help to ensure that tea, coffee and water are available.

- There might then be brief introductions. The mediator may wish to introduce himself or herself, though this might commonly have been done beforehand, formally or informally. If everyone knows everyone else, no further introductions are necessary; but often lawyers or other professionals have not met the other parties, and introductions are in order.

- The next step would be to consider the Agreement to Mediate and to check that everyone has understood and accepted its terms. This should have been done in advance; but if there are any residual queries, they can be dealt with at this stage. The mediator may wish to draw attention to key terms, particularly the evidentially privileged (without prejudice) nature of the process, and the rules relating to confidentiality. If there are any other particular terms that need discussion, the mediator should comment on these. The formality of signing the agreement is then undertaken, and each party will usually receive a signed copy, with one also being retained by the mediator.

- The mediator might then outline the intended procedure for the mediation. The mediator explains that each party or their legal representative will be asked to make a presentation. They should expect that, having been forewarned to prepare for it. The mediator will explain that after the presentations (and any questions, if these are to be allowed), the joint meeting will end and that the mediator will then meet the parties privately in their separate rooms. The mediator will outline (either at this stage or after the presentations) how these separate, private meetings will be held, and what the confidentiality rules are.

- The length and style of this opening stage will be a matter for the mediator's judgment. It will depend on the mediator's personality, style and approach, the nature of the issues, the requirements of the parties and their previous experience, if any, and expressed perceptions of mediation, and the mediator's sense as to the pace and detail needed at this stage.

- The mediator can now turn to the substantive mediation.

The way in which this opening stage of a commercial mediation is **9–046** conducted can influence the way the mediation progresses. This is because parties may often make early judgments about the mediator, and form a view as to whether the mediator's judgment can be respected, and whether he or she will manage the process firmly and fairly and help to achieve an agreed outcome. The mediator should try from the outset to be an effective manager of the process, a wise judge of the requirements of the parties and a competent facilitator, but ultimately, mediators can do no more than be themselves, albeit armed with the skills, techniques and strategies that they have learned.

Stage 5: Establishing the issues and setting the agenda

The mediator establishes the issues between the parties in a number of ways. **9–047** First, each party will submit a written statement outlining the issues and their comments on them. Secondly, the bundle of documents will usually clarify and amplify the issues. Thirdly, the parties will in many cases make an oral presentation to the mediator further clarifying their position and the issues as they see them.

The individual oral presentation by or on behalf of each party has a **9–048** number of useful functions:

- It allows a summary of each party's case to be presented, with such emphasis as may be considered appropriate, to ensure that the mediator understands the relevant factual, legal or technical issues and that the necessary focus is given to those aspects which the presenter feels are most important.

- If the mediator has any queries about the facts of the case, these can be raised and the position clarified in the context of the presentation.

- It allows the other party or parties to hear, sometimes for the first time, an oral presentation of the issues as perceived from the other side's point of view, and to experience the strength of opinion or feeling that may lie behind the presentation.

- Parties often have an emotional need to have their "day in court", which can to some extent be met by putting their case to a neutral third party, even if that person has no power to make any determination about the case. In any event, the parties are bound to want the mediator to understand their point of view, and will want to ensure that the case is forcefully and clearly put.

- From the presentations, the mediator can gain information about the parties, their interests, concerns and aspirations. The mediator may observe the parties as the presentations are made, discreetly note their reactions, and gain an impression of the dynamic between the parties.

- The parties will observe the mediator listening to the presentations. Does the mediator listen with care to what is being said? Is there a sense that the points are understood, whether or not they are agreed with? Can the parties trust the mediator to deal with the forthcoming negotiations in an even-handed way? Does the mediator manage the process firmly and fairly, for example, by not allowing interruptions? Can the mediator be empathetic with each party without showing favour or alienating the other?

9–049   The length of time allocated to each party for presentation will depend on the complexity of the issues and the time available for the whole process. In some cases five or 10 minutes may be sufficient for each presentation, especially where these are informal and the issues straightforward. In other cases, hours may be needed on each side (though such long presentations may prove to be counter-productive and should be avoided as far as possible). A 20 to 30 minute presentation on each side will usually be ample.

9–050   Once each side has made a presentation, it is not usual to allow a further response by each, though there is no reason why a mediator should not allow the parties to reply briefly in appropriate cases. Responses, however, are not necessarily a constructive use of available time, especially as they merely serve to continue the polarisation of the parties, where the next stage is going to be to try to bring them closer together. In any event, they will have the opportunity to respond to any aspects of the presentations with which they may disagree in the separate meetings with the mediator, which will commonly take place next. This point can be made to the parties if they seek to reply and the mediator prefers them not to do so in the joint session.

9–051   The presentation can be made by the parties or by their lawyers if they are legally represented in the mediation. The method of presentation is a matter for each presenter. It is usually done as an address, highlighting relevant matters which may already have been mentioned in the written submissions. Other devices may also be used: for example, flip-charts, projectors, videos, maps, plans, photographs, or indeed anything else within reason, can be used or referred to. The mediator can guide the way in which the presentations might be made. In preliminary discussion with the parties' lawyers, when explaining what is required, the mediator can, if appropriate, indicate that the presentation should be explanatory rather than confrontational. It may, for example, be necessary to reduce the level of conflict. In such event, it can help for the mediator to suggest that the presenters might not only outline their case, but also indicate in general terms what they hope the mediation might achieve (though obviously not so as to compromise their position).

9–052   Some clarifying questions may be allowed if the mediator thinks that they would be helpful. If the mediator is doubtful about their value, questions should be deferred until they can be raised in the separate sessions.

9–053   In some circumstances, presentations might not be appropriate. For example, in a family business dispute involving relatives who are already hostile to one another and who have been through the issues innumerable times, the mediator may feel that presentations will just inflame the position. They would be better dispensed with. Another example of a case where presentations might be inappropriate would be where a party's sensitivities are so raw that presentations would just cause distress without serving any positive purpose.[24] Presentations can often be useful for the reasons outlined above, but should not become ritualised.

Having established the issues, the mediator will need to construct an agenda.[25] That may be done formally and explicitly, in discussion with the parties; or it may be implicit from the issues that have been raised. Where the issues are narrow and limited, the agenda will be simple and straightforward. Where, however, the issues are complex, and especially if the parties have each brought different issues, the mediator may need to identify and prioritise the issues for resolution.[26]   **9–054**

As observed in Chapter 8, the presenting issues sometimes conceal underlying issues that emerge as the mediation develops. For example, in a shareholders' dispute about a family business, what appeared to be an argument about company administration developed in some respects into a question about the validity of a will in which a parent left shares to one of the children. Although not alleged in the documents, there were inferences of undue influence and even fraud in the execution of the will. Underneath this, there were unspoken questions about sibling favouritism and which child the parents had preferred. Many of the underlying issues in a mediation cannot necessarily be addressed by a mediator, but it can be necessary to understand them in order to help with the presenting issues.[27] Underlying issues do not only exist in family disputes, but commonly also in other relationship disputes such as partnerships, shareholder disagreements, professional negligence claims and other working and personal relationships. They may also be found in other civil and commercial issues.   **9–055**

Stage 6: Information gathering
In civil and commercial mediation, a mediator needs to know the following to be able to help effectively: **9–056**

- What are the issues in dispute?

- What is each party's contention or position on each of the issues?

- Has litigation or arbitration started? If so, what is its present status?

- Is there any relevant documentation that may throw light on the issues?

- How far have the parties got in trying to settle the issues themselves?

---

[24] *e.g.* where a claim against a health authority related to a particularly traumatic death, a presentation of the allegations and the defence would have caused renewed and quite pointless distress. A short and general opening presentation by each lawyer was sufficient in those circumstances.

[25] See Chap. 8 at paras 8–075 *et seq.* for consideration of the agenda.

[26] *e.g.* in a case involving multiple issues, with numerous claims and counterclaims including allegations of negligence and trust maladministration that could not hope to be concluded before one party was due to emigrate a few days later, it was essential to identify and prioritise the issues.

[27] See also Chap. 1 on the distinction between the justiciable issues that a mediator can deal with, and the behavioural issues that are the province of a counsellor, therapist or management consultant.

- What is the relationship between the parties? Have they had a relationship that has broken down, and if so, what do they each feel about the future?

- Are there any relevant underlying issues, apart from those disclosed?

- Will the mediator need to have or acquire any specialised knowledge or expertise to assist in understanding and helping with the issues?

- Is there any other information that might be relevant to the mediation?

The issues in dispute and the parties' positions and contentions

9–057   The mediator obtains an understanding of the relevant facts and issues in different ways. First, it will be through each party's initial written statement of submissions. Secondly, the documents submitted to the mediator will amplify the submissions. Thirdly, if court or arbitration proceedings have commenced, the mediator may wish to have copy statements of case and other formal documents. Fourthly, each party will commonly make oral presentations at the initial meeting. Fifthly, the mediator may ask clarifying questions either in the joint session, or in the separate meetings with each party.

9–058   In these ways, the mediator also establishes the contentions and positions of each party. There is commonly a divergence between a party's stated position and his or her private one. Ideally, once the mediator is able to establish the true and private positions of each party, it should be possible for the mediator to help find terms that bridge their positions. It would be most helpful if each party gave their true aspirations and "bottom lines" to the mediator, who could use that private knowledge to help them "design" settlement terms.[28] In practice, it seldom works that way. That is because although some parties may disclose their true positions and aspirations to the mediator, most are reluctant to do so right away. That may be because they are not ready to move to what they may perceive as their worst outcomes right at the start, even though the mediator has undertaken to maintain that confidentially. They may, whether in hope or as a matter of strategy, prefer to hold as close as they can to their public positions. Consequently, establishing the true positions of the parties may be a slow process that develops during the mediation, especially as trust develops and a negotiating pattern emerges. In any event, aspirations and positions tend to shift as negotiations develop, new perspectives emerge, differences and gaps narrow and solutions are formulated.

The status of any pending litigation or arbitration

9–059   If proceedings are pending, the mediator ought to be informed about this, including whether any material court orders have been made, or hearings are due to take place. Copies of statements of case, affidavits, orders and other relevant documents should be furnished to the mediator.[29]

---

[28] See de Bono's concept of a third party "design idiom" at paras 9–084, n. 35 and 18–142.

[29] To those not steeped in the culture of litigation, court pleadings and particulars were seen as opaque documents written in an obscure legal style that obfuscated rather then clarified the issues. Under the Civil Procedure Rules that came into force in April 1999, "pleadings"

There is no reason why mediation should not take place parallel with pending proceedings.[30] Indeed, the existence of a hearing date can often act as a spur to negotiations. Sometimes though, if more time is needed or the parties prefer to lift the threat (and defer the cost) of a hearing, it may be preferable to adjourn proceedings either generally or, if appropriate, to a fixed date while the mediation takes place.

9–060

Any other relevant documentation

The mediator does not need or expect to have all the extensive documents that might be furnished in the case of a formal trial. It is unnecessary, and usually wasteful, to have a full disclosure process, involving large quantities of documents. Instead, the parties are invited to select those documents that they think will be helpful to the process. Ordinarily, they will between them ensure that key documents are placed before the mediator. Sometimes they can agree on the bundle of documents. If they cannot agree, each can produce their own bundles, even if there is an overlap.

9–061

The mediator must become familiar with the documents before the start of the mediation. The parties are entitled to no less, and in any event, it is necessary and valuable to do so. If the mediator thinks that any documents are missing (for example, where replies are sent to letters but the letters themselves are missing and seem material) it would be sensible to seek the documents before the start of the mediation meeting. Once the meeting is under way, it may not always be possible to obtain further documents without what may be an unwanted adjournment.

9–062

The status of prior settlement negotiations and underlying issues

It is perhaps strange that more emphasis is not given to this aspect. While some parties may of their own accord include in their written submissions the current status of settlement negotiations, or may reflect their proposals, that is not usually a specific mediation requirement, and it does not always happen. Consequently, the mediator may well enter the substantive meeting with no information about whether the parties have attempted to settle the issues, and if so, how such attempts have fared.

9–063

There is an argument for the negotiations starting afresh, rather than just continuing in the mode in which they were stuck before the mediation but it is not inconsistent with a fresh start to know the position reached by the parties before they agree to mediate. It can be galling for a party and awkward for a mediator if the negotiations get under way in the mediation, only to find that one party has decided to submit settlement proposals that are a step backwards from where the bilateral negotiations left off. That situation is exacerbated where the mediator, unaware of the earlier negotiations, carries those "new" proposals to the other party and is faced with indignation and disappointment.

9–064

---

became "statements of case" and should be simpler, more factual and less technical. That is a very welcome reform.

[30] Mediation can take place at any stage. The appellate mediation pilot scheme in the Court of Appeal, for example, deals with cases where judgment has already been given, and an appeal is pending. In those circumstances, the mediator is given details about the case and the judgment.

9–065   There may be something here for mediation organisations to learn from the divorce pilot scheme, the Ancillary Relief Pilot Scheme,[31] in which a district judge conducts a privileged Financial Dispute Resolution (FDR) process, acting as a neutral, non-binding evaluative facilitator. Under that procedure, each party is required in advance of the FDR meeting to disclose the state of "without prejudice" proposals including the latest offers made by each party. Civil and commercial mediators could benefit from having similar information.

9–066   Where the mediator does not have that information, and in any event, even where it is available, it is often helpful for the mediator's initial separate meeting with each party to be a fact-finding one, rather than immediately entering into the exchange of proposals. The mediator can take this opportunity to listen to each party, establish their thoughts and aspirations, and glean the status of past negotiations, if any. Although this may not yet enable the mediator to carry any proposals to the other party, it can be time well spent.

9–067   The information that a mediator acquires during this stage may not necessarily be in the form of hard or relevant facts, but it may nevertheless inform the mediator about the concerns and interests of the parties and provide a backdrop against which negotiations are conducted. This information does not necessarily come to the mediator in a clearly identified form, but may rather be gleaned through careful and shrewd observation, by listening with sensitivity to the parties, by asking pertinent questions and by observing non-verbal communication, or body language.[32]

The relationship between the parties

9–068   In some cases, there is no pre-existing relationship between the parties. That would be the situation, for example, in a claim for damages following a motorcar accident. In many cases, however, there is or has been some kind of relationship. It may be personal (such as relatives in a family business dispute or neighbours in a boundary dispute), professional (such as a doctor/patient or lawyer/client relationship in a negligence dispute) or commercial (such as business/customer, franchisor/franchisee, principal/agent, present or former partners or shareholders).

9–069   The nature of the relationship will invariably be clear from the submissions and documents furnished to the mediator. If not, the mediator would probably find it helpful to establish the position. What can sometimes be more difficult, however, is to identify what the parties want or expect with regard to the restoration or ending of the relationship, and what the mediator's role can be in that regard.

9–070   Where, for example, the dispute is between siblings or parent and child (as it commonly is in family business issues) or between business or professional partners, or between neighbours, the presenting dispute may well just be "the tip of the iceberg". In such cases, and indeed sometimes in cases that do not overtly appear to have any emotional content, there may well be a history of

---

[31] See Chap. 3.
[32] See Chap. 15 for consideration of the skills of a mediator, including those of listening, observing non-verbal communications and questioning.

conflict and emotional entanglement that could significantly affect the dispute and its possible resolution.[33]

The mediator should be aware of the emotional implications of the issues and the relationships between the parties. These are likely to affect the process directly, and the mediator would be disadvantaged in not being aware of their existence and effect.   **9–071**

Parties will not usually flag up their emotions or their expectations about their relationship with the other party. Obviously though it is material to know whether any past relationship may be restored, or whether there is scope for some acknowledgement to be given as part of an ending. Mediators will have to establish this information from discreet observation and questioning, and from seeing how the negotiations and discussions unfold.   **9–072**

Other substantive knowledge or expertise required
A mediator is an expert in dispute resolution process. He or she may or may not also be an expert in the subject-matter of the dispute. Process expertise indicates knowledge and understanding of the mediation process, and implies the availability of the attributes and skills of a competent mediator. Substance expertise may include legal or any other technical knowledge and expertise about the subject-matter of the dispute.   **9–073**

Ideally, a mediator will have both process and substance expertise. Where, however, it is not possible or practicable to engage a mediator who has both of these, process expertise is undoubtedly more important. Substance expertise can be introduced into the mediation in a number of ways but a substance expert who lacks process expertise and the relevant mediation skills and experience is likely to have difficulty in managing and making progress in the mediation. If a mediator needs to obtain expertise from other sources, for example, from technical, legal or other professional advisers, this can be achieved in a few different ways: **9–074**

- The mediator can liaise with the relevant experts engaged by the parties. If the experts differ in their respective views, however, the mediator may not be in a position to know which view should prevail. This may or may not matter, depending on the extent to which expertise is critical to the outcome of the mediation and to what extent the process is evaluative.

- By arrangement with the parties and at their shared cost, the mediator can consult an independent expert, introducing such expertise for the benefit of the parties jointly.

- In appropriate cases, the missing expertise can be furnished by using the co-mediation mode. For example, if the dispute involves complex legal, fiscal and accounting principles, it may be decided to have a lawyer and accountant as co-mediators, rather than either as a sole mediator consulting with the other.[34]

---

[33]Scratch below the surface and a mediator will often find this background of conflict and emotions. For consideration of this emotional aspect, see paras 8–119–122, 8–136–138 and 9–104 *et seq.*
[34]See the discussion about co-mediation at paras 7–080 *et seq.*

9–075 The mediator will have to establish any other relevant information. For example, it may be important for the mediator to know.

- Whether in a case involving a number of issues, there are any that either party considers more important than others. Single issue cases, such as a disputed claim for payment, can be more difficult to resolve creatively than complex cases, in which there may be scope for trading-off some issues against others.

- Whether issues of confidentiality or publicity affect either party.

- Whether third parties' views or decisions may affect the outcome of the mediation. If, for example, insurers or a governing board need to approve settlement terms or to provide funds, the mediator should be aware of this as it may affect who attends the mediation or how it is to be approached.

- Whether there are significant disputes of fact causing an absence of trust and belief by either party in the other. Where there is a direct conflict of fact such that one or other party must be lying, with no possibility of misunderstanding or other explanation, it can be more difficult to reach a settlement. The mediator may have to work with both parties to find creative ways of dealing with that situation.

The mediator will decide in each case what other information is needed to help the parties conduct their negotiations constructively and effectively.

Stage 7: Managing and facilitating discussions and negotiations
9–076 In this stage, the mediator assists the parties with their substantive discussions and negotiations towards settlement.

9–077 By this juncture, most of the earlier stages will have been completed, though some residual information gathering may still have to continue.

9–078 The mediator must now decide how much can be achieved by continuing with the joint meeting, and when to hold separate and private meetings (caucuses) with each party. If the parties are communicating productively and are exchanging thoughts and ideas constructively, or perhaps even while they are expressing their emotions in a way which seems necessary and which is not counter-productive, the joint session can continue. Where there is a personal relationship between the parties, as in the case of a family business dispute, the joint session may be a useful forum in which to explore options, rather than the separate meetings which can sometimes have an isolating and divisive effect.

9–079 It is, however, generally through the separate meetings that the mediator can best facilitate negotiations in civil/commercial mediation.

The first separate meetings
9–080 The mediator must decide whom to see first. This decision will be made on the basis of the mediator's judgment of the parties and the issues, and his or her sense as to who is more likely to get negotiations more productively

under way. Some mediators decide to start by seeing the party who appears to be bursting to be heard. Others choose to see the claimant first, which is a sequence that can always be logically explained to the parties. Alternatively, where one party carries a key to the resolution, it may be sensible to meet that one first.

If there are tight time constraints, or if the mediator wishes to get directly **9–081** into the negotiations, the first meeting will be used to start formulating settlement terms immediately. Significant benefit can, however, often be obtained by using the initial meeting simply to acquaint the mediator with the parties and their thoughts generally. In that event, proposals would not be immediately formulated, but the mediator would rather get a broad view of the position and of each parties' ideas, interests, concerns and aspirations. This gives the mediator a sense of the dispute and a feeling for the underlying issues, as well as those presented. The mediator can tell the parties that the first separate meeting will be used to help get an understanding of respective positions, rather than to formulate specific terms. That will avoid the parties having unrealistic expectations of the initial session.

The mediator should watch the timing of the first sessions. It is very easy **9–082** for these to run at length, as each party takes the opportunity to explain his or her position. The mediator has to bear in mind that the other party will be getting increasingly anxious and impatient and that it can become counter-productive to spend a long time with either party at this point. The mediator may therefore have to ask questions thoughtfully and selectively, and be able to help each party to express his or her thoughts and feelings while being contained in time and content.

The appropriate time for the initial sessions will depend entirely on the **9–083** needs and circumstances of each individual case. On average, an initial session of 20 to 30 minutes with each party should usually suffice.

Initiating discussions and negotiations

When the mediator has obtained a preliminary feeling for the parties' **9–084** positions, it will be necessary to start the negotiating process with a view to constructing settlement terms.[35]

In some cases, the parties will be ready to commence substantive **9–085** negotiations right away. They may already have started to do so with one another, and been unable to settle; or they may be clear about the kind of settlement terms and approach they have in mind. In this event, there are alternative ways to negotiate in the mediation forum.

The one way is for each party to formulate terms and submit them to the **9–086** mediator, so that neither sees the other's terms first, but the mediator has both. In this event, the mediator can see what common ground there is, and what areas of difference there are. With those insights, the mediator can then submit proposals to both parties. Alternatively, and more commonly, the mediator will arrange for one of the parties to start the negotiations by

---

[35] Edward de Bono refers in his book *Conflicts: A better way to resolve them* (Penguin 1985) to a constructive "design idiom" through which the neutral can help the parties to design their own outcome to the problem. This may be seen as helping the parties to "craft" settlement terms out of the material that they provide but cannot themselves manage.

submitting proposals. The mediator will carry these to the other party. In this event, negotiations take place sequentially, with the mediator shuttling between the parties carrying proposals and counter-proposals, and trying to narrow and eliminate any differences.

9–087   Each approach has its own advantages and disadvantages. Sequential negotiation is more familiar to many mediators and parties, and allows differences to be narrowed as discussions develop. On the other hand, it may tend not to allow sufficiently for a problem-solving approach, nor for creative solutions, but rather to follow the traditional bargaining mode, with its limitations. Having both parties furnish their proposals to the mediator to extract settlement terms also has pros and cons. It has the benefit of ensuring that neither party gets an advantage from seeing the other's proposals before formulating their own; and it gives the mediator greater scope to create a framework of composite terms. On the other hand, it can be difficult for the mediator to reflect the differences that inevitably exist, bearing in mind that the mediator's function is to help the parties with their negotiations rather than to become a personal principal in the negotiations.

9–088   Where both sets of proposals are furnished to the mediator, one way forward would be to "craft" a framework of outline terms based on the proposals furnished by the parties, showing where appropriate the parameters for negotiation. Having given that to the parties, negotiations can thereafter be conducted on a sequential basis.

Option development and reality-testing

9–089   Where parties are not able to formulate settlement terms, or where a fresh approach is desirable, the mediator is likely to encourage the parties each to explore possible options for settling the issues. The mediator should help the parties to develop as many options as they can, and to examine them to see which are realistic and which are not.

9–090   There are different ways of thinking about options. One is in the traditional mode, which might result in a set of terms being formulated for submission to the other party, with some expectation that bargaining would follow. Another would be in the problem-solving mode, which might result in the parties seeking creative solutions to what they accept is a problem that they need to address jointly and individually, and not antagonistically. This is the mode that mediators try to encourage; but in practice, it may be difficult to shift parties to this mode to any substantial degree (though they can benefit from edging towards it).[36] Another mode is Edward de Bono's idea of dropping the word "conflict" and designing an outcome that fits the needs of the situation.[37] Yet another is the transformative approach, in which the mediator takes no responsibility for the outcome of his or her intervention, but reminds the parties of their own power to make decisions, and asks questions to help them to make and evaluate options.[38]

9–091   The parties usually develop the options, but there is no reason why the mediator should not help them to do so, provided that any options that the

---

[36]See Chap. 6 for the different modes of negotiating.
[37]*ibid.*, p. 41–43 and 81–91.
[38]See paras 1–040 and 21–132–134 for further information about the transformative approach.

mediator puts forward are not presented as "the mediator's solution". One way to assist with option development is through brainstorming, where all ideas are noted without initially rejecting or commenting on any, for later evaluation.

Options can be discussed, narrowed and converted into concrete proposals, or they can be put to the other party more generally to encourage a response in a similar mode. Eventually, of course, terms will have to be extracted from them.   **9–092**

The mediator serves a reality-testing function at various stages. One of these is to help parties to appreciate the factual situation, rather than the misconceptions that can often arise when conflict exists. Another is to help them to consider whether options that they are exploring, and proposals into which these may translate, are realistic. In this way, they can act as a sounding board for ideas and possible solutions which each side may be considering putting to the other, indicating ways in which this could most effectively be done and encouraging movement.   **9–093**

Shuttle mediation

As previously indicated, the mediator commonly uses a form of shuttle mediation to move between the parties, carrying messages and proposals from one side to the other and trying to assess how proposals could be varied or amplified to make them more mutually acceptable.   **9–094**

While the mediator is engaged in a private meeting with one party, it can be helpful if there is a genuine task for the mediator to ask the other party to undertake. That uses time effectively, and lessens the opportunity for the party who is left alone to become too anxious about what is happening in the other room. Parties who have been left alone often comment on how long the mediator has been away. Mediators should be aware of this, so that if they find that they are spending longer with one party than they expected, they can pop in to the other and briefly indicate how long they expect to be. If a session is likely to take a long time, the mediator may wish to indicate this in advance to the other party, who can take an agreed break.   **9–095**

If the mediator has his or her own room, it can be useful to pause in it occasionally between shuttle meetings, to collect his or her thoughts and to consider how best to help the parties to move forward.   **9–096**

Shuttle mediation can continue as long as it is proving to be useful in narrowing differences.   **9–097**

Although it is usual to shuttle between parties during the course of the mediation day, this can take place over a more extended period. In one case, the day fixed for the mediation had ended without a settlement, but with terms still being discussed. Instead of adjourning to another fixed date (which would not have been practicable for some time), arrangements were made for the mediator to shuttle between the parties at their respective lawyers' offices from time to time over the following week. This resulted in a settlement.   **9–098**

Working with professional representatives and advisers

Although many parties may be unrepresented in the mediation process, it is common for parties to have their lawyers with them at civil and commercial mediation sessions, especially where litigation is pending or threatened. They   **9–099** may be solicitors or barristers. Parties may also bring other advisers to mediation sessions, for example, their accountants or property advisers, where appropriate.

9–100 During the negotiation stage, it is a matter for the represented parties whether they wish to deal with the negotiations themselves or through their lawyers. Mediators should respect the parties' decision, but should also be aware that unlike traditional proceedings they do not need to be hidebound by the convention of only communicating through representatives. To the contrary, the mediator is likely to address the party directly where appropriate, or the party and representative jointly, rather than the latter exclusively.

9–101 In some situations, the mediator may wish to meet the lawyers without the parties present. While that is a proper option, the mediator should use it with care, as the parties may be concerned about what is being discussed. This option can be helpful to arrange timetables and procedural rules, particularly towards the end of a session that is to be adjourned. If lawyers are posturing for their clients, the mediator may want to separate them briefly to enable them to deal more candidly with issues that need to be straightforwardly addressed.

9–102 Sometimes it can help to arrange for each party's professional advisers to meet separately or to communicate with one another, either during the mediation or during any adjourned period. For example, where the issues relate to accounting matters, and the accountants cannot agree, the mediator may propose that they meet together to consider and identify their differences, and to consider ways of resolving these (for example, asking them to try to agree conflicting records, accounts or valuations). They may not be able to resolve the differences themselves, but they may, for example suggest machinery for doing so. Similarly, other experts or valuers may be able to find ways of narrowing their differences.

9–103 Professionals accompanying their clients in the mediation are there to support, not to undermine a negotiated outcome. If they seem not to appreciate the adverse effects of negative interventions, the mediator may wish to discuss this with them (though respectful of the fact that the representative is there to protect the client's interests).

Dealing with emotions: the myth of rationality in civil and commercial disputes

9–104 There is a widespread notion that, unlike parties in family disputes, civil or commercial disputants tend to deal with matters in a reasonable, businesslike and rational way without what is seen as the diversion of emotions. While sometimes true, this is in many cases a myth.

9–105 Many civil and commercial disputes involve strong feelings. In some kinds of cases, this may be obvious. For example, family business or partnership disputes are highly likely to be emotional. This may be extended to most situations in which a working relationship existed but has broken down. So, for example, disputes between shareholders in private companies, such as claims for unfair prejudice under the Companies Act[39] can be highly charged.

---

[39] Ss. 459–461 of the Companies Act 1985 give the court power to grant relief to a member of a

So can disputes between former principals and their agents, franchisors and franchisees, manufacturers and their former distributors or employers and former employees.

Where the relationship breakdown arose because of an actual or alleged **9–106** breach of duty by either party, and negligence in particular, the sense of grievance and distress can be great. So, for example, a clinical (medical) negligence dispute commonly contains elements of patient anger, distress, anxiety and blaming by the patient. The medical practitioner in turn may experience many other possible emotions including anger and disappointment at the patient's apparent disloyalty, indignation at being accused of error in often difficult circumstances, fear, regret and distress. Similar feelings may arise in negligence actions against other professionals, and perhaps in most fields of activity.

There may similarly be strong feelings where contractual relationships **9–107** have ended in dispute. An apparently straightforward construction dispute may involve disagreement, anger, frustration and ill will between, for example, a contractor's manager and an employer's representative or the engineer. What appears to be a straightforward disagreement about a technical matter may disguise an element of personal blaming and conflict between individuals.

Even if a disagreement itself might initially have been a straightforward **9–108** issue capable of rational disposal, the way in which it developed can have created antagonism and distress. For example, excuses and attempts by parties to exculpate themselves and avoid liability may create hostility that did not initially exist. Factual disputes can cause anger (and denials in statements of case, though perhaps technically justified in a narrow sense, can exacerbate antagonism). The challenging tone adopted by some insurers and litigation lawyers can result in reasonable people becoming entrenched in their adversarial positions.

Parties who hold strong feelings may or may not demonstrate these in the **9–109** mediation and may not necessarily even be aware of their existence. Whereas overt anger can be addressed, suppressed anger is far more difficult to deal with, especially if the party concerned does not acknowledge its existence. Yet suppressed anger can sabotage deals. The anger may manifest itself indirectly, surfacing unexpectedly and in disguise. It may come out in snide comments, unwillingness to co-operate with the mediation, criticism of the mediator or the process, or resistance to agreeing terms.

Sometimes the emotional responses that occur in a civil dispute can mirror **9–110** those in family disputes. It is interesting, for example, to note that some of the same factors that arise in the breakdown of a commercial relationship are almost identical to those in the breakdown of a couple's relationship. This is especially so where one party or both (or all) remain emotionally entangled in the continuation of the relationship. As in the family field, a number of factors indicate the existence of emotional non-separation from the relationship. These include ambivalence about ending the relationship; continuing conflict and dispute; high levels of blaming; ineffective

---

company who can demonstrate that the company's affairs are or have been conducted in an unfairly prejudicial way.

communications, even if extensive; reactive rather than pro-active negotiations, tending towards opposite and polarised positions; third parties drawn into taking sides; and difficulty in making reaching agreements or in implementing any that are reached.[40]

9–111   Mediators need to be aware of how parties' emotions can be a block to resolution of their issues. Mediators should be sensitive to these as far as they can. Every individual copes differently with the expression of feelings, or with managing certain kinds of feelings, such as anger. A few guidelines might be helpful:

- It may not help to try to contain the expression of emotions. Many mediators find that this merely bottles up the problem, which then surfaces in some other form and inhibits resolution.

- If emotional issues arise in a joint meeting, it can sometimes be important for the other party to experience the strength of feeling that exists. However, this may be something that the other party has previously experienced and may not wish to have recurring in the mediation forum. The mediator must use his or her discretion in deciding how far to allow these feelings to be expressed in the joint meeting. Up to a point, it may be important to allow. Beyond that point it may become unhelpful to everyone.

- The mediator can give sympathetic acknowledgment of the emotions (though not necessarily of the factors causing it), taking care not to compromise his or her neutrality. The mediator may need to mutualise by acknowledging the emotional effect on both the parties, if indeed this is the case.

- If, however, the expression of emotions is causing undue distress to any other party, or looks likely to destabilise the process, the mediator should try, with the necessary sensitivity, to bring the more emotional party back to task.

- In any event, when either or both parties have expressed strong emotions, it is commonly a relief to them if the mediator gently and non-judgmentally brings them back to the task of seeking a solution to their substantive issues. That, after all, is the purpose of the mediation and the task of the mediator.

- It is often easier to manage strong feelings when these are expressed in the separate meeting with a party. The mediator then only has to deal with the party concerned, and not with both or all parties. For this reason, it may be better to defer issues likely to arouse strong feelings until the separate sessions. However, mediators must remain balanced and impartial, and must take care not to be drawn into the emotional maelstrom, or to overreact in empathising with either party.

- The mediator may perhaps meet the parties without their professional advisers, for example, where personal or emotional aspects need to be

---

[40]For a comparison with the family field in this regard, see paras 10–158–160.

privately aired. This should, however, be undertaken with the greatest caution, if at all. Some mediators decline to meet parties separately from their lawyers under any circumstances, though they might meet the lawyers alone for some issues.

- Where it is clear from the papers that emotional aspects have significantly affected the dispute to date and seem likely similarly to affect the mediation, the mediator may consider touching on this in a joint meeting, for example, in the opening discussion at the start of the mediation. Where properly judged and sensitively delivered, and where everyone realises that it is a factor, it can sometimes help to acknowledge this openly. In such event, it can be normalised, for example: "It is clear from reading the papers that there are some very strong feelings on both sides. That is not surprising, given that this dispute has been running for the last x years. Indeed, it would be surprising if that were not the case. I am just mentioning this, because in my experience strong feelings can sometimes block settlements and I would like to be able to come back to this if necessary."

- There are risks in the mediator airing emotional aspects at the outset. First, parties may wish to try to use the mediation process as an opportunity to avoid their usual patterns of emotional response, and an introduction referring to their feelings may be inappropriate. Secondly, if one party has stronger feelings than the other, both may perceive the mediator's remarks as being aimed at one party notwithstanding that it may be expressed as applying to both. Thirdly, the parties may not be ready to hear this, and may question the mediator's judgment. It may often be safer to hold such observations until they become obviously appropriate in the separate meetings. At that stage, it would be a matter of judgment for the mediator to decide whether and to what extent to touch on them.

- Mediators are not expected to be counsellors or to resolve personal hostility that may surface in mediation. Sometimes this may be resolved as a by-product of the mediation, either within the process or (more usually if it happens at all) in the fullness of time after the dispute has ended. Nor can mediators provide emotional support for parties or help them resolve emotional issues, which may well be complex and seldom exclusively related to the dispute. They have a specific and limited role, to help the parties to resolve the dispute. If strong feelings get in the way of this, the mediator can acknowledge the feelings without acknowledging correctness of the causes. The mediator can help the party to feel heard. The mediator can sometimes also help parties to an awareness of the effect of their feelings on negotiations, but only if this would be helpful and with the greatest of caution. The mediator's empathy can be helpful to unblocking emotional obstacles to negotiation. With sensitivity to these aspects, the mediator can help bring parties back into the process of businesslike negotiation.

Using facilitation and communication skills

9–112 The mediator will facilitate communication and negotiation between the parties and the formulation of concrete proposals that reflect their interests, concerns and requirements, and will assist them in maintaining a practical, businesslike approach.

9–113 Throughout the process, and especially during this stage, the mediator will use communication and other mediation skills. This will include listening carefully to the parties, reframing their communications to enhance constructive dialogue, acknowledging movement, mutualising concerns and interests, questioning each to clarify, probe and test how realistic their ideas are, helping to develop options and generally facilitating negotiations.[41]

9–114 As the mediator demonstrates an authentic involvement in the process and a patient commitment to helping the parties, they are likely to develop increasing trust in the mediator and the process. This in turn can have a positive effect on the movement towards resolution.

Adopting an evaluative mode[42]

9–115 Most mediators try to help parties to resolve their issues using all the facilitative procedures outlined above. Sometimes these do not prove to be sufficient, especially where parties have different perceptions of the strengths of their case, and make different assessments as to the likely outcome. In such cases, some models of civil and commercial mediation provide for an element of evaluation to be used.

9–116 Many mediators do not introduce evaluation at all, while others might perhaps do so unwittingly. There are many misconceptions about what evaluation involves. It seldom involves a formal declaration by the mediator as to the likely outcome of the case if it were to be taken to trial. Rather, it may (and commonly does) involve a questioning of parties' certainties, or a reference to relevant case law or precedent, or an informed challenge to assumptions of outcome.

9–117 Mediators who are willing to introduce an element of evaluation into their mediation are well aware that this is likely to antagonise one of the parties and that it could compromise the mediator's role. Evaluation is therefore not lightly undertaken.

9–118 There is another concept that is sometimes referred to as evaluation. This is the strategy of the mediator, at the request of the parties and if he or she is willing to do so, informing the parties of the settlement terms that he or she considers appropriate in the circumstances. This is not ordinarily part of a mediator's facilitative function; but some evaluative models allow it, particularly but not necessarily when the mediation is on the point of ending without a resolution.

Post-caucusing

9–119 When the mediator feels that the separate meetings have served their purpose, either because matters have been substantially or totally resolved or

---

[41]See Chap. 15 for the mediator's skills and attributes.
[42]For a more detailed consideration of evaluation, including specifically evaluative models of mediation, see Chap. 16.

because nothing further is likely to be achieved by continuing with them, the mediator may decide to meet the parties again in joint session.

Where agreement has been reached, the joint meeting can serve as an opportunity to summarise and check the terms and to discuss the formalities that will be followed to record and implement the agreement. Where the joint meeting serves as a continuation of the negotiations, the mediator may summarise the current position, using facts that are authorised to be released, and may then try to encourage negotiation movement in the joint meeting. At some appropriate stage, separate meetings could be resumed. The mediator may indeed have as many joint or separate meetings as he or she sees fit, being guided primarily by a judgment as to how useful either would be.

9–120

Stage 8: Employing impasse strategies
Where progress in negotiations comes to a halt and the parties are deadlocked, the mediator may need to use impasse strategies to help regain movement. In amplification of those previously mentioned,[43] the following may be particularly relevant to civil and commercial mediation:

9–121

Risk assessment (BATNA/WATNA)
As already noted, a useful method is to help the parties to examine their best and worst alternatives to reaching a negotiated agreement in the mediation.[44] This involves:

9–122

- Facilitating the examination by each party of their best alternative to an agreement in mediation, assuming the realistic best outcome in any other forum such as litigation. In assessing this, positive and negative factors need to be taken into account; for example, allowance must be made for the additional costs that would be incurred including those which would be irrecoverable. Delay and publicity factors, and any other relevant considerations, would be taken into account. Each party will then have some idea of the best result that could be achieved if agreement is not reached.

- Similarly, facilitating the examination of the worst alternative to an agreement, assuming the realistic worst outcome in any other forum such as litigation. Here again, all relevant factors must be taken into account, including total costs payable by the losing party to his own solicitor, and likely costs payable to the winner. Delay and publicity factors, and other relevant considerations, are again taken into account. Each party will then have some idea of the worst result that might follow if agreement is not reached.

- In those models using evaluation, perhaps helping each party to assess the likelihood of winning or losing in the event of adjudication. Where evaluation is not undertaken, or if the mediator considers evaluation inappropriate in these circumstances, the mediator can

---

[43]See Impasse Strategies generally in Chap. 8.
[44]See paras 6–011 *et seq.* for this subject generally.

facilitate the parties and their lawyers arriving at their own assessments.

- Helping the parties to review the negotiations with the benefit of the parties knowing their best and worst alternatives and having a shrewd idea of their prospects of success.

9–123 In some cases, the best and worst alternatives can be discounted by reference to percentage prospects of success. For example, Smith claims, say £60,000 from Jones. Smith considers that he has a 60 per cent prospect of recovering the full £60,000 at trial. After deduction of irrecoverable costs, he would receive £50,000 net. That would make his notional settlement target 60 per cent of £50,000, *i.e.* £30,000. Jones might believe that he has a 70 per cent prospect of defeating Smith's claim. His risk would be 30 per cent of paying £60,000 plus all costs, say another £50,000, that is 30 per cent of £110,000, or £33,000.

9–124 Using this wholly unscientific method of calculation, settlement parameters would lie between £30,000 and £33,000. There are some obvious logical defects where risk is discounted in this way, but it provides another way of looking at settlement terms.

9–125 The BATNA/WATNA exercise produces results that many practitioners may well arrive at intuitively. It is nevertheless a potentially useful exercise for each party to undertake. It sometimes throws up surprising results, demonstrating the pointlessness of seeking a determination in another forum. It will be clear that it is not something that can ordinarily be undertaken by the parties jointly.

9–126 This intelligence, whether general or using percentages, may help negotiations to get back on track. If it leads the parties to decide to abandon the negotiations and to seek adjudication, that will have been based on their respective risk assessments and that decision must be respected.

Managing differences of legal or risk perception

9–127 An impasse can sometimes arise or be perpetuated by the nature of the advice or support being given to a party by his lawyer, accountant or other professional adviser. It is entirely proper and appropriate for the adviser to have a supportive role that is partisan.[45] However, in some cases, the adviser may have difficulty in confronting his or her client with options or views that the client is set against wanting to hear. The adviser may need support in dealing with this issue, and the mediator may need to accept the role of a scapegoat in helping to achieve a necessary shift.[46]

9–128 Mediators who do not evaluate can raise questions that challenge the party's perceptions (though this itself may be a form of evaluation); but this may not necessarily resolve the impasse. It can be more helpful, and may sometimes be necessary, to challenge perceptions more directly, for example

---

[45] See the value of the partisan role in *Partisans and Mediators* by Gwynn Davis (1988).

[46] One role of the mediator is sometimes to be a scapegoat for the decisions that the parties need to make. If a party can "blame" the mediator for having to reach a particular decision, the mediator will need to have sufficiently broad shoulders to accept that as part of his or her function.

by asking how they reconcile their views with particular legal provisions or judicial precedents, or by referring to aspects of the case put forward by the other party. Evaluation does not need to be specific; it can and often is more oblique.

In challenging parties' perceptions, mediators would not want to undermine individual lawyers or other advisers. When the mediator raises such a challenge in a private meeting, it is common to find the lawyer quite relieved and even supportive of the mediator. The lawyer may well have issued cautions to his or her client, but might not have wanted to press these too strongly. The lawyer may not want to have been perceived as being too negative or may have wanted to support the client in maximising the client's position, while looking for settlement opportunities. **9–129**

A mediator may feel that an impasse exists because the lawyer or other professional adviser is (in good faith but mistakenly) over-stating the strength of the party's position or prospects. The party may thus have a false impression of the risk of adjudication, creating an impasse. Here again, a mediator can raise questions (and in an evaluative model can indicate views, albeit tentatively) that may help the party and the adviser to reassess their views and to shift stuck positions. **9–130**

Written notes, summaries and analyses

Where parties are deadlocked, it can help for the mediator to prepare written notes for the parties to consider: **9–131**

- The mediator may produce a summarised analysis of the issues, reflecting those aspects on which there is some measure of agreement and those where there are differences, with the range of solutions put forward by each party.

- The mediator may add his or her own thoughts on the possible ways in which stuck issues can be approached consistently with the aspirations of each of the parties. This can be done non-judgmentally, merely by outlining available options; or if the circumstances necessitate, the mediator could add his or her views as to the direction which the negotiations could take to become more effective.

- Depending on the specifies of the situation, the mediator may create a written note that creatively assesses the stuck aspects. The key requirements of such a strategy would be, first to bring a greater awareness of the issues to the parties, and secondly to offer some constructive ways to overcome the deadlock.

Examining underlying issues

If it is not apparent what is causing the deadlock, the mediator may wish to consider what underlying issues may be inhibiting resolution. In civil and commercial mediation, one might expect the issues to surface straightforwardly, but that will not necessarily be the case. For example, in a clinical (medical) negligence case, the claimant may not be satisfied merely with financial proposals, as much as those would be welcomed. There may be a strong need for some form of acknowledgment, explanation or apology **9–132** that would move matters forward. Or in a dispute under section 459 of the Companies Act 1985 (relating to allegations of unfair prejudice to the interests of shareholders), a minority shareholder may be distressed and angry about the way he or she was treated and may need some form of vindication besides a mere cash or shareholding adjustment.

9–133   The mediator may need to probe gently with each party to establish the underlying issues and requirements. Once these are identified, the mediator can try to consider with the parties what would need to be done or said that would satisfy those underlying issues and concerns. This can help to unblock stuck attitudes.

Making non-binding settlement recommendations

9–134   In some models that allow for this, the mediator can offer to furnish the parties with written non-binding recommendations for settlement in the event of impasse. These would not be binding on the parties. The mediator should make it clear that the recommendations are a suggested negotiation outcome and not an expert opinion, evaluation or non-binding determination.[47]

9–135   Some organisations, such as the City Disputes Panel, use this as a part of their substantive process. Others would see this as something to be expressed only at the end of the mediation, or in writing afterwards. As a matter of practice, parties should preferably be told to inform the mediator if they accept his or her recommendations, rather than contacting one another. The reason for this is that if one accepts and the other does not, the mediator can still maintain the necessary confidentiality, and the refusing party need not be told of the other's willingness to agree.

Addressing other causes of impasse

9–136   Deadlock can arise for various other reasons, such as the terminology being used, the symbolic implications of the dispute or its resolution, differing perceptions of fairness or facts, or emotional blocks. The mediator's approach to dealing with these and other problems is dealt with elsewhere in this book.[48]

9–137   A basic impasse strategy that should not be overlooked is simply that of pausing and reflecting. That should be fundamental. The mediator may need time and space to reflect on the cause of the deadlock, and why it is so difficult to overcome that cause. Self-examination is part of this process: the mediator may find that his or her own attitudes and assumptions are contributing to the problem, rather than helping to overcome it. This may, for example, concern the way the mediator relates to one of the parties. The mediator may have to change his or her approach or attitudes to create a new dynamic.

---

[47]The Centre for Dispute Resolution (CEDR), *e.g.* has a term of its model mediation procedure that provides: "If the Parties are unable to reach a settlement in the negotiations at the Mediation and only if all the Representatives so request and the Mediator agrees, the Mediator will produce for the parties a non-binding written recommendation on terms of settlement. This will not attempt to anticipate what a court might order but will set out what the Mediator suggests are appropriate settlement terms in all the circumstances."

[48]See "Impasse Strategies" in Chap. 8.

Preparing for adjudication

If attempts to resolve the impasse are not successful, the mediation may have **9–138** to end. The parties will have reserved their right to proceed to adjudication. Sometimes coming face to face with that serves as an effective impasse strategy itself, and brings parties back into negotiation. However, a mediator should not use this as a strategy unless genuinely intending to end the mediation if there is no further movement: this should not be used by way of brinkmanship, but rather as a genuine last resort.

Even where the mediation is to end, the mediator can serve a useful **9–139** function in helping the parties to prepare for adjudication in as constructive a way as possible. Issues and formal arguments can be addressed and simplified, and the parties can be encouraged to view the adjudication as a way of resolving the dispute by getting a third party to make a determination, rather than as an act of hostility.

Phase Three: The end of mediation and afterwards

Stage 9: Concluding mediation and recording the outcome

As in all other fields of mediation, the process will end either when an **9–140** agreement has been reached, or when the parties or the mediator conclude that, although complete resolution may not have been reached, nothing further can be achieved in the mediation process.

At this stage, the mediator will have to consider and perhaps discuss with **9–141** the parties whether a written record of the outcome is needed, and if so, in what form and by whom it should be prepared.

It is a first principle of civil and commercial mediation that if agreement **9–142** has been reached, a written memorandum of settlement terms should immediately be prepared and signed by the parties before they leave.[49] It will ordinarily be immediately binding, and this should be clear and explicit. If it is only to become binding after some further stage has been reached, such as after ratification by a board of directors or confirmation by an insurer, this must be clearly stated. It must also reflect any conditions in the case of a conditional agreement.

The memorandum should contain all the material terms of settlement, with **9–143** no missing or vague essential elements, however complex this makes the memorandum and however long it takes.[50]

Lawyers representing the parties may undertake or help with the necessary **9–144** drafting. The mediator's role may be to undertake the drafting, to lead or support it, to review it or perhaps just to receive a copy of the agreement.

Where the parties are not legally represented in the mediation, or where for any other reason the mediator needs to be more closely involved in

---

[49]For drafting guidelines and precedents, see Appendix II.

[50]One of the authors mediated a longstanding and complex family business dispute. Settlement was reached at the end of the afternoon. With both lawyers working co-operatively with the mediator, it took until 4 a.m. to conclude and sign the detailed agreement. On the way, it almost broke down twice as drafting threw up problems. Had it not been concluded in minute detail, new issues would almost certainly have emerged in the morning. In the event, the parties stayed for the signing, and the deal was concluded and later implemented to their mutual satisfaction.

drafting (for example, where the mediator has kept notes that will facilitate drafting) the mediator may be primarily responsible for preparing the agreement. If only partial resolution has been achieved, the mediator might prepare a non-binding without prejudice summary of the position for the parties. The summary could usefully indicate the common ground and the differences between the parties, to facilitate further discussion in the future.

9–145   Where court orders or arbitration awards are required as part of the settlement, the mediator would not be expected to draft the relevant order or award. Indeed, on current practice it would probably be inappropriate to do so. This would be the responsibility of the parties' lawyers. The memorandum might, however, need to record in clear terms what kind of order is needed and what time-scale, formalities and procedures are envisaged for obtaining and implementing the agreement.

Stage 10: Post-termination

9–146   The mediator can assist in various ways with any settlement the parties may enter into. For example, the mediator may supervise implementation of the settlement terms, act as stakeholder, mediate any issues that may arise, or perhaps even act in an adjudicatory capacity in relation to the implementation of the settlement.[51] Some of these functions may be undertaken by the ADR organisation that arranged the mediation.

9–147   The extent to which the mediator or the ADR organisation that arranged the mediation can have a post-settlement role in relation to civil and commercial mediation will depend on a number of considerations, including for example:

- The needs of the settlement terms, and whether and to what extent they involve a deferred implementation, or one that would benefit from neutral supervision or involvement.

- The relationship between the mediator and the parties including the level of trust established and the readiness of the parties to allow a third party a supervisory role in the implementation of their settlement.

- The additional cost factor of having further neutral involvement, balanced against the perceived benefits of such involvement.

9–148   A supervisory function could be useful, for example, in the implementation of a construction industry dispute where the work is continuing, or in the supervision of some physical activity which forms part of a settlement, such as the stocktaking of a business. The mediator might retain documents in escrow or care for physical items pending the payment of funds payable on completion of a transaction, to be released on specified terms.[52]

---

[51] This would not be med–arb in its usual sense, as the adjudicatory function would relate to the settlement terms and not the original dispute. Nevertheless it changes the nature of the neutral's role, and care would be needed in agreeing these provisions, drafting the terms of adjudication and implementing them.

[52] For example, in one mediation it was a term of settlement that confidential documents held by a party had to be lodged with the mediation organisation that arranged the mediation, for

The mediator's post-settlement functions may either be contained in the written terms of settlement[53] or might be arranged on an ad hoc basis when the need arose.

9–149

4. CASE EXAMPLES

Mediation has been used extensively for a range of civil and commercial cases, varying enormously in scale and content.

9–150

At the one end of the spectrum, a case described as one of the largest and most complex pieces of litigation ever seen was settled by mediation under the auspices of CEDR in January 1999. This was the action brought in the English High Court by accountants Ernst & Young, as administrators of British & Commonwealth Holdings (B&C), against a number of defendants, notably BZW (now Barclays Capital), N. M. Rothschilds, and accountants Spicer & Oppenheim and Coopers & Lybrand. B&C were at one time the United Kingdom's largest financial services conglomerate. The original claims, reported to be for over £850 million, arose following the collapse of Atlantic Computers, which in turn resulted in the collapse of B&C itself.

9–151

The court trial in the B&C case had been scheduled to start in May 2000 and was expected to run for up to 15 months, with a likely appeal after that. CEDR were approached and two mediators were appointed, the retired law lord, Lord Griffiths and Jonathan Marks of the U.S. dispute resolution organisation, Endispute Inc. They conducted private meetings with the parties over an intense period of days, and the mediation was successfully concluded within a month. According to reports, settlement sums of over £116 million were agreed. Confidentiality clauses prevented details of the mediation from emerging, but lawyers involved in the process are reported as observing that this case was "a striking vindication of mediation" and that "tens of millions of pounds of costs have been saved".[54]

9–152

This was a similar experience to the earlier mediation of a major dispute, the De Lorean case in the Commercial Court, which was also resolved by mediation. Large construction and other disputes, both domestic and international, have similarly been resolved by using mediators.

9–153

At the other end of the scale, mediation has helped to settle county court disputes and consumer issues that would not necessarily have been cost-effective to litigate.

9–154

CEDR report that during the year 1997–98, case values handled by them ranged from £5,000 to billion pound matters with a combined claim value of over £4 billion.[55] Within this range, the largest segment of cases, amounting to about a third of the total, each had values of between £50,000 and £250,000.

9–155

The following is an example of how mediation assisted in the resolution of a family business dispute.

9–156

---

destruction after the terms of settlement had been fully implemented (but not before).
[53]For a precedent of such terms, see A2–169, cl. 5.
[54]See the reports in *The Times,* January 8, 1999, *Solicitors Journal* of January 15, 1999 and *Commercial Lawyer* of February 1999.
[55]*CEDR Highlights* 1997–98.

Family business dispute

9–157   Differences existed between two co-shareholders and co-directors of a family business, who were also farming partners. There were High Court actions pending between them dating back over a decade. The issues included the validity of share transfers, the implications of working procedures and accounting practices and the valuation of shares and properties. Court injunctions limited their freedom of action. Settlement negotiations between their lawyers had been inconclusive.

9–158   Lawyers and accountants represented both parties in the mediation. Each lawyer made a short oral presentation and each group then moved to separate rooms for separate confidential meetings with the mediator. The mediator shuttled between them, getting to understand their concerns and aspirations, exploring settlement possibilities, and carrying proposals and responses between them.

9–159   It became increasingly clear that different opinions expressed by the respective accountants gave rise to one of the major areas of disagreement. Consequently, while shuttling between the parties, the mediator arranged for the accountants to meet one another to try to narrow their differences and to identify information that could be provided. They worked out a timetable for furnishing such information.

9–160   The parties both accepted that it was not feasible for them to continue together in business and that settlement discussions had to focus on the separation of their interests, the extent and value of which were in issue. Different settlement options were explored: the permutations of land transfer, cash adjustment, share transfer and other factors depended on which of three or four farms (each having different attributes and values) would be transferred to the parties by way of settlement.

9–161   The mediator and the lawyers worked out a schedule and timetable for exchanging accounting and other information and proposals, covering some months. Three specific settlement routes were identified and would be explored.

9–162   Accounting information and valuations were obtained and the three settlement routes narrowed down to two, based on the possible transfer of two alternative farms, each with different ancillary terms and implications. The next meeting explored the payment and other terms that might attach to each option. One idea was for one party to take one specified farm, farming it for an agreed period to see if he found it satisfactory, and having an option to sell it by a specified date, with the other guaranteeing any shortfall on sale below an agreed level.

9–163   Two further meetings were held to explore and develop options further. After extensive probing and challenging, the parties eventually agreed settlement terms. These were based on transferring one of the farms to the other later that year, after harvesting, with various ancillary terms relating to share transfers, company loan accounts, indemnities, gaining early access to the farm, dealing with possible future property development and other matters.

9–164   In this case, the parties were eventually personally reconciled. That is sometimes a by-product of settling commercial disputes such as family business disagreements by mediation, though not an invariable one. What may often happen, however, is that the resolution of the issues in an agreed and reasonable way creates the conditions for later reconciliation where the parties have a continuing personal relationship.

CHAPTER 10

DIVORCE AND FAMILY MEDIATION AND OTHER FAMILY PROCESSES

1. INTRODUCTION

10–001 The process of divorce in England and Wales has been through momentous and continuing change, of which mediation and counselling form a significant part.

- The concept of no-fault divorce was supposed to have been embodied in the law before the passing of the Family Law Act 1996. The existence, however, of "facts" such as adultery, behaviour or desertion meant that an element of fault was inherent in divorce practice and attitudes. The Family Law Act introduced a genuine no-fault basis to divorce law.[1] The Lord Chancellor announced in June 1999 that the no-fault reforms would be withdrawn but that the position would be reviewed in the future. Divorce practitioners will continue with the divorce laws as before, but know that future changes are inevitable.

- The Family Law Act also introduced the concept of counselling and mediation as processes that stand alongside the legal process in dealing with the consequences of marriage breakdown. These have been retained in principle, though the changes in the law to which they were initially attached have been dropped.

- Mediators and counsellors now fall within the ambit of state funding through legal aid.

- Pilot court schemes have been developed and extended to make matrimonial proceedings more expeditious, less costly and less acrimonious.

- A national family mediation umbrella organisation, the U.K. College of Family Mediators, was established in 1996 to advance public education about mediation, to develop and maintain professional

---

[1] This said, individual attitudes were always likely to take time to catch up with the law. It is not possible to legislate that people should not feel aggrieved about the ending of a relationship.

standards in family mediation practice, and to maintain a register of member mediators.

- While family lawyers have long been involved in the development of all-issues mediation, an increasing number are training and practising as mediators, and working more closely with counsellors. The Law Society has developed recommended standards of training and a Code of Practice for family lawyer mediators, and is establishing a specialist panel of family solicitor mediators.

- The Council of Europe, in a major conference on family law, has recommended the introduction, promotion and strengthening of family mediation in its Member States.[2]

While family mediation is a form of ADR, it differs from other dispute resolution processes in that it does not necessarily focus on disputes as such, but rather deals with the consequences of relationship crisis or breakdown. Mediators will generally be as engaged in helping parties to make decisions that affect their futures and those of their children, and to formulate ways of adapting to changed circumstances in their lives, as in dealing with straightforward dispute resolution.   **10–002**

There is accordingly a different culture in the field of family and divorce mediation than in other ADR fields. Nevertheless, there is also a substantial overlap of process.   **10–003**

2. THE RANGE OF PROCESSES FOR FAMILY ISSUES

Couples or families have a range of professional resources from which to select a process most appropriate to their needs.[3]   **10–004**

Currently these processes are treated as separate and discrete from one another. Mediation is generally regarded as putting the traditional legal process on hold. If an agreement does not result, the mediation ends and the parties revert to the legal process, though there is scope for the processes to work together more fluently and for couples to be able to move back and forth between them as appropriate. So, mediation may help the couple to deal with certain issues, while solicitors deal with others. Alternatively, the couple may wish to revert to mediation after certain sticking points are addressed in the legal process or in counselling. Constructive exchanges between lawyers during the course of a mediation, and parallel with it, may enhance the mediation.[4]   **10–005**

---

[2]See "Text of Recommendation No. R (98) 1 of the Committee of Ministers to Member States on Family Mediation and its Explanatory Memorandum" (1998), also Janet Walker's "Text of Recommendation No. R (98) 1 of the Committee of Ministers to Member States on Family Mediation and its Explanatory Memorandum" (1998)

[3]The resources outlined in this section are not necessarily ADR processes. This section takes a wide and "holistic" view of all processes relevant to family issues, whether or not strictly ADR. That reflects the spirit of taking a broad approach to family issues, and supports a networking concept.

[4]Proper boundaries are necessary, but more creative thought needs to be given to considering the overlap and the boundaries between the processes.

10–006   Processes to help families and couples to deal with such issues can probably be divided into the following categories:

Counselling/psychotherapy

10–007 The consequences of relationship breakdown may involve dealing with a mixture of personal and emotional issues, matters concerning the future of the children, practical questions of housing and finance, and coping at a personal and pragmatic level with substantial change, as well as trying to decide on respective "rights". This often occurs against a background of different perceptions of fairness and conflicting legal advice.

10–008   Counselling and psychotherapy have long been available to help families, couples and individuals to examine difficult personal issues and to cope with the personal consequences of ending the relationship. Public perceptions are changing in their increasing readiness to avail themselves of these resources, though much misconception remains about them and their objectives.

10–009   Counselling is still regarded by some as a process to help a couple to save their relationship. While that may well be its consequence, its objective is not generally so prescriptive. Rather, it helps people in a non-judgmental and non-directive way to explore their issues and to arrive at their own outcome, whatever that may be.

10–010   There are also those who think of counselling as undertaken by well-meaning amateurs whose role is to offer words of wisdom and comfort to the parties, or to advise them what they should do. Fortunately that perception is changing. Virtually all therapy and counselling organisations and regulatory bodies require their counsellors to be properly trained and to demonstrate a high degree of professionalism, usually subject to some form of supervision. In the United Kingdom, the regulation of counselling and therapy is in the process of development by a number of regulatory bodies.[5]

10–011   The distinction between counselling and psychotherapy is not clear. Counselling generally tends to help with shorter term and more focused issues, whereas psychotherapy may deal over a longer term with more fundamental personal issues. Having said this, therapy is available on a short-term basis, and may deal with specific issues; and longer-term counselling may deal with fundamental life issues and not just focused aspects. "Counselling" often embraces specific areas of problem or difficulty. Counsellors may deal with relationship endings, sexual problems, grief, addiction and other defined aspects. Perhaps the distinction is less important than establishing what a particular counsellor or therapist offers, how he or she works, over what period, and whether the party or couple feel that he or she can establish an effective and empathetic relationship. Given that the terms "counselling" and "therapy" may still connote some sense of malfunction, the concept of seeking "professional support" in times of personal crisis may help to introduce people to available resources.

---

[5] *e.g.* The British Association for Counselling (Tel: 01788 550899); the UK Council for Psychotherapy (Tel: 0207 436 3002); and the British Confederation of Psychotherapists (Tel: 0208 830 5173). There is a strong movement in favour of registration of psychotherapists and counsellors. For an opposing view, see *The Case Against Psychotherapy Registration: A Conservation Issue for the Human Potential Movement* by Richard Mowbray (Trans Marginal Press, 1995).

Some counsellors and therapists only work with individuals, others **10–012** undertake individual, couples, family or group work. Each serves a different function. There is some concern that where only one of a couple undertakes counselling or therapy, this can feel threatening rather than supportive to the other, unless the other wholly supports the counselling or therapy initiative.[6] Couple's counselling or therapy tries to maintain the balance, helping both to explore necessary changes.

Counselling and therapy may be undertaken from different theoretical **10–013** approaches, which may be difficult to identify. A number of books have been written which help with this identification[7]; but the problem remains of assessing which approach is most helpful and appropriate for a particular couple or individual. The problem about seeking this answer from an "expert", however, is that "almost all of them will give advice that is self-serving to some degree, while none will be in possession of more than a small part of the truth."[8] That may be harsh: counsellors and therapists will provide guidance and where appropriate may well direct a client to a different practitioner. Kovel is however correct that counsellors and therapists choose to work in a perspective that they consider most effective. Few work on a sufficiently eclectic basis to meet all individual needs.

Theoretical perspectives include the following, from which dozens of **10–014** subgroups may emerge:

- *The psychodynamic approach.* This is based principally on a psychoanalytical theory of personality development and human relationships, as developed by Freud and latterly Melanie Klein, or analytical psychological theory and practice developed by C. G. Jung. Change brought about by this approach can occur at both conscious and unconscious levels.

- *The rational-emotive approach.* This therapy, established in 1955 by an American psychologist Albert Ellis, identifies marital disturbance, examines how this arises from irrational beliefs and seeks to replace these with rational alternatives.

- *The behavioural approach* involves addressing specific behavioural problems and helping the person to modify that behaviour by establishing a set of clear and observable goals. It does not attempt to uncover unconscious processes. Its techniques include positive

---

[6]Robin Skynner and John Cleese in their important work *Families and how to survive them* (Methuen, London, 1983) identify how individuals hide awkward emotions behind a "screen" (repression) and that many couples are secure in not looking behind their own or one another's screens. Healthy couples will help one another to bring feelings out into the open. However, if one is determined to change while the other resists change, that will inevitably lead to stresses in the relationship.

[7]*e.g. Marital Therapy in Britain* edited by Windy Dryden (Harper & Row, 1985); *A Complete Guide to Therapy* by Joel Kovel (Pantheon Books 1976, Penguin Books 1991); *Individual Therapy* edited by Windy Dryden (Open University Press, 1990); *Handbook of Family Therapy* edited by Alan S. Gurman and David P. Kniskern (Brunner/Mazel, 1981); and *Marriage and Marital Therapy* edited by Thomas J. Paolino Jr and Barbara S. McCrady (Brunner/Mazel, 1978); *Introduction to Counselling and Psychotherapy* edited by Stephen Palmer (Sage, 1999).

[8]Joel Kovel, *A Complete Guide to Therapy* at p. 292.

reinforcement by mutual "rewards" which has developed into more sophisticated approaches including communication improvement and helping to modify inappropriate beliefs and perceptions.

- *Systems approaches.* These view the couple as part of wider systems, and consider that individuals, couples and families interact in accordance with the systems to which they belong.

- *The humanistic approach.* This describes a wide range of approaches, generally adopting a holistic approach to the whole person, including mind, body and spirit, and acknowledging the capacity of people to assist in their own process of healing. The work of Carl Rogers, who established the concept of non-analytical, client-centred therapy, requires a special mention as it has influenced many models of neutral intervention. It emphasises the therapist's role, through his or her own sincerity and empathy in helping the individual to reflect upon himself and find his own, positive self-perception.

10–015

A practitioner in the field of marital breakdown will need to be aware of the implications and availability of different counselling and therapeutic resources.[9] Many lawyers and mediators will develop networks of counsellors and therapists, both individual and organisational, who may be able to assist in dealing with marital breakdown and stress, and their consequences.

Mediation

10–016   Mediation may be used for various different kinds of family issues. By far the most common is for couples facing the ending of their relationship, who are going through or contemplating the process of separation or divorce. It is this usage that will be primarily addressed in this chapter. Family mediation is, however, also available and used to help with other kinds of issues, such as those between siblings, gay and lesbian couples, family business disputes, child abduction issues, and elder mediation.

10–017   Mediation between couples may take place at any stage, from the time when they are still considering the possibility of separating, through to a time when they may have resolved virtually all issues (whether by adjudication or agreement) but wish to mediate outstanding points, or to review existing arrangements.

10–018   The way in which family mediation is conducted will be a product of a number of different factors. These may include the mediation model and Code of Practice followed by the mediator, the ethos and practice of any mediation organisation to which the mediator belongs and the personal approach, style and professional disciplinary background of the mediator.

10–019   All models and family mediation organisations tend to combine the fundamental principles of impartial facilitation with an awareness that parties mediate "in the shadow of the law".[10] Parties are likely to have regard to

---

[9]See n. 5. Other resources include Relate Marriage Guidance (Tel: 01788 573241 national); London Marriage Guidance (Tel: 0207 580 1087); the Institute of Family Therapy (Tel: 0207 435 1651); and the Tavistock Marital Studies Institute (Tel: 0207 435 7111).

[10]A concept based on Robert Mnookin and Lewis Kornhauser's "Bargaining in the Shadow of the Law, The Case of Divorce" 88 Yale L.J. 950 (1979).

their legal rights, though these will not prevail and they will consider other factors as well.

Separating or divorcing couples may bring certain specific matters to mediation, such as the future of the relationship, or matters affecting the children, property, finance or any other aspect of their affairs. In the United Kingdom, some mediators only deal with children issues and others cover the whole range of issues that may arise. Mediation dealing with the whole range of issues is known as "all-issues mediation"

10–020

Legal representation

This almost certainly remains the principal approach taken by the public, and undoubtedly it will continue for many years to be viewed as key to any resolution, even where other processes are also used.

10–021

Lawyers representing individual parties can be brought into the picture at virtually any stage, and can perform a wide range of possible roles, including:

10–022

- Giving a party preliminary advice about rights, options and available processes before that party makes any decisions, whether substantive or procedural.

- Supporting the client in mediation, for example by helping to select a mediator, outlining the mediation process and helping the client to prepare for it, assisting with collating financial particulars and advising the client as the mediation progresses.

- Advising the client at the end of a mediation by reviewing the mediation summaries including financial particulars, making recommendations about the proposed settlement terms, recording them and helping with implementation.

- Where mediation does not take place, or if it does not result in an agreed outcome, representing the client in communications and negotiations with the other party or their solicitor. Commonly this involves the exchange of financial information, and the negotiation of settlement terms. This may be done either prior to proceedings being brought, or parallel with them.[11]

- Representing a party in any adjudication or enforcement of a party's rights.

- Solicitors will also generally support their clients indirectly. This may, for example, involve giving emotional support and practical advice, or helping to refer the client to the solicitor's network of other professionals, such as counsellors or therapists, accountants or tax or financial advisers.

---

[11]Subject to the Ancillary Relief Pilot Scheme in areas where it operates and from June 2000, nationally (see paras 3–049 *et seq.* and 22–073).

Neutral non-binding evaluation[12]

10–023   In traditional matrimonial practice, parties will invariably obtain opinions (evaluations) of their respective legal positions from their lawyers before agreeing or even starting to negotiate financial settlement terms. A party would be regarded as rather foolhardy if he or she thought of settling matrimonial issues without having had some such opinion.

10–024   It is almost impossible for legal advisers, particularly in the rather complex system of English family law, to fix entitlement with precision. This is because rights are not based on any accurately measurable or quantifiable basis,[13] but on a range of different and sometimes competing principles and criteria. Some of these are fixed by statute and others have been developed by judicial precedent.

10–025   Although financial entitlement cannot be accurately assessed, a skilled and experienced family lawyer can form a judgment as to the parameters likely to be applied by a court to any couple. This information enables parties to ensure that they are negotiating within realistic legal parameters. Parties remain entirely free to move outside those parameters if they choose to do so on an informed basis.

10–026   Each party may obtain an evaluation from his or her solicitor or from specialist matrimonial counsel. Alternatively, the couple may jointly seek a non-binding third party evaluation of their issues from a neutral family lawyer.

10–027   Some lawyers working as mediators will inform the parties if they are proposing an outcome which falls outside of the limits that a court would be likely to approve (but without asserting what a court might order). This is not really an evaluation.[14]

10–028   Some evaluation may be made by a district judge under the Financial Dispute Resolution (FDR) procedure introduced in the Ancillary Relief Pilot Scheme.[15] With the development of the FDR in the courts, there seems to be no reason why a form of private FDR should not become available from experienced lawyers.

Arbitration[16]

10–029   Arbitration is a widely used process for the adjudication of civil and commercial disputes by a privately appointed arbitrator outside of the court system, employing such simplified rules of procedure as may be agreed. It is, however, not generally used in relation to family proceedings. Issues which affect the status of marriage and arrangements for children are not regarded as arbitrable issues on public policy grounds. It is unlikely that arbitration

---

[12]See Chap. 16.

[13]A notable exception to this is child maintenance fixed by the Child Support Agency (CSA) under the terms of the Child Support Act 1991. This is done by a prescribed calculation. Even child maintenance is not always simple, however, because of exceptions to the use of the CSA, by allowing top-up orders beyond the scope of the Act through the court, and excluding certain kinds of cases from the Act, and because underlying figures may not always be accurate or consistent.

[14]See para. 16–025.

[15]This pilot scheme is to be extended to the whole of England and Wales from June 2000. It is intended to provide stricter court control and improved procedures to reduce delay, limit costs and facilitate settlements. See Chap. 3.

[16]For the principles of arbitration generally, see Chap. 4.

has much of a role to play where children are concerned. Aside from public policy issues parties may be willing to resolve critical issues about children by agreement or through courts, where judges can be expected to apply accepted standards and where a right of appeal exists to redress aberrant decisions. They might be less likely to entrust such critical decisions to a private adjudicator (though it is arguable that some arbitrators with extensive skills, experience and judgment are likely to have at least the wisdom of many judges).

Perhaps similar considerations prevail in relation to the resolution of money claims by arbitration in the matrimonial context. There does, however, seem to be some scope for the use of arbitration for financial disputes on divorce.[17]   **10–030**

Med–arb[18]

Med–arb (mediation–arbitration) refers to a process in which attempts are made to resolve issues by mediation, and if this fails then the issues are determined on a binding basis by arbitration. Usually this is taken to mean that the same person who acted as the mediator would change role at some stage and become the arbitrator. However, because of concerns that this would be likely to compromise both the mediation and the arbitration processes, med–arb has been developed in some jurisdictions (though by no means in all) to mean that when the mediation ends, a different person will act as the arbitrator.   **10–031**

In the family field in the United Kingdom an attempt has been made to introduce med–arb but there is no record or anecdotal evidence of this having been taken up.[19]   **10–032**

Private judging[20]

In some jurisdictions, the court may refer a case to a person chosen by the parties to decide some or all of the issues, or to establish any facts needed to enable the court to decide the issues. Although conducted as proper judicial trials, privately judged cases may use a simplified and expedited procedure. Special legislation is needed for this private judging procedure. It has been enacted in various states in the U.S., such as Texas, California, New York, Ohio and Oregon. It has not been introduced in the United Kingdom nor are there thought to be any plans to do so.   **10–033**

Adjudication by the court

Ultimately, if none of the procedures for out-of-court resolution enable the issues to be resolved, the matter may need to be adjudicated upon by the court.   **10–034**

There is a public policy principle "that parties should be encouraged so far   **10–035**

---

[17]The Institute of Family Mediation and Arbitration, established in 1996, for a short while offered a training and practice programme for lawyers in family mediation, arbitration and med–arb.

[18]For the general principles of med–arb, see Chap. 7.

[19]See n. 17 above.

[20]For the general principles of private judging, see paras 18–037 *et seq.*

as is possible to settle their disputes without resort to litigation...."[21] That accords with the conventional wisdom of most family lawyers, who generally strive to reach settlements for their clients, while safeguarding individual clients' interests and concerns. There are those in the United States and the United Kingdom, mainly academics, who consider that lawyers have allowed the pendulum to swing too far in favour of settlement. They consider that lawyers treat adjudication as an option that feels like a failure, rather than a proper choice to have the issues decided by the court.[22]

10–036   Practitioners are aware of the financial and personal cost of litigation and the adverse effect it can have on relationships, particularly but by no means only where children are concerned. Their preference to see matters settled is not misplaced. However, the option to have issues adjudicated where necessary and appropriate should be respected, and practitioners should assist couples to achieve this in the least acrimonious and most effective way possible.

3. SOME ISSUES IN FAMILY MEDIATION PRACTICE IN ENGLAND AND WALES

Court and publicly funded mediation or private sector mediation

10–037   The history of family mediation in England and Wales has been chronicled by a number of writers.[23] It has developed in both the public and private sectors.

10–038   In essence, family mediation in the United Kingdom started in the late 1970s in the public sector with the courts and voluntary services providing mediation (then called conciliation) primarily for children's issues. District judges (then called registrars) and court welfare officers mainly provided court services.[24] The voluntary services, working largely but not exclusively alongside the courts, were similarly geared in the main to child issues.

10–039   Most voluntary services were, and currently still are, affiliated to National Family Mediation (NFM).[25] Initially under their 1983 Code of Practice, property and financial issues could be discussed in outline in mediation only where these were inextricably linked with issues relating to children; otherwise they were to be referred to solicitors. Over the years, many of these voluntary services moved to offering all-issues mediation though many mediators in these services still primarily deal with children issues only.

10–040   In England and Wales, the development of conciliation services in the courts has been uneven. A conciliation scheme has been operating in the

---

[21]*Cutts v. Head* [1984] Ch. 290 at 306.

[22]See, *e.g.* the views of Gwynn Davis in *Partisans and Mediators: The Resolution of Divorce Disputes* (Oxford, Clarendon Press, 1988) and of Prof. Owen Fiss.

[23]See for example *Divorce Reform: A Guide for Lawyers and Mediators* by Bishop *et al.* (1996); *Family Mediation* by Lisa Parkinson (1997); *Mediation in Family Disputes* by Marian Roberts (1997); and "Family Mediation" by Janet Walker in *Rethinking Disputes: the Mediation Alternative* edited by Dr Julie Macfarlane (1997).

[24]By a Registrar's Direction dated July 28, 1986, if conciliation fails "any report which is ordered must be made by an officer who did not act as a conciliator."

[25]Previously called the National Family Conciliation Council and the National Association of Family Mediation and Conciliation Services.

Principal Registry of the Family Division in London since January 1, 1983. It was modified by a Practice Direction of October 18, 1991 to reflect the changes brought about by the Children Act 1989. It provides that when an application is made to the court for a residence or contact order under section 8 of the Children Act, such application must be referred for conciliation. The leave of the court may be sought to bypass conciliation in appropriate circumstances. Where the application is for a prohibited steps or specific issue order, it is to be referred for conciliation only if the applicant so requests. The district judge may refer a summons for wardship to conciliation where orders under section 8 are sought.

The procedure for conciliation in the Principal Registry is set out in the **10–041** October 1991 Practice Direction. Parties and their legal advisers having conduct of the cases are required to attend. The issues are outlined to the district judge and a welfare officer, and the couple may move to a private room with the welfare officer to try to reach agreement. All such discussions are privileged. Children of nine years of age or over should be brought to the conciliation appointment. If one child is over nine, younger children may also attend. If a conciliation is successful, appropriate orders may be made; if not, the district judge will give directions for the hearing; and that district judge and court welfare officer will not be further involved in that application. Currently, mediation by the court deals with children's issues only. Issues involving finance and property are referred to outside mediation bodies. **10–042**

The concept of dealing in mediation with all issues, not just child-related, was developed in a pilot scheme undertaken by a small group of practitioners. This led to the establishment in 1988 of the Family Mediators Association (FMA) which primarily served the private sector. Its membership comprised family lawyers and counsellors, psychotherapists, social workers and other professionals working with couples or families. **10–043**

Other mediation organisations subsequently entered the field. These include the Solicitors' Family Law Association (SFLA), whose main objective is the encouragement of sensitive, efficient and economic handling of family issues. It offers a family mediation training and practice programme. Other groups such as the British Association of Lawyer Mediators (BALM), LawWise, Professional Development and Training (PDT) and the Academy of Experts similarly offer lawyer mediators training and practice support. Solicitor mediators are supported by the Law Society, which has developed recommended standards of training and a Code of Practice for solicitors who practise as family mediators, and which has committed itself to maintaining standards and regulating the practice of mediation by its members.[26]

The distinction between court, voluntary and private mediation blurs to **10–044** some extent, because all family mediation processes in England and Wales follow broadly similar principles and Codes of Practice,[27] though some

---

[26]See paras 21–014 *et seq.* for further information about the Law Society's interest and involvement in mediation.

[27]Two main Codes of Practice are in use in England and Wales. (See Appendix II.) The U.K. College of Family Mediators has created one, the Law Society the other, adopted by the SFLA. There is much overlap between the two, but the Law Society's Code is geared to cover the practice and ethical requirements of solicitors.

details of practice and theory may vary. Distinctions blur further because voluntary services will act for private clients, and many private mediators will work on a legally-aided basis, to offer mediation to the widest possible public.

Voluntary or mandatory

10–045   Referral to mediation is prescribed by the court in certain circumstances, though the mandatory nature of this is blunted by the fact that parties may decline to attend and cannot be compelled to do so. Even if parties do attend the mediation, however, there can be no compulsion on them to reach an agreement, and there is no coercion. However, where parties are legally aided, the failure to use mediation effectively may affect their entitlement to receive funding for any further proceedings.[28]

10–046   All family mediation, voluntary or mandatory, will only continue as long as the parties wish it; and the parties must be allowed in any mediation to end the process when they wish. Mandatory mediation can only mean making acceptance of the process mandatory, and not the acceptance of any proposed resolution.

Sole or anchor mediation and co-mediation[29]

10–047   As in other fields, mediators can work as sole mediators or together with another as co-mediators. Within family co-mediation, further choices exist. A lawyer may work with a professional from a different discipline, experienced in couple and family dynamics. This model was originally adopted by the FMA, and is still one of the FMA's and SFLA's ways of working. Another option is for two lawyers to work together, ideally one of either gender. This model has been initiated by the SFLA as an occasional alternative to its main model of sole mediation.

10–048   If neither co-mediator is a family lawyer, the mediators refer to lawyers in one of a number of different possible ways, such as bringing in a solicitor for a particular session, or having a solicitor as an occasional consultant.[30]

10–049   The idea of "anchor mediation" evolved to allow one mediator to see the couple initially and to bring in a co-mediator later, if necessary. However, someone brought in after the process has started suffers various disadvantages. He or she enters an established dynamic as an "outsider", may be perceived as some kind of "expert" which is not necessarily help ful, and does not have all the necessary information. It may also raise questions for the couple about the initial mediator's ability to cope with the process.[31]

10–050   Family co-mediators must have regard to ethical, organisational and

---

[28]See s. 29 of the Family Law Act 1996. See also "No Legal Aid Without Mediation—Section 29" by Andy King in Fam. Law 1998, 28, 331.

[29]See the general discussion on this subject at paras 7–080–088.

[30]This raises issues about the solicitor's ethical responsibility. Is it to both parties, with their different interests? If it is to the mediator or the mediation service, on what basis and information is it provided? What is the couple told about the consultant's role? Solicitors understanding this role may wish to have their responsibilities and position clarified by the mediation service, and be guided by the Law Society.

[31]It might help for the mediator to indicate at the first enquiry that he or she generally mediates alone but that he or she might later suggest bringing in a co-mediator if that seems advisable.

insurance considerations. Where they belong to the same organisation, rules are likely to exist regulating co-mediation between members. They may be covered by a group insurance policy (as in FMA) or by their respective professional indemnity policies (as in SFLA) or perhaps by individual policies.

Where mediators from different family mediation organisations wish to co-mediate, there has to be an understanding as to whose Code of Practice is to apply, which practice documents and procedures will be used for that mediation, and what insurance arrangements are in place so that both mediators are properly covered. These principles should be agreed between the main family mediation organisations, so that their members can co-mediate without having to negotiate these matters individually.

10–051

Lawyers and rights in family mediation

Some mediators have an uneasy relationship with the question of rights and the role of lawyers in family mediation.

10–052

- All organisations accept that couples have rights which they are not expected to give up just because they choose to enter the mediation forum. They negotiate "in the shadow of the law".[32] Yet there is no consensus about how to ensure that mediators properly handle the question of rights within the mediation process, or indeed whether they should do so at all.[33]

- Mediation organisations differ as to the perception of lawyer mediators. Some consider that the fact that they are lawyers should be made clear to the couples. Others consider that professional disciplinary backgrounds are irrelevant to the couple and that mediation is effectively a new profession.[34]

- All organisations accept that the ultimate professional responsibility for a party's acceptance of settlement terms lies with that party's individual lawyer, yet in many models parties' lawyers are excluded

---

[32] In the sense that they can leave mediation and seek to establish and enforce their rights in the legal process. See n. 10 above.

[33] Janet Walker, in her *Report to the Fourth European Conference on Family Law* (1998) says that most family mediators appear to share a common set of principles. These include party responsibility for formulating their own agreements "based on their own circumstances, with an emphasis not on rights and wrongs but on establishing a workable solution". The concept of "rights" here could be ambiguously interpreted. Party responsibility is paramount and "rights and wrongs" as in past conduct are not the main focus. However, dividing capital equitably and fixing maintenance may not be possible for the couple to agree without some reference to rights. Different principles may apply where the marriage was long or short, or where parties made significantly different contributions, or where other material factors exist.

[34] Some regard mediation as "a distinct and autonomous professional activity" (Marian Roberts in the Summer 1997 issue of *Family Mediation Gazette*, the official journal of the U.K. College of Family Mediators). The U.K. College has, however, indicated that solicitors may mediate as part of their legal practices if they do so in a different role from their traditional advisory one. The Law Society of England and Wales and the SFLA see mediation as part of the professional activity of a lawyer or any other professional, to be conducted under appropriate ethical rules and Codes. All agree that it needs to be conducted differently from the lawyer's traditional advisory role.

from the mediation process and their interventions, however potentially constructive, are not encouraged or welcomed.[35]

10–053 There is a consensus between mediators of all disciplines, including lawyers, that rights should not dominate the mediation process. It is generally accepted that mediators should not advise parties on their rights or try to indicate what the outcome might be if litigated in the courts. Mediators should also not direct the parties towards any particular outcome, but may provide even-handed legal and other information to assist couples in making informed decisions.[36]

10–054 Some lawyer mediators inform couples if the settlement terms they are proposing fall outside the parameters that a court might approve.[37]

10–055 Lawyers may be involved in the mediation process:

- *As a preliminary information provider.* Under the Family Law Act, preliminary information was to be provided to parties about the alternative processes available to them, particularly mediation, counselling and the legal process.[38] People of different backgrounds, including solicitors, were able to do this. Following the abandonment of information meetings on a statutory basis, solicitors will continue to provide information to their clients about mediation and other resources, as part of their advisory function.

- *As a mediator.* Family lawyers have knowledge of law and procedure, and experience of working with family issues and negotiation. They can provide information without influencing couples towards any particular outcome or advising. Those with a directive approach will have to "unlearn" this through mediation training. Their skills can then be reassembled in a non-directive way that recognises and respects the couple's autonomy.

- *As a lawyer advising either party engaged in the mediation.* They have many possible functions. They can provide information and advice on process and substance, assist with financial disclosure, review and advise on settlement proposals and deal with any formalities to implement the terms. Parties' solicitors might also participate directly in the mediation, for example in caucusing sessions.[39] They might also communicate with one another parallel with the mediation, in a way that is sensitive to the mediation.

---

[35] *e.g.* Paul Foster describing "The Lawyer's Role Alongside Mediation" in the *Directory and Handbook of the U.K. College of Family Mediators* 1997/98 refers explicitly to " ... the lawyer's role during, but *outside* the mediation process." (Foster's emphasis).

[36] This is accepted in Principle III(x) attached to the Council of Europe's Recommendation No. R (98) 1 of Family Mediation (1998).

[37] See para. 10–027.

[38] S. 8 of the Family Law Act 1996 required parties to attend an information meeting before filling a statement for divorce. The information meetings were, however, said to be unsuccessful (though reports on this varied). In the event, the Lord Chancellor has abandoned the concept and practice of information meetings.

[39] Parties' solicitors do not commonly participate in the mediation process, but there is no reason why they should not do so where the couple and the mediator think that it would be helpful. It can help to cut through negotiations and avoid delay. As to solicitors' role in caucusing, see paras 8–095 and 19–092.

- *As a lawyer advising the mediator.*[40] The details and implications of this role need to be clear and specific.[41] The solicitor could not, directly or indirectly, advise both parties, as this is precluded by the Law Society's ethical rules. Nor could the solicitor participate in the mediation except as a mediator. The role would be one of meeting mediators for general discussion from time to time, and of having ad hoc discussions as required.[42]

Involving children in mediation

There is no unanimity of practice as to involving children directly in the mediation process. Mediators recognise that there can sometimes be advantages in doing so, but that there are also concerns and potential difficulties that need careful consideration. **10–056**

If children attend a mediation meeting, they might do so together with their parents, or they might see the mediator alone, perhaps prior to a joint meeting with parents. Where a meeting with children is considered appropriate, the mediator must ensure that the parents are agreed about the objectives of the meeting and how it will take place. Everyone should be properly prepared for it, and issues such as confidentiality must be considered and resolved. Although their wishes and feelings are being established, the children should not be asked (or believe that they are being asked) to make any decisions about any issues. Parental authority must not be undermined. The nature of the communications with the children will need to be appropriate to their ages. **10–057**

Many mediation organisations and individual mediators take the view that a mediator should not bring children physically into the mediation process unless there is a good reason to do so and the mediator has had specialised training in working with children. They consider that the disadvantages and risks of working with children, especially without specialised skills, might outweigh any possible benefits.[43] Where, however, the mediator has those special skills, the children and parents may benefit from the children's views being heard and reflected to the parents in a thoughtful and sensitive way.[44] **10–058**

---

[40] NFM uses "legal consultants" to help non-lawyer mediators to understand areas of law that may be less familiar to them, such as pensions or inheritance, as well as the general way in which divorce law operates.

[41] The propriety of this role will depend on the functions of the solicitor and the way in which the solicitor's role is explained to the couple. See n. 30 above.

[42] The solicitor has an educative function, reacting to issues identified by the mediators. The solicitor cannot be accountable for the mediator's decisions or standards of practice. There is concern among some lawyer mediators that mediators who are not lawyers might inadvertently overlook aspects that lawyer consultants, not present in the process, might not have any way of picking up, and which might unwittingly affect the rights of either party.

[43] There is a consensus that children's views and feelings should be taken into account. The question is how this can best be achieved. There is a strong view that parents should do this themselves, with professional support if required. If the parents cannot deal with this, then counselling or family therapy may be helpful. Marian Roberts in *Mediation in Family Disputes* (2nd ed., 1997) analyses the arguments for and against direct involvement of children in mediation. She says (at p. 146) that while children may need help (*e.g.* through counselling) in coping with the separation of their parents, a mediator should not do this.

[44] In *Family Mediation* (1997) Lisa Parkinson considers reasons for and against involving children in mediation. She concludes that consulting children to establish their views, feelings and needs can be too limited and that there is also a function in conveying reassuring messages to

10–059   The conciliation scheme in the Principal Registry of the Family Division specifically provides for children to be brought to the conciliation appointment.[45]

10–060   To some extent, this question reflects a wider debate. One view is that parents are the best people to make decisions for their children and that professionals should not intrude on that process. The other view is that parents should be supported in their decision-making, but that at times, for example of stress, they may need some help in doing so. In both views, there is agreement that parents should be left with the ultimate responsibility for such decisions, except where outside agencies need to be involved, for example, in the case of child abuse.

10–061   Other aspects of this debate go beyond the scope of this book. They are contained in other works and articles on this subject.[46]

Reconciliation implications

10–062   In the years before 1978, when conciliation services first began to be established in the United Kingdom, conciliation commonly took the form of "reconciliation", that is, an attempt by the parties to re-establish their relationship. This historical background and the similarity of terminology has led to there being some confusion between the terms "conciliation" and "reconciliation".

10–063   Apparently, none of the mediation models in the United Kingdom or elsewhere is used as a vehicle specifically to promote reconciliation by assisting the couple to restore their relationship once it has broken down. It may be that if parties find that their communications are improved and that the dynamic between them has changed, as often happens in mediation, they may wish to give their relationship another chance. This is an occasional consequence of the process, but it is not the specific object.

10–064   There is a duty to keep the possibility of reconciliation under review throughout mediation.[47] This does not create an obligation to use the mediation to try to achieve reconciliation. If the mediator considers that possibilities of reconciliation exist, this should be explored and the question of counselling might appropriately be considered.[48]

10–065   Family mediation is usually neutral in relation to reconciliation. If the

---

[45]See 10-041 above.

[46]See, *e.g.* Lisa Parkinson, *Conciliation in Separation and Divorce* (1986) and *Family Mediation* (1997); Marian Roberts *Mediation in Family Disputes* (1988 and 1997); Julia Ross's article "The Scottish Scene: A Summary of Recent Development in Conciliation Throughout Scotland" in *Mediation Quarterly* No. 11, March 1986; and Donald Saposnek's article "The Value of Children in Mediation: A Cross-Culture Perspective" in *Mediation Quarterly* Vol. 8, No. 4, Summer 1991.

[47]S. 27 of the Family Law Act 1996, amending the Legal Aid Act 1988, provides that a mediator's Code (where legal aid is involved) must include such a provision. The U.K. College of Family Mediators' Code of Practice contains a provision reflecting this requirement (Para. 6.2), as does the Law Society's (s. 11.3). In both cases, the Code's provision is of general application and not limited to legally-aided cases.

[48]Emanual Plesent describes in an article "Mediation for Reconciliation" in *Mediation Quarterly* No. 21, Fall 1988, how to mediate with a raised consciousness and sensitivity towards this area. However, mediators should take care to respect the boundaries between mediation and counselling.

mediator has a private agenda of what he or she feels the parties should aim for, such as reconciliation, there is a risk of corruption of the integrity of the process. If, however, both parties specifically sought mediation to try to establish a reconciliation, that would be their agenda, and that might be a proper matter for mediation (though in practice counselling or therapy might be more appropriate).

Issues around mediating with domestic violence or abuse
A mediator is responsible for providing a safe and secure environment, **10–066** addressing power imbalances and ensuring fairness of process Most Codes of Practice also require mediators to prevent manipulative, threatening or intimidating behaviour by either party. It is thus inherent in the mediation process that it cannot take place effectively if one party conducts himself or herself in such a violent or abusive way that the process cannot be fairly or effectively carried out.

A duty also exists under section 27 of the Family Law Act 1996 (which **10–067** amends the Legal Aid Act 1988) under which mediators must comply with a Code requiring the mediator to ensure that parties participate in the process willingly and without fear of violence or harm. Any such cases are required to be identified as soon as possible.[49]

Concerns have been expressed whether mediation can protect the interests **10–068** of those who are vulnerable to abuse and threat. There is a view that an abuser and victim can never negotiate on an equal footing. There is also concern that mediation may allow an abuser to avoid accountability for his behaviour. It is essential for mediators to be sensitive to such issues, which reflect a legitimate concern about power imbalances that most mediators would share.

Mediators should be aware of the different kinds of abuse that there may **10–069** be. These obviously include direct violence, physical and sexual abuse and threatening or harassing behaviour. They also include *emotional* abuse such as ridicule and humiliation or any behaviour designed to undermine confidence or self-respect; *economic* abuse such as unilaterally closing a joint account, cutting off sources of cash or cancelling credit or bank cards; *social* abuse such as being insulting or offensive to friends, neighbours or family; and *psychological* abuse, where someone behaves subtly in a way that knowingly causes distress but which is not overtly objectionable, then dismisses the complaint as unreasonable or irrational. The last category includes for example "gaslighting", named after the film *Gaslight* where one person falsely denies his behaviour, and suggests that the other is becoming mentally disturbed.

Mediators must have a screening mechanism for identifying cases where **10–070** abusive behaviour exists that could affect the safety of a party or impact on the fairness and effectiveness of the mediation process. Screening may take place at different stages. First indications may arise in the initial phone calls which provide an opportunity for preliminary enquiry. They may then be found in the preliminary information forms that the parties send to the

---

[49] Here again, both the U.K. College of Family Mediators (Paras 4.20 and 4.21) and the Law Society (ss. 6 and 12, with commentaries) make provision in their Codes of Practice for this.

mediator, which might have direct or indirect questions to help identify abuse.

10–071   Some mediators see the parties separately at the start of the mediation, which allows individual screening to take place. They find this to be a good practice because it allows a vulnerable party to discuss abuse more easily than would be possible in a joint meeting. It does, however, raise questions about confidentiality and practicalities that need to be considered.

10–072   Others do not start with separate meetings but keep a watch for signs of abuse during the joint meetings. Mediators should be on the lookout for signs of possible violence or other abuse at all stages of the process. These may, for example, include physical signs, or the demeanour of the parties, especially where one is dominant and the other is submissive (though of course, that does not necessarily indicate abuse). Mediators must be watchful for indications that are combined with a readiness by one party to make concessions or admissions that seem inappropriate. If the mediation is started in joint session, it may be possible to move into separate meetings if indications of possible abuse arise.

10–073   Where a mediator suspects violent or abusive behaviour, direct or indirect questions could be raised to check the position. Signals or halting revelations or admissions need to be gently eased out. People who are subject to abuse will not necessarily acknowledge this: they may be afraid or ashamed to do so. If a direct approach is necessary, this might take the form of asking each party whether he or she or the other has difficulty in coping with the stressful situation in the home. They may also be asked how they handle their own or the other's anger. It is ultimately necessary to establish whether one party is afraid of the other and how that affects the ability to arrive at decisions in the mediation fairly and effectively.

10–074   While the views and feelings of individuals who do not wish to enter mediation once there has been any violence should be respected, the question of suitability for mediation may involve wider considerations including especially the following:

- *What is the severity of the abuse and in what circumstances did it occur?* There are qualitative differences between a minor one-off incident in a moment of anger and mutual provocation, and a pattern of serious and severe assaults. There is also a question as to the ability of the abuser to control his behaviour. Where, for example, an abuser is socially or emotionally dysfunctional, or suffers from alcoholism or substance abuse, mediation is most unlikely to be appropriate (unless undertaken in conjunction with counselling, therapy or treatment for the problem condition, and then only with great care).

- *Does the perpetrator admit the abuse?* If the abuser acknowledges that abuse took place (even if details are not fully agreed) it allows the mediator and the parties to consider the possibility of mediation and any conditions. If however there is a dispute of fact about whether the occurrence took place or not, then mediation is unlikely to be possible.

- *What is the genuine view of the victim of the abuse or threat in relation to the continuation of the mediation?* By ending the mediation, the mediator may force the couple into the courts, which may be the last thing that the victim wants. On the other hand, even a relatively "minor" incident may have a profound effect on someone sensitive to any such situation. The victim of abuse or threat may not be free to express a view, and therefore the mediator may not be able to establish whether a decision to continue is genuine.

- *How does the abuse relate to other power issues between the couple?* Abuse is a blatant, crude and immediate form of power imbalance between a couple. It is likely in most cases to outweigh all other kinds of power disparities. Sometimes however other power issues may re-balance the abuse.

- *Is there a risk to the victim (or the mediator) if the mediation continues?* If the mediator believes that there is a real risk of harm to the victim or the mediator, that is the strongest indication that mediation is inappropriate.

- *Could the mediation continue if parallel steps were taken to protect the victim?* The parties may be able to agree on protection for either or both of them. For example, the perpetrator may agree to give undertakings to the other or through the court not to do certain things, or perhaps may consent to an injunction being taken out, even in agreed terms.[50] It may be helpful in appropriate cases to arrange for each party to have their lawyer present in the mediation to provide support and re-balance power.

A person who has been subjected to abuse may well wish to have **10–075** independent advice on whether or not mediation should take place. Other support services, including counselling (for either or both parties) may be available. A mediator who continues with the mediation where there has been violence or abuse must remain personally non-judgmental while making it clear to both parties that domestic violence and significant abuse are not acceptable. There must be a commitment to ending them; but the mediator can nevertheless continue working impartially with the couple to help them find their solution to the issues facing them. Mediators should have regard to continuing safety issues[51] such as ensuring that couples are not left together unsupervised and that a victim of abuse is allowed to leave the mediation first. Machinery can also be established in the mediation to reduce the risk of conflict and to monitor arrangements for avoiding abusive behaviour.

---

[50] This must be properly done, and must not become an abuse of court process. There are now limitations by virtue of the Family Law Act on the giving of undertakings.

[51] See Sherri L. Schornstein's *Domestic Violence and Health Care: What Every Professional Needs to Know* (Sage Publications, 1997) at pp. 117–135. Her concerns relate to hospitals and health care institutions, but the principles are adaptable to other circumstances. See also *Domestic Violence: Picking up the Pieces* by Helen L. Conway (Lion Publishing plc, 1997) which deals with issues concerning domestic violence and outlines options available for victims.

Mediation and counselling/therapy distinguished

10–076   Family mediation is not counselling or therapy and is not likely to be muddled with either of these. The differences of aim, method, role, duration and other features have been clearly identified in many works and articles; and these differences should be clear in training and practice.[52]

10–077   However, these differences are not always understood. Working with a couple and helping them to communicate better can have a therapeutic effect. Some counsellors and therapists also work as mediators and even if they keep their roles separate, there may be a mistaken assumption that there is a connection. Furthermore, some therapy and counselling notions and terms have been usefully incorporated into mediation, such as "working within a family system", "acknowledging", "mutualising" and "reframing".[53] Some writers have commented on links that they perceive exist.[54]

10–078   Clearly there should be no hidden agenda to provide therapy or counselling for people whose contract is for family mediation; nor is it likely that properly trained family mediators will confuse these roles.

10–079   This does not mean that strategies and approaches developed in systems theory or in any other kind of therapeutic intervention should automatically be rejected for mediation. On the contrary, there is scope for different kinds of processes to learn from one another, and to be imported and adapted with sensitivity and respect. The fact that some ways of working with couples may usefully be adapted to another process does not mean that all the principles of the initial process are imported lock, stock and barrel into the latter.

Family issues other than separation and divorce

10–080   Family mediation largely covers married couples in relation to separation and divorce. That is the main focus of this Chapter. However, there are also many other kinds of issues of a family nature which it can cover, including for example:

- Issues between unmarried cohabiting couples. There is no difference in principle or process in mediating between couples who are married and those who are not, save perhaps that aspects of information gathering may need to be adapted.

---

[52] See, *e.g. Divorce Mediation* (1988) by Folberg & Milne at pp. 6–10; *Mediating Divorce* (1989) by John Haynes & Gretchen Haynes at pp. 5–9; and *Mediate your divorce* (1985) by Joan Blades at pp. 50–52. A useful table of distinctions between the roles of counsellor, therapist and family mediator is contained in *Family Mediation* (1997) by Lisa Parkinson at pp. 85–87.

[53] *e.g.* Lisa Parkinson, in *Family Mediation* (at p. 90) describes systems theory as offering "helpful ways of understanding family structures, relationships and patterns of behaviour". John & Gretchen Haynes note in *Mediating Divorce* (at p. xiii) that "the basic systems theory of family therapy is evident in John M. Haynes's work". Both Parkinson and Haynes are clear about the lines to be drawn between mediation and therapy. See, e.g. p. 9 of Haynes's work, where he says that "reorganising interpersonal dynamics is the work of a therapist, and negotiating agreement over issues is the work of a mediator".

[54] *e.g.* in *Divorce Mediation and the Legal Process* edited by Dingwall and Eekelaar, Simon Roberts (at p. 145) describes "therapeutic intervention" as one of three basic models of family mediation. In Marian Roberts's *Mediation of Family Disputes* (2nd ed.) she argues that "the assumptions, objectives and methods of these two modes of intervention [are] incompatible" and that "there also seem to be a number of hazards associated with attempts to apply family therapy approaches to mediation".

- Issues between other cohabitants including, for example, gay and lesbian couples.[55]

- Disagreements relating to family businesses. In practice this is treated as commercial mediation, with family implications, as commercial mediation processes generally lend themselves more satisfactorily to issues of this kind. Nevertheless, many of the issues and dynamics will be familiar to a family mediator.

- Issues arising from parental abduction of children.[56]

- Differences between parents and children, siblings and other family members. Although information gathering will be different from matrimonial work, all facilitation aspects will follow the same broad approach as other forms of family mediation.

Other family mediation distinctions

Although there are many fundamental points of similarity, models of family **10–081** mediation and approaches differ from one mediation organisation to another. Such differences have been outlined in this chapter where practicable, but that cannot be comprehensive. The following are some further distinctions:

- Some mediators will see each party separately for a brief discussion before meeting the couple jointly.[57] This has the advantage of allowing each party to identify areas of concern without the other present. This may also be helpful as part of a process of screening for possible domestic violence.[58] On the other hand, it has the disadvantage that even before the couple have met the mediator, he or she is having private discussions with each, which may create concerns about the mediator's ability to be impartial.[59]

- Where the issue is child-related only, mediation may take place in one lengthy session, rather than in a series of meetings.[60]

---

[55]See, *e.g.* "Mediation for Lesbian and Gay Families" by S. Bryant (1992) 9(4) M.Q. 391. See also "Gay Parents and Child Custody: A Struggle Under the Legal System" by Douglas H. McIntyre (1994) 12(2) M.Q. 135, "Mediation as an Alternative to Court for Lesbian and Gay Families: Some Thoughts on Douglas McIntyre's Article" (1995) 13(1) M.Q. 47 by Isabelle R. Gunning; and "Mediation of Children Issues When One Parent is Gay" by Alan Campbell (1996) 14(1) M.Q. 79.

[56]In the U.S., Child Find of America, Inc. has developed a programme using mediation to help prevent and resolve parental abductions. See Helen D. Millar's article "Resolving Parental Abduction: Child Find of America's Mediation Program" (1996) 13(3) M.Q. 207. The Council of Europe in its Text of Recommendation No. R (98) 1 on Family Mediation (1998) refers at para. 22 to "a body of mediators in France [that] has substantial experience of mediation in child abduction cases across Europe". In Principle VIII(b) it cautions that in such cases "international mediation should not be used if it would delay the prompt return of the child".

[57]See also "caucusing" at paras 8–094 *et seq.* and 10–166 *et seq.*

[58]As to the question of violence and abuse, see paras 10–066 *et seq.*

[59]Those who use this procedure generally express satisfaction with it. Those who do not use it express concern about it.

[60]Single session mediation may be suitable for a single issue such as contact. However, it is inappropriate for all-issues mediation. People need time to absorb and consider ideas and changes, and time is invariably needed between sessions to exchange information and reflect on developments and proposals.

- Some mediators will hold separate meetings (caucuses) with the parties where they feel that these would be helpful. Other mediators do not do so.

It will be seen that family mediation, particularly in relation to separation and divorce, has a range of organisational and methodological variations.

4. THE STAGES OF FAMILY MEDIATION

10–082 The following outline, using the ten stages set out in Chapter 8, will reflect various of the methods and approaches, rather than one distinct model.[61]

Phase One: Before mediation

Stage 1: Engaging the parties in the mediation forum

10–083 The first stage of family mediation involves helping parties to decide whether mediation is likely to be appropriate and suitable for them.[62] They may prefer to seek counselling, individually or jointly, or to use the traditional legal process.

10–084 Information is likely to be provided by family lawyers, mediators, counsellors, therapists, mediation bodies, Citizens' Advice Bureaux and other referral agencies.

10–085 Family mediation organisations and individual mediators, supported by the media, have been active in raising public awareness of the availability of mediation for family issues. This is done through the publication of articles, newsletters and brochures; the holding of conferences, seminars, workshops and training courses; radio, television, newspaper and magazine articles, reports and programmes; advertising in journals and directories; and in other ways.

10–086 Enquiries made at this initial stage will generally be dealt with through a range of methods. These may include a personal meeting, telephone discussion, e-mail communication or providing the inquirer with written explanatory material. Usually mediators will assist the inquirer in engaging the other party if required. For example, they may furnish information or written particulars of the process to the willing party to pass on to the other, or they may explain the process to the other, in writing or by telephone. However, they might not ordinarily initiate a call to a party who has not indicated a wish to have such information.

10–087 Individual mediation bodies commonly have brochures and other

---

[61] It is generally based on the processes used by the Family Mediators Association, the Solicitors' Family Law Association and PDT.

[62] This may be viewed as a stage of mediation, *e.g.* s. 26 of the Family Law Act 1996, in amending s. 13A of the Legal Aid Act 1988, defines "mediation" (for the purpose of legal aid) as including "steps taken by a mediator in any case (a) in determining whether to embark on mediation; and (b) in preparing for mediation....". Most issues and parties are potentially suitable for mediation, except where domestic violence or abuse makes it impossible to contemplate mediation. However, some parties may be unable to negotiate with one another under any circumstances and they would be unsuitable.

information packs that they can make available to inquirers. They may also advise their members how to respond to requests for information. The U.K. College of Family Mediators has as one of its main objectives the advancement of public education about family mediation; and the Law Society of England and Wales is committed to a policy of educating its members about mediation.

Ideally, a trained mediator should deal with the initial inquiry, who can **10–088** respond patiently, sensitively and in an informed way to specific inquiries about the process. Mediators who act as contact points for mediation groups develop the experience of dealing with inquiries, and become more familiar with this process, which requires particular empathy and skills: people inquiring may be anxious, distressed and uncertain about the process or the best way to proceed.

If it is not possible to have a trained mediator deal with preliminary **10–089** inquiries, it would be advantageous for the person concerned to have some basic training or understanding of the process. In any event, he or she should refer any particular inquiries to a mediator to ensure that accurate information is given to inquirers.

Some mediation organisations provide specifically for an "intake" session, **10–090** in which the process is explained, preliminary information obtained, and questions answered. This is a specific requirement for legally aided cases.[63] There is a view that an initial session should where possible commence the process substantively. That is the best way for the couple to understand the process, and is more likely to be helpful and cost-effective. It might be frustrating and ineffective if the initial session was limited only to preliminary information. Consequently, apart from legally-aided cases, intake sessions are not very common, unless they lead straight into substantive mediation.

Some private sector mediators offer a short introductory meeting as an **10–091** option for couples to discuss the process, seek information and provide preliminary particulars. If the couple want to convert that into a substantive opening session, they may do so.

Whatever intake procedure is followed, it is particularly important at this **10–092** stage for both parties to appreciate the impartiality of the mediator. There may be a tendency for a party who did not initiate the mediation to suspect and perhaps reject the idea simply because it comes from the other, and the mediator or agency may need to help that party understand the process and the integrity of the mediator.

The substance of the issues should not be discussed with either party **10–093** making inquiries at this stage. Discussion should be limited to explaining the nature of the process and dealing with practical questions such as cost, timetable, procedure and arrangements.

Both parties should confirm that they wish to proceed with the mediation. **10–094** Most mediators would be reluctant to commence the process merely based on one party making the arrangements, without hearing from the other. That is

---

[63] The Legal Aid Board has issued rules and guidelines for the practice of family mediation. The mediator must establish that the parties feel safe together and that the legally-aided party is financially eligible.

not purely a matter of form. The process is more likely to be (and to be seen to be) even-handed and to be more effective where both have given a clear commitment to it, rather than where one has acted as a mouthpiece for both. There is also a risk of misunderstanding where the mediator has only spoken to one person.

Stage 2: Obtaining commitment and agreeing mediation rules

10–095 It might seem self-evident that mediation can only take place if both parties voluntarily enter into the process. In the private sector, that is indeed the position. It is, however, somewhat different where either party is legally aided, or where court rules require the parties to undertake mediation. In these cases, parties are expected to participate in the mediation, notwithstanding that there can be no compulsion on them to arrive at an agreed outcome.

10–096 Where mediation arises as a consequence of court rules or practice requiring them to seek mediation,[64] the question arises whether they will have "contracted" to mediate, and if so, on what terms. To avoid doubt or misunderstanding about this, it is desirable to ask them to make their contract explicit, by signing a prescribed form of agreement, which would effectively be based on the Code of Practice of the mediator. If that is impracticable, then alternatively both parties should be furnished with written terms of mediation, which would be likely to bind them to those terms by implication.

10–097 In private mediation, the notion of a contract to mediate is essential. It may be written or oral or perhaps implied by the act of attending the mediation. A written contract may not be essential where there are limited issues, for example relating to disagreements about children. In all-issues mediation, it is good practice to have a written agreement between the parties and the mediators or the mediation agency recording the terms under which the mediation is undertaken.[65]

10–098 Such a contract need not be formal or daunting in style. It may be in the form of a Letter of Agreement sent to each party before the first meeting, which sets out the ground rules of the process as well as practical matters such as charging rates. This document is discussed at the first meeting and is signed as a contract between the parties and the mediator.

10–099 The written contract can indicate the main aspects of the relevant Code of Practice either by reference or perhaps by informally incorporating the relevant provisions. It records matters such as confidentiality (for example, excluding this where anyone is apparently at risk of significant harm), privilege, payment and other practical aspects including the ground rules for the process. It requires each party to give a considered commitment to the mediation and to provide full information relevant to their financial circumstances. It informs the couple that the process will be conducted in a

---

[64] The Family Proceedings (Amendment No. 2) Rules 1997 (S.I. 1997 No. 1056) inserted new rules 2.71 to 2.77 into the Family Proceedings Rules 1991. Para. (1)(d)(iv) of r. 2.74 provides that the district judge may in an application for ancillary relief where the Ancillary Relief Pilot Scheme applies direct that "the case be adjourned for out of court mediation or private negotiation . . .". This scheme will be applied nationally from June 2000.
[65] See sub-para. 6.3 of the Code of Practice of the U.K. College of Family Mediators (1997/98) (at para A2–101 below). See also s. 4.1 of the Law Society's Code of Practice for family mediators (1998) (at para. A2–065 below).

professional and business-like way. It can clarify the mediator's professional capacity, for example, if a solicitor does not act in that professional capacity but only as a mediator.

In the absence of a written contract, there is a risk that the parties may misunderstand or inaccurately remember the basis on which the mediation is undertaken. This could be particularly unfortunate if a court subsequently dealing with any issue wishes to be informed about matters covered or thought to have been covered in the mediation process or by the mediation agreement.

10–100

Stage 3: Preliminary communications and preparation

At this stage, the mediator obtains preliminary information from the parties, commonly in a form that is sent to the parties. This form may include personal information, details about children, initial data about finances, particulars of pending proceedings and legal representation, the matters that each wishes to deal with in the mediation, and other details.[66] Usually this form is sent to each party for completion and return before the initial session. A comparison of both parties' forms will assist the mediator in preparing for the initial session and identifying issues on a preliminary basis. It is not uncommon to make it clear that confidences will not be maintained, so preparing the parties for an exchange of forms if appropriate. However, it is not essential for the forms to be physically exchanged: the mediator would though be likely to inform both parties at the first meeting of the general thrust of the forms, and to try to resolve any discrepancies.

10–101

During this phase, practical arrangements are usually made with the parties for the initial meeting, and any procedural questions that they may have can be answered. This is generally done on the telephone. The frequency and length of the mediation meetings will usually be discussed with the parties in advance. Some models may involve one or two meetings, particularly where issues concerning children are exclusively or primarily required to be dealt with. In all-issues mediation, five or six sessions of one-and-a-half to two hours each are common. These may take place at agreed intervals, commonly fortnightly. Where the issues and financial circumstances are complex and/or the parties have particular difficulty in reaching agreement, more meetings may be needed.

10–102

Couples are not usually asked to make written submissions outlining their claims and the issues. It is also generally unhelpful to ask them to provide documents in advance, which if prematurely sought could meet with resistance or misunderstanding.

10–103

Where either party is legally represented, there may be communications with the respective solicitors at this stage. Mediators would not want to discuss the substantive issues with the solicitors, but rather to focus on procedure and timetable. Sometimes a meeting between the mediator and the solicitors might be a helpful initial step, if this was what both parties wanted. This could usefully allow the solicitors to satisfy themselves as to the aspects that the mediation was going to cover, could identify any reserved issues,

10–104

---

[66] Legally-aided mediation may require further information to be obtained including enquiries to establish financial eligibility for legal aid.

could clarify the role of the lawyers, and could generally enable procedural matters to be aired. An initial meeting with lawyers is not common in family mediation in the United Kingdom, though it sometimes occurs. It is accepted in some other jurisdictions.[67]

10–105   Once an appointment has been made, the mediator would ordinarily write to the parties confirming the venue and details and sending the preliminary information form and draft Agreement to Mediate if this had not already been done. The mediator would then make the practical arrangements to ensure that a suitable room was booked and that ample time was allowed for the session. The mediator is now ready for the substantive phase of the process.

Phase Two: During the substantive mediation

Stage 4: Establishing the venue and meeting the parties

10–106   The environment in which family mediation ideally takes place is a room with a sympathetic but business-like ambience. As this will often be an office, there may not be much scope for softening the feeling of the room, apart from removing files and perhaps having pleasant pictures, flowers or plants.

10–107   The reception arrangements should ensure that the mediator is notified as soon as each party arrives, so that they are not left along together for any length of time (and where tensions are high or there is any risk of confrontation or abuse, not at all). Some mediators have two separate reception areas so that where appropriate, couples could be kept apart at this sensitive and sometimes volatile stage. Few practitioners have that facility, so that if there is any suggestion of possible abusive conflict, the first party to arrive might be shown straight into the mediation room while the other waits in the reception area.[68] Couples will usually be on their own, without legal representatives.

10–108   As to seating arrangements, where no table or only a small coffee table is used, the couple will usually face the mediator, with both chairs turned slightly inwards.[69] Where the mediation includes financial issues, it is more practical and business-like for the parties to be seated around a conference table, which they can use for their papers.

10–109   The mediator should have all necessary equipment and material in the

---

[67] *e.g.* Landau, Bartorelli & Mesbur say in their *Family Mediation Handbook* (Butterworths, 1987) that in Canada "where both parties are represented at the outset of mediation, it is desirable to hold a meeting with both counsel present prior to beginning the mediation..." (at p. 48). In the United States, lawyers do not usually meet with the mediator. However, in a 1994 survey of family lawyers in Florida, a relatively small responding sample indicated that over 55% attended some mediation sessions with their clients, and that 14.8% only did so for the first session to satisfy themselves about the mediator's training, skills and experience. ("Why Attorneys Attend Mediation Sessions" by Susan W. Harrell, (1995) 12(4) M.Q.)

[68] Few private sector mediators have more than one reception area, so it is ironic that the Legal Aid Board expects mediators undertaking legally-aided mediation to have such facilities. This must be seen as an aspiration rather than a prerequisite.

[69] See the general discussion about seating and personal space at paras 8–058–059.

room. This may include a flip-chart and marker, calculator, tissues, diary and reference material such as information and tax tables.

Offering tea or coffee at the beginning of the meeting can help to relax the couple, and make the process slightly less formal. Doing so by arrangement part way into the meeting, when it can serve as a natural break, can relieve any tension that may have built up. **10–110**

The mediator will welcome the parties, acknowledge the forms that they have sent in, and will usually explain the ground rules for the mediation, especially concerning privilege and confidentiality. The Agreement to Mediate will be discussed, any questions answered, and it will be signed. If the mediator thinks that the use of first names would be useful, which it commonly is, this should be checked and agreed with the parties. **10–111**

If the mediation is undertaken on the basis that no agreement arrived at by the couple in the mediation is to be binding until they have both had an opportunity to take independent legal advice at the end of the process, that will be explained and agreed. Most parties understand the benefits of this, but some are concerned in case the independent solicitors try to undermine the proposed resolution. They can be reassured that solicitors are not generally obstructive, and that when matters need to be referred to independent lawyers, there will be a discussion to assist them both in dealing with that aspect. **10–112**

Stage 5: Establishing the issues and setting the agenda

In most divorce mediation, parties are not ordinarily asked to make presentations of their respective positions, as parties in civil or commercial mediation would be. These could well be contentious and inflammatory. Bearing in mind that the couple may be finding it difficult to meet together, and may need help in managing the conflict between them, any decision to focus on their differences, especially in a presentational form, could well be counter-productive. **10–113**

The mediator does not usually seek the reasons for the breakdown of the marriage, though these may be established at some stage if this becomes relevant.[70] The dynamic between the couple and the factors leading to their differences often become apparent during the course of the mediation. **10–114**

In some models the mediator meets each party to hear their views without the other one present. In legally-aided cases, there might be a separate intake meeting with the parties before the commencement of the substantive mediation. Sometimes the intake meeting might become substantive. **10–115**

The mediator establishes the parties' issues in a number of ways. They may briefly be mentioned or inferred during the initial phone inquiry. Then parties may be invited to say in the preliminary information form what they hope the mediation will achieve. This should give a clear indication of the likely issues. **10–116**

The main occasion for establishing the issues will be when the mediator first meets the couple. The mediator will elicit the issues from the parties and **10–117**

---

[70]See however the references to transformative mediation at paras 1–040 and 21–132–134. Some mediators, whether or not they accept the value of future-focus, place value on parties being able to talk about past issues that have been important to them in forming present attitudes.

establish an agenda, either formally or as an informal guide. The issues will then be prioritised according to the preference of the parties.

10–118   If the mediator has more than one meeting with the parties, which is usual, then it is good practice to check the agenda with them on each occasion. It is common for new issues to emerge or for priorities to change.

Stage 6: Information gathering

10–119   The culture of family mediation is especially different from other kinds of mediation in the information-gathering stage for a number of reasons:

- There is in the United Kingdom a policy of information disclosure in the family field generally. In particular, financial arrangements are not normally made without complete reciprocal disclosure of financial means and circumstances.

- A court asked to make an order on financial aspects will ordinarily require an outline of the parties' respective financial positions to be provided. If the court reviewing a proposed order has any query it may decline to make the order until having clarified and resolved any such query.

- Any financial arrangements may be vulnerable to being set aside if a material non-disclosure or misstatement is subsequently discovered.

- Information gathering may be particularly important to enable the couple to make informed decisions about their futures and those of any children.

- In the nature of the relationship between couples, it is not uncommon for there to be a discrepancy of knowledge about finances between them, necessitating a redress through the information exchange stage.

10–120   Mediation is not a soft option so far as disclosure is concerned. Couples are expected to make the same full disclosure as they would in traditional adversarial proceedings. Mediators cannot undertake to verify such disclosure, though they will ordinarily provide the opportunities for such disclosures to be discussed and tested. They may mention ways in which verification can, if required, take place, for example by the production of documentary evidence or through the couple's own solicitors or on oath, as may be appropriate.

10–121   There are different kinds of information in family matters. Some will be factual, such as facts about the marriage, children and financial circumstances. Some will be technical, such as valuations of property, insurances or pensions, tax implications and legal considerations. Some may underlie the observable facts, such as the relationship between the parties and with their children, the underlying emotions of the parties and their respective aspirations, expectations, wants and needs. Inevitably parties will agree on some information, and not other, and there will be views and perceptions that differ.

10–122   One area where a particularly structured approach is taken to information gathering is that of finance. There are different ways of gathering this information; but whichever method is used, it is essential that this should be carefully and effectively garnered and pooled.

Parties are ordinarily each given a form of financial memorandum which **10–123** embodies an extensive questionnaire covering all aspects of their financial affairs in considerable detail.[71] This is completed at home and returned to the mediator. The information which each party furnishes in completing this form is jointly considered, displayed on a flip-chart[72] and used as the basis for any amplification or particularisation that may be required, and for the further discussions and negotiations that will then take place.

Information may continue to emerge throughout the mediation. Facts, such **10–124** as those concerning finance or family circumstances, may be supplemented, amplified and amended as the process continues. Obtaining underlying information, and data gathering generally, are part of a continuing and unfolding process. Details or documents which are not initially available may come to hand; valuations may be obtained to replace estimates; assets may be sold or acquired; circumstances may change; underlying factors may surface. As in other fields of activity, the mediator also obtains information through the observation of non-verbal communications.

Care must be taken that the parties do not make substantive decisions **10–125** before sufficient information is available. This does not mean until total and complete particularisation is achieved. There is no reason why discussions cannot take place while the information is being collected together, and preliminary directions and options can be examined parallel to the information-gathering process.

Stage 7: Managing and facilitating discussions and negotiations

This is the substantive stage of mediation. The mediator helps the parties to **10–126** communicate with one another and to negotiate acceptable terms. This is usually done with the couple in joint sessions.

This stage has a number of facets, which may be summarised as follows:[73] **10–127**

Option development

One of the mediator's primary functions is to help parties to identify and **10–128** develop options for dealing with their issues, and then to narrow these down to those that both would find acceptable.

If the issue under discussion appertains to the future of the relationship, **10–129** the options might, for example, be to continue as they are now, or to stay together while seeking professional help such as counselling, or to separate temporarily while doing so, or to plan long-term separation or a divorce.

If the couple are considering a separation, the practicalities and **10–130** consequences of this may be explored and fully discussed. This may include, for example, who will leave the matrimonial home and when; and what

---

[71] Under the Ancillary Relief Pilot Scheme, a standard disclosure form (Form E) is used in divorce practice. That form is now used by some mediation organisations in the interests of standardising disclosure in both the traditional process and mediation (with some changes to headings and endings). It is likely to be increasingly widely used in mediation.

[72] For the use of a flip-chart, see para. 8–083. Also, electronic screens may now replace flip-charts and facilitate copying of data.

[73] Though these are used extensively in this stage, they are not peculiar to this phase but will arise throughout the mediation.

interim arrangements will be made about the children, finance and any other matters.

10–131   Where housing arrangements are being considered, the mediator might help the couple to explore a range of possibilities. For example, the family home may be retained or sold (if it is owned). If retained, the options may include either party remaining in it, and in that event, either indefinitely or for a limited period. There are options as to the nature of the limitation. If it is sold, there will be options for dealing with the proceeds of sale to enable both parties to acquire new housing.

10–132   If the issues relate to children, different parenting possibilities can be explored. These do not have to be limited by the legal concepts of "residence" and "contact". Other options for each having proper time and good communications with the children may be considered. Parents usually share common concerns about the well-being of their children, and it can help to focus on this and to acknowledge the mutuality of these concerns. It can also help to establish that neither parent wishes to exclude the other. Quite often, as parents start to acknowledge one another's parenting, even if they can no longer remain together as partners, anxieties ease and a freer and more flexible discussion can take place.

10–133   Whatever issues are being discussed, the generation of options is a freeing exercise. Options would usually be put forward by the parties, through brainstorming[74] or in the course of discussing possibilities generally. They need not, however, be limited to the parties' ideas: the mediator can add to the options (and indeed sometimes has to do so) provided that the mediator's options are not seen by the parties as recommendations.

Providing legal and other information

10–134   All family mediators agree that their role includes some element of providing an educative function for the parties.[75] There seems little doubt that mediators can provide some kinds of information, though individual mediators differ as to the proper nature and extent of such information.

10–135   Information provided by the mediator can often help the couple. A line must, however, be drawn when that information becomes "advice", which is not an acceptable part of the mediation process. Similarly, legal information may be acceptable whereas legal advice would not be.[76] The following principles may be helpful in considering the distinctions between legal information and advice:

- Family mediation does not try to anticipate what a court would order, but allows parties to consider other factors and values that they feel

---

[74]See paras 8–102–104.

[75]The U.K. College of Family Mediators in its 1998/99 *Director* says (at p. A139) that "information giving involves maintaining a relationship of impartiality with the client(s). It involves setting out information as a resource without recommending which course of action/ option to choose".

[76]See the Law Society Code of Practice Commentary to Section 1 (at para A2–052 below) which distinguishes between legal advice and legal information. The U.K. College of Family Mediators in its 1998/99 *Directory* says (at p. A139) that "advice giving is inseparable from a partisan relationship with the client. It includes evaluation and the recommendation of a particular course (or courses) of action."

are relevant and important. Rights are relevant but constitute only one of a number of factors to take into account.[77]

- A couple may agree on the principles and values applicable to their circumstances without focusing on the law. However, where they hold differing views, they may wish to be guided by the principles that a court might apply. General principles would be regarded as proper information that can be given to them by the mediator; but if the mediator tries to anticipate what a court would order in their particular circumstances, that would be advice not information, and would not be proper, non-evaluative mediation practice.

- Some models provide for the parties to be informed if the mediator considers that their proposals fall outside the parameters that a court would be likely to approve.[78]

- Even if a couple do not inquire about their legal rights, the question arises whether they can properly arrive at a resolution without being aware of those rights. As a general principle, decisions in family mediation, as in the traditional system, should be made on an informed basis. Consequently, most if not all models of all-issues family mediation in the United Kingdom provide for parties to obtain legal advice or information in some way.

- A mediator may also, where appropriate, indicate the range of solutions that the courts have used in the past for certain kinds of issues. This may for example relate to dealing with the family home, pensions, inheritances or a business.[79]

- Parties may seek legal advice from their own lawyers during the course of the process on specific issues as necessary. In any event, most divorce mediation in the United Kingdom, at least where all-issues are involved, provides that any resolution arrived at is not binding until the parties have had the opportunity to take advice from their own legal advisers and have thereafter decided to become bound. If a party's solicitor should raise any queries or have any reservations, these can be brought back to the mediation for consideration.

It is difficult for anyone, even in the traditional process, to predict with any certainty what a court may decide in any particular case. The parameters in family work may be wide. Parties will often be thrown back upon themselves, with the assistance of the mediator, to resolve the issues, having

10–136

---

[77]See paras 10–019 and 10–052–053.

[78]See s. 4(10) of the Law Society and SFLA Code of Practice (1998) at p. xxx below. In Canada, the mediator may raise concerns about the fairness of the proposals: See Landau Bartoletti & Mesbur's *Family Mediation Handbook* (1987) at p. 146.

[79]See, however, the *Mediation Quarterly* article "Mediation and Therapy: An Alternative View" by John Haynes, (1992) 10(1) M.Q. 21, who says at p. 33 that "legal thinking is not useful in mediation because it is based on the judicial system that has as its goal disposal rather than settlement of cases." In this view, the legal system disempowers parties by taking over from them the right to define the problem. Lawyer mediators need to be alive to the need to leave this to the parties.

regard not only to legal factors but also to such other considerations as they may consider relevant.

Using communication skills[80]

10–137 These skills are used throughout the mediation but are particularly relevant here. To facilitate discussion and negotiation, the mediator has to be able to listen effectively and to help the couple to hear one another. He or she needs to be able to summarise and reframe effectively, sensitively and accurately. The mediator will need to acknowledge parties from time to time, and to help one another to do so where appropriate. Mutualising concerns and interests and normalising their feelings and anxieties may be necessary at this time.

10–138 Communication skills include the ability to help the parties to engage with one another. The mediator may try to help them with this. To start with, the mediator may communicate with each party directly and attract direct responses. Gradually, the couple may be encouraged to address one another, and the mediator may decide not to intervene even where direct exchanges become more emotional, as long as both parties seem able to cope with them.

Dealing with the expression of emotions

10–139 Inevitably, when a marriage is going through the crisis of breakdown, parties will experience many emotional reactions. These will obviously vary between individuals, and will shift from time to time and sometimes rapidly within each individual.

10–140 Emotions commonly experienced may include anger, disbelief, grief, distress, sadness, loss, humiliation, hatred, hurt, fear, anxiety, guilt, blaming, self-doubt and relief. Some people may be in a state of denial about what is happening, as their way of coping. Some may suffer depression, which is manifested as an inability to feel other emotions. Others may feel a loss of self-confidence and self-worth.

10–141 People may experience many of these emotions within the mediation forum, especially during this phase of substantive discussions. The intensity of such feelings will depend on various factors including how much time has passed since the breakdown arose, how well each person has adjusted to it, whether they have had professional support such as counselling or therapy, and how differentiated they are.[81]

10–142 Where any of these emotions are manifested in the mediation, mediators have to be able to respond appropriately. Their personal attributes, including empathy and sensitivity, will help, as will their training and professional background.

10–143 In essence, expressions of emotion should be acknowledged and treated as normal and should neither be suppressed nor stimulated by the mediator. The following guidelines might be helpful:

---

[80]See paras 8–108–109 and 15–096 *et seq.*
[81]Undifferentiated couples are those who have not succeeded in separating emotionally from one another. See paras 10–159 *et seq.* for impasse strategies in dealing with such couples.

- Expressing emotion should be normalised. This will be evident from the mediator's response, whatever words might be used. Acknowledgment may sometimes be unspoken but clear.

- Where the emotions are so intense that either party is adversely affected or the mediation seems to be placed at risk, the mediator should try to help the person to contain them.

- The mediator should also be aware of his or her own limitations in coping with the parties' intense emotions, and will need to respect those limitations.

- Even if the mediator's background is counselling or therapy, but especially if not, the mediator should remember that the process is not counselling but helping the couple to deal with specific issues, and should help bring the couple back to task. Generally, that is what they will want and appreciate.

Managing the process

The mediator needs to be a proficient manager of the mediation process. This necessitates having an agenda for each session, albeit informal; controlling the procedure; constantly making decisions what to address; setting an appropriate pace for the process; controlling negative or abusive behaviour; and generally acting as a firm but fair chairperson. **10–144**

If a mediator loses control of the management of the process, whether by allowing any party to dominate the proceedings or merely by a general inability to maintain authority, trust and confidence is likely to be eroded. The corollary of this is not domineering regulation by the mediator, but gentle, firm, impartial and effective management control. **10–145**

Helping with reality-testing

The mediator's function may relate to different aspects: **10–146**

- A party may have a misconceived impression about the other or about any factual situation. The mediator can help to redress distortions of fact, by ensuring that accurate information is brought into the process.

- A party may have a misconceived idea about the implications and effect of proposals that he or she is making or considering, or of a course of action under consideration. The mediator can help the parties to consider such proposals and to try to ensure that they are realistic. This may be done in joint meetings. If done in separate meetings, the mediator can help to filter such proposals by acting as an informal sounding board for the party thinking of putting them forward.

Reality-testing arises throughout the process, but is likely to become more focused during the stage of negotiation and discussion, when ideas and proposals are being exchanged. Care must always be taken to ensure that the mediator is not imposing his or her version of reality on the couple. **10–147**

Facilitating negotiations and decision-making

10–148   Certain common themes run through all kinds of issues. These are facilitating communications; encouraging a problem-solving approach; helping with the generation, development and exploration of options; and assisting in translating needs, interests and concerns into concrete proposals and terms.

10–149   The mediator can also help in many practical ways. For example, if a divorce is being discussed, the mediator can help the parties to consider who will file the petition, when and on what grounds, and may also discuss the actual contents of the petition so that when received it will not be viewed as a hostile document.

10–150   If the issues relate to property and finance, there are a number of possible approaches. One way to assist the couple is to invite them to examine their respective accommodation and other needs. Another is to review their capital, income and expenditure with them and to help them explore how their respective future living plans can be financed. Where there is a shortfall of financial resources, the mediator can assist the couple to examine how that will be met; and where there is a surplus to both of their needs, a division needs to be discussed which is acceptable to both.

10–151   These approaches are by no means free from difficulty: individual perceptions of fairness may vary, and legal principles may not necessarily accord either with notions of fairness or with respective needs.

10–152   In assisting the couple with their negotiations, mediators will generally need to encourage a problem-solving approach and to use all the skills and techniques mentioned in the general chapter on mediation practice[82] and in the chapter outlining the function, role and skills of a mediator.[83]

Stage 8: Employing impasse strategies

10–153   An impasse strategy is one designed to help a couple to resolve deadlock. The general principles and strategies outlined in relation to mediation generally may be similarly applicable to family mediation. It will also be helpful to consider some impasse strategies specific to family mediation.

Pausing and reflecting

10–154   When an impasse surfaces, the mediator may want to pause and consider what it is about. What has caused it? Does it arise because of the parties' personal or emotional needs, or is it a matter of substance? Has the mediator contributed to the impasse by his or her comments or attitude? Might the mediator's approach or attitude towards either party fuel rather than resolve the dispute? Although the temptation may be great to try to find a quick solution to the impasse, it will usually help just to take time to pause and reflect on it.

Allow the parties to absorb the progress

10–155   Sometimes parties need time to absorb the progress that they have made. Each may feel that he or she has gone too far and given away too much. It may help just to review the position, to acknowledge the progress that has

---

[82]See Chap. 8, Stage 7: Facilitating negotiations.
[83]See Chap. 15.

been made, and to mutualise by making it clear that both have shifted from their original positions (which is invariably the case). Instead of pressing them, the mediator may more beneficially give them time to reflect on the position. The deadlocked issue might temporarily be put to one side and some other issue addressed.

Addressing underlying fears and concerns

An impasse may be caused by a party being blocked, often unwittingly, by **10–156** his or her underlying fears and concerns. For example, a deadlock about a "clean break" settlement, where maintenance is not required, but nominal maintenance is sought by one but refused by the other, may actually be broken down into a concern by one about future security and by the other about giving open-ended commitments. Once this is identified, the underlying concerns can be addressed. In this example, the mediator can try to help the couple to examine future circumstances in which one party's insecurity may arise, and may explore alternative possibilities such as insurance. The other party's concern about open-endedness may be explored by examining possible "backstop" dates, and guidelines regulating the circumstances in which future maintenance might become payable in the absence of a clean break, and the implications of payment.

An impasse may mask anxiety about the future. Will I be able to cope, **10–157** will I feel very lonely, will it be possible to maintain a proper relationship with the children? These may not be articulated in these ways, but they may be the concerns that are blocking progress. The mediator may articulate these and examine them with the couple. By helping underlying issues to surface, the mediator can put them into perspective and help to see that they are addressed.

Addressing unresolved emotional blocks

In some cases, the impasse may arise because of unresolved emotional blocks **10–158** that prevent the mediation from continuing effectively. These may arise from either party or both of them. The mediator should consider whether he or she can deal with this in the mediation or whether it is appropriate to discuss with the couple the possibility of their seeing a counsellor or therapist, either together or separately. In either event, the mediator may decide to discuss this with the couple openly and directly.

One of the most difficult kinds of couples to deal with are those where **10–159** either or both of them have not emotionally separated from one another, yet they are in the process of physical, legal or financial disengagement. They have been referred to as "undifferentiated" or "enmeshed" spouses. Undifferentiated couples can be among the most difficult to mediate because commonly their boundaries are blurred, their objectives are confused, their communications are intense but superficial, their ability to make and implement decisions is poor and their emotions are raw.[84] These difficulties may be even more intense where one party is emotionally ready to separate

---

[84]For an overview of this subject and reference to the literature on it, see "Couples from Hell: Undifferentiated Spouses in Divorce Mediation" by Richard D. Mathis, (1998) 16(1) M.Q. 37. Mathis's analysis and recommendations have been adopted and adapted in this section.

and divorce, but the other remains emotionally connected and unable to negotiate for separate and autonomous lives. Conflict and polarised positions are likely to be highest with such couples.

10–160   The mediator dealing with such couples needs to be pro-active and maintain firm control of the process, providing a clear structure and highly defined rules for their interaction. It may be essential to address directly and explicitly the problems of lack of differentiation before being able to approach the issues in dispute, while avoiding turning the mediation into therapy. Professional support in therapy or counselling may be necessary. Sometimes formal adjudication may be essential for such couples.

Dealing with cyclical patterns of behaviour

10–161   Patterns of behaviour that operated during the relationship are likely to be repeated in the mediation process, such as cycles of conflict and mutual recrimination. One of the mediator's functions is to identify such patterns and help the couple to break from them and use the mediation more effectively. In appropriate situations the mediator may draw the couple's attention to their patterns and ask them if they would create their own rules for overcoming those patterns which block their objective of arriving at an agreed resolution.

Considering perceptions of fairness

10–162   An impasse may exist because of different perceptions of fairness. The problem is that it is very difficult to help people to agree on fairness when they start from different viewpoints. It may help to discuss the issue in terms of fairness. What aspect is not fair? What would need to be done to make it fair? If these differences of perception cannot be reconciled, it may nevertheless make it clear to the couple how people can see things in different ways, and that this is not unnatural or wrong. Perhaps they may each have to maintain their own view of fairness, but may have to deal with the issue more pragmatically.

Recognising the power of words and symbolism

10–163   Sometimes deadlocks arise because of terminology or the symbolic implications of some aspect of the proposed agreement. "Residence" and "contact" in relation to children could be such words. A party may want something akin to equality of time with children. It may be possible to work out terms on the basis of the time the children spend with each parent and the nature and quality of their relationship and communications, rather than referring to "residence" and "contact".

10–164   Similarly, certain items or events may have a symbolic meaning to one party, not necessarily identified in the mediation (perhaps not even appreciated by the party). A relatively minor point may be fought over just so that each can show the other who was actually right about the ending of the marriage.[85]

---

[85]See the ginger jar factor, at para. 8–132, n. 51.

Short-term experiments

If there is disagreement about a proposed course of action, the parties could **10–165** test it out over a short term before deciding whether to commit themselves to it. They could give reciprocal assurances as necessary; and a review date could be agreed when they could examine how matters worked during the test period. This may feel less threatening and more creative than immediately implementing untested proposals, about which one party is unhappy.

Caucusing (separate meetings with each party)

Although some models of family mediation in the United Kingdom involve **10–166** having separate meetings with each party, this is not a widely used procedure in family mediation, particularly in the negotiation phase. It may on some occasions, however, be a useful impasse strategy. This may extend into shuttling between the two and carrying messages and proposals. This forum may also allow the mediators to examine the underlying issues and concerns more carefully.[86]

Caucusing needs to be used with great circumspection and care in family **10–167** mediation. Issues of confidentiality and ethics have to be considered.

On confidentiality, the mediator can agree to maintain no confidences **10–168** between the couple, but paraphrase all aspects for the parties. At the other end of the spectrum, he or she will maintain strict confidentiality on each side save for any aspects that the parties will authorise the mediator to disclose to the other. The SFLA has a midway position, appropriate to its policy of distinguishing between open disclosure of financial information but privilege for negotiations. In it, the mediator will maintain confidentiality about each party's private reflections and comments which, if conducted in joint session, would be privileged. However, where open information (financial disclosure) is given to the mediator, then the mediator will not keep that confidential but will disclose it to the other.[87]

Caucusing tends to emphasise separateness rather than joint decision- **10–169** making. It may consequently be less useful for issues such as parenting, which need to focus on the improvement of communications and the strengthening of joint discussions. It can, however, be useful to resolve issues such as property and finance, especially where these are complex and each party wants more time on his or her own to consider matters and perhaps to reality test with the mediator.

Some practical suggestions may enhance caucusing as an impasse strategy: **10–170**

- Caucusing is more time-consuming than joint meetings. Ample time should be allowed for it. Where a joint session of one-and-a-half hours may suffice, at least three or more hours should be allowed for a series of separate meetings.

---

[86]See "The Caucus: Private Meetings That Promote Settlement" by Christopher W. Moore (1987) 16 M.Q. 87 which outlines when private meetings are appropriate and how they should be conducted.

[87]Under consideration is the concept of extending this to cover also material facts. For more detail on caucusing, with particular reference to confidentiality, see para. 8–095.

- Long caucusing sessions tend to be counter-productive where a party is on his or her own. They may be more effective where their solicitors accompany the parties, especially if the solicitors support the mediation process.

- The most productive caucusing sessions tend to take place after the issues have been aired and narrowed, when caucusing is a last resort. Where caucusing is used to try to accelerate the process before joint meetings have run their course, outcomes tend to be less productive.

10–171   Caucusing can be a useful resource, but can also create concerns for the parties. Furthermore, it moves away from the notion of the parties dealing directly with one another and improving communications, and it places greater power in the hands of the mediator. It should be used as an occasional exceptional resource.

Managing differences of legal perception

10–172   An impasse may arise if the parties have received conflicting advice from their independent legal advisers. On the assumption that the conflicting positions are such that it would not be possible for both views to be correct and upheld by the court, the mediators could consider a number of possible strategies for helping the couple to resolve this impasse without undermining the individual advisers:

- The mediator could help the parties to formulate questions to take to their lawyers. For example, the lawyer might be asked to indicate percentage prospects of success and how he or she would expect the opposing side to be advised. Other questions could relate to the likely costs of proceeding to trial and whether there is any prospect of having to pay the other party's costs; and establishing what the delay factor would be. These particulars can help the parties to evaluate whether or not it is worth continuing in mediation.

- An option for both parties might be to seek a second opinion through their solicitors, for example from a barrister, on the points in issue. The mediator can help the parties to formulate the questions to be raised with counsel.

- Alternatively, the mediator could assist the parties in getting a joint opinion on the issues causing the deadlock from a third party such as a neutral barrister or a solicitor. This could be done through the parties' own solicitors by their collaborating on jointly briefing counsel. Instructions could be jointly agreed by the couple in mediation, perhaps (if required) coupled with an addendum from each party outlining their respective contentions. Such a non-binding evaluation could help the parties and their advisers to shift from entrenched positions and negotiate more realistically. Counsel or the solicitor giving the opinion should understand the mediation process to be able to formulate the opinion in a manner useful to the parties in the mediation context. If appropriate, the mediators and the parties could attend a conference with counsel. The non-binding opinion would be brought into the next mediation meeting and could serve as a helpful basis for further discussion and for movement.[88]

- Alternatively, the mediator may perhaps be able to instruct counsel or the neutral solicitor direct.[89]

- The mediators might suggest that respective solicitors attend a mediation meeting with the couple to examine matters more fully. Both solicitors could then expand on their respective views, and discuss the position with everyone present. They would, however, be encouraged thereafter to move into a problem-solving mode, and the opportunity could be taken to explore ways of resolving the deadlock, including caucusing if necessary.

Using draft summaries

The mediator can prepare a draft summary of the position to date, and send it to both parties, for use at the following meeting. This would cover the issues already resolved and those remaining in contention and unresolved, in the latter case outlining alternatives based on ideas already put forward. By seeing what has already been achieved, and having an outline of what remains outstanding, with parameters for discussion, parties have a clearer visual grasp of what needs to be done. It has been found useful to have the unresolved aspects in italics, to identify them clearly. This has the added advantage that as issues get resolved, and updated summaries are sent to the couple, the italics get replaced by regular print, visually indicating the progress that is being made. **10–173**

Risk assessment (BATNA/WATNA)[90]

The mediator may suggest that the parties each examine their best and worst alternatives to reaching agreement in the mediation. BATNA calculates the position if everything went in the best way in an alternative forum. It explores outcome, cost, time factors, effects on family and relationships, and all other factors if that party chose to go down a different route from settling in mediation. **10–174**

The WATNA exercise calculates the position if things went badly in an alternative forum for a party who decided not to settle in mediation. Assuming the worst result, it explores the outcome, cost, time factors, effects on family and relationships, and all other factors if that party chose to go down a different route from settling in mediation and was unsuccessful. **10–175**

---

[88]There was a scheme, now discontinued, for obtaining non-binding evaluations from barristers, somewhat inappropriately named the Family Bar Conciliation Scheme. Such evaluations can be obtained by way of opinion from any individual family law barrister or solicitor. There is also scope for developing a private equivalent of the FDR—see paras 16–125–127.

[89]Solicitor-mediators mediating within their practices can instruct counsel. However, mediation practice has not developed in the direction of mediators themselves instructing third party neutrals such as barristers. For other mediators, it would be a matter of Bar ethics as to whether instructions could be accepted from them. It is understood that the Bar has resolved to accept instructions from mediators whatever their professional background.

[90]BATNA is the Best Alternative to a Negotiated Agreement, and WATNA is the worst alternative. See paras 6–011 *et seq.*

10–176   With the benefit of best and worst alternatives, calculated separately by each party, they will have a better idea of what faces them at best and at worst if they decided not to settle. This can help them to re-examine any stuck issues.

Preparing for adjudication

10–177   Where an impasse cannot be resolved, the mediators can sometimes use available time in a session to assist the couple to prepare themselves for adjudication in a constructive way. This may involve narrowing the issues, and helping them to take a non-hostile view of the fact that a third party adjudication is needed. That, after all, remains their right and is an entirely appropriate choice in some circumstances. In some cases, dealing with the deadlocked issues in this way can also serve as an impasse strategy in its own right.

Phase Three: The end of mediation and afterwards

Stage 9: Concluding the mediation and recording the outcome
Concluding the mediation

10–178   Family mediation may be ended by either party or by the mediator, whether or not any resolution is arrived at. The process will ordinarily end when the parties have resolved their issues. It may end, however, without the parties reaching consensus on all issues. There may be a number of reasons for this. The parties may have reached an intractable impasse, and they may wish to have the outstanding issues dealt with by their respective solicitors, and through the court if necessary. In this event, they may decide to endorse the partial agreements reached in the mediation, limiting their dispute only to the unresolved points; or they may want to disregard the partial resolution and deal in the adversarial process with all issues. Whichever way they proceed, parties often find that the mediation will have helped them in various ways. For example, the mediation may have dealt with information gathering, and may have narrowed the issues. Settlement possibilities discussed in the mediation, although initially rejected, often come back into focus at a later stage. Mediation may also have helped them to communicate better with one another despite some or even all the issues still needing adjudication.

10–179   The mediation may end or be suspended because the parties decide to go to counselling or therapy. Mediators must in some circumstances under English law keep the possibility of reconciliation in mind.[91] Counselling may address the possibility of reconciliation, or it may aim to help couples with other issues, such as coming to terms with the separation or considering children's needs.

10–180   Alternatively, mediation may be discontinued because the couple have gone as far as they can or want to at that time, perhaps deferring any further discussion pending the happening of a certain event such as a child completing a particular stage of education, or the couple first selling a property.

---

[91] See para. 10–064, n. 47.

In some cases, the mediator may initiate the termination. This could **10–181** happen if, for example, he or she felt that it was inappropriate to continue with the mediation for any reason such as one party abusing the process or the couple reaching a stage where it became clear that no further progress was likely. Most Codes of Practice will specify circumstances in which mediation should be discontinued by the mediator.

Preparing summaries and memoranda

Where the parties have resolved all their issues, the mediator will usually **10–182** prepare a document summarising their agreement or proposals. Whether this document records a binding agreement, or whether it is prepared as a non-binding summary of their proposals or a memorandum of understanding will depend upon the parties wishes and intentions and also on the model of modiation being used.[92] The most common procedure is that the mediator drafts a non-binding memorandum of understanding[93] on a without prejudice basis, as well as an open summary of financial information, which the couple can take to their respective solicitors.

Where the mediation ends without complete resolution, it may still be **10–183** appropriate and helpful to the parties for an off the record written memorandum or summary to be prepared. This can set out the issues that were resolved and those that remained unresolved, perhaps indicating the alternative options put forward by each and the parameters of any outstanding disagreement. This can serve both as an informal note to prevent misunderstanding as to the status of any partially resolved aspects, and as an agenda for any settlement discussions that the respective solicitors may wish to enter into.

Mediation memoranda and summaries are usually written in non-legal **10–184** style, informal but clear, precise and sufficiently specific to avoid any ambiguity or misunderstanding. A memorandum of understanding is not usually written in the manner of a Deed of Separation or a court order. It should though cover all points in such a way that the independent lawyers acting for the parties can prepare any necessary documents based on its clarity and sufficiency of information. Lawyer mediators do not draft the legal documents flowing from the mediation.[94]

The parties will then each have the opportunity to consult their own **10–185** lawyers with the summaries, which should provide a substantial picture of the parties' financial circumstances and their joint proposals. Each solicitor will then advise on an individual basis, and may liaise with the other party's

---

[92] Care needs to be taken in relation to the concept of "agreement". The court may decide to consider an agreement, albeit expressed as conditional. Furthermore, once there is agreement, without prejudice communications may be treated as open. It is therefore advisable, until mediation privilege has been firmly established, to avoid the notion of "agreement" until parties are ready to bind themselves, having had independent legal advice.

[93] Terminology has varied. The term "memorandum of understanding", imported from the U.S., is recommended by the U.K. College of Family Mediators and is now widely used. "Summary of proposals" is preferred by some, but has been abandoned for the sake of national consistency.

[94] They might help the couple to draft otherwise contentious aspects, such as behaviour clauses in divorce petitions. Where solicitors mediate as part of their solicitor's practice, the question is bound to arise as to their being able to prepare Deeds of Separation and draft court orders. The ethical and practical implications of this question remain to be considered.

solicitor to arrange for the preparation of any formal documentation or court order and for any necessary formalities to be complied with.

Concluding formalities

10–186   Any query or reservation about the proposed terms may be resolved between the parties themselves, or by the respective solicitors. Where the mediation process has been conducted with proper care and detail and on the basis of full financial disclosure, then if the parties' solicitors should raise concerns or queries, the parties themselves will understand their proposals clearly and will usually be able to respond satisfactorily to those concerns.

10–187   In general, while respective solicitors will examine proposals and may raise questions, they are not generally obstructive of their client's wishes. If solicitors do raise matters which seem to merit some review of the proposed agreement, these can be brought to another mediation meeting for discussion; and if necessary, the respective solicitors can be invited to attend the meeting. In such event, the mediators might ask the solicitors to assist in adopting a problem-solving approach to help find ways to allow the parties to achieve an agreed resolution while accommodating as far as possible any concerns raised.

10–188   Mediators may be willing to discuss the summaries with the individual solicitors, but should obtain the consent of both parties to do so, and any such discussions should be to facilitate drafting and not to debate the merits of the proposals. With the approval of the parties, there is no reason why the mediators cannot clarify any drafting or process questions that may be raised by the parties' solicitors.

Stage 10: Post-termination

10–189   After the mediator has sent the couple the final summaries or a memorandum of understanding, and the couple have seen their separate legal advisers and dealt with any necessary formalities, the role of the mediator will usually be at an end.

10–190   Family mediators may in some circumstances continue to be involved with a couple after the conclusion of the mediation. For example:

- Certain issues concerning the children may be subject to later review. The couple may seek help in working out or revising arrangements for the children if they find that they cannot effectively do so themselves.

- Financial issues may also be subject to later review, including for example, maintenance provisions. This may be particularly necessary where future incomes are unpredictable, or where future changes of circumstances are contemplated but cannot be accurately forecast.

- Making short-term rather than long-term arrangements can sometimes be helpful to a couple.

- A couple may resolve to return to mediation if at any time they find that any continuing aspect of their affairs is causing contention between them which they cannot resolve themselves. However, the experiences of communicating effectively with one another within the mediation may make it easier for some couples to do so by themselves and to resolve issues outside mediation without the need for further neutral third party assistance.

- Couples sometimes agree that if there is any problem with the implementation of settlement terms they will revert to the mediator to assist them in overcoming the problem rather than risking it escalating into a dispute.

5. DIVORCE REFORM: THE FUTURE

Given the profound social and individual importance of marriage and family, their disruption and breakdown will inevitably engender strong feelings, both at societal and individual levels. **10–191**

Legislators face conflicting pressures. Some people are, understandably, concerned about the role and sanctity of marriage and are concerned about any move that might in their view damage the marriage bond. For this view, parties who are "innocent" of any matrimonial fault should not have to face divorce; and divorce procedures should be stringent to prevent marriage being able to end too casually. Equally understandably, there are those who are concerned about a system that effectively compounds the problems and anguish of marriage breakdown rather than supporting couples who are struggling to cope with major transitions in their lives. On this view, the marriage relationship is too complex to allocate "fault" and trying to do so merely exacerbates relationship problems. The issue is not one of making divorce easy or difficult, but rather providing appropriate support systems to help manage the consequences of breakdown. **10–192**

While these views are often polarised, there is also an overlap. Opponents of no-fault divorce accept that divorce is necessary and inevitable; and proponents of no-fault divorce agree that marriage and families should be supported as far as possible. Between these views, many other thoughts and concerns exist about how marriage breakdown should be addressed. **10–193**

Professionals working in the field of marriage and cohabitation breakdown, including especially lawyers, counsellors, therapists and mediators, are generally aware of the damaging effects and the cost (both financial and personal) of adversarial proceedings. This is a recurring reason given by those wishing to train as mediators. They are also aware that many people tend to think of relationship breakdown in terms of fault. They will commonly experience couples who blame one another for the breakdown. The question for many professionals is whether the system is able to devise processes that can help couples to move forward constructively with their lives, while accommodating the need of those who wish to examine the reasons for the breakdown. **10–194**

Apart from ideological and pragmatic issues, legislators also face fiscal pressures in creating a system that will satisfy legitimate societal and individual needs. There seems little doubt but that strains on the legal aid budget influenced the shape of the Family Law Act 1996 and the legal aid **10–195** provisions that accompanied it. In any event, there is an increasing awareness of the need to have procedures that are reasonably economic, whether privately or publicly funded. It cannot be acceptable for couples to spend considerable sums of their or the State's money on arguing relationship breakdown issues, and particularly not on the potentially damaging argument as to who was more responsible for the breakdown of the relationship. Under the Woolf reforms, the issue of proportionality has assumed importance, and it must surely be especially relevant to couples trying to establish new family arrangements in circumstances that are inevitably strained and difficult.

10–196   The Family Law Act 1996 was an attempt to create a constructive system to support marriage while removing the issue of fault where an ending was inevitable. Its underlying principles were substantially sound. Unfortunately, however, in trying to find a compromise between opposing views, the law fell between two stools and lost much of its initial value. It sought to be all things to all people. Its no-fault provisions upset those who saw this as a home-breaker's charter. Its long-winded and cumbersome provisions, which enabled the Lord Chancellor to reassure opponents that it was actually supporting marriage and making divorce a more difficult and thoughtful procedure, apparently proved to be unacceptable to many of the general public. Ancillary provisions, for rigidly controlled information meetings for example, were unpopular; and the public and profession did not support the procedures for trying to steer couples into mediation.

10–197   The future is uncertain in many respects, and this is especially the case for those in England and Wales concerned about divorce reform, both substantive and procedural. As a vision of how reform might affect the future of couples, we venture the following thoughts:

- More serious and authentic preparation for couples entering marriage, with a greater awareness of its implications and the support systems available if it encounters difficulties. This is almost universally rejected on the grounds that it is inappropriate (and unromantic) to raise issues about possible relationship problems with couples embarking on marriage. This view may need to be re-examined.

- More support for couples undergoing relationship problems. Organisations such as Relate and London Marriage Guidance need more support, and counselling needs to be seen as a professional resource that can readily be used, not a process that indicates personal failure. (There were reports that the provision for counselling through legal aid funding envisaged by the Family Law Act might only have covered a single session of one hour. If that is true, it signals a misconception about the nature and value of counselling, and would pay no more than lip service to the concept of providing support).

- Greater networking between the professionals dealing with relationship breakdown, especially lawyers, mediators, counsellors and therapists. New and improved ways should be found to provide more rounded support services for couples.

- Substantive divorce law reform to allow couples the opportunity to explore their problems and the nature of the breakdown of their relationship in a way that does not involve mutual blaming (hence no-fault) but which allows them also to articulate and examine the reasons for the breakdown, for those who wish to do so. This indicates a "process over time" along the lines of the Family Law Act, but adapting the procedures and times to make them more acceptable.

- National support during the divorce process from mediators able to deal with all issues arising on divorce, or limited issues such as children's arrangements.

- Legal aid for those requiring and qualifying for it, without being forced to go through mediation, but supported in doing so. This may mean directing couples to try mediation, but not penalising them if it does not result in an agreement. It almost certainly also means that those in mediation should have the support of their individual lawyers throughout the process as well as after it has ended.

Reform can take many shapes and has many components. The primary concept may, however, be to understand marriage breakdown as a process of family transition rather than as something involving blame and dispute. If processes reflect this and support the couple and family, the reforms are likely to succeed. **10–198**

CHAPTER 11

EMPLOYMENT MEDIATION AND CONCILIATION

1. OUTLINE OF CURRENT STATUS OF EMPLOYMENT DISPUTE RESOLUTION

11–001 As will be seen from the historical introduction that follows, the use of mediation and conciliation in the field of employment and industrial relations dates back well over 100 years. It has a long and honourable record, and significantly pre-dates the use of these processes in other areas of activity such as for civil and commercial dispute resolution, family issues and neighbourhood disagreements.

11–002 It is therefore somewhat surprising to observe that mediation and conciliation in relation to employment and industrial relations have had such a relatively low profile among those concerned with dispute resolution generally. It is of course widely known that ACAS[1] undertakes conciliation for employment disputes. However, information about mediation and conciliation in the employment field is sparse, compared with the volume of writing that exists on the use of these processes for other disputes. This is particularly surprising in view of the large volume of conciliation cases undertaken by ACAS and the wealth of experience there must be.

11–003 Indeed, the authors of this work turned to ten significant works on employment law published within the last three or four years, to check what references they had to mediation or conciliation. Looking up these terms in the index and table of contents of each work, they found that "mediation" was not mentioned at all in nine of those 10 books. "Conciliation" had a brief mention in four of the works, not in the others.

11–004 In the event, the last decade has seen substantial changes in the field of employment dispute resolution, even to the adoption of this terminology in the Employment Rights (Dispute Resolution) Act 1998. Following pressures caused by the increasing volume and complexity of cases, and against a background of complaints about delays and the growth of legalism, and perhaps concerned about costs considerations, the Employment Department (as it then was) undertook an internal review of the tribunal system in 1994. This led to the publication of a Green Paper in 1994,[2] which was part of the consultative process that led eventually to the 1998 Act.

---

[1] The Advisory, Conciliation and Arbitration Service. See below.
[2] "Resolving Employment Rights Disputes: Options for Reform".

One of the changes brought about by the 1998 Act was the renaming of **11–005** Industrial Tribunals as "Employment Tribunals".[3] These tribunals have provided the foundation for the adjudication of employment disputes, designed to be less formal and more expeditious than the court system.

More substantially, the Act has addressed the question of improving **11–006** employment tribunal procedures and encouraging alternative dispute resolution methods. Against the dearth of references to "mediation" and "conciliation" previously mentioned, it is interesting to note that in a book on the new employment law there is now a chapter entitled "Alternative Dispute Resolution".[4] In referring to ADR, the Act does not necessarily envisage the full range of processes ordinarily understood by this term. The elements of ADR that are envisaged (as alternatives to employment tribunals) are as follows:

- *Individual conciliation.* This relates to the resolution of individual disputes, for example in relation to claims for unfair dismissal or other complaints by individuals that their rights under employment protection legislation have been infringed. It is described as "a vital element in the process of handling employment rights issues".[5] It accounts for about two-thirds of ACAS operational resource.

- *Collective conciliation.* This relates to the resolution of collective disputes, for example, concerning pay or working conditions where employers and trade unions are in dispute. These are usually referred by trade unions or employers, separately or jointly, though occasionally ACAS may at its own initiative offer conciliation to disputing parties.

- *Dispute mediation.* A distinction has recently been developed in employment issues separating "dispute mediation" from what is being called "advisory mediation".[6] Dispute mediation is a similar process to conciliation, "but the mediator, or board of mediation, makes formal but non-binding, proposals or recommendations intended to provide a basis for settlement of the dispute".[7]

---

[3] The Donovan Report in 1968 is reported in *Employment Tribunals: the New Law* by Brian J. Doyle (1998) as having suggested that industrial tribunals might be designated as "labour tribunals". Doyle comments that this proposals has never been acted upon "and would now look equally out of place in modern employment rights litigation". The authors of this work have noted the shift in terminology and have abandoned the previous chapter title of "Labour Mediation".

[4] Chap. 4 of Doyle's *Employment Tribunals: the New Law,* see n. 3 above.

[5] ACAS Research Paper 1: Jane Lewis and Robin Legard, *ACAS individual conciliation* (ACAS, circa 1998). (A number of ACAS publications such as this do not indicate anywhere the year of publication, which seems unsatisfactory.)

[6] See, *e.g.* the 1998 ACAS Annual Report, dealing with "advisory mediation" at p. 52 and "dispute mediation" at p. 69.

[7] The quoted words are extracted from an ACAS publication *Preventing and resolving collective disputes.* Interestingly, mediation is linked in the pamphlet with arbitration, not conciliation, and the explanation for mediation states that "mediation involves a similar process to **arbitration**" (our emphasis). This does not appear to be a misprint, but a fundamental difference in concept between mediation, as it is known and used in all other fields, and mediation in employment disputes.

- *Advisory mediation.* This term is widely used in ACAS literature.[8] It refers to the facilitation of joint discussions and procedures between employers, employees and employee representatives and by the use of joint working parties and workshops.

- *Arbitration.* Although, as its name indicates, ACAS has always had the power to offer arbitration for industrial disputes, this power has only just been extended by the 1998 Act to cover individual employment disputes concerning unfair dismissal. The proposals for an arbitration scheme are "underpinned by the Arbitration Act 1996".[9] Arbitrators would make awards binding on all parties. By entering into an arbitration agreement, parties would contract out of the jurisdiction of the employment tribunals.[10]

11–007   The concept of ADR in employment disputes is developing in its own way. Some of the processes, like those included within the concept of "advisory mediation" (namely joint working parties and workshops) are very similar in principle to those used in public policy mediation. Conciliation is widely used, in its most facilitative form. Mediation for the resolution of disputes is infrequently used, and, as previously indicated, is conceived as a different kind of process from its usage in most other areas of activity. Arbitration for individual unfair dismissal disputes is now being made available. How and to what extent it will be used and how effective it will be remains to be seen.

2. HISTORICAL INTRODUCTION

11–008   Industrial conciliation in Britain dates back to the time of Pitt the Younger, with a series of statutes in the second half of the nineteenth century, the so-called "pretentious legislation" of 1867 and 1872. These failed, however, in their aim of preventing disputes or industrial action arising from disputes.

11–009   The Acts were repealed in 1896 by the Conciliation Act, which for the following 80 years provided the legal basis for voluntary conciliation services provided by the State. During the last three decades of the nineteenth century there was greater local recognition of conciliation. Parliament abandoned attempts to find dispute settlement procedures within a quasi-judicial framework, and the voluntary element remained in the ascendancy. This voluntary principle stood alongside another principle, namely that of respect for autonomous institutions existing within particular industries.

11–010   The fillip required by the legislature in the nineteenth century was provided by the success of such autonomous machinery in the north of England. A. J. Mundella, an early industrial entrepreneur, established joint boards for the hosiery industry in Nottingham, with the proposition that

---

[8]See n. 6 above. See also ACAS Occasional Paper No. 55 *Joint problem-solving* by Ian Kessler and John Purcell (undated) which is subtitled "Does it work? An evaluation of in-depth advisory mediation". The term "advisory mediation" is also used in the ACAS publication *The ACAS Commitment*.

[9]See ACAS Consultation Document, *ACAS arbitration scheme for the resolution of unfair dismissal disputes,* July 1998.

[10]S. 8 of the Employment Rights (Dispute Resolution) Act 1998.

"masters and men should get around the table and 'talk it out' on a footing of equality".[11] By equality, he meant that employers and employees would participate in equal numbers. His casting vote was removed as an indication of the spirit of agreement seen as necessary in the continuing relationship.

The experience in Nottingham was one of reduced strikes, lock-outs and industrial violence, which encouraged the spread of these boards into other areas and other industries. Even when the boards were overtaken by developments in industrial relations, notably the rise of the national trade unions, the agreements the boards had achieved remained. The boards were almost always replaced by a different form of autonomous dispute resolution machinery, which enjoyed early TUC support. In its 1888 Congress, the TUC noted that they "increased understanding and peaceful settlement". These early experiences set the agenda and established the basis for future industrial dispute resolution.

11–011

Parliament's approbation of a voluntary system of industrial dispute resolution reflected the fact that many aspects of employment law were not legally grounded. For example, a prominent role was given to custom in defining the employer/employee relationship, including the duties of fidelity and mutual trust and confidence.

11–012

The Industrial Courts Act 1919, which had marked similarities to the 1896 Act, also sounded the death knell for the last remnants of State laissez-faire in industrial relations and industrial disputes. The new role for the State would be a hands-off approach, encouraging without forcing, by supplying the means, funding and if necessary the location for conciliation.

In the twentieth century it was clear that both employers and employees would react with indignation to any State involvement in their disputes. State policy is still largely unchanged today, that is, to encourage autonomous institutions with the option of recourse to a standing, independent arbitration and conciliation service funded by the State. Notwithstanding the institutional expansion of government regulatory agencies, including employment (formerly industrial) tribunals (established in 1964), the Central Arbitration Committee, and ACAS, it remains true to say that most disputes are conducted outside State-supplied machinery. Parliament remains largely committed to this self-regulation in most sectors of industry.

11–013

The twin considerations of effective dispute resolution and cost effectiveness are obviously applicable in the employment context, but are overshadowed by the principle of "good industrial relations", that seems the *raison d'etre* of legislation in this area throughout the twentieth century. Conciliation and mediation offer the means to have disputes listened to and dealt with independently and impartially.

11–014

3. TERMINOLOGY

As already mentioned, the employment sector in the United Kingdom uses some terms with a different meaning or in a different way from most other

11–015

---

[11] Sharp, *Industrial Conciliation and Arbitration in Great Britain* (1949) at p. 466.

areas of activity. That does not matter, as long as everyone is clear what its terminology means.[12]

11–016   The term "conciliation", which was more widely used in the 1970s, has in many other fields given way to the term "mediation". These terms are elsewhere often used interchangeably. Where both terms have survived, some organisations use "conciliation" to refer to a more pro-active and evaluative form of process. However, the reverse usage is sometimes employed; and ACAS falls into this category.

11–017   In relation to employment, the term "conciliation" is used to refer to a mediatory process that is wholly facilitative and non-evaluative. The definition of conciliation formulated by the International Labour Organisation in 1983 has been followed by ACAS, namely that it is:

> " ... the practice by which the services of a neutral third party are used in a dispute as a means of helping the disputing parties to reduce the extent of their differences and to arrive at an amicable settlement or agreed solution. It is a process of orderly or rational discussion under the guidance of the conciliator."[13]

11–017   Mediation, however, in this context, involves a process in which the neutral mediator takes a more pro-active role than the conciliator in the conciliation process, making his or her own recommendations for the resolution of the dispute, which the parties are free to accept or reject.

11–018   ACAS distinguishes between mediation and conciliation as follows:

> "Mediation ... may be regarded as a half-way house between conciliation and arbitration. The role of the conciliator is to assist the parties to reach their own negotiated settlement, and he may make suggestions as appropriate. The mediator proceeds by way of conciliation but in addition is prepared and expected to make his own formal proposals or recommendations, which may be accepted as they stand or provide the basis of further negotiations leading to a settlement. Such recommendations may be similar in form to an arbitrator's award, but the crucial difference is that the parties do not undertake in advance to accept them."[14]

11–019   The employment sector has also coined the term "advisory mediation", which is not generally used elsewhere. Some would say that it was a contradiction in terms, in that mediators do not ordinarily give "advice" as such, and many in other areas of activity are precluded by their Codes of Practice from doing so.

11–020   "Dispute mediation" is used by ACAS to refer to pro-active mediation used to settle existing disputes. "Advisory mediation" tends to be used by

---

[12]"When I use a word" Humpty Dumpty said, in a rather scornful tone, "it means just what I choose it to mean—neither more nor less." Lewis Carroll's *Alice Through the Looking-glass.*
[13]"Industrial relations disputes: the ACAS role" by the Advisory, Conciliation and Arbitration Service, in *A Handbook of Dispute Resolution: ADR in Action* (1991) by Karl Mackie (ed.) at p. 104.
[14]ACAS, *The ACAS role in Arbitration, Conciliation and Mediation* (1989).

ACAS to refer to its role in the prevention of disputes. This kind of mediation covers the following techniques[15]:

- *Joint Working Party (JWP)* involving the establishment of a working party comprising management and employee representatives to deal with issues on a joint problem-solving rather than adversarial basis.

- *Workshops* involving discussion and working groups from management and the workforce to articulate and deal with specific employment issues.

4. RATIONALE FOR ADR IN EMPLOYMENT DISPUTES

Employers and employees are in a special relationship, which will invariably have to continue after the dispute has been resolved. Their disputes are not necessarily amenable to judicial pronouncement, especially where complex and many-sided agreements are concerned and where it may not be appropriate for the solution to involve having one party as a winner and the other a loser, as occurs in most traditional court litigation. **11–021**

It is generally accepted that the best solutions to disagreements between employers and employees are those arrived at through negotiated agreement usually through an element of mutual give and take. Such agreements can be tailored to the needs of the parties, rather than imposed upon them. This creates the optimum conditions for a satisfactory continuing working relationship, whereas litigation is more likely to lead to a hostile working environment. **11–022**

Many people are affected by an employment dispute: the employers, the employees, their families and sometimes even the surrounding geographical area or associated industries, making an agreed settlement the most desirable outcome. **11–023**

Disputes may often be about the very agreements that sought to avoid industrial action. Again, it is preferable that these be resolved by agreement. **11–024**

In the United States, as in the United Kingdom, it was in the field of industrial disputes that conciliation and mediation were initially used, dating back to the nineteenth century. Disputes in this field generally fall into two categories: grievance disputes, which arise in relation to the application of collective bargaining agreements or complaints by individuals about alleged breaches of employment terms or conditions; and collective bargaining, which involves issues regarding the terms of proposed new collective agreements.[16] **11–025**

As will be observed, grievance disputes tend to relate to existing rights, whereas disputes concerning collective bargaining agreements relate to prospective and not existing rights, and consequently are viewed as interests rather than rights. This distinction between rights and interests affects the nature of the dispute resolution machinery that may be employed. In relation **11–026**

---

[15] *Joint problem-solving* at p. 14 (see n. 8 above).

[16] See Murray, Rau & Sherman, *Processes of Dispute Resolution: the Role of Lawyers* (1989) at p. 309.

to rights resolution, the neutral deals with the interpretation and application of the terms of an existing agreement, whereas in relation to interest resolution, the neutral is required to determine the terms that will apply in the future.[17]

11–027   While arbitration remains the principal procedure used in collective bargaining agreements in the United States, mediation plays an increasing role there both in the bargaining process leading up to an agreement and in relation to disputes arising from alleged breaches of those agreements.[18] Mediation has commonly been used in disputes over interests in the context of negotiating collective bargaining agreements. However, its extension into the rights context in the United States has been described as "one of the most promising innovations ... in the grievance procedure prior to arbitration."[19]

11–028   Arbitration, despite its advantages over litigation of relative informality and specialised knowledge of the context of the dispute, still involves the same limitation as other forms of adjudication including litigation. This is that it must provide a winner and a loser, without scope to create a resolution that takes into account the varying needs, interests and concerns of the different parties and the nuances so often inherent in a complex consensual settlement. The confrontational context of arbitration and its win–lose outcome can often have negative consequences in terms of parties' satisfaction, perceptions of fairness and compliance with decisions.[20]

11–029   Furthermore, in the United Kingdom, doubts have been expressed as to who will find arbitration advantageous in its proposed new application to individual disputes. The advantage of privacy is often mentioned; but in the relatively small number of cases where privacy is an issue for one party, it is likely that the other party will see an advantage in maximising publicity. Concerns exist as to whether all arbitrators will adopt similar principles and tests or whether different arbitrators will use different principles and tests from one another. These are matters that will no doubt be addressed, but (perhaps not surprisingly where new procedures are being introduced) concerns remain.

11–030   There has been an increasing usage of conciliation and mediation in the industrial arena in the United States and in the United Kingdom and elsewhere, including Canada[21] and South Africa.[22] Conciliation is viewed as a preliminary step to be undertaken before arbitration is commenced, and used after the ordinary negotiation stage has been found to be inadequate but before parties turn to adjudication.

---

[17] See Murray, Rau & Sherman, *ibid.* at pp. 404–409, quoting also from Craver, "The Judicial Enforcement of Public Sector Interest Arbitration" at 21 B.C.L. Rev. 557, 558 n. 8 (1980).

[18] See Murray, Rau & Sherman, *ibid.* at p. 308; at p. 421 quoting from the U.S. Department of Labor "Characteristics of Major Collective Bargaining Agreements" (1981) that an estimated 96% of U.S. collective bargaining agreements provide for the arbitration of grievance disputes.

[19] See Deborah M. Kolb's article "How existing procedures shape alternatives: the case of grievance mediation" in the *J.D.R.* Vol. 1989 at 73.

[20] See Kolb, *ibid.* at p. 72.

[21] See Kolb, *ibid.* at p. 73.

[22] IMSSA, the Independent Mediation Service of South Africa, has been in the forefront of industrial mediation activities in that country, and has been instrumental in the resolution of a number of major disputes, including those with significant economic, political and social implications such as a potentially crippling rail dispute.

In the United Kingdom, ACAS received 1,301 requests for collective **11–031** conciliation during 1998, and managed to avoid industrial action in 95 per cent of the cases. In relation to cases involving individuals during 1998, there were 113,636 requests for individual conciliation. The most commonly claimed jurisdiction was unfair dismissal with 40,153 cases during 1998, slightly down on the 1997 figure of 42,771. There were, by comparison, significantly fewer requests for arbitration (not yet of individual disputes) and dispute mediation, curiously lumped together, namely 51, compared with 71 in 1997. The vast majority of these referrals were for arbitration, indicating that (dispute) mediation is hardly used in the employment sector as compared with conciliation: perhaps not surprisingly so, when the concept of employment mediation is so unclear.

5. ADVISORY, CONCILIATION AND ARBITRATION SERVICE (ACAS)

Although, as already noted, a voluntary conciliation and mediation service **11–032** has been provided by government since the turn of the century, criticisms about the link with government led to the Conciliation and Arbitration Service being established in 1974 as a separate service "at arm's length from government".[23] This was established as a statutory body in 1976 by the Employment Protection Act 1975 and renamed the Advisory, Conciliation and Arbitration Service (ACAS).

ACAS is impartial and independent from government notwithstanding the **11–033** annual report to the Secretary of State at the Employment Department. It has a general duty to promote the improvement of industrial relations, which it does across four key areas of activity:

- preventing and resolving disputes

- conciliating in actual and potential complaints to employment tribunals

- providing information and advice

- promoting good practice.[24]

The ACAS mission is "to improve the performance and effectiveness of **11–034** organisations by providing an independent and impartial service to prevent and resolve disputes and to build harmonious relationships at work".[25]

ACAS is a Crown body, and its staff, though not the members of its **11–035** Council (which includes three part-time members appointed after consultation with the Confederation of British Industry, and three after consultation with the Trades Union Congress) have the status of civil servants. Its services are sought from both sides of industry.

The staff of ACAS undertake most of the organisation's functions, **11–036** including conciliation. In this latter regard, ACAS provides training in

---

[23]See the ACAS article in Mackie, *Handbook of Dispute Resolution* at p. 100.
[24]*ACAS 1998 Annual Report* at p. 37.
[25]All ACAS pamphlets including *The ACAS Commitment*.

conciliation for its more experienced staff, helping them to develop their judgment, sense of timing and self-confidence in the process, and to reflect their trustworthiness, impartiality and independence in practice.[26] Dispute mediation is, however, usually referred to an independent outside person, or (more rarely) to a Board of Mediation.

11–037   The arbitration of trade disputes is referred to an individual arbitrator or occasionally in some major issues to a Board of Arbitration. That arbitrator would not be a member of the ACAS staff, but appointed by ACAS to a panel of arbitrators from which the ACAS secretariat assigns arbitrators to individual cases.

11–038   Under the proposed arbitration scheme for individuals a separate panel of arbitrators will be established. They will not be on the staff of ACAS. The central feature of the scheme will be freedom from legalism, with an inquisitorial rather than adversarial approach. The arbitrator will rule on his or her jurisdiction and on procedural and evidential matters. To give the arbitration finality, appeals will be limited to allegations of serious irregularity.[27]

11–039   ACAS's approach has changed over the years. It has been increasingly concerned to develop a distinctive niche.[28] The emphasis that it developed was on "jointness". This concept of joint problem solving, with its focus on an integrative, non-adversarial approach rather than distributive, conflictual style of negotiation[29] has characterised the ACAS approach. It has led to the development of processes such as joint working parties and workshops that form the main thrust of its advisory mediation.

6. CONCILIATION PRACTICE

11–040   As already indicated, there are two kinds of conciliation which may be undertaken by an Industrial Relations Officer (IRO), the one being collective conciliation and the other individual conciliation. The conciliation process is likely to be used by parties who may be contemplating or who have commenced action including perhaps arbitration, and in entering into this process, the parties reserve their right to continue with such action if that becomes necessary.

Conciliation procedure

11–041   Conciliation meetings can be set up quickly as the arrangements to be made are informal. The machinery and methods used by the IRO are likely to be quite similar wherever the conciliation is undertaken, partly due to ACAS's success with those methods and partly by reason of a history of shared traditions and training. There will obviously, however, be differences of detail depending upon the needs of the individual case and the approach of the individual conciliator. Officers will invariably have their own individual styles. A qualitative evaluation of individual conciliation undertaken by

---

[26] *ACAS*, Mackie *ibid.* at pp. 105–106.
[27] *ACAS Arbitration Scheme* consultative paper, foreword. See n. 9 above.
[28] See ACAS Occasional Paper 55, *Joint problem solving*, at p. 12 (see n. 8).
[29] For a distinction between distributive and integrative bargaining see Chap. 6.

ACAS reflected that the officers "varied in the extent to which they are active, persistent and enthusiastic in initiating contact with parties or representatives, and in responding to contact. . . . A distinction was also drawn between an administrative or reactive style of conciliation, and an analytical or proactive style."[30] The evaluation also indicated that while some officers were relatively non-interventionist, others were said to be "more discursive or persuasive in their approach, discussing the strengths and weaknesses of the case, challenging assessment of the case, and being creative in suggesting ways of resolving the case without a hearing."

The IRO, at an early stage of the process, will explain his or her functions and role and the independent nature of the role. He or she must also gather information about the issues and establish, as far as possible, the interests of the parties, including, in many cases, their underlying interests as well as the hidden boundaries of the dispute. What is at stake for the parties may not always be readily apparent.   **11–042**

Most contact in ACAS conciliation takes place over the telephone. This is generally regarded as satisfactory by large employers and representatives, and by some parties. However, in some cases telephone contact does not satisfactorily meet parties' needs, especially where legal information is complex or parties are conducting the discussion in difficult circumstances, for example at work.   **11–043**

IROs will also meet with parties personally, particularly in the early stages of cases or where parties are unrepresented. In such event, they use three kinds of meetings. The process is commonly started by way of separate meetings with each party, at which the facts and issues are established and the conciliator's role is discussed. These comprise the most common form of approach, enabling parties to speak freely to the IRO on a confidential basis (though the IRO may seek authority to discuss with the other side matters raised in such separate meetings).   **11–044**

Secondly, there is the joint meeting, at which the parties meet together with the IRO; though these are rarely held because of the concern that they may in many situations, especially of high tension, be counter-productive. There is experience that such meetings can help to break deadlock, but that the ACAS officer needs to play an active role for the meeting to be successful.   **11–045**

Thirdly, there is the "caucus" meeting at which negotiators from each side have a private session with the IRO, perhaps to discuss some technical or drafting point or issue, or where negotiations seem to be foundering and the IRO considers that such a meeting would be helpful.[31]   **11–046**

The conciliator may not make any evaluation of the case, nor express a view about its merits, but rather should try to help the parties themselves to reach agreement based on their being as fully informed as possible of the legal position and the options available to them. In helping to inform them, the IRO may provide the parties with relevant data about the legal position, including legislation and case law, and about procedural matters.   **11–047**

---

[30] Research paper 1: *ACAS individual conciliation* at p. 11. See n. 5 above.

[31] The term "caucus" in this context has a more limited usage than the general mediation context, where it refers to separate meetings with each party, just negotiations.

11–048   The IRO's conciliation role may be conducted within the space of a telephone call or two, or may involve several meetings and phone calls. When meeting the parties separately, the IRO is likely to adopt a peripatetic role, moving between the separate rooms accommodating each of the parties, trying to establish common ground and to narrow the issues between the parties. In the absence of authority to impose or even to suggest any solution, the IRO must depend upon personal and process skills, on developing the co-operation of the parties, and on an ability to help them to address and reconcile their respective interests if a resolution is to be achieved.

11–049   While making sure to avoid giving an opinion, the IRO may caution parties about the risks of proceeding with any action, for example in a tribunal; and may perhaps indicate whether he considers that a party is being conciliatory or that a proposal is generous. The IRO provides feedback to the parties, and in doing so must invariably act with care as to what can properly be said in order to be helpful without entering into an evaluative mode or unduly influencing the parties.

Compromise agreements

11–050   If the parties are able to settle their dispute, the terms are recorded in writing. Although this recording may not be thought to be part of the substantive dispute resolution process, it is an inherent part of it, and indeed the rules governing these agreements have an effect on the approach taken to the processes themselves.

11–051   Some brief background to this issue may be helpful. In the 1980s, employers increasingly chose to record settlement terms in a form (COT3) that precluded a claim from being made to tribunal, especially but not only where settlement negotiations took place at the time of actual termination of employment. In 1990, conciliation officers became concerned about exceeding their statutory powers and ACAS practice concerning COT3 settlements was standardised. Conciliation officers would only use COT3 in limited circumstances, in particular, where the employment had already terminated, and where there was a clear employment dispute; and where the parties had not already reached a *de facto* settlement agreement between themselves before involving ACAS. In practice, this had the effect of making the rapid and efficient resolution of employment disputes with the assistance of ACAS more difficult to achieve. The consequence was that fewer disputes were resolved at an early stage and more claims were presented to tribunals.

11–052   The "compromise agreement" represented an attempt to address the problem of the increasing number of employment disputes. Before 1993, the only way to achieve an agreement ousting the jurisdiction of the employment tribunal was by using ACAS conciliation. Under the Trade Union Reform and Employment Rights Act 1993, written compromise agreements under certain conditions became effective to oust the tribunal's jurisdiction in relation to "particular complaints". This would apply even if they were entered into before proceedings had been issued. The requirements for a compromise agreement to be binding included provisions that the employee must have had independent legal advice from a "qualified lawyer". That lawyer must have had an insurance policy covering him or her, and the advice must have covered the terms and effect of the proposed agreement and the employee's ability to continue tribunal proceedings.

Sections 9 and 10 of the 1998 Act extend the provisions for compromise agreements. They substitute an "independent adviser" for an independent qualified lawyer, and they clarify that insurance includes professional indemnity insurance cover. **11–053**

While compromise agreements are very popular, some uncertainty remains about the extent of their scope, with some awareness emerging that they might be more limited than anticipated. There are views that the pre-1990 procedures were simpler and more effective than they have become in the ensuing decade. **11–054**

7. MEDIATION PRACTICE

Dispute mediation

If a dispute is to be referred to mediation, three statutory conditions must be met: the consent of all parties is required; any agreed procedures should be fully used; and parties are expected to have made every effort first to resolve the matter through conciliation.[32] **11–055**

A mediator appointed in relation to an employment dispute may use all the same methods and procedures utilised by a conciliator. The fundamental difference between the two processes is that the mediator can in addition make recommendations to the parties for the resolution of those aspects that they cannot themselves settle. The parties are under no obligation to accept the mediator's recommendations. **11–056**

Parties will generally, but not invariably, provide written statements of their case to the mediator and to one another before the mediation process is commenced. They will also furnish a bundle of relevant documents. If this course is to be followed, it should be done reasonably well before the date fixed for the first mediation meeting so that the mediator can obtain supplementary information if required. This may perhaps include meeting separately with the parties or with individual employees, or making such other inquiries as he may consider useful and appropriate. **11–057**

As with conciliation, the mediator may hold separate, joint or caucus meetings, and may use a range of skills and techniques to try to assist the parties in arriving at an agreement. He will seek to establish a constructive ambience for negotiation, will create an acceptable agenda and try to work to it, will manage the process and chair the proceedings, will control any personality conflicts that may occur, and will generally try to facilitate a settlement. **11–058**

At the conclusion of the mediation, the mediator will prepare a report and submit it to ACAS to be sent to the parties. If the issues have been resolved, the report will contain the terms of settlement but if they are unresolved, then the report is the vehicle in which the settlement recommendations of the mediator are contained. Parties may accept the recommendations, or reject **11–059**

---

[32]*Encyclopaedia of Employment Law and Practice* by Frank Walton, published by Professional Publishing.

them and go to a tribunal or take other proceedings, or may revert to conciliation through an ACAS conciliator using the recommendations as a basis for further discussion and negotiation.

11–060   Mediation is not generally regarded as suitable for straightforward distributive conflicts such as annual pay claims. It is appropriate, however, for those cases where a form of conciliation is required, but it is felt that a higher level of intervention is needed than conciliation allows. It can also be more appropriate than arbitration for complex and interdependent issues, such as major reorganisation of jobs.[33]

Advisory mediation

11–061   In accordance with the principles of joint problem solving adopted by ACAS, advisory mediation mainly uses two processes for providing assistance. *Joint workshops* provide "a non-negotiating forum for parties to explore problems and identify appropriate courses of corrective action, including an agreed agenda for taking matters forward. *Joint working parties* are non-negotiating bodies, typically chaired by ACAS staff, through which employer and employee representatives work together, adopting a structured problem solving approach—problems are defined, information is gathered and considered, options are evaluated, and solutions are agreed and implemented".[34]

11–062   Advisory mediation is used as a tool both for preventing disputes and for helping to resolve them. An evaluation of the use of joint working parties[35] considered the methods used in establishing and working with these. It found that joint working parties rarely involved external full-time trade union officers. A number of managers tended to be involved, rather than just one manager from personnel. The scheme was more likely to succeed where a range of organisational members participated in the process of problem-solving, consensus-building and implementation.[36] The participation of employee representatives was high throughout the process, but especially during information-gathering, analysis of issues and formulating recommendations. "Problem-solving in 'smoke-filled rooms' between skilled negotiators was *not* a feature of ACAS advisory mediation. It involved a wide range of individuals as well as people acting in a representative capacity."[37] Research outcomes in the evaluation indicated a high level of success in the use of advisory mediation, including "surprisingly successful" outcomes in non-union organisations. "If customer satisfaction seen in benefit to the organisation is used as an outcome measure, then our survey provides unequivocal evidence of positive value. If 86 per cent of managers tell us that their organisation benefited a fair amount or a lot from the ACAS work, we presume a positive outcome in cost-benefit terms unless proved otherwise."[38]

---

[33] See ACAS article in Mackie, *Handbook of Dispute Resolution* at p. 111. As to the suitability of mediation for complex, interdependent issues, see the note on polycentricity in Chap. 14.
[34] *ACAS 1998 Annual Report* at p. 53.
[35] See n. 8 above.
[36] For similarities with consensus building in public policy issues, see Chap. 14.
[37] See nn. 8 and 35, *Joint problem solving* at p.23.
[38] *ibid.* at p. 32.

CHAPTER 12

MEDIATION OF COMMUNITY AND NEIGHBOUR DISPUTES

1. DEVELOPMENT OF COMMUNITY MEDIATION

Community mediation has developed in Britain with the aim of bringing **12–001** disputes arising within local communities under community control. The concept is that the legal system should not have to be used to deal with inter-personal or social disagreements. This is based on the notion of "grass-roots community self-help schemes" using local volunteers to bring disputing parties "face to face to discuss their allegations and grievances in a controlled way" and "to explore ways in which they could get on in future without conflict."[1]

Community mediation is well established in the United States, Canada and **12–002** parts of Australia (particularly New South Wales) and now in Britain. The idea was imported by the United States from Third World societies (such as the Indian panchayat) and older European village moots, which have survived in Norway, for instance, in the shape of "conflict councils". Various European countries, notably the United Kingdom, France and Finland, re-imported the community mediation idea from the United States.

The adaptation of these traditional concepts to modern Western culture has **12–003** inevitably been accompanied by radical changes in the process. It has become more informal, individualised (or private), and imbued with values (such as gender equality, acceptance of change, inter-group tolerance) not necessarily characteristic of the traditional manifestations.

2. DISPUTES COVERED BY COMMUNITY AND NEIGHBOUR MEDIATION

Although it may be assumed that "community mediation" covers all disputes **12–004** arising within a community, the position is not quite so simple. This is because other kinds of mediation exist, which may well overlap with one another. So a dispute within a community may involve family members, and may be more appropriate for family mediation. Or a dispute between a

---

[1] See *Reparation, Conciliation and Mediation* (1984) by Tony Marshall published by the Home Office Research and Planning Unit.

shopkeeper and a customer may be referred to commercial or civil mediation. Or a disagreement about environmental issues within a community may be appropriate for environmental mediation.

12–005   Certain kinds of issues commonly arise in community and neighbour mediation. These are listed separately, but there may often be an overlap between them, as one problem becomes the basis for disagreement or conflict in another field.

Noise problems

12–006   In cities, this tends to be the most frequent cause of disputes, particularly between neighbours. There may be a genuine absence of awareness that a problem exists. Lack of consideration and poor noise insulation may commonly be substantial contributory factors to the problem. Mutual frustration and aggressive responses may exacerbate actual events, and misconceptions and prejudices may feed reciprocal antagonism. Sometimes, one person does not realise that a noise problem exists and is faced with hostile behaviour by his neighbour. This is how they may become embroiled in a dispute, the one about noise and the other about aggression.

Harassment

12–007   Harassment may take different forms. It may constitute verbal abuse or threats; or it may comprise actions such as breaking windows, daubing walls with paint or engaging in other vandalism. It is usually aimed at a specific person, family or group (perhaps because of their race, culture or sexual orientation). Sometimes the harassment is by adults, who might become the principals in any mediation; but sometimes it may be by children, in which case whole families may be drawn into the dispute and the attempts to resolve it.

Children's behaviour

12–008   Children's behaviour may of course also give rise to complaints, even where it does not constitute harassment. Playing ball against a neighbour's wall, mischievous behaviour or excessive exuberance can create conditions in which antagonism can fester. This is most common where the "disturbed" party is elderly and may be afraid to approach young people about their behaviour. The lack of interaction between them may lead to the young people being projected as perhaps criminal or aggressive; and if this results in the police being called in, the conflict escalates. Also, people who do not have children in their household may sometimes have a different perception of "normal" levels of noise from family households where there are children. This can similarly lead to conflict.

Pets and other animals

12–009   Problems with animals can create enormous conflict between neighbours. These may, for example, include dogs that bark late at night or early in the morning or that are not kept under proper control, cocks that crow at dawn in urban or suburban areas, or birds that are fed excessively and create a nuisance to surrounding properties.

Boundary issues

The way in which neighbours maintain their property boundaries, and indeed **12–010**
the siting of such boundaries, can provoke anger and distress. One person
may consider that a fence encroaches on his land, even by just a few inches,
and he retaliates by moving or damaging it. Another objects to the height of
the fence, which she perceives as a deliberately offensive act. Trees overhang
a boundary wall and create problems, or are not trimmed and block a
neighbour's light. Common walls are not properly maintained. Disputes such
as these have involved people in costly litigation.

Eyesores and other environmental issues

People who do not maintain their properties acceptably, who erect unsightly **12–011**
signs or unusual structures on their property, or whose taste in colour or style
cause upset in the neighbourhood, may find themselves involved in dispute.
A man who truly enjoys allowing his garden to become overgrown with
weeds may contend that "his home is his castle" but his neighbours may
become aggrieved. Issues of hygiene may arise where there is serious lack of
care.

Where these issues affect individuals as between themselves, they would **12–012**
be likely to be appropriate for community or neighbour mediation. Where,
however, they affect the community as a whole, or sections of it, for example
where there are planning or more general environmental issues involved, then
that might be more appropriate for environmental mediation. (There could be
blurring, as where community mediators offer environmental mediation; or if
planning issues are very local and only affect neighbours, community
mediation would probably be more appropriate.)

Parking and other neighbour issues

Parking can become a cause for disagreement for example where a common **12–013**
driveway is blocked. Rights of way can also become contentious, both as to
the way in which they are entitled to be used, and their abuse. Almost any
issue that involves contact between people who live in close proximity to one
another can give rise to problems and misunderstanding.

3. OTHER KINDS OF COMMUNITY MEDIATION

In addition to neighbour disputes, community mediation may also embrace **12–014**
issues such as domestic quarrels, landlord and tenant disputes, conflicts
between estate residents and groups of youths, complaints against
organisations and conflicts within local organisations. Other kinds of specific
mediation should also be mentioned:

Mediation in schools and peer mediation

In the United States there are many school-based mediation schemes, in **12–015**
which pupils have been selected and trained to act as mediators in school
conflicts.[2] The National Association for Mediation in Education (NAME),

---

[2] See Charles T. Araki's article "Dispute Management in the Schools" (1980) 8(1) M.Q. and the

founded in 1984, has for example been actively developing programmes in conflict resolution and management in thousands of primary and secondary schools.[3] U.S. research as at 1997 indicated that peer mediation programmes in schools were successful in reducing disciplinary problems and violence and in improving the overall atmosphere. Reports showed that the programmes among adolescent pupils also produced an improvement not only in behaviour and attitudes, but also academic results.[4]

12–016   A number of mediation schemes in Britain have been introduced to schools, training both pupils and teachers in the skills of handling conflict. This is used for example to help children to deal with playground problems and bullying on a peer basis. Teachers and other school staff such as meal supervisors may also be able to act as mediators within a school.

12–017   In deciding on a schools programme, it must be decided whether conflicts other than those between pupils could be encompassed, such as those between pupil and teacher or between parent and school. The general learning effects of school mediation are regarded by many as being as important as the facility for resolving specific interpersonal disputes: improving school management with regard to handling conflicts, changing the attitudes of pupils and teachers, and giving children skills that enable them to avoid violence and fighting.[5]

Mediation of social conflicts and inter-group disputes

12–018   Community mediation services may from time to time be asked to assist in relation to major social conflicts, including for example environmental disputes, planning negotiations, racial conflict, police-community antagonisms and public policy issues. Further particulars are set out in Chapter 14 "The mediation of public policy issues and social conflicts".

Mediation involving older people

12–019   A mediation service geared specifically for older persons was established in 1991. The Elder Mediation project deals with conflicts affecting older people. These may be community conflicts (music played too loudly), family conflicts (generational disagreement involving grandparents), residential care conflicts (for example care staff operate rules too rigidly) or special conflicts (for example when old people become confused and are inconsistent in their ability to make decisions).[6]

Mediation dealing with complaints against doctors

12–020   There have been moves for mediation to be used to deal with complaints against doctors and other professionals. In 1991, the Leicestershire Family

---

references listed in that article.

[3]See the article by Karen Khor "Violence-plagued schools turn to conflict resolution" in *Consensus* No. 25 of January 1995. See also the article in the same issue "But do these programs really stop violence?" reporting on the generally positive outcome of research on these projects between 1990 and 1995 in schools around Ohio.

[4]See the article "Conflict Resolution in America's Schools" by Kay O. Wilburn and Mary Lynn Bates in the American Arbitration Association's *Dispute Resolution Journal* of January 1997.

[5]For an example see Valerie Marshall's article "Big Wayne and the White Gang" (Spring 1992) *Mediation* 9.2.

[6]Information extracted from the Elder Mediation Project pamphlet.

Health Service Authority established an informal conciliation service for patients with complaints against their doctors.[7] In 1996 the National Health Service introduced a new complaints procedure which includes a mediation option,[8] and pilot projects were instituted to deal with medical negligence claims by way of mediation.[9]

Other community mediation

Victim–offender mediation, which was the forerunner of many of the community mediation developments, is dealt with in Chapter 13. Other kinds of community conflict resolution services include a students' mediation service at the University of Portsmouth; a service in Plymouth concentrating on mediating where domestic violence exists; conflict resolution training in Leicester to help people deal with the problem of prostitution in a residential area; a mediation service in London to help young people who are estranged from their families; and a multi-faith and multi-cultural mediation service specialising in dispute resolution in situations of religious, spiritual or racial conflict.

12–021

4. COMMUNITY MEDIATION SERVICES

In Britain the first community mediation centres were set up in the early 1980s, initially in Newham, London (the Conflict and Change Project). There has been a significant increase over the last decade in the number of community mediation services operating in the United Kingdom, and as at 1997 the number has been estimated at 135 services.[10] Most inner London boroughs are now served, and they are particularly prevalent in other metropolitan areas around the country such as York, Leeds, Cambridge, Manchester, Plymouth, Liverpool, Brighton and Leicester.

12–022

Mediation services are common in all types of districts, not just inner city areas, although rates of conflict in the latter can be relatively high because of the population density and the general stresses of life there. Newer services are being established in small towns and rural areas, which have their own kinds of issues.[11]

12–023

Many services adopt a wider brief than merely offering mediation facilities. They will for instance give advice to people who are in conflict, provide training in the handling of conflict for local residents, police officers and social workers and work with local groups to develop a sense of

12–024

---

[7] See the article "Doctor, I have a complaint—about you" by Rachel Carmichael in (1994) 10(3) Med.

[8] The NHS calls this "conciliation". Access to conciliation is a statutory requirement for all complainants who choose to make a formal complaint through the NHS Complaints Procedure.

[9] See the article "Mediation in a Health Context" by Alison Campbell in (1997) 13(4) Med.

[10] This estimate is contained in *Community & Neighbour Mediation* by Marian Liebmann (ed.), Cavendish Publishing (1998). It compares with a figure of 100 services as at 1996 (as estimated by Mediation U.K. in their *Guide to Starting a Community Mediation Service* 2nd ed., 1996).

[11] See the Chap. "Community and Neighbourhood Mediation: A UK Perspective" by Marian Liebmann in *Rethinking Disputes: The Mediation Alternative* by Dr. Julie Macfarlane (ed.), Cavendish Publishing, 1997.

community or to combat racial tensions. This provides them with greater flexibility when responding to clients' needs or desires.

12–025   The Newham project saw itself as having very wide aims concerned with community development in a multi-racial area, although mediation has remained one of its central planks. As a grass roots initiative, run by local residents themselves, the project has pioneered a very informal approach to mediation, which puts as much emphasis on educating local people in how to manage their own disputes as on helping to settle specific cases. Many community mediation services espouse similar aims, but more recently established ones have tended to take a somewhat more formal approach to mediation, especially when they have been set up on an inter-agency basis or by local authorities. These two strands of community mediation run parallel with one another. The one focuses on volunteer-based services working at a grass roots level aimed at improving understanding. The other tends to be agency-led, using paid staff and some volunteers, concentrating on problem-solving and effectiveness of outcome.[12]

12–026   Where volunteers are used from the local community, they can bring to their mediation knowledge of that community, its cultures, facilities and problems, and experience of living there. This is a valuable asset. It enables them to speak "on the same wavelength" as the disputants and understand the unspoken undertones of their arguments. It makes them more acceptable to the clients, as being "one of us". It also sets a ready example that people "like us" can cope with conflict in a civilised and reasonable fashion.

12–027   There are now many different styles of mediation services in terms of structure and management. All are likely to have common membership in the national umbrella body, Mediation U.K., which has drawn up a common code of practice and an accreditation scheme that have general acceptance.[13]

12–028   Community mediation services may operate as independent services, usually with charitable status; or they may be part of a statutory agency. There are various sources of funding, such as Community Trusts or other charitable trusts, local authority funding, or special Government schemes.[14] In some instances, parties can contribute a voluntary donation after mediation if they wish.[15]

---

[12]See *Community & Neighbour Mediation* at pp. 80–81, which expresses concern at the danger perceived by some people that the agency-led model will lead to the process becoming too solution geared, rather than recognising the importance of helping people to achieve greater mutual understanding. Prof. Chris Mitchell anticipated this dichotomy in the formative years of Mediation U.K., when, for example, in his talk in 1988 to the Annual General Meeting of FIRM (Forum for Initiatives in Reparation and Mediation, the former name of Mediation U.K.) he warned against the professionalisation of community mediation. However, not all community mediators share this view of two strands, nor in particular does this mean that objectives or potential outcomes differ.

[13]Mediation U.K. offers an Accreditation Pack to mediation services for a nominal charge (£10 in 1997).

[14]For further details of funding sources, see Mediation U.K.'s *Guide to Starting a Community Mediation Service*.

[15]There are various mediation schemes being piloted by the courts. If community mediation services receive court referrals, a fee may need to be paid by the court, perhaps recouped from the parties or from legal aid.

5. THE MEDIATION PROCESS IN COMMUNITY DISPUTES

Neighbourhood disputes tend to be highly marked by emotions and personal prejudices, which means that mediators may have to spend time on allowing parties to express their feelings and paying as much attention to psychological healing as material agreements. In some cases, the original material dispute may have entirely disappeared with the passage of time, but the conflict continues to escalate through acts of animosity and revenge.[16] **12–029**

Two co-mediators commonly carry out community mediation. This provides support during the mediation, and allows newly trained mediators to obtain experience in conjunction with more seasoned colleagues. It also allows differences between disputants to be matched, for example if one is black and one is white, or one is male and the other female. This may be helpful to the parties' perceptions of empathetic understanding from the mediators if there are issues in the dispute related to the racial, gender or age differences between the parties.[17] **12–030**

The process of mediation of community disputes will be described using the broad framework of 10 stages outlined in Chapter 8.[18] **12–031**

Stage 1: Engaging the parties in the mediation forum
Referrals to community mediation services tend to come from individuals themselves, or from a range of community agencies, such as Citizens' Advice Bureaux, the police, environmental health or housing departments of the local authority and solicitors. **12–032**

The first step is to discuss the issues with the person who raised the issue and to get some understanding of the problem. This might be the complainant or the person who is being complained about (who may well wish to have the issue resolved).[19] If mediation is considered appropriate, the mediators will explain the process and inquire whether the mediators may approach the other party to suggest and explain mediation. If the initial party is unwilling for the mediators to make such an approach to the other party, the mediators can help the person analyse their situation dispassionately. This may present a new perspective that helps the person resolve the issue or at least to come to terms with it. Merely listening actively can help relieve tensions and anger that prevented that person from directly approaching the other party. **12–033**

If the first party is willing, the mediators attempt to contact the other party and introduce the idea of mediation. In some cases, the second party may be **12–034**

---

[16] See Tony Marshall's article "The power of mediation" (1990) 8(2) M.Q. 115–124.

[17] However, some mediators feel that such "matching" may be a token practice, especially if there are no issues in the dispute relevant to such racial, gender or age differences. While it may be positive if it enhances the disputants' perception of mediator impartiality, it may sometimes avoid a need for mediators to examine their own perceptions and prejudices about different cultural groups.

[18] These 10 stages are used as a framework for all mediation reviewed in this book. Mediation U.K. in its training programme identifies 7 stages of community mediation: see its *Training Manual in Community Mediation Skills* (1995). All of the stages set out in this chapter should be supplemented by reference to the general principles outlined in Chap. 8.

[19] Services tend to call parties "Party 1" being the person who approached them, and "Party 2" being the other party. Most disputes involve counter-allegations of one kind or another, so the term "complainant" is not necessarily useful or relevant.

quite unaware that a conflict exists, because the first party has been too afraid to raise the issue directly with him. Some disputes can be quickly resolved at this stage, once the mediators contact the second party to establish that person's concerns and views.[20] In other cases, the second party does not want mediation and the mediators must fall back on simply assisting the first party with reviewing and analysing the situation. Mediators would not in these (or any other) circumstances give advice to either party; but they may give information about where to go for support or for legal advice, such as a Citizens' Advice Bureau.

12–035   For mediation to take place, both parties must of course agree to it.

Stage 2: Obtaining commitment and agreeing mediation rules

12–036 Both parties' agreement to mediation will constitute the initial commitment to the process. It remains necessary to consider with each party whether there will then be a joint meeting, or whether either of them prefers not to have a face to face meeting. In the latter event, the mediators may offer to shuttle between the parties (though many community mediators find that if parties are unwilling to discuss a dispute, shuttle mediation is unlikely to be any more successful).

12–037   If a joint meeting is agreed, an informal arrangement will be made as to the place and time for the mediation. If shuttle mediation is to take place, the mediators will liaise with the parties as to convenient times for doing this.

12–038   Unlike many models of family, civil or commercial mediation, parties in community mediation are not ordinarily asked to sign an agreement setting out the terms and ground rules on which the mediation will take place. They may, however, be given or sent a note outlining the procedure and ground rules. As a rule, participation in the process is voluntary and informal.

Stage 3: Preliminary communications and preparation

12–039 As previously indicated, in some cases, because of the intensity of the emotions involved, it will not be possible to contemplate an immediate meeting of the parties. In such event, the mediators will talk separately to each party. This may result in an agreement without a face to face meeting occurring at all, especially if the parties do not need to have any significant contact with one another in the future. Alternatively, the shuttle mediation may lay the groundwork for an eventual meeting.

12–040   The parties are not asked to prepare written summaries of their positions or to produce documents in advance. If they have relevant papers that they wish to mention in the mediation, they may be asked to bring them to the meeting if this is thought appropriate. This would not, however, be dealt with in a formal or legalistic way.

12–041   Much of the preparation will have been covered by the preliminary

---

[20] There are differences of practice between services as to whether the second party is informed of the problem, as indicated by the first party. While some may do so, others feel that the second party visit has the same function as the first party visit, namely to hear of any concerns that person may have about their neighbour. Whichever approach is followed, the mediator would need to guard against being seen as an advocate for the first party rather than an impartial intermediary.

discussions with each party, and establishing their wish to mediate. The mediators may send them procedural information. By the time the parties reach the mediation forum, they should understand what is involved and be committed to trying to deal with the issues there.

Stage 4: Establishing the venue and meeting the parties

Joint mediation sessions in the community context are informal in style. They should take place in a neutral venue. Usually the parties and the mediators sit in a circle. The placing of the parties has to be considered in advance in the light of the information gathered by the mediators on the state of the relationship between them. Apart from seating, mediators should check that they have tea or coffee, water and other facilities available, that they have agreed the applicable smoking regulations, and that they are clear about their opening statement and procedure.[21]   **12–042**

In some cases, the mediators will be different from those who prepared the case: practice in this respect differs between services.   **12–043**

Where the nature of the premises allows, parties may be able to wait in different ante-rooms when they arrive, but much depends on whether difficulties are anticipated, and the availability of space.   **12–044**

The conduct of a mediation session itself is similar to other types of mediation in other fields. The mediators will make a brief introductory statement, outlining the process. They may re-affirm their neutrality, and the parties may be asked to confirm that they wish to proceed if any reservations are expressed. Ground rules are established and agreed. Some mediators ask parties, as a sign of good faith, to confirm that they are present to try to resolve their dispute. This co-operative act can then be built on as the mediation progresses.   **12–045**

Stage 5: Establishing the issues and setting the agenda

Following the introductions, each party in turn will be given a chance to give their own account of the dispute. The mediators will not allow these presentations to be interrupted. The mediators during this phase will try to ensure that parties express their feelings as well as the material facts of the case as they see them, but they will deter abusive, harassing or threatening remarks. They will generally summarise each presentation by way of feedback, to ensure that the parties are satisfied that they have each been heard correctly.   **12–046**

At some convenient point, clarification may be sought on points of detail. This is unlikely to be done before both parties have completed their presentations, in order to avoid an imbalance in the time given to either party, especially for example one who is less articulate or who has brought more issues. Mediators will be aware of the build-up of frustration while parties wait to make their own presentations, and will avoid exacerbating this by inappropriately timed questions.   **12–047**

---

[21] These matters and community mediation practice generally are covered in *Peacemaking in Your Neighborhood: Mediator's Handbook,* (Friends Conflict Resolution Programs, Philadelphia, 4th rev., 1990) (ed. by Jennifer E. Beer); also in *Community & Neighbour Mediation* by Marian Liebmann (ed.) (see n. 3 above) and in Mediation U.K.'s *Training Manual in Community Mediation Skills* (1995).

12-048   Consideration will be given as to who should make the first presentation. It has been suggested that that the timid participant or less articulate or powerful person might feel more comfortable if given the opportunity to speak first, or that an agitated party may need to be asked to start. The mediator may otherwise decide to ask the original complainant to commence, or may ask who wishes to start. Speakers should be limited in time, or asked to summarise if they become repetitive.[22]

12-049   An agenda is likely to be implicit from the issues raised by the parties, rather than necessarily explicitly decided upon. The mediators may however discuss fixing an informal agenda, especially where the issues identified by the parties are complex; or at least they should identify the parties' priorities.

Stage 6: Information gathering

12-050   This is not done as a distinct stage but rather information is gathered as the process unfolds. The mediators will obtain some relevant information during their initial communications with the parties, some in separate meetings with them, and some during the course of the process itself.

12-051   One of the most useful ways of gathering information in informal mediation of this nature is through effective questioning. This may help to elicit the necessary information and clarify any areas of misunderstanding. It is not, however, in the nature of cross-examination. The mediators will need to listen with care to what is being said, and should pay attention to body language and other non-verbal communications.[23]

Stage 7: Managing and facilitating discussions and negotiation

12-052   After the presentations, there will be a phase of free discussion and exchange, exploring differences and clarifying the nature of the principal issues. During this phase the mediators will try both to establish a common view of the nature of the problem and to ensure that the parties are able to communicate freely and constructively. They will attempt to identify common ground as well as differences, the nature of each party's real needs (as distinct from their negotiating positions), their priorities, any underlying problems that need to be encouraged into the open and emotions that may have to be addressed.

12-053   This stage may sometimes be quite heated, or parties may become distressed. The *Mediator's Handbook* suggests that the mediators should handle this stage calmly, asserting control over the framework of the process as necessary, involving anyone who is not participating, and allowing feelings to come up but not pressing people to discuss these.[24]

12-054   It should now be possible to enter the phase of generating and examining options for settlement and working towards arrangements that would best meet all needs.

12-055   All the skills of facilitation outlined in Chapters 8 and 15 are relevant to this stage. The mediators need to help the parties to adopt a problem-solving mode. They will also need to maintain control of the process, keep

---

[22]See *Peacemaking in Your Neighborhood: Mediator's Handbook* at pp. 25–26.
[23]See "Non-verbal communications" in Chap. 15.
[24]*Peacemaking in Your Neighborhood: Mediator's Handbook* at pp. 31, 32, 38.

discussions focused, provide a model for the conduct of the parties, balance negotiating power if necessary, maintain a constructive climate for discussions, and where necessary "confront problem behaviour".[25] The generation by the parties of suggestions and options for solving the problems is a key part of the process.

As in other mediation, this process is generally "future-focused" to move **12–056** the parties from past grievances towards new ways for the future. There is, however, some tension between this approach and the "transformative" one described by Folger and Bush in their work *The Promise of Mediation*.[26] The latter approach questions the emphasis on future-focus and problem-solving, concentrating instead on helping disputing parties to a better understanding, and empowerment.[27]

Stage 8: Employing impasse strategies

When parties are stuck, it can help to move to other issues and to try to **12–057** generate progress there. If separate meetings with the parties have not been held, the mediators may try these. Sometimes it can also help for the mediators to acknowledge that they are stuck and to invite the parties' ideas. Some mediators may offer their own ideas, but if this is done it should be "impersonally, not as advice".[28] Mediators should not, however, try to press their solutions on the parties.

Many of the impasse strategies outlined in Chapter 8 may be equally **12–058** relevant to community disputes. Care should always be taken by the mediators to avoid exercising authority which may inhibit the parties from reaching their own conclusion or choosing to move to other alternatives, including use of the courts if that is what they wish.

Stage 9: Concluding mediation and recording the outcome

Where the mediation results in an agreement, the mediators should **12–059** acknowledge the parties' achievement. They may then need to formalise the agreement. Where no agreement is reached, they may want to consider with the parties what further options they have, and may offer further help in the future if required.

In most neighbourhood disputes the issues are not clearly separable. Facts **12–060**

---

[25]*ibid.*, at pp. 33–37: the confrontation of problem behaviour merely means that it needs to be identified and corrected, in a firm but not imperious way, and with sensitivity to possible loss of face.

[26]*The Promise of Mediation: Responding to Conflict through Power and Recognition* by Robert A. Baruch Bush and Joseph P. Folger (San Francisco, Jossey Bass, 1994).

[27]This tension is identified by Marian Liebmann in *Community & Neighbour Mediation* at p. 81. She relates this dichotomy to the two strands in community mediation: see para 12–025 and n. 12 above. She does, however, also emphasise that there are factors that suggest that the situation is not "either/or" but that both approaches have the aim and effect of increasing understanding between people. Other community mediators agree with this latter emphasis, rather than the two-strand concept, as the potential outcomes in mediation are the same under either strand.

[28]See *Peacemaking in Your Neighbourhood: Mediator's Handbook* at pp. 48–49. The authors urge care in doing this, to avoid giving too much authority to the idea, *e.g.* by offering two or three suggestions at once. However, there is a strong alternative view that even this is not good policy in community mediation, having the effect of disempowering the parties, and perhaps affecting their view of the mediator's impartiality. Many community mediators prefer alternative methods of genuine inquiry, without putting forward any preconceived solutions.

and feelings may be interrelated, and care needs to be taken to prepare an agreement that similarly balances the issues and parties' obligations, not identifying clear winners and losers. The agreement should also include provisions for future disputes, for example "If A is disturbed in future by B's dog, than A agrees to tell B about this in a calm manner, and not go straight to the police".

12–061   Although in some cases the parties may not require any written record of the understandings reached by them, agreements are normally recorded in writing and signed by the parties, because this acts symbolically as an assurance of the parties' sincere intentions. Such an agreement is not normally intended to carry any special legal status but of course it might have legal consequences and should therefore be drafted with care.[29] The position would be different if a solicitor or a court referred the case with the express purpose of formulating a legal agreement. In such a case, the settlement would need to be binding if so required by the parties. In this event the parties may in some cases want their legal advisers to review it before they sign it, though obviously much depends on what issues and obligations are involved. Where legal rights are actually or potentially involved, the mediators may in any event advise parties to seek legal advice before entering into any agreement.

Stage 10: Post-termination
12–062   It is accepted as good practice for the mediators to offer a follow-up service by getting in touch with the parties after a specified time to see whether the agreement is working successfully, and if not to offer further mediation. Such follow-up contacts would normally only take place, however, if the parties gave prior agreement to them.

General observations
12–063   Many difficulties may occur in this kind of mediation because of the various extrinsic factors that may impinge upon a resolution of the problem. These may include the nature and history of the relationship between the parties, the influence of common acquaintances, the nature and culture of the area where they live, personal and social problems unrelated to the immediate issues, power struggles, attitudes and styles of living. A dispute may sometimes occur because of the isolation of one of the parties and their use of complaints to stimulate some kind of personal relationship, even if it is a negative one. Parties may blame one another for a problem caused by a third party, such as local authority housing with party walls that provide inadequate sound insulation.

12–064   Power imbalances may need to be addressed by the mediators by ensuring parity of opportunity in discussion, or helping less articulate parties to express their needs or opinions. In extreme cases, mediators may decide to discontinue mediation because there is no way in which a fair outcome can result.[30]

12–065   Sometimes it will be necessary to involve other parties in the mediation

---

[29]See Stage 9 of Chap. 8 and Appendix II for the principles applicable to such drafting.
[30]See Chap. 21, Ethics, fairness and power balance.

because the ramifications of the dispute make it insoluble for the original parties alone. Racial and other cultural animosities may be present, which are particularly difficult for mediators to deal with; but much experience has been accumulated in relation to such problems, and special training programmes are available on handling prejudice.

The complexity and diffuse character of community disputes necessitate a **12–066** high degree of flexibility and informality in the structure of such mediation. Periods of face to face discussion may be interspersed with separate meetings. For community mediation, mediators need to be trained in the principles and skills of conflict resolution, and not a rigid set of procedures, so that they are able to adjust action to the exigencies of each dispute.

CHAPTER 13

VICTIM–OFFENDER MEDIATION AND REPARATION

1. MEDIATION AND REPARATION IN THE CRIMINAL JUSTICE SYSTEM

13–001 A form of mediation has been developed in the field of criminal justice, combining concern for victims and the rehabilitation of offenders with the notion of reparation. Mediation and reparation schemes for certain victims of crime and their offenders have been established in many parts of North America and Europe, including the United Kingdom. As at 1998, there were believed to be 315 such programmes in the United States and over 700 in Europe (43 of them in England).[1]

13–002 Under these schemes, victims meet their offenders in the presence of a third party in order to afford them an opportunity for discussion and to arrive at agreed terms for restitution, whether financial or by way of services to be performed for the victim or the community. These were known in Britain as "reparation schemes" and in the United States as "victim–offender reconciliation programs" (VORPS). However, in both countries the term "victim and offender mediation" schemes or programmes is now more commonly used; and the generic term "restorative justice" covers these schemes.

Restorative justice: The rationale

13–003 The criminal justice system is largely based on the proposition of crime being an offence against the State. Consequently, the State prosecutes offenders and exacts retribution by way of punishment. This, however, overlooks the relationship that the victim has with the crime and the offender and sometimes neglects the victim in the process. For this reason, the system has re-balanced itself over the last decade or two by introducing the concept of victims' rights and support.[2]

13–004 Restorative justice is based on the inter-relationship of the victim, the

---

[1] See the "National Survey of Victim–Offender Mediation Programs in the United States" by Mark S. Umbreit and Jean Greenwood in M.Q. 16(3) of Spring 1999 at pp. 235–237.

[2] Concern for the victim developed in the 1970s and early 1980s, and manifested in the Victim Support movement and the National Association of Victim Support Schemes. See "The Victim Support Perspective" by Helen Reeves in *Mediation and Criminal Justice: Victims, Offenders and Community* edited by Martin Wright and Burt Galaway (1989). See also the *Victim & Offender Handbook* compiled by Deidre Quill and Jean Wynne (1993).

offender and the State. It involves a different way of viewing crime, by focusing on the injury to the victim and the community, rather than to the State, and by aiming for restitution rather than punishment as a primary goal. The breach of State law is seen as a secondary element.

The following definition is said to have been adopted by a United Nations   **13–005**
Working Party on Restorative Justice: "Restorative justice is a process whereby all the parties with a stake in a particular offence come together to resolve collectively how to deal with the aftermath of the offence and its implications for the future."[3] The aim of restorative justice has been described as "repairing (as far as possible) or making up for the damage and hurt caused by the crime."[4]

With the development of concern for victims of crime came the   **13–006**
development of the concept of compensation, which had in fact been promoted some decades earlier by Margaret Fry of the Howard League for Penal Reform.[5] Fry had been prominent in seeking compensation for victims of crime, a campaign which is said to have influenced the development of criminal injuries compensation in 1964.

The following are the main principles of restorative justice: **13–007**

- The offence is primarily against the victim and secondarily against the State.

- Restitution is important in restoring the relationship between victim and offender.

- Restitution may be achieved by way of reparation, usually in the form of compensation or some form of community service.

- Reconciliation between victim and offender is also seen as an important objective of restorative justice, but not universally so. Some people feel that victims should not be pressed to forgive and become reconciled with their offender until they are ready to do so. (This is one of the main reasons why victim–offender reconciliation programs in the U.S. changed their name to victim–offender mediation programs.)

- Communication and negotiation between the victim and offender is possible and often desirable to consider how to redress the wrong.

- Offenders are required to take responsibility for their actions and are given the opportunity to make amends.

These broad principles of restorative justice are promoted as an alternative   **13–008**
to the present criminal justice system based on punishment and deterrence.

---

[3]Restorative Justice Overview: on the Internet at *http://www.restorativejustice.org/rj1overview.htm*
[4]Martin Wright, *Justice for Victims and Offenders: a restorative response to crime* (1991) at p. 41 (as mentioned in *Victim–Offender Mediation: Limitations and Potential* by Gwen Robinson (1996).
[5]See Robinson, *op. cit.* at p. 10.

Restorative justice programmes

13–009   Restorative justice is translated into practice through a number of programmes based on its principles:

Victim–offender mediation programmes

13–010   These programmes allow victims and offenders an opportunity, either directly or indirectly, to work with a mediator to discuss the crime, its consequences and effects, and to consider how the offender can best make amends for the offence. This may be by way of apology, reparation, community service or any other agreed form.

13–011   The history of these programmes has been traced in a number of works and articles.[6] The forerunner of victim–offender reconciliation programmes in North America is said to have been an experiment conducted by a court in Kitchener, Ontario, in 1974. In that case, a probation officer invited the court to see whether the victims of a vandalism spree would be willing to meet the offenders to discuss the crime. This first experiment resulted in the offenders making restitution to the victims, and "was successful beyond everyone's expectations".[7] These concepts developed in North America into Victim–Offender Reconciliation Programmes and latterly Victim–Offender Mediation Programmes.

13–012   In the United Kingdom, interest in victim–offender reparation schemes developed in the 1970s. Compensation orders were introduced into the substantive law by the Criminal Justice Act, 1972. Community service schemes started around the same time sponsored by the Home Office, to help offenders re-integrate with their communities by carrying out acts of service. But it was only in the 1980s that actual reparation schemes began to be created. By then, there was an increasing awareness of victims' rights and needs, and the National Association of Victims Support Schemes had been launched. The Home Office established four experimental reparation schemes. These were in Coventry (where funded by the Cadbury Trust, Martin Wright carried out a feasibility study, which was the first of its kind in England), Wolverhampton, Carlisle and Leeds.[8]

13–013   Home Office interest in the experimental schemes moved towards reparation as an additional sanction of the court, rather than as a voluntary instrument of reconciliation. This was not approved by the experimental schemes. Home Office funding ended, and schemes found alternative sources

---

[6] See, *e.g.* Tony Marshall's *Reparation, Conciliation and Mediation,* (London: Home Office Research & Planning Unit, Paper 27, 1984); Marshall & Walpole, *Bringing people together: Mediation & Reparation Projects in Great Britain* (London: Home Office Research & Planning Unit, Paper 33, 1985); Marshall & Merry, *Crime and Accountability* (London: HMSO, 1990); Wright and Galaway (eds.), *Mediation and Criminal Justice: Victims, Offenders and Community* (London: Sage Publications Limited, 1989); Wright, *Justice for Victims and Offenders: a restorative response to crime* (Milton Keynes: Open University Press, 1991); Gwen Robinson's *Victim–Offender Mediation: Limitations and Potential* (Oxford: Centre for Criminological Research, University of Oxford, 1996) and the bibliography mentioned there.

[7] See "The Kitchener Experiment" by Dean E. Peachey in Wright and Galaway (eds.), *Mediation and Criminal Justice: Victims, Offenders and Community* (1989).

[8] For a more detailed history of these schemes, see the chapter in Wright and Galaway (1989) "Reconciling Mediation with Criminal Justice" by John Harding, who had directed one of the U.K.'s first community service schemes. See also the West Yorkshire Probation Service/Save the Children Fund handbook (1991), and Quill & Wynne (1993) which gives more information about the Leeds service.

of funding and support. Many of these developed into the victim–offender mediation programmes now in existence.[9] The umbrella organisation, Mediation U.K., (which began in 1985 as the Forum for Initiatives in Reparation and Mediation), has been a strong supporter of victim–offender mediation programmes since its inception. It provides a code of practice, helps develop training for mediators, stimulates and helps plan new schemes, and helps protect against threats to the neutrality and aims of mediation organisations.[10]

This chapter will describe this form of mediation more fully.   13–014

Family group conferencing

A conference is described as "a structured meeting between offenders,   13–015
victims and both parties' family and friends in which they deal with the consequences of the crime and decide how best to repair the harm. [It is] neither a counselling nor a mediation process....".[11] These conferences have mainly been used for juvenile offenders, to allow victims the chance to confront the offender and express their feelings, and to allow the offenders the chance to apologise and make amends. A facilitator, rather than a mediator, will assist the process.

According to a two-year study, Family Group Conferences have produced   13–016
high levels of satisfaction, with 94 per cent compliance with commitments made at the conference.[12] Tony Marshall (of the Home Office Research Unit and the first Director of Mediation U.K.) sees the conferences as "an exciting idea which could become a central practice in a system of 'restorative justice' complementary to the courts system.... full of vast practical potential at the leading edge of a new conception of justice."[13] However, Marshall warns of potential pitfalls. These include the risk that the process will be undertaken by facilitators without highly specialised training in mediation, and that police officers or social workers might take on the role of facilitators instead of parties. He also warns of the need for careful and detailed preparation, and of the need to ensure that victims play a full part in the process, balanced against offender's rights being safeguarded. Families involved in the process might need to receive support.

Young offenders projects

These are Restorative Justice projects geared specifically for juveniles, and   13–017
merit some special attention because of that specific focus.

The Thames Valley Police have successfully conducted a pilot Restorative   13–018
Justice scheme for young offenders. The results of the pilot scheme were reported to be startling to senior officers as well as groups dealing with young offenders. They showed that whereas national figures suggested that a third of young people would reoffend after receiving a caution for their first

---

[9]See Gwen Robinson (1996) and Davis, with Messmer, Umbreit & Coates, *Making Amends: Mediation and Reparation in Criminal Justice* (1992).
[10]See Chap. 1 of *Victim & Offender: Mediation Handbook* by Quill & Wynne, (1993).
[11]"Real Justice", on the Internet at *http://www.realjustice.org/Pages/what-is.html*
[12]"Real Justice", see n. 11.
[13]See his articles "Criminal Justice Conferencing: Calls for Caution" in (1997) 13(1) Med. published by Mediation U.K., and (1997) 13(2) Med.

offence, the pilot scheme changed the reoffending rate from about 30 per cent to just four per cent.[14] As a result, the pilot scheme has been extended, and there have been calls for the programme to be adopted nationwide.[15]

13–019　　The Thames Valley pilot scheme dealt with almost 400 young offenders during the period April 1995 to October 1997. Participation was voluntary, and was available only to offenders facing a caution in the court. One of the main elements of the scheme was to confront offenders critically with the consequences of their actions.

13–020　　The Chief Constable of Thames Valley Police suggested to a conference in March 1997 that second and third time offenders should be referred to community conferencing. This would bring together not only the victim and offender but their families, mentors, secondary victims such as neighbours, and community representatives, to discuss the incident, its causes and effects, to invite a response from all parties, concluding with a restorative agreement.[16]

13–021　　The Thames Valley Police Project uses the restorative conference as a key feature of its work. Typically, those present at the conference would include victims and their families and friends, offenders and their families and friends, and, if appropriate, representatives of the community affected by the crime. A trained person chairs the conference and facilitates discussion. In this way, offenders hear the details of the harm that they have caused. The conference usually provides the opportunity for an agreement to be reached about reparation, which "may include an embarrassed, yet sincere, apology to the victims; a subsequent written apology; or some form of financial compensation or work in kind."[17]

13–022　　Thames Valley Police describe restorative justice as consistent with a "problem-solving style of policing". One way of tackling the causes of crime is to seek community-based solutions. Restorative justice, in their view, gives communities a voice and ensures that offenders are faced with the consequences of their behaviour. It provides a means for offenders to change their behaviour, instead of facing what the Thames Valley Police brochure calls the "depersonalised, technical nature of the proceedings and the mitigation process" in the courtroom setting.

13–023　　Conferences are also used as an opportunity to give a caution to an offender where this is the appropriate way to deal with a case. Whereas an instant caution may be given where the impact of the crime on the victim or the community is minimal, a restorative caution may be given where the impact is more significant. In such cases, all parties concerned would first be contacted to check that this was the most appropriate way to proceed. If a victim wished to participate in a face to face meeting with the offender, this would be done at a conference, where a trained police officer would give the formal police caution.

13–024　　As at May 1999, Thames Valley Police had trained 277 members of staff, comprising police and other agencies, in restorative justice conferencing.

---

[14]*The Guardian*, October 18, 1997.

[15]Although important, recidivism is not the only issue in this kind of mediation. Other benefits exist apart from reducing re-offending rates.

[16]Wright, *op. cit.*

[17]Thames Valley Police brochure: "Restorative Justice: A balanced approach".

Over 500 restorative justice conferences were carried out between May 1998 and May 1999. The scheme is being evaluated[18] but early indications show a significant reduction in recidivism. Clearly, reducing recidivism is an important feature of the scheme. Other benefits may also exist, which cannot perhaps be so easily quantified.

Another similar project is SACRO's Young Offenders Mediation Project, **13–025** which was established in Fife, Scotland in 1996. The model used in this project was derived from SACRO's experience in victim–offender mediation for adults. SACRO state that it is based on three distinctive features. These are early intervention, victim perspective and voluntary reparation.[19]

The Fife project is geared to offenders considered to be potentially at risk **13–026** of further offending. Victims are contacted by a project mediator, as are offenders and their parents. Reparative work is arranged through voluntary groups and community councils.

It is interesting to note that although face to face meetings between victim **13–027** and offender only took place in 10 per cent of the cases in Fife, around 90 per cent of the offenders felt that the project had helped their understanding of their behaviour and had changed their thinking about getting into trouble. 75 per cent of victims said that they would recommend participation in the project to other victims. Apart from direct meetings between victims and young offenders, the project had various other outcomes. These included written explanations and apologies (13 per cent), reparative work for the victim (eight per cent), reparative work for the community (27 per cent), an agreement not to approach or harass the victim (eight per cent) and a discussion programme (20 per cent). Many victims appreciate the young offender undertaking reparation work. Equally important and satisfying to the victims is that they have been consulted and allowed to express their views.

The restorative justice consortium

In May 1999, the Restorative Justice Consortium was launched as a forum of **13–028** national organisations with a common interest in promoting a fully restorative criminal justice system. It includes all major voluntary organisations and professional organisations involved in criminal justice, for example, the Association of Chief Officers of Probation, the Association of Chief Police Officers, the Police Foundation, the Prison Governors' Association, the Howard League for Penal Reform, Mediation U.K., Victim Support National Office and the National Association for the Care and Resettlement of Offenders.

The Consortium has endorsed the value of restorative justice in "bringing **13–029** balance to criminal justice" so as to be more effective in healing victims, preventing re-offending and healing communities. It seeks a wider discussion about the principles of restorative justice so that these may be "more widely understood and debated, monitored and evaluated, and sensitively developed".[20]

---

[18]The Oxford Centre of Criminological Research is undertaking this.
[19]SACRO, *Young Offenders Mediation Project: Annual Report 1997/1998* (Edinburgh: SACRO, 1998) and related paper.
[20]Restorative Justice Consortium Public Launch pamphlet, May 20, 1999.

Referral sources

13–030   Referrals to victim–offender mediation come from a variety of agencies, usually police liaison panels, courts, defence solicitors, Citizens' Advice Bureaux, environmental health or housing departments of the local authority, probation officers and social workers. Victim Support schemes in some areas take an interest in such work, and referrals are now received from these schemes as well.

13–031   In North America and Australia, community mediation centres also receive referrals of cases involving inter-personal disputes from the civil and criminal courts. Proceedings are discontinued while the mediation takes place. If the case is resolved, it may not need to go back to court.

13–032   Victims may be of any kind, both personal and corporate, and may have different objectives in meeting the offender. The victim may desire information (why did you do it? why did you pick me?), to express anger, or to impress on the offender the personal consequences of the crime.

Kinds of offences dealt with by mediation programmes

13–033   The various victim–offender mediation schemes each have their own policy about the nature of the offence that can be brought to them. Many exclude serious violent and sexual offences, though some have no restrictions and may even gear themselves to cases that are more serious.[21] Mediators will be careful to screen out parties who are too emotional or disturbed to handle direct meetings.

13–034   There may be a relationship between seriousness of offence and stage of proceedings at which it is brought into a scheme. A crime diverted before prosecution will tend to be less serious than one brought into the scheme following prosecution or sentence.[22]

13–035   Offenders may be subject to an official caution, currently in the course of being prosecuted, or already sentenced. They will all have admitted guilt: mediation is not appropriate where this is in dispute. They may be feeling remorse to variable extents prior to the meeting. Those with obviously cynical attitudes will not be accepted. One of the intentions of a meeting with the victim is to create a realisation of the personal harm caused and to encourage the offender to accept responsibility, so that some degree of change of attitude can be expected, often quite considerable, at least in the short term. The offender may be glad of the chance to apologise and to set the record straight, often also to offer reparation.

13–036   Some believe that it is in more serious cases, such as aggravated burglary or sexual assault, that victims may have most to gain from being able to express their feelings and come to some sort of resolution of the aftermath of the crime. Mediation has even been used in manslaughter and murder cases between the offender and relatives of the victim (usually some considerable time after the event). Mark Umbreit, writing about the transformative and healing power of mediation, observes that these powerful, if controversial to some, qualities of mediation have been observed in the use of mediation and

---

[21]See Robinson (1996) at p. 23, referring also to Davis (1987).
[22]The possibility of using mediation more extensively by probation officers preparing reports for the courts in relation to sentencing is examined in an article by Maria R. Volpe and Charles Lindner, "Mediation and Probation: The Presentence Investigation" (1991) 9(1) M.Q. 47.

dialogue in the United States between parents of murdered children and the offender.[23]

A significant proportion of crimes involving personal victims are committed by someone who is acquainted with the victim. A Home Office study[24] showed that in half the cases it considered the victim and the offender already knew one another, at least by sight. Even if not, commonly they lived in the same neighbourhood, in either event creating the potential for dispute, especially in those cases where desire for revenge (by victim or offender) was a factor. Such situations offer opportunities for better understanding and reconciliation through mediation.   **13–037**

The Fife Young Offender Mediation Programme lists theft as the main crime brought into its scheme. Other offences mainly dealt with are vandalism, assault and road traffic offences.[25] The Thames Valley Scheme specifies that only those offenders facing a caution are able to take part. The scheme is voluntary. Robinson suggests that "police-based projects are inevitably concerned with less serious offences whilst court-based schemes can be expected to deal with the upper range of the magistrates' court caseload".[26]   **13–038**

Thames Valley Police provide a case study in their brochure of two drunken teenagers who smashed their way into a memorial hall in an Oxfordshire village in 1997. When arrested, both admitted the offence. Neither had previous convictions. The Parish Council initially wished to prosecute but agreed to participate in a conference. In the conference, the councillors outlined how the hall had become unusable and had closed down. Village groups had been affected. The young men's parents said how appalled they were at their sons' behaviour. The teenagers were very ashamed and offered to make amends by paying for the damage and helping by redecorating the hall. An agreement to this effect was signed, and the councillors, teenagers and their parents were all able to enter into discussions. The parish councillors said that they felt great satisfaction in having been able to participate. They and the local police were pleased with the outcome.   **13–039**

Voluntariness

The voluntary element of victim–offender mediation is critical to its use. However, there are risks that this voluntary element will not be whole-hearted or that it may arise through direct or indirect pressure to participate.   **13–040**

For the offender, there might be coercion from the criminal justice system to take part in the process. Alternatively, the offender might hope for some benefit from taking part, such as a more lenient sentence if the mediation takes place before sentencing. For the victim, the pressure might be direct, or it might be more subtle, as where the victim expresses a willingness to participate and the victim finds it difficult not to agree to do so.   **13–041**

There is general agreement among writers and practitioners that genuine   **13–042**

---

[23]"Humanistic Mediation: A Transformative Journey of Peacemaking" at M.Q. 14(3) 203, Spring 1997.

[24]By Marshall and Merry, see n. 6 above.

[25]See *SACRO Annual Report 1997/1998.*

[26]Robinson (1996) at p. 22.

voluntariness is required for the process, albeit that this is difficult to ensure. Coercion of any kind "can inhibit personal responsibility and impede a free-flowing dialogue".[27]

Mediator training

13–043   Bringing together a victim and an offender can obviously only be contemplated in the context of control by a skilled facilitator, whose role is similar to that of any other mediator, involving comparable principles and skills. Training for this role is essential.

13–044   Training in victim–offender mediation is similar to that for community mediation in duration, but includes study of the nature of crime, how the criminal justice system operates, and victims' needs. While professionals trained in social work will already have many relevant skills (such as listening and communication), they need reorientation in relation to those conditions of mediation that are different from social work, such as the maintenance of neutrality and minimal intervention.

13–045   Mediators working with juveniles will require particular skills and knowledge, and a specialist training course will be needed.[28]

13–046   Mediation U.K. has taken a lead in developing standards of mediation practice, producing publications, working with agencies concerned with victim–offender schemes and publicising conferences and training courses and workshops.

2. PROCESS OF VICTIM–OFFENDER MEDIATION

13–047   There is a variety of practice across British victim–offender mediation schemes, in terms of management, control and the recruitment of mediators. Some schemes are police-based, or are linked to the courts or criminal justice agencies. Others are independent of the criminal justice agencies. They work as an alternative to police involvement, or if referred after the criminal justice aspect has been completed, (for example, after sentencing) offer no penal benefits to offenders.

13–048   Mediation U.K. has drawn up a Code of Practice and recommendations for the structure and management of victim–offender mediation. It accepts all kinds of models but draws attention to the need for more safeguards of mediator neutrality in the case of schemes run by existing agencies, where there may be a possibility of conflict of interest for professionals acting as mediators.

13–049   The process of victim–offender mediation is similar to other fields of mediation, though there may be more intensive pre-mediation work than in commercial mediation and some community mediation schemes. It may be undertaken by a single mediator or by co-mediators.

---

[27] See, *e.g.* Sally Engle Merry's chapter "Myth and practice in the mediation process" in Wright and Galaway (1989) at p. 244.

[28] See, *e.g.* the Leeds Mediation & Reparation Service training outlined by Quill & Wynne, (1993) at pp. 65–101.

Indirect mediation

If either party does not want to meet the other directly, the mediator may still   **13–050**
be involved in passing communications between them, such as conveying the
grief and harm felt by the victim, or offers of reparation from the offender.
This can be done on a shuttle basis. Using this approach, the mediator has
the opportunity to assess the victim's concerns and needs and to put these to
the offender. The mediator can confront the offender with these, and carry
back the offender's response.

It appears that a majority of parties prefer the indirect approach. For   **13–051**
example, of 84 mediation cases completed by the Leeds scheme in 1993,
direct meetings took place in only 16 per cent of them.[29] Face to face
mediation is not necessarily offered in many cases.

The process outlined below relates to direct mediation.   **13–052**

The stages of victim–offender mediation

The process of direct victim–offender mediation will be described using the   **13–053**
broad framework of ten stages outlined in Chapter 8.

Before mediation

Stage 1: Engaging the parties in the mediation forum

It is essential to ensure that both parties voluntarily and without coercion   **13–054**
wish to enter into mediation, and understand the process and implications.

Procedures differ between schemes as to how to screen cases to see that   **13–055**
they are appropriate, and to approach parties to establish whether they wish
to be involved in the mediation. The approach may be done by telephoning
or writing to the parties or by calling on them. The mediator may do this, or
probation officers or victim support workers.[30] Whoever deals with this, they
need to explain the ground rules of the mediation to both the victim and
offender and make sure that they agree to these. It is sensible to check with
the offender first, to ensure that he or she is willing to meet the victim and to
discuss making restitution. This precludes the possibility that the victim
agrees, only to find that the offender does not agree.

The parties' attitudes, emotional readiness and objectives should also be   **13–056**
checked in greater detail. Some parties, such as a particularly angry, upset or
fearful victim, or an inarticulate offender, may need guidance or counselling
before being able to take part. The mediator may provide this, especially if
he or she is a trained social worker or it may be passed to victim support
volunteers or the offender's probation officer. Given the emotional nature of
victim–offender meetings, parties need to be well prepared for them: and in
particular, one party's tendency to see the other in wholly negative terms
may need to be addressed to allow for a productive discussion.

The issue of engaging parties in the victim–offender mediation forum   **13–057**
continues to be important. A study undertaken in the U.S. using data

---

[29]Robinson (1996) quoting the Leeds Annual Report, 1993.
[30]See Martin Wright's chap. 4 in Quill & Wynne (1996). For a more detailed procedural outline,
see Mark Chupp's chapter "Reconciliation Procedures and Rationale" in Wright & Galaway
(1989).

collected between 1989 and 1997 has considered the factors that facilitate and inhibit participation in this process. One of its findings is that in general, parties are more likely to participate in relation to offences against property if contacted sooner than they are at present. However, the opposite position applies to personal or violent offences. In these cases, parties are more likely to participate if contact with them is delayed for a longer period. The study suggests other avenues for exploration of the predictors of client participation.[31]

13–058 ## Stage 2: Obtaining commitment and agreeing mediation rules

If both parties agree to mediation, an informal oral agreement will be made as to the place and time for the mediation. Written agreements to mediate are not required, and indeed might be counter-productive to the informality of the process. A standard form letter though might be written confirming that the mediation is to take place with details of time and venue and any other information considered helpful.

The mediator will have spoken to both parties and will have obtained their oral commitment to the process. The applicable ground rules will also have been discussed and broadly agreed.

13–059 ## Stage 3: Preliminary communications and preparation

This stage blurs and merges with Stages 1 and 2. The preliminary communications with the parties are necessary to establish the appropriateness of the process for the case and the parties' willingness to participate. That leads to an agreement to mediate and a commitment to the

13–060 process.

After the parties have agreed to mediate, it will be necessary for practical arrangements to be made for the mediation, a venue and appointment will have to be established, and details notified to the parties and checked with

13–061 them.

Parties do not prepare written summaries of their positions or produce documents, though if they have relevant papers that they need to mention in the mediation, they may be asked to bring them to the meeting for informal consideration if this is thought appropriate.

13–062 As in all mediation, the venue for the mediation needs to be neutral, and acceptable to both parties. Some writers have accordingly questioned whether it should take place, for example, at the probation officer's premises, in case this is identified as being too associated with the offender. Church halls or community centres may be used. The mediator must try to ensure that both the victim and offender feel safe: it is essential that neither should feel threatened or physically insecure.

13–063 If either party has any special needs, these will be discussed and the necessary arrangements will be made. These may relate, for example, to interpreters for foreign languages or for people with impaired hearing, or to building accessibility.

[31] See Wyrick and Constanzo "Predictors of Client Participation in Victim–Offender Mediation" 1999 M.Q. 16(3) 253.

During the substantive mediation

Stage 4: Establishing the venue and meeting the parties
The mediation venue needs to be prepared for the parties. This usually   **13–064**
involves ensuring that the reception and seating arrangements are properly
prepared, and that the parties have a comfortable and secure environment in
which to work.

Sometimes, parties may be fetched at their homes and accompanied to the   **13–065**
mediation meeting. This may be helpful and reassuring, especially where a
party is particularly anxious. Otherwise, parties will meet at the venue. As in
other kinds of mediation, reception arrangements should be in place to ensure
that they do not have to wait alone together. Either the mediator should be
available to welcome them each as they arrive, or the first one to arrive
might be asked to wait in an ante-room, if one is available.

In the mediation room, consideration must be given to seating, which   **13–066**
needs to be balanced. The victim and offender may sit opposite one another
in some arrangements, though this may be regarded as somewhat
confrontational.

The mediator will welcome the parties, thank them for attending and will   **13–067**
usually discuss the ground rules and mediation procedure to allow the parties
to raise any questions before formally agreeing to continue. The voluntary
nature of the process and its confidentiality will be reiterated. The mediator
should deal with these matters in a relaxed but professional manner, putting
the parties at their ease as far as possible.

Stage 5: Establishing the issues and setting the agenda
The equivalent of establishing the issues in victim–offender mediation is   **13–068**
allowing each party to explain themselves and their feelings. There may not
be a formal agenda as such, but the goal and aims of the session need to be
clearly understood. These may be to allow a party to apologise or to offer
some form of reparation, or to help an offender to understand the effects that
the offence had on the victim, or to allow opportunities for reconciliation, or
some combination of these.

Following the introduction, each party in turn will be given a chance to   **13–069**
speak without interruption. Some mediators might ask the parties who would
like to speak first.[32] Others suggest that the victim usually begins.[33] In either
event, after they have both spoken, each should have an understanding of the
other's position.

Stage 6: Information gathering
Information gathering is largely undertaken at an early stage, before the   **13–070**
parties meet with one another. Some data will be furnished with the referral.
It will then be a matter for the mediator to establish a better picture during
the initial communications with each of the parties.

The mediator will need to have certain basic facts. These include   **13–071**
information about the offence including whether any violence was involved

---

[32]See Quill & Wynne (1993) at p. 44, outlining the West Yorkshire training model.
[33]See Chupp (1989) at p. 61.

or injuries caused and what loss the victim sustained. The mediator needs to judge whether any safety issues have to be considered.

13–072   Further information will be obtained from the meetings with the victim and the offender. Their genuine attitude towards the possibility of mediation can be established, both from what they say and from any other indications that they may give, which should be sensitively reviewed. There may be cultural, racial or gender issues in the case, and if so, this needs to be known. As previously mentioned, the emotional readiness of each person to enter mediation has to be considered.

13–073   Some information will, by its nature, emerge during the course of the mediation. The ability of the offender to make reparation and the way in which this can be done may be discussed during the meeting (or in the course of shuttling in an indirect mediation). The effects of the offence, both on the victim and any others who may have been touched by it, are also likely to emerge at that stage.

Stage 7: Managing and facilitating discussions and negotiations

13–074   Victim–offender mediations may involve fewer issues for creative resolution than other types of mediation. The fact that the offender has been apprehended, has admitted guilt and has been, or will be, punished will have already resolved some issues. Negotiation is often restricted to the amount and details of reparation, which may already have been explored by the mediator before the meeting. The meeting itself will be likely to allow the victim to ask questions and to confront the offender with the personal effects of the offence, and allow the offender the opportunity to express feelings of remorse and to apologise. There could be discussion about how the offender might keep out of further trouble, and in appropriate cases, parties may need to resolve their future relationship, and deal with the issue of possible future revenge.

13–075   The most frequent problem encountered in victim–offender mediation is the difficulty in creating a comfortable atmosphere and in breaking down the natural animosity or detachment of the parties. This requires the mediator to foster a good flow of communications and constructive attitudes. It is important for the mediator to help the parties to see one another as individuals.

13–076   A mediator undertaking victim–offender mediation will need all the skills of communication and facilitation outlined in Chapter 15, and must be able to be empathetic to both victim and offender. Those working with juveniles will require particular skills and knowledge, to be able to communicate and work effectively with juveniles without patronising them.

Stage 8: Employing impasse strategies

13–077   Some impasse strategies will be relevant to victim–offender mediation. These could include, for example, pausing and reflecting, to assess why the process is stuck. They could also include considering whether the parties are deadlocked because of any symbolic act or any form of words.[34]

13–078   There is, however, a case for saying that if parties to victim–offender

---

[34] See Chap. 8 "Impasse strategies" for a wider consideration of this subject.

mediation cannot reach agreement, and if reasonable attempts to facilitate have not helped, the mediator should not persist in trying to press them to find a resolution. Possibilities might still remain for the mediator to convert the process into an indirect mediation, and to explore with them separately how to find the best solution.

Stage 9: Concluding the mediation and recording the outcome

Agreements, usually concerning reparation, are normally recorded in writing and signed by the parties. With the consent of the parties, usually sought before the mediation commences, these agreements will be copied to referring agencies, who may take them into consideration when further dealing with or sentencing the offender.[35] **13–079**

Many mediators like to end victim–offender meetings with some symbolic expression of the reconciliation that has been achieved, whether some positive remark about the efforts each party has made, or a handshake. There is though a danger of artificially constructing such "good endings", and such rituals should generally emerge naturally from the exchange rather than be imposed. **13–080**

Stage 10: Post-termination

Normally parties are asked immediately after the meeting whether they wish the mediation scheme to contact them again later to find out how the agreement has fared. Such follow-up, if parties agree to it, is recommended as good practice. It has been found that some victims begin to doubt the value of the meeting as the memory becomes less vivid. Having gone through the emotional experience of the meeting, it may seem something of an anti-climax never to hear anything about the case again. Many, for instance, like to know what has happened to the offender since the meeting, while others prefer to put the whole experience behind them. **13–081**

---

[35]Mediation U.K.'s Code of Practice stipulates that the mediators should get the parties' agreement for the outcome of the mediation to be given to another agency.

CHAPTER 14

MEDIATION OF ENVIRONMENTAL AND PUBLIC POLICY ISSUES

1. PUBLIC ISSUE MEDIATION

14-001   Mediation and other co-operative dispute resolution procedures have increasingly been used in the field of public law and policy decision making, and to tackle social and inter-group conflicts.

14-002   In the United States, people have used mediation for a variety of issues, sometimes very complex. These relate, for example, to environmental matters, civil rights, racial conflict, planning and land use, site clean-up activities, housing allocation and management, the farm debt crisis, the management of major metropolitan areas, and police-community problems.

14-003   In the United Kingdom, mediation is just starting to be used for environmental issues and other matters of public concern. This usage was initiated by Environmental Resolve, an undertaking of the Environmental Council, an independent charity which describes itself as "dedicated to protecting the U.K.'s environment by promoting effective dialogue and a collaborative approach to finding sustainable solutions to environmental issues".[1] A number of United Kingdom mediators now work in this field of activity.

2. CONSENSUS-BUILDING APPROACH

14-004   Public issue mediation differs from commercial, family or neighbourhood mediation in many ways, but especially in one important respect. Whereas in these forms of mediation, the disputants are clearly identified and are usually limited in number (though occasionally private disputes may involve a multiplicity of parties), the parties to a public issue mediation may not necessarily be easily identified and there may be a large number of them. Some may share common interests, others may have opposing interests, and others may have varying or overlapping interests. These parties, known as

---

[1] See pp. 210–217 of *Resolving Disputes Without Going to Court* (1995) written by Andrew Acland, one of the pioneers of environmental mediation in the U.K. and a trainer for Environmental Resolve. See also the Environmental Council's website at *http:// www.greenchannel.com/tec/tec.htm*

"stakeholders", are likely to emerge as the issues become publicly identified.[2]

The challenge for public policy mediation is not only to ensure that all stakeholders participate in the process, but that they can all be effectively heard and their views taken into account. This process of involvement, participation and collaborative problem-solving is known as "consensus-building".   **14–005**

This consensus building approach may be difficult to achieve. Not only might it be difficult to identify the stakeholders, but many of them may not be interested in participating in the process. Others might seek to impose conditions on taking part. Issues are often complex and interests are likely to diverge very considerably. Public officials concerned with these issues may co-operate with the process or may prefer a more traditional approach. Despite these difficulties, there is an impressive record of successful outcomes of public policy issues being resolved through the employment of consensus-building strategies.   **14–006**

Consensus building arises not only in the context of dealing with contentious public issues, but may be harnessed to support non-contentious community projects. So, for example, a small county in Hawaii used consensus building to address major community concerns following the destruction and disarray that resulted from a severe hurricane and the frustration that subsequently followed. The mayor carried out a series of town meetings, using facilitators to help local communities to express their concerns and feelings about the relief effort that had been perceived as inadequate. As a result, unfounded rumours could be dealt with, public officials could learn from the communities and respond to them, and a sense of unity within the community could be re-established.[3]   **14–007**

3. ENVIRONMENTAL ISSUES

Kinds of environmental issues mediated

Dealing with environmental issues forms a substantial part of public policy mediation. In so far as these are concerned, the variety of situations in which mediation has been found to be helpful was listed by Gail Bingham in 1985 in her analysis of the outcome of over 160 environmental mediations.[4] She found that the primary issues in dispute fell into six broad categories: **14–008**

- Land use (neighbourhood and housing issues, commercial and urban development, parks and recreation, preservation of agriculture land, facility siting and transportation).

---

[2] See the article "Multi-Party Public Policy Mediation: A Separate Breed" by Lawrence Susskind in *Dispute Resolution Magazine* of Fall 1997. Professor Susskind, President of the Consensus Building Institute, has written and practised extensively in the field of public policy mediation in the U.S. He points out that "there are almost always a great many parties, and not all of them are obvious. Indeed, it is hard to know exactly who the stakeholders are and who can speak for them".

[3] See *Consensus* No. 21 of January 1994.

[4] See Gail Bingham, *Resolving Environmental Disputes: A Decade of Experience* (1986).

- Natural resource management and use of public land (fisheries, mining, timber management and wilderness areas).

- Water resources (supply and quality, flood protection and thermal effects of power stations).

- Energy (siting of hydro-electric plants, conversion from oil to coal, geothermal development).

- Air quality (odour, acid rain, development of legislation).

- Dealing with toxic substances (regulation of chemicals, removal of asbestos, pesticides and the clean-up of hazardous materials).

14–009   In the United States, there has been extensive use of mediation and consensus–building to deal with environmental issues. The following are examples of these:

Snoqualmie River Dam mediation

14–010 In a major public policy mediation in 1973, the proposal to build a dam for flood protection on the Snoqualmie River near Seattle started as a dispute between the State Governor and environmentalists. In reality, it affected various parties in complex ways. One set of stakeholders were the farmers, whose land was liable to flood damage and yet who did not want the value of their land to rise excessively with the development potential because of their fears that they would be forced to sell out to land developers. Another group comprised the environmentalists, who believed the land below the dam would become urbanised in a damaging way. Yet another group was made up of the people who used the river for recreational purposes such as walking and kayaking. The public downriver were concerned they might be deprived of water in years to come. Land developers wanted to build on the newly protected land. Finally, there were the government authorities, who wanted to build the most efficient flood protection possible. The issues were complex, public interest competed against private benefit, short-term needs against the interests of future generations, and practical questions of maximising benefits, avoiding delay and cost-effectiveness all needed to be addressed.[5] This was done in mediation.

New Haven Bridge mediation

14–011 Traditional methods of public contribution to decision-making did not prove to be sufficient in relation to the proposal to build a bridge to carry Interstate 95 over New Haven Harbor in Connecticut. Community reaction to the project was described as "swift and sharp": both the local political leadership and neighbourhood organisations expressed concern about severe disruption, and environmental groups had expressed strong views.[6] The State

---

[5] See Dembart and Kwartler, "The Snoqualmie River Conflict: Bringing Mediation into Environmental Disputes" in *Roundtable Justice* (1980) by Robert Goldmann (ed.), in Goldberg, Green & Sander, *Dispute Resolution* (1985) at pp. 415–428.

[6] See the article by Emil H. Frankel, who was at that time state Commissioner of Transportation responsible for the project, in *Consensus* No. 28 of October 1995 entitled "Public outcry prompts collaboration at New Haven's 'Q' Bridge".

Commissioner of Transportation set up a collaborative planning process involving all the major stakeholders most likely to be affected by the project. These included the City authorities, the Metropolitan Planning Organisation, the Chamber of Commerce, neighbourhood organisations, environmental advocacy groups, historic preservationists, the highway and bridge construction industry, relevant trade unions and major user groups such as the automobile association and the motor transport industry. The bulk of the cost of the exercise was met by the Federal Highway Administration.

A professional facilitator was appointed to manage and direct the process, **14–012** which spanned a period of two years. Alternative options were considered and narrowed. All groups remained in the process, which culminated in consensus being reached on the kind of bridge required, with provision for the enhancement of parallel public transit facilities and high occupancy vehicle capacity on the new bridge. There was also agreement on efforts to preserve adjacent neighbourhoods and to mitigate impacts on natural resources and parks.

Groveland water pollution mediation

A complex dispute in which parties had been locked for 14 years was settled **14–013** by the use of environmental mediation. The issues related to charges of water pollution made against four local manufacturers in Groveland, Massachusetts, who denied liability.[7]

The Federal District judge who was to have dealt with the case **14–014** recommended mediation, which took place over an eight-month period. The mediation was conducted on an evaluative basis, with the primary litigants' experts making informal presentations, and the joint mediators assessing the strengths and weaknesses of each position.

Under the mediated settlement, the town of Groveland received U.S.\$1 **14–015** million over a six-year period to upgrade its water supply, with a considerable saving to all parties of legal costs and years of delay. In this case, the judge is said to have played "an instrumental role at critical junctures of the case", urging and encouraging the parties in their discussions and "helping them bridge the gap when difficult issues arose".

In the United Kingdom, environmental mediation and consensus building is **14–016** at an earlier stage, but there have been some activities in that area, including for example the following:

Dialogue on the transport of nuclear fuel in Cricklewood

A consensus building dialogue has been arranged during 1999 through the **14–017** Environment Council to deal with concerns relating to the transportation of used nuclear fuel through the area of Cricklewood in London.

Stakeholders in this dialogue include British Nuclear Fuels Limited **14–018** (BNFL) and Direct Rail Services (DRS), who transport the fuel, and those affected by the transportation, including local authorities (Barnet, Brent and Camden), local health authorities, residents' associations, Chambers of Commerce and commercial firms, environmental groups such as Greenpeace and Friends of the Earth and many other organisations and individuals.

---

[7]See *Consensus* No. 24 of October 1994.

14–019   As at June 1999, the status of the dialogue was that a draft list of questions to BNFL and DRS has been prepared by the Environment Council to inform the dialogue that is to take place to examine the issues in more detail. These questions cover the routing of trains, safety, security, monitoring and emergency procedures.

Brent Spar

14–020   When Shell's Brent Spar North Sea oil rig had completed its functions and needed to be decommissioned, a substantial dispute arose as to the method of its disposal. Environmental groups were concerned about the potentially damaging effects of disposing of it at sea.

14–021   An inaugural seminar was held in London in November 1996, which was participative and interactive. Participants were both technical and non-technical. Its aim was to obtain information about possible solutions, which at that stage numbered some thirty outline options, and to consider them with a view to Shell producing a shortlist for further discussion.

14–022   Further seminars took place during 1997 at Copenhagen, Rotterdam, Hamburg and London. At the first of these, Shell produced a shortlist of 11 possible solutions, which participants evaluated. At the following seminar, the evaluation process was further considered, assisted by the showing of short videos to describe each of the proposed solutions. Participants discussed the proposals and considered what criteria should be included in the evaluation process, including non-scientific or quantifiable criteria such as public acceptability and precedent setting. Participants identified the advice they wished to give to Shell.

14–023   The concluding seminars were held over a three-week period in October 1997. An independent evaluation body, DNV, provided the results of their evaluation and participants were given the opportunity to discuss these. Those discussions covered both technical aspects and value judgments between different criteria, such as safety and environment, greenhouse gases and marine pollution.

14–024   Shell's eventual decision took into account the concerns and issues raised by stakeholders in the dialogue process. According to the Environment Council, who expressed themselves delighted by the decision, the outcome "would satisfy key stakeholders".[8] The participants at the various seminars included environmental groups, consumer bodies, trade unions, fishing representatives, engineers and academics from a range of disciplines.

The use of environmental mediation for United Kingdom planning procedures

14–025   In the first edition of this book, the authors considered whether and to what extent environmental mediation might be relevant to land use in the United Kingdom, with particular reference to the local system of planning.

14–026   Some attributes of mediation have been adopted in planning practice, though not overtly. Two specific areas may be interpreted as being biased

---

[8]Information about the Brent Spar and Cricklewood dialogues has been obtained from the Environmental Council's website: see n. 1 above.

towards a mediatory form as against the more common form of adjudication in planning inquiries.

First, in minor issues the parties have the option of an informal hearing as an alternative to either a formal public inquiry or written representations. Where both parties agree to an informal hearing the inspector takes a more active role in the inquiry. The inspector initiates a discussion and elicits information with the aim of the parties reaching mutual agreement rather than having a decision imposed. These proceedings are more relaxed and the procedures followed less formal than those of a public inquiry.   **14–027**

This process has not, however, been widely used. The informal hearings were intended to be less formal, quicker and cheaper than a public inquiry. They were not intended to usurp the public inquiry. Even with an informal hearing, the decision would be imposed (by the inspector). This decision-making function of the inspector means that he cannot really be considered as a mediator, but the approach is mediatory and the principles not wholly distinct from those used in the United States in negotiated rule-making.   **14–028**

The second area where a mediatory process takes place is the pre-inquiry meeting held in major inquiries under the Town and Country Planning (Inquiries Procedure) Rules 1988. The inspector, acting as a moderator, discusses the real issues with the participants. His role is to define the areas of conflict, set the agenda, and control the areas that are discussed.   **14–029**

The pre-inquiry meeting was set up to shorten the public inquiry, which in major issues may run into months. The inspector sets the parameters that are agreed before the meeting. The pre-inquiry meeting was not intended to replace the public inquiry, but rather to aid the process of adjudication.   **14–030**

Although the informal hearing and pre-inquiry meeting have tentative mediatory elements, both are an adjunct to and not a replacement for the public inquiry. From a process viewpoint, both have a basic flaw: neither takes place until planning permission has been refused. It is only after refusal that any dialogue begins.   **14–031**

If any form of mediation is to work effectively within the planning system, contact needs to begin before an application has been decided, and not afterwards.   **14–032**

An English environmental land-use planning lawyer, John Harrison, has written that a "dialogue of the deaf pervades so much of the English planning system".[9] He points out that the rules governing English planning and environmental policy go further than other governmental rule-making in England in giving the public opportunities to have a say in both formal and informal settings. Nevertheless, he considers that they fall far short of the U.S. model of consensus building. Procedures do not bring stakeholders face to face in dialogue, nor are neutral facilitators used to find negotiated solutions to difficult and conflictual situations.   **14–033**

The English planning process, although consultative, stops short of the kind of negotiated dialogue used in the U.S. Proceedings tend to be adversarial in a process that is, according to Harrison, "an inefficient if not impossible mechanism for maximising mutual gains or winning consensus.   **14–034**

---

[9]"Dialogue of the deaf: English land-use planning often ignores public input" in *Consensus* No. 31, July 1996.

By this stage, the parties have locked into entrenched positions; the opportunities for creative bargaining have passed."

14–035   In the Heritage Trust Lecture,[10] Professor Larry Susskind gave examples from the United States of the effectiveness of early intervention and mediation. Harrison considers that the "mutual gains" approach used in the U.S. does much more than the English policy of having one's say and going home. It "facilitates discussion between opposing parties, allows them to explore shared interests and very often produces imaginative solutions that everyone can support." Andrew Acland, who has been involved in the work of Environmental Resolve since its inception,[11] considers from his discussions with environmentalists, business people and "some enlightened officials" that "our present planning resource allocation and policy-making procedures do not always meet the needs of those who take part in them". Nor do they serve the needs of "those upon whom they impact, or of the environment as a whole—or indeed of the planners and policy-makers themselves".[12] Many indications exist of the need for change in English planning procedure to introduce greater dialogue and consensus building processes.

14–036   The arguments against the use of mediation are first, that inquiries are not unique to planning but are the backbone of the appeals system in administrative law (*e.g.* immigration and social security) of which planning forms a part. Secondly, mediation before refusal of a planning application would require additional funding, and an extension of the statutory period for determination of a planning application. Thirdly, it was public demand that moved the appeal system away from an informal hearing to a more formalised public inquiry headed by an inspector with the ultimate decision of the Secretary of State, or the courts on legal issues. Fourthly, it has been said that the system of public participation in the public inquiry process counters the American need for mediation in this field and that in practice the inspector usually strains to give all an opportunity to be heard.

14–037   The question is not whether mediation through dialogue and consensus building should wholly replace existing methods of inquiry, but whether and to what extent it could supplement them. The process of informed and constructive dialogue involving all stakeholders and the legislature or agencies concerned with decision-making may be viewed as a valuable tool to reduce misunderstanding and narrow down the issues. While decisions might ultimately need to be imposed in many cases, that does not diminish the value of dialogue and consensus where it can be achieved.

4. Other Kinds of Public Policy Issues

14–038   Public issues requiring mediation can arise at various stages. The first stage would be as policies are being created and shaped, when the mediation process facilitates exchanges of views between interested parties and groups.[13] The second stage would be as policies are being implemented and

---

[10]"Environmental Siting Disputes: avoiding the NIMBY syndrome". January 21, 1992.
[11]See n. 1 above.
[12]*Resolving Disputes Without Going to Court* (1995) at p. 211.
[13]*Mediation Quarterly* No. 20, Summer 1988, is wholly devoted to the subject of "Using

enforced, when mediation can similarly be used to improve communication between interested parties; and where actual disputes and problems in the social context have arisen, when mediation can assume its role of dispute resolution.

Shaping public policy

Mediation is used in the United States to assist those government and other agencies responsible for the formulation of rules and even statutes to do so in a way which has due regard to competing groups and interests. This is done through policy dialogues that are held between the agencies concerned and these various groups and interests.   **14–039**

Policy dialogues tend to be complex discussions, involving numerous parties representing a wide range of interests, dealing with the resolution of policy issues, and facilitated by neutral mediators.[14]   **14–040**

One example of policy dialogue arose in 1982, when it was decided that, as many of the rules made by federal agencies were being subsequently challenged in court, federal agencies should use negotiated rule-making to try to ensure that rules were made as far as practicable on a consensual basis.[15] This became known as "negotiated rule-making" or "regulatory negotiation" ("regneg"). The rule-making agency is a party to the process, and consequently its consent is needed to the final form of any rules to be made. If agreement between the participants is not reached, then the agency has ultimate responsibility for making the rule. Experience has, however, shown that with the benefit of the negotiating process, the agency is more likely to appreciate the needs of the interested parties and groups, and less likely to create regulations which will be challenged.   **14–041**

Ehrmann and Lesnick[16] describe a three-stage process in the policy dialogue: **14–042**

- The first phase involves entry, in which the mediators, assisted perhaps by an advisory committee, make initial contact with the parties and examine the issues.

- The second phase designs the process, including venue, timetable, agenda and structure.

- The third phase is the substantive one in which the mediators facilitate the discussions, keeping the parties focused, helping them to reach agreement, and dealing with questions of implementation.

As this process has been shown to be effective, its use has increased, and it is now used not only for a multitude of environmental issues including land use and waste management, but also for energy and health issues   **14–043**

Mediation to Shape Public Policy". Edited by James H. Laue, it contains nine articles on this subject, covering process, substance, principles and a bibliography and list of U.S. resources.

[14] See "The Policy Dialogue: Applying Mediation to the Policy-Making Process" by John R. Ehrmann and Michael T. Lesnick in (1988) 20 M.Q. 93–99.

[15] See Leah V. Haygood's article "Negotiated Rule Making: Challenges for Mediators and Participants" in (1988) 20 M.Q. 77–91.

[16] See n. 14 above.

including AIDS.[17] It has moved from being a loose discussion forum to becoming a highly structured and valued process.

14–044   The governors of several U.S. states have established public dispute resolution programmes and have urged others to do so. In Oregon, for example, a controversial health plan, providing different ways of paying for medical procedures, was accepted where something similar had been highly contentious at national level. The Oregon spokesperson said "it won wide acceptance within Oregon because of the collaborative process we used to create it".[18]

Examples of public policy issues

14–045   Although environmental issues including land use form a large part of public policy mediation, the range of other kinds of issues is substantial and the following can only serve as examples of mediation dialogue and consensus building:

Health care issues

14–046   Mediation has been used in relation to health care on many occasions. Reference has been made to the acceptance of a controversial health care plan in Oregon.[19] Another example is the Bioethics Mediation Project in New York and a pilot mediation project involving 25 nursing homes in Virginia, Maryland and the District of Columbia.[20]

14–047   Two New York hospitals, the Montefiore Medical Center and the Beth Israel Medical Center, ran their project for over two-and-a-half years to 1994, working out a structure for resolving acute care disputes, in which both had often been involved and a training programme for staff concerned. This included bioethical issues, raised by questions such as "Was enough done for the patient?" or "Was the treatment too experimental?" Increasingly, such disputes would usually be referred to ethics committees or bioethical consultants. The project finally produced a report *Mediating Bioethical Disputes* (written by Nancy Dubler of the Montefiore Medical Center and the project facilitator, Dr Leonard Marcus) dealing with the mediation of bioethical disputes in institutional settings.

14–048   In New Jersey, consensus-building techniques were used to develop accord on health care funding issues. The New Jersey Coalition for Health Care Reform negotiated consensus on a wide range of issues. Stakeholders in the dialogue included the New Jersey Hospital Association, the New Jersey Business and Industry Association, the New Jersey AFL-CIO (American Federation of Labor - Congress of Industrial Organisations), physician and nurse associations, insurers, Blue Cross/Blue Shield, Health Maintenance Organisations and consumers. After months of meetings and the use of both large groups and intensive small work groups, the Coalition produced "Points of Consensus" which formed the basis of New Jersey's comprehensive health care reform law.[21]

---

[17]See Ehrmann & Lesnick, *ibid.* at p. 95.
[18]See "Governors electing more mediation" by Paul Katzeff in *Consensus* No. 38, April 1998.
[19]See n. 18.
[20]For particulars, see *Consensus* No. 26, April 1995.
[21]See the article by Patricia Warlock Moore, the mediator in the New Jersey Coalition, in

South African transition dialogue

One of the many contributing components of South Africa's peaceful transition to democracy was a dialogue that took place between 26 parties to the Multi-Party Negotiating Conference that took place in 1994

14–049

The participants comprised all political parties including those who were then perceived as radicals, such as the South African Communist Party and the Pan African Congress. The only party excluded was a right-wing group opposed to the negotiations, who subsequently tried to disrupt the process. Despite walkouts and many difficulties, agreements were reached on a range of subjects that helped to move the country's political transformation forward.

14–050

Racially based public conflict

In the aftermath of the 1992 Los Angeles riots in which 58 people were killed and more than U.S. $1 billion of property destroyed, enormous efforts were needed to rebuild the community. To this end, the Ford Foundation commissioned an assessment of the capacity of mediation services to deal with complex racial disputes. Washington D.C.-based practitioner, Michael Lewis of ADR Associates was appointed to undertake this and focused on the broad public policy questions that elicited racial tensions, rather than individual disputes. He liaised with African-Americans and Korean-American community members and merchants, trying to assess the position. He found that it would be necessary to introduce multi-racial teams of mediators and established training programmes to achieve this.[22]

14–051

Public conflict may apparently be about other issues, such as police violence or housing conditions, but race may well be a factor. The barrier to finding an effective solution is greater when parties are not willing to acknowledge that there is a racial issue in addition to the presenting problem. Mediators dealing with these issues indicate that the common strategy to overcome such barriers is education, including discussing specific experiences and practising and teaching active listening.[23]

14–052

Disputes concerning gaming laws

Eric E. Van Loon of JAMS-Endispute outlines the use of mediation to deal with a dispute that arose in 1995 between the U.S. National Indian Gaming Commission and those concerned with running or sharing revenue from a bingo casino in Milwaukee, Wisconsin (a businessman and a non-profit community school).[24]

14–053

In that dispute, the Commission alleged many violations of federal Indian gaming laws at the casino. The businessman and school repudiated these allegations and brought lawsuits of their own. The situation was, however, complicated by the fact that the Indian tribe that owned the casino had not

14–054

Consensus No. 19; July 1993. That issue of *Consensus* also reports on the use of facilitated negotiation to design and implement a Medicaid long-term care reimbursement system in Ohio.

[22]See *Consensus* No. 30, April 1996.

[23]See n. 22.

[24]See the American Bar Association's *Dispute Resolution Magazine* of Fall 1997, focusing on public policy disputes, including at p.11 Van Loon's article, "Bingo, Business and Bureaucracy".

been included in any of the litigation because of tribal sovereign immunity, and that the Commission's interests were in some respects derived from the tribe's.

14–055   Van Loon as mediator first sought to understand the broader context of the mediation, visiting the tribal centre, the school and the casino. Cultural sensitivity was clearly a critical factor. While financial considerations were significant, sometimes other issues were more important, including respect, control, autonomy, sovereign immunity and deep feeling about land.

14–056   The parties were given an opportunity to hear one another's views, to discuss these and to evaluate one another's positions and proposals. Negotiations took place through caucusing sessions in a phase that lasted about two months. Van Loon had to facilitate discussions within the tribe itself, as it was represented by five separate counsel, each of whom represented different tribal authorities with different responsibilities and agendas. He also had to report to the tribe's General Council, often attended by over 100 participants.

14–057   Matters were finally settled in mediation in a multi-faceted agreement that ran to 58 pages plus exhibits, requiring approval by the court and by government agencies. Van Loon could not anticipate the settlement's ultimate durability, but is certain about the effectiveness of mediation for resolving complex multi-party disputes having multiple public policy dimensions.

HIV/AIDS prevention planning

14–058   A group called Coloradans Working Together: Preventing HIV/AIDS (CWT) was formed in early 1994 to produce a plan for the state of Colorado for the prevention of HIV. It was convened by the Colorado Department of Health, with guidance from the Centers for Disease Control (CDC).[25]

14–059   The first meeting of CWT attracted 110 participants, including those who had contracted the HIV virus (and some who also had AIDS), gay rights advocates, community activists, Latinos, African-Americans, health care specialists and members of religious groups including Christian evangelicals.

14–060   During 1994, a number of meetings were held, starting with process and moving to data gathering and information about current strategies used to stop the transmission of disease. From there, the group moved to an analysis of the data and had extensive discussions on a collaborative problem-solving basis. By the end of 1994, they had come to understand, listen to and respect one another and were able to write and revise the core elements of a plan, which became the State of Colorado's 1995 HIV Prevention Plan.

14–061   The process was not an easy one, with sometimes strained relationships between different groups. One of the joint mediators, Michael Hughes, writes that "it is difficult to do justice to the depth of grief and fear that permeated CWT's work...CWT members responded brilliantly, sharing their experiences and responding to one another with concern and support". Hughes attributes the success of CWT's efforts largely to the thoughtfulness, respect and honesty that members brought to the process. Despite the

---

[25] For particulars, see *Consensus* No. 28, October 1995, Practitioner's Notebook for an article by Michael Hughes of CDR Associates, who was joint mediator with Derek Okubo of the National Civic League.

seriousness of the task, members were able to celebrate together when they reached their concluding meeting. Hughes describes the project as a "remarkable example of collaborative planning and conflict resolution".[26]

5. THE RATIONALE FOR PUBLIC ISSUE MEDIATION

Exploration of alternative approaches for resolving disputes in this area stems largely from dissatisfaction with the more traditional decision-making process. Under the traditional process, parties are often unable to deal satisfactorily with the real issues in dispute, interested parties have difficulty in influencing the outcome and concerns exist about fairness and efficiency. **14–062**

The appropriateness of mediation in relation to public issues and social conflicts is based on two assumptions. These are, first, that the parties involved are good judges of the real issues and as to whether the proposed policies or solutions are adequate and effective. Secondly, the voluntary nature of the process allows the parties to exercise their judgment freely both in the decision to participate and in whether to concur in the agreement. **14–063**

Public policy issues have their own distinct features that necessitate special procedures being adopted: **14–064**

- The issues are often complex and polycentric (or "many centred") and any change to the situation will create a new set of complicated tensions.[27] They may comprise value judgments about various questions, such as: what is meant by "reasonable living standards"? What is a fair time for compliance with new regulations? What is a reasonable level of penalty for temporary noncompliance? Should such judgments be made by the people they affect or by society as a whole?

- The nature, boundaries, costs and participants of a dispute are often unclear. There is often a variety of participants who each believe that they represent the public interest or a section of it, many of whom act on principle rather than self-interest. The atmosphere may be public and highly politicised. The media may take a keen interest.

- There are many possible outcomes to a dispute and a premium is placed on the search for creative and consensual solutions.

- The standards adopted by society may change as understanding, values or technology develop; and both the process of efficiently managing the reaction to those changes and the ability to implement the agreement reached over a period of time are likely to be as important as the agreement itself.

---

[26]See n. 25.
[27]As to polycentricity, see Prof. Lon Fuller, "Forms and Limits of Adjudication" 92 Harv.L.Rev. (1978) quoted in Murray, Rau & Sherman, *Processes of Dispute Resolution: The Role of Lawyers* (1989) at pp. 26–29 and 36–37. Prof. Fuller considers that polycentric problems are generally outside the proper limits of adjudication.

14–065   Andrew Acland outlines the reasons for using consensus-building.[28] He considers that present procedures do not meet the needs of the people concerned or of the environment. These procedures often produce compromises, but, he says without necessarily achieving mutual understanding and often as dictated by the most powerful party. Awareness raising needs to move to the task of finding solutions, which consensus-building helps to achieve. Consensus-building encourages commitment and mutual understanding, and provides an outlet for frustrated energies and abilities.

6. PUBLIC POLICY MEDIATION: ASPECTS OF PRACTICE

Preliminary aspects

14–066   Although the sequence may vary, the following are the matters that will initially need to be addressed in public policy mediation:

Analysis and assessment

14–067   An analysis of the conflict needs to be undertaken by a neutral facilitator,[29] to include considering who is inviting the mediation and why; and whether the mediation has realistic prospects of reaching a consensual outcome. The facilitator will be conscious of the need to maintain demonstrable neutrality towards and independence from any particular party or interest group, and will wish to ensure that the process is not likely to be abused by any individual or group for political or other advantage.

14–068   This preliminary assessment is usually undertaken through individual interviews with actual or potential stakeholders and may involve a review of the history of the issues. The facilitator is likely then to make an evaluation of the data and the issues, to enable the commissioning party and the stakeholders to consider how they might wish to proceed.

14–069   The facilitator's preliminary report may make recommendations how to proceed or how to approach the formulation of any policy decisions that need to be made. It will address the question whether mediation is appropriate and may propose a structure for the conduct of the mediation process. The suitability of mediation may not be immediately apparent. The facilitator may need to consider whether the parties have an incentive to negotiate an agreement and whether it is feasible to think that mediation of the particular issues will achieve anything. Facilitators will need to guard against being over-optimistic. Public mediation needs to be preceded by a careful fact-finding phase to establish the limits of the conflict objectively, and facilitators and mediators should avoid finally committing themselves to the process until they are able to make a dispassionate assessment of the chances of success.

14–070   In considering this question, the facilitator may wish to establish whether there are unadmitted political agendas. Parties may be superficially co-

---

[28]See n. 12.

[29]Or by a team of facilitators. Most organisations will offer individuals or teams, as the situation requires. The Environmental Forum, a division of JAMS-Endispute in the U.S., *e.g.* suggests that team mediation can reduce overall cost and add value to the process and outcome. See its web site at *http://www.jams-endispute.com/why/environmental/index.htm*

operative but one group or another may be entering into the process cynically in order to "demonstrate" that another party is unco-operative (as will be "evidenced" by a failure to get to an agreement) or in order to ensure that no agreement is reached.

Who should attend the mediation?

These will include individuals or organisations directly involved in the dispute, who are likely to be readily identified, as well as those representing interests that bridge the main parties, or those with a stake in community peace rather than any particular outcome to the negotiations. **14–071**

As negotiations generally occur between groups rather than individuals, this raises questions of representation and who can properly speak for a wide constituency. The time and resources needed for public issue mediation, which may include elaborate information-gathering, may be very considerable and delegates may need to be found who have the resources and commitment to devote to the process and who will act in a proper representative manner. **14–072**

Where decision-making power vests in an individual or an institutional group, successful implementation of any agreement invariably requires those with such power, as well as those responsible for the implementation of their decisions, to be involved in the mediation process. As they gain a stake in the agreement, they have a commitment to work with it. **14–073**

Individuals' elected officials may sometimes, however, have different interests to their voters, for example the desire to be seen as taking quick decisive action in relation to an issue rather than ensuring full consultation. Other parties have found it difficult to take responsibility for deciding what would be the appropriate position on a particular issue, preferring simply to provide critical analyses. **14–074**

Absent parties or groups

A common problem in public mediation is that it may not always be possible to involve all the interested parties. Just one group may refuse to be involved, yet an agreement without their participation may be useless. **14–075**

Mediators will need to assess how crucial such omissions might be on an individual case by case basis. Are the uninvolved groups capable of sabotaging any agreement? In modern democratic societies, the answer to this question is usually that they can. Even ensuring that the perspective of such groups is represented in the negotiations, despite their lack of direct involvement, may not be sufficient. Uninvolved groups have been known to undermine agreements that, from an objective viewpoint, were apparently in their interests. **14–076**

Are all the parties equally able to represent their case?

Significant differences in power are normal in public mediation; while some parties may be able to organise themselves well and represent their case effectively, mediators may need to help others to settle their constituencies, choose representatives, gather information to bolster their case, and formulate clear policies. If doing so would jeopardise the mediators' actual or perceived neutrality, they may need to find some other competent person to assist such parties. **14–077**

14–078 Groups may also have other needs, ranging from practical requirements such as information and research facilities to less tangible needs such as empowerment, trust-building and reassurance. A local university or technical college may need to be brought in to provide independent technical advice to parties unable to fund their own research.

Funding the process

14–079 The mediators will have to consider a large number of complex issues, co-ordinate a large number of parties and marshal a complex process, and they are likely to require substantial funding resources. Also, all parties with an interest in an issue need to be represented and given sufficient physical and intellectual backup to enable them to participate fully, and that will require funding resources which may not be readily available.

14–080 Discussions as to who will fund the initial assessment are likely to be difficult and the sums involved considerable. In the Snoqualmie River case,[30] the mediators undertook six months of exhaustive research and discussions with the parties before satisfying all parties that mediation might be appropriate and should be explored.

14–081 Under-resourced intervention may exacerbate the situation more than help resolve it. It is good practice, indeed essential, for the mediators to establish secure funding for the mediation. This may require preliminary negotiations with the major parties on how the mediation is to be financed and how the costs are to be shared or otherwise met. If one party bears all or most of the costs, as may occur, for instance, in an environmental dispute between a commercial company and voluntary groups, the mediators must assess the possible effect of their neutrality, and upon public perceptions of that neutrality.

14–082 In the United States, development of public policy mediation has largely occurred by virtue of patronage from charitable foundations and public bodies. Whether a similar level of support will be given in Britain for these purposes remains to be seen.

Proceeding in imperfect circumstances

14–083 Circumstances for conducting public issue mediation are seldom ideal. How are the mediators to decide whether and when to go ahead with the process, or to stop the preliminary discussions and inquiries and to decide that mediation will not be appropriate?

14–084 Public mediators may find themselves having to compromise on some basic principles: for example, they may have to proceed without the involvement of one interested party, or without cast-iron independence, or despite the existence of unresolved power differences between parties. They may need to do so because these issues cannot be resolved until the mediation is under way, at which stage changes can be made as necessary to the conditions for the mediation. Non-participating groups may then decide to become involved, the mediators can establish conditions to ensure their independence and other modifications to the process can be made.

---

[30] See n. 5 above.

Designing the mediation process

The first collaborative phase of the mediation is likely to relate to agreeing   **14–085**
the structure of the mediation process. Disputes frequently revolve round a
large number of complex and inter-related issues against the background of a
lack of clear legal standards. The following matters need to be considered:

- Clarity of process is essential. The mediator will need to get
  agreement on procedures and agendas at each stage, even if these are
  changed as the process moves on. The parties must have clearly
  defined and agreed structures for each stage of the mediation.

- Agreement needs to be sought on conditions for the mediation, before
  tackling the issues in dispute. Who should facilitate the mediation
  process? How should meetings be organised to ensure fair
  participation? What is the broad timetable? How often should the
  parties meet? How is media interest to be handled? These and many
  other procedural questions need to be considered.

- Decisions may need to be made as to whether any particular
  information and training will be required by some or all of the parties
  to enable them to participate productively, and if so, what kind, and
  who should provide it.

- In public mediation, the mediator often has less control over the
  process conditions. This fact, the multiplicity of parties, and the social
  implications of the conflict, all mean that there are more extrinsic
  uncontrollable influences and consequently more things that can go
  wrong. The public mediator has to be prepared for setbacks, and
  consequently for rethinking strategy.

- A corollary of this is that the mediator should be careful not to over-
  promise in the way of results. "Building a basis for discussions" may
  be a better preliminary objective than "resolving the conflict".

- The mediator may have views on process, agenda and timetable, but
  cannot proceed without the agreement of all the parties, who may
  have other process preferences. Mediation among church groups may
  therefore look very different from mediation among commercial
  companies.

- The outline agenda may provide for the process to commence by the
  parties identifying and defining the problems and to continue with the
  provision of information, expertise, the search for possible outcomes,
  questions of implementation and future planning and developments.

Facilitative processes

The following processes are all inter-related or overlapping, but each may   **14–086**
have its own particular attributes or emphasis:

Dialogue facilitation

The dialogue between stakeholders is an integral and essential part of any   **14–087**
public policy mediation process. Sometimes this dialogue has to take place

before stakeholders can agree whether or not they want to proceed any further, for example to mediation.

14-088   The parties will usually need assistance in getting to learn and understand one another's viewpoints and concerns, so that they can more effectively address the issues that they are all facing. The facilitator will help the parties with this dialogue.

Consensus-building

14-089   The Consensus Building Institute Inc. defines consensus-building as a process that "involves informal, face-to-face interaction among representatives of stakeholding groups. It aims for 'mutual gain' solutions, rather than win–lose or lowest common denominator outcomes. It complements, rather than replaces, the traditional decision making activities of agencies, courts, and legislatures. It generates solutions that are fairer, more efficient, better informed, and more stable than those arrived at by more conventional means".[31]

14-090   The Conflict Management Group (CMG)[32] describes the role of consensus-building as looking beyond emotional argument to uncover and balance the interests of all parties and crafting fair and equitable solutions.

14-091   A consensus building approach is universal in its application. Its use is justified not only by virtue of its efficacy, but also as it is perceived as a more socially responsible way to arrive at decisions in an increasingly complex and pluralist society.

Partnering

14-092   As described in Chapter 6, "partnering" is a voluntary, non-binding collaborative process that focuses on solving common problems between different groups working on the same project or sharing a common purpose. This is done in various ways, such as by developing teams with common goals, establishing and implementing project action plans and establishing conflict resolution machinery.

14-093   Partnering has been used in a public context to facilitate major projects, for example the construction of public buildings such as schools and the cleaning up of military sites.[33]

Facilitating negotiations in mediation

14-094   Once the extensive preparation for public issue mediation has been done and the process is under way, the process of communication and negotiation will follow a broadly similar pattern to other forms of mediation, subject always to the special needs and circumstances of this field of activity.

14-095   There are many elements common to all mediation. These include seeking common ground, encouraging mutual respect and understanding, and facilitating communication and negotiation. The mediator may undertake

---

[31]For more information, see the web site of the Consensus Building Institute Inc. (CBI) at *http://www.cbi-web.org/about/dispute.htm*

[32]A U.S. organisation founded in 1984 to provide the negotiation approach developed at Harvard Law School. It is supported by leading academic experts including Roger Fisher and Howard Raiffa. See its information web site at *http://www.cmgonline.org/cmginfo.htm*

[33]For an extensive consideration of the use of partnering, see *Consensus* No. 36, October 1997.

caucusing, deal with emotional issues, help with the generation and exploration of options, test the efficacy of proposed solutions and reality-test generally. The process is also likely to cover encouraging creative solutions, brainstorming, and various of the other skills, techniques and strategies of mediation.[34]

Confidence in the process, and in the mediator, is crucial, and can only be built slowly in situations where the parties are unused to mediation. The mediator in a public mediation is always a potential party and must be continually aware of this, and avoid having that neutrality compromised. **14–096**

Public issue mediation effectiveness

The factors that affect the success of public issue mediation have been considered by a number of American writers, including Gail Bingham[35] and Philip J. Harter.[36] **14–097**

An analysis of the success of public issue mediation is difficult. One measure is to examine the number of agreements reached at the end of the process. Overall, Bingham found that agreement was reached in 78 per cent of the cases researched by her. Another is to look at the implementation of those agreements. Here she found that 80 per cent of the agreements in relation to site-specific issues were wholly implemented with another 13 per cent partially implemented, as against 41 per cent of agreements reached in the more general policy dialogues, with another 18 per cent partially implemented. **14–098**

Bingham attributes the lower rate of implementation to the fact that those with the responsibility for implementing the decisions had generally not been part of the mediation process. She and Harter both identify a number of factors that are likely to affect the success of reaching agreements and having them implemented in relation to public policy issues: **14–099**

- Both writers take the view that the agency concerned with implementation should be directly involved in the negotiating process. Where Harter takes this view "on balance",[37] Bingham regards this as the "most significant factor in the likelihood of success" in getting agreements reached in the process implemented.[38]

- Bingham ascribes the relatively high success rate in reaching agreements as being probably due to the work done by the mediators

---

[34]For more information about the process, see Susskind and Cruikshank (1987) *Breaking the Impasse: Consensual Approaches to Resolving Public Disputes* and Christopher W. Moore (1986) *The Mediation Process.*

[35]See n. 4 above.

[36]"Negotiating Regulations: A Cure for Malaise" 71 Georgetown L.J. 1 (1982); "Regulatory Negotiation: the Experience So Far" *Resolve* Winter 1984 in Goldberg Green & Sander, Dispute Resolution at p. 428; "Government ADR Policies and Practices" in *Report of the Administrative Conference of the United States* (1987); and "Analysis of the Environmental Protection Agency's Negotiated Rule-making for a New Source Performance Standard for Residential Woodstoves" (1988) in Leah Haygood's article—see n. 15 above.

[37]See "Regulatory Negotiation: the Experience so far" in Goldberg Green & Sander, *Dispute Resolution* (1985), p. 433.

[38]Goldberg Green & Sander *ibid.* at p. 412.

in the preparation for each case, in relation to the assessments and ground rules discussed at the outset.

- Both point out that the interest groups that have to decide whether or not to be involved in the process will decide whether they can achieve more through a consensual approach, or through the traditional processes. If a party feels that its views cannot be accepted, then it may decline to participate. Harter considers it necessary to make it clear that "consensus" means that without acceptance by all, the result will not be regarded as an agreed outcome.

- The way in which the proceedings are conducted seems to be an important factor. Interest-based and problem-solving approaches are found to be more helpful than positional bargaining.

- Other factors do not clearly indicate the likelihood of success or otherwise. Deadlines, coalitions, incentives and other factors may influence the outcome, but these seldom all point in the same direction, and may well mitigate the effect of one another.

14–100   Other aspects of success are not easily quantifiable. Were all those with a stake in the decision represented? If not, the agreement may not have addressed their concerns. Does the agreement comply with community norms of fairness? Are the agreements technically sound? Have the parties considered how to deal with unanticipated problems that may arise during implementation? If not, then it may be that one party may force the whole issue back before the court. Indeed even if the primary aim of the mediation, reaching an agreement, was not achieved, have other benefits been realised such as the development of a relationship that will enable the parties to resolve future disputes between themselves?

Criticisms of public issue mediation

14–101   The development of mediation into the area of public policy-making has not been without its critics both as to principle and as to particular processes and practices. It has been suggested that it encourages accommodation when certain rights and public interests should simply not be compromised. Some disputes, for example, involve issues that parties consider to be non-negotiable matters of principle (such as nuclear power plants) and therefore there is no possible area of compromise and no scope for good faith negotiation and mediation.

14–102   Others suggest that it may, however, be better to ensure direct participation of all interested parties and a better understanding of the technical and policy issues involved amongst those who are likely to be affected so that they can decide whether compromise is possible or desirable.

14–103   There has also been controversy whether mediation simply reinforces the power imbalances that already exist between the parties. Large companies, government or landowners may be lined up against citizens' groups, tenants or individuals, the rich and sophisticated against the poor and inexperienced. Proponents claim that experienced mediators have a role in equalising the power imbalances or addressing them directly, which cannot necessarily be achieved in the traditional processes.

Claims have been made that public policy mediation provides a cheaper **14–104** and quicker process for the resolution of disputes than the traditional process. This has been criticised. Certainly, the mediation of complex issues is likely to take a long time and the complexity of the issues to be addressed means that the resources of the mediators are likely to have to be substantial and therefore costly. However, many disputes can be rectified or prevented by the timely use of available alternatives, and often this will save or reduce costs.

Finally, the question of the accountability of public issue mediators has **14–105** been debated with differing views as to whom they should be accountable.

The proponents of public policy mediation consider that an effective range **14–106** of processes is available to assist in dealing with public issues and policies and social conflicts, which allow for creative, consensual outcomes. They do not argue that they should be used for all purposes or that they can or should replace traditional processes, but rather that they effectively supplement existing procedures.

In recent years, these criticisms have tended to be significantly **14–107** overshadowed by the extent or support in favour of the use of dialogue, consensus-building and mediation for the resolution of public policy issues. Consensus-building is "a conscious and deliberate attempt to help people to become engaged in making the decisions which affect their lives".[39]

---

[39] Acland (1995) at p.217.

CHAPTER 15

ON BEING A MEDIATOR

15–001   Many factors affect the quality of the mediation process. The model of mediation, the Code of Practice upon which it is based and the techniques and strategies used by the mediator: all of these are highly relevant. But arguably one of the biggest single factors is the quality of the mediator.

15–002   Being a mediator involves a significant personal and professional commitment. It demands a new approach from virtually all occupations of origin. Existing attributes and qualities may need to be re-examined and new understandings will be needed. Practical skills are likely to be used in a different way. A new ethical awareness has to be developed. Mediators need to draw on existing experience in a new way, and may have to discard some old habits. Most people find it a challenging process.

15–003   This chapter will examine what it means to be a mediator. To facilitate this, a "mediation construct" has been created, which summarises the essential aspects of being a mediator. The mediation construct is merely a device to assist in graphically identifying some of the main features of what a mediator ideally brings to the process. It cannot and does not pretend to be a comprehensive and exhaustive chronicle of all relevant attributes and qualities of a mediator. To some extent, these are covered in other parts of the chapter, which amplifies the construct. It should also be borne in mind that mediators from different fields, disciplines and approaches are likely to work in different ways. This chapter will seek to extract common principles that run through all kinds of mediation.

1. THE MEDIATION CONSTRUCT

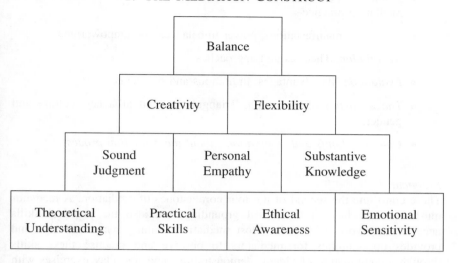

The concept of the construct

There are four fundamental cornerstones to the construct, which form its base. These are the basic elements of the process: theoretical understanding, practical skills, ethical awareness and emotional sensitivity. Next, the mediator brings sound judgment, personal empathy, and substantive knowledge of legal, technical or practical aspects of matters relevant to the dispute. Next, the mediator needs to be creative and flexible. Through all of this, the mediator needs to have balance: an impartial, balanced and even-handed approach to the issues and the parties. Each of these ten elements will be considered.

15–005

Theoretical understanding

There is no single theory of mediation. Each field, model and approach may have different theoretical orientations. However, the following are some examples of matters of which a mediator should have theoretical knowledge:

15–006

- *A theoretical perspective.* For example, mediation as a set of stages or a communications perspective, or a transformative theory of mediation.

- *The mediator's role and function.* The essence of impartiality and even-handedness.

- *Conflict and dispute.* Their basis, management and resolution.

- *Adversarial and consensual dispute resolution processes.* How mediation fits in.

- *The principles of mediation.* Common principles run through all kinds of mediation.

- *Confidentiality and legal privilege.* The principles that regulate mediation practice.

- *Power.* Its manifestations, power imbalances and empowerment.

- *Negotiation.* Theories and approaches.

- *Evaluation.* Its advantages, limitations and problems.

- *The dynamics of mediation.* Triangulation and alliances, culture and gender.

- *Cautions, limits and reservations about the mediation process.*

Practical skills

15–007 These constitute the second of the four cornerstones of mediation. A mediator must not only have a theoretical grounding, but also the practical skills necessary to work effectively. Most mediation training recognises this and provides opportunities for mediators to observe and practise these skills through a combination of videos, demonstrations and role play exercises with feedback from trainers and participants.

15–008 Practical mediation skills comprise a combination of management and facilitation abilities. The mediator must be able to manage the process firmly but not autocratically, and with due sensitivity. He or she must also be able to facilitate movement and negotiation, culminating in the resolution of the dispute. Once this has been achieved, the mediator has to be able to ensure that the outcome is properly recorded as the parties and process require. This demands appropriate drafting skills.

15–009 This chapter will outline the practical skills of the mediator, and the role and function that this involves.

Ethical awareness[1]

15–010 The role of mediator carries considerable responsibility, not only to provide effective assistance to the parties, but also to do so in an ethically proper manner. A mediator intervenes in a private dispute and has significant power and opportunity to affect the outcome. Indeed, that ability to change the course of the dispute is what leads disputants to engage the mediator. Mediators must undertake their practice with awareness of that responsibility and of the ethical issues that this entails.

15–011 Mediators should have regard to the following ethical considerations in carrying out their functions:

- The Code of Practice under which they mediate. This will usually provide clear ethical and practical guidelines for their practice.

- The ethical rules of any professional body to which they belong. So, for example, solicitors who mediate within their practices will have to comply with the Law Society's ethical rules as well as the regulations of their mediation body.

---

[1] For a fuller consideration of ethics, see Chap. 21.

- Fairness: The extent and limitations of the mediator's responsibility for fairness.

- When not to mediate: there are circumstances in which it would be inappropriate for the mediator to mediate, or having started, to continue.[2]

- Mediators should be aware of cautions and reservations that have been expressed about mediation, so that they can ensure that they do not fall foul of these.[3]

- Mediator training should provide an inherent appreciation of the mediator's ethical responsibilities. These may, for example, include issues about the mediator's duties towards people who may be identified in the mediation as being vulnerable to harm. They may also include matters concerning non-discrimination and other such issues.

Emotional sensitivity

The fourth cornerstone of mediation practice is the mediator's ability to work in a way that is sensitive to any strong feelings that may be expressed by the parties.   **15–012**

Emotional sensitivity does not mean that the mediator must have the skills and expertise of a counsellor or that the mediation should be confused with counselling or any process that deals with the resolution of personal emotional issues. It rather means that the mediator can offer the parties some of the following: **15–013**

- An ability to cope with the emotions expressed by the parties in the mediation in a way that accepts them normally and non-judgmentally.

- An ability to work sensitively with parties in exploring issues and concerns underlying those that they present in the mediation.

- Recognition of the possible impact of the emotional aspect on the process, and an ability to acknowledge parties' feelings in a non-patronising way.

- Assistance in getting back to the task of finding a resolution to the issues when the parties or any of them are caught up with the strength of their feelings.

- An understanding of the network of resources available to help parties where the strength of their emotions is so great that it impairs their ability to resolve matters in the mediation.

These are the four fundamental qualities that a mediator offers: theoretical understanding of mediation and its dynamics; practical mediation skills;   **15–014**

---

[2]See, *e.g.* paras 18–112 *et seq.* for circumstances in which the mediator should not mediate; also paras 21–071 *et seq.* for situations of conflict of interest.

[3]For cautions and reservations about mediation, see Chap. 18.

ethical awareness; and emotional sensitivity. The next three qualities supplement these.

Sound judgment

15–015 This is a subjective attribute that might be honed with practice, but cannot easily be taught or learned. It is nevertheless an extremely important one for mediators to have and to use. Mediators who are used to exercising their judgment are likely to have developed this facility and to be able to bring it into play for the benefit of disputants.

15–016 There may be a link between the exercise of sound judgment and an ability to trust intuitive responses. Many professionals, especially lawyers, place a high premium on the value of logic and are loth to acknowledge the significance of intuition. In truth, both of these have their places in the exercise of judgment. Intuition is probably more immediate; logic and reason probably underpin decisions based on intuition.

15–017 Every step in the mediation process demands the exercise of judgment. Should the mediator limit the time allowed to each party to make a presentation of their case? Which party should the mediator ask to make a presentation first? How should the mediator handle interruptions or provocative statements? How indeed should the mediator handle each aspect of the process? If the mediator does not proceed with good judgment, this is likely to be reflected in the way the mediation develops. Mediators must be able to offer sound judgment to the parties.

Personal empathy

15–018 This is also an attribute that cannot readily be taught, though it is possible to develop an attitude that makes it easier to be genuinely empathetic to parties even when one does not readily find them likeable.

15–019 Empathy is defined in the Shorter Oxford dictionary as "the power of identifying oneself mentally with (and so fully comprehending) a person or object of contemplation". A mediator tries to identify with both or all parties and to "fully comprehend" their positions, concerns and aspirations. Yet such identification has to be properly boundaried, to maintain the necessary professional balance.

15–020 Parties can generally sense whether a mediator is genuinely empathetic. If they appreciate that the mediator is trying to help them to achieve an outcome that tries to meet their requirements, they will feel able to work with that mediator. The fact that the mediator is also seeking the same outcome for the other side does not diminish that willingness to co-operate. If, however, they sense that the mediator does not understand or comprehend their situation and cannot relate to them, their willingness to work constructively with that mediator is bound to be affected.

15–021 Inevitably mediators will come across parties who conduct themselves in a way that the mediator may find unattractive. It can sometimes be difficult to be empathetic towards parties whose behaviour and approach feel offensive to the mediator's sense of justice and propriety. Yet if a mediator is to function effectively it is essential to maintain that empathy with all parties. That does not mean that the mediator abandons all personal values and feelings, but rather that the mediator develops an understanding of the positions of all parties and approaches the mediation with that balance.

Sometimes it may be necessary for a mediator consciously to review his or her attitude towards a party. One of the impasse strategies outlined in Chapter 8[4] requires the mediator to consider whether he or she is "perpetuating the problem by perhaps being stuck in one approach or by unwittingly supporting one position?" The strategy requires the mediator to reflect on what to do to change the dynamic. This reflects the problem that can arise where a mediator unwittingly starts to support one party's view and position. In that situation, the mediator has lost balance and almost certainly empathy with all parties, and the result may be that the mediation goes off track. Balance and empathy are probably related in this way.

15–022

Substantive knowledge

There is a truism that, given the choice between process expertise and substance expertise, one would always choose to engage as a mediator someone who is skilled in the mediation process rather than someone who is an expert in the subject-matter of the dispute.

15–023

While reiterating the validity of that proposition, the position in practice is that many fields of activity require the mediator to have substantive knowledge in addition to process expertise.

15–024

Substantive knowledge can mean detailed expertise in a particular specialist field. So, for example, a mediator may be an engineer with detailed and specialist knowledge of bridge construction. Alternatively, it can mean a general awareness of the culture and practice in a broad area of activity. So, a mediator may be a lawyer who has no specialist knowledge of engineering, but who understands the general principles of contract, of commercial relationships and of disputes in the commercial world. Both of these bring substantive knowledge to the mediation, and either might be appropriate to be selected as a mediator in a construction industry dispute. Parties given the choice might prefer to have as a mediator the specialist engineer; but if the issue was primarily contractual, they might prefer to have the more general lawyer mediator. They would be unlikely to choose a mediator who worked in a neighbourhood and community context and who had neither specialised knowledge of their industry nor even general knowledge and experience of working in a commercial context.

15–025

Similarly in the family field, mediators bring substantive knowledge into the process. They may have expertise in working with children or may be therapists or counsellors with a specialist knowledge about relationship breakdown or they may have a background as a family solicitor with experience in dealing with separating and divorcing couples and their children. Some may not have a background in working with families, but might have been specifically trained to do so, being given a knowledge base about couple's dynamics, children's needs and legal issues. The required substantive knowledge base might in some cases be very specific.[5] It would

15–026

---

[4] At 8–130.

[5] The Legal Aid Board for example has some very specific requirements as to the knowledge that it expects mediators to have, including knowledge of or access to relevant social security legislation.

not be seriously thought that general mediators with no substantive knowledge of issues facing couples or families should undertake divorce mediation involving children, finance and the other issues that couples bring into the process.

15–027 In the community and neighbourhood field, mediators are largely drawn from members of the local community and are not usually professionals. In a sense, though, they could be said also to have "substantive knowledge". They are likely to know about the local community, to have experience of the kinds of problems that local people face, and to understand the needs of the disputants better than, for example, a specialist construction industry mediator. It is possible that in the field of local neighbourhood disputes, the need for substantive knowledge is less than in the fields of civil and commercial disputes, or family issues especially on separation and divorce, or criminal reparation issues, or environmental issues. In most fields of activity, a well-rounded mediator will bring substantive knowledge to the table, and will be expected by the parties to do so.

Creativity

15–028 Edward de Bono considers creativity to be an essential part of the process of designing dispute resolution outcomes.[6] In his view, people in dispute and involved in dialectic argument are least likely to be able to adopt a creative approach to the resolution of their issues. That is likely to be the experience of most practitioners.

15–029 The neutral practitioner who is brought in to help parties in dispute will ordinarily be in a good position to help them to see beyond the confines of their argument. That role is expected of the mediator or other ADR neutral. One of the benefits of ADR is its ability to help parties to examine matters beyond their immediate dispute, and to consider their wider interests. Certainly, disputes may be resolved by finding a point somewhere between their respective positions, and that is a perfectly good and honourable way to settle many differences. However, many other situations call for a more thoughtful and creative approach, necessitating a wider look at the issues, the underlying needs and concerns and the surrounding circumstances.

15–030 Creativity may manifest itself in many ways. A property dispute involved partners in having to allocate properties between themselves. One party was tentatively interested in accepting a farm, but was unsure whether it was really the best course. Deadlock loomed. The mediator tested with the parties a possible solution by which the party would accept the farm for a year and would see whether it was acceptable. If it proved not to be right, then it would be sold on the open market, and the price achieved would be credited towards the settlement payable to that party. That simple and creative course helped to break a deadlock and to resolve the issues. Perhaps the parties would have arrived at this solution themselves in direct negotiation, but that

---

[6] *Conflicts: A better way to resolve them* (Penguin, 1986) at p. 114. He prefers the term "lateral thinking" because of the vagueness of the term "creativity" and its artistic connotations and value-laden perception. Whereas he says that creative people can be rigid in their thinking, lateral thinking escapes from existing perceptual and conceptual patterns and opens up new ways of looking at things and doing things. Nevertheless, he uses the term "creativity" in his work.

was unlikely because the nature of their conflict and antagonism inhibited the exploration of creative solutions. It is often up to the mediator to develop creative ideas, taking care to test them tentatively with the parties and not to promote them if the parties are not interested in them.

Flexibility

One of the great advantages of ADR is its flexibility. Instead of facing the rigid structures of litigation, disputing parties have the benefit of processes that are adaptable to their specific needs. An ADR practitioner can create a process that responds to the requirements of the parties and their issues. This is the origin of the various hybrid processes of ADR.[7]   **15–031**

This flexibility extends not only to the creation of processes, but also to the way in which each process is conducted. While some framework is helpful, there is scope for flexibility and creativity within that framework. The ADR practitioner can work in a way that the situation requires.   **15–032**

In the course of a commercial mediation, a mediator may for example decide to suspend separate meetings with the parties and have a joint meeting with their financial advisers. Separate meetings with the parties' lawyers might follow this, and then a joint meeting with everyone to review progress. Or in a family mediation, the mediator might help the couple to explore a much wider range of permutations of options than lawyers in the traditional adversarial process would conceive of doing. This flexibility of approach is inherent in ADR.   **15–033**

There cannot be flexibility of process without flexibility on the part of the person responsible for administering the process. One of the hallmarks of a good mediator is the ability to be flexible where the situation requires it.   **15–034**

Balance

Poised at the top of the construct, balance is the mediator's critical quality. This involves impartiality and even-handedness between the parties. It demands an ability to see both sides of the conflict, and to maintain that even-handedness at all times.   **15–035**

A mediator maintains a centred position in relation to the parties, showing favour to neither. This even-handedness does not mean that the mediator might not lean one way or another in the course of the process: on the contrary, this is almost inevitable as the mediator probes here, questions there, prevents abusive behaviour, perhaps from one person and then from the other. However, balance involves the mediator always maintaining and returning to a centred position.   **15–036**

Another concept of balance refers to the mediator being in a balanced frame of mind. A mediator who is personally off balance is likely to be less effective. This reference to personal balance in mediation has led to some comparisons with the practice of the form of aikido, a Japanese martial art, which requires a practitioner to be balanced, centred, perceptive and decisive, moving responsively with the flow of the challenger.[8]   **15–037**

---

[7] See Chap. 2 for an outline of hybrid processes.

[8] Thomas Crum, a U.S. martial arts expert and a dispute resolution practitioner, draws on the principles of aikido in his theories and practice of conflict resolution. See his interesting books *The Magic of Conflict* (1987) and *Journey to Center* (1997). He believes that a neutral who is

2. OTHER MEDIATOR ATTRIBUTES

15–038 In addition to the qualities identified in the mediation construct, a mediator will ideally also have other attributes. There can be no definitive list of these nor can they be easily distinguished in practice because of their overlap. The way in which a mediator acts will be an amalgamation of inherent attributes, qualities and predilections, of learned and intuitive skills and techniques, of cultural and professional influences, and of the circumstances and requirements of the parties and their issues. There will also be other extraneous factors such as the model of mediation being used and the code of practice being followed.

15–039 Attributes are the inherent traits and qualities that a person has, rather than the skills that are specifically employed in the process. They are a product largely of personality and psychological make-up. In addition to those already identified, the following attributes are important in a mediator:

15–040 *Understanding:* The ability to understand with sensitivity the issues, often complex, and the concerns and aspirations of the parties, explicit and implicit.

15–041 *Intuition:* An ability to sense information without any rationalisation, obtained through a perceptiveness to verbal and other signals received.

15–042 *Trustworthiness:* Integrity coupled with a sense that trust can be reposed in the mediator.

15–043 *Authority:* A firmness of touch in managing the process effectively and constructively.

15–044 *Constructiveness:* A practical turn of mind that sees positive possibilities and can motivate the parties to deal constructively with settlement options.

15–045 *Independence:* This includes an ability to work autonomously, without support or feedback, and to maintain a neutral and independent stance.[9]

---

centred is more likely to be stable and sensitive and better able to deal effectively with conflict. Another mediator, Donald Saposnek, describes in an article "Aikido: A Systems Model for Maneuvering in Mediation" (1987) 14/15 M.Q. 119 the parallels between the two processes, including the stages of defence: perception, evaluation, decision and reaction.

[9] In his 1983 paper "The psychology of a mediator" (SPIDR Occasional paper 83–1), Jerome T. Barrett mentions isolation as one of the psychological ingredients of the mediator's job. The mediator, he says, does not have the support, reassurance or understanding of a colleague or supervisor. Most family mediation organisations in the U.K., however, provide for mediators to be supported by supervisors or consultants, at least until accreditation and to some extent even afterwards. Nevertheless, sole mediation is a demanding solitary activity.

3. MEDIATION SKILLS

The mediator's skills

In addition to the attributes mentioned above, the mediator also needs to use various skills in conducting the mediation. These skills may be learned or intuitive, largely enhancing communication, negotiation flexibility and creativity within a secure, well-managed environment, and include the following:

15–046

Listening

This is a fundamental but often neglected communication skill. It involves allowing the parties to speak without interrupting, anticipating or contradicting them, and then absorbing those words and ideas before responding. Some people, while listening to a sentence or idea, are thinking of a response, perhaps even responding before the speaker has finished the sentence. To some this may be viewed as a strength. As a mediator, however, except where the circumstances require the mediator to interrupt a party or to stop a line of discussion for a specific reason, it is important to exercise patience and restraint, to listen carefully and to hear what is being said before responding.

15–047

Observing non-verbal communications

A skilled mediator will have highly tuned antennae which can pick up things that have not only been said, but are merely hinted at. A grimace or flicker of the eye may lend a clue as to how a party feels about some issue, and an observant mediator will notice this and either respond to it in some way, or perhaps store it as data received.

15–048

Much has been written on how non-verbal communications such as "body language" can inform one about a person's underlying feelings.[10] This includes eye signals, facial expressions, gestures, body postures, tone of voice and maintenance of personal space.[11] The mediator needs to draw on all kinds of skills, and to supplement the information formally provided by the parties with additional data that may not be volunteered but which may be relevant to the resolution of the issues. An ability to pick up non-verbal as well as verbal communications can be most helpful. An intuitive mediator who is sensitive to the parties, their issues, concerns and motivations will be alive to the subtleties of their responses without needing any theoretical base.

15–049

---

[10] A simple introduction is contained in *Body Language: How to read others' thoughts by their gestures* by Allan Pease (1981). See also Knapp, *Non-verbal Communication in Human Interaction* (2nd ed.) Holt, Rinehart & Winston (1976); Desmond Morris's various books: *The Naked Ape* (1967), *The Human Zoo* (1969), *Intimate Behaviour* (1971) and *Manwatching* (1977); and Eric Berne, *Games People Play* (1964) which describes ways in which people programme themselves into procedures and rituals.

[11] Allan Pease (see n. 10) refers to personal space, comprising zones determined by cultural factors, status and personal factors. These are the intimate zone (into which only those emotionally close to the person are allowed); the personal zone (acceptable for social occasions); the social zone (for communicating with people not well-known to the person); and the public zone (relevant to addressing a group of people). He identifies social rules and rituals relating to such zones. He also deals with "Desks, Tables and Seating Arrangements", including co-operative and competitive positions; and he comments on seating, table sizes and shapes.

15–050   There is a corollary. The mediator will be engaged with taking notes, asking questions and managing the process. If as a result of this, the mediator becomes so insensitive to the nuances of the parties' communications that he or she is not able to listen carefully to the parties and note their unspoken responses, something of value in assisting the resolution of the issues may be missed.

Helping parties to hear

15–051   People do not always hear what is being said, especially when they are in a stressful situation. They may hear the words, but they are so caught up with what they are planning to say, or with their own perceptions of the position, or are so emotionally troubled in relation to issues or to the person speaking that they cannot necessarily take in what has been said. In the traditional process, lawyers will be familiar with the client who does not remember some point being made or advice being given in a meeting, which the solicitor clearly remembers saying.

15–052   The situation is not unfamiliar where, in the course of an exchange between disputing parties in a joint mediation meeting, the one may make some concession, and this will go unnoticed by the other.

15–053   In a situation where one party makes an unheard concession, or says something relevant which passes unnoticed, the mediator can ensure that it registers with the other. This can be done, for example, by reiterating the statement, by acknowledging it, or perhaps by asking it to be repeated.

15–054   Similarly, the mediator needs to ensure that parties do not misunderstand one another. The mediator has a role to help people to hear and to understand one another.

Questioning

15–055   Skilled questioning is a fundamental tool of the mediator. Questions can be used for a number of purposes, for example:

- They can help the mediator to gather information and get a better understanding of the issues, to clarify facts and to probe unclear aspects.

- They can help to get a party to examine whether his position or assessment or his understanding of the issues is realistic, or whether a proposed option or course of action is workable in practice. Confronting a party's perceptions, positions or preconceived notions with questions that present alternative ways of viewing the situation may be essential in getting necessary and proper understanding and movement.

- They can help to promote reflection by a party on any aspect of his or her circumstances or proposals and thus to become more fully aware of the issues involved in any situation.

- Questions may be used to encourage a party to review a position or to focus on specific issues.

- They may redirect the way in which discussions are moving, and may be used as a form of intervention in conflict management to divert parties away from a heated discussion into a more productive field.

- A question may be strategic, where the mediator knows the answer but wishes the party to arrive at the answer himself.

- Instead of a mediator expressing a personal view on a situation, questions can be asked which allow parties to consider issues needing to be examined without compromising the mediator's neutrality.[12]

John Haynes points out that the mediator accomplishes most of his or her **15–056** work through questions. Haynes draws attention to the value of questions in allowing the mediator the opportunity to frame statements as questions, minimising the scope for mediator error and giving parties the opportunity to correct invalid assumptions. This also allows the parties to shift their positions themselves as they review the problem after answering questions.[13]

Questions may take different forms: They may be *open,* allowing for any **15–057** kind of answer, or *closed* and more specific, usually calling for a yes or no response. They may be *general* or *focused.* They may be *directed* to a specific party, or may be *undirected,* allowing any party to respond. They may be *circular* as where one asks a party "How do you think that Fred would answer that?" They may be in the form of *minimal prompts* to parties to develop more fully what they are saying, such as the mediator merely saying "yes" or "I see" or even just nodding, or repeating as a question a word or phrase used by a party.[14]

Mediators need to be aware of the range and power of questions. Some **15–058** mediators say that they do not influence parties because they do not express views but only ask questions. But clearly questions can have enormous power.

Summarising

Summarising can be very important and helpful. First, it helps the mediator **15–059** to ensure that he or she has a correct understanding of what has been said. Secondly, the mediator can be seen to have understood what has been said, which helps to establish confidence. Thirdly, it crystallises and focuses the issues to facilitate decision-making. Summarising is not, however, mere parroting what has been said, but involves careful and accurate paraphrasing.

It is obviously not necessary or appropriate to summarise everything a **15–060** party says to the mediator. That would be excessively laborious and probably rather annoying. There are times, however, when a mediator may find it

---

[12]But see Chap. 16 for the possibility of questions and reality-testing being used as a vehicle for evaluation. This is not necessarily inappropriate, but needs to be undertaken with care, awareness and responsibility.

[13]See John M. Haynes and Gretchen L. Haynes, *Mediating Divorce* (1989) at pp. 32–34. Their section on question forms is applicable to all kinds of mediation, and not merely family disputes. Haynes acknowledges the pioneering work of Karl Tomm in "Interventive Interviewing: Intending to Ask Lineal, Circular, Strategic, or Reflexive Questions" (1988) 27(1) *Family Process,* pp. 1–15.

[14]See *The Skilled Helper: A Systematic Approach to Effective Helping* by Gerard Egan (1986) at pp. 112–115, which in turn refers to Hackney and Cormier, *Counseling Strategies and Objectives* (1979) who suggest the "accent" which accentuates a word repeated as a question, and the use of minimal prompts.

useful to summarise. For example, the mediator may do so at the end of a party's presentation of his case particularly if complex issues have been covered that need to be checked, when concluding a separate meeting with a party, or selectively during the course of discussion.

Acknowledging

15–061　One of the mediator's functions can be to hear a party's views, feelings and grievances about the issues, even though the mediator's role is not to adjudicate on them. Sometimes what is needed is an acknowledgment that they have been heard and recognised. This does not mean that the mediator needs to agree with them: on the contrary, that may not be at all appropriate and could damage neutrality. It also does not mean patronising the party. A simple acknowledgment that the mediator has heard and understands the views or feelings will usually suffice.

15–062　　Other forms of acknowledging may be appropriate during the mediation. If one party makes a creative suggestion or is willing to make even a small concession, it may be worth acknowledging the helpfulness of that, again without being patronising. Acknowledging may often be no more than a nod of response to a party, an indication that he or she has been heard.

Mutualising

15–063　It is no surprise that parties to a dispute tend to see the issues from their own point of view, and that each is likely to have quite different perceptions of the same facts. One way that a mediator can help to bridge this discrepancy of perception is to make observations that tend to show that there are similar concerns or interests on both sides. So, for example, where one party feels that he has been making all the concessions, the mediator might observe that both have actually been doing so, and that both probably share similar feeling about this. Mutualising each side's concerns can help to remove the focus from the party's own position and serve as a gentle reminder that similar concerns exist on both or all sides.[15]

15–064　　The term "mutualising" is not a familiar one and is sometimes dismissed as jargon. While the word itself may feel uncomfortable, the concept should not be dismissed. It means clarifying that the other party shares a similar feeling, and that concerns are mutually felt. A simpler alternative term may be preferred, as long as the concept is retained, which is a valuable skill for mediators.

Using language effectively and reframing

15–065　Mediators have to take special care with the words they use. Language needs generally to be neutral, and the mediator should not adopt the words or images of one party. The mediator has to avoid language directing parties ("I think you should . . . "). The mediator may need to acknowledge a party, but must take care that this is not patronising. Some words and ideas are best avoided: for example, asking for a "bottom line" in negotiation is unhelpful,

---

[15]John Haynes refers to mutualising statements as "powerful creators of doubt" about individual positions, bringing the focus back on overlapping self-interests. See *Mediating Divorce* by John and Gretchen Haynes (1985).

because the words carry a connotation of ending the negotiations if the proposed terms are not agreed.

It is difficult enough to conduct the mediation process, with the hurly-burly **15–066** this sometimes involves, without also having to watch every word with care. Nevertheless, it is essential to be aware of the importance of how language is used. It quickly becomes second nature to do so.

Words also have to be used with care when carrying messages, ideas and **15–067** proposals between parties in the course of shuttle mediation. Sometimes it is necessary to do so in the exact words of the party. Sometimes, however, paraphrasing is necessary without distorting the meaning of what has been said. A party might for example tell the mediator privately that he considers a claim to be grossly inflated and typical of the claimant's greed, and that he will not pay it, but that he might explore settlement at a more realistic level. The mediator need not parrot those words back to the other party. It might be more productive if the mediator were to paraphrase this into something like "It may not surprise you to hear that X does not agree with the level of your claim. He thinks that it is much too high; but he tells me that he would be willing to explore settlement possibilities at a rather lower level, which he thinks would be more realistic..." Re-wording in such circumstances is sometimes called reframing, but this is not strictly correct technical usage of the term "reframing".

The term "reframing" has been adopted from the language of family **15–068** therapy. It refers to a technique that assists people to change the frame of reference against which a person views an event, so that the judgment placed on that event takes a different meaning or perspective. So, for example, in a partnership disagreement, professional partners may see one partner's actions as constantly and deliberately provocative. If, however, the "provocative" partner is anxiously trying to force the partners to confront certain issues which are damaging to the firm as a whole, and this can be made clearer to all concerned, the actions in question may be seen in a somewhat different light. This is the essence of reframe.

The use of reframing in mediation does not distort the meaning of a **15–069** party's actions, but rather allows those actions to be seen in a positive rather than negative way. It is essential that a reframe should resonate with all parties if it is to be effective. If the mediator reframes in a way that does not sound right to the parties, they will reject the reframe.

Normalising

This is another jargon word that refers to a helpful skill. Parties to a **15–070** mediation may feel that their situation is an unusual and rather extraordinary one that no-one else could have encountered and that may be beyond their (or the mediator's) capacity to resolve. In a divorce, for example, a couple may feel very troubled and distressed about particular aspects and may not realise that such feelings are not unusual. The mediator may want to reassure them of the normalcy of such feelings, while taking care not to minimise or be dismissive of those feelings. That can help to put their minds at rest, and allow them more easily to address the issues facing them.

A mediator should not try to "normalise" inappropriately, and should be careful not to patronise parties. The effective use of normalising, however, can be a relief to parties.

Managing conflict and the expression of emotions

15–071   As some element of conflict is invariably likely to be inherent in mediation, a mediator will need to have some proficiency in the skill of conflict management. This involves the ability to intercede between two opposing sides and to channel their energies, which may have been devoted to sustaining the conflict, into a more productive and creative mode. This role is not required by a neutral adjudicator, such as a judge or arbitrator, in the traditional adversarial process: he may suggest to the parties that they should try to settle, but must protect his judicial role and cannot enter into the maelstrom of the dispute itself.

15–072   Sometimes the parties need to be diverted from their conflict on an immediate basis, when they are engaged in a high level of conflict with one another during the meeting. A mediator may need to be able to distract the parties from their immediate altercation and to direct them towards a more productive line of discussion.

15–073   This leads to the question of the mediator's ability to allow a party to express his feelings arising from the dispute without damaging the mediation process or losing the other party. Situations of conflict and dispute can involve a high level of emotional content. This is not limited to family and inter-personal disagreements: whenever relationships break down or are under strain feelings can run high, as anyone involved in a business or professional partnership dispute or a professional negligence claim will confirm. Indeed, some level of personal antagonism or other feelings probably exist in a significant percentage of commercial and civil disputes.

15–074   In such situations, a mediator needs the skill of handling parties in conflict. If a party is upset or angry, or is experiencing any other strong feelings, it may be necessary for the mediator to allow those feelings to be expressed rather than trying to keep them bottled up. If this happens in a private meeting, the other party is unlikely to be affected, at least directly. If, however, it happens in a joint meeting, there is a risk that the other party may also become upset, angry or emotional. That may also be necessary. At some point, however, the expression of emotions may move from being necessary and sometimes cathartic and restorative, to being unhelpful to the process and even destructive.

15–075   The mediator needs to allow parties to express their emotions, but must remember that the object of the exercise is dispute resolution not counselling. The mediator will have to judge how far emotions can be allowed to be expressed before the party is gently, or if necessary briskly, brought back to the business at hand. Until a party has been able to express the feelings he or she is experiencing, discussions and negotiations may often be unproductive; but afterwards matters may settle down more easily into a constructive mode.[16] It is equally important in a joint meeting that the other party should understand that such expression of feelings will not continue unchecked but will be eased towards an end. There is a balance to be struck.

Highly conflictual situations may be defused in a number of ways. This may call on the mediator's empathetic skills, or may involve acknowledgment, mutualising or other skills as outlined in this section. The expression of feelings may be necessary, or distraction may be required to divert a crisis. A short break may be needed to let feelings cool, or a light or humorous touch to help break the tension, where appropriate.[17]

15–076

Managing the process

Distinct from conflict management, the mediator needs to be a proficient manager of the mediation process itself. This necessitates maintaining control of the procedural aspects, making and implementing the agenda and deciding how best to deal with the issues. It involves acting as a firm but fair chairperson of the process and ensuring that time is used effectively.

15–077

If a mediator loses control of the management of the process, whether by allowing any party to dominate the proceedings or merely by a general inability to maintain authority or effectiveness, the trust and confidence of the parties is likely to be eroded. This will have potentially adverse consequences on the outcome of the process. The corollary of this is not domineering regulation by the mediator, but gentle, firm, impartial and effective management control.

15–078

Lateral thinking

This term, invented by Edward de Bono, involves thinking in a different way from the usual method, by changing perceptions and concepts and seeking new perspectives, ideas and alternatives.[18] This is what mediation is often largely about, and so the development of skills that enhance these processes must be valuable.

15–079

De Bono identifies methods of developing lateral thinking skills. These include finding ways of generating alternatives; challenging assumptions; suspending judgment; "fractionation" (his term for breaking situations down to their basic components in order to restructure); using a "reversal" method of standing ideas on their heads; brainstorming; and designing problem-solving solutions.

15–080

---

[16]Most mediators, especially interpersonal, recognise the need to address emotional aspects, if only to be able to move forward from them effectively. CDR Associates in Colorado, *e.g.* have devised the concept of a "Circle of Conflict." This provides that value problems, relationship problems (including emotional and communications issues) and data problems (lack of information or misinformation) need to be dealt with before substantive issues (interests and structural problems) can be addressed. Parties tend to move back and forth between the two areas.

[17]Humour can be valuable in mediation. This does not mean facetiousness; but a warm, apt, humorous remark can sometimes help to defuse tension and give parties an opportunity to step back from tense and hostile confrontation.

[18]See de Bono, *Lateral Thinking: A Textbook of Creativity,* (1970); also *Lateral Thinking for Management, Practical Thinking, The Use of Lateral Thinking* and his many other works.

Understanding triangulation and avoiding coalitions

15–081   A mediator entering the arena of the dispute creates a new dynamic by his or her very presence. That dynamic contains both risks and benefits.

15–082   A third person can have an impact in different ways on two others (whether the two are united, conflicted or fluctuating between these states). A reflection on these differences and their implications may constitute a theory of triangulation.

15–083   Counsellors and psychotherapists will be aware of the risk of triangulation during the course of their professional work. Mediators need similarly to be aware of this risk. The issue of triangulation ties in closely with that of coalitions, which are formed through alliances between two parties against the third.

15–084   A coalition between the mediator and one party may happen consciously, but more usually develops unwittingly. It must inevitably have adverse implications for mediator impartiality, and is likely to be damaging to the process and its effectiveness, as well as the perceptions of both parties. Mediators must therefore be alive to the risk of being triangulated into a coalition, and the need to avoid this conscientiously.

15–085   When a mediator believes that a power imbalance is occurring in the mediation, and takes steps to redress that imbalance, a risk of a coalition with the weaker party exists. A party may deliberately or unconsciously try to engage the mediator on his or her side, on the basis of establishing rapport based on same gender, or common interests or background, personal or occupational.

15–086   A mediator may develop an antagonism or competitive attitude towards one of the parties. This might, for example, happen if the party is perceived as withholding full co-operation with the process. Where the other party overtly or covertly looks to the mediator for support in these circumstances, triangulation can occur.

15–087   Parties may form an alliance against the mediator ("We'll show the mediator how stuck we are!") leaving the mediator feeling excluded or ineffective. This is rarely done as a deliberate act, but can be defence mechanisms of couples, business partners or others with a personal or working relationship.

15–088   Coalitions and alliances may not necessarily be long-term. A brief alliance could happen, for example, where something is said which results in one party giving a knowing glance at the mediator. For that unspoken moment, there could be an alliance between the mediator and that party. This can be difficult to avoid, but the mediator needs to understand what is happening to prevent this from developing into a pattern.

15–089   Triangular thinking has benefits as well as risks and cautions. Edward de Bono has coined the term "triangular thinking" which he uses where a third party helps the disputing parties to create a design for the resolution of their issues. He distinguishes this method of conflict resolution from both the confrontational approach and from the negotiating or bargaining approach. He believes firmly that conflict resolution requires such a "design idiom" to avoid existing systems which he considers to be inadequate and dangerous. He believes that a third party role in conflict resolution is essential because parties to a dispute usually cannot undertake problem-solving themselves simply because of the nature of conflict situations and as they are not generally trained in lateral thinking and the problem-solving mode. He does not view the third party merely as a go-between but as an active participant in the creative process of designing appropriate solutions.[19]

Encouraging a problem-solving mode[20]

While some parties may enter mediation receptive to a problem-solving mode of negotiation, many others tend to be in a competitive mode, because of their strong views or feelings about the dispute or because they believe that to be the most effective way to negotiate. One of the mediator's skills is to help the parties to move towards a more creative and problem-solving negotiating approach.

15–090

This is not to suggest that parties are expected to abandon their self-interest when they enter the mediation process: that would be nonsense. It rather means that the mediator helps the parties to realise, and where appropriate to reinforce the awareness, that eacy party's aspirations may be more readily achieved in the context of an approach which seeks imaginative and resourceful solutions that can benefit both or all parties. As indicated by Lax and Sebenius[21] negotiation even in a problem-solving mode will still involve tensions between the needs, wants and aspirations of the parties. That will not disappear in mediation. Hard bargaining will inevitably and understandably continue even in the mediation context. One of the skills of the mediator lies in creating a balance between these different negotiating tensions.

15–091

Centring

This term has two different usages. In the first one, a mediator maintains a centred position in relation to the disputants, showing none of them more favour than the others. This even-handedness does not mean that the mediator will not lean one way or another in the course of the process. On the contrary, this is almost inevitable as the mediator probes here, questions there, challenges one and then the other, and prevents abusive behaviour perhaps from one side and then from another.

15–092

The second notion of centring is the mediator being in a balanced frame of mind, unflustered and in personal control. A mediator who is knocked off balance by the parties, and who stops being centred within himself or herself is likely to be less effective in working with the parties.[22]

15–093

Being silent

There are times when a mediator may want to respond to a statement, make a comment or offer an opinion, when it would be better to maintain silence. Professionals whose traditional roles involve giving advice or assistance may

15–094

---

[19]See de Bono, *Conflicts: A better way to resolve them* (1985), which develops the concept of "triangular thinking" and argues for the "design idiom". He puts forward interesting and challenging notions as well as practical ways of working.

[20]See the reference to the problem-solving mode of negotiation in Chap. 6.

[21]See Chap. 6, at para. 6–034.

[22]For more information about centring, see the books by Tom Crum, n. 8 above.

find this a difficult skill to develop, but an essential one on many occasions.[23]

15–095 For example, there may be a significant moment in a joint meeting when one person tells the other something critically important and perhaps personal. That may need time and silence to absorb, especially if it is painful. Some professionals may want to leap in at such a time with words of comfort or digression, to rescue the party from the pain. Yet that would be inappropriate: mediators must be able to allow people the space they need, including time to hear and to take in what is said. Quiet empathy may follow.

15–096 At other times, there may need to be a silence while a party is considering the position and the options, or simply needs time to think. Mediators must be able to respect silence when it is appropriate.

Constructive facilitation

15–097 This summarises the essence of the mediator's role: to prioritise issues, devise and implement strategies to help the parties to communicate and negotiate effectively with one another, encourage them to develop and consider options, and help to direct the process towards a consensual resolution.

15–098 The way in which a mediator communicates with the parties will depend in part upon the level of facilitation adopted by the mediator. A mediator playing an active facilitation role may want to be pro-active in discussion, inviting options or brainstorming, asking questions and stimulating discussion. Alternatively, the mediator may prefer a lesser role, allowing the parties themselves to reflect and initiate thoughts and ideas. The degree of facilitation will reflect the style of the mediator, the preferences of the parties, express or perceived, the needs of the situation, the strategy decided on by the mediator and the model of mediation being followed.

15–099 There is also a relationship between the parties' perception of the mediator's trustworthiness and commitment, and the way in which the parties communicate with the mediator. Where the mediator is seen as competent, honest, empathetic, committed and authoritative the scope for a productive dialogue is enhanced.

15–100 The obvious implication of this is that a mediator who is genuinely concerned about the issues and the parties, who is scrupulous about maintaining trust, and who works effectively, is likely to find it easier to communicate productively with the parties than one who lacks that commitment.

15–101 There is, of course, no set of right ways to communicate. Those mediators who are experienced in dealing with people in dispute or distress will no doubt deal instinctively with the parties to a mediation. On the other hand, in this relatively new way of working as a neutral, an awareness of the considerations mentioned in this chapter can help to expand instinctive responses and to develop useful additional skills.

---

[23] See the Friends Conflict Resolution Program publication *Peace-making in Your Neighbourhood: Mediator's Handbook,* (ed.) by E. Beer (1990) at p. 34.

4. THE MEDIATOR'S ROLES AND FUNCTIONS

Mediators perform a number of different roles and functions at different **15–102** times during the mediation process, sometimes consecutively, sometimes simultaneously. Some may be more relevant to one model of mediation than another; nor are they as clearly defined in practice, where they overlap and blur, as they may be in theory.

The mediator as manager of the process[24]

There are various ways in which the mediator manages the mediation process **15–103** and when doing so needs to exercise management skills and authority:

- By making the practical arrangements for the initial mediation meeting (in those cases where this function is not carried out by an ADR organisation). This administrative role may cover matters such as arranging the venue for the meeting, how it should be conducted, what documents are required and other practical matters.

- By acting as an informal chair of the meetings and ensuring that when the parties meet with him or her there is an orderly and reasonably secure environment in which discussion can take place effectively and constructively.

- By assuming responsibility for the conduct of the mediation process in accordance with ground rules accepted by the parties.

- By formulating, implementing and varying as necessary an agenda for the mediation, where appropriate in consultation with the parties.

- By managing the meetings, regulating the time spent on different aspects under discussion, deciding whether and when to meet parties separately, deterring abusive conduct, allowing or preventing interruptions, and generally assisting the parties in using the time productively.

Newly practising mediators, conscious of their neutral, facilitative role, are **15–104** sometimes uncertain about the extent of management authority they should exercise. This may depend on the model of mediation being used, the culture within which it is taking place and the style and strategy of the mediator. It is, however, generally accepted that the management of the mediation process is the mediator's responsibility; and this needs to be authoritatively, even if gently, asserted in order for the process to be most effective.

The mediator as information gatherer

The mediator needs to establish the issues, usually by collecting commonly **15–105**

---

[24]The notion of the mediator having control of the mediation process is inherent in various works, including, *e.g.* in John Haynes and Gretchen Haynes, *Mediating Divorce* (1989), at pp. 16–17 and Lisa Parkinson *Family Mediation* (1997) at p. 400. But see the process of transformative mediation at paras 1–040 and 21–132–134, in which even the process and its management may follow the parties' wishes.

available information and by receiving supplementary information from each of the parties.

- The mediator may ask the parties to furnish relevant copy documents. Where the model allows confidentiality between the parties, there must be a clear distinction as to which documents are shared between the parties and which are confidential to the party supplying them. It may be prudent initially to seek only commonly available documents, especially if these are supplied in advance of the first meeting.

- In some models, parties send written submissions to the mediator and to one another, setting out the facts and issues that each party considers relevant and material, and their contentions on the issues.

- In joint meetings with the parties, the mediator can seek clarification and amplification of any unclear aspects, being careful to maintain neutrality in doing so.

- Where each party makes an oral presentation in the joint meeting, appropriate questions can be asked which may help to inform the mediator and to clarify or highlight matters for the other party.

- In private meetings with each party, the mediator may receive information on a confidential basis. Any information received on this basis must of course be maintained confidentially, but the mediator may seek permission to make some disclosure to the other party if this may assist with the negotiations.

15–106 The mediator also receives information in a more indirect way, through hints given by the parties, body language and other non-verbal communications, and through data obtained from third parties such as experts and advisers.

15–107 To enable the mediator to facilitate effectively, careful neutral information-gathering and proper disclosure is necessary.

The mediator as facilitator

15–108 This is the mediator's primary role. Views differ as to how active the mediator should be. At one end of the spectrum is the minimalist view that a mediator should do little more than create the necessary conditions for the parties to meet and to conduct their own negotiations, with a relatively low level of intervention. At the other end, some would see the mediator making settlement proposals and actively encouraging parties to accept these. There is a broad consensus that a mediator can and should be an active facilitator, but that a mediator should not try to coerce the parties into accepting his or her preferred outcome.

15–109 The following are some of the facilitative functions that a mediator can perform:

- Helping each party to understand the other party's position.

- Prioritising the issues and helping to guide the parties through the range of issues brought to the mediation.

- Helping the parties to generate, explore and narrow options for resolving the issues, encouraging brainstorming, and consistently seeking ways to create additional resources that may assist in achieving a resolution.

- Acting as a sounding board for a party to test whether possible proposals may be useful and viable before they are communicated to the other party.

- Examining common interests and aspirations, and possibilities for future relationships where appropriate, and endeavouring to seek common ground between the parties which will facilitate resolution.

- Examining mutual concerns, including underlying issues and anxieties, and exploring how these can most effectively be dealt with.

- Allowing the parties to express their feelings such as anger, distress or frustration about various aspects of the dispute or towards the other party, without letting this become counter-productive to the process.

- Reframing statements when communicating them from one party to another, to put them into a more understandable context or to minimise the risk of polarisation where a negative statement has to be communicated.

- Acknowledging the strength of views and feelings held without necessarily agreeing with these.

- Using other communication skills and strategies.

- Suggesting such outside resources as may assist the parties, such as their seeking valuations or specialist third party advice or expertise relevant to the issues.

- Using impasse strategies if the parties are deadlocked.

- Exploring the alternatives to negotiated resolution and their implications.

- Helping parties to consider and prepare for adjudication.

The mediator as reality-tester and evaluator

Testing the realism of a party's views, position or proposals is a different **15–110** function from evaluation, though there can be a continuum between them.

A mediator may wish to check whether a party is being realistic about the **15–111** viability of proposals for resolution, the strength of his position, or any other aspect. Helping the parties to test their realism is widely regarded as being an integral part of the mediation process, even following an exclusively facilitative model in which no form of evaluation takes place. This may involve no more than asking the parties questions ("What if ...?") to help ensure that they have correctly understood the matter or proposal under discussion and its implications and consequences.

15–112   An evaluation goes further than mere reality-testing and involves the mediator in considering and expressing a view on the respective merits of any one or more of the issues between the parties, or of any matter under discussion. It may be based on the mediator's own expertise and knowledge, or on third party expertise imported into the mediation.[25]

15–113   The mediator's evaluative view has no binding effect, but may influence the parties to adjust their respective negotiating positions, and their settlement aspirations, to accord more closely to what they perceive to be their respective rights and obligations. For this reason, where evaluation is undertaken at all, it needs to be done with the utmost care and sensitivity, and with responsibility.

- The mediator may test one party's views or perceptions by reference to the other party's position and views, to objective criteria where these are known, or to the mediator's own perceptions of the position. Under a model that uses evaluation, there is a view that the parties may need to have a more accurate appreciation of their respective strengths and weaknesses in order to be better able to achieve a realistic settlement.

- Even if an evaluation of the issues is not explicitly requested by the parties, the mediator may in some situations want to make some evaluative comments, perhaps informally, or to ask probing questions to help parties to recognise valid points and to get them to reassess positions that might otherwise become entrenched.

- The mediator may be specifically asked by the parties in some cases to make an evaluation of the position. This may range from a formal opinion in the nature of a non-binding judgment, to merely giving an informal indication of strong and weak aspects to help guide subsequent negotiations.

- There is always a risk that an evaluation will damage the perceived neutrality of the mediator. A mediator will need to consider in the circumstances of each individual case whether or not it would be appropriate and helpful to provide any such evaluation, and if so, in what form and at what stage of the process.

The mediator as scribe

15–114   A mediator may have a number of possible tasks as a scribe in the mediation proceedings.

- While the process is under way, the mediator should maintain notes of certain aspects, for example, matters that need to be further investigated or researched; undertakings given by the parties in the course of the proceedings; or the terms of alternative settlement proposals under discussion.

---

[25]See Chap. 16 for discussion about neutral, non-binding evaluative processes.

- The mediator may provide the parties with a note of outline settlement proposals under consideration with the object of this being used to focus the parties on the details of the proposals and to maintain an impetus towards resolution.

- Where the issues are resolved, one of the mediator's tasks may well be to prepare a note of the terms of settlement or heads of agreement for the parties to sign.[26] This may be required to be signed immediately, before the parties leave the meeting (as usually happens in civil/commercial mediation), or it may be subsequently prepared for later execution (which is more common in family mediation). In some models, particularly where the parties do not wish to be bound right away, this may comprise a summary of the proposed terms which the parties may wish to consider further, either by themselves or with the benefit of professional advice.

- It may be left to the legal representatives of the parties to draft the agreement, particularly if they attended the mediation proceedings. The mediator may assist with the drafting of the settlement agreement or may wish to check its drafting to ensure that it correctly reflects the position. Alternatively, the mediator may prepare a first draft, or heads of agreement, for the parties' own lawyers to finalise.

The mediator as settlement supervisor
The mediator can assist in various ways with regard to the supervision or implementation of any settlement the parties may enter into: **15–115**

- The mediator (or the ADR organisation appointing him or her) may act as a stakeholder, with explicit directions as to the circumstances under which the stakeholding may be released.

- The mediator may be appointed to supervise a settlement and to ensure in a specified way that the terms of settlement are being properly implemented.

- If any dispute arises in the course of implementing a settlement, the mediator can be given authority to liaise with the parties in order to resolve that issue.

Under some circumstances, the mediator can be given limited or general **15–116** adjudicatory powers to deal with matters arising during the implementation period.

---

[26] For discussion about drafting, and for precedents, see Appendix II.

CHAPTER 16

NON-BINDING EVALUATIVE ADR

1. INTRODUCTION TO EVALUATIVE PROCESSES

16–001   As indicated in Chapter 2, dispute resolution processes may be viewed along a continuum with negotiation at the one end and litigation at the other end. These processes may be divided into two main categories, *adjudicatory* (where a binding decision is made by the neutral) and *consensual* (where parties control the decision-making).

16–002   All consensual ADR processes are based on the principle of the parties being helped to arrive at agreement by third party intervention and facilitation. A significant number of these consensual processes may include the neutral also helping the parties to evaluate or to review their evaluation of the merits of their dispute. That neutral assistance informs and empowers the parties, so that they can arrive at decisions with a better awareness of their respective rights. It is non-binding and leaves decision-making control with the parties. These non-binding evaluative processes, falling squarely within the consensual category of ADR, include in particular:

- Evaluative models of mediation

- The mini-trial (Executive Tribunal)

- The summary jury trial

- The neutral fact-finding expert

- Early Neutral Evaluation

- Non-binding court-annexed arbitration

- The Financial Dispute Resolution (FDR) procedure under the Ancillary Relief Pilot Scheme

- Ombudsman

Before examining each of these processes individually, it is necessary to consider the motivation for evaluation and what it entails.

Reasons for evaluating

16–003   If parties are unable to settle their issues by direct negotiation, impartial third party intervention may help them. This is the essence of mediation and virtually all other ADR processes.

Purely facilitative processes can be enormously helpful to many parties. Practitioners using such processes can help the parties to communicate and negotiate, to adopt problem-solving rather than competitive approaches, and to explore options for resolution based on interests, needs, concerns and considerations other than just legal rights. **16–004**

For many other parties, however, that may not be enough. There may be different reasons for this. For example, parties may wish to achieve settlement terms that broadly accord with their respective rights (which would be a perfectly proper aspiration) and may wish to have an indication from a bona fide neutral what those rights might be. Or they may have had different advice from their respective lawyers and may not be able to agree what those rights are. Or one party may be unrealistically refusing to accept reasonable terms because of a mistaken perception as to the strength of his rights. **16–005**

Parties to a dispute may want to try to establish from a neutral practitioner on a non-binding basis whether their perceptions of their rights and strengths are broadly correct. Alternatively, they may wish to use a facilitative process, but may welcome the introduction of an evaluative element to help break a deadlock arising from their different perceptions of the strength of their respective positions. ADR has a number of processes that can help parties towards realistic settlement terms by combining facilitative procedures with elements of non-binding evaluation. **16–006**

As will be amplified in this chapter, evaluation as part of an ADR process has potential advantages and disadvantages, and must be carried out with great care and sensitivity. Subject to cautions, ADR processes can help parties to evaluate their positions in appropriate cases and situations. **16–007**

What constitutes neutral evaluation?
Evaluation may be defined as a non-binding expression of opinion about the merits of issues between parties. **16–008**

Where this evaluation is undertaken for a party by that party's adviser, it is partisan, though if it is to have any value, it will need to be as objective as possible. Each party needs to obtain an objective assessment to be able to analyse the strength of his or her case. This in turn assists parties in deciding whether to risk proceeding to adjudication if necessary, and what level of terms might be appropriate for the purpose of settlement. It is a well-known feature of dispute resolution in the United Kingdom that parties may arrange through their solicitors to consult a specialist barrister for an opinion on the merits of the dispute. Such an opinion is (and is perceived as) giving the party a realistic assessment of his or her rights and strengths, even if unwelcome, so that a correspondingly realistic strategy and course of action can be formulated. The fact that it is partisan does not prevent it from indicating views that the party may have preferred not to hear. **16–009**

A non-binding evaluation provided neutrally for both or all parties to a dispute is obviously not partisan. However, the indications given by the neutral evaluator will invariably support one party more than the other, and this may create some ambiguity about the evaluator's neutrality and **16–010** impartiality. Can an ADR practitioner express a view on the merits and remain neutral and impartial?

16–011   There seems little doubt that the expression of a view on merits does not of itself erode a practitioner's impartiality. A judge or arbitrator may rule on an interim or final aspect of a case while retaining impartiality and without becoming partisan. The question is not one of objective fact, but rather of subjective perception. If a party forms a view that the ADR practitioner is no longer neutral and impartial, that will inevitably damage the process, possibly fatally.

16–012   Some people tend to have their own particular ideas of what neutral non-binding evaluation entails. This perception may vary from one person to another, because such evaluation can take different forms. Its object is not that a practitioner should sit in judgment but rather that the evaluation should help parties to view the case with a better awareness of the merits of certain aspects. A neutral, non-binding view may be expressed in a number of different ways:

- An evaluation may involve giving a detailed or comprehensive opinion on the respective prospects of success of the parties.

- It may involve the evaluator in expressing a preliminary and qualified view, perhaps with appropriate reservations. For example: "I have now been able to reflect on the statements and documents that you have both sent me and to liaise with each of you. You have asked me to express a preliminary view on this aspect of A's claim, and I do so very tentatively, bearing in mind that I cannot anticipate what a court would decide after detailed enquiry and argument. Although I understand the strength of B's feeling, it seems from what you have both submitted that A might well be able to establish this aspect, though he would have to quantify it properly. However, other factors could emerge that might change this preliminary view."

- An evaluation may relate only to some part of the case, and not necessarily the outcome if adjudicated. For example, it may relate to a preliminary aspect or to an application for interim relief; or it may cover just one of a number of points in issue that would not decide the whole case.

- Without expressing a view, an evaluator may set himself or herself up as "devil's advocate" and postulate counter-arguments, either hypothetical or actually put forward or expected to be submitted by the other party.[1] Some may feel that this does not constitute

---

[1] See the article by Jonathan Marks, Vice-Chairman of JAMS-Endispute, a primary ADR organisation in the U.S.: "Evaluative Mediation—Oxymoron or Essential Tool": *http://jams-endispute.com/articles/evalmed.html*. Marks is the mediator who, with Lord Griffiths, helped resolve the largest case mediated in the U.K., the *British & Commonwealth* case: see Chap. 9 at para. 9–151. He says that although in most cases he does not have to express a view, in a substantial minority of cases, skilful questioning and focused devil's advocacy are not sufficient to shift parties from their outcome predictions. In those cases he says "I think the mediator's responsibility is firmly to step over the threshold from facilitator to evaluator. If, but only if, the parties agree (and have so stated in a pre-mediation agreement), I'll tell them (with reasons) what I think a fair settlement is and what I think will happen in court if they

evaluation; but insofar as this expresses a point of view that might well (and is often intended to) influence a party to change his or her opinion on the merits, it would arguably fall within a broad definition of evaluation.

- Similarly, an evaluator may confront a party's views by asking questions that challenge that party's assessment of the merits of his or her case. Some practitioners believe that questioning is a non-directive way of working with parties. It certainly is a less direct challenge to parties, but depending on the questioning, it may be just as directive and just as evaluative. "Have you read the latest case on this point, *X v. Y?*" may be just as evaluative as outlining the principles of that case. Or "Are you seriously holding to the view that you can succeed on this application?" may convey a neutral's views as surely as spelling it out. There are shades of grey, but practitioners who challenge parties' views on merits by questioning may find that they are evaluating. Even the choice of questions and the concept of "reality-testing" may well reflect the neutral's judgment of the position and constitute an element of evaluating, albeit subtle, indirect and hidden.

It appears that the divide in process is not so much between facilitative and evaluative processes, but between adjudicatory and consensual. Facilitative processes, even if they contain a non-binding evaluative element, fall within the consensual category. Within the consensual grouping, a practitioner may provide degrees of assistance to the parties. These may range from pure facilitation to the neutral informing the parties of his or her opinion on aspects of the merits of the case.   **16–013**

Relationship between evaluative and facilitative processes

It will be seen that some mediators and other ADR practitioners who view themselves as purely facilitative may find that they are actually introducing an element of evaluation into their work, albeit subtly and often unwittingly.[2]   **16–014**

No clear line exists as to when questions or reality testing become evaluative. The test is probably whether the neutral's intervention conveys a view, whether expressed directly or indirectly, which may influence a party to change his or her opinion or position on the merits of the dispute or the possible terms of settlement.   **16–015**

If questions, reality-testing or any comments by the neutral have this effect, whether or not intended, then arguably the process has an evaluative element. Mediators who believe that because they only ask questions and do not offer comments, they do not influence the parties, may be avoiding the responsibility that in fact they have. It would be better to recognise and   **16–016**

---

don't settle."

[2] In Prof. Hazel Genn's Evaluation Report of the Central London County Court Pilot Mediation Scheme (July 1998), she found that "many mediators were explicitly evaluative during the course of mediations, despite their introductions which stressed their merely facilitative role." (Para. 7.6.4).

acknowledge that responsibility and to ensure that it is exercised with due care and propriety.

Considerations relevant to neutral non-binding evaluation

16–017   The following matters are relevant to neutral non-binding evaluation:

- The main aim of neutral evaluation is to help parties to gain a more objective and realistic view of the position, and where appropriate to shift from unrealistic positions. They can if they wish try to arrive at a resolution that broadly (or more substantially) approximates to the likely outcome if the matter were to be decided in an adjudicatory forum such as the court.

- Some ADR processes are specifically designed with the aim of providing the neutral evaluation before any facilitation is undertaken. Examples of these are the mini-trial (Executive Tribunal), evaluation, summary jury trial, and early neutral evaluation (ENE).

- Other ADR processes place their primary focus on facilitation, and introduce an element of evaluation mainly to assist the facilitative process. This is the position in some evaluative models of mediation. If the parties can resolve the matter on the basis of their interests, concerns and their own evaluations of the issues, then a neutral evaluation is unnecessary.

- Some practitioners are purely facilitative, others specifically add an evaluative element. That division is clear. However, some practitioners may introduce an indirect and sometimes unwitting evaluative element to their facilitation, blurring the distinction between facilitative and evaluative processes.

- If a mediator or other ADR practitioner personally makes an evaluation, then depending on its nature, there is a risk that he or she may be perceived as having lost some element of his or her neutrality. The more specific and definitive the view expressed by the neutral, the greater this risk would be.

- An outside neutral other than the mediator or ADR practitioner third party may be brought in to undertake the evaluation (for example a barrister or other lawyer jointly instructed by the parties for this purpose).[3] This may make the evaluative element more acceptable in that the mediator or other ADR practitioner has not personally expressed a view and can retain (and be seen to retain) an impartial role.

- A neutral evaluation as to the likely outcome of the case may help the parties to become more realistic. It does, however, also contain serious inherent problems in that it might well entrench or even harden the position of the party in whose favour it is made. That

---

[3] See, *e.g.* the engagement of a third party lawyer to provide an opinion to both parties as an impasse strategy in family disputes: para. 10–172.

might make it more difficult rather than easier to arrive at a negotiated resolution. The value of the evaluation also depends on the level of expertise of the evaluator.

- Evaluation does not necessarily involve expressing a specific view. A continuum exists between at the one end expressing a specific view and at the other end merely asking questions that have the effect of challenging a party's perceptions. There are many shades of grey in between.

- Many mediators who are willing to evaluate under some circumstances would not automatically do so in every case. On the contrary, mediators will commonly try to resolve the dispute through facilitation and only consider using the evaluative mode as a last resort. They would not doubt want to know that both or all parties wanted them to undertake some form of evaluation, and would need to be satisfied that it was both right and timely to do so.

- There is a substantial responsibility in altering the parties' perceptions of their respective positions by an evaluation that is necessarily personal and that is not subject to independent review.

- If the practitioner gives an evaluation to the parties separately, there is a risk that they may understand what he says differently, especially as he may use different words with each party. To preserve integrity, any evaluation should be given consistently to each party, even if the manner of presentation varies.[4] It is not, however, essential for a practitioner to discuss the same issues with each party. Indeed, where separate confidential meetings are conducted with each of them, it is likely that separate confidences will be maintained. In this context, it may be appropriate for evaluative challenges to be made to one party without necessarily informing the other that this has been done.

- Many mediators do not consider evaluation to be a proper part of a mediator's function, and will not undertake it at all.

2. MEDIATION: EVALUATIVE MODELS

The concept of evaluation in mediation

By its nature, mediation is a facilitative process. The introduction of an evaluative element does not change that. Consequently, the division of mediation into "facilitative" and "evaluative", which the first edition of this work adopted, may have created some misunderstandings. Evaluation is an optional extra that may in some circumstances be added on to the facilitative process of mediation. **16–018**

One of the authors has the experience of negotiating in a Malaysian street market for the purchase of a sarong. With no idea of local value, he was given a price and invited to make an offer, which was then ridiculed as **16–019**

---

[4] A mediator undertaking evaluation should not give inconsistent views, *e.g.* suggesting to each in turn that they are likely to fail in litigation, in order to try to persuade each to settle.

wholly insufficient. In the negotiations that followed, he used his negotiation skills to press the vendor eventually to accept a figure much closer to his original offer than the vendor's counter-response. His negotiating triumph was short-lived when he subsequently found that the article was available at the official tourist centre for less than he had originally offered. Negotiation skills are of limited value if the negotiator has no true idea of the "market value" of what he or she is negotiating.

16–020 This anecdote contains an object lesson for mediators. It is not feasible to expect people to negotiate with one another in mediation unless they have some realistic idea of the value of the subject-matter of their negotiations. "Value" does not necessarily mean financial value, but might refer to the weight to be placed on the claim or obligation.

16–021 Nor is it sufficient to contend that parties place their own value on the subject-matter. If one party discovers that there is an objective or measurable value, and that he or she has negotiated in ignorance of that, there could well be an understandable sense of subsequent disappointment, coupled with a feeling of having been let down by the mediator or the process.

16–022 In some cases, value may be irrelevant, for example, in neighbourhood or community disputes, such as those relating to noise or environmental issues. The same would probably apply to interpersonal issues, where parties are trying to resolve disputes that would not be likely to be adjudicated. In many other cases, however, assessing the value rights of the parties may be necessary to enable effective negotiations to take place. In some circumstances, it may be difficult for parties in mediation to assess such value.

No idea where to start

16–023 Parties may have no real idea of the parameters within which to negotiate. This might be the case, for example, in divorce mediation where a party may not know what level of capital, income or other financial adjustment is appropriate.

16–024 In English law, legislation and precedent prescribe various factors to be taken into account in dealing with financial issues on divorce. These would apply if the issues were to be resolved in the traditional adversarial process. Parties commonly wish to be guided by what these are likely to be before they agree on terms to settle their own issues. This necessitates an evaluation, generally made by the parties' own advisers outside the mediation.

16–025 If, however, parties do not engage lawyers (at the start of the mediation in any event), they may expect some kind of guidance from the mediator. Some models that are purely facilitative would not regard it as appropriate for mediators to give such guidance. Others, despite also being virtually entirely facilitative, might offer some help, for example.

- The mediator could provide information about the legal principles applicable to the couple's circumstances, without trying to predict what the court would be likely to order in their particular case. This does not constitute evaluation. An awareness of the applicable legal principles, and perhaps some indications of how the courts have tended to apply them generally, might help the couple to arrive at their own preliminary assessment of the position.

- The mediator could inform the couple if the proposals they are considering seem likely to fall outside the parameters that a court might order or approve. This does constitute a form of evaluation; but the mediator, having informed the couple of the position, would not ordinarily elaborate by indicating his or her view as to the likely court order. It would be up to the parties to seek their own advice or to decide to settle outside court parameters. At least they would do so consciously and not unwittingly.

Assistance and an element of evaluation may be appropriate and helpful in circumstances such as those outlined in this example, where required by the parties. The mediator would have to be suitably qualified, and would need to act with circumspection and care, being sure not to promote any particular outcome over any other.[5]   **16–026**

Deadlocked by differing outcome perceptions

During the course of mediation, parties may become deadlocked because of their different views as to the likely outcome if the case were to be adjudicated. All attempts to achieve an agreed resolution may be frustrated by the strength of these respective perceptions. In these circumstances, it may be necessary for the mediator, particularly in civil or commercial mediation, to introduce an evaluative element to help break the deadlock.[6]   **16–027**

It is interesting to note that parties may have unrealistic outcome perceptions notwithstanding having been given realistic advice by their lawyers. Perhaps the parties do not want to hear negative advice about their case. Perhaps the lawyers present negative advice too gently, aware of the need to introduce clients to adverse outcomes with care. Whatever the reason, mediators will know that when they challenge and confront a party's outcome perceptions in a separate meeting, the party's lawyer will not uncommonly support the mediator and indicate a sense of vindication of advice given previously. It is as though the party needed to hear the reservations from a neutral person, despite having already heard it from his or her own lawyer. In such circumstances, shifts can occur in the negotiations.   **16–028**

Family mediators are far less likely to want to introduce their own views, and may be precluded from doing so by their Codes of Practice. Some will introduce evaluation by bringing in outside neutrals to provide the evaluative element, such as a neutral barrister's or solicitor's opinion. This would keep the mediator personally out of the actual evaluation. Other do so indirectly by the way they ask questions and deal with "reality-testing". More discussion is probably needed as to whether, when, in what circumstances   **16–029**

---

[5]Both of these examples of assistance and evaluation are offered by mediators working under the aegis of the Solicitors' Family Law Association. SFLA mediators are family lawyers and qualified to provide the information and evaluation. Parties will probably expect solicitor mediators to provide legal information and assistance of at least this kind.

[6]As described by Jonathan Marks, see n. 1 above.

and how family mediators might introduce evaluative elements into family issues.

Evaluation specifically required

16–030　　One model of commercial/civil mediation involves the mediator in establishing the facts and the issues, and expressing a preliminary view as to possible terms of settlement before the start of substantive negotiations. The mediation is then conducted against the background of this early assessment.[7]

16–031　　The City Disputes Panel offers a conciliation process, in which the conciliator may express a view on the merits and may suggest how a settlement might be constructed.[8]

16–032　　Where parties specifically require this form of mediation, there is no reason at all why it should not be provided.

16–033　　Evaluation is at the heart of appellate mediation, which takes place in the context of a legally binding decision having been given by a judge at first instance. In these circumstances the mediator will need to form a view on the parties' respective chances on appeal and will need at the appropriate moment to offer his own view. It may be possible to avoid expressing an opinion, but that will depend on the positions adopted by the parties. If, for example, one party is obdurate and believes that the judge's findings will be upheld, the mediator may need to express a view in order to break the impasse.

Mediators' responses to evaluation in mediation

16–034　　The idea of offering evaluation as part of the mediation process tends to provoke different responses from mediators:

- Some consider evaluation to be inconsistent with the principles of mediation. They are concerned about the impact on mediator impartiality and on the concept of party empowerment. They would not wish to evaluate under any circumstances.

- Some have no difficulty with the principle of evaluating if required by the parties, but are concerned that the parties will then no longer perceive them as neutral. If this practical issue could be resolved, they would consider evaluating in appropriate circumstances.

- Some would be quite willing to evaluate if the parties specifically agreed that this was required, and if they felt satisfied that it would be helpful.

- Some regard evaluation as an essential part of the mediation process.

- Organisations offering or regulating mediation vary in their positions. The Centre for Dispute Resolution has tended not to favour evaluative elements in mediation, but does offer recommendations of settlement terms in some circumstances. It does, though, now discuss the evaluative model. The City Disputes Panel provides both for purely

---

[7] A well-known proponent of this model is Kenneth Feinberg, who has apparently achieved some very good results with it.

[8] *City Disputes Panel Handbook 1997–8.*

facilitative mediation (called "mediation" by it) and an evaluative model (which it calls "conciliation"). The Law Society recognises both kinds of models and allows for either, with qualifications.[9] The Solicitors' Family Law Association offers facilitative mediation, but its mediators will inform parties if their proposed terms are thought to fall outside the parameters that a court would order or approve.

- The notion of mediators evaluating by the way they question or test the realism of the parties has not been addressed, but clearly it has implications for mediator attitudes to the issue of evaluation.

Mediators who favour incorporating an element of evaluation in mediation are generally cautious about its use, but consider it essential in certain cases. Jonathan Marks writes that "Effective mediation in cases where outcome prediction is a critical barrier requires the mediator to go beyond facilitation. The secret to success is understanding and using a variety of tools along a 'facilitation/evaluation' continuum."[10] Another mediator, John Bickerman, similarly writes that "Without sacrificing neutrality, a mediator's neutral assessment can provide participants with a much-needed reality check. Counsel will often look to a mediator to reduce a client's expectations by providing frank assessments of the risk. Parties do not lose trust in mediators or consider them biased because mediators talk frankly with them about their cases.... While pure facilitative mediation may work in certain contexts, parties often want—and expect—a mediator to explore strengths and weaknesses of the case."[11] **16–035**

An opponent of evaluation in mediation, writing to resist an extension of the mediation rules in Florida, says that if mediators can give advice and opinions during a mediation, that would damage the present structure of mediation. Mediation, in his view, "could, and probably would, quickly devolve into an undelineated combination of mediation, arbitration, early neutral (or perhaps not so neutral) evaluation, early expert (or perhaps not so expert) evaluation and private judging".[12] The author of that article considers that all the forms of ADR outlined by him are potentially effective and appropriate, but that they "should not be used under the guise of mediation." **16–036**

To some extent, a mediator's attitude to the introduction of evaluation into mediation will be influenced by a combination of his or her personal predilection, experience, view of the culture of mediation and ADR, professional and organisational background, and mediation training. **16–037**

---

[9]The Law Society's Code of Practice for civil/commercial mediators for example, provides in the commentary to s. 1 that the section "does not preclude the mediator, at his or her discretion and with the consent of the parties, from expressing an opinion or from providing some elements of non-binding evaluation in those models of mediation that are not purely facilitative but also evaluative. The mediator should not however advise parties in the sense of asserting what their rights are and recommending how those rights should be translated into settlement terms."

[10]See n. 1 above.

[11]See "Evaluative mediator responds" in *Alternatives* published by the CPR Institute for Dispute Resolution, Vol. 14, No. 6, June 1996. Bickerman is an attorney and adjunct professor at Georgetown University Law Center.

[12]Charles N. Castagna, in an article "Mediation: Leave Well Enough Alone" in the November 1997 newsletter of the Clearwater, Florida, Bar Association. These concerns are widely shared among mediators in many countries.

Practitioners who see ADR as a flexible process, offering parties a range of options that might mix elements of non-binding evaluation with mediation and negotiation are likely to accept an evaluative element in mediation with relative equanimity. Others properly prefer to keep the processes separate. There does not seem necessarily to be a "right" answer to this issue, but rather a number of possibilities, each with its own validity and reservations. Perhaps the different views can be reconciled by having a range of ADR processes, facilitative, evaluative and hybrid, but ensuring that they are clearly distinguished from one another for the benefit of consumers.

3. THE MINI-TRIAL (EXECUTIVE TRIBUNAL)

The mini-trial concept

16–038   The term "mini-trial" was coined by the *New York Times* in a report on the first known case using that procedure: a major patent infringement action between Telecredit Inc. and TRW Inc. which took place in the United States in 1977. This name is not really apt, since it is not a trial but a non-binding ADR process which assists the parties to a dispute to gain a better understanding of the issues, thereby enabling them to enter into settlement negotiations on a more informed basis.

16–039   The concept of traditional negotiation is that each party, with his lawyer next to him, faces the other party and his lawyer across the table. Notionally, the mini-trial changes this arrangement by putting both parties, or in the case of corporations, their chief executive decision-makers, on the same side of the table, and the lawyers on the other side of the table. By virtue of this change, the parties effectively become a "tribunal", assisted in most cases by a neutral expert who sits between them; and the lawyers take turns to present an abbreviated version of the case to them, in accordance with procedural rules devised and agreed in advance.

16–040   No determination is made, though the neutral will ordinarily express a non-binding opinion to the parties about the case. In this way, the parties have an opportunity of "hearing" the case and forming their own views about it, with the benefit of the neutral's assistance, enabling them to convert the problem to a business one rather than a purely legal one. They can then bring their business judgment into the settlement discussions that usually follow the presentations.[13]

16–041   Those subsequent settlement discussions are enhanced by the parties' understanding of the issues and by bringing their business sense into play. Here again, the neutral can have a significant role, as far as may be required by the parties, by acting as a facilitator of their negotiations.

16–042   This notion of the parties constituting the tribunal to listen to the

---

[13] This brief outline is based on an informal explanation given to one of the authors of this work by Jonathan Marks (see also n. 1 above). Marks was a lawyer in the original mini-trial case (TRW and Telecredit, 1977) and helped to design the process together with Prof. Eric Green, whose article "Growth of the Mini-trial" (U.S.) 9 *Litigation* 1 (Fall 1982) helpfully describes the process. Prof. Green wrote the *Mini-trial Handbook* published by the CPR Institute for Dispute Resolution, USA. Another counsel involved in the original case has written a description of the procedure used in it: Olson "An Alternative for Large Case Dispute Resolution" (U.S.) 6 *Litigation* 22 (Winter 1980).

presentations and to formulate their views on the case has led CEDR (the Centre for Dispute Resolution) to give this process the name of "Executive Tribunal".

The mini-trial is really an elaborate and stylised form of evaluative mediation.[14] In a sense, it is the ultimate kind of evaluative process because the evaluation is so formal, specific and inherent in the process.   **16–043**

There is still no evidence of the mini-trial having been used in the United Kingdom to any significant degree since the concept of ADR started to develop. Perhaps that will follow once the use of mediation becomes more widespread, and the culture of designing dispute resolution processes rather than just adjudicating everything becomes more widely accepted.   **16–044**

The mini-trial procedure
Appointment of neutral adviser
The neutral adviser, who may be a neutral lawyer, a retired judge or any other person with authority in the field of the dispute, is a very important figure in this process, some might say a key figure.   **16–045**

A view does exist, however, that the neutral is not essential to the process, and that a mini-trial can be conducted without a neutral adviser assisting the parties. In this event, the parties would alone comprise the tribunal. Indeed, in the United States mini-trials are sometimes conducted in this way. Where the nature of the issues or the approach of the parties makes the presence of a neutral expert less important, then there are still benefits to be obtained from using the mini-trial process without the neutral. Indeed, this approach may be favoured by some parties or lawyers, both because of cost-effectiveness and because they may prefer to have all the opportunities offered by the process without a neutral expert expressing a view on the merits or otherwise interceding.   **16–046**

The concept of the mini-trial is that it allows the parties to hear the presentations and to obtain an informed neutral view about the merits of the case. The role of the neutral adviser in chairing the process, asking appropriate questions, helping the parties to a better understanding of the issues and if necessary forming and expressing a view on the merits, is thus widely regarded as being a central one. While noting that the process can be conducted without a neutral adviser, the procedure that follows will assume that a neutral adviser is required.   **16–047**

A number of United Kingdom organisations offer to arrange mini-trials and to provide neutral advisers. These include CEDR, the Chartered Institute of Arbitrators and the Academy of Experts.   **16–048**

Organisations in the U.S. which offer the mini-trial as part of their dispute resolution processes include the AAA (the American Arbitration Association) JAMS-Endispute Inc. and the CPR Institute for Dispute Resolution. Other organisations elsewhere include the Australian Commercial Disputes Centre, the Hong Kong International Arbitration Centre, the Chamber of Commerce in Zurich, Switzerland and other dispute resolution organisations and companies.   **16–049**

---

[14]Prof. Eric Green, one of the originators of the mini-trial, has informally described it as "a kind of evaluative mediation".

16–050   Parties will either need to agree upon an organisation to appoint the neutral adviser, or they may appoint an individual of their own choice without engaging an organisation. In either event, a contract will be needed, following the general form of the mediation agreement[15] but adapted to reflect the more specific and detailed requirements of the mini-trial.

Preparation

16–051 For a mini-trial to be most effective, it needs to be carefully planned, with the neutral adviser and the parties' lawyers centrally engaged in such planning. If an organisation is arranging the mini-trial, it will usually take responsibility for the necessary planning and preparation.

16–052   The following matters need to be considered:

- The venue and date(s) for the mini-trial.

- The length of time allowed for the process, allocating a time frame to each component part.

- The form and time-scale within which each side will provide written submissions before the presentations. This is likely to be by way of written statements of fact and submissions, sent to the neutral and to one another. It may include copy statements of case, or extracts, where the case has already commenced in the courts.

- What documents will be furnished by way of an agreed bundle or individual bundles to explain and amplify the case. This will usually be an abbreviated bundle, containing the essential documents, rather than a comprehensive bundle.

- The time to be allowed for the claimant's advocate to present the claimant's case, and a corresponding time for the defendant's advocate to present his case; and for other parties to be similarly heard where the case involves a multi-party dispute.

- Whether technical experts will be called, and if so, how many on each side and what time each may have; and whether and how questions may be put to the expert.

- Whether any other witnesses will be called, and if so, similarly what limited questions may be put, and how. The usual rules of evidence do not apply to mini-trials.

- Whether any further information should be furnished, and if so, what and how. It will generally be left to the individual advocates to present their cases as they each see fit, and the details do not have to be agreed in advance. The advocates may choose to use charts, plans, slides, films, overhead projectors, photographs or such other devices as they may wish, and this would not ordinarily be disclosed or agreed in advance, so long as it fell within the advocate's agreed presentation time.

---

[15]See Appendix II for a form of contract to mediate. For a precedent minitrial agreement, see (1985) 3(5) *Alternatives* 8 published by the CPR Institute for Dispute Resolution.

- What time should be allowed for each of the advocates to make responding statements after initial presentations have been made and witnesses, if any, heard.

- Who should attend the mini-trial to represent corporate parties. While parties cannot select or influence the choice of other parties' representatives, it is important that the representatives of each party should be senior personnel used to making decisions, and authorised to make binding decisions about settlement within their own discretion, albeit within any fixed limit of authority. It is also preferable that they should be detached from the dispute, rather than involved in it, though this may not always be practicable.

- What the role of the neutral adviser is to be: in the mini-trial; afterwards, in explaining the issues and his or her views to the parties; and in relation to any subsequent settlement negotiations.

- Practical arrangements for the settlement negotiations that would ordinarily follow the mini-trial.

- The non-binding, confidential and privileged nature of the proceedings would be confirmed.

- Practical matters need to be clarified such as responsibility for costs, which are usually shared between the parties equally. Other matters might include temporary suspension of pending litigation if applicable; an agreement not to call the neutral adviser in any subsequent proceedings; and whether the mini-trial process can be terminated before it has run its full course, and if so, by whom and under what circumstances.

- Any other matters specifically relevant to the individual case may need to be discussed and agreed.

As many of these matters as practicable should be resolved in advance to **16–053** make the process as smooth and effective as possible. It is not essential, however, for every point to be individually debated and agreed. The ADR organisation or the neutral adviser can stipulate a procedure and timetable which covers the process; and as long as the parties accept this, the mini-trial can proceed. These matters can usefully be included in the agreement between the parties to use the mini-trial procedure.

The conduct of the mini-trial
The actual progress of the mini-trial itself will ordinarily follow the **16–054** procedure and timetable agreed by the parties with the neutral adviser. One of the great advantages of the process is that, like most ADR forms, it can be structured to meet the individual needs and nuances of the actual case.

The following is a typical example of how a mini-trial might proceed **16–055** (though the procedure and time-scale would vary from one case to another, depending on the complexity of the issues and the requirements of the parties and the neutral adviser)[16]:

- The neutral adviser welcomes the parties and addresses them about the process, reminding them about the procedures that are to follow, which have of course already been agreed, and of the confidential, privileged and non-binding nature of the process. The neutral adviser then chairs the proceedings which follow.

- The claimant's lawyer presents the claimant's case, summarising the evidence, and making legal submissions. Use may be made of photographs, films, charts and other devices in making this presentation. This may take an agreed period of, say, three hours.

- An expert then summarises the technical position on behalf of the claimant, similarly using projectors, diagrams and any other devices that may be useful to explain and clarify the technical aspects. This may take an agreed period of, say 90 minutes.

- A key witness may be called to outline relevant aspects of the claimant's case. (Alternatively, the lawyer may instead summarise the proposed evidence in his or her presentation.)

- The neutral adviser may ask the claimant's lawyer and witnesses any questions to clarify the case. This is not generally done either by way of cross-examination to seek to damage the claimant's case, or by way of help to make good shortcomings in the presentations, but rather by way of genuine inquiry to assist the parties and the neutral in understanding the case properly. Of course, such questions may have a probing effect. If the parties have any questions, they may put these through the neutral, or if so agreed, directly to the lawyer. The defendant's lawyer may be permitted to ask some questions of the claimant's lawyer and in some cases to the witnesses, if this has been agreed.

- The defendant's lawyer then presents the defendant's case, similarly using any useful devices, and also taking the agreed period of, say, three hours.

- The defendant's expert summarises the technical position on behalf of the defendant, similarly using functional devices to explain and clarify the technical aspects. This may also take 90 minutes.

- The defendant may call a key witness.

- The neutral then asks the defendant's lawyer and witnesses any questions that help to clarify aspects of the defendant's case, similarly

---

[16] In his article in the *Journal of Dispute Resolution (Missouri)* Vol. 1987, p. 133 "Whose Dispute Is This Anyway?: The Propriety of the Mini-trial in Promoting Corporate Dispute Resolution", Lewis D. Barr outlines the key features found in the mini-trial, referring for elaboration to Eric Green's *CPR Mini-trial Handbook* (see n. 13 above). Barr suggests that the presentations, made in the lawyers' best and most concise fashion, should usually take no more than 6 hours for the case in chief and 2 hours for the rebuttal.

taking care to do so only by way of genuinely enhancing understanding. Reciprocal arrangements will apply to questions by the claimant's lawyer to the defendant's lawyer and witnesses.

- If so agreed, time may be allowed for the experts to have a brief dialogue in front of the tribunal, perhaps responding to questions asked by one another.

- The claimant's lawyer then makes a winding-up statement, taking an agreed period of, say, one hour.

- The defendant's lawyer does the same, also taking, say, one hour.

- The neutral adviser thanks the participants, and adjourns with the parties to discuss the matter.

The neutral adviser's role

The role of the neutral during the mini-trial has already been indicated. It takes the form of acting as a chairperson, managing the process, keeping the lawyers to their time-limits, asking pertinent questions and generally obtaining sufficient information to be able to form a view about the issues and to assist the parties in doing the same.   **16–056**

At the end of the presentations, the neutral may adjourn with the parties in order to discuss the presentations with them. The neutral may then give an indication of his or her view of the respective strengths and weaknesses on each side. This may cover aspects of the case which were clear or which were uncertain, aspects where cross-examination or other probing in an actual trial might affect the outcome and those which would be unlikely to be affected, and any other matters which may be thought to be relevant. The neutral will answer questions put by the parties, and will give any information and views that may help them to gain a better understanding of the issues and the merits.   **16–057**

If required, the neutral adviser will provide an oral or written opinion as to the merits of the case as presented, on a privileged and non-binding basis. The object of this is to give the parties a neutral and expert assessment of the case.   **16–058**

The settlement discussions following the mini-trial are likely to be held between parties and lawyers, without necessarily requiring the intervention of the neutral. If required, however, the neutral may have a further role: that of facilitator of the negotiations, in the mediator mode.   **16–059**

As an alternative, if it is not considered appropriate for the neutral adviser to act subsequently in the capacity of mediator, then a second person may be engaged to act as mediator. That person would, in such event, also attend the mini-trial. It would be more costly to have two people rather than one undertaking these separate functions; but if the issues are substantial and there is a preference to separate the expert function from the mediatory role, this may be considered to be a worthwhile expenditure.   **16–060**

The settlement negotiations

These take place on a without prejudice basis between the parties after the conclusion of the mini-trial. One object of having a senior executive   **16–061** decision-maker of corporate parties attend the presentation and the negotiations is to bring into the process the kind of commercial judgment which a top decision-maker generally has. Chief Executive Officers of companies make commercial decisions on a wide range of matters, but where there is a legal dispute, they need to be guided by their legal advisers. The mini-trial allows them to supplement legal advice received from their lawyers with judgments that they can personally form based on the presentations and the neutral adviser's input. They can then bring into the negotiations their own commercial judgment and, working with their lawyers, can help to find a realistic business-like solution to the dispute.

16–062   It follows from this that the parties themselves are likely to play a greater role in the settlement negotiations following a mini-trial than they would in traditional without prejudice negotiations between solicitors. This does not diminish, but rather alters, the nature of the solicitor's role, which is to support and assist the client in negotiations. Whether the solicitors conduct the actual discussions, with their clients closely involved, or the parties do so with the solicitors in close support, is something that may vary from one case to another.

16–063   Time should be built into the overall process to allow these negotiations to take place, either directly or soon after the mini-trial has concluded.

16–064   If the matter is settled, all the principles that apply to the resolution of a mediated dispute or any other settlement will similarly apply to the mini-trial. The terms of settlement will be recorded in a formal agreement; and if there is a case pending in the court or in an arbitration tribunal, a formal consent order or award may be obtained.[17] If the matter is not settled, all rights will have been reserved, and the parties can revert to the adjudicatory system for the resolution of their dispute. They will not ordinarily be allowed to refer in such formal process to any of the matters that arose in the mini-trial.

16–065   Experience in the United States has shown that if the mini-trial and subsequent negotiations do not result in a settlement, a "cooling-off" period can be useful before litigation is commenced; and that during this period, settlement is often achieved.[18]

16–066   Something similar seems to have occurred in what is understood to be the first United Kingdom mini-trial. Litigation had commenced in respect of a "relatively substantial claim" concerning the laying of an oil pipeline, which had problems and needed to be dug up and treated or replaced. There were a large number of disputes involving about 11 parties and extensive discovery. Costs were expected to run to over a million pounds. The parties agreed to have a mini-trial, without a neutral adviser. In the event, it did not settle in the discussions following the mini-trial, but it did settle "shortly afterwards", following the pattern of settlements occurring soon after the conclusion of negotiations, as experienced in the United States.[19]

---

[17]See Stage 9 of the mediation process, "Concluding mediation and recording the outcome" at Chap. 8 for the general position, and Chap. 9 for the resolution of civil/commercial disputes. See also Appendix II for a section on drafting.

[18]See "A Primer on Mini-trials" by John H. Wilkinson in *ADR Practice Book* (1990) at p. 173.

[19]See the transcript of an address given in December 1988 by Philip Naughton Q.C. for the Chartered Institute of Arbitrators, the Inns of Court and the Bar Council. His outline of the case and of the mini-trial, in which he was involved, contains some interesting, helpful and positive comments. However, another lawyer engaged in that mini-trial has expressed the view

Kinds of cases suitable for mini-trial

Mini-trials are used most often in the United States for substantial business disputes covering mixed issues of fact and law, and also those involving technical disputes. They are also tailored for other kinds of cases, for example, as summary jury trials in which cases are presented to mock juries, who make findings which help the disputants to obtain an indication of what a real jury might find, to inform them prior to settlement negotiations.[20] Mini-trials have been used in cases involving contract, tort, infringement of patents, insurance claims, construction disputes, and many others.

16–067

Where the parties are in deadlock because of a good faith disagreement, or by reason of emotional barriers caused by the parties' or their lawyers' personal antagonisms, or because they cannot construct a settlement which reflects their respective perceptions of their rights, the mini-trial is particularly apt.[21] Indeed, it is suitable for most kinds of issues that could be settled by negotiation; but because of the cost of preparing for and running the mini-trial, it would normally only be used where the costs are justified relative to the amount in issue. This accords with the developing concept of "proportionality" of costs.

16–068

The mini-trial is unsuitable for cases which turn exclusively on credibility and which necessarily have to be tested by way of cross-examination; or for cases which turn exclusively on points of law, which may need to be judicially resolved; or for cases in which a binding precedent is required; or where fundamental non-negotiable rights are concerned. It is, like most other consensual ADR processes, unsuitable if either party does not genuinely wish to settle but has an interest in delay or in abusing the process. It is also unsuitable if a party cannot produce "an effective decision-maker who can negotiate a settlement".[22]

16–069

Timing of mini-trial usage

A mini-trial can take place at any stage of a dispute, from the initial disagreement before proceedings have been initiated, through to the eleventh hour, shortly before a formal trial is due to take place.

16–070

Some disputants prefer to wait until after statements of case have been delivered and all documents have been disclosed. They consider that this provides the best balance between on the one hand identifying the issues and documents under the strict rules of the adversarial system, and on the other hand obtaining the benefits of the mini-trial relatively early, before steps are taken and costs incurred in preparing for trial.[23] In this event, the formal statements of case and an abbreviated bundle of relevant documents are then used in the mini-trial.

16–071

---

that the process did not contribute to the settlement that followed.

[20] See para. 16–078 *et seq.*

[21] See *Dispute Resolution* by Goldberg, Green & Sander (1985) at p. 272. The mini-trial focuses on the legal merits while "reconverting into a business problem" what has become a legal fight.

[22] *per* Philip Naughton Q.C., December 5, 1988, see n. 19 above.

[23] See Barr, *ibid.* at p. 139. He considers that the issues need to be sufficiently developed for the mini-trial hearing to be useful, and that the more complex the subject-matter of the dispute, the more documentary disclosure will be necessary before using the abbreviated discovery of the mini-trial.

16–072   A mini-trial can however be effectively run at an early stage of the dispute.[24] This not only maximises cost savings, but allows the parties to consider the position with greater flexibility, before attitudes have hardened and become entrenched. It would ordinarily, however, be premature to do so before the issues have clearly crystallised, unless it was felt that the process would help to focus parties on the issues and that the advantages of using it at an early stage outweighed any disadvantages.[25]

General observations about mini-trials

16–073   Mini-trials are said to be substantially successful in the cases in which they are used. Wilkinson says that they result in "prompt settlement in more than 95 per cent. of the instances where used."[26] In 1986, a survey of 19 lawyers and a former judge who had participated in mini-trials reflected that 24 out of 28 cases using this process had ended in settlement, with 16 of the 19 lawyers satisfied with the process and enthusiastic about using mini-trials again.[27]

16–074   It is also said that most parties who have been engaged in mini-trials feel that even if the case does not immediately settle, they do not regard the money spent on it as wasted, because the focused work done on it is so useful as a preparation for the trial.[28] Philip Naughton Q.C. says of the mini-trial in which he was originally involved, that he initially regarded it as a "one-off affair" but that he has come to the view that the potential of the mini-trial process can be "quite considerable".[29]

16–075   On the other hand, there are also disadvantages. The cost factor is relatively high compared to conventional without prejudice negotiations, though relatively low compared to the costs of a full-scale trial and its preparation, which may be averted. There is also a high time investment required by the parties, and where these are corporations, by their senior personnel. A risk exists that parties may inform their opponents of their trial strategies and of the weaknesses in their opponent's case, enabling the opponents to anticipate the trial more accurately and to make good at the trial any shortcomings disclosed by the mini-trial.[30] This is, of course, a reciprocal disadvantage; and is generally felt to be outweighed by the potential advantages of an early and effective settlement, and by the ability of most experienced lawyers to conduct a mini-trial effectively without

---

[24]Philip Naughton Q.C. expressed the view (see n. 19 above) that it was not essential to wait for disclosure to conduct a mini-trial. He suggested that there could be a limited disclosure of documents identified to be relevant. He cited the Industrial Tribunal as a precedent for this.

[25]Barr, *ibid.* at p. 139, quotes Eric Green in "Corporate Alternative Dispute Resolution" 1 Ohio St J.D.R. 238–46 (1986) as suggesting that parties should base their decision as to timing on a cost/benefit analysis on the value of obtaining additional information.

[26]See n. 18, *ibid.* p. 180.

[27]See Barr, *ibid.* p. 134, referring to "The Effectiveness of the Mini-Trial in Resolving Complex Commercial Disputes: A Survey" published in 1986 by the American Bar Association's Litigation Section, ADR Sub-committee.

[28]Goldberg, Green & Sander, *Dispute Resolution* (1985) at p. 277.

[29]See n. 19.

[30]Annie Billings mentions this in her article "The mini-trial: misunderstanding and miscommunication may short-circuit its effective use in settlements" published in (1990) 2 J.D.R. 417.

giving away any strategic information, but rather using it with considered judgment.

The absence of probing the case by cross-examination and the need to **16–076** present it in an abbreviated form, may also result in some important elements being missed; but here again, these are matters which can be guarded against by lawyers alive to risk.

Like all ADR, the mini-trial is not a panacea and is not suitable or helpful **16–077** for all cases.[31] As observed by Philip Naughton Q.C., "miracles are not made at mini-trials". It is, however, a substantially useful and effective process: it "returns the dispute to the businessmen, educates them, and then allows them to use their developed skills—assessing risk and negotiating—to resolve the dispute."[32]

4. The Summary Jury Trial

The mini-trial procedure can be adapted as required. One American variation **16–078** (principally used in the Federal rather than the State courts) is the "summary jury trial", which is a mini-trial conducted before a mock jury who give a verdict which is not binding, but which helps to inform the parties of the likely reaction of a real jury. This is used in relation, for example, to personal injury cases, and reflects the American constitutional and personal preference for jury trials.

Texas, for example, has a statute governing ADR including summary jury **16–079** trials, which explains the procedure as a "forum for early case evaluation and development of realistic settlement negotiations".[33] The statute provides a skeleton outline of the procedure. Each party and counsel present their position to a panel of six jurors, or such other number as may be agreed. The panel may issue an advisory opinion as to liability or damages or both, which is not binding.

In some jurisdictions,[34] after an advisory verdict is returned, the lawyers **16–080** may ask questions of the jury through its foreperson. This is intended to assist the parties to understand the jury's reasoning and reactions. It is consistent with the principles underlying neutral non-binding evaluation. Parties should be helped by the process to gain a better and more realistic insight into the merits of their case and its prospects in the event of adjudication, so that they can negotiate settlement terms on a more informed basis.

Two articles in the Donovan, Leisure, Newton and Irvine: *ADR Practice* **16–081** *Book* (1990) express different views about the summary jury trial. Federal District Judge Hon. Thomas D. Lambros, in whose court the process was first used in 1980, describes its benefits. However, in the chapter "Personal Experiences with Corporate ADR", Howard J. Aibel and Edwin A. Kilburn, both counsel to ITT, describe having found the summary jury trial unsatisfactory and prefer the mediation process. That divergence of view was

---

[31] See Barr's analysis of the criticisms of the mini-trial process, in his article, *ibid.* (n. 16).
[32] Olson, see n. 13.
[33] Texas Civil Practice and Remedies Code, Sec. 154.026.
[34] *e.g.* in Northampton County, Pennsylvania.

replicated in articles that appeared in the *Journal of Dispute Resolution* in 1995, in which one writer, Ann E. Woodley supported the process[35] and a U.S. District Judge, Avern Cohen, raised a caution, stating that her experience and that of her colleagues suggested that "the drawbacks of summary jury trials outweigh the benefits".[36] A third article, written by a U.S. Magistrate Judge, Alexander B. Denson, supported the summary jury trial procedure, suggesting how it could be used in a more effective way, including in particular by careful case selection. He pointed out that not every case was suitable for the process.[37]

16–082   The summary jury trial is unlikely to be relevant in the United Kingdom because of the limited use of civil jury trials. It does, however, demonstrate how ADR processes can be adapted to meet particular needs, whether of procedure generally or of individual disputes.

5. EARLY NEUTRAL EVALUATION

16–083   Early Neutral Evaluation (ENE) is a system of case evaluation begun in 1985 in the United States District Court for the Northern District of California. It proved to be a success, and has been extended to other jurisdictions.

16–084   Under the U.S. form of ENE, cases are referred to a third party lawyer for non-binding evaluation. Commonly this is done on a voluntary basis. The mandate of the early neutral evaluator is to look at the strengths and weaknesses of the case, and to consider how best to conduct the litigation rapidly and economically. The scheme was initially designed to force parties to confront the merits of the case more carefully and to develop an efficient approach to the issues and to discovery. Subsequently settlement facilitation was added to the scheme, and the evaluator now has the authority at the evaluation session to help the parties, in joint or separate meetings, to explore the possibility of settlement. Another function of ENE is to consider whether the case can be disposed of more effectively and expeditiously by other means than litigation.

16–085   The types of cases referred to ENE are wide, including disputes arising in contract, tort, labour law, intellectual property, civil rights, securities and banking. In some jurisdictions, certain kinds of cases are excluded, such as social security cases, deportation cases and cases involving the constitutionality of federal, state or local statutes or ordinances. There is no upper limit to the amount in issue between the parties.

16–086   For the purpose of the evaluation, the parties furnish the evaluator with the pleadings that have been filed and statements specifically obtained from each of them, setting out relevant information and submissions. The evaluator is required to consider these and to convene an evaluation session within a prescribed period (in California, 90–160 days).

16–087   At the evaluation session, the parties themselves, or their legal representatives, each make an oral presentation, and the evaluator then

---

[35] "Saving the Summary Jury Trial: A Proposal to Halt the Flow of Litigation and End the Uncertainties", (1995) 2 J. D. R. 213.
[36] "The Summary Jury Trial—A Caution" in (1995) 2 J. D. R. 299.
[37] "The Summary Jury Trial: A Proposal From The Bench" in (1995) 2 J. D. R. 303.

frankly assesses the relative strengths and weaknesses of the case, explaining his or her reasoning for the views expressed. The evaluator helps the parties to devise plans for conducting discovery, sharing material data and expediting procedures. Settlement facilitation and, if required, exploration of alternative processes then also take place. A maximum of about five hours is allowed in most cases.

The evaluation session and its related material are "off the record" and **16–088** privileged, and no communication made in the ENE may be disclosed or used in any pending or subsequent proceedings. If the evaluator thinks that it might be helpful and appropriate to have any follow-up activities after the initial session, these can be arranged. Usually, they would be in the form of written or telephone communications, and perhaps, with the consent of the parties, a second evaluation meeting.

The ENE procedure has been extensively researched in the United States **16–089** and the findings show that the process works satisfactorily, and that it is widely viewed as being fair and valuable, though some aspects still need improvement and development.[38] The positive benefits include making parties and their lawyers examine the case more carefully and systematically; giving them a better understanding of the issues; improving information exchange; improving communications; and creating opportunities for early settlement discussions to be conducted. Apparently, a major benefit of this scheme has been a more economical approach to the disclosure of documents and a speeding up of the conduct of cases.

While the research reflected that most parties found the evaluations reliable **16–090** and useful, some parties did not understand how the evaluator arrived at his conclusion, and were disappointed by it despite the policy being to ensure that parties hear and understand what is being said about their cases. Conclusions could not be reached about the cost-effectiveness of ENE as compared with other ADR programmes, such as court-annexed arbitration.

6. CASE EVALUATION

The City Disputes Panel offers evaluation (or "case evaluation") by an **16–091** authoritative panel, which makes a reasoned or graded evaluation of the dispute. It is not a judicial or arbitral process, but written and oral submissions can be made to it, and witnesses can be heard and cross-examined. The evaluation is non-binding and without prejudice to all rights, claims or defences. Its evaluations may then be used as a basis for settlement discussions, through conciliation if required.[39]

Case evaluation was successfully used in the major reconstruction and **16–092** renewal plan for Lloyd's insurance syndicates. Part of the process necessitated valuing reinsurance cover, which would have been almost

---

[38]See Prof. David I. Levine's articles "Early neutral evaluation: a follow-up report" in *Judicature* Vol. 70 No. 4, Dec–Jan 1987 and "Early Neutral Evaluation: The Second Phase" in the (1989) J. D. R. 1.

[39]The City Disputes Panel's range of dispute resolution services includes conciliation, which it reflects as more pro-active than mediation. Under CDP rules, a conciliator may express a view on the merits and may suggest how a settlement may be constructed.

impossible with many disputes pending. An expeditious process was needed, which was provided by a case evaluation procedure, involving a group of some 15 senior lawyers and market experts co-chaired by Lord Ackner and Lord Templeman. From this group, panels dealt with individual disputes, evaluating them on a range between "very strong" and "hopeless". Evaluations were based on documents submitted, and in some cases, a one-day hearing. They did not affect the parties' legal rights.[40]

7. NEUTRAL FACT-FINDING EXPERT

16–093 Where a case involves technical, scientific, accounting, economic or any other specialised issues, the parties and the court will generally be dependent on expert advice and evidence in arriving at a proper conclusion.

16–094 Where, as in most instances, the individual parties engage different experts, those experts are expected and required to maintain professional objectivity.[41] Such objectivity may sometimes itself help to get matters resolved, especially where their contributions are significant to the outcome and where they are prepared and able to co-operate with one another in discussing the issues and endeavouring to arrive at a consensus between themselves. In practice, however, this has not historically happened as commonly as might have been hoped. There are a number of reasons for this. Parties and their lawyers are unlikely to select an expert who disagrees with their case and may therefore seek out experts who support their positions. Not all experts have consistently maintained the objectivity that some people might have hoped for; and opportunities for the experts to exchange views in a constructive and creative way have not always readily existed. Consequently, courts have had to choose between or reconcile the views of experts expressing opposing opinions.

16–095 In such complex, technical cases requiring the specialised gathering, collation and analysis of information and the expression of an expert opinion, the appointment of a single neutral fact-finding expert can help considerably in its resolution. Not being partisan, such an expert can make a neutral evaluation of the facts, which can be of assistance to a court in adversarial proceedings, and can help the parties by narrowing the issues and promoting settlement.[42]

16–096 The role of experts in England and Wales has changed under the reforms introduced by Lord Woolf,[43] and the possibility of appointing a sole expert to report on a neutral basis has been enhanced.[44] In the reformed system, the

---

[40]See the article by Sarah Scarlett in *Insurance Day* of February 25, 1997 "Use of ADR in Lloyd's R&R plan". The Lloyd's process was dealt with by the City Disputes Panel, using its case evaluation procedures.

[41]See especially the rules for experts introduced in England and Wales under the Woolf Reforms. Experts will be required to follow an Experts' Protocol, regulating the way they function.

[42]In the USA, the Federal Rules of Evidence may lend themselves to the appointment of such an expert. For a detailed consideration of the subject of court-appointed neutral experts, see Prof. Eric Green's "The Complete Courthouse" in *Dispute Resolution Devices in a Democratic Society*, pp. 44–51 (1985 Roscoe Pound ATLA Foundation, Washington D.C.).

[43]See Pt 35 of the new Civil Procedure Rules.

[44]In an article "On experts and protocols" in the *Law Society's Gazette* of January 6, 1999, District Judge Frenkel says that in recent personal injury cases, he has suggested the

court controls the nature and amount of expert evidence to be given in a case. The expert's duty is to the court, to which any expert report must be addressed. The new rules envisage the possibility of a single expert being appointed in a case, though there is unlikely to be a significant shift to single experts in the short term.

Where the parties participate in the selection of the expert and in the formulation of his instructions, this itself can help to narrow and define the issues. A neutral expert's brief and functions should be clearly specified. **16–097**

In the U.S., when the neutral expert has concluded his inquiries and his consideration of the issues, he advises the parties of his findings, which gives him an opportunity to play a facilitative mediatory role if required. It is therefore helpful if the expert also has training in ADR generally. **16–098**

The neutral fact-finding procedure is non-binding. The parties commonly agree that the expert's opinion will be admissible in any court proceedings between the parties, but that it is not conclusive. If this is agreed, it allows each party to adduce any other expert evidence to try to controvert the neutral expert's views. This gives the neutral expert's opinion a persuasive quality without making it decisive. It is this factor which keeps it a non-adjudicatory form of ADR, and distinct from private judging. The information provided by the neutral expert will quite commonly cause either or both parties to reassess and perhaps modify their estimate of their probability of success, with consequent impact on settlement attitudes. **16–099**

Clearly, the appointment of a neutral fact-finding expert, whose role and functions are either prescribed by the court, or more satisfactorily by the parties themselves, and who provides a non-binding but persuasive opinion, can also be a very helpful adjunct to court procedures. With the Woolf reforms in their infancy, there is scope for developing a neutral expert procedure that provides the benefits of the U.S. procedure while complying with English procedural rules. **16–100**

Professor Eric Green of Boston University, who has conducted a survey on the use of the neutral expert by United States federal trial judges, has found this process under-used. He believes that this may be partly because of lack of knowledge of the potential benefits of the process, but that it may also relate to a concern by judges, and indeed lawyers, that the neutral expert may take power away from them by "destroying the judge's monopoly on neutrality and the parties' control of the expert information and opinion". He suggests that the traditional role of judges and lawyers "should give way slightly if adjustments will rationalise the adjudicatory process, making it fairer and more efficient".[45] **16–101**

8. COURT-ANNEXED (OR COURT-ORDERED) ARBITRATION

Distinguished from arbitration under court rules

In order to avoid confusion of terminology and concepts, it is essential to distinguish between two different kinds of arbitration through the courts. **16–102**

---

appointment of a joint expert and that this has always been accepted.
[45]See n. 42: from "The Complete Courthouse".

16–103   In England, a binding arbitration may be effected by a commercial court judge; or the county court may order that a small claims dispute be dealt with by binding arbitration by a district judge or a third party, with the force of a court order. These forms of arbitration by the court may be useful and valuable, but in this book they are not included in the terms "court-annexed arbitration" or "court-ordered arbitration", and will not be further addressed in this chapter.

16–104   There is also a different procedure, used in the United States, Australia and elsewhere, but not yet in England, by which the court orders a case to be dealt with by way of arbitration by a third party, whose finding is initially non-binding. Either party may require a re-hearing by a judge, but if neither does so the award becomes a binding court order. However, if the case is re-heard by a judge, and the judge's decision does not result in a better award to the person who applied for the re-hearing, then there may be sanctions applied to that party (where such sanctions are constitutionally allowed). It is this process that is interchangeably called "court-annexed arbitration" (the term which for convenience this book will henceforth use) or "court-ordered arbitration".

16–105   Although court-annexed arbitration is not available in England, it has become established in a number of other jurisdictions as an effective way of dealing with disputes without having to embark on full-scale litigation.

Non-binding court-annexed arbitration

16–106   Non-binding court-annexed arbitration was first established in Pennsylvania in 1952. Since then, it has been increasingly widely used and many jurisdictions in the United States now use some form of court-annexed arbitration.

16–107   Court-annexed arbitration has been viewed as a successful alternative to litigation achieving two goals: " . . . [providing] prompt, relatively inexpensive, fair and less formal resolution of a great many civil cases; and [preserving] at the same time the procedural and substantive rights of citizens involved in law suits."[46]

16–108   Court-annexed arbitration might be less effective if a significant proportion of disputants chose to have a re-hearing. The award must therefore be as fair as possible and applications without merit for a re-hearing need to be discouraged, while preserving an effective right to do so. One such sanction in the United States is a costs award against the applicant for a re-hearing who does not improve his position at a trial. Such a "fee-shifting" provision has been held to be invalid in Michigan by reason of being outside the trial court's rule-making authority;[47] but the Washington and Florida ADR statutes make specific provision for fee-shifting, and Washington state's intermediate appellate court has upheld such provisions.[48] In England, where costs would ordinarily be ordered in any event, the award of costs might be a sanction, though not necessarily a substantial one; but perhaps costs might be awarded on a full indemnity basis, including those of the arbitration. Alternatively, the

---

[46]First U.S. National Conference Report, 1985.
[47]*Tiedel v. Northwestern Michigan College* 865 F. 2nd 88 (6th Cir. 1988).
[48]*Colarusso v. Petersen* 61 Wash. App. 767; 812 P. 2nd 862 (1991).

arbitration might be with no order for costs either way, but a re-hearing would require the loser to pay the costs of the second or both hearings.

The court-annexed arbitration procedure can also facilitate settlements **16–109** because, after the non-binding arbitration, realistic settlement discussions can and do take place, which necessarily have regard to the non-binding award made by the arbitrator and the fact that the losing party may wish to seek a re-hearing.

The level of jurisdiction and the nature of subject-matter appropriate to **16–110** court-annexed arbitration is generally fixed by the relevant statute or rules: this process tends to be used for lower levels of dispute and not for cases involving more substantial sums.

If court-annexed arbitration were to be introduced in England, it would be **16–111** necessary to have a panel of arbitrators approved by the court and available to undertake this form of arbitration. These could, but would not necessarily have to be lawyers, but some form of acceptable training and qualification would no doubt be required. In the United States, the court generally pays arbitrators' fees.

Normally, in the United States, the hearings are informal. Some take place **16–112** in the court, others do not. Rules of evidence may be relaxed. Parties may be advised about conducting document disclosure prior to the arbitration. Hearings tend to be brief and summary. The arbitrator will usually make an immediate decision. Procedures vary as to the power of the arbitrators. Unless otherwise agreed, any re-hearing of the case would ordinarily (but not necessarily) be fresh and without reference to the arbitration evidence.

The results of a number of studies indicate that most litigants are satisfied **16–113** with this process and that it achieves a high rate of success. A study of one American programme considered whether the process might deliver "second-class" justice and surmised that critics' standards of "first-class" justice might include "the full panoply of judge-and-jury trial and due process safeguards that are provided by our traditional adversarial process". However, it was clear from their interviews that litigants shared " ... neither the critics' concern that the quality of justice is denigrated by arbitration, nor their standards for evaluating." A further observation was that the average citizen's notion of "fairness" did not require:

" ... the judicial robes, formal procedures, or the various components of
due process that are the hallmark of trial. But his notion of fairness is not
simply cheap, quick dispute resolution. Rather, the average individual
seems to believe that a 'fair' dispute resolution procedure is one that
provides an opportunity for a hearing of the facts of the case before a
neutral third party adjudicator. Our data suggests that ability to appeal the
arbitration award contributes to individuals' perceptions that the process is
fair ... ".[49]

---

[49]Adler, Hensler & Nelson, "Simple Justice: How Litigants Fare in the Pittsburgh Court
Arbitration Program" (1983) at pp. 629–637 of Murray, Rau & Sherman, *Processes of Dispute
Resolution: The Role of Lawyers* (1989).

Variations: Moderated settlement conference and Michigan mediation

16–114   In the United States there are variations based on the court-annexed arbitration principle. One of these is the moderated settlement conference, under which a panel, usually comprising three impartial lawyers, follows a procedure similar to court-annexed arbitration. Where a panel rather than an individual arbitrates, and in those jurisdictions where a costs sanction against non-meritorious applications for re-hearing is not unconstitutional, such sanction might only apply if the panel's evaluation of the claim is unanimous.

16–115   Another variation is "Michigan mediation", which was adopted in the Michigan Supreme Court, and which has been described as a blend of mediation and arbitration in which a panel meets the lawyers of parties separately to seek an agreed settlement. Failing agreement, the panel makes its own settlement proposals, which become binding if not objected to within a specified period. The use of the term "mediation" is now said by its proponents to be misleading and is being dropped in favour of "evaluation", henceforth "Michigan evaluation".

Adapting court-annexed arbitration principles

16–116   If England were to introduce a system of court-annexed arbitration, adapted from the experience of other countries, then specific legislation would be needed to do so. There are many examples on which such legislation could be based.[50] There are a number of aspects that would need further consideration such as the binding or non-binding quality of the arbitration, and the provisions for a re-hearing by the court, as well as the training of arbitrators and the administration and funding of the scheme generally.

16–117   In England, claims falling within the prescribed jurisdiction might be referred to arbitrators. Arbitration might take place, for example, in the arbitrator's office during an evening or at a weekend, bringing the process of dispute resolution more effectively into the community, while preserving the role of the court.

16–118   As an alternative to the introduction of the court-linked process of court-annexed arbitration as described above, and in the absence of legislation, an informal procedure in which the parties contractually agree upon a similar process, has been suggested in England. This process has been named "concilio-arbitration" by its proponent, Rowland Williams.[51] The suggested procedure is for a concilio-arbitrator to examine the case informally, consider the evidence, hear the parties' representations and make a non-binding award. If both parties accept the award, it becomes binding. If one party does not accept then the case proceeds to litigation; and if the party who refuses to accept the award does not achieve a significantly better result at the trial, there is a costs penalty.

---

[50] *e.g.* the Arbitration (Civil Actions) Act 1983, No. 43, with amendments, of New South Wales, Australia; or, perhaps less likely because of its different cultural approach, the Texas Civil Practice and Remedies Code which deals with a range of alternative methods of dispute resolution.

[51] See an article by Rowland Williams in the *Law Society's Gazette* of November 23, 1983 "Concilio-Arbitration: A New Proposal for the Quick and Inexpensive Resolution of Dispute". See also "Concilio-Arbitration: the Service Commences" by the same author in the *Law Society's Gazette* of May 28, 1986.

It will be apparent that court-annexed arbitration differs from ordinary **16–119** arbitration by virtue of the fact that it is not binding in the first instance, and that disputants do not lose their right to have the matter heard by the court. Also, the awards, once accepted, become as effective as orders of the court. These differences appear to make them more acceptable to the public than traditional binding arbitration.

9. THE FINANCIAL DISPUTE RESOLUTION PROCEDURE (FDR)

FDR under the ancillary relief pilot scheme[52]

The Ancillary Relief Pilot Scheme was set up in the United Kingdom to **16–120** explore new and improved procedures and stricter court control for the resolution of financial and property issues arising in family cases. The aim of the scheme was to reduce delay, limit costs and facilitate settlements.

One of the innovative procedures introduced under the scheme is the **16–121** Financial Dispute Resolution (FDR) appointment. This meeting is held with a district judge on an evidentially privileged basis to explore possibilities of settlement.

The FDR meeting is conducted as an evaluative ADR process, albeit with **16–122** a higher level of evaluation than in many other ADR forms. The concept of it is that the judge meets the parties and their lawyers with a view to helping move them in what the judge considers to be a sensible settlement direction. The judge in question would not hear the case itself if the parties do not settle: it would be appointed to some other judge. Consequently, in an evidentially privileged environment, the judge can comment on the proposed terms and can, if appropriate, indicate what judgment he might give on the issues generally or any particular aspect, if he or she were to be hearing the case.

As with other non-binding neutral evaluative processes, the evaluation is **16–123** intended to help the parties and their lawyers to address settlement realistically. Early experience of this new process is that it can help the parties to get a better idea of what a court might be likely to order. However, some inconsistencies still exist between district judges in the way they exercise their powers.

It has become clear in this process that a judge dealing with parties in the **16–124** FDR meeting must have a very good grasp of the facts and issues before offering any comment. Trying to nudge parties towards settlement by giving indications based on a superficial reading of the case can be damaging rather than helpful.[53]

---

[52]See Chap. 3 for further information about the scheme.

[53]One of the authors mediated a case that had been close to settlement when the parties attended an FDR meeting. The district judge suggested a capital payment that was less than the offer that one party had already made. That party then withdrew the offer and replaced it with the lower figure. This led to a breakdown in negotiations. The parties entered mediation as a last resort to avoid the litigation that then seemed inevitable. The matter was settled in mediation, though the judge's comments proved the biggest obstacle to resolution.

A private FDR process?

16–125 With the development of the FDR in the courts, there seems to be no reason why a form of private FDR should not also be made available. Experienced lawyers could provide this privately, to supplement bilateral negotiations or mediation. This process may be a useful option for parties who wish to be guided in their discussions, with or without the benefit also of using a mediator.

16–126 Because of the importance of the neutral's evaluative role, it would be essential for the neutral to have the necessary expertise. After all, one of the strengths of the court-based FDR is that the evaluation is made by a judge, whose indications are likely to be regarded with the necessary authority and respect. In a private equivalent, the neutral could be a lawyer who has been appointed as a deputy district judge,[54] or might be a retired judge, or a specialist family barrister, solicitor or legal executive with the requisite expertise and experience.

16–127 Mediators have been careful to ensure that the FDR process should not be confused with mediation. If, however, a private equivalent were to develop, consideration would need to be given to how this could most effectively be used in both the traditional and mediation contexts.

10. OMBUDSMAN

Ombudsman's role[55]

16–128 An ombudsman is usually an independent person whose role is to deal with public complaints against administrative injustice and maladministration, with the power to investigate, criticise and make issues public. Although having no power to alter a decision when a complaint is found to be justified, he may persuade the relevant department or authority to alter its decision or to pay compensation to the complainant.

16–129 Arguably, the ombudsman does not fall strictly within the ADR ambit, because his functions are the examination of grievances rather than the resolution of disputes. As the role includes investigative and mediatory functions, however, it may properly be included under the broad heading of ADR.[56]

16–130 The office of ombudsman was originally established in Sweden early in the nineteenth century and from there moved to various other countries in Scandinavia, New Zealand, Australia, Germany, parts of the United States and elsewhere. In the United Kingdom the first ombudsman was appointed

---

[54]In England and Wales, some experienced practising lawyers are appointed to part-time judicial posts as deputy district judges.

[55]For a list of all ombudsmen and complaints adjudication systems in Britain and Ireland, with details of their roles, powers and procedures, see the *A-Z of Ombudsmen: A Guide to Ombudsman schemes in Britain and Ireland* published by the National Consumer Council in 1997.

[56]The U.S. Society of Professionals in Dispute Resolution (SPIDR) includes the ombudsman procedure as part of its work. See the article by Michael P. Mills "Mediation is Ombudsmanry" in *Beyond Borders* (SPIDR 1991 Proceedings, 19th Annual Conference). See also the chapter "Complaints mechanisms in administrative law: recent developments" by Patrick Birkinshaw in *A Handbook of Dispute Resolution* ed. by K. Mackie (1991).

under the Parliamentary Commissioner Act 1967, with the title of Parliamentary Commissioner for Administration, with lesser powers than the ombudsman under the Swedish system. He receives complaints about Government departments and other public sector bodies, not from members of the public directly, but through a Member of Parliament. The commissioner may not inquire into matters of policy, nor does he investigate complaints where the complainant has recourse to any other tribunal. Consequently, there is inevitably some overlap between the functions of the commissioner and the courts.

The ombudsman concept has been extended both by statute and voluntarily **16–131** into other administrative areas. The National Health Service Reorganisation Act 1973 set up the offices of Health Service Commissioner for England and Wales. In 1974 the ombudsman system was extended from central to local government (Local Government Act 1974). Commissioners for Local Administration appointed under the Act investigate administrative actions taken by local authorities and other bodies such as the Commission for the New Towns and new town development corporations, urban development corporations, police authorities and water authorities. Certain matters are expressly excluded from investigation by a local commissioner, such as the institution or conduct of civil or criminal proceedings before any court of law, action taken to prevent crime, certain contractual transactions, various specified matters concerning employment conditions and a list of other specified exclusions. The procedure for complaint and investigation is set out in the Act; and the commissioner has powers similar to those of a High Court judge with regard to the attendance and examination of witnesses and the production of documents. The commissioner will furnish a written report to the complainant and the authority or body concerned. If the commissioner concludes that there has been an injustice, the authority or body must inform the commissioner of the action taken or to be taken in response to the report. If it fails to do so, that becomes the subject of a further report. This may lead to a payment being made or benefit being given to the person who has suffered the injustice.

The ombudsman system has also extended outside of the statutory regime, **16–132** and in the voluntary sector has moved into fields such as building societies,[57] insurance,[58] banking, pensions,[59] funerals, estate agencies, and legal services. As to the last category, the Courts and Legal Services Act 1990 made provision for the setting up of two new ombudsmen: the Legal Services Ombudsman (section 21) and the Conveyancing Ombudsman (section 43).

The Legal Services Ombudsman investigates the manner in which a **16–133** complaint relating to a member of the legal profession has been dealt with by the relevant professional body. In her report at the end of the investigation she may, *inter alia,* recommend that compensation be paid to the complainant. There is provision for publicity in relation to any failure to

---

[57] The Building Societies Ombudsman Scheme was established in 1987 as the first statutory scheme in the private sector.

[58] But in 1994 the Insurance Ombudsman's Bureau lost a scheme allowing the public to lodge complaints about life assurance and related products up to a value of £100,000. It was given to the new Personal Investment Authority (with a reduced ceiling).

[59] The remit of the Pensions Ombudsman, Dr Julian Farrand, was substantially extended in 1997.

comply with the ombudsman's recommendations, and for the ombudsman to recover certain items as a civil debt.

16–134   Alongside the ombudsman system, and closely related to it, is the complaints adjudication system. So, for example, the Registrar of Companies in the United Kingdom appointed a Complaints Adjudicator in 1995 to act as a referee between Companies House and its consumers. There is also an Adjudicator for Inland Revenue, Customs and Excise and the Contributions Agency, who deals with complaints about the way in which a department has handled the affairs of members of the public. Certain complaints about the police can be referred to the Chair of the Police Complaints Authority, and complaints about treatment of the public in relation to television and radio can be referred to the Chair of the Broadcasting Standards Commission.

Developments of the ombudsman function

16–135   There may be scope for an ombudsman to work within the civil justice system. For example, it has been suggested that a legal costs ombudsman could deal with complaints of cases having been excessively litigated, rather than expeditiously settled. There could perhaps even be ways in which an ombudsman might act as a watchdog over the practice of dispute resolution processes, both traditional and alternative. Doubt has, however, been expressed by the government and by members of the legal profession as to whether any ombudsman would be qualified to comment on the workings of the court.

16–136   There may also be scope for extending the ombudsman's role in the private business sector. For example, businesses could appoint ombudsmen to investigate consumer complaints, or particular industries could appoint them to investigate a range of matters from complaints about quality to procedural grievances. Such appointments and investigations would not be in substitution for, but rather supplemental to, the rights of parties to seek their redress in other forums, but might well be effective in reducing the demand for more formal methods of dispute and complaints resolution. Obviously, the fact that the ombudsman is appointed by the organisation or industry concerned would inevitably lead to some limitations on the ombudsman's authority and perceived neutrality and efficacy. There is though a view that "when an ombudsman is diligent and secure, there is a likelihood that justice will be done."[60]

16–137   Meanwhile, the office and functions of the ombudsman continue to develop. A new Financial Services Ombudsman has been created, to bring together five financial ombudsman schemes, including insurance, pensions and personal investments. The Independent Housing Ombudsman has agreed to use a panel of mediators from CEDR (the Centre for Dispute Resolution) to resolve housing related disputes. A code of practice is planned by the British and Irish Ombudsmen Association. New challenges are being addressed, such as those posed by the European Convention on Human Rights.[61]

---

[60]*per* Robert Coulson, President of the American Arbitration Association, in Wilkinson, *ADR Practice Book* (1990) at p. 6.

[61]Art. 6 of the Convention stipulates that all hearings must be "fair and public", which is likely to affect the way in which ombudsmen have been operating and introduce lawyers more

In an age of increasing technological development, it is perhaps inevitable **16–138** that there should be an "Online Ombuds Office". This is a pilot project, established at the Department of Legal Studies, University of Massachusetts, to deal with conflicts in cyberspace.[62] This Online Ombuds Office is said to be "an attempt to allow the Ombuds model to migrate one more time, from the educational, commercial and governmental institutions in which it is now embodied, to cyberspace." The pilot scheme is a project jointly undertaken by the author of the article, Ethan Katsh, whose background is described as being in "networks and computers", and Janet Rifkin, "an experienced ombudsperson and a scholar of alternative dispute resolution". The article describing the pilot project indicates that its authors have considered various aspects relevant to the new milieu in which they are operating. This includes, for example, the establishment of a web site,[63] a data base of online disputes and cases and materials, consideration of the role of the neutral and the difficult aspect of confidentiality, and familiarity with the tools of the new technology. This pilot scheme should be seen in the context of a developing array of dispute resolution processes geared to the world of cyberspace and e-commerce.

---

widely, changing the character of the process.

[62] See the article by Ethan Katsh, "The Online Ombuds Office: Adapting Dispute Resolution to Cyberspace" at *http://www.law.vill.edu/ncair/disres/katsh.htm*

[63] Located at *http://www.ombuds.org/*

CHAPTER 17

ADR: INFORMATION TECHNOLOGY, THE INTERNET AND CYBERSPACE

17–001   It is trite to observe how rapidly information technology (IT) has been developing, as well as Internet activity, electronic communications and electronic commerce. There is a view that legal rights and liabilities in this field and the enforcement of any rights, will take a considerable time to catch up with technological developments, and may not do so at all.

17–002   Those interested in dispute resolution have not neglected the opportunities and challenges that these new fields offer. They have entered this arena in different ways and with different objectives:

- Some organisations in the field of dispute resolution are using the new technology to promote and market their ADR and traditional services, for example, by establishing web sites and offering information and communications through the Internet and e-mail.

- Some organisations are offering to use new technology to address disputes that arise in the "real" world.

- Some organisations are offering to use ordinary ADR processes such as mediation to address disputes arising out of the new technology.

- New ideas are being developed and tested to use new technology and electronic processes to address problems arising in cyberspace[1] and the "virtual" world.

17–003   Telephone conferencing, for example, has been used in the Patent Court and document imaging is used in U.S. courts.[2] This may easily be incorporated into ADR use. The availability of video-conferencing makes ADR processes accessible even if the parties and the mediator cannot be together at the same time.[3]

---

[1] The term "cyberspace" covers communication through the Internet and through other kinds of networks including cellular telephones and satellites. Because of the transitory nature of cyberspace communications, references in this section and elsewhere in this work to web-sites and Internet addresses may change or cease to be available.

[2] See the article "IP and IT—the way forward" by Kate Swaine in "In Focus Intellectual Property Newsletter" No. 46 of June 1998.

[3] Lord Woolf is reported as having described it as a "vital tool" in case management. See Kate Swaine's article, n. 2 above.

Online dispute resolution

A number of articles might be helpful to introduce the concept of dispute resolution on the Internet. Some are to be found in print.[4] Others are located on the Internet.[5] For many dispute resolvers this is new territory; but there are indications that it is a rapidly widening territory. Indeed, as one writer has observed, as the Internet grows it will increasingly be perceived "as a place" as actual physical places are displaced and become less used.[6]

17–004

There is experience of successfully mediating over the Internet.[7] Professor Krivis, an established U.S. mediator, dealt with what he describes as "a relatively simple contract claim brought by a United Kingdom franchiser against his most successful franchisee in the western United States". There was a binding arbitration clause, but Professor Krivis suggested mediation in the first instance. For practical geographical reasons, a long-distance mediation was proposed and the parties agreed to use electronic mail as the basis for mediation communications.

17–005

In his article, Professor Krivis outlines the frustrations of dealing through a medium that takes time for each communication, rather than having instant reactions and observing body language. E-mail allowed each party to take time and use language that was not conducive to settlement. He found it necessary to undertake online "listening". Eventually, Professor Krivis prepared a neutral evaluation with settlement proposals, allowing them 48 hours to respond. Both parties accepted the terms.

17–006

Professor Krivis suggests that online mediation is best used for parties living in different time zones, who seek neutral help in a relatively convenient manner and keeping costs contained. He offers "ten tips for on-line ADR" including, for example, creating credibility through a personal biography; having the parties enter into an agreement covering confidentiality and incorporating online procedures and ground rules including time-limits; setting an early agenda; and filtering angry or emotional replies. He favours case evaluation, carefully undertaken; and makes the obvious but critical point of ensuring that a correct e-mail address is used.

17–007

E-commerce

Electronic (or online) commerce covers various commercial activities. It might involve commercial transactions undertaken through the Internet, or transactions with specialised online institutions. Or it may involve using electronic communications for traditional commercial business.[8] It has been described as "a general term applied to the use of computer and telecommunications technologies, particularly on an inter-enterprise basis, to

17–008

---

[4] See, *e.g.* Prof. Eugene Clark's article "Arbitration, dispute resolution and the World Wide Web" [1998] A.D.R.L.J. 3, which introduces the Internet, sources of information, legal sites and Internet resources on dispute resolution.

[5] See, *e.g.* the On-line mediation service of the University of Maryland School of Law: *http:// www.mediate-net.org/frequent1.htm*

[6] See the article by Ethan Katsh, "The Online Ombuds Office: Adapting Dispute Resolution to Cyberspace" at *http://www.law.vill.edu/ncair/disres/katsh.htm*

[7] See Prof. Jeffrey Krivis's article "Mediating in Cyberspace" [1998] A.D.R.L.J. 19 (and "Alternatives" Vol. 14, No. 10 November 1996).

[8] See "The role of alternative dispute resolution in online commerce, intellectual property and defamation" by E. Casey Lide [1998] A.D.R.L.J. 31 (and *Ohio State Law Journal on Dispute Resolution* 1996).

support trading in goods and services. Electronic commerce uses a variety of technologies, such as electronic data interchange, electronic mail, facsimile transfer, continuous acquisition and life cycle support and electronic catalogue and directory systems."[9]

17–009   Journals are being established to deal specifically with legal issues arising in electronic business[10]; and the European Union Commission is considering the introduction of specific laws for electronic business. In this context, the European Commission has proposed a Directive to establish a coherent framework for the development of electronic commerce within the European Union. As part of this initiative, a dispute resolution procedure is planned in order to encourage the development and use of "effective, alternative cross-border dispute settlement systems for on-line services".[11] Cyberspace custom is expected to play a large role in the development of "cyber-law" particularly with reference to intellectual property.[12]

Online neutrals and ADR provision

17–010   Online mediation specialists are readily found on the Internet.[13] So are mediation and ADR organisations, some being dedicated to online dispute resolution and others to traditional "real world" dispute resolution marketed online, with resources for providing information and communications online.

17–011   Some examples of these include the following:

- The World Intellectual Property Organisation (WIPO) not only has arbitration and mediation schemes and panels, but has an Online Dispute Resolution resource. It is described by WIPO as "an online, Internet-based system for administering disputes". Its scheme involves digital communication tools that allow disputants to use electronic forms and to submit documents through secure channels. These will supplement audio and video facilities.

- A Cyber Tribunal has been established as an experimental project by the *Centre de recherche en droit public* (CRDP) in Montreal, Quebec, which deals with "the prevention and resolution of conflicts arising in cyberspace". It aims to "meet the needs of cybernauts . . . " and " . . . to determine the feasibility of using alternative mechanisms to resolve cyber-conflicts which cannot be covered adequately by the traditional means of state law." It offers its services in French and English.[14]

- The University of Massachusetts has established a "Center for Information Technology and Dispute Resolution". It also runs the

---

[9]Clark, *op. cit.* at p.16, quoting from *Electronic Commerce: Commonwealth Government Statement of Direction* (Canberra, AGPS, April 1995).

[10]*e.g. Electronic Business Law* and *E-Commerce Law & Policy*.

[11]See *Electronic Business Law* Vol. 1 No. 1, February 1999 at p. 2.

[12]Lide, *op. cit.,* at p. 40.

[13]See, *e.g.* "Internet Neutral" which says that it teaches mediation and Internet communication skills and maintains a panel of qualified, experienced mediators. See: *www.internetneutral.com* It has also published on the Internet a set of "Internet Neutral Mediator Rules" that will apply to all mediation conducted by the "Internet Neutral".

[14]See *http://www.cybertribunal.org/english/html/project.asp*

"Online Ombuds Office", which seeks to adapt the ombudsman's role to cyberspace issues.[15]

- Family mediation is offered online by "Maryland's On-Line Mediation Service". This is a trial service administered by Professor Roger Wolf, the Director of the Program for Dispute Resolution at the University of Maryland School of Law, and Richard Granat, the Director of the Center for On-Line Mediation Inc. Initially it is only accepting family disputes arising under Maryland law, but it is planned to extend this in due course. The process is conducted initially by e-mail, after which they may use various electronic communication tools including electronic conferencing, on-line chat sessions, video-conferencing (where parties have access to the required equipment) and telephone if agreed. The process has significant evaluative elements, in that after information-gathering the mediator will present proposed settlement terms by e-mail to both parties and will liaise separately with each on their responses.[16]

- The Virtual Magistrate is a specialised, online arbitration and fact-finding system for disputes involving users of online systems, those who claim to be harmed by wrongful messages, and System Operators (as recipients of claims or demands). Virtual Magistrate is operated by the Cyberspace Law Institute (which directs policy), the American Arbitration Association (which administers cases), the Center for Information Law and Policy (which operates the service) and the National Center for Automated Information Research (which funds the project). Its services are available to computer networks anywhere in the world, provided that the interested parties all agree to participate.[17]

- Nova Scotia Southeastern University in Florida has established "Alternative Dispute Resolution Resources on the Internet", which contains a wealth of information for dispute resolution practitioners. For example, it contains a list of over 230 web sites of organisations concerned with conflict resolution and dispute resolution, linked for immediate access. It also provides links with online discussion groups, contains ADR online papers, and has a communication, conflict and conflict resolution database.[18]

- Another helpful site has been established by Archie Zariski, Managing Editor of *E-Law—Murdoch University Electronic Journal of Law*, Perth, Western Australia. It contains links with over 80 conflict and dispute resolution organisations, as well as his Academic Space, containing student resources, links for online publications, webspaces and WWW topics.[19]

---

[15] See *http://128.119.199.27/center/Default.htm* See also information about the Online Ombuds Office under "Ombudsman" in Chap. 16.

[16] See *http://www.mediate.net.org/frequent1.htm*

[17] See *http://vmag.vcilp.org/*

[18] At *http://www.nova.edu/ssss/DR/adrwww.html*

[19] Archie Zariski's Conflict and Dispute Resolution Links can be found at *http://*

387

17–012   These are just examples of online resources, and are merely representative of them. Many others can be located through online search engines, and more specifically through specialist sites, such as Alternative Dispute Resolution Resources on the Internet and Archie Zariski (mentioned above), the Mediation Training Institute International,[20] or ConflictNet.[21]

17–013   Discussion groups and listservs are useful Internet features, where specific topics can be discussed online, or by way of e-mail. Links to these can be obtained through "Alternative Dispute Resolution Resources on the Internet"[22] or direct, for example, the Discussion List for Dispute Resolution.[23] By subscribing to specialist lists, it is possible to engage in on-line discussion, to share information, obtain details of conferences and other announcements and generally get information about other relevant sites.[24]

Some practical issues in cyberspace dispute resolution
Confidentiality

17–014   Rules regulating confidentiality in mediation or other dispute resolution process conducted in cyberspace should be agreed before the process is started. This should cover both a contractual commitment to confidentiality by the parties and technological assurances about confidentiality and privacy in the process.

17–015   Maryland's On-Line Mediation Service, for example, commits itself to a policy that all communications to the service, and between parties, will be supported by a secure Netscape Commerce Server, said by the service to be "totally secure for all practical purposes."

17–016   Technological developments, such as digital signatures using encryption technology, are likely to improve levels of security and confidentiality, both in relation to e-commerce and more specifically to online ADR processes.

Enforcement

17–017   According to E. Casey Lide, the enforceability of arbitration awards and ADR outcomes should not be a problematic issue as long as procedures are fair. Judicial recognition and enforcement of ADR decisions has increased.[25]

17–018   Lide considers that "the second major tool of enforceability could be a threat in the form of 'co-operation exile'...grounded in contract." The concept would be of establishing a network of system administrators and users who would "exile" any party failing to comply with an ADR decision. This route of enforcement is at the present time aspirational, to say the least. Lide acknowledges that it "would require an extraordinary degree of co-

---

www.staff.murdoch.edu.au/ ~ zariski/bookmark/adrbook.htm His Academic Space is at *http://carmen.murdoch.edu.au/ ~ zariski/*

[20] At *http://www.qni.com/ ~ mti/links.htm#search engines*

[21] A conflict resolution network at *http://www.igc.org./conflictnet/*

[22] See n. 18.

[23] At *listserv@listserv.law.cornell.edu* To subscribe, the message "subscribe dispute-res your name" must be sent.

[24] A site that provides details and links to listservs and that recommends the web sites of small groups and individual dispute resolution professionals is "ADR Resources" at *http://adrr.com/adr0/links1.htm* See also *CataList*, the official catalogue of listserv lists, located at *http://www.lsoft.com/lists/listref.html*

[25] Lide refers to S. Gale Dick, "ADR at the Crossroads" Disp. Resol. J., March 1994 at pp. 52–53.

operation, but might be eased by some sort of technological improvement ... "

As in practice, enforcement would depend on having a contract or award **17–019** that would be recognised by a "real" court: this issue should be considered and agreed in any contract to undergo "online" ADR.

Law and jurisdiction
Until cyberspace establishes its own enforceable rules and jurisdiction, all **17–020** indications are that parties contracting on the Internet or elsewhere in cyberspace would be well advised to agree on a legal system that will be applicable to their transaction. It would also be sensible to agree on any territorial jurisdiction that would apply, though some of the benefit of using online ADR processes might be to avoid jurisdictional problems.

Practitioners may find that the disputants have already agreed these issues **17–021** in their contract that forms the subject-matter of the dispute. Providers of goods or services through the Internet might well have stipulated that certain terms regulate the transaction. Such terms might either have been explicitly agreed, or may be deemed to have been implicitly accepted by virtue of their having been mentioned and the parties thereafter having entered into the transaction. In many cases, the transacting party might not have been consciously aware of the provisions, but might well be bound by them. It is very easy for Internet users to agree standard terms as a formality without studying and negotiating them.

The consequence of parties having agreed law and jurisdiction in their **17–022** contract would be to make these binding, unless a court found the provisions to be unenforceable for any reason. This though begs the question of which court would be used to challenge the contractual law and jurisdiction provisions. The object lesson is that all Internet users and people transacting in cyberspace should take great care to read and be satisfied about the terms that apply to any commercial transaction into which they may enter.

There is not yet a sufficient body of case law and precedent or statutory **17–023** provision to regulate these matters. Territorial jurisdiction is commonly established by concepts of residence or the carrying on of business; but these are not relevant to the virtual world. Until internationally accepted principles emerge and are adopted, or case law becomes clear and generally accepted, dispute resolution is likely to depend on the principles of contract. It is encouraging that the European Union is proposing to establish dispute resolution procedures for e-commerce.[26]

---

[26] See n. 11.

CHAPTER 18

CHOICE AND TIMING OF PROCESS USE

18–001   It is a central theme of this book that effective dispute resolution involves an informed choice of the process most suitable to the individual dispute. This chapter is intended to assist practitioners in making such choices by providing a brief comparative summary of the key features of each process.[1] It will also guide practitioners on the optimum timing for the use of ADR processes, and the principles affecting the reservation of rights while ADR is being used. Finally, it contains some cautions about the use of ADR and the effect of triangulation and alliances.

1. GENERAL PRINCIPLES GUIDING CHOICE

18–002   Negotiation is generally the simplest, most cost-effective and most satisfactory way to resolve disputes. If a disagreement can be settled through bilateral or multilateral negotiations between the parties or their representatives, that should be explored before any other process is considered.

18–003   If, however, negotiation fails or is not appropriate, other methods of dispute resolution may need to be considered. These will either be adjudicatory or consensual.

Adjudicatory processes

18–004   For most disputes, if an adjudication is needed, the main choice is most commonly between litigation and arbitration, since private judging is not currently available in the United Kingdom, and expert determination and contractual adjudication are primarily used in relation to certain specific circumstances. For this purpose, court-annexed arbitration[2] will not be considered as it is not currently available in the United Kingdom, and in any event, even if it were, it would not necessarily be relevant to the voluntary choice of process facing practitioners.

18–005   There are certain kinds of cases for which consensual ADR processes would be unsuitable, and adjudication, usually litigation rather than

---

[1]*Dispute Resolution* by Goldberg, Green & Sander (1985) contains an analytical table at pp. 8–9 distinguishing the different characteristics of the main primary and hybrid processes used in the U.S.

[2]As described in para. 16–014.

arbitration, would be appropriate. These are cases in which a party lacks the capacity to contract; cases where constitutional principle, civil rights or other fundamental issues are in contention; cases where enforceable binding decisions or precedent are essential; cases in which there are intractable issues requiring adjudication; cases where rights may be lost or prejudiced by delay; cases where the power imbalance between the parties is too great; and generally any case which is inappropriate for settlement.[3] In any of these cases, litigation should be considered as a first option.

In some circumstances, adjudication may be needed but the parties may require the privacy, neutral's expertise and/or expedition which arbitration can offer, and in such event, arbitration or one of the other adjudicatory processes may be more appropriate than litigation. **18–006**

The advantages of arbitration are to be found in the ability to use more flexible procedures, and with these it is said, "speed and a saving of costs".[4] The parties can decide to have an inquisitorial rather than adversarial procedure, and can agree to follow abbreviated, simplified rules, including, for example, a determination based on documents only. The arbitrator, chosen by the parties or nominated on their behalf, will invariably be a specialist in the field of the dispute, thus minimising the need for expert contributions and technical explanations. The proceedings are private and confidential, which is invariably an advantage (unless either party in any particular case may consider the publicity inherent in litigation to be an advantageous factor). The venue and timing of the proceedings can be fixed to meet the convenience of the parties. Where international elements are involved, arbitration will avoid any reservations which a party may have about litigating in the national courts of the opponent. Arbitration is said to be "acceptable to many States which, for reasons connected with national prestige, would never consider any submissions to the jurisdiction of a foreign court, but would have confidence in the independence and privacy of an arbitration."[5] **18–007**

Whether regarded as an advantage or disadvantage, arbitration does not carry an automatic right of appeal against the decisions of the arbitrator. The principal intention of the legislature in passing the 1979 Arbitration Act (which, *inter alia*, swept away the case stated, the consultative case and the court's jurisdiction to review for errors of fact or law on the face of the award) was to encourage finality in arbitration awards. The 1996 Act further limited appeals against arbitrators' awards.[6] **18–008**

Arbitration is not necessarily cheaper than litigation, however, where all the procedures of litigation are replicated, with legal representation on both sides, and a full-scale hearing. On the contrary, it may be more expensive, since in addition to each side's own costs they will also have to meet the **18–009**

---

[3]But in some cases, factors that may appear to exclude ADR could be overcome if parties want to use ADR, *e.g.* where urgent injunctive relief is needed, this could be obtained by agreement, perhaps even in the context of the ADR, and the issues then dealt with by ADR.

[4]For the advantages of arbitration, see the article by Margaret Rutherford, "Arbitration: be there dragons?" in the *Law Society's Gazette* of 2 September 1987, at 2423.

[5]Rutherford, *ibid.* n. 6.

[6]See *B.T.P. Tioxide v. Pioneer Shipping Ltd and Armada Marine S.A. (The Nema)* [1982] A.C. 724 and *Antaios Compania Naviera S.A. v. Salen Rederierna A.B. The Antaios* [1985] A.C. 191, HL. For the position since 1996, see Chap. 4.

costs of the arbitrator, or in some cases three arbitrators, and the costs of the venue and the recording and transcription of the evidence.

18–010 Fast-track adjudication involves an interim finding that binds the parties pending either their reaching agreement or taking the issues to formal arbitration. It is particularly helpful in those cases where the parties are engaged in a business relationship that needs to continue in effect without the disruption caused by disagreement on pending issues. So, for example, an adjudicator can make a finding in relation to a pending construction contract that allows the work to continue on the basis of the interim decision, while not precluding the parties from arriving at a subsequent negotiated settlement on any other terms or taking the matter to a full-blown arbitration.

18–011 Expert determination may allow parties to chose an expert to settle their technical issues, or to assist them in resolving management or other impasses, without necessarily having to follow all the procedures inherent in litigation or arbitration.

18–012 All adjudicatory forms of dispute resolution can be used in conjunction with consensual processes. Indeed, it is quite common for mediation and other ADR forms to be used parallel to adjudicatory processes, sometimes but not necessarily on the basis of a suspension of adjudicatory activity.

Consensual (non-adjudicatory) ADR

18–013 Any case that could be settled in the traditional adversarial process is generally suitable to be dealt with by way of consensual ADR, since these processes may be regarded as methods of facilitating settlement.

18–014 Mediation is the primary consensual ADR process, and is likely to be suitable for most disputes. Depending upon the facts of each individual case, the ground rules for the mediation can be discussed and adapted. If required and appropriate, the mediator can perhaps provide an evaluative element or may agree to recommend settlement terms if the parties cannot agree on settlement terms themselves.[7]

18–015 Some substantial and complex commercial or technical disputes may be more suited to the mini-trial or to the appointment of a neutral expert or an evaluator. Alternatively, the particular requirements of the parties or the issues may indicate that hybrid processes need to be specifically designed for the individual dispute.

18–016 The main objectives of consensual processes are as follows[8].

- To provide the services and the additional dynamic of a third party neutral with skill and expertise who can help the parties to reach an agreement by facilitating negotiations between them.

- To provide a structured forum and a secure environment in which the parties can generate and explore settlement options in a constructive, businesslike way, and seek terms for the resolution of the dispute

---

[7]See Chap. 16 for the introduction of evaluative elements into mediation.

[8]These are the objectives of the providers of the processes and presumably also of those who use them. Some users may have other objectives, *e.g.* those who are emotionally enmeshed may use these as new forums for continuing their struggles. Providers may also have other objectives, *e.g.* some see mediation as an opportunity to provide a transformative process for users.

which meet their needs, interests and concerns. Settlements arrived at through these processes tend to have a flexible, creative and mutually compensatory character, with nuances within the terms which cannot easily be achieved even in bilateral or multilateral negotiations.

- To provide an opportunity for the parties themselves to be directly involved in the dispute resolution process, resulting in their maintaining a greater responsibility for their own issues and a greater control over outcome.

- To enhance direct communication between the parties where practicable, or, in some models, to provide for separate meetings and a system of confidential shuttle mediation where this is considered more helpful.

- To allow scope for testing the realism of parties' views, perceptions and proposals. A neutral can help to bring a sense of realism into the matter and into settlement negotiations. Parties can also use the confidentiality of the separate meetings, where these are part of the process, and the overview of the neutral to test intended settlement proposals before communicating them to the other party.

- Where the dispute is between people who have a business, professional and/or personal relationship, to enhance the possibility of that relationship continuing in the future, if necessary on new terms to be agreed. Where that relationship has ended or needs to end, it can help them to do so on mutually beneficial terms.

- To save or limit the costs of litigation.

- To avoid the delays of litigation.

- To avoid the risks and stress of litigation by seeking to resolve the matter in a way which is acceptable to both or all parties.

2. SOME CONSIDERATIONS IN CHOOSING BETWEEN LITIGATION AND MEDIATION

In choosing between litigation (or any other form of adjudication) or mediation (or any other non-adjudicatory ADR process) the following points of difference may be noted: **18–017**

- In litigation or other adjudication the parties delegate to their respective lawyers, and ultimately to the court or the adjudicatory tribunal the function of resolving the dispute. In mediation and other consensual ADR processes, they retain this function themselves, because any resolution depends upon their agreement.

- Mediation and other ADR processes allow parties to seek solutions that accommodate all needs and interests, allowing more flexibility than adjudication, which provides an outcome with a winner and a loser.

- Litigation is ordinarily a public process, whereas arbitration, mediation and other ADR forms are private and confidential.

- Whereas litigation necessarily involves elements of delay, ADR can proceed at whatever pace the parties require and are able to agree upon. Arbitration can sometimes involve similar delays to litigation; but where there are specialised organisations with experience of arbitration, they can often operate expeditiously, or parties can agree to use procedures that are more expeditious.

- Mediation costs can be much lower than those of litigation. If, however, mediation does not result in an agreement, then the mediation costs will be in addition to the litigation costs. They may not be wasted since mediation may well have provided some benefits, perhaps in information gathering or in narrowing issues, or in helping the parties to move towards a later settlement.

- Litigation and inter-lawyer communications within the adversarial system have a tendency to escalate antagonism (although with care this can in some cases be avoided), whereas mediation and consensual processes tend to minimise this and to seek more co-operative approaches.

- Litigation offers the enforcement of its judgments and orders, whereas a mediated or other ADR agreement will usually be binding in contract only. However, where court proceedings are pending or intended, ADR agreements can be made into consent orders of court.

- In litigation, the adjudicator is a qualified lawyer who follows objective standards of practice and known or ascertainable rules of law and procedure. In mediation, the mediator's qualifications and standards of practice may need to be individually established.[9]

- Litigation deals with power imbalances between parties by providing an impartial forum.[10] Mediation relies on the skills, training and integrity of the mediator.

- In litigation and arbitration, experts tend to be engaged in a partisan capacity, though under court reforms that have been introduced, this is likely to change. In consensual processes, they may have other roles of a neutral nature. They may for example work as neutral evaluators, mediators or neutral experts.

- If a case turns solely on legal issues, evaluation might be helpful, but litigation would be necessary if a binding judgment or precedent were needed.

- If credibility plays a pivotal role, then litigation may prove to be

---

[9] Accreditation and regulatory procedures have been developed in most countries, including England and Wales, to try to ensure that mediators achieve and maintain acceptable professional standards. See Chap. 24.

[10] However, despite the notion that courts can redress power imbalances, these may sometimes still continue within litigation. As to power imbalances generally, see Chap. 21.

necessary. Significant credibility issues create a lack of trust that can inhibit parties from feeling able to negotiate effectively with one another. They do not render cases incapable of settlement or of being mediated, especially as there are often other and more complex issues. However, they can tend to be contra-indicators to the use of consensual processes.

- ADR may not necessarily be helpful where litigation is instituted or defended purely for tactical reasons. Some cases may not be capable of settlement, as where they are brought to make a political point or to gain publicity. However, some tactically brought or defended cases might need to settle at some stage. It may be difficult to judge in each individual case whether a party whose proceedings are tactical is ready or willing to try to settle.

3. COMPARATIVE SUMMARY OF PRINCIPAL DISPUTE RESOLUTION PROCESSES

There now follows a brief comparative summary of the main dispute resolution processes, both traditional and alternative. **18–018**

Litigation
Availability in United Kingdom: Litigation is available through the formal court system. The agreement of parties to participate is not required, as participation can be compelled. **18–019**

Summary of procedure: Court rules prescribe the formal procedures. Respective submissions are contained in written statements of case and other documents. Documentary and oral evidence is presented, subject to questioning and probing through prescribed procedures. The trial hearing is usually public. **18–020**

Form of outcome: Binding determination, applying legal principles, judicial authorities and precedent, generally subject to appeal. **18–021**

Role of neutral: The neutral is a court appointed judge, district judge, master or other legally qualified official, who hears the parties and makes a binding decision. **18–022**

Indicators for usage: Litigation is available for virtually all kinds of disputes, especially those needing a binding precedent and/or enforcement by the court, for example, on an injunctive basis. It is also needed where constitutional, civil or other non-negotiable rights or issues of principle are concerned or where power imbalances between parties are substantial and can best be redressed by the court. It is also required where any party has a legal disability such as mental incapacity; or in circumstances where no negotiated **18–023** settlement can realistically be anticipated. Litigation may provide the spur to settlement negotiations.[11]

18–024 *Contra-indicators against usage:* Where the dispute can be resolved by negotiation, especially where the parties have a business, professional or personal relationship which could be preserved; where a public hearing and publicity are not desired; where a speedy resolution is needed; where the costs of litigation and the risk of liability for costs cannot be sustained; where the neutral must have a specialised technical knowledge of the subject-matter of the dispute; where the issues relate to inter-personal or other conflicts not readily amenable to judicial resolution; or where for any other reason judicial intervention would be inappropriate.

Arbitration

18–025 *Availability in United Kingdom:* Arbitration is available in the United Kingdom through various specific arbitration and ADR organisations; professional, trade and other associations; and from individual practitioners.

18–026 *Summary of procedure:* Procedures are prescribed by the Arbitration Acts or rules of arbitration organisations, but can be varied by agreement. United Kingdom procedure historically tended to be similar to litigation but less formal. However, the position was significantly improved by the Arbitration Act of 1996. There are written and may be oral submissions; documentary and oral evidence is presented, subject to questioning and probing at a confidential hearing.

18–027 *Form of outcome:* The arbitrator makes a determination that is binding on the parties. The award is generally not subject to appeal but may be subject to review by the courts in certain limited circumstances.

18–028 *Role of neutral:* Adjudicator agreed upon by the parties, or appointed at their joint request by a nominee, who in making his decision applies legal principles, judicial authorities and precedent, and draws on his special expertise. In some jurisdictions the arbitrator may also have the power to decide *ex aequo et bono.*

18–029 *Indicators for usage:* Arbitration is available for many kinds of disputes. It is especially suitable for disputes where a neutral with a highly specialised knowledge of the subject matter of the dispute is needed; or where the parties' business relationship makes the publicity and formality of the courts unsuitable.

18–030 *Contra-indicators against usage:* As for litigation.

Expert determination

18–031 *Availability in the United Kingdom:* Expert determination is available through professional, trade and other associations; from the Academy of Experts; and from individual experts.

---

[11]Parties generally negotiate "in the shadow of the law", *i.e.* in the knowledge that litigation is an available option.

Summary of procedure: Procedure is explicitly or implicitly fixed by the   **18–032**
contract establishing the process. Rules of evidence do not apply.

Form of outcome: The expert makes a binding determination that is not   **18–033**
subject to appeal.

Role of neutral: The neutral is an expert with an informal adjudicatory   **18–034**
function, agreed upon by the parties or appointed at their joint request by a
nominee.

Indicators for usage: Available and suitable for all disputes where an expert   **18–035**
knowledge of the subject is necessary, especially where the parties have a
continuing relationship which may give rise to specific issues needing
resolution such as the proper level of payment to be made by one party to
another, taking into account prescribed factors; or how a technical,
management or other decision is to be made.

Contra-indicators against usage: Where the dispute can be resolved by   **18–036**
negotiation; where a more structured procedure is needed including each
party to be fully heard; where neutral specialised expertise does not add
anything to the resolution process; where there are significant issues of
credibility; or where the issues relate to inter-personal or other conflicts
which are not readily amenable to third party determination. Also as for
litigation.

Private judging
Availability in the United Kingdom: Not available in the United Kingdom. It   **18–037**
would require special legislation to be introduced.

Summary of procedure: The case is conducted similarly to conventional   **18–038**
litigation, except that a judge is privately appointed, who may with the
agreement of the parties introduce simplified and expedited procedures.

Form of outcome: Binding determination, applying legal principles, judicial   **18–039**
authorities and precedent, which becomes an order of the court, and is
subject to appeal.

Role of neutral: Private adjudicator appointed by the court to act as a judge,   **18–040**
with all judicial powers but excluding the contempt power.

Indicators for usage: In those jurisdictions where the procedure is available,   **18–041**
can be used for such disputes as may be prescribed; where the parties want
to choose their own adjudicator, with special expertise if appropriate, to hear
the matter without being subject to court delays; and where, unlike
arbitration, they want to preserve a right of appeal.

Contra-indicators against usage: This procedure is not available in the   **18–042**
United Kingdom and there are no indications that it might be introduced. In
those areas where it is available, it is generally only suitable for substantial

cases, as it usually involves the parties in sharing the costs of the private judge in addition to their own trial costs. Other contra-indications are as for litigation.

Court-annexed arbitration

18–043 *Availability in the United Kingdom:* The ADR form of court-annexed arbitration (that is, distinguished from arbitration under the court rules)[12] is not available in the United Kingdom and would require special legislation to be introduced.

18–044 *Summary of procedure:* The court appoints a neutral third party to act as an arbitrator, using informal procedures at a hearing at any venue and at any time, to make a determination which is initially non-binding. If neither party applies for a court hearing, the determination becomes binding. If either party wants a court hearing, that supersedes the arbitration decision. The non-binding determination may help parties to arrive at an agreed settlement.

18–045 *Form of outcome:* Initially non-binding, but at either party's instance can be re-heard *ab initio* by the court. There may be a penalty for seeking a court hearing if this does not exceed the arbitration award, but this may be unconstitutional in some jurisdictions.

18–046 *Role of neutral:* Adjudicator appointed by the court to act as non-binding arbitrator, applying legal principles, judicial authorities and precedent, and drawing on personal expertise.

18–047 *Indicators for usage:* In those jurisdictions where the procedure is available, it is used for all kinds of disputes, but usually limited to those below a certain specified sum.

18–048 *Contra-indicators against usage:* At present court-annexed arbitration is not available in the United Kingdom. Where used, it is not available for disputes above a certain level of jurisdiction.

Evaluation

18–049 *Availability in the United Kingdom:* There are two main kinds of evaluation standing in their own right as ADR processes (as distinct from forming a part of some other process). The one is Early Neutral Evaluation (ENE), which is used in California and other parts of the U.S. That form is not generally used in the United Kingdom, though it could be adopted. The other form is case evaluation, which can take place at any time. This kind of evaluation is being used in the United Kingdom, particularly for substantial financial disputes.

18–050 *Summary of procedure:* In ENE, an evaluator meets parties at an early stage of a case and makes a confidential assessment of the dispute. This helps parties to narrow and define the issues, and may promote settlement efforts.

---

[12]The ADR form of court-annexed arbitration is outlined in para. 16–104.

In case evaluation, a case is submitted to an evaluator or panel, who consider submissions, may hear witnesses and then evaluate the case for the parties.

Form of outcome: Non-binding determination, applying all principles that would be used in the event of a formal adjudication. Allows parties to obtain a neutral evaluation without the cost, formality and risk of a trial. May be used as a precursor to settlement negotiations, where parties want to settle broadly in accordance with their rights.   **18–051**

Role of neutral: The neutral hears the matter substantially as an arbitrator might, and applies similar principles to arriving at a decision. That decision, however, is merely intended for the guidance of the parties and is not binding on them. Obviously the neutral needs to be authoritative for the evaluation to be acceptable. The City Disputes Panel offers this process in the United Kingdom using an expert panel. It offers the option of a graded evaluation, *e.g.* very strong; strong; medium; weak; or hopeless.   **18–052**

Indicators for usage: Suitable for cases where parties have different perceptions of the relative strengths of their cases and cannot therefore agree settlement terms. Especially helpful for good faith disagreements (though not limited to these). Technical or complex issues can be assessed without the need for a trial.   **18–053**

Contra-indicators against usage: Not appropriate where parties seek resolution based on factors other than their rights or where they (or any of them) would not shift position whatever the evaluation might be.   **18–054**

Mediation
Availability in the United Kingdom: Through mediation and ADR associations and networks, in different areas of activity, for example commercial, family or community; and from individual mediators.   **18–055**

Summary of procedure: The mediator meets the parties, together and/or separately, and helps them towards a consensual agreement by facilitating their communications and negotiations, in many models shuttling between them.   **18–056**

Form of outcome: Any resolution is based exclusively on agreement between the parties, recorded as a binding contract, or as a court order by consent if appropriate.   **18–057**

Role of neutral: The mediator acts as a facilitator with no adjudicatory or advisory function, though in some models he or she may sometimes have a non-binding evaluative role.   **18–058**

Indicators for usage: Mediation is suitable for any issues capable of being settled by negotiation between the parties, especially for disputes where the parties have or have had a business, professional or personal relationship. It   **18–059** is used for commercial, civil, employment, family, inter-personal, community, and a wide range of other disputes.

18–060 *Contra-indicators against usage*[13]: Where consensual ADR processes would not be appropriate including, for example, where constitutional principles, civil rights or other fundamental issues are in question or where remedies available only from the courts are needed, such as injunctions. It is also unsuitable where precedents must be obtained; where a party lacks the capacity to contract; where rights may be lost by delay in bringing proceedings; or where for any other reason attempts to settle would not be appropriate.

Med–arb

18–061 *Availability in the United Kingdom:* Med–arb is available through some commercial ADR associations and from some individual mediators who also work as arbitrators. Many practitioners, however, view the process with caution and are disinclined to use it, at least, where the same person is to act in both capacities.[14] However, the notion of moving from mediation to arbitration using different neutrals is widely accepted.

18–062 *Summary of procedure:* The mediation procedure is first followed; if this is inconclusive, the same person then becomes an arbitrator and makes a binding determination of the issues.

18–063 *Form of outcome:* For the mediation phase, see the mediation outcome above; for the arbitration phase, see the arbitration outcome above.

18–064 *Role of neutral:* First a mediator, then an arbitrator. Alternatively, an arbitrator may adopt a mediatory role to try to help resolve the dispute by agreement between the parties. In some models, the mediator may stand down (after giving a non-binding advisory opinion at the end of the mediation). In other models, the mediator may move into an arbitration mode only if the parties at that stage re-confirm their agreement to his or her doing so.

18–065 *Indicators for usage:* Med–arb is used in the United States for labour contract negotiation disputes. It may also be used for any dispute requiring mediation, but where the parties wish to proceed to arbitration if the mediation is inconclusive.

18–066 *Contra-indicators against usage*[15]: Med–arb is not suitable in any cases where either mediation or arbitration would be inappropriate; or for any case

---

[13] Some of the contra-indicators mentioned here may be qualified as there are circumstances in which mediation may still be suitable, but with particular caution.

[14] See the cautions expressed about med–arb in Chap. 7. It may, though, be easier for an arbitrator to move into mediation mode, and then out again, than for a mediator to become an arbitrator in relation to the issues in the mediation. That would be closer to the concept of a judge who tries to help the parties towards settlement.

[15] Most practitioners will not use this process because of their concerns about its adverse effect both on the neutral's mediatory and adjudicatory functions.

where the parties may want to disclose confidential information to the mediator which might compromise them if the mediator were to become an adjudicator.

Mini-trial

Availability in the United Kingdom: Offered by various commercial ADR associations including CEDR ("Executive Tribunal").　　　　　**18–067**

Summary of procedure: The parties or their senior executives in the case of corporations and a neutral adviser hear abbreviated non-binding case presentations. These, with the views of the neutral if required, enable them to assess their relative strengths and weaknesses, so that they can then enter into business-like settlement negotiations.　　　　　**18–068**

Form of outcome: As for mediation.　　　　　**18–069**

Role of neutral: Expert in the subject-matter of the dispute and with relevant process skills who helps the parties to assess the presentations and evaluate the case. May be asked to provide a non-binding opinion and/or act in a mediatory capacity to facilitate negotiations.　　　　　**18–070**

Indicators for usage: Suitable for any issues capable of negotiation especially substantial commercial or technical disputes with mixed fact and law issues; including patent, construction and contract disputes, product liability, joint venture disagreements and many other kinds of cases. Particularly suitable where senior executives (frequently not involved in the genesis of the dispute) wish to bring their business judgment into settlement negotiations with the benefit of a thorough analysis of the case.　　　　　**18–071**

Contra-indicators against usage: It is not suitable where the case turns exclusively on issues of law or credibility. It is generally used for substantial cases and not for smaller disputes where the cost and time factors would not be warranted.　　　　　**18–072**

Neutral fact-finding expert

Availability in the United Kingdom: Although expertise is available through the Academy of Experts, other ADR organisations and from individual experts, this particular usage of experts is not yet common in the United Kingdom.　　　　　**18–073**

Summary of procedure: Neutral expert investigates legal or technical issues and submits a non-binding report.　　　　　**18–074**

Form of outcome: Non-binding report that helps parties to reassess their positions. It may assist the court if it is agreed to be so used without being definitive.　　　　　**18–075**

Role of neutral: Neutral expert has an initial function of investigating into　　　　　**18–076** technical matters and reporting to the parties jointly. If parties require, the neutral's role can then change to a facilitator of negotiations between them.

18–077　*Indicators for usage:* Suitable for cases with technical issues that would benefit from neutral expert appraisal and reporting. Kinds of issues include patent infringement, medical or other professional negligence, product liability cases and other technical matters.

18–078　*Contra-indicators against usage:* Not appropriate where there are no technical, scientific or specialist issues requiring expert involvement, nor where witness credibility is crucial and would render technical appraisal irrelevant.

Ombudsman

18–079　*Availability in the United Kingdom:* Ombudsmen have been appointed in relation to certain specific fields of activity.

18–080　*Summary of procedure:* An aggrieved person makes a complaint to the ombudsman, who investigates and deals with it, for example by making a public criticism, making issues public and sometimes, in limited circumstances, awarding compensation.

18–081　*Form of outcome:* The outcome is limited by the prescribed powers of the individual ombudsman. Commonly the outcome takes the form of publicising injustice or maladministration

18–082　*Role of neutral:* Independent person appointed by the state or by quasi-official body or organisation; deals with complaints by the public against administrative and organisational injustice and maladministration in certain specified areas.

18–083　*Indicators for usage:* Grievances and public complaints in certain specified fields of activity, for example local authorities, financial services, legal services and conveyancing.

18–084　*Contra-indicators against usage:* Only available for certain limited kinds of issues. Not a substitute for resolution of grievances through the courts and other tribunals or organisations.

4. RESERVING RIGHTS WHILE USING ADR

18–085　Where parties decide to deal with their issues through a binding adjudicatory process such as arbitration, they will invariably do so on the basis of waiving their right to have these issues determined by the court by way of litigation.[16]

---

[16]The court may nevertheless assert the right to deal with the dispute notwithstanding an agreement between the parties to accept arbitration. See Chap. 20.

Where, however, parties use a non-binding, consensual form of ADR such **18–086** as mediation or the mini-trial, they will implicitly or explicitly have reserved their rights to have the matter resolved by adjudication, whether litigation or arbitration, in the event that no agreement is reached in the non-binding process. This would be similar to the position in relation to without prejudice settlement negotiation. That is fundamental to the ability of parties to use a non-binding method, otherwise there would be the absurd position of parties losing their right to have the issues determined by adjudication, but unable to compel others to resolve the matter by agreement.

A reservation of rights applies even where parties hope to use an ADR **18–087** process as a complete alternative to litigation. The knowledge that litigation may follow if agreement cannot be reached is inherent in the non-adjudicatory ADR process, and serves as a sanction against unreasonable non-co-operation. The existence of the court and its rulings as a backdrop to settlement negotiations has led to the use of a phrase which effectively sums up the position, namely that parties bargain "in the shadow of the law".[17]

An interim injunction does not preclude referring a case to an ADR **18–088** process any more than the issue of a writ would. Pressing claims and protecting positions formally on the one hand, and seeking consensual solutions on the other hand are by no means mutually exclusive. On the contrary, where robust action may require parties to pause and re-examine their respective circumstances and the possibility of stepping away from the brink, ADR offers them the machinery for doing so.

It is a matter for individual decision in each case whether formal **18–089** proceedings should be suspended or continued while ADR processes are pursued. The following factors are relevant:

- *Whether there are time constraints affecting the case, such as limitation being imminent, or a hearing date approaching.* If limitation is a factor, a party may decide to serve proceedings to protect the position, perhaps even by agreement with the defendant, or the parties may specifically agree in writing (and perhaps under seal) to suspend the operation of the limitation period for an agreed time in consideration of the agreement to engage in ADR.[18] As far as hearing dates or other deadlines are concerned, these may be kept in place as a spur to the negotiations, or they may be adjourned where considered appropriate.

- *Potential prejudice.* If the case is at an early stage where there would be little or no prejudice to a party to suspend proceedings while the ADR process takes place, that may indicate suspension. If, however, a party wished to maintain a momentum, the ADR procedure may need to be structured around a timetable that allows the case to continue in the meanwhile. There are natural delays in the litigation process, for example after statements of case have been filed and a trial date is

---

[17] Mnookin and Kornhauser "Bargaining in the Shadow of the Law, The Case of Divorce" 88 Yale L.J. 950 (1979).

[18] See CEDR research paper RP2 (1991) by William Marsh for a discussion paper on limitation of actions.

fixed and awaited, during which ADR processes can be used without creating delay and without a need to agree on suspension.

- *Creating a settlement-conducive climate.* While a deadline may impel negotiations, settlement prospects may also be enhanced by the creation of a climate favourable to exploring agreement. This may be achieved in various ways, for example, encouraging the parties to approach the process in a constructive and creative way. An agreement to suspend proceedings while the ADR process is under way can help in this respect.

- *The cost factor.* The saving on costs is often one of the considerations in favour of settlement, and it may be helpful for the parties to agree to suspend formal action and keep costs to a minimum while ADR is in progress. Other factors may, however, override the cost savings consideration.

5. TIMING OF ADR USAGE

18–090   ADR processes can be used at virtually any stage of a dispute, between the first glimmerings of disagreement and the hearing of an appeal against judgment given in a case. Indeed, an Appellate Mediation pilot scheme is being conducted in England, in which parties submit the issues to mediation while the appeal is pending.

18–091   There can be distinct advantages in bringing ADR processes into play at an early stage of a dispute:

- Issues can be nipped in the bud. Also, where appropriate, for example in a continuing relationship, early remedial action can be jointly considered and agreed. There is greater scope for damage limitation.

- The parties may not yet have established themselves in positions that they believe they have to defend. The longer parties uphold a position, the more entrenched they tend to become. Consequently, there is greater scope for a creative and flexible problem-solving approach if ADR is used early on.

- Legal costs, if any, will probably still be at a relatively low level and the potential savings may be greater than if the process is used closer to a trial.

18–092   Because of these advantages of early intervention, some contracts provide for the appointment of a neutral mediator, adjudicator, disputes adviser or disputes review board. In the construction industry there has been an increasing trend to provide for informal dispute resolution procedures, rather than merely to rely on formal processes. Such a notion of "intermediate dispute resolution" allows the neutral to deal with issues as they arise using whatever informal procedure may be considered most appropriate, and falling back on either arbitration or on a less formal adjudication if the parties cannot reach agreement through any consensual procedure.

A neutral dispute review board in a construction project may be appointed   **18–093**
at the commencement of the contract, and will ordinarily be fully informed
about it and kept up to date with developments as the project proceeds.[19] It
will meet informally at fixed intervals, perhaps with site inspections, briefings
and round-table discussions, and will consider disputes as they arise,
requiring explanations and particulars as necessary. Such a board may
represent "the most positive prospect for a good, well-managed construction
engineering process that will provide some kind of equity to both parties".[20]
The rights of the parties to proceed to a formal adjudicatory process such
as arbitration would not be overridden by the existence or actions of
the board, but many interim issues could be resolved. Even if some
issues needed to be adjudicated upon, there would at least be an interim
process to regulate the parties' actions pending the outcome of the
adjudicatory process.

There are, however, also some disadvantages in trying to resolve matters   **18–094**
through ADR processes at too early a stage of the dispute:

- Elements of the issues may not yet have properly crystallised, and
  attempts to resolve them may be premature. For example, the
  implications of a course of action may not yet be clear or the extent
  of damage or loss may not have been established.

- There is a view that until statements of case have been filed and
  documents exchanged through the disclosure process, it might be
  premature and unsafe to commence ADR proceedings. There is,
  however, an alternative view that the issues can be informally stated
  at an early stage, and that a preliminary bundle of essential documents
  can easily be assembled.

- Sometimes settlement discussions may not succeed because they take
  place too early in the dispute. Parties going through the adversarial
  process who experience some of its delays, costs and uncertainties,
  often begin "cooling off" and become more receptive to the
  possibilities of settlement. This follows the view that there is a time
  when a dispute becomes ripe for attempts to settle it, and that trying
  to do so too soon may be less effective.

These factors militate in favour of using ADR later rather than sooner. On   **18–095**
the other hand, however, the adversarial system may have different effects:
while sometimes it may be seen as softening an opponent, it may on the
other hand achieve the contrary, and attitudes and positions may harden.
Costs will have increased, and may sometimes be a further impediment to
settlement. If any remedial action was possible in relation to the issues, it

---

[19] See the paper by Kenneth Severn "Progressive Mediation in the Construction Industry" in
  Alternative Dispute Resolution, Euro Conferences Limited 1991. See also the section on
  Contractual Adjudication in Chap. 4.
[20] In the Channel Tunnel project a panel of five members was established, with a permanent
  president who selected two of the four other members. Parties could refer issues to this panel,
  which was required to make a decision within 90 days. See the paper by Jack Lemley, Chief
  Executive of the Channel Tunnel Consortium, "Dispute Resolution Provisions in International
  Construction" in *Alternative Dispute Resolution*, Euro Conferences Limited 1991.

might have had to be unilateral rather than agreed, and damage limitation may not have had maximum effectiveness, thus widening possible differences.

18–096   There is no standard ideal time for mediation or other ADR processes, as much depends on the circumstances of each case and the readiness of the parties to engage in the process. As a general principle, it is probably better to engage in the process sooner rather than later. There is no reason, however, why ADR should not be used at any time right up to the trial of an action, and indeed the imminence of an approaching trial date can act as a positive impetus towards using ADR.

ADR processes are settlement-facilitative and help to break down barriers to settlement. They can therefore be used at any time when either party would like to try to settle, and perhaps sooner than might be thought possible in the traditional system.

6. CAUTIONS AND RESERVATIONS ABOUT ADR

18–097   ADR assists with the process of dispute resolution, but is not a panacea that will remedy all the ills, actual or perceived, of litigation. Indeed, there are circumstances when ADR processes would be inappropriate, or in which ADR forms, once commenced, might need to be discontinued. Sometimes they should be employed only with the utmost circumspection. ADR practitioners need to be alive to the cautions and reservations applicable to ADR processes, so that they can be employed only when they are proper and appropriate.

18–098   Reservations about a concept do not discredit it, but rather allow healthy and open debate to take place. Confronting reservations and concerns about the principle or detail of ADR and its individual processes is necessary and important if it is to develop and continue to mature.

Are settlements necessarily preferable to adjudication?

18–099   The view that settlement is a desirable outcome to litigation is prevalent among most lawyers, based on their experience of the litigation system and its costs, risks, delays and uncertainties.[21] ADR processes are largely based on this premise of helping disputants to find better, more efficient and expeditious ways of arriving at settlement

18–100   A school of thought in the United States and the United Kingdom, however, questions the premise that settlements are necessarily to be preferred to litigation. In essence, and with some variations, the criticism of the settlement process, and therefore implicitly of ADR processes, which assist settlement, is that settlements are not necessarily preferable to resolution of disputes by adjudication. On this view, people should be encouraged to use an adjudicatory approach rather than be deterred from it: they should not have their rights to obtain the decision of the court eroded by alternative means of dispute resolution.

---

[21] See Chap. 22 for the public policy consideration that it is in the public interest for disputes to be settled and litigation avoided.

So, for example, Professor Lon Fuller, an American academic, suggests, **18–101** broadly speaking, that disputes should generally be resolved by the adjudicatory processes of the courts, and that mediation, while it may sometimes be helpful, is the antithesis of a rule-based system of law. In his opinion, where an underlying relationship is best organised by "impersonal act-oriented rules", mediation is generally out of place and should not be used except to create or modify rules. He considers that mediation is wholly inappropriate in some situations, such as where more than two parties are involved.[22] Professor Fuller takes the view that adjudication should be the standard instrument of dispute resolution in a society regulated by laws, and should be seen as a form of social ordering. One of Professor Fuller's criticisms against mediation is that "it is all process and no structure".

Another American academic, Professor Owen Fiss, also considers that the **18–102** courts should be more effectively used, and has expressed the view that settlement is not a desirable end to a dispute, being often coerced and lacking in justice, especially where there is an imbalance of power between the parties. He likens settlement to plea bargaining, and describes it as "a capitulation to the conditions of mass society and should be neither encouraged nor praised".[23] He sees civil litigation as necessary to achieve the ideal of bringing to the people "all that the law promises".

Professor Marc Galanter, without taking an "anti-settlement" position, **18–103** questions some of the arguments used in favour of settling rather than litigating.[24] He concludes that settlement, like litigation, is "not intrinsically good or bad" and suggests that more consideration needs to be given to tackling the dynamics of the various species of settlements and to trying to assure the quality of settlements. In his interesting article "The Quality of Settlements", he suggests that this is a task not only for the negotiators themselves, but also for those who intervene in them, for example mediators, as well as those involved in creating policy in this connection.[25]

Similar concerns have been expressed by a United Kingdom academic, **18–104** Gwynn Davis, in relation to the divorce process. He fears that the emphasis increasingly placed on settlement "could lead to an erosion of the parties' right to seek judicial determination". Parties may be placed under pressure, both through the courts and through the mediation process, to arrive at settlements by way of compromise, which may not be soundly based. He is troubled by the possibility that settlements are sought to minimise judicial determinations as "a form of rationing" and believes that the trial process itself needs to be transformed and made less alienating and less expensive, and that there should be more trials and less settlements.[26] He observes that "new approaches" may not be used to acknowledge the limitations of

---

[22]See, *e.g.* Fuller, "Mediation—its forms and functions" 44 S.Cal.L.Rev. 305 *et seq.* (1971). However, ADR has been used extensively and successfully for multi-party disputes: see Chap. 7.

[23]See "Against Settlement" by Owen Fiss, 93 Yale L.J. 1073.

[24]See Prof. Galanter's article "The Day After the Litigation Explosion" at 46 Maryland L.Rev. 3, pp. 32–37 (1986) in Murray, Rau and Sherman, *Processes of Dispute Resolution* (1989) pp. 46–49.

[25](1988) J. D. R. 55–84.

[26]His aspirations have since been largely achieved with the reforms that have taken place in the U.K. in the legal process.

professional expertise but "to extend the boundaries of professional dominance and control".[27]

18–105   The view that disputes should be resolved by litigation is not one supported by most lawyers, nor would their clients necessarily appreciate it. Such a view can be understood and would certainly be endorsed in relation to certain kinds of issues, such as those involving fundamental human and civil rights. It is, however, more difficult to sustain in the context of a legal system that allows individuals to resolve their disputes as they see fit. The fact is that litigation involves costs, delay, risk, uncertainty, anxiety, a serious potential for the escalation of hostility and results which are not always as satisfactory as those which might have been achieved consensually.

18–106   Other writers and practitioners have responded to the views outlined above. For example, Professor Eric Green has described Professor Fiss's views as "a bizarre mixture" of the "traditionalist" view of the courts, and the "adaptationist" view, which sees courts as adapting to current social needs "within the limits of due process".[28] Professor Green agrees with the principle that large, important public issue cases, relating for example to school desegregation and prison reform, are unsuitable for ADR. However, he distinguishes such cases from civil and commercial cases, which he suggests, can quite properly be dealt with by negotiation and ADR. Lewis D. Barr, in an article in the *Journal of Dispute Resolution* (Missouri)[29] analyses and responds to Professor Fiss's criticism. He takes the view that Professor Fiss's "virulent opposition" to alternative dispute resolution mechanisms may stem from his "misconception" that ADR proponents "make no effort to distinguish between different kinds of cases . . . (and that) they lump all cases together."

18–107   Any notion that there may be some kind of conspiracy to ration cases going to trial by pressurising people into settlements does not accord with the reality of the mediation process.

18–108   Acknowledging the benefits of mediation or other ADR forms does not question the value of adjudication. The litigation process has shortcomings and it is unsuitable for many cases; but it also has advantages. There are cases for which it is not only suitable but essential. This needs to be borne in mind at all times. People should not be made to feel that they have failed if they do not settle their dispute but prefer to have it resolved by adjudication.

18–109   Adjudication by the court needs to be distinguished from the whole adversarial legal system with the escalation of hostility that so often accompanies it. If adjudication could be achieved without that escalation, on the basis that parties have bona fide differences that they cannot resolve and that a neutral third party will make an informed, rational and principled decision for them, that might make the adjudication process more acceptable and less hostile. ADR practitioners can help parties to approach adjudication in this way in those cases where they are unable to reach a conclusion in the

---

[27]In *Partisans and Mediators* (1988) at pp. 12–13 and 202–210.

[28]See Eric Green's "The Complete Courthouse" (1985) in *Dispute Resolution Devices in a Democratic Society*, Roscoe Pound Foundation–American Trial Lawyers Association at pp. 58–59.

[29]"Whose Dispute Is This Anyway?: The Propriety of the Mini-Trial in Promoting Corporate Dispute Resolution" Vol. 1987 at p. 133.

ADR process itself and may be able to use the ADR process to discuss, narrow and define the real issues for adjudication.

Whatever view may be taken of the notion that litigation is preferable to settlement, Gwynn Davis's view that the adjudication process should be made more acceptable and less hostile must be right. Reforms of the system that achieve this end must be welcomed. **18–110**

ADR practitioners including those who also practise as litigation lawyers would not be able to function effectively if they subscribed to the view that settlements were to be avoided. It is essential, however, that practitioners should use ADR selectively, and should be aware of the situations in which ADR is not appropriate and when litigation should be viewed as the proper dispute resolution process. **18–111**

When non-adjudicatory ADR is not appropriate

It is not practicable to list the circumstances in which non-adjudicatory ADR is inappropriate. Practitioners need to have a constant awareness that situations may exist, arise or become apparent, in which attempts to achieve a consensual resolution are not suitable and the parties should instead be referred to adjudication. The following may be useful guidelines in this connection. **18–112**

ADR processes that depend on the parties reaching agreement with one another are inappropriate where a party lacks the necessary capacity to contract, for example being a minor or mentally incapacitated. (If representatives on their behalf conduct the process, it may be subject to such ratification by the court.) **18–113**

Cases involving issues of constitutional principle, civil rights or other matters of substantial public importance are generally unsuitable for ADR, and should invariably be resolved by judicial determination. There are some matters of public policy decision-making which may well be amenable to a form of public policy mediation,[30] but disputes where rights or principles need to be tested, clarified or affirmed should be taken to the judicial authorities for binding determination. **18–114**

Where parties need a binding decision enforceable as an order of the court or which has value as a precedent, litigation will be the proper way to proceed. ADR might be used if the agreed resolution can be made into an order of court by consent or in any other way serve the required purpose. **18–115**

Where either party's rights may be lost or prejudiced by using ADR, then it should not be used. If, for example, a limitation period is approaching or delay might prejudice a party, litigation might be needed. The parties might though agree to overcome the problem within the ADR format, such as by suspending or interrupting statute-barring, or by agreeing that a writ should be served and then the case held in abeyance. Injunctive relief may have to be obtained through the court; but having done so, ADR might not necessarily be ruled out. **18–116**

Where one party materially abuses the ADR process causing actual or potential prejudice to the other party, it would not ordinarily be appropriate for the process to continue. A failure by a party to negotiate in good faith **18–117**

---

[30] See Chap. 14.

may, but would not necessarily, be such an abuse; but it would be so if, for example, the party misled the neutral and the other party to try to gain an improper advantage, or it became clear that the party was using the process for delay or for any other motive without any real intention of achieving an agreed resolution.

18–118 Where a power imbalance between parties is so great that a fair agreement cannot realistically be reached between the parties, or where one party adopts and persists in maintaining an abusive, harassing or threatening approach making consensual resolution virtually impossible, the process should ordinarily be ended. However, there are some power imbalances in most situations and this is not itself necessarily a reason to terminate ADR.[31]

Effects of informal third party intervention

18–119 It will be apparent from the reservations outlined above that there is concern about the informal intervention of third party neutrals in replacement of the more formal, rules-based and reasoned decision-making process of the courts.[32]

18–120 Other writers are also concerned about the fact that third parties who intervene in a private dispute can change the relationship between the parties, as well as their expectations and the nature of the resolution of their issues, without being directly accountable or subject to question or appeal. This concern is expressed, for example, by Professor Simon Roberts who says that in the mediation process power over the outcome of the dispute may not pass to the parties in the way that is believed, because mediators may "profoundly alter the course of a simple bilateral exchange". By the intervention of the mediator, and especially if that intervention is directive or by a person of dominant rank or specialist skill, the parties' views may change through "arguments, choices and evaluations" that they may not have been aware of, and through pressure and persuasion. This power of the mediator is not open like a judge's, but covert and unregulated.[33]

18–121 Professor Roberts has consequently promoted what he calls "a minimal form of alternative intervention". Under this the mediator would establish and maintain contact between the parties, provide a forum for their discussions which the mediator would support neutrally, and stimulate discussion; and arguably also provide ground rules for the meeting, help the parties to articulate their issues, and identify available options. A mediator using this approach would not go beyond these functions.[34]

18–122 Mediators need to be alive to the potential they may have to influence the

---

[31]With regard to power imbalances, see Chap. 21.

[32]ADR's informality is part of the criticism directed at it. See *e.g.* Richard L. Abel, *The Politics of Informal Justice* (1982) who is concerned that disadvantaged groups may be diverted by informal processes from properly asserting their rights.

[33]See "Towards a Minimal Form of Alternative Intervention" by Simon Roberts in M.Q. No. 11 (March 1986) at p. 36. See also his article "Mediation in Family Disputes" in *Modern Law Review* (September 1983) at p. 550.

[34]In *Dispute Processes: ADR and the Primary Forms of Decision-Making* (1998) Professor Roberts and Michael Palmer say (at p. 126) that "even a minimalist mediator may influence the process of dispute resolution by characterising the issues in a certain manner, clarifying factual difficulties, encouraging the parties to consider various options and so on."

outcome of the dispute in which they have been asked to intervene. In this connection the following points may be noted.

A properly trained and skilled mediator should respect the need for the parties to retain power over the decision-making process and should not try to influence them away from their own decisions. In helping them to test whether their decisions were appropriate for them and workable, a mediator would need to bear in mind the effect that this could have on the decision-making process and must act with care and circumspection. A mediator might draw on his or her expertise or experience, but must not have a hidden agenda to provide any indirect form of persuasion. **18–123**

Parties may have inappropriate expectations. So, for example, if they want counselling, they should be directed to a counsellor. Similarly, if they require evaluation in a model of mediation that does not offer this, they need to be redirected to an evaluative model or process that can facilitate realistic settlements by having regard to rights as well as interests and concerns.[35] It would be extraordinary if parties in dispute could try to resolve that dispute bilaterally with the benefit of each having independent advice and expertise, but could not agree to bring in a neutral expert to help them to do so. ADR practitioners, however, have the potential to influence parties, and need to exercise their functions with care and integrity. **18–124**

Other reservations

ADR practitioners have themselves expressed reservations, in the course of improving existing processes and ensuring that any shortcomings are addressed. **18–125**

Questions have been raised about the notion of judicial officers entering the settlement arena. These doubts do not extend to their encouraging the parties to try to settle, which is a long-standing judicial prerogative, but rather to their actually mediating, even if informally, by meeting the parties and discussing proposals, options and suggested settlement terms. The concerns are that parties may feel coerced into settlement by the weight of judicial authority. The further concern is that if this does not result in settlement, parties may feel prejudiced by the judge knowing their positions or facts that might have emerged in these informal discussions. However, pilot schemes where district judges have been used as facilitators have been well received, where those judges would not hear the case if it was not settled.[36] **18–126**

An adjudicator may be given authority to try to settle a dispute without having to make a binding decision. So, for example, in Hong Kong, the Arbitration Ordinance allows the arbitrator to mediate and then to revert to the arbitral role in the absence of settlement.[37] In the United States, Judicial settlement conferences in state and federal courts, conducted by a judge who negotiates between the parties' lawyers, are common.[38] **18–127**

---

[35] See Chap. 16 for evaluation in ADR.
[36] See the Financial Dispute Resolution procedure in the Ancillary Relief Pilot Scheme, Chaps 3 and 10.
[37] S. 2B of the Hong Kong Arbitration (Amendment) (No. 2) Ordinance 1989.
[38] See Deborah R. Hensler, "Court-annexed ADR" in Wilkinson, *ADR Practice Book* (1990) at pp. 352–354.

18–128   Related to this question is the role of a person in some authority mediating, even if not the same person who will adjudicate later. This question arises, for example, in relation to the role of a court welfare officer who may subsequently prepare a report for the court if there is no agreed outcome. Concern has been expressed as to whether, if such a person mediates, he or she should be allowed to influence the court in any subsequent litigation. This question has been considered in the United Kingdom and the United States, and different views have been expressed.[39] Court welfare officers do not necessarily view their role as being quite so narrowly defined as having to choose between either assisting the parties towards a conciliatory approach or assisting the court by providing a report. They are alive to the tensions between these different approaches.

18–129   Questions have occasionally been raised as to whether mediators coming from particular professional backgrounds can sufficiently disengage from their usual disciplines in order to be able to function properly in the neutral, impartial role of a mediator. This question is directed at solicitors and barristers, steeped in the culture of adversarial proceedings and generally accustomed to adopting a partisan role; to psychotherapists and counsellors, whose background may incline them to view mediation in a therapeutic mode; to social workers, whose ethos may be feared as being too interventionist; and to any background profession which might be perceived as inconsistent with the principles of mediation.

18–130   These cautions also need to be noted. It would indeed be inappropriate for a lawyer mediator to bring a partisan mode into the neutral function as it would for a therapist mediator to have a hidden agenda for therapy. A social worker mediator should not to be unduly intrusive in the mediation; nor should a mediator of any other discipline import into the mediation practices that are inimical to the principles of the process. On the other hand, mediators invariably will properly and beneficially draw on their skills, expertise and experience gained in all aspects of their lives, including notably their occupational backgrounds where appropriate, in the interests of the parties and the effective resolution of their dispute.

18–131   Lawyers, therapists, counsellors, social workers and mediators from a wide range of background occupations are currently mediating successfully and effectively in Britain and elsewhere. The key to their doing so in a proper and effective way is closely linked to their training, translating their existing skills into a new mode. In this regard, the Law Society's Report on ADR comments that:

> " . . . solicitors, with their experience of litigation and negotiation, are generally able to adapt to ADR processes. That adaptation will involve learning how to apply their experience and skills differently, learning some new skills, principles and procedures, and 'unlearning' those ways which may be incompatible with the ADR mode. To this end, specific ADR training is generally essential."[40]

---

[39] See also, *e.g. Family Mediation* by Lisa Parkinson (1997) at pp. 69–70, and *Mediation: A Comprehensive Guide to Resolving Disputes Without Litigation* by Folberg and Taylor (1984).
[40] See the *Law Society Report on ADR* (1991) by Henry Brown for the Courts and Legal Services Committee, para. 11.6.

In those models of ADR that involve a summarisation of the evidence, **18–132** such as the mini-trial, the query is sometimes raised as to whether a sufficiently comprehensive or accurate picture can be obtained without the opportunity to test the quality of the evidence and the credibility of the witnesses. A summary can rarely be as effective for the purpose of completely testing evidence as a full-scale trial, so if a case turns solely on credibility, parties may well wish to go to trial. However, in all cases that settle before trial the parties do so without testing the quality of the evidence or the credibility of witnesses. Parties in ADR processes may actually have a greater opportunity to probe, challenge and question the other side than they are likely to have in bilateral negotiations. Ultimately, however, if a case is not appropriate for settlement, then it is likely to be similarly inappropriate for ADR.

One of the concerns periodically expressed about ADR is the extent to **18–133** which it is relevant where there is unequal bargaining power between the parties. There is a notion that the courts can more effectively redress any such imbalances than the informal ADR processes. Some inequality in power exists in almost every situation, yet that does not necessarily preclude parties from negotiating settlements, either bilaterally or in mediation or other ADR processes. The question of the balance of power is addressed in Chapter 21.

These reservations are undoubtedly not exhaustive, but they do serve to **18–134** show that, like litigation, ADR cannot be assumed to suit all cases and satisfy all needs. The issues raised are likely to generate further discussion and debate, and will serve to keep practitioners sensitive to the need to proceed with new processes with proper caution and circumspection.

7. TRIANGULATION

The notion that underpins triangular thinking is that of a third person having **18–135** to confront two others who are either united or in opposition. A third person may affect or relate to two others (whether united, conflicted or fluctuating) in different ways.

Triangulation: the pitfalls
Counsellors, psychotherapists and others who work with two parties will be **18–136** aware of the risk of triangulation during the course of their professional work. ADR practitioners need similarly to be aware of this risk. The issue of triangulation ties in closely with that of coalitions, which are formed through alliances between two parties against the third.

A coalition between an ADR practitioner and one party may happen **18–137** consciously, but more usually develops unwittingly. It must inevitably have adverse implications for mediator impartiality, and is likely to be damaging to the process and its effectiveness, as well as the perceptions of both parties. Practitioners must therefore be alive to the risk of being triangulated into a coalition, and the need to avoid this conscientiously.

Coalitions may not necessarily be long term. A brief alliance could happen, **18–138** for example, where something is said that results in one party giving a knowing glance at the practitioner. For that unspoken moment, there could be an alliance between the mediator and that party. This can be difficult to avoid, but the mediator needs to understand what is happening to prevent this from developing into a pattern.

18–139   Dealing with triangulation does not mean that the mediator should never support one or the other party on specific issues. Rather it means that any support should be even-handed, and with a clear basis of impartiality. Also, it should be noted that triangulation can occur even within a larger framework, for example where two people out of three within a group of four develop a coalition (so there can be triangulation even within co-mediation).

Triangles: the benefits

18–140   The introduction of a third person to adjudicate the issues between two people (such as a judge or arbitrator) constitutes a form of triangulation. This is, however, a beneficial intercession in the sense that the parties cannot resolve the matter themselves and the third party will make a decision for them to end the problem.

18–141   In the same way, the intercession of a neutral mediator turns a dispute between two people into a beneficial triangle. The mediator brings skills and impartial facilitation into the picture, assisting the parties to deal with issues that they have been unable to resolve by way of bilateral discussions.

18–142   Edward de Bono has initiated the term "triangular thinking".[41] He uses this where a third party helps the disputing parties to create a design for the resolution of their issues. He argues that parties to a dispute usually cannot undertake problem-solving themselves simply because of the nature of conflict situations and because they are not generally trained in lateral thinking and the problem-solving mode. For this reason he believes that a third party role in conflict resolution is essential. For him, the third party is not merely a go-between, but an active participant in the creative process of designing appropriate solutions (in what he calls the "design idiom").

Triangulation: balancing advantages against risks

18–143   ADR practitioners bring a positive third party force into situations where two people are stuck and unable to sort out their own issues. That third party element can become damaging if instead of being used impartially it is used in alliance with one of the parties against the other, however unwittingly.

18–144   That requires a practitioner to be sensitive to the risk and problem of triangulation. If it has occurred or there is a perception that it might have done, the practitioner may need to address this in some specific way. This might be simply by taking particular care to avoid the occurrence; or it might be necessary to discuss this with the parties (though obviously with care and sensitivity). In situations that are more serious, it may perhaps be met by introducing a co-mediator. These issues can, however, be avoided by maintaining an awareness of the danger of being compromised by being drawn into a triangular coalition.

---

[41] In *Conflicts: A Better Way to Resolve Them* (Penguin Books Limited, 1985).

CHAPTER 19

LAWYERS' ROLE REPRESENTING PARTIES IN MEDIATION

1. INTRODUCTION

This chapter considers how lawyers can best represent their clients in mediation. Similar principles will apply to representing parties in other kinds of non-adjudicatory ADR processes.

19–001

Representing a client in mediation does not change the lawyer's basic duty to act in the best interests of the client. There are, however, differences in the way in which that duty can most effectively be carried out. First, the lawyer must have regard to the fact that the client has chosen to try to resolve the dispute in a consensual and not an adjudicatory manner or forum. This necessarily means that the lawyer needs to be acquainted with the chosen process and to work within its rules and principles. Secondly, the client has selected an approach which requires if not an abandonment, then at least a suspension, of the adversarial mode of practice, with its related potential for the escalation of differences. Thirdly, results can be achieved for the client in a way that does not necessarily involve having to defeat the other side but rather by seeking solutions that are mutually beneficial, as far as this is possible. These all involve a difference of approach on the part of the lawyer.

19–002

On the other hand, each party will invariably still wish to achieve the best possible result in mediation, and strong positions and tough negotiations may well take place. The lawyer's task is to balance these competing requirements and tensions in a way that produces the best outcome for the client.

19–003

Differences between civil/commercial and family mediation

There are differences of both process and culture between civil/commercial mediation and family mediation, which will be reflected in the way that lawyers represent their clients in each field of activity.

19–004

So, for example, lawyers do not generally participate directly in family mediation, though they might do so in some circumstances. In civil and commercial mediation, on the other hand, they are more likely to do so as a matter of course. However, proposals arrived at in commercial and civil mediation are likely to be converted into binding agreements in the mediation. In family mediation, they will generally be non-binding until the

19–005

parties have had an opportunity to obtain independent legal advice outside the mediation and have thereafter agreed to be bound.

19–006   In this chapter, general principles and practice applicable to both fields will be stated. Differences between the two fields will be indicated where applicable.

2. DECIDING ON THE MEDIATION FORUM

19–007   Lawyers representing clients who are engaged in a dispute need to consider with their clients in what forum the dispute can most effectively and appropriately be addressed. It is no longer acceptable to assume that litigation will automatically be required, though this is inevitably the litigator's first thought.[1]

Is the dispute suitable for mediation?
19–008   To assess whether a dispute is suitable for mediation, some of the following questions may need to be considered:

- Is it essential to have a court order? Clearly, mediation would be inappropriate in cases where a court order is needed, for example, to create a binding precedent or to obtain an injunction regulating behaviour. Some issues, relating to constitutional rights or personal freedom, are not amenable to mediation at all. Sometimes mediation may be possible after or in conjunction with the obtaining of an interim injunction or a court order.[2]

- Is there a time-limit within which litigation must be started? If a claim has a statutory limitation period within which it must be brought, a lawyer may find it necessary to bring court proceedings to prevent the claim being statute-barred (time-barred). However, once limitation is interrupted, for example by the institution of proceedings, a choice of fora for dealing with the issues may again be available.

- Is the case being brought or defended for strategic reasons? Are there objectives that cannot be met through settling, such as attracting public interest or delaying the fulfilment of obligations? These are contra-indicators to mediation, though sometimes objectives such as these can be met through a mediated outcome.

- Are the issues capable of negotiated settlement? If so, one of the advantages of mediation is that it can accelerate the time frame for addressing settlement possibilities. The strategy of developing adversarial postures before being ready to negotiate is not always necessary or cost-effective.

- Does the dispute involve a past or present relationship that has broken

---

[1] Eric Green remarks that "If the only tool you give a person is a hammer, do not be surprised if all he can see are nails".

[2] For further consideration of the advantages and disadvantages of litigation, mediation and other dispute resolution processes, see Chap. 18.

down? This may be a personal, professional or working relationship. In such event, mediation is usually strongly indicated. Cases of this nature may for example include marriage or cohabitation breakdown, medical or any other professional negligence claims, partnership and shareholder disputes, construction disputes and breach of contract claims. However, mediation is also suitable for most other kinds of issues. It is merely that relationship issues tend to be particularly amenable to resolution by mediation.

- Are there any other indicators or contra-indicators to mediation? Factors that may bear on the decision include for example, whether the case turns exclusively on credibility. Where each party directly accuses the other of distorting the truth, it can be more difficult for them to find common ground on which to base a settlement (though pragmatism may rule and settlement terms may nevertheless be found). Where the issues are raw and recent, parties may not be ready to enter into negotiations to resolve them. Where parties want to find a solution quickly and economically, mediation must be a primary option.

What kind of mediation is required?

As will be apparent from Chapter 7, "mediation" is a generic term covering different ways of working, styles and approaches. Some thought needs to be given to what kind of mediation is required, in so far as choices are available. **19–009**

Parties and their lawyers need to know whether the mediator will try to facilitate a settlement based on the parties' interests and needs rather than their rights. In such event, the mediator will not express any view as to the merits of the issues, leaving it to the parties to obtain these views from their individual advisers. Purely facilitative mediation of this kind is very common. It does not preclude the mediator from challenging parties' perceptions, but the mediator would not indicate what his or her views were. **19–010**

Alternatively, the mediator may be one who introduces an evaluative element into the process. This could involve anything between a formal evaluation expressed to both or all parties, or, more usually, an informal evaluation expressed to either, both or all of the parties.[3] **19–011**

Parties may expect the mediator to give some indication of his or her views of the merits and might be disappointed to find that this was not done, especially if resolution is blocked by unrealistic outcome expectations.[4] Expressing views does however carry the risk that the mediator may then be suspected of bias in favour of one party. **19–012**

It may also be worth establishing in advance whether the mediator will, if asked, be willing to consider making settlement recommendations. Many mediators will not wish to do so. However, some commercial mediators, for example those appointed under the standard terms of the Centre for Dispute Resolution in the United Kingdom, will consider doing so, though usually **19–013**

---

[3] See Chap. 16.
[4] See the views expressed by some participants to the Central London County Court Pilot Scheme, who felt that some evaluation would be helpful. See paras 3–063 *et seq.*

only as a last resort if the mediation is being ended without an agreed outcome. Family mediators will almost always decline to do so.[5] Some mediators, for example those working under the aegis of the Solicitors' Family Law Association, will, however, undertake to inform parties if settlement terms that they are proposing would, in their view, fall outside the range that a court would order or approve. Parties remain free to agree such terms, but would do so on an informed basis and not unwittingly.

Does the mediator need to be an expert?

19–014   As indicated elsewhere, the most important requirement of a mediator is to be an expert in the mediation process. If a choice has to be made between process expertise or expertise in the subject matter of the dispute, then process expertise will always prevail.

19–015   It may, however, be possible to engage a mediator who has expertise in the subject matter of the dispute, as well as process expertise. That could be helpful, especially but not only, if any element of evaluation is expected. Although a competent general mediator of civil/commercial disputes could effectively mediate on a range of issues (as a competent general litigator could deal in litigation with a range of issues), some parties may feel more comfortable with a competent mediator with a specialist knowledge and experience in the field of activity of their dispute. However, mediation process expertise in one field does not indicate expertise in another: one would not, for example, expect a family mediator to undertake commercial disputes unless he or she was trained in both fields.

Commercial and civil disputes

19–016   So, for example, people involved in construction disputes are more likely to choose a mediator with specialist knowledge of the construction industry. A mediator with a background in engineering, architecture or surveying (a chartered surveyor or a quantity surveyor) might be required. Or the parties may prefer a lawyer with experience in dealing with disputes in the construction industry.

19–017   Similarly, there are specialist mediators in most civil and commercial fields of activity. These include, for example, mediators working in clinical (medical) negligence, intellectual property, disputes in the financial sector, shareholders' and family business disputes, computer software and other information technology areas, property disputes and many others.

19–018   Some organisations specialise in particular fields. The City Disputes Panel, for example, has mediators who specialise in substantial disputes within the financial sector. The World Intellectual Property Organisation (WIPO) offers mediators who specialise in disputes arising in relation to intellectual property issues. Other organisations, such as the Centre for Dispute Resolution, offer both generalist mediators and specialists in particular fields of activity.[6]

---

[5] But see the possibility for parties engaged in dealing with family issues to obtain a neutral evaluation outside the mediation, for example, from a private equivalent of the Financial Dispute Resolution procedure used in the Ancillary Relief Pilot Scheme. See paras 16–125–127.

[6] For a list (necessarily non-comprehensive) of some of the organisations offering civil and commercial mediation in the U.K. and various other jurisdictions, see Appendix I.

If legal expertise is required, for example where there are legal issues or implications, lawyer mediators may be appointed who have experience and expertise in the area of the dispute. **19–019**

Where the substance or complexity of the dispute warrants it, co-mediators might be considered. For example, a medico-legal issue might benefit from having a team comprising a doctor and a lawyer. Or an accountant and a lawyer might be appropriate as a joint appointment for a complex corporate dispute. **19–020**

Family issues

There are two different views about the relevance of the mediator's background expertise in relation to the mediation of family issues, including in particular those arising on separation and divorce. **19–021**

One view is that mediators who have an aptitude for mediation and who are properly trained, will be able to acquire sufficient generic skills to enable them to work effectively with couples.[7] On this view, mediation is a profession in which the mediator's background expertise (if any) is irrelevant. While therefore mediators may be drawn from legal, social work, counselling or other professions concerned with families, they may also be drawn from any other background irrespective of its relevance to family issues. Couples would not necessarily be aware of the mediator's background profession. **19–022**

The other view shares the conviction that mediators must be properly trained as such, but acknowledges the relevance and value of the mediator's professional background. On this view, family lawyers may mediate as part of their legal practices (or outside of them if they prefer), and bring their experience and legal knowledge to bear in the way they mediate. Similarly, counsellors, psychotherapists and others with experience and expertise in working with families, couples and children are recognised as bringing additional knowledge and awareness into the mediation process.[8] **19–023**

Even where the mediator has relevant background professional expertise, he or she would not seek to influence the couple as an "expert". This would be inappropriate on any view. Rather, the mediator could draw on his or her professional background experience to provide even-handed legal or other information to the couple, to help develop options, and to help couples check whether their ideas and proposals are effective, workable and (where appropriate) within the parameters that a court would approve. **19–024**

Parties and their lawyers may wish to consider whether they would prefer to have a family mediator with legal, counselling or other background professional skills and expertise. This may be especially relevant where the parties require "all-issues" mediation, namely dealing with the issues that arise on separation and divorce. These may include separation and divorce **19–025**

---

[7] National Family Mediation (NFM), which operates through services that employ mediators, tends to subscribe to this view.

[8] Family mediation organisations subscribing to this view include the Solicitors' Family Law Association (SFLA), the British Association of Lawyer Mediators (BALM) and LawWise, which trains many BALM mediators, and Professional Development & Training (PDT). The Family Mediators Association (FMA) also subscribes to this view, drawing its mediators from practising family lawyers, counsellors, therapists and other professionals with experience of working with couples or families.

arrangements, accommodation plans, arrangements for children and property adjustment, maintenance and other financial issues. They may also wish to ensure that the mediator subscribes to a mediation Code of Practice and is subject to an accreditation and regulatory regime provided or approved by a reputable mediation organisation.

3. ENGAGING THE OTHER PARTY IN MEDIATION

19–026   Mediation may be considered in either of the following circumstances:

- It may be a mandatory requirement, either stipulated by the dispute resolution provision in a contract or by a court rule or direction of a judge. Alternatively it may be quasi-mandatory for example, where parties are obliged to consider and in some cases try to use it as a prior term before an application for legal aid will be considered. In these circumstances, both or all parties are equally faced with the obligation, and neither is in the position of asking the other to mediate.

- It may be a voluntary, ad hoc decision by the parties after a dispute has arisen. In this event, it is likely that one party or their lawyer will first consider mediation and will test the possibility of mediating with the other.

19–027   This section will address the issues facing lawyers who may wish to suggest mediation to their counterparts.

19–028   In jurisdictions where the mediation process is reasonably well established, it may be unnecessary to have to explain it to the other side. Having observed this, the experience of many mediators in England, where civil and commercial mediation has been practised for around a decade, is that the majority of lawyers are still unaware of the details of the process. No assumptions can be made that they will fully understand what is being proposed, except in general terms. Awareness of the mediation process increases exponentially. It starts slowly, limited initially to a few proponents, then slowly widens over the years as more mediators are trained, more mediation is gradually undertaken and public, professional and judicial awareness increases. In England and Wales, court reforms have also influenced the growth of mediation and ADR generally.

19–029   Some lawyers are concerned that proposing mediation might send the wrong signal to the other party by implying too great a willingness to compromise. Inasmuch as mediation does imply some willingness to find a mutually acceptable solution, there would be little point in suggesting it if there were no willingness at all to compromise. In an evaluative model of mediation (and perhaps even in a purely facilitative model) it might however be worth suggesting it even if one is very confident of succeeding at trial, if only to allow the other party a graceful and low-cost opportunity to withdraw from the litigation. The conventional approach is to indicate that one is sufficiently confident in one's prospects of success to agree to a mediation. If there is no evaluation, the prospect of settling without some realistic compromise is less likely.

If parties are both, or all, willing to seek a compromise solution, which **19–030** certainly does not automatically mean "splitting down the middle" but rather trying to find a mutually acceptable resolution, then mediation can offer a real opportunity to find a settlement. It can be accompanied by expressions of confidence in one's case, in the same way that this is done when entering into bilateral negotiations.

Civil and commercial disputes

ADR organisations commonly have case managers who will provide **19–031** preliminary information to the parties about the process including timing, procedures, costs and other matters. If one party contacts an organisation, their case manager is likely to be willing to approach the other party to offer mediation, provide information and deal with any queries.

Organisations will usually also have panels of mediators, who might be **19–032** generalists or specialists. The case manager will help parties to select a short-list of potential mediators suitable for their dispute. The organisation will also arrange the venue and facilities, provide the framework for the mediation including its rules and agreement to mediate, and will deal with all necessary formalities and practicalities.

Parties choosing an individual mediator directly, rather than through an **19–033** organisation, will usually make a joint approach, because of his or her specialist experience or reputation. If only one party contacts the mediator, the mediator may be willing to contact the other party, but is less likely to wish to do so than an organisation's case manager, because a party contacted by an individual mediator is likely to be more suspicious of the mediator's neutrality. The mediator may though provide information and promotional material for both or all parties.

Family issues

Family mediation organisations in the private sector do not usually set up the **19–034** mediation, as commercial ADR organisations do. More usually, they will provide a mediator or list of mediators approved and regulated by them, leaving it to the parties to contact the individual mediator direct. It is then up to the parties and the mediator to discuss process and requirements, and to make the necessary arrangements direct.

In the voluntary sector, couples are more likely to contact a family **19–035** mediation service as such, rather than seeking out individual mediators. The service will then set up the mediation and make all the necessary arrangements. In either case, services and individual mediators are likely to have information and material helpful to couples in outlining the process and its attributes and explaining mediation rules and procedures. In some cases, information about the individual mediators will also be furnished.

4. UNDERSTANDING THE MEDIATION PROCESS

Mediators commonly and not surprisingly find that the lawyers representing **19–036** the parties are unfamiliar with the mediation process. It is the mediator's function and responsibility to explain it and to try to ensure that parties and their lawyers participate fully and effectively. It is consequently not essential for participating lawyers to be fully conversant with the process before deciding to use it.

19–037   It is, however, helpful for lawyers representing parties to understand the principles and procedures of mediation. This will enable them to use it to best effect, knowing when and how to adapt negotiations to the needs of each situation, to enter the problem-solving mode without necessarily having to concede individual advantage and to gain the maximum benefit from using the dynamic of mediator intervention.

19–038   As a device to assist in considering the process, this book divides mediation into three phases, covering ten stages. The first phase covers the procedures that apply before the substantive mediation starts. The second phase covers the substantive process. The third phase applies after the substantive mediation ends. This breakdown is used to explain both civil/commercial mediation and family mediation.

19–039   The fundamentals of mediation are outlined in Chapter 7. The stages applicable to all forms of mediation are dealt with in Chapter 8. Subsequent chapters cover mediating in different fields of activity: civil and commercial issues in Chapter 9 and family issues in Chapter 10. Distinctions between civil/commercial mediation and family mediation will be identified throughout this chapter where they are significant.

Phase One: Before the substantive mediation starts

19–040   The stages of this phase include selecting the mediation forum and the mediator, which has been addressed, agreeing the rules and procedures for the mediation and preparing for the mediation, including dealing with the documentation and preliminary exchange of information.

Agreeing the mediation rules

19–041   It is generally accepted that parties should enter into a mediation agreement before the process begins. This serves various purposes, including determining the ground rules that will regulate the mediation.

19–042   Lawyers for the parties should ensure that they have an opportunity to consider the agreement and to discuss it with their clients before either of them attends the mediation meeting. If they have any queries, these should be discussed and clarified with the mediation organisation or the mediator who sent the document to the parties. The parties may be expected to sign the agreement at the commencement of the mediation meeting, sometimes as a symbolic opening act, and that would be rather late for raising significant queries.

19–043   The agreement may usually also deal with practical matters such as confidentiality, mediation costs, time allocated to the process and complaints procedures.

Dealing with the documentation

Civil/commercial disputes

Two kinds of documents are needed for a civil or commercial mediation. The **19–044** first is a statement of each party's case. The lawyer in consultation with his or her client will usually prepare this. It will set out, in simple and non-legal terms, the relevant facts and issues, and each party's submissions. As it is a legally privileged document, it can also outline the party's thoughts and position regarding the "off the record" negotiations, if that is thought to be helpful.

If the mediation process is likely to include any element of evaluation, it is **19–045** likely that the written submissions will include an outline of the legal propositions and facts supporting parties' respective contentions. These should not, however, dominate the document. If the mediation model is entirely facilitative, legal propositions are less relevant, though parties are still likely to include them if only to inform the other side of their views and contentions. The statements may not always be relevant to the mediator's function, but may well influence the other party in the settlement negotiations.

The lawyers should establish from the mediator or mediation organisation **19–046** what length of statement is required, and what arrangements are to be made for exchanging statements. It is usual for one copy to be sent to the mediator and one copy simultaneously to the other party. Commonly this is done as a simultaneous exercise, rather than sequential.

The second kind of documentation is the creation of a bundle or selection **19–047** of documents relevant to the issues. Where possible, the parties through their lawyers should try to agree a common bundle of documents, ensuring that copies of these are furnished to the mediator and to one another.

The bundle of documents does not have to follow the selection or **19–048** disclosure process that would be used in traditional litigation. It is not necessary to include every document that could possibly have some bearing, nor is it essential to disclose documents that a party thinks may be prejudicial. Selection is based rather on including documents that my clarify the position or persuade the mediator (in an evaluative process) or the other party (in any event) that a party's case has merit.

If parties cannot agree on a common bundle, each party may prepare their **19–049** own separate bundle, copying them by arrangement to the other side and the mediator.

Where a case is pending in the court or in an arbitral or other adjudicatory forum, the mediator may wish to have a set of the court or arbitral documents, or at least those that outline the respective cases such as statements of case. Lawyers should check this with the mediator or mediation organisation.

Because civil/commercial mediation is conducted within a specified time **19–050** frame, usually consecutive hours or days, all necessary documentation should be exchanged before the mediation starts, or should be available at the mediation meeting. Occasionally a party may show a mediator a document on a confidential basis. The mediator should respect this in the same way that the confidentiality of a remark would be respected. Once the mediation is under way, it may not be practicable for supplementary documents to be obtained.

Family issues

19–051   It is usual but not invariable for family mediators to obtain preliminary information from the couple before starting the mediation. Most commonly, this is done by sending each person a standard form to complete and return. This form provides basic information about the parties and any children, and about any other relevant matters such as an initial indication of the status of their relationship, their financial circumstances and their legal representation. It can also serve as an initial step in the process of screening for domestic abuse.

19–052   Parties and their lawyers should be aware that this preliminary information form may well be disclosed to the other party, as many family mediation organisations will not maintain separate confidences, at this stage in any event[9] Addresses and telephone numbers may however be confidentially maintained.

19–053   Unlike civil/commercial mediation, a bundle of documents would not be prepared at this preliminary stage. Documents tend to play a smaller part in family mediation, and are more likely to be limited to supporting financial disclosure, by agreement, during the course of the mediation. As family mediation is usually undertaken through a series of meetings held at intervals, there is more opportunity to discuss what documents are needed and to arrange for them to be furnished for a later meeting.

19–054   Where property or other financial issues are to be dealt with in the mediation, a detailed financial disclosure is generally required. This is, however, usually discussed and arranged during the mediation rather than required in advance of the initial meeting.[10]

Preparing for the mediation

19–055   Differences between civil/commercial mediation and family mediation become increasingly apparent during this stage. In the civil/commercial process, lawyers will often attend the mediation meeting, which is fixed for as long a block of time as is needed. Extensive preparation is accordingly required. In the family process, however, lawyers are unlikely to attend the mediation, which in any event, is likely to be spread over a number of meetings Legal preparation is accordingly less relevant, though some preliminary discussion between lawyer and client is useful.

Preliminary lawyers' meeting with mediator

19–056   In some cases, the mediator may hold a preliminary meeting with the parties'

---

[9] Special confidentiality rules may in some cases be agreed if the mediator conducts separate meetings with each party. See Chap. 10.

[10] The experience in England of trying to obtain detailed financial disclosure before the first meeting has not been good. Couples generally need time to meet the mediator, discuss the process and talk through the question of financial disclosure before being asked to provide detailed and sometimes complex financial particulars.

lawyers. This may take place in civil/commercial cases if the mediator thinks it would be useful, or in family cases though this is rare.[11]

The preliminary meeting may serve a number of functions: **19–057**

- It allows the lawyers an opportunity to form a preliminary view about appointing the mediator to deal with the matter (if this has not been firmly done)

- The mediator can explain the process and deal with any procedural queries or concerns.

- The mediator and the lawyers can discuss and agree procedural aspects such as preparing and submitting the parties' statements and a bundle of documents, and the mediation timetable. In family mediation, they may be able to agree on the way in which financial disclosure and particularisation (if required) can be made.

- In those civil/commercial cases where the lawyers will be attending the meeting, the mediator can outline what kind and length of presentation is expected at the hearing. The lawyer usually makes this presentation, but it may alternatively be done or supplemented by the party personally.

- It may be helpful for the lawyers to give the mediator a preliminary sense of the issues and the parties and to outline any relevant personal or business considerations.

Preparation of civil/commercial cases

In a conventional bilateral negotiation, the more strongly lawyers can present **19–058** their clients' case, the greater the prospect usually is of achieving satisfactory settlement terms. The more concerned a party becomes about prospects of success in the event of a trial, the greater the likelihood of that party making concessions to achieve a settlement.

In the same way, the better able a party is to persuade the mediator and **19–059** the other party of the merits of his or her case, the more likely it is that the outcome for that party will be positive. This signals a need to prepare carefully and thoroughly for the mediation, with an ability to demonstrate on facts, law and any technical aspects reasonably good prospects of success at a trial.

The lawyer will be expected to prepare and present his or her client's case **19–060** competently and effectively, perhaps having to condense considerable material into a relatively short time. An experienced American litigation lawyer who acts as a mediator and an advocate for parties to mediation considers that "skimping on preparation for a mediation is myopic."[12] In view of the high percentage of cases that settle in mediation, he questions "what better quality time" could be spent than in preparing for what will

---

[11] In some jurisdictions, however, preliminary meetings involving lawyers in family cases are more common. Landau, Bartoletti and Mesbur describe this process from a Canadian perspective in their *Family Mediation Handbook* (1987).

[12] See Randall W. Wulff's article "A Mediation Primer" in Wilkinson, *ADR Practice Book* (1990) at p. 124.

probably be "the most important event of the case". Another senior U.S. mediator who works with JAMS/Endispute and as counsel to a law firm, Dina R. Jansenson, points out that "mediations are less formal than arbitrations or hearings, but they require no less preparation. Not only should the client be thoroughly prepared for the mediation, but every statute, case deposition transcript and document supporting the party's position should be brought to the mediation. For the mediation to work, you will have to be forthcoming. The more information you are willing to divulge, the more likely the mediation is to succeed."[13]

19–061   If the process involves any element of evaluation by the mediator, a lawyer will want to present and substantiate the case as fully and competently as possible to maximise the prospect of obtaining a positive evaluation, so as to achieve the best possible result for his client. However, even in a purely facilitative mediation, proper preparation is essential as the mediator, though not evaluating, will carry messages, proposals and thoughts between the parties, and the sense of having a meritorious case is likely to be conveyed directly or indirectly.

19–062   This preparation and ability to argue the client's case is not inconsistent with the lawyer joining the mediator and the other party or parties in adopting a problem-solving approach to the issues. As observed in Chapter 6, there is an "essential tension" between a problem-solving approach that seeks joint gains, and a competitive approach that seeks the best outcome for each party individually.

19–063   As the mediation develops, the parties are likely to rely on their lawyers to advise them in relation to the negotiations and on possible settlement terms. The lawyer will need to be fully conversant with the facts, issues, strengths and weaknesses of the case to be able to assume an effectual role.

Preparation of family cases

19–064   As lawyers would not expect to attend family mediation meetings, except in special circumstances, and as there is no presentation of case or legal argument, the preparation for family mediation is very different from civil and commercial mediation.

19–065   In many instances, perhaps most, there is no preparation at all. The parties simply attend the initial meeting with the mediator and deal with matters over a series of meetings, obtaining legal advice and support from their individual lawyers from time to time as matters develop.

19–066   It is, however, good practice, and in many cases necessary, for a party to have preliminary advice from his or her lawyer before attending the initial mediation meeting. While lawyer mediators will in many cases be willing to offer legal information on an even-handed basis, this is not a substitute for each party being advised individually and specifically as to their legal position and rights. Awareness of rights does not mean that the party should not enter the process with a commitment to trying to resolve family issues in a reasonable and sensitive way. The lawyer's role at this stage is to give the client a preliminary understanding of the legal position and of the mediation

---

[13]"Representing Your Clients Successfully in Mediation: Guidelines for Litigators" in *The NY Litigator*, Vol. 1. No. 2 (November 1995).

process, to help support the client in the mediation. Further meetings are likely to be necessary as the process develops and especially as prospective terms of settlement are formulated.

Phase Two: The substantive mediation process

During this phase, the mediator will welcome the parties and the substantive mediation process will take place. In most models, the mediation will start with a joint meeting. In family mediation, this is likely to continue throughout the process, though in some circumstances separate meetings may take place. In civil and commercial mediation, it is usual for the parties to break into separate meetings and for the mediator to undertake shuttle mediation between them, after the conclusion of the preliminary joint meeting.   **19–067**

During the initial stage, the agreement to mediate will usually be signed, and the mediator will explain the process. In civil and commercial mediation, the parties will ordinarily be asked to make an oral presentation of their respective cases, but that is not usually done in family mediation.   **19–068**

Presentation of the case in civil/commercial mediation

Ordinarily, where a party is represented by a lawyer in the process, the task of presentation of the case will fall to the lawyer, although there is no reason why in appropriate circumstances the party should not personally present or support the case.   **19–069**

One of the key questions which a legal representative must consider in relation to any such presentation is: at whom is this presentation aimed? The answer to this will help to guide and inform the lawyer as to both the substance of the presentation, and its style and tone.   **19–070**

In adjudicatory processes, the primary object of presenting the facts and contentions is to persuade the adjudicator to make a determination in one's favour. Whether the concentration is on facts, law, technical aspects or equitable principles, the presentation will be focused towards the adjudicator, since that is where the decision making power lies. There may well be a secondary objective of persuading the opponent of the merit of one's case, especially if that may make the opponent more amenable to a reasonable settlement, but that is seldom the primary objective.   **19–071**

That focus shifts in non-adjudicatory forms of dispute resolution because the decision-making power does not lie with the neutral, but with the other party or parties. Certainly, the neutral retains a very important role in this connection. The mediator will need to understand the issues to be able to work effectively. The parties may feel that the mediator has a moral authority even if not determining the issues, and some parties may seek vindication of their position from the mediator. The mediator's role is especially significant if the mediation has an evaluative element. However, it is ultimately the other party who has to be persuaded by the presentation and by any supplementary argument.   **19–072**

The shift in approach from an adjudicatory process means that the presenter of the case, while addressing the mediator, will have a more   **19–073** complex agenda. He or she must present the argument in such a way that it is persuasive but not aggressively contentious. The aim is not only to persuade the mediator of the rightness of the case, but also to raise sufficient doubts in the mind of the other party to create a climate for negotiations in which the other party will consider making reasonable concessions.

19–074   The following practical observations may be helpful in formulating a strategy for presenting a party's case in mediation:

- In the adversarial forum the advocate's personal style and demeanour is usually of minor relevance to the outcome, since the judge or adjudicator can disregard this in making a determination; and an advocate may be expected to assume a contentious posture in the nature of adversarial proceedings. There must, however, be some risk that a pugnacious approach could be counter-productive in a non-adjudicatory forum where the parties themselves are going to have to arrive at their own resolution. This does not mean that the case should not be forcefully presented or that the strength of a party's views and feelings should not be made entirely clear. On the contrary, it is the advocate's duty to do so, and it is important that this is heard on both sides. Rather, it means that there must be an awareness of the effect that the presentation can have on the other parties. The object of the exercise is persuasion rather than belligerence, and exacerbating personal antagonisms by the content, manner or style of presentation is unlikely to have a beneficial effect on the process that will follow.

- A presentation is more likely to influence the other party if it is based on a version of the case which that party can understand and recognise, rather than a version which is contentious and perceived to be misrepresented. Of course, where there are substantial issues of fact and credibility, these cannot be ignored in the presentation. Even then there is scope for considering how the presentation can be effective, confronting those issues, yet maintaining an overview of the case that puts them into an understandable context. Differences may arise because the parties or the witnesses have good faith disagreements, recollections or perceptions; different technical opinions; values or ideas of fairness which do not accord with one another; miscommunications and misunderstandings. Presentations can be made in a context that allows and helps the parties to appreciate the possible validity of conflicting viewpoints.

- Consideration should be given to ways of supporting or enhancing the presentation, where appropriate. For example, the advocate may cross-refer to documents and correspondence in the bundle furnished to the mediator. Pivotal evidence may be outlined or a party may supplement the advocate's presentation. Technical devices may be used to help illustrate the case, such as flip-charts, audio-visual devices, slides, overhead projectors or the like (though it would be prudent to arrange this with the mediator in advance). Legal or technical references may be quoted and maps, plans, diagrams, schedules or other aids to understanding may be produced. In most mediations presentations will be substantially by way of summary of the case, in the nature of a lawyer's address to a court or an arbitrator; but there is no reason why they should necessarily be limited in this way.

- Because of the focused and abbreviated nature of the process, the approach by the lawyers to the presentations should be to concentrate on the main issues and not to diffuse energy, time or attention in dealing with peripheral issues or technical procedural points, which can be reserved if considered appropriate.

- Time-limits agreed between the parties or stipulated by the neutral should be observed as closely as possible, and time used efficiently and effectively by addressing the issues crisply, clearly and directly.

- It is unusual to have responses following the initial presentation. Most mediators prefer not to move towards the adversarial mode that this procedure would emulate. Lawyers should not expect or insist upon the right of response unless there is some special reason to do so. Usually there will be an opportunity to deal in the separate meetings with matters raised by the other side.

Presentations in family mediation

Unlike civil and commercial mediation, there is not usually a presentation of the case in family mediation. Nor is this an issue for lawyers, as they will not ordinarily attend the mediation meetings, save in certain circumstances. **19–075**

Family mediation is often said to be "future focused" so that the history of issues and grievances that arose in the marriage are not primarily addressed. Rather the mediator will help the parties plan for the future. However, it is sometimes essential to look at past issues, because they may contain the reasons for present positions and attitudes. Indeed, there is a view that it is essential to allow the past its space in working out the future. In either event, neither a lawyer nor a party will ordinarily be required to make a presentation as such in family mediation. Relevant past issues will emerge during the course of the mediation. **19–076**

In some situations, the parties' lawyers may attend a mediation meeting after the parties themselves have had some sessions, and perhaps if they encounter an impasse that the mediator thinks can best be addressed by having the solicitors present. In such event, the lawyers may sometimes be asked to give a brief outline of the position, as the solicitor sees it. This would require the lawyer to balance two competing priorities. The one is to present the client's case clearly and strongly, to show its merit. The other is to avoid being unnecessarily contentious, which may not help the negotiating process that will have to take place. **19–077**

Providing information

In civil and commercial mediation, relevant information is provided at the outset, through the written statement and the bundle of documents. The mediator may obtain supplementary information as the process develops. In family mediation, information is provided at different stages. Some is **19–078** obtained in the preliminary telephone conversations, some through the preliminary information form, some through more detailed financial forms, and some through documents that are provided and questions that are asked during the substantive mediation.

19–079   Dina Jansenson suggests that "mediation may not be appropriate for parties who do not want to reveal information for fear of tipping their hand, or who suspect that their adversaries are participating in mediation simply to obtain free discovery".[14] These are less likely to be concerns in the United Kingdom, where there is little to be gained from participating in mediation simply to gain advance sight of the documents that in any event will need to be disclosed in the adversarial process.

19–080   A mediator will also obtain information through probing questions and by observation of the parties.

Negotiating and communicating during the mediation

19–081   One of the strengths of mediation is it lends itself so well to the use of problem-solving approaches to negotiation rather than the purely competitive approaches which so often typify adversarial proceedings.[15] Where parties in bilateral negotiations may sometimes find it difficult, for tactical and personal reasons, to introduce a problem-solving mode into the discussions—though undoubtedly this is done in many cases—the intercession of an impartial third party makes this a more possible approach.[16]

19–082   On the other hand, parties do not easily or naturally fall into a mode of negotiating which may well be unfamiliar and which may not appear to serve their best interests. In fact, in some situations, there may be no scope at all for adopting a problem-solving approach, and a competitive approach may well result in the toughest negotiator achieving the best result. Consequently, the tendency will generally be to negotiate in the most familiar way. Where creative thoughts from the mediator or from any party allow the negotiations to assume a constructive direction towards an integrative outcome in which all parties can benefit, this will invariably be generally welcomed. Problem-solving and competitive approaches are however likely to co-exist within any ADR process, requiring a lawyer to be able to shift between them as necessary.

19–083   The fact that in mediation an outcome can only be achieved if all parties reach agreement obviously affects the way in which negotiations take place. There is less room for a brinkmanship approach (although at some point, where parties have genuinely reached their limits, they will adopt a "take it or leave it" position; and ultimately all bargaining takes place "in the shadow of the law").[17] The following points may be helpful in conducting negotiations and communications in mediation:

---

[14]See n. 13.

[15]See Chap. 6 "Negotiation"

[16]Edward de Bono in *Conflicts: A Better Way to Resolve Them* (1985) considers that certain functions, relating to "the design of an outcome" must be carried out by a third party. This is because he considers that the parties themselves, for practical reasons and flowing from the logic of their maintenance of opposing positions, generally cannot do so themselves.

[17]Mnookin & Kornhauser: see para. 18–087, n. 17.

- Even if using a competitive or positional negotiating method, lawyers should be aware of the problem-solving approach and should be willing to consider constructively with their clients any approaches that enable all parties to gain an advantage from a suggested outcome.

- When considering making settlement proposals, lawyers and their clients should examine these from the vantage point of all parties and not just their own. What is the incentive to the other party to accept the proposals? Can anything be added or varied to make the offer more acceptable to the other party without eroding any aspect that the client wishes to maintain intact? Is there any outcome that could bring gains to all parties? Are there any beneficial side-effects to resolving the dispute which could be incorporated into the proposals, such as the continuation or extension of an existing business relationship? A constructive and creative approach does not need to be at the expense of the client's best interests, and a problem-solving method can be mutually beneficial.

- It is usually unhelpful for a negotiator in ADR processes to bargain on the basis of "bottom lines" or "final offers" unless these are genuinely meant. The problem about taking positions is that it is often very difficult to move from them, and parties will not wish to lose face or to feel discredited by having to extricate themselves from a position that was previously reflected as immovable. Positional bargaining does not necessarily produce the best results, and parties may prefer in many cases to engage in principled negotiation aiming for a fair outcome using objective criteria.[18]

- The confidential separate meetings that a mediator may have with the parties in most models of civil or commercial mediation will provide a good opportunity for the parties and their lawyers to test settlement ideas and options in discussion with the mediator, without being committed to developing them. The mediator may be able, with the benefit of his or her overview and obviously within the constraints of confidentiality, to indicate whether a particular line of thought is helpful or not, or whether intended proposals might more effectively be structured in an alternative way. Negotiators should use this resource to maximum effect.

- Lawyers are likely to have a business-like relationship with their opposite numbers, sometimes cordial and sometimes belligerent, depending on personal and tactical circumstances. As to the lawyers' relationship with the other parties, they will not usually have direct dealings with them in the traditional processes, and a lawyer's attitude will be likely to reflect his client's perspective. In the ADR mode, similar conditions may apply, but the effect of the relationship may be more marked. Belligerence, derision, aggression or insults may provoke similar responses and set the whole process back. Courtesy,

---

[18]See Fisher & Ury, *Getting to Yes: Negotiating Agreement Without Giving In* (1981) and the discussion about this work and the various theories of negotiations in Chap. 6.

respect for opposing views even while disagreeing firmly with them, a willingness where appropriate to acknowledge the correctness of an opposing position and perhaps to shift one's own position, and the establishment of common ground can be of positive assistance in creating the climate for progress.

- A key element in successful negotiation is for the lawyer to have an understanding of and respect for his client's position, concerns and interests and for the client to trust the lawyer sufficiently to appreciate that the lawyer may sometimes need to give advice which the client will find unwelcome. That relationship can be as important for a lawyer as his negotiating skills. The lawyer will need to prepare for the mediation by analysing the case, understanding its strengths and weaknesses and expressing a frank and honest opinion to the client. Supporting the client does not involve taking an inappropriately optimistic view of the position, but rather identifying with the client's aims and concerns and trying to achieve the best result realistically and properly consistent with these.

19–084   The availability of the mediator can assist the lawyer in the task of helping the client to assess the position realistically. Where the client has reservations about the lawyer's advice, or perhaps where the lawyer is tentative about views that the client may not be happy to hear, the lawyer may raise such issues with the mediator in caucus in order to get the mediator's reactions to these. This may allow both the lawyer and the client an opportunity to consider and discuss the issue, with the benefit of the mediator's comments where the mediator is willing to give these.

19–085   Ultimately, while bearing these matters in mind, negotiators will be guided by their own experience, instincts and instructions to conduct effective negotiations, and will do so in their own individual styles. They will probe where they perceive weaknesses, will make judgments about the way in which their clients' proposals are made and the timing of them, and will draw conclusions from what is said to them and will react as they then consider proper. They will, in short, be themselves in the new forum, drawing on all the skills which they have, but aware that there are additional benefits that can be achieved by working more flexibly and creatively.

Strategies

19–086 Negotiators in the traditional process are likely to have a negotiating strategy of some kind, even if informal. They will know what their clients' aspirations are, what the other side's expectations are likely to be, how they envisage movement might proceed, at what point they will call off discussions and generally at what pace and in what direction they wish to move. The situation is similar in mediation negotiations, though the mediator's role and function may change the dynamic of negotiations.

19–087   The following points arise for consideration:

- Is it possible that either side is strategically using the mediation to achieve some gain that would not have been available in the traditional process? If this gain is mutual, then that would be acceptable and indeed a desirable part of the process. If, however, the gain is unilateral and arises from an exploitation or abuse of the process, then the opposing lawyer will want to guard against this, as will the mediator. Obviously, a plaintiff will be alive to the risk that the mediation may be used to delay litigation; and if this is a concern, then terms may have to be agreed, for example fixing a time-limit or arranging that court proceedings will run parallel to the mediation. Or if the concern is that a party may only wish to use the ADR process to establish how the case will be argued at the trial and not to engage in good faith negotiations, then this may affect the way in which the case is presented. Negotiations may be discontinued if there are no signs of bona fide movement.

- In mediation the mediator may invite the parties in the confidential separate meetings to indicate areas of concern, proposals for settlement and parameters for negotiation. The question arises: should the party tell the mediator his outer limits right away, even if restricting the mediator's authority to use that data, so that the mediator will be in a position to have an overview of settlement possibilities? Or should the party rather hold back on his true position, aiming for the best outcome and only easing gradually into improved offers as and when pressed by the mediator? There are no absolute answers to these questions. While co-operation with the mediator requires genuine negotiation, nothing requires a party to go to his most extreme position right at the outset. In practice, it is unlikely that parties will make their best offers initially, even if asked by the mediator to do so. A natural inclination must exist to test the process and the possibilities. If, however, in the judgment of the party and the lawyer, that party's best interest will be served by confidentially telling the mediator the best offer right at the outset, even if still controlling the pace at which that is released to the other side, that would be a matter of individual judgment. Of course, negotiations can develop their own dynamic, with new ideas emerging as time passes; so it would be understandable if parties moved slowly forward, waiting to see how far they needed to go, where time and other factors permitted.

- Mediation can be conducted relatively informally, and mediators are usually willing and sometimes keen to communicate as freely with the parties as with their lawyers. Consideration may be needed as to how far the client should play a leading role in the process and to what extent it is to be lawyer led. This decision will be based on a judgment as to effectiveness of the lawyer or the client leading the negotiations, which in turn will depend at least in part on the client's skill as a negotiator, the nature of the issues, and the relationship between lawyer and client. In many cases the lawyer will lead the negotiations, but this cannot be assumed in every case.

- Ultimately a decision will have to be made as to whether the result achievable in the mediation is acceptable to the client; and in case of doubt, whether the client should end it and turn to adjudication. That decision will be made on the basis of two analyses that will have to be made: one is to assess the client's best and worst alternatives to a negotiated outcome[19]; and the other is to analyse the client's realistic prospects of success in litigation. On the basis of those assessments the client, with his lawyer's assistance, can make a considered decision. In this, the responsibility of the lawyer is no different from traditional bilateral negotiations: to advise the client competently and professionally, guiding and counselling him as may be required.

The lawyer's role during substantive family mediation

19–088   After the lawyer has given preliminary advice to his or her client and the client has gone off to family mediation, there is likely to be a period of silence while the mediation takes place. Some mediators will write to the parties' lawyers as a matter of courtesy, and will be willing to discuss procedural matters but not substantive issues.

19–089   Family mediation takes place with the couple directly and the lawyers do not have a participatory role during this phase. That can feel uncomfortable for some lawyers, who are more used to controlling the process. They may feel anxious on their client's behalf, especially if the client is perceived as vulnerable and the other party as strong or manipulative.

19–090   In the early days of mediation, it was unclear what the lawyer's role might be while the client was engaged in mediation. There was, and sometimes still remains, some notion that if the client consulted with the lawyer between meetings, that might constitute an unwarranted and somehow unfair intrusion into the process. That is a misunderstanding of the lawyer's role. Perhaps the following principles might be more relevant to the representation of clients engaged in family mediation:

- Family mediation involves an element of personal empowerment of the parties by working with them individually and without constant recourse to their professional advisers. Lawyers will no doubt wish to respect that element, and allow their clients to formulate their own thoughts and ideas how to resolve their issues, as far as they may wish to do so.

- On the other hand, clients may not be choosing mediation in order to empower themselves, but rather to achieve the resolution of their issues in a fair, effective and expeditious way. They may wish to be supported by their lawyers through the process. In that event, lawyers have a duty to support their clients in achieving this.

- Lawyers should therefore be available to advise and support their clients as required through the mediation process. Some clients may wish to discuss matters between every meeting, and get guidance as it progresses. Others may prefer to consult their solicitors only as specific issues arise.

---

[19]See BATNA and WATNA in Chap. 6.

- Some mediators will recommend to the parties that both should get independent advice at certain points during the process. They should, however, leave it open to the parties to seek advice at any time, and not just when this is suggested to them.

- There are some important points at which the lawyer should be consulted. The first might be for a general indication of the position before embarking on mediation, and perhaps to consider whether mediation is appropriate. The lawyer might wish to explain the nature of the process to the client, and check whether this is what the client requires. The next important stage is usually the formulation of the financial disclosure form. Many parties complete this without getting legal advice, and generally that is satisfactory. However, parties should feel free to get advice from their lawyers on the completion of this document, especially if the form or their financial circumstances are at all complex.[20] Other stages may arise as specific issues are addressed; and a consultation may well be indicated when settlement terms are being formulated.

- Lawyers should bear in mind that their primary responsibility is to their client, and not to the mediation process. Of course, as their client has chosen that process and is committed to working in it, the lawyer should support and not undermine that decision. If, however, they believe that the process is prejudicing or damaging their client in any way, then they should be explicit in advising their client accordingly. Some way may need to be found to rectify the problem so that the process can be more effective and fair. In the final analysis, they may need to suggest to the client that the process is inappropriate and should be ended.

Lawyers are often uncertain whether it is proper for them to communicate **19–091** with the mediator about any issues concerning them or their client while a family mediation is pending. They might be uncertain about the propriety of writing to the mediator. This is not surprising, since mediators do not readily welcome communications from lawyers, especially if they concern matters that the party might have raised personally at a mediation meeting. If there is any aspect that a lawyer feels should be introduced into the mediation, it is ordinarily preferable for the client personally to do so. If, however, the issue feels too sensitive or the client feels unable to raise it, then it may well be necessary for the lawyer to communicate with the mediator direct. It must though be borne in mind that this may have to be on a non-confidential basis, and that any such communications may well have to be shared with the other party. An exception would be if this was done pursuant to an agreement between the parties that the mediator could have separate and confidential

---

[20] In some courts in England, a complex form, Form E, is now used. This is to be extended nationally. See the Ancillary Relief Pilot Scheme in Chap. 3. Lawyers should probably assist their clients in completing this form especially if it becomes more widely used in mediation, as it is in the traditional process. Also, where finances are complex or substantial, or where maintenance may depend on how the expense lists are formulated, independent advice may be indicated.

communications with each party, which is sometimes agreed in the context of caucusing.

19–092   Lawyers may be invited to attend mediation meetings, though this is unusual and generally occurs only in an impasse between the parties or where a lawyer has advised at the end of a mediation that proposed terms are unacceptable. In such event, the lawyer should check with the mediator what is expected of him or her at the mediation meeting. A short, non-contentious presentation might be required, or the lawyer might just be invited to support the client without having a dominant role. If separate meetings are to be conducted, these may follow the pattern of separate meetings in civil and commercial mediation, save that special confidentiality rules might need to be agreed.[21]

Phase Three: After the substantive mediation

Drafting and formalising

19–093   At the end of the mediation, if total or partial resolution is achieved, some record of the terms will have to be prepared. In civil and commercial mediation, it is generally regarded as essential for a note of the agreement to be signed before the parties leave the meeting. The usual object of this is to have a binding document executed as part of the process. In family mediation, it is usual for the mediator to prepare the record of the terms after the parties have left the meeting, and to send it on to them for consideration. In this case, parties would not ordinarily be bound until they have had the opportunity of taking independent legal advice on the proposed terms.

19–094   The drafting of the settlement agreement in civil and commercial mediation will either be done by the mediator, in which event the role of the parties' lawyers is to check and approve the draft; or more commonly it will be left to the parties' lawyers to draft the necessary documentation. In the latter event, the mediator will usually have a supporting role, perhaps providing notes and comments, and checking drafts as they are prepared.

19–095   The settlement agreement must be drafted with care and precision, even if it is informal in style: the parties have just resolved a dispute and will not want to have any later arguments or misunderstandings about the terms of settlement.[22]

19–096   The following checklist may be helpful to a lawyer drafting the settlement terms:

- Check that the terms of settlement are understood and agreed.

- Are the terms to be binding immediately? If not, when and under what circumstances do they become binding?

- Are the terms unconditional? If not, what are the conditions applicable to them: these need to be clear, specific and unambiguous.

---

[21] See paras 19–081–087.

[22] See Appendix II and the framework precedent for a civil or commercial settlement agreement.

- Are all dates, periods, amounts, methods of calculation and other directions and formulae clear, specific and unambiguous?

- What are the consequences of non-compliance with the settlement agreement? Do these need to be specified?

- Check the terms of the Agreement to Mediate. Does it specify any terms which may be relevant to the settlement agreement (for example, as to consequences of non-compliance)? Do any such terms need to be varied or reflected in the settlement document?

- What format is appropriate for the settlement agreement? A formal document, heads of agreement, a letter of agreement, a deed or some other?

- Do the parties envisage that a further and more comprehensive document will be entered into later, perhaps to be amplified and drafted by counsel? In such event, what is the status of the document meanwhile being entered into? What will the effect be if no such further document is executed?

- Is an order of the court required? If so, are its terms to be drafted and agreed immediately or will this be done later, and with what consequences if there is a later problem in relation to the drafting and finalising? Who will deal with the formalities of getting the order made?

- If proceedings are pending in any court, is the settlement agreement clear as to what is to happen with such proceedings? Are they to be discontinued? Is there any agreement as to costs?

- If an existing relationship is to continue, is this on the same terms as at present, or are these to be varied, and if so, are the new terms clear and explicit?

- Does confidentiality need to be confirmed or is this already explicitly covered? Are there any special requirements as to confidentiality of the settlement terms?

- Are there any aspects that involve a neutral third party role after execution of the agreement, such as acting as a stakeholder? Are documents to be held in escrow or items to be retained pending completion? Is there to be any supervision by the mediator? Do these need to be provided for in the agreement?

- Does the agreement need to specify which country's laws are to apply to the construction of the settlement agreement or to any aspect arising from it? Do the parties wish to submit to the exclusive or non-exclusive jurisdiction of any court? Or provide for arbitration or any other form of adjudication if any further disagreement arises? Or for further mediation?

- Will the parties be executing the agreement in personal or representative capacities? In the latter event, do the signatories have the necessary authority?

- Check draft agreement with other parties, lawyers and mediator before finalising.

19–097　　The role of the lawyer in finalising and formalising any settlement arrived at in mediation is similar to the role where the parties have arrived at an agreement following without prejudice bilateral negotiations. However, the mediator adds a significant resource in helping with the drafting and in overcoming any obstacles to finalisation.

Vetting family mediation proposals

19–098　　One of the principles of family mediation is usually that parties will have the opportunity before finalising any agreement to take independent advice from their solicitors about the acceptability or otherwise of the proposed terms. For this reason, agreements as such are not reached in family mediation (in England and Wales in any event), but rather a concept of mutually acceptable proposals, which are subject to independent advice.

19–099　　To enable parties to obtain such advice, the mediator will usually prepare summaries that each party will take, in identical terms, to his or her own lawyer. These summaries should comprise an open statement of financial particulars (where there are financial issues for resolution) with such supporting documents as might have been considered appropriate, and a privileged summary of settlement proposals, commonly known as a Memorandum of Understanding.

19–100　　Where the lawyers have been involved in the mediation from an early stage, the proposed terms should not come as any surprise, and the lawyer should be able to advise on them without difficulty. It is to be hoped that in such circumstances, the lawyer would be able to support the client in agreeing the proposals. Obviously, there could be circumstances where a lawyer, despite having been involved throughout, does not feel able to do so.

19–101　　It is generally more difficult for a lawyer who has had little or no role in advising the client during the mediation, who is faced with a client expecting the lawyer to endorse the settlement terms. The difficulty is twofold. Firstly, the lawyer has not had the benefit of working through the process and understanding the reasons for the terms having been arrived at. A good mediation summary will help to explain these reasons, but this can at best only be in abbreviated form. Secondly, the lawyer has legal responsibility for the terms, and might be liable in negligence if he or she allowed the client to enter into disadvantageous terms; yet the lawyer could well be regarded as obstructive or "spoiling" if he or she advised against agreeing such terms.

19–102　　Despite any such difficulties, the duty of the lawyer is clear. It is to advise fairly and effectively on the proposed terms and to draw attention to any deficiencies. The client will often be able to explain why certain terms were accepted, and the lawyer will no doubt wish to respect decisions that are well considered. There are, after all, many reasons for agreeing terms that may be perceived as less than ideal, and many parties have found themselves doing so "at the doors of the court". A client may choose to accept terms in the face of advice that better terms might be achieved in court. Lawyers may wish to protect against negligence claims by recording their advice in writing, as they would do in similar circumstances in traditional negotiations.

The whole point of deferring the finalisation of agreements to allow parties   **19–103** to seek independent advice is to give them a genuine opportunity to review their proposals. In most cases, these are confirmed; but where a lawyer believes that they should not be confirmed, that should be readily accepted as part of the process. Many mediators will invite parties to return to mediation for further discussion if either lawyer considers the proposals inappropriate. Some will also invite the lawyers to attend, if that is thought to be helpful. Having lawyers vet proposed terms is the safeguard built into the family mediation process, and lawyers should not shy away from challenging terms where they are patently inappropriate or out of order. Equally, they should where possible and appropriate support clients who have gone through an arduous process and who have arrived at terms that they wish to accept.

CHAPTER 20

JURISDICTION, FORUM AND LAW

1. ADR JURISDICTION

20–001   In traditional litigation, the courts obtain their jurisdiction from legislation, from rules made pursuant to such statutory provisions and from the concept of inherent jurisdiction. Non-adjudicatory ADR processes, however, depend largely on the agreement of the parties for their authority, though sometimes this is derived from mandatory procedural requirements that parties should attempt consensual processes before seeking adjudication.

2. AUTHORITY ARISING FROM STATUTE

20–002   It is easier to make statutory provision for dispute resolution processes that produce binding outcomes than for processes that are consensual and depend on the agreement of the parties to produce a binding outcome. The reason for this is that although machinery can be provided for a consensual process, people cannot be forced to reach an agreement if they do not want to do so. Consensual processes may not necessarily result in an agreed outcome, whereas adjudicatory forms will necessarily produce a result in every case.

20–003   Furthermore, procedures for adjudicatory forms are easier to prescribe. Consensual processes vary and generally involve greater participation in the process by the neutral practitioner than adjudicatory processes. Consequently, the skill, style and approach of the neutral can play a greater part in the process. For legislators, adjudication can be more easily regulated, whereas mediation and other consensual ADR is more difficult to control and regulate.[1]

20–004   ADR (including, for this purpose, adjudicatory forms) based directly or indirectly on statutory provisions may be divided into the following categories:

- Compulsory binding arbitration of relatively minor disputes imposed

---

[1] Regulatory bodies do try to regulate the mediation process, but they run the risk of over-controlling it, inhibiting creativity and flexibility in the interests of maintaining uniformity, without necessarily achieving better outcomes.

440

by the Civil Procedure Rules 1998 I/CPR/26..6. In this case, the arbitrator will be a district judge or other court official.

- Statutory arbitration, arising under various different English laws.

- Court-annexed (or court-ordered) arbitration.[2] This kind of arbitration is not at present available in the various jurisdictions operating within the United Kingdom.[3] Whether the arbitrator's decision is binding on the parties, or whether it is initially non-binding but can become binding under certain circumstances, and what rules or limits to jurisdiction will apply in relation to such arbitration proceedings, will depend upon the model of court-annexed arbitration provided for by the statute.

- Voluntary submission to binding arbitration by a judge of the Commercial Court.

- Arbitration in the United Kingdom under the Arbitration Act 1996. Although the procedures are governed by statute, amplified by common law and judicial precedent, arbitration requires the agreement of the parties in order for this procedure to be used. Once parties have agreed to arbitrate, either by way of general consent before any dispute has arisen or specifically in relation to a particular dispute after it has arisen, the arbitrator will have authority to consider the dispute and to make a binding decision. This is subject only to the discretion of the court to intervene in the very limited ways permitted by the Arbitration Act 1996, for example, under sections 67, 68 and 69.

- Private judging.[4] This procedure for the appointment of a third party neutral referee with various prescribed judicial powers requires specific legislation. It is used in certain jurisdictions such as California and Texas. It has not been introduced in the United Kingdom.

- Mandatory (court-imposed) mediation is stipulated in some jurisdictions in different parts of the world, for example in California, Texas and Florida,[5] the latter two covering not just family but also civil disputes. Australia has statutory mediation and court-annexed

---

[2] See Chap. 5 for a description of this process. In the U.S., it usually refers to arbitration by an outside arbitrator appointed by the court, not being a judge or court official, who hears the parties and makes a determination. If neither party appeals, the decision becomes binding. If either party appeals, the decision is non-binding and a fresh hearing takes place before a judge. There may be sanctions for seeking a further hearing and not achieving a better result. This form of arbitration has proved to be popular.

[3] As at the summer of 1999. Jurisdictions that use court-annexed arbitrations include many states in the USA and New South Wales in Australia, though there are indications that in the U.S. court-annexed arbitration is not as well regarded as court-annexed mediation.

[4] See paras 18–037 *et seq.* for a description of this process.

[5] California's Mandatory Mediation Act entered the California Civil Code as Section 4607 in 1981. It relates to issues of child custody and visitation (contact). For a detailed discussion of the California code, see the article by Lester Cohen "Mandatory Mediation: A Rose by Any Other Name" in (1991) M.Q. Vol. 9(1). Florida's court-ordered mediation is available not just in a family context, but for all civil matters. See Bruce W. Talcott's article "Court-Ordered Mediation in Florida" in (1989) 23 M.Q. In Texas, the Civil Practice and Remedies Code covers a range of ADR processes.

systems in a number of areas and courts.[6] Mandatory mediation can only oblige people to attempt the process. It cannot force them to agree. There is no mandatory mediation in England and Wales, though there is a requirement that conciliation must ordinarily be attempted in family disputes involving children; but this cannot be compelled.[7]

- Mediation may be voluntarily entered into, but then regulated by statute, rules and regulations. A number of jurisdictions, but not England and Wales, have enacted ADR legislation which does not compel parties to enter into those processes, (and certainly cannot compel them to use them effectively by concluding agreements) but which governs the way in which such processes are employed within that jurisdiction. For example, Hong Kong provides for conciliation within the arbitration ordinance[8]; and South Africa has enacted an ADR statute.[9]

3. AUTHORITY ARISING FROM AGREEMENT

20–005 Save where there is statutory or court-imposed provision for arbitration or mediation, ADR processes generally require the consent of all parties for the process to be used. In the absence of such agreement, litigation is the usual way for a dispute to be determined.

20–006 Agreement to engage in mediation or any other ADR process can be given before any dispute is envisaged, for example stipulated in a contract as a dispute resolution procedure to be used in the event of any dispute arising on that contract. Alternatively, it can be agreed in relation to a specific disagreement after it has arisen, that is, on an ad hoc basis.

Contract clause stipulating for ADR

20–007 Once a dispute arises in relation to a contract, there is commonly a tendency for the parties to assert their respective positions, with little inclination by either of them to suggest meeting with one another to explore creative and constructive ways of trying to resolve their differences. The usual reason for this disinclination is that neither side wishes the other to gain an impression of weakness which it is feared is how any suggestion of willingness to talk about the matter may be perceived. Consequently, both sides often feel they must pursue their respective positions through the adversarial process, even if

---

[6]For particulars of court-annexed processes in the U.S. and Australia, and developments in Canada and New Zealand, see Chap. 5 above and the references cited there.

[7]See the Practice Directions in Appendix II. Note, however, that there are requirements to undertake mediation in the family field as a prerequisite to being granted legal aid, unless a party falls within certain specified exemptions. This does not make mediation mandatory, but it has resonances to a mandatory regime.

[8]In Hong Kong the Arbitration (Amendment) (No. 2) Ordinance 1989 makes provision for the appointment of a conciliator and for a duly appointed arbitrator to act as a conciliator, within specified rules.

[9]The South African Act is the Short Process Courts and Mediation in Certain Civil Cases Act No. 103 of 1991. ADR practitioners in South Africa felt that the concept behind this legislation, fixing statutory rules for the conduct of mediation and appearing to limit it to minor cases, was inappropriate and untimely. Nevertheless it has remained on the statute book.

privately they may hope for an opportunity to be able to discuss settlement without having to indicate weakness or to lose face.

Of course, not all disputants respond with this concern, and there are many **20–008** who are well able to initiate a settlement discussion without loss of face. There are reports that an increasing number of disputants are responding with a mature approach to addressing problems and disagreements by discussion instead of immediate threat and action. It remains, however, a sufficiently common phenomenon to merit seeking some way to overcome this reservation about opening communications.

One way to obviate this problem is to insert in the initial contract a **20–009** dispute resolution clause, which either side can invoke without any suggestion of weakness or lack of confidence. This offers machinery for dealing with disagreements at an early stage before the parties become too entrenched in their respective positions.

Such a clause may be limited to providing for arbitration instead of **20–010** litigation. In such event, while this transfers the dispute into an arbitral forum, it does not address the problem of providing a way for the parties to discuss disputes at an early stage. To meet that need, the clause has to go further and to provide that parties are not to pursue arbitration until having endeavoured to resolve the issues through a stipulated non-adjudicatory ADR form.[10]

While non-adjudicatory ADR procedures are being engaged, all rights are **20–011** ordinarily reserved to revert to adjudication. If court proceedings need to be started or pursued in the meanwhile, this may well be done parallel to ADR. For example, it may be essential to start proceedings to avoid statute-barring by limitation, or injunctive remedies may need to be pursued without delay. In any such event, parties would ordinarily wish to protect their positions through court proceedings without necessarily precluding the possibility of trying to resolve matters through ADR; and their ability to do so would depend upon the terms and enforceability of the relevant ADR clause in the contract.

Arbitration clause

If there is an arbitration clause in the contract, parties will generally be held **20–012** to the arbitration procedure, and the courts will ordinarily decline to deal with the issues and require the parties to use the arbitration procedure that they have agreed upon.[11] In some circumstances the court may, however, override such agreement and nevertheless accept jurisdiction.[12]

An arbitration clause can take various forms. The principal requirements **20–013** are that the parties must commit themselves clearly and unconditionally to

---

[10]For arbitration and ADR clauses in contracts see Appendix II. See also *The Freshfields Guide to Arbitration and ADR: Clauses in International Contracts* (1993) by Hunter *et al.*

[11]Such a clause may but need not necessarily be in the form of a *Scott v. Avery* clause, which makes the award of the arbitrator a condition precedent to the right to litigate in the courts to enforce the rights under the contract.

[12]The court will do so where all parties agree that despite the arbitration clause, the court should deal with the matter. Where one party wishes to abide by the arbitration clause, but another wants to be released from it and prefers the court to adjudicate, the court will examine all relevant considerations and will decide whether or not to override the arbitration clause and to accept jurisdiction.

arbitration of the issues as stipulated in the clause and that the issues are arbitrable. If there are any limitations on the kinds of issues that may be so referred, this should be explicit. An arbitrator may be specifically identified, by name or by reference (such as a person nominated by the President for the time being of a stated professional body). If any system of law or institutional or ad hoc arbitration is to apply, that should also be stated (such as the rules and regulations of the International Chamber of Commerce or the UNCITRAL rules). If this is not done, the provisions of the Arbitration Act may apply where the parties are subject to English law and procedure. In international contracts, it is vital to provide for a venue.

20–014   For a specimen short form for arbitration, see Appendix II.

Clause for non-adjudicatory ADR

20–015   Where the parties wish to go beyond merely having an arbitration clause, and want to stipulate in their contract for a non-adjudicatory form of ADR, often but not necessarily mediation, they may use various alternative forms. Specimen forms are set out in Appendix II.

20–016   Clauses may reflect the sequence of process that the parties intend to follow to try to resolve any dispute. First they will usually negotiate, then mediate or undertake any other agreed ADR form, and if that does not succeed, then they will turn to arbitration. Of course, the initial negotiation provision can be deleted, and so can the concluding arbitration provision if litigation through the court is preferred. It is advisable to specify what form of adjudication is to be followed.

20–017   Dispute resolution clauses in contracts may be in a short form, just setting out the fundamental requirements. In this event, the commitment to the process is given and sufficient information to give the clause meaning, but procedural and other details are left for the parties or the neutral practitioner to resolve in the event of a dispute. Alternatively, they may be in a longer form, setting out procedural details and other relevant information in advance. Whether to use a short form or a long form is a matter of judgment. The advantage of the short form is that it makes simple provision for ADR, leaving it to the parties to work out and agree the details if a dispute arises. The disadvantage is that the detailed machinery is not settled, and it may be difficult to agree this later; also the less detailed the form, the less the prospect may be of having it enforced by a court.

20–018   On the other hand, a long form will minimise later scope for procedural disagreement and may enhance the possibility of a court treating it as enforceable. The disadvantages, however, are that the details may not necessarily be appropriate to the actual dispute when it arises; and trying to agree detailed dispute resolution provisions in advance, which may never arise in practice, rather than a general provision, may not be considered commercially desirable by parties when entering into a contract.

20–019   A further question arises as to whether or not it is necessary to provide specifically that a party is free to take formal action if this is for example necessary to prevent limitation, or seeking injunctive relief, notwithstanding the existence of an ADR clause. Arguably, this is inherently possible, notwithstanding the existence of a reference to ADR. In view, however, of a possible trend to try to enforce ADR clauses and to prevent litigation until they have been followed, it may be desirable, where appropriate, to insert such a provision for the avoidance of doubt.

Clauses in contracts need to be devised with due regard to the specific requirements of the parties. The model clauses in Appendix II are not intended to be comprehensive or exhaustive. They merely serve as specimens of the sort of clauses that are currently being used and need to be appropriately adapted. The following matters may be considered for such a clause[13]: **20–020**

- A description of the kinds of disputes and differences covered by the clause.

- Provision for the parties first to try to negotiate in good faith, using their best endeavours, perhaps with a time-limit.

- Provision for the dispute then to be referred to mediation or to some other ADR form, perhaps listing the other possibilities and allowing the parties to choose.

- If the name of the mediator or the organisation providing the mediation or other ADR services is agreed, this may be specified; alternatively, the machinery for appointing a neutral practitioner should be stated.

- The rules, regulations, procedures and/or code of practice that will apply to the mediation or other ADR form could usefully be specified, either in specific terms or indirectly, by reference, for example to an ADR organisation.

- It may be specified that the mediation or other process will be confidential, and any other terms relating to it may be indicated. If the parties agree that the process should be treated as without prejudice or otherwise privileged that should be stated.

- The clause can specify if the mediator is required to provide a report, opinion, recommendation or evaluation, which would be off the record and non-binding.

- The timetable for the mediation or ADR process can be specified, providing also for it to be extended or amended by agreement.

- Provision can be made, if required, for an obligation on the parties to negotiate in the process in good faith and to co-operate with the reasonable requirements of the mediator.[14]

- The clause can stipulate whether an agreement arrived at in the process is to be binding and if so whether it needs to be reduced to writing and signed by the parties, or any other such requirements.

- The rights of the parties can be reserved in the event that no

---

[13]See Precedent 8 in Appendix II.
[14]See Chap. 6 regarding the implications and efficacy of a commitment to negotiate in good faith.

agreement is reached. It can specify that parties are free to pursue formal steps if required to protect their positions and that this will not prejudice the continuation of the mediation.

- If the process does not result in an agreement within a specified period, to be extended or amended by agreement, the clause can specify the adjudicatory process that is to follow, for example, arbitration (or litigation).

- If the clause provides for arbitration, it may specify the name of the arbitrator or how or by whom such arbitrator is to be appointed and in international contracts the venue should be specified. It may also specify the rules of arbitration which are to apply and confirm that such arbitration is to be final and binding.

- The contract will usually stipulate which system of substantive law applies to the contract, but in case not, this may need to be specified in this clause.

ADR agreement after dispute has arisen

20–021 If parties in dispute have not agreed in advance what procedure is to apply to the resolution of their differences, then it will ordinarily automatically follow that their dispute, if it cannot be settled by negotiation between them, can be determined by the courts under usual litigation procedures.

20–022 However, parties are free at any time to agree to some alternative procedure for the determination or resolution of their dispute. If they wish to have it privately adjudicated on a binding basis, they may agree that it should be submitted to arbitration or to some other form of adjudication such as expert determination. If they first want to try to resolve it by agreement with the help of a neutral facilitator, they can agree to attempt mediation or any other non-adjudicatory form of ADR, while reserving their right to revert to litigation or arbitration if the consensual process is unsuccessful.

20–023 The form of an agreement to submit to arbitration after a dispute has already arisen will closely follow the form used to contract for arbitration. It will, however, need some adaptation to the actual requirements of the case.

20–024 The form of an agreement to submit to mediation or any other ADR process will also broadly follow the contractual forms discussed above. It will usually need to be more detailed, to include for example the agreed terms relating to confidentiality, privilege, timetable, whether or not agreements reached in the process are immediately binding, non-liability of mediator (if applicable), terms of payment of mediator's fees and various other such matters.[15]

20–025 Two specimen agreements are contained in Appendix II, providing for parties to enter into mediation after a dispute has arisen between them.[16] They will need to be adapted to individual requirements. A wide range of

---

[15]Contracts providing for mediation or other non-adjudicatory forms of ADR are more likely to be effective if these detailed terms are agreed in advance, either specifically or by reference to the standard terms of agreement or practice of a specified ADR organisation.

[16]The terms of contract may affect the mediator's professional indemnity insurance. The level of risk inherent in the terms on which the mediation is undertaken may affect the level of premium.

possibilities exists as to what matters may be covered by the agreement, whether to have a simple form and perhaps just append a code of practice, as to drafting style and as to the terms of engagement.[17]

4. JURISDICTION OF COURT TO OVERRIDE ADR PROVISIONS AND CONCLUSIONS

This covers two separate aspects: **20–026**

- whether and to what extent a court would either enforce or override a contractual agreement between parties that they will use an ADR process before instituting proceedings in court or through some other form of adjudication; and

- whether and to what extent a court would enforce an agreement reached by parties using an ADR process.[18]

Enforceability of ADR clauses in contracts

The enforceability of an agreement to mediate or to enter into any other kind **20–027** of consensual ADR process has not yet been tested in the courts of the United Kingdom. Mustill and Boyd point out that the court "has an inherent power to stay any action which it considers should not be allowed to continue" and that "this power could, in an appropriate case, be employed to deal with an action brought in breach of an agreement to arbitrate."[19] By analogy, it seems irresistible that the court must have a similar inherent power to stay an action brought in breach of an agreement to mediate.

It is clear that under English law an agreement to enter into negotiations is **20–028** not an enforceable contract. This was decided in *Courtney and Fairbairn Ltd v. Tolaini Brothers (Hotels) Ltd,* where Lord Denning M.R. said that it was "too uncertain to have any binding force".[20] After being followed in a number of subsequent cases, this decision was challenged in *Walford v. Miles* in the House of Lords, which, however, confirmed that "a bare agreement to negotiate has no legal content" and is unenforceable.[21] In that case, Lord Ackner also said that the concept of a duty "to carry on negotiations 'in good faith' is inherently repugnant to the adversarial position of the parties when involved in negotiations." This could be distinguished from an agreement "to use best endeavours" which could be enforced.[22]

It remains unresolved whether an ADR clause would be enforced by the **20–029** English courts if it were to specify a machinery for dispute resolution

---

[17]See Appendix II for some of the matters that could be included. Some mediators specify their agenda and timetable in detail, indicating the approximate time that they expect to spend on each stage of the process, that they require good faith co-operation from the parties and confidential disclosure of all relevant matters including strengths and weaknesses, whether or not evaluation is required and if so at what stage it will be provided, and various other practical matters.

[18]As to enforcement of agreements arrived at through ADR, see Chap. 21.

[19]*Commercial Arbitration* (2nd ed.) (1989) at p. 461.

[20][1975] 1 W.L.R. 297 at 301–302.

[21][1992] 2 W.L.R. 174, *per* Lord Ackner at 181–182.

[22]*per* Lord Ackner at 181.

covering mediation in the first instance followed by arbitration if necessary thereafter. If the ADR provision is clear, certain and reasonably detailed in its terms, and especially if it is an inherent part of a process which involves a stipulation for an eventual determination if the negotiation and mediation phases do not resolve the issues, there would seem to be no reason why a court should not regard it as being as enforceable as it would in relation to an arbitration clause.

20–030 When the English courts are faced with a question of the enforceability of an ADR clause, it is to be hoped that the approach set out by Lord Justice Kerr in the *Tubeworks* case[23] (a case of adjudication) will be followed. In that case Lord Justice Kerr approved and applied the principles enunciated in *Northern Regional Health Authority v. Derek Crouch Construction Co. Ltd*[24] in order to uphold and enforce the dispute resolution mechanisms upon which the parties had agreed.

20–031 In 1998, in the case of *Beaufort Developments (N.I.) Ltd v. Gilbert-Ash N.I. Ltd and another*,[25] the House of Lords overruled the Court of Appeals decision in *Northern Regional Health Authority v. Derek Crouch Construction Co.* Arguably, however, this 1998 decision did not undermine the principle that parties may agree on the dispute resolution machinery regulating their contractual relationship. Indeed, Lord Hope of Craighead observed (at 794) that "the whole question as to the extent of [the arbitrator's] powers rests upon contract. So it is necessary that the agreement should set out all the powers which he is to have in order that he may determine all the matters which are in dispute." He went on to say (at 799) that "...the Court of Appeal in the *Crouch* case, having started from the correct principle, fell into error in its application to the facts".

20–032 Other jurisdictions have addressed similar issues. Two Australian cases, *Allco Steel (Queensland) Pty. Ltd v. Torres Strait Gold Pty. Ltd*[26] and *Reed Constructions Pty. Ltd v. Federal Airports Corporate*[27] produced two different outcomes. In the former of these cases, the court decided that an ADR clause in the relevant contract, providing for the parties to try to resolve their dispute through ADR before litigating, was not enforceable. In effect, it was held that the parties were not bound to attempt ADR before litigating. However, in the latter case, *Reed Constructions*, where a differently formulated ADR clause provided for an arbitration procedure which included as one of the mandatory steps an attempt to mediate the dispute, it was ruled that the parties had to comply with the whole arbitration clause before litigation could begin.[28]

20–033 Some American courts have enforced agreements to submit to ADR procedures other than arbitration. In *DeValk Lincoln Mercury Inc. v. Ford*

---

[23]*Tubeworks v. Tilbury Construction Ltd* (1985) 30 B.L.R. 67.

[24][1984] 1 Q.B. 644; [1984] 2 All E.R. 175.

[25][1998] 2 All E.R. 778.

[26]Unreported, Queensland Supreme Court, March 1990: see paper by Justice Andrew Rogers "ADR in Construction Disputes: the Experience in Australia" to I.B.A. Hong Kong, Sep./Oct. 1991.

[27]Unreported, New South Wales Supreme Court, December 1988: see Rogers, *ibid.* n. 22.

[28]See also the article analysing the *Allco Steel* decision, "Alternative dispute resolution clauses: are they enforceable?" by Robert S. Angyal in the *New South Wales Law Society Journal*, February 1991.

Motor Co.[29] the court upheld a contract clause that required mediation before any litigation. In *AMF Inc. v. Brunswick Corp.*[30] the court held that an agreement to submit a dispute to a third party for an advisory opinion was enforceable under the Federal Arbitration Act[31]; and in *Haertl Wolff Parker Inc. v. Howard S. Wright Construction Co.*[32] the court upheld a provision requiring that disputes be submitted to a third party for a recommendation.[33]

It is questionable whether a party would necessarily seek to insist upon **20–034** any other party being compelled by law to enter into negotiations where the latter can effectively frustrate all attempts to resolve the matter by simply declining to agree to anything substantively. That raises the question whether in such event an ADR clause has any value at all. The answer must be affirmative. An ADR clause may well have legal effect. It certainly contains a moral and ethical requirement to comply with the terms of the contract in good faith. It has the practical value of providing an agreed machinery which requires the parties to seek a resolution, without having to examine this question afresh and perhaps either side being concerned that referral to a dispute resolution process might be construed as a sign of weakness. Furthermore, parties who have agreed to use mediation or any other ADR process to settle their dispute, if held to that commitment, may well find that it does indeed achieve that purpose. It should at least be attempted in order to give effect to the original intention of providing a means to avoid adjudication if possible.

5. ADR Forum

The notion of a forum in which a dispute is resolved is fundamental to the **20–035** traditional processes of litigation, in that without first deciding upon the forum there cannot be an adjudicator or rules governing the process. The parties may have agreed in their contract which forum would apply to the resolution of disputes. They might, for example, stipulate that "The Courts of England shall have exclusive jurisdiction to resolve any dispute or disagreement arising from or by virtue of this Agreement". Or they might provide that "All disputes arising in connection with the present contract shall be finally settled under the Rules of Conciliation and Arbitration of the International Chamber of Commerce by one or more arbitrators appointed in accordance with the said Rules. The venue of the arbitration shall be Geneva, Switzerland."

In the absence of agreement, whether private or by the application of a **20–036** convention such as Brussels, various factors may apply to the choice of forum for traditional litigation. Where there are competing claims, as for example where the courts of more than one country might arguably or in fact have jurisdiction, the forum will be the one which according to the relevant

---

[29] 811 F.2d 326 (7th Cir. 1987)
[30] 621 F.Supp 456 (E.D.N.Y. 1985)
[31] 9 U.S.C. <D188><D188> 1 *et seq.*
[32] U.S. Dist. LEXIS 14756 (D. Or. 1989)
[33] U.S. Dist. LEXIS 14756 (D. Or. 1989)

principles of law,[34] is judged to be the most appropriate: the *"forum conveniens"*.

20–037 In arbitration of international disputes, agreement on the venue is vital, for upon that choice may depend the enforceability of the arbitration agreement itself, the efficacy of the arbitral process and the ease of enforcement of any award. Increasingly, parties to international contracts do stipulate a venue. If they do not, then the venue will depend either upon the decision of any arbitral institution upon which the parties may have agreed or upon the decision of the arbitrator or arbitrators themselves who have been appointed. A court may become seized of the matter if, for example, one or other of the party seeks to enforce the arbitral agreement in a given jurisdiction and the court in question exercises supportive powers to give effect to the intention of the parties to arbitrate.

20–038 In ADR, the forum for the process is necessarily a matter for agreement between the parties. For this purpose, "forum" may mean the kind of process, the arena in which the ADR process is conducted, and the venue where this happens. This may have been agreed in the original contract. Where ADR is being agreed ad hoc, forum is obviously a matter to be considered. In practice, this will generally be inherent in the choice of process and its ground rules and the choice of the neutral or organisation undertaking the process.

6. APPLICABLE LAW

20–039 The use of ADR does not necessarily remove the need for the parties to know the substantive legal system within which they are operating, as it may be vital to their rights and obligations, which may differ under different systems of law, apart from the procedural implications of such system.

20–040 As to procedure, where the parties are using an adjudicatory form, the legal system of the venue may regulate such procedure, as for example applying the Arbitration Act 1996, rather than the arbitration laws of some other country. Where they are using a consensual, non-adjudicatory form, the legal system may be less relevant, as the process will often have its own procedures, which may not be dependent on the applicable legal system. The organisation or practitioner responsible for implementing the process is likely to have a set of rules and procedures, perhaps in the form of a code of practice or a contract. Nevertheless, the legal system may as a matter of public policy prescribe what kinds of procedures are permissible and enforceable, and so the system does always have a relevance even to procedure.

20–041 Parties may agree which country's laws will apply to their transaction, and it is commonplace for a contract involving international aspects, such as parties based in different countries or performance to cover different territories, to contain a provision stipulating which system of law is to apply to their agreement. This is quite a different matter from which court is to

---

[34]For a statement of the applicable principles of English law in such cases see *Spiliada Maritime Corp. v. Cansulex (The Spiliada)* [1987] 1 Lloyd's Rep. 1.

have jurisdiction to hear the case, or whether disputes are to be resolved by arbitration, and if so how and where. So, for example, the contract may provide for disputes to be resolved by arbitration under the rules of arbitration of the International Chamber of Commerce, the arbitration to take place in Geneva, and for the system of law applicable to the contract to be English.

If the parties to an ADR contract have not stipulated for an agreed system **20–042** of law, then if there is no international aspect and the parties are both or all in England and Wales, English law will generally apply; or if both or all in Scotland, Scots law. If, however, there is an international element, then the question as to which law applies to the provision for ADR will be resolved by the principles applicable to the conflict of laws. The factors that will primarily be taken into account will be the relevant international conventions and agreements, including those which affect Member States of the European Union in so far as these may be applicable, the countries in which the parties reside or carry on business, and the places where the terms of the agreement are to be performed.

CHAPTER 21

ETHICS AND VALUES, FAIRNESS AND POWER BALANCE

21–001 Providing impartial third party assistance in the field of dispute resolution or management raises a number of ethical questions for practitioners, which will be addressed under the following heads:

21–002 *Rules of underlying professional bodies:* Professional issues concerning dispute resolution practice may arise from the rules of a practitioner's traditional practice, for example, Law Society rules relating to solicitors who mediate or Bar Council rules relating to barristers who do so.

21–003 *ADR ethics and Codes of Practice:* Professional questions may arise in relation to the practitioner's ADR practice, whether arising from a code of practice or from ethical standards that should be inherent in any neutral dispute resolution practice.

21–004 *The practitioner's values, attitudes and beliefs:* These could affect issues of fairness, practice and ethical responsibility. What does "neutrality" or "impartiality" mean in this context?

21–005 *Fairness:* The question arises whether and to what extent a practitioner has responsibility for the agreement which parties may reach including responsibility for the fairness of its terms and for fairness of the process.

21–006 *Conflicts of interest:* The impartiality and the parties' perceptions of the impartiality of mediators and other practitioners are critical to the mediation process. Conflicts of interest, imputed bias and situations that suggest a lack of impartiality need to be avoided.

21–007 *Ethics of confidentiality:* This relates to the issues and dilemmas facing practitioners in dealing with sensitive information received on a confidential basis.

21–008 *Power imbalances:* This relates to the question whether, to what extent, under what circumstances and how a practitioner can and should deal with the question of power imbalances between the parties.

1. RULES OF UNDERLYING PROFESSIONAL BODIES

Professional organisations have rules and guidelines regulating the conduct of **21–009** their members in their professional capacities. Insofar as any dispute resolution practice may overlap the traditional practice of the practitioner, consideration may have to be given to ensuring that there is no conflict between the two sets of practices. For example, the Law Society regulates the way in which a solicitor may practise; and the basis on which the practice of mediation is permitted under the Law Society's rules and guidelines will be relevant to the concerns of a solicitor who also works as a mediator. Similar concerns will apply to all other ADR practitioners whose own traditional professional bodies may have rules that could affect their dispute resolution practice.

The legal profession is the main profession whose members engage in **21–010** dispute resolution, and the rules of the Law Society and the Bar will be considered. Other professional bodies may also regulate their members who engage in dispute resolution, and this may need to be checked.

The Law Society of England and Wales
General provisions

Before considering the specific rules of the Law Society which relate to **21–011** mediation, there is a general provision relevant to this subject, namely Rule 1 of the Solicitors' Practice Rules 1990 which reads as follows:

"Rule 1 (Basic Principles)

A solicitor shall not do anything in the course of practising as a solicitor, or permit another person to do anything on his or her behalf, which compromises or impairs or is likely to compromise or impair any of the following:

    (a) the solicitor's independence or integrity;
    (b) a person's freedom to instruct a solicitor of his or her choice;
    (c) the solicitor's duty to act in the best interests of the client;
    (d) the good repute of the solicitor or the solicitor's profession;
    (e) the solicitor's proper standard of work;
    (f) the solicitor's duty to the Court."

These general rules may apply in a number of ways. A solicitor has a duty **21–012** to ensure that any dispute resolution activities undertaken comply with the requirements as to integrity, independence and standards. When representing a client in traditional practice, he or she must also act in the best interests of that client, by being aware of all appropriate processes available properly advising the client about them so that an informed choice can be made.

The question arises whether it may be remiss, and possibly negligent, for a **21–013** solicitor not to advise a client about all relevant resolution processes. An analogy might be the failure of a solicitor to advise a client about the availability of legal aid in circumstances where it is available and could be appropriate. Whatever the strict legal situation may be, clients need their solicitors to be able to advise them on the whole range of processes available for their disputes, and not automatically assume that adjudication, and especially litigation, is appropriate. In some parts of the United States cases have been initiated against lawyers on the basis of their failing to advise their clients about the availability of alternative processes; but there is no information of similar claims yet having been initiated in the United Kingdom.

Specific mediation provisions

21–014 Law Society policy has developed significantly over a decade or so on the position of its members who wish to mediate.

21–015   Initially, in the mid- and late-1980's, there was some uncertainty about solicitors who mediated. Mediation was a new concept and the question was raised whether solicitors who mediated might perhaps be infringing the rule precluding them from acting for both parties to a dispute. To avoid this becoming an issue that might inhibit the practice of mediation by solicitors, the initial pilot scheme (Solicitors in Mediation) agreed with the Law Society that there would be no problem if solicitors did not undertake mediation as part of their practice as solicitors.

21–016   Solicitors mediating outside their practice are not allowed to refer to themselves in this context as "solicitors" and are not covered by their solicitors' professional indemnity insurance. The Law Society does not regulate them in their mediation practices, though it retains control over solicitors who fundamentally breach ethical rules.

21–017   After a few years, as the practice of mediation became more widespread and its implications became clearer, the Law Society reviewed the position. Solicitors pointed out that when mediating they were not representing or advising both parties and that there was no ethical dilemma. Solicitors had long adopted neutral roles that could be distinguished from their traditional advisory roles. In particular, they were able to act as neutral arbitrators within their practices as solicitors without breaching ethical rules. As a result of more considered reflection the Law Society had no difficulty in deciding that solicitors were free to mediate as a part of their practice as solicitors. That is clearly a correct decision and it remains its current policy.

21–018   However, by the time of that review, a number of family mediators were already mediating outside their practices, and the Family Mediators Association had been established on this basis. The Law Society's policy since then has been that solicitors may choose either to mediate as part of their legal practice or outside their practice as solicitors[1], as long as they make it clear to the parties, orally and in writing, of the basis on which they are mediating.

21–019   In a major further development, the Law Society decided to create specific requirements for solicitors who mediated as part of their legal practice. To this end, the following steps have been taken:

- The Law Society has stipulated that solicitors who mediate within

---

[1] This does not necessarily mean the law firm in which they work, but more generally, in their capacity as solicitors in legal practice. Solicitors may undertake work unrelated to legal practice, which they do outside legal practice and which is therefore not regulated by the Law Society.

their legal practice will be expected to undertake specific training in mediation.

- It has been through an extensive consultation process with family mediation bodies and training organisations to identify and publish a set of training standards that solicitors who mediate family issues in their practices will be expected to have followed.

- It has published a Family Mediation Code of Practice for solicitor mediators to observe.[2] This, too, has been through a process of consultation and of harmonisation as far as possible with the U.K. College of Family Mediators, to try to achieve a consistent form of code throughout England and Wales.

- The Law Society has also published a draft Code of Practice for civil and commercial solicitor mediators, which has similarly been subject to extensive consultation. It follows the format of the Family Mediation Code, but the differences from that Code reflect the differences in practice and culture between the two fields of practice.

The Law Society's Family Mediation Panel

The Law Society has expressed a commitment to regulating its solicitor members who mediate. To this end, it has taken steps to establish a specialist panel of family mediators, and is looking at the composition and qualifications of panel members. It proposes to establish confidence testing criteria, in consultation with other bodies including the U.K. College of Family Mediators and the Legal Aid Board. **21–020**

This is consistent with the Society's policy of creating specialist panels for solicitors working in specialist fields. The Family Mediation Panel joins, for example, the Family Law Panel, the Children Panel, the Immigration Panel, the Insolvency Panel and various others. **21–021**

Criteria for membership of the panel have not yet been finalised. The Law Society has appointed a Chief Assessor, with the power to appoint supporting assessors, whose responsibility will include establishing and implementing criteria and evidential requirements for panel membership. **21–022**

Provisionally, the intention is to have two-tier panel membership, following the broad approach of the U.K. College of Family Mediators and the (U.S.) Academy of Family Mediators. The first tier is intended to provide for those who work and have experience in family law practice and who have completed the designated training (General Members). The second tier is intended to cover those who have completed an accreditation process involving prescribed practice, consultancy, peer group and further education requirements (Practitioner Members). It is envisaged that mediators who have been appropriately trained and accredited by mediation organisations whose training and criteria are Law Society approved will be "passported" onto the panel. The Society's assessment team will assess those who apply independently of such an organisation. **21–023**

---

[2] The Code is reproduced in Appendix II at para. A2–046 *et seq.*

The Bar

21–024   The General Council of the Bar has not yet published any ethical standards specifically for barristers acting as mediators. Its view was that the standards applicable to barristers contained in the Code of Conduct would apply whatever their function, be it as barristers in practice or barristers acting in any part-time judicial function. However, changes have been taking place within the profession. An increasing number of barristers have been trained as mediators, and it is expected that ADR will be taught as part of the Bar Vocational Course. The Bar is accordingly reviewing its position on the Code of Conduct and it is probable that specific provisions for barristers undertaking mediation will be made in the near future.

The CPR-Georgetown Commission on ethics and standards in ADR

21–025   This project is an important part of the discussion concerning the role of law societies and bar associations in regulating those of their members who mediate as part of their law practices.

21–026   In April 1999 a Commission established by the prestigious U.S. dispute resolution organisation, the CPR Institute for Dispute Resolution and Georgetown University Law Center published a draft "Proposed Model Rule of Professional Conduct for the Lawyer as Third Party Neutral".[3] This was sponsored by them jointly and supported by the William and Flora Hewlett Foundation, which has financially supported many organisations and projects concerned with conflict resolution.

21–027   The proposed Model Rule addresses the ethical responsibilities of lawyers serving as third party neutrals and is designed to be incorporated into lawyers' ethical codes. It deals with the lawyer as mediator, arbitrator, evaluator or in any other neutral role and does not attempt to cover the lawyer's other roles, such as representing parties as an advocate in an ADR process.

21–028   This project relates only to lawyers, and does not address cross-disciplinary issues. Model Standards of Conduct for Mediators from different disciplines were agreed in 1994 between the American Arbitration Association (AAA), the American Bar Association (ABA) through its Section of Dispute Resolution (but apparently not yet ratified by the ABA Board of Governors) and the Society of Professionals in Dispute Resolution (SPIDR). Those AAA-ABA-SPIDR rules apply on a cross-disciplinary basis but according to the CPR-Georgetown Commission, do not adequately provide for the specific role of the lawyer as neutral practitioner.[4]

21–029   As the draft Model Rule points out at pages 3 and 4, "modern lawyers serve (these) values of justice, fairness, efficiency and harmony as partisan representatives and as third-party neutrals.... Contemporary law practice involves lawyers in a variety of new roles within the traditional boundaries of

---

[3]The Commission comprised 69 members, including prominent practitioners and academics such as its chair, Prof. Carrie Menkel-Meadow, Prof. Frank Sander, Prof. Nancy Rogers, James Henry (founder of CPR), Hon. Wayne D. Brazil of the U.S. District Court in San Francisco, Michael D. Young of JAMS/Endispute and Michael K. Lewis of ADR Associates in Washington D.C. It included members of law firms such as Irell & Manella; Milbank, Tweed, Hadley & McCloy; Latham & Watkins; and Skadden, Arps, Slate, Meagher & Flom.
[4]See p. 2 of the Proposed Model Rule draft of April 1999.

counselors,[5] advocates and advisors in the legal system. Lawyers now commonly serve as third party neutrals, either as facilitators to settle disputes or plan transactions, as in mediation, or as third party decision makers, as in arbitration.... When lawyers act in neutral, non-representative capacities, they have different duties and obligations in the areas addressed by this Rule than lawyers acting in a representative capacity."

There has been a continuing debate over whether mediation constitutes the practice of law and articles have been written from both viewpoints.[6] The Model Rule provides ethical guidance without seeking to resolve this controversy.

21–030

The main aspects covered by the proposed Model Rule are:

21–031

- *A requirement for diligence and competence.* Diligence recognises that while settlement or resolution is the main goal of most processes, the outcome rests with the parties and a lawyer-neutral should not coerce or improperly influence a party. In an adjudicative or evaluative capacity a lawyer-neutral should exercise independent judgment and be guided by judicial standards of diligence and competence. As to competence, a lawyer-neutral must only accept an appointment if he or she has sufficient knowledge and skill regarding the process and subject-matter to be effective. Factors relevant to such sufficiency include the parties' reasonable expectations, the complexity of the matter, the lawyer-neutral's ADR experience and training, legal experience and subject-matter expertise, ability to prepare and feasibility of employing experts or co-neutrals if appropriate.

- *The need for confidentiality.* ADR confidentiality is "distinctly different from lawyer-client confidentiality" and the extent of the protection provided by it "can be determined by contract, court rules, statutes or other professional norms or rules".[7] The Model Rule outlines proposals for confidentiality, which in essence preserve confidences save as may be considered "necessary to prevent death or serious bodily injury from occurring, or substantial loss from occurring in the matter at hand as the result of a crime or fraud that a party has committed or intends to commit". As ADR confidentiality can be governed by different and sometimes conflicting sources of law and ethical duties, the Model Rule reflects the importance that this be discussed and that the parties and the neutral understand the extent and uncertainties of the ADR confidentiality protections. Information provided privately to a lawyer-neutral in a separate meeting or caucus

---

[5] This is, of course, the American usage of the term as legal counsellors and does not imply counselling in a therapeutic sense.

[6] A list of these is set out in n. 12 at p. 5 of the draft Model Rule. They include Professor Geoffrey Hazard's contention that ADR activities can be considered "ancillary" functions of the lawyer, "When ADR is Ancillary to a Legal Practice, Law Firms Must Confront Conflict Issues" in 12 *Alternatives* 147 (1994); Prof. Carrie Menkel-Meadow's comments "Is Mediation the Practice of Law?" in 14 *Alternatives* May 1996 at p. 57; and Bruce Meyerson, "Lawyers who Mediate are not Practicing Law" 14 *Alternatives* June 1996 at p. 74.

[7] See p. 13, n.1 of the draft Model Rule.

is to be maintained confidentially in the absence of authority to disclose it.

- *The requirement of impartiality.* A lawyer who serves as a third party neutral "should conduct all proceedings in an impartial, unbiased and even-handed manner, treating all parties with fairness and respect".[8] There is an obligation to disclose circumstances that may affect the parties' perceptions of the mediator's impartiality, erring if necessary on the side of disclosure. To prevent the erosion of impartiality, the Model Rule provides that "after accepting appointment and while serving as a neutral, a lawyer shall not enter into any financial, business, professional, family or social relationship or acquire any financial or personal interest which is likely to affect impartiality or which might reasonably create the appearance of partiality or bias, without disclosure and consent of all parties".

- *The avoidance of conflicts of interest.* This provides for lawyer-neutrals to be disqualified from establishing interests or relationships during the course of proceedings that would conflict with their duties of impartiality. Rule 4.5.4(a)(2) further provides that "a lawyer who has served as a third party neutral shall not subsequently represent any party to the ADR proceedings (in which the third party neutral served as neutral) in the same or a substantially related matter, unless all parties consent after full disclosure". Lawyers affiliated to disqualified lawyers are similarly affected by the disqualification, in the absence of adequate screening and subject to other provisions to protect the parties.

- *Arrangements regarding fees.* Lawyer-neutrals are required to send a written communication to the parties specifying the basis, rate and allocation of fees. Contingent fees (said to be relatively common) are mentioned, and while not outlawed, are said to give the neutral a direct financial interest in settlement that may conflict with the parties' possible interest in terminating the proceedings without reaching settlement. Lawyer-neutrals must consider whether such arrangements might give an appearance or actuality of partiality.

- *Fairness and integrity of the process.* There is an obligation to try to conduct the process fairly and not to engage in any process or procedure not consented to by the parties. Lawyer-neutrals should be attentive to the basic values and goals informing fair dispute resolution. These include party autonomy and choice of process and fairness in the conduct of the process. There is also a duty to try to ensure that the agreement is entirely voluntary and not coerced. However, the neutral cannot under the Model Rule be "the guarantor of a fair or just result".[9]

21-032   It is interesting to note that the Law Society of England and Wales had,

---

[8] Rule 4.5.3 at p.17 of the draft Model Rule.
[9] See p. 27 of the draft Model Rule.

well before publication of the CPR-Georgetown Model Rule, embarked on a regulatory programme more than fully implementing its spirit and letter.

2. ADR ETHICS AND CODES OF PRACTICE

Acting as an impartial practitioner in a dispute resolution process carries with it a substantial ethical obligation to act in a responsible, competent and effective way with principle and integrity. It would be easy for practitioners to influence the course of proceedings by the way in which they conduct the process, the questions they ask and the options they help the parties to examine. However, they must not, directly or indirectly, try to impose their own views or settlement terms on the parties. An abuse of this ethical rule could be harmful rather than beneficial, and could bring the practitioner's reputation and that of the process into disrepute.   **21–033**

Practitioners need to comply with rules and agreements about confidentiality and legal privilege, and generally need to observe high ethical standards in the way that they conduct the process and themselves within it.[10]   **21–034**

There may be a number of sources of these ethical standards: **21–035**

- As observed above, the practitioner's traditional occupation may stipulate standards and requirements.

- Mediation and other dispute resolution organisations generally stipulate the standards of conduct required of their members, which may be informally regulated, or may be in the form of a Code of Practice or Model Procedure to which members are required to subscribe.

- Individual practitioners may subscribe to their own practice and ethical rules, either informally or as part of an agreement with the parties.

- Properly trained practitioners should be aware of the ethical considerations and the need to work with integrity and should do so as part of a personal ethos irrespective of any formal document regulating these activities. They should be imbued with a sense of the need to conduct the process in a fair, effective and even-handed way.

A Code of Practice is likely to reflect an organisation's ethical values and practical ground rules. It may outline the organisation's policy or guidelines on various matters such as mediator qualification, mediation practice, values and principles underlying practice, confidentially and privilege. It is likely to address other ethical issues such as conflicts of interest and circumstances in which the mediation should be ended and practical matters such as payment of fees and indemnity insurance for the mediator.   **21–036**

The Codes of the U.K. College of Family Mediators and the Law Society are both included in Appendix II to this work by way of example.   **21–037**

---

[10] For detailed ethical requirements, see the CPR-Georgetown Commission's Model Code at paras 21–025–031 above and the Codes of Practice and the Model Procedure in Appendix II.

Similarities will indicate the many areas of shared values and practices between the two bodies, and the harmonisation discussions that have taken place. Differences between the Codes will no doubt reflect the fact that the Law Society's Code has been drafted specifically for lawyer mediators whereas the U.K. College's Code covers mediators from a wide range of backgrounds. The Model Procedure of the Centre for Dispute Resolution, CEDR, is also included in the Appendix as an example of a commercial procedural guide.

21–038   Ethics constitute one of the cornerstones of ADR practice. A third party is given substantial power to influence the resolution of disputes, in many cases affecting the lives of the people concerned. That person's practice is carried out largely privately, out of the public gaze, and without the same kind of protections provided by the court system, such as the possibility of getting reasoned judgments and of appealing. Practitioners owe it to the public and to their profession to observe a strong sense of ethical awareness. Training programmes have a moral obligation to include ethics in their courses, and in many cases, a regulatory requirement to do so.

21–039   Given the range of fields within which ADR is practised and the variety of skills, styles, cultures and approaches that it encompasses, some controls are desirable in the public interest. In the interests of diversity, however, those controls should not be rigid practising controls, seeking to detail every permissible step and outlawing every forbidden step. That would replicate the rigidities and problems of the legal system that ADR sought to avoid. Rather, the controls should be maintained by a keen and clear sense of ethical propriety. If an ethical framework is in place, practitioners have a sound theoretical understanding, and are practised in facilitative skills, there should be scope for creativity and flexibility.

3. THE PRACTITIONER'S VALUES, ATTITUDES AND BELIEFS

The concept of neutrality

21–040   The term "neutral" runs through the literature on ADR. It is extensively used both as a noun, to refer to the impartial practitioner ("the neutral") who works in ADR, and as an adjective, to refer to the "neutral" quality of the practitioner or as a part of the process, as in "early neutral evaluation". It is used in both ways in this work. However, there is a widespread view that nobody can be strictly "neutral" because they cannot function in any way as human beings without bringing their own personal values, attitudes and beliefs into what they do, whether consciously or not. Hence they cannot truly operate strictly "neutrally".

21–041   For this reason, there has been some reaction against using the word "neutral" inappropriately. Instead of referring to "neutrality" in relation to the ADR practitioner's role, many people prefer to use the terms "impartiality" and "even-handedness", which refer to an absence of bias or partiality and do not imply any reference to the presence or absence of the practitioner's values. The authors of this work accept that neutrality is a concept that cannot imply an absence of personal values, and commonly use the word "impartial" rather than "neutral". However, the word "neutral" and the concept of neutrality continue to have a significant relevance and usage. Firstly, the term "neutral" has a widespread acceptance and use and it would be artificial to try to avoid it in the context of processes that are inherently described as "neutral". Secondly, most people adopt its Oxford dictionary usage as "not helping or supporting either of two opposing sides, especially states at war or in dispute". This definition is a broad one, and does not concern itself with the underlying values that "neutral" practitioners invariably have. Thirdly, even among those who use "neutral" selectively, there is a general acceptance that a practitioner can quite properly be neutral as to the outcome of the process, and indeed can and should be neutral in that respect. Consequently, the term "neutral" continues to be used in this work, albeit with some selectivity.

Personal values, attitudes and beliefs

Mediators and other dispute resolution practitioners working in a neutral role will inevitably have values, attitudes and beliefs that affect their approach to their work. Rather than imagining that they can abandon all of these, it is probably more useful for practitioners to be fully aware and conscious of them. With that awareness, they can try to ensure that their values, attitudes and beliefs do not impinge on the process and unconsciously affect what they do and how they work.   **21–042**

Various aspects can usefully be brought into awareness: **21–043**

Attitude to conflict

Practitioners bring into the dispute their underlying views and responses to conflictual situations. These will generally have started to be formed in their families of origin, based on early experiences. If family conflict was well managed, the practitioner may be able to address conflict in later life more easily. If conflict was avoided, commonly by one member of the family (perhaps even the practitioner) being the peace-maker, the practitioner may in later life tend towards adopting a conflict-avoidance approach to conflict management and resolution. If conflict in the family commonly resulted in high levels of anger or distress, and felt destructive, the practitioner may view all conflict as dangerous and potentially destructive.   **21–044**

These and other related attitudes, developed over years, will invariably affect the practitioner's approach to particular disputes. Will the practitioner be able to tolerate joint meetings of disputants where the conflict is visible, or will he or she prefer separate meetings where the conflict can be more contained? Will the practitioner make assumptions about the consequences of parties' behaviour based on personal experience of conflict? Can the practitioner enter the conflict arena and feel comfortable in it?   **21–045**

It is not necessary for a practitioner to formalise this self-inquiry, but rather to consider his or her attitude to conflict on a reflective basis. Formal tests do exist. For example, the Myers-Briggs Type Indicator (MBTI) classifies 16 psychological types, which it identifies through a specific questionnaire. Some people find that this typology helps towards self-understanding and to identify sources of conflict. Less formal self analysis generally suffices, though guidance in undertaking it can always be helpful. With the benefit of these insights, a practitioner's ability to address   **21–046** conflictual situations can be improved. Also, practitioners may remind themselves that their attitudes and responses are not universal, and that each party may be better able, or less able, to cope with the conflict than the practitioner.

Rationality-emotionality

21–047   Practitioners may also find it helpful to have an understanding of their broad positioning between rational and emotional responses, on a notional continuum.

21–048   There are, however, inherent risks in referring to rationality-emotionality on this basis. Firstly, people are more complex than this, and may at times be rational and at other times emotional (and sometimes both): there is unlikely to be consistency. Secondly, it is easy for people to make generalised gender assumptions. Some people tend to identify general principles of emotionality with women and rationality with men.[11] Social conditioning and other factors may result in patterns that have observable gender similarities; but it is risky and unsustainable to create theories or generalisations based on any such patterns. Thirdly, there is no real continuum between rationality and emotionality.

21–049   Parties, especially in inter-personal disputes including marital issues, but also in a range of other conflicts, may well have their own different positions on this notional spectrum. Family mediators will be familiar with the rational-emotional divide. One party may seek a calm, logical and ordered approach to resolving the issues, whereas the other party may be more emotional and unready to resolve matters purely on the basis of a business-like approach, preferring to deal with personal issues. A mediator in such a situation who adopts a rational, business-like approach is in some respect failing to acknowledge the party who is more emotional. Correspondingly, if the mediator resonates with the more emotional approach, the "rational" party may be troubled. Practitioners (not just in the family field) need to be aware of this division and of their own natural inclinations in response.[12] They may need to find an approach that recognises and acknowledges the validity of both ways of functioning.

21–050   Practitioners also need to be aware of their own individual capacities to cope with the emotions of the parties. People vary in the way in which they can handle these, and should take care not to exceed their own limits. Some people can tolerate parties' anger, distress or frustration more easily than others. They should have this awareness when entering the field of conflict. They should also remember that the parties themselves may well have different tolerances from one another and from the practitioner. These limitations need to be borne in mind when following the skills process of "allowing parties to express their emotions".[13]

---

[11]Writers such as John Gray have commented on gender differences along similar lines to these, *e.g.* in his book, *Men are from Mars, Women are from Venus* (1993). Works such as his may offer some insights into gender differences, but run the risk of all generalisations, namely that they do not apply universally.

[12]The authors wish to acknowledge Neil Dawson and Brenda McHugh, family therapists and mediators, for their contributions to these insights.

[13]The term "venting" emotions is commonly used in dispute resolution literature. Although not intended to be disrespectful to the parties, it could have that connotation. The "expression" of

Much that practitioners do in conflict and dispute resolution is intuitive. **21–051**
Many lawyers and other professionals tend to place a premium on logic and
rationality, but in fact have well-developed intuitive responses that are not
readily acknowledged. They may have a sense that something is not quite
right or a feeling about what they are being told. Skilled questioning relies
on this sense about what to pursue and what to leave unasked. Similarly,
skilled mediation involves intuitive as well as reasoned responses. There is a
balance to be struck, which the mediator hopes to achieve.

Values, beliefs and assumptions

All people have their own individual values and belief systems, on which **21–052**
their assumptions about behaviour are based. It is impossible to divorce
ethical awareness from individual beliefs, if ethics are to be observed at a
fundamental level.

People start forming their values and beliefs from the earliest age and **21–053**
develop them as they grow older. Many factors will shape these. They
include, of course, individual experience, the culture of one's nuclear and
extended family, community and religion, the influence of schools and
teachers, and the media. Practitioners enter the conflict arena with an array of
beliefs, assumptions, biases and in some cases prejudices. It will not be easy
to identify these with particularity, but at least the practitioner should
understand that they exist, to be ready to guard against the effect that they
may have if they intrude on the dispute resolution process.

John Crawley says that "belief systems are sensitive, personal and **21–054**
absolutely necessary. They provide us with a basic framework from which to
relate to the people and situations we encounter. An effective conflict
manager possesses a strong set of positive values about other people, but also
needs to examine and be in control of his or her own beliefs, assumptions,
stereotypes and prejudices".[14] An ADR practitioner cannot function
effectively unless aware of his or her biases, stereotypes and prejudices.
Merely controlling them may not be sufficient: prejudices tend to surface
indirectly and are likely to become obvious even if attempts are made to hide
them. They can be addressed with awareness, knowledge and understanding.

4. FAIRNESS

Fairness of process or fairness of outcome

An issue that commonly arises directly or indirectly is whether and to what **21–055**
extent the mediator is responsible for fairness in mediation. The principles
that apply to mediation will generally apply to other forms of consensual
dispute resolution.

It is a fundamental principle of mediation that the parties are the **21–056**
negotiators and that the mediator serves as a facilitator. The parties are
responsible for all their decisions including their settlement terms. In arriving

---

emotions does not just happen in family and interpersonal issues. Underlying emotions can be
strong in many civil and even commercial disputes.
[14]*Constructive Conflict: Managing to Make a Difference* (1992/95) at p.31.

at their decisions, the parties may have regard to any considerations they may consider relevant. A common thread that runs through all models of mediation in all fields of activity is the principle that the mediator does not impose his or her decisions or preferences on the parties. The mediator may provide information and may in some models help with evaluation; but none of this allows a mediator to influence the parties unduly in their decision-making.

21–057   In these circumstances, given that parties make their own decisions however much the mediator may have a different view, it is clear that mediators cannot be responsible for the fairness of the outcome agreed between the parties. This is not always understood. Anecdotal reports have been heard of senior government officers expressing the view that family mediators "will ensure that the parties enter into a fair agreement". That is not within the power or function of the mediator.

21–058   What mediators can do and need to do, however, is to establish fairness of process. This means that they should manage the mediation process in such a way that the procedure is as fair as possible to both or all parties. When people refer to mediation being a "fair" process, it is this quality of procedural fairness to which they refer and not necessarily fairness of substantive outcome.

21–059   Fairness of process implies certain requirements:

- Participation in the process must be voluntary and parties must not feel coerced into arriving at settlement terms. This may raise questions as to whether mediation can be mandatory. The authors of this work would contend that mandatory mediation is not necessarily a contradiction in terms, and that it is not inherently unfair to stipulate procedures that require parties to try in the first instance to resolve their issues through mediation. Parties can for example be required to use settlement facilitative procedures as a prerequisite to using the courts, provided that there are proper safeguards for parties or cases that should not be in mediation. As a further proviso, there should be no coercion to settle, but merely a requirement to try the process. Parties should not be penalised by the withholding of legal aid if they try to use mediation and do not find it helpful.

- Mediators must be even-handed and impartial in their dealings with parties. If a mediator adopts any partiality towards any of the parties, that would not be fair. This does not mean that the mediator may never say anything that one or other party may not like to hear. At times a mediator may need to challenge one party or the other. This does not imply partiality, which should be viewed in the round.

- Mediators should create conditions in which both or all parties can be properly heard. If one party dominates the process, that would ordinarily create a sense of unfairness. In some situations, more attention may need to be given to one of the parties than to another; but that should ordinarily be done on a consensual basis.

- Power imbalances exist in most situations, and are likely to continue in all forms of dispute resolution. Mediation cannot and does not pretend to eliminate power imbalances, but mediators may have strategies to help prevent these from distorting the process. Mediators may address power imbalances where appropriate, but should decline to mediate where the power imbalances are so severe that the mediation process cannot be fairly or effectively conducted. In the United States, some states address this specifically. Under the Oklahoma Supreme Court rules[15], for example, a mediator must avoid bargaining imbalances that occur when one party has legal or negotiating assistance and the other does not. In domestic relations mediation in Iowa, mediators must "assure a balanced dialogue and must attempt to diffuse any manipulative or intimidating negotiating techniques utilized by either of the participants."[16] In England, especially in relation to family issues, practice codes commonly provide for power imbalances to be addressed.

- If any party to the mediation is unduly influenced in decision-making, the mediator needs to take steps to address this to ensure as far as practicable that parties negotiate and decide freely. If there is any harassment, abuse or violence, the mediator must take steps to deal with that to ensure that negotiations are voluntary and not induced by fear or made under duress. If that is not possible, the mediation would have to be ended. In family mediation an appropriate screening process should be in place to try to establish whether parties are being unduly influenced in their decision-making. In practice, many people are influenced by fears and concerns in reaching agreements. They may be afraid of the risks and costs of litigation, or of the animosity that proceedings may cause. They may fear that their losses will be even greater if they do not concede during negotiations. Threats may be implicit albeit not explicit. The mediator's job is to carry out his or her functions in a way that allows fears to be addressed as far as practicable, and that a party is not forced into a decision by improper pressure or duress.

- Mediators should not unduly influence the parties in their decision-making, either directly or indirectly. A comment is periodically heard from mediators that they do not influence the parties because they do not make statements, but primarily work through questions. However, the way in which questions are used and the choice of questions can be very influential. Mediators cannot avoid responsibility by suggesting that questions are inherently neutral.

- Parties must be capable of decision-making and of understanding the issues. If any party, through illness, mental incapacity or for any other

---

[15]Oklahoma Supreme Court Rules and Procedures for the Dispute Resolution Act, Rule 12; Code of Professional Conduct for Mediators, Oklahoma Supreme Court Rules and Procedures for the Dispute Resolution Act, app. A.

[16]Rules Governing Standards of Practice for Lawyer-Mediators in Family Disputes, adopted by the Iowa Supreme Court on December 21, 1986.

reason cannot properly participate in the process, it should not take place.

- A sense of fairness and respect should permeate the whole process. The mediator should be aware of this in his or her interventions, questions and comments; in any information provided, in the procedures used; in the arrangements made for meetings; and in the conduct of the process generally.

21–060   In some models, such as the transformative approach,[17] mediators do not use a fixed structure for the mediation, but "follow the parties". In this event, parties may be said to control the process as well as the substance. This differs from the approach in which parties control the substance and the mediator controls the process. Questions may arise as to whether mediators, in using a model in which parties control process, can still be responsible for fairness of process. Arguably, the mediator must remain responsible for this in all models. If a mediator were to believe otherwise, it would be necessary to consider whether the parties had made an informed choice of process.

What constitutes fairness?

The parties' views guiding fairness

21–061   The fairness applicable to mediation is the parties' sense of fairness and not that of the mediator. This means that if the parties regard a resolution as fair, the mediator should not be troubled by the fact that it does not accord with his or her sense of fairness. The mediator may wish to check that the terms and their implications are fully understood by the parties; but subject to doing this, the mediator's views as to their fairness would not be relevant.

21–062   This is not a difficult proposition for mediators to accept. The problem, however, is that parties in dispute often find it difficult to agree on a mutual definition of fairness in their circumstances. They may have different perceptions of fairness. How, then, does a mediator address fairness? What are the criteria or factors that apply?

Legal principles guiding fairness

21–063   The legal system is concerned with justice and fairness. Unfortunately, two problems exist in this connection. First, while these principles constitute an ideal, the system in many countries, including England and Wales, has found that it cannot always deliver on its promise of these principles. The system's inability to do so effectively and economically has led to the major reforms brought about by Lord Woolf. In the United States, a similar cry is heard: the legal system simply cannot provide solutions in a consistently effective, economic and equitable way. Secondly, the principles of fairness adopted by the law are not necessarily the principles adopted by people generally. Lawyers tend to use legal principles of fairness as their starting point for testing fairness; yet many agree that this is an inadequate measure.[18]

---

[17] See paras 1–040 and 21–132 *et seq.*

[18] In family mediation training courses, lawyers who are asked whether they think that the courts can be relied upon to provide consistently fair outcomes almost always respond in the negative. The standard response tends to be that the courts are sometimes fair and sometimes not.

As mediation is conducted "in the shadow of the law" and parties can **21–064** generally turn to the court system for redress if they are not satisfied with the mediated outcome, legal principles and rights tend to guide parties in deciding what they think is fair. Yet this may not meet parties' needs in all cases. So, for example, in a financial dispute on divorce, a couple may have agreed during their marriage to share finances equally; but if on divorce one person has many millions of pounds, a court would not necessarily split the capital equally. Rather, the courts have developed their own principles for awarding provision for housing and income, and having regard to other considerations such as contributions. The principles of equality that might have guided the couple in their lives together would not necessarily be adopted. This is an example of the court using principles that parties might not have adopted as their own.

Workability guiding fairness

Mediators sometimes take the view that fairness is an elusive concept, and **21–065** that all that they can do towards helping the parties towards fairness is to test the workability of proposals. If proposals are viable and workable in practice, that is as close to fairness as mediators may feel that they can take matters. Mediators would test workability by asking the parties questions about implementation, in the form of "reality-testing".

Legal representation guiding fairness

Where parties are both or all represented by lawyers in the mediation **21–066** process, a mediator may perhaps not consider it necessary to be concerned about the fairness or otherwise of the terms of the settlement. There is a view that lawyers create an equality of bargaining power, and can help their client to assess all relevant factors in deciding whether or not to accept settlement terms. It is true that legal representation for all parties tends to help reduce certain kinds of power imbalances, but it cannot achieve full equality of power nor can it guarantee fairness.

Other fairness considerations

Other attempts are sometimes made to devise fair principles to guide dispute **21–067** resolution negotiations. An example is the mathematical formula devised by Steven J. Brams and Alan D. Taylor in their work, *Fair Division: From cake-cutting to dispute resolution*.[19] The authors have adapted the cake-cutting procedure of "I cut, you choose" with mathematical formulae to try to create what they call "envy-free" allocations. Their procedures are somewhat complex but it is understood that they have produced a computer programme to make their work more accessible. Whether and to what extent their procedures will be helpful in practice to dispute resolution remains to be seen.

Sometimes practitioners can do no more than allow parties to express their **21–068** views of fairness, try to help them to hear and understand one another, and then, if necessary, to agree to differ.

---

[19]Cambridge University Press, 1996. For a brief outline, see Chap. 6 at para. 6–037 above.

Manifest unfairness

21–069   Mediator views are divided as to the responsibility of the mediator where there is not merely a perception of unfairness in the outcome, but manifest unfairness. What is the mediator's responsibility in these circumstances?

21–070   Many mediators take the view that however unfair the settlement of the issues might seem, that is a matter for the parties. Others would not wish to participate in a resolution that they felt to be manifestly and fundamentally unfair, even if both parties agreed to it. This must ultimately be a matter for the mediator's individual conscience. However, some Codes of Practice provide for contingencies such as this. The Family Mediation Code of Practice of the Law Society of England and Wales provides at Paragraph 5.10 that if the parties "are proposing a resolution which appears to the mediator to be unconscionable or fundamentally inappropriate, then the mediator should inform the parties accordingly and may terminate the mediation, and/ or refer the parties to their legal advisers".

5. CONFLICTS OF INTEREST

21–071   Impartiality, even-handedness and the mediator's neutrality to the outcome of the mediation are essential components of mediation. It is vital to the integrity of the process that mediators should neither have any conflict of interest, nor should they be perceived as having any interest or potential bias, even if no actual conflict of interest exists.

21–072   Three aspects need to concern mediators. Similar principles will apply to practitioners in other kinds of consensual processes:

- *Actual conflicts of interest*, where the mediator has or has previously had another role or relationship that is inconsistent with his or her impartial, even-handed and neutral function as mediator.

- *Potential conflicts of interest*, where a conflict does not yet exist but the possibility of it arising is inherent in the situation.

- Situations or relationships that do not constitute actual or potential conflicts of interest as such, but which nevertheless may cast doubt on the mediator's ability to act impartially and give rise to imputed bias. For ease of reference, these will be referred to as *"perceived conflicts"*. (Impartiality means that the mediator will conduct the process fairly and even-handedly, will not favour either party over the other, and has no personal interest in the outcome of the mediation.)

Defining and regulating conflicts of interest and perceived conflicts

21–073   Mediators need to have rules regulating whether or not they can mediate where a conflict of interest exists. Generally, subject to the possibility of obtaining informed consent, they should not ever do so; and they should carefully observe the restrictions and qualifications on mediating in situations where perceived conflict exists. The U.K. College of Family Mediators and the Law Society have rules that regulate conflicts and perceived conflicts. In addition, professional bodies such as the Bar Council, British Association of

Counselling, British Confederation of Psychotherapists and U.K. Council for Psychotherapy may have their own stipulations regulating conflicts of interest that their members may face. The Legal Aid Board also has rules that need to be observed where appropriate.

The wider net covering conflicts and perceived conflicts

Rules that regulate actual and potential conflicts and perceived conflicts do not apply only to the mediator personally. They may also affect other people who are, or are perceived to be, in certain kinds of close relationships with the mediator, including those that involve a sharing of information. In certain situations, information known by one person is deemed to be known by others who have an actual or potential information-sharing relationship with that person. That will apply whether or not information is actually shared: the fact that it could be shared is sufficient to make it vulnerable.   **21–074**

For example, all members of a law firm or other partnership are deemed to have knowledge that one member of that firm or partnership acquires, notwithstanding that the person with actual knowledge may be at pains to keep it confidential from others within the firm or partnership. The principle that applies is that "Chinese walls" to keep information confidential cannot ordinarily be erected within a relationship where there are possibilities or duties of information-sharing.[20]   **21–075**

Similarly, there will be other working relationships, such as mediation services and certain kinds of consortia, where knowledge of facts by one person may create the presumption that all other members of that service or consortium similarly have that knowledge. The effect of this is that if one member of the firm, service or consortium is precluded from acting as a mediator because he or she has relevant information about the parties, then all other members of the firm, service or consortium will be similarly precluded.   **21–076**

The term "firm, service or consortium" includes the following: **21–077**

- All partnerships, associations or consortia in which people hold themselves out as partners (but not generally including a consortium of practitioners who are clearly independent of one another but who merely join together in a loose association for mutual marketing or support).

- Any other association or relationship which involves people working or co-operating with one another in a way that includes actual or potential sharing of profits and/or access to one another's confidential information.

---

[20] See the landmark House of Lords case of *Prince Jefri Bolkiah v KPMG (a firm)* [1999] 1 All E.R. 517 relating to the unqualified duty that attaches to confidential information imparted during a professional relationship that has to be retained confidentially after the ending of that relationship. Lord Millett referred to the "Chinese walls" that are "widely used by financial institutions in the City of London and elsewhere .... for managing the conflicts of interest which arise when financial business is carried on by a conglomerate". He expressed the view that "an effective Chinese wall needs to be an established part of the organisational structure of the firm, not created *ad hoc* ... " (at 530).

Absolute and relative bars to mediating by reason of conflicts and perceived conflicts

21–078   In some situations, mediators will be absolutely barred from mediating even if the parties wish to release the mediator from that bar. In other situations, it may be possible for the parties to decide that they do want the mediator to mediate for them notwithstanding the existence of a perceived conflict. In the latter case, however, consent to mediate can only be effectively given by parties who are fully aware of the circumstances of the perceived conflict. Consent can only be effective if it is informed consent.

21–079   Each organisation or regulatory body needs to formulate rules that apply to each of these kinds of situations. The following are examples of how such rules might be adopted, but are not intended necessarily to be definitive:

Absolute bar to mediating

21–080   It is suggested that a mediator ought not to mediate for parties in the following circumstances even if the parties specifically request him or her to do so and purport to give consent:

- Where the mediator or member of his or her firm, service or consortium has a personal or financial interest in the outcome of the mediation.

- Where the mediator or a member of his or her firm, service or consortium has at any time provided legal, counselling or any other professional advice, support or representation for any party in relation to issues that may arise in the mediation.

- Where the mediator has or at any time has had a therapist/client or counsellor/client relationship with one of the parties.

- Where the mediator or a member of his/her firm, service or consortium advises or acts for or has previously advised or acted for either party on a matter unrelated to the likely issues in the mediation, as long as the other party is unaware of this.

- Where the mediator or a member of his or her firm, service or consortium advises, acts for or counsels or has previously advised or acted for any third party whose interests may conflict with those of either party to the mediation (such as the trustees of a family trust of which either party is a beneficiary, discretionary or otherwise).

- Where the mediator is aware that for personal or other reasons he or she will not be able to mediate in an impartial way, or notwithstanding informed consent is likely to be perceived as being unable to do so.

21–081   This last category covers all situations in which the mediator finds himself or herself in a position where his or her duties and responsibilities to the parties are or may potentially be compromised. This may arise by having (actually or potentially) an interest that is incompatible with the neutrality and impartiality owed to the parties. Alternatively, it arises where his or her impartiality is likely to be perceived as being compromised (imputed bias), even if there is no actual or potential conflict.

A mediator may feel unable to mediate impartially, for example, if he or she has such strong feelings about a situation or about any of the parties that he or she feels unable to be impartial and neutral. It is obviously to be hoped that mediators will be trained to overcome personal blocks of this nature; but there may well be times when this is not the case, and in such event the mediator will be acting properly in declining to mediate.   **21–082**

Another example of the mediator's inability to mediate impartially would be if the mediator subscribed to certain views about the pending issues that would be perceived as being likely to affect impartiality. In such a case, even if the mediator felt that he or she would be impartial and even if the parties agreed, the mediator should decline to act. The test for the mediator must be whether the perception is likely to continue to exist that he or she will not be able to maintain impartiality. It is not practicable to try to list all situations in which an actual or potential conflict of interests exists. There are many possible examples of this and individual facts and circumstances may vary substantially.   **21–083**

Qualified bar to mediating

It is suggested that in the following circumstances, a mediator ought not to mediate for parties unless they specifically request him or her to do so and give informed consent: **21–084**

- Where the mediator or a member of his or her firm, service or consortium advises or acts for or has previously advised or acted for either party on a matter unrelated to the likely issues in the mediation and the other party is aware of this.

- Where the mediator or a member of his or her firm, service or consortium has acquired information relevant to any issue likely to arise in the mediation, then the mediator should not act unless the nature and source of such information is known to all parties and they consent to the mediator acting.

- Where the mediator or a member of his or her firm, service or consortium advises, acts for or counsels or has previously advised, acted for or counselled any third party on a matter related to the likely issues in the mediation and the parties are aware of this. (However, where the third party's interests may conflict with those of either party to the mediation, it is suggested that there should be an absolute bar on mediating.)

- Where the mediator has a social or other personal relationship with either party to the mediation, or with any third party materially affected by the mediation, the mediator should not act unless full disclosure is made to the parties and they consent to the mediator acting.

- Where circumstances exist and are known to the mediator in which a party aware of such circumstances might reasonably be concerned about the mediator's ability to act impartially as a mediator, but which do not constitute an actual or potential conflict of interest. In such event, if full disclosure of the circumstances is made to both parties and they give informed consent, the mediator should be able to act as such.

21–085   The concept of informed consent means that the parties are all aware of all facts relevant to the decision to ask the mediator to act as such. So, for example, if a mediator knows that he or she is socially friendly with one of the parties, or with someone else materially close to one of the parties, the mediator should inform the parties of that fact. They may want to know more about the relationship. If, with such knowledge, they decide that they want the mediator to mediate, then he or she may do so.

21–086   The distinction between the absolute bar and the qualified bar to mediate must be clearly understood. In the case of an absolute bar, the conflict of interest or perceived conflict is so fundamental that it cannot be overcome, even with the consent of the parties. It is inherent in the situation that the mediator cannot act as such. In the case of a qualified bar, however, the conflict, potential conflict or perceived conflict, while serious enough to raise concerns, is capable of being accepted where all parties agree to do so, with full knowledge of all relevant facts and concerns.

21–087   This allows parties proper freedom of choice, where a mediator might be entirely suitable and is not conflicted out, but where circumstances exist that the parties can properly overlook if they choose to do so. For example, a solicitor may have acted for both parties on the purchase of their home. With consent, they should be able to appoint that solicitor to act as a mediator. Or a solicitor may have acted for one party on entirely unrelated aspects, such as a debt collection, and the other party with full knowledge of that, may agree to that solicitor acting as mediator. If, however, the solicitor incidentally also advised the party on an issue that might arise in the mediation, then he or she could not act as mediator. Or if the solicitor gained material information about the party's circumstances, even while acting on an unrelated aspect, that would have to be disclosed to the party for the consent to be informed.

Conflicts or perceived conflicts arising or identified after mediation has started

21–088   If a mediator starts to mediate in the good faith belief that no conflict or perceived conflict exists, and either of these subsequently arises or is identified, the mediator must be guided by his or her organisation's rules as to whether he or she can continue to act.

21–089   Where there is an absolute bar to mediating, the mediator must withdraw from the mediation. Where there is a qualified bar, the mediator must either withdraw or inform the parties of all relevant facts and circumstances relating to the conflict or perceived conflict, and should establish whether the parties wish him or her to continue mediating. If they do, then the mediator can continue to act as such. In some circumstances, the mediator may consider that even where a qualified bar exists, he or she should not continue to act as mediator. In such event, the mediator should withdraw from the mediation. Mediators should not withdraw lightly where there is only a qualified bar and the parties wish him or her to continue, especially if they have already spent significant time or made significant progress in the mediation.

Changing roles after the conclusion of mediation

Organisations and regulatory bodies need to make it clear whether mediators **21–090** can change role after the end of the mediation. Some bodies provide that the mediator may not represent, advise or counsel the parties to the mediation or either of them in relation to any issues dealt with in the mediation. This would mean that a solicitor mediator could not act as solicitor for either party, or for the parties jointly, in relation to any matter that arose in the mediation. In such event, he or she could not bring court proceedings in any consequent divorce or deal with the conveyancing of any property that was required to be transferred from one to the other.

There seems to be a broad consensus, though not necessarily unanimity, **21–091** that a mediator should not be precluded from subsequently acting in another role (such as solicitor) for a party to the mediation in relation to any issue or matter that is unrelated to the issues in the mediation. However, he or she should not do so or even discuss or agree to do so until the settlement terms have all been implemented. This would ensure that the parties are able to revert to mediation if any problems or issues arise during the course of implementation. It would be invidious and improper for a mediator during the mediation to agree or even to discuss the possibility that he or she will after conclusion of the mediation act for one party albeit in an unrelated matter.[21]

6. ETHICS OF CONFIDENTIALITY

The legal implications of ADR confidentiality are dealt with in Chapter 22. **21–092** However, certain ethical issues arise in relation to the subject of confidentiality which, although they overlap with the legal aspects, will be considered separately from them in this Chapter. These arise, first, in relation to the broad issue of confidentiality within the ADR process, and secondly, in relation to the subject of maintaining confidences in the holding of separate meetings with different parties.

Ethics of confidentiality in ADR generally

An ethical issue may arise where a practitioner is bound by an agreement to **21–093** maintain confidentiality in ADR proceedings and comes across a situation in which he or she feels morally or ethically obliged to breach that duty of confidentiality. This may, for example, arise where parties in a mediation inform the mediator in confidence that a public structure or a product being marketed is unsafe or a couple tell the mediator confidentially that a child is being subjected to physical or sexual abuse.

Whether or not there is a legal obligation to maintain confidentiality will **21–094** depend upon the conditions under which the process takes place, and on the

---

[21] See also para. 21–031 above for the Model Rule 4.5.4(a) proposed by the CPR-Georgetown Commission.

applicable law in the jurisdiction governing the process. So, for example, in some states in the United States there is an obligation on the part of the mediator to report to the authorities any serious allegations of abuse or neglect in family mediation.[22] In some cases, the terms of the agreement to mediate or the relevant Code of Practice may exempt the mediator from maintaining confidentiality in relation to certain kinds of information.[23]

21–095   If there is no legal duty of confidentiality, or if the circumstances of the matter and a legal duty of disclosure override the obligation to maintain confidentiality, the mediator will be able to consider the ethical position without legal constraints. The mediator's dilemma will, however, arise where there is a legal duty to maintain confidentiality with no clear exemption from that duty, and yet the facts are such that the mediator feels obliged to make a disclosure. There is no standard answer to that dilemma. The mediator must be guided by the applicable law; the terms of the agreement to mediate; the terms of any relevant Code of Practice; his or her duties to the parties; the nature, seriousness and implications of the information; any applicable public policy considerations; and ultimately the mediator's own conscience.

21–096   This moral issue has been addressed in an article by an American mediator, Kevin Gibson, "Confidentiality in Mediation: A Moral Reassessment".[24] He challenges a perception that exists among some writers that everything in mediation is necessarily strictly confidential and incapable of being examined. He believes that few mediators are "absolutists" with regard to the question of confidentiality, but rather that there is a broad spectrum of opinion about what should be revealed" and with what justification.

21–097   The Code of Practice under which a mediator works may guide this question, particularly if it is incorporated explicitly or by indirect reference into the contract for mediation between the mediator and the parties. It follows that organisations establishing such codes or individuals creating their own contracts could make their own choices as to what degree of freedom from confidentiality they wish to provide. So, for example, the Law Society's Family Mediation Code of Practice provides at Section 7.1 that:

"**7.1** The mediator must maintain confidentiality in relation to all matters dealt with in the mediation. The mediator may disclose:

7.1.1 matters which the parties and the mediator agree may be disclosed;
7.1.2 matters which the mediator considers appropriate where he or she believes that any child or any other person affected by the mediation is suffering or likely to suffer significant harm (and in such case, the mediator should so far as practicable and appropriate discuss with the parties the way in which such disclosure is to take place); or
7.1.3 matters where the law imposes an overriding obligation of disclosure on the mediator."

---

[22]See, *e.g.* the article on "Confidentiality and Privilege in Divorce Mediation" by Jay Folberg at p. 323 of *Divorce Mediation—Theory and Practice* by Folberg and Milne (1988).
[23]See Chap. 22 at paras 22–020 *et seq.*
[24](1992) *Journal of Dispute Resolution* at p. 25.

The Mediation Council of Illinois, in its Professional Standards of Practice for Mediators published in a revised version in 1996, provides for confidentiality in Paragraph 11. It then goes on to say that "Where there is a clear and imminent danger to an individual or to society, the obligation of the mediator to maintain confidentiality will not apply". Other mediation bodies have adopted similar exclusions.[25]   **21–098**

Different codes make different provisions in this regard. For example, a code might exempt from confidentiality any information obtained by a mediator "that a criminal offence has been, or is likely to be, committed". However, the less confident parties feel about the confidentiality of the information provided by them, the less useful the process may be considered to be, and the less ready parties may be to use it, effectively or at all. Some mediators may feel that they should not be free to report, say, a tax evasion notified to them, but that they should be free to report, say, child abuse. Where the line is to be drawn is a matter for individual mediators or organisations to consider.[26]   **21–099**

Gibson's article considers the moral aspect of confidentiality, including the distinctions between the law and morality, where "legal acts are sometimes immoral, and moral acts are sometimes illegal".[27] Consequently, "mediators who face difficult or novel questions about whether or not to disclose client confidences are unlikely to find plain guidelines in the law" though an examination of the law may be helpful.[28] Gibson analyses the various bases for mediator confidentiality and decides that these "do not support a clear-cut rule for mediators to always keep their client's confidences."[29] He analyses the cases where there may be a duty to break confidences, for example, warning victims of intended violence, child abuse and public interest and concludes that "mediation confidentiality is only as strong as the justifications that can be made on its behalf.... There are two (crucial) elements... one is the policy element which supports the institution of mediation and the related role obligation; the second is the mediator's own ethical judgment." He argues for public accountability, substantial and adequate rather than absolute confidentiality, an external review mechanism and a review of codes of practice to allow mediators more scope to make their own considered judgments about disclosure. In the years since his article was written, that seems to be the trend of codes and agreements.   **21–100**

Ethics of confidentiality in private meetings

Caucusing is the process of meeting the parties separately and privately in the mediation process, often combined with "shuttle diplomacy" in which   **21–101**

---

[25] See also the CPR-Georgetown Commissions' Model Rule, as mentioned at paras 21–031 *et seq.* above, and the release from confidentiality as necessary "to prevent death or serious bodily injury from occurring, or substantial loss from occurring in the matter at hand as the result of a crime or fraud that a party has committed or intends to commit".

[26] Gibson, see n. 24 above, refers for example to the Code of Conduct for the Colorado Council of Mediation Organisations, which covers child abuse or where "a probable crime will be committed that may result in serious psychological or physical harm to another person..."

[27] At p. 31.

[28] The legal, as distinct from the ethical and moral, issues concerning confidentiality are dealt with in Chap. 22. In practice, the law on public policy disclosure and the contractual provisions increasingly inserted into Agreements to Mediate may well cover many situations.

[29] At p. 49.

the mediator moves backwards and forwards between the parties, carrying messages and helping to facilitate their negotiations with one another.

21–102   The holding of separate meetings with the parties is not used in all models of mediation. Some mediators only have joint meetings with the parties. However, where separate meetings are held, there are three principal ways of dealing with the confidentiality aspect. In one, the matters discussed in the separate meetings are brought back by the mediator into a subsequent joint meeting based on full disclosure. In the second, the mediator undertakes to each party to maintain confidentiality about any matters discussed in the separate meetings and not to disclose anything to any other party without specific authority. The third way involves partial confidentiality. The ethical aspects of each of these ways of working will be considered.

Disclosure of information from separate meeting into joint meeting

21–103   The object of this procedure is that it enables each party to speak more freely to the mediator in the separate meetings, while maintaining the principle that all matters discussed will be made available to all parties. The mediator has the duty to bring the separate information into the joint meeting, having perhaps discussed with each party separately how this will be done.

21–104   Although this model can work effectively, ethical problems can arise. For example, notwithstanding that the mediator may have agreed that there would be disclosure in the joint meeting of matters discussed with each party separately, a party may say something in the separate meeting which he or she does not want the mediator to disclose to the other. This may place the mediator in a difficult position, especially where the information could be embarrassing or inflammatory. In that situation the mediator would have to discuss the problem with the party who made the statement, explaining the need to disclose the information according to the agreed procedure, and perhaps helping to deal with any concerns relating to such disclosure. If the party is adamant that there cannot be disclosure, the mediator may feel unable to continue acting in that mediation. The mediator can avoid such a situation by emphasising the need to bring back all information to the joint session and that no separate confidences can be maintained.[30]

21–105   Mediators using this model will not necessarily report back verbatim to the joint meeting, but will commonly summarise and paraphrase. Many consider that they do not need to repeat non-material statements. This is understandable and generally unobjectionable; but it does leave the discretion as to materiality with the mediator and carries the risk that potentially material information might be withheld.

21–106   There may also be some risk that the mediator, in carrying the information back from the separate meeting to the joint meeting, may summarise or paraphrase it inaccurately and consequently not fully comply with the agreement for disclosure. Although this may become an ethical problem, it can be overcome by the mediator ensuring that communications are carefully and accurately conveyed when this model is used.

---

[30]Some agreements allow some separate confidences even where all information is to be shared, *e.g.* that addresses and telephone numbers may be kept confidential if required.

Agreement to maintain confidentiality of separate meetings

This is the most common way of working in civil and commercial disputes, **21–107** and the practice of maintaining such confidentiality is integral to most models of commercial mediation.

For those unfamiliar with this method of working, there may be questions **21–108** about the notion of a practitioner being placed in the position of having confidential information from both sides, and moving between the parties releasing information as authorised to do so. There is, however, no practical or ethical reason why the practitioner should not be able to do so, and this is common and well-accepted practice.

Ethical dilemmas can also arise in this method. One example is where the **21–109** mediator receives confidential information in the separate meetings, and is subsequently required to evaluate formally (in those models where that is part of the process). Can the mediator evaluate using confidential information not known to the other side? There are a few possible answers.

If the mediator is required to give a reasoned evaluation to all parties, **21–110** permission will have to be sought to use confidential information in the evaluation. If it would help to resolve matters, such permission is likely to be given, albeit perhaps with qualifications. Alternatively, the mediator may evaluate but decline to provide details or reasons. This could be unsatisfactory, as the confidential information would remain unknown and untested. Further alternatively, the mediator might adopt a more informal approach to evaluation (which in any event is more common), discussing the issues with each party informally, taking care to make useful evaluative comments without breaching any confidences. Finally, if a party providing significant information refused to allow it to be used, the mediator might decline to evaluate.

Another ethical dilemma could arise where the mediator receives **21–111** information from one party in the separate meetings which indicates to the mediator that another party is under a misapprehension about some matter, whether as to the legal or factual position or as to the consequences of any proposed course of action. If the mediator is not able to disclose that confidential information to the other, any such misapprehension may not be able to be remedied. Clearly, the mediator would not wish to allow any such misunderstanding to remain if it arose as a result of anything said by the mediator or the party that was directly or indirectly misleading. The situation might however be more complicated if the error arose without any fault or misleading element on the part of the mediator or any other party, and if the mediator was required to maintain strict confidentiality about the correct position.[31] In that event, the mediator might seek permission to correct the misunderstanding (being sure not to breach any confidence the other way round). The mediator might perhaps point out where relevant that the maintenance of the erroneous understanding by the other party could result in an unsatisfactory and unworkable agreement being reached. If confidentiality was still insisted upon, and the misunderstanding was significant and material, the mediator would have to consider whether or not to continue

---

[31] See the discussion in Chap. 6 about the duty to negotiate in good faith, and the way in which this may have to be interpreted.

with the mediation. This would depend on the circumstances, the nature of the misapprehension and its effects, whether the party was being professionally advised, and other relevant factors.

21–112 Another ethical dilemma might arise where a mediator learns confidentially from one party that he would pay more than the sum that the other party has told the mediator privately he would be willing to accept. How does the mediator deal with the surplus? Concluding on either the higher or the lower amount would achieve a settlement, but would result in the mediator aligning with one party or the other. What is the mediator to do? Is, for example, the mediator justified in taking a figure somewhere in the middle? Or should the mediator ignore the information and leave the parties to reach their agreement? Views have been expressed that it would be appropriate to discuss the dilemma with the parties and to see whether they would "split" the surplus.

21–113 Ethical dilemmas of this kind occur infrequently. The mediator can invariably deal with them by following sound principles and acting with personal integrity. It is important, however, for practitioners to be alive to these issues and to be prepared to deal with them in a proper and principled manner.

Partial confidentiality of separate meetings

21–114 Parties can agree any permutation they wish between on the one hand having the mediator report everything back to them, and on the other hand, maintaining total confidences. Such a procedure has been developed by the Solicitors' Family Law Association for separate meetings conducted by SFLA mediators. It allows the mediator to maintain total confidence about settlement options, negotiations and discussions (that is, anything that would be without prejudice in the SFLA's model). However, the mediator is obliged to inform the other party of any financial information disclosed in the separate meeting (that is, anything that would be open and available to the court). This allows the mediator to discuss possible settlement terms with parties confidentially in the separate meetings, without eroding the principle that all financial information must be shared on an open basis.

21–115 An adaptation of these rules is to extend the obligation of disclosure to include any material factual information that a party may tell the mediator in a private meeting. That would therefore oblige a mediator to inform the other party if one party told the mediator privately that he was about to leave the country permanently, or that he was about to remarry. (In English law, an intention to remarry is relevant financial information in any event.) The SFLA and other organisations are considering this extension.

7. POWER IMBALANCES

Forms of power

21–116 The issue of power understandably gives rise to many concerns. It is perhaps summed up by the question "How does ADR, which depends upon consensual resolution, deal with the situation where one party to a dispute is more powerful than another and can accordingly use that power to influence the outcome of the dispute?''

To deal with this question, it is first necessary to consider the notion of power in dispute resolution.[32]   **21–117**

Power may superficially seem easy to describe and identify, but in practice it is rarely so, because it exists in different forms and is often subtly exercised. It is affected by the perceptions which parties have of their own power and the power of others, which may or may not be accurate. Power is not necessarily static, but may shift as circumstances change. Power relationships may be complex, and different elements of power may reside in different ways in the parties to provide a more complicated balance than may be obvious.   **21–118**

This will be revealed by analysing any dispute. For example, in a commercial dispute between a multi-national corporation and a small franchisee, there is apparently a clear power imbalance. The multi-national company is likely to have very substantial resources to fight a case, will engage top lawyers, and may be unaffected by the outcome where the small franchisee may be crippled by an adverse outcome. That could well be the true power position. Other factors might, however, balance the power between them. For example, the legal merits of the dispute might favour the franchisee, so that the franchisee might well succeed in a trial. There may be other franchisees interested in the way the multi-national company deals with its franchisees, which could make its handling of the situation politically sensitive. The multi-national company might also be sensitive to adverse publicity if it crushed a small company in what could be portrayed as a "David and Goliath" encounter. The financial collapse of the franchisee in the event of the multi-national company winning at a trial might be a less satisfactory outcome for the multi-national company than working out a solution that allowed the franchisee to continue in business. The circumstances and factors comprising the total power relationship between the parties might not be as one-sided as first impressions might have suggested.   **21–119**

In this example, mediation of the dispute between the parties could well provide them each with what they need, namely a mutually acceptable, agreed resolution of their differences. The suggestion sometimes made that litigation would be more effective in redressing power disparities would not necessarily be valid in this situation. The power imbalance would be manifest in litigation, which might operate to favour the multi-national company with its ability to extend and prolong the dispute. The smaller company would perhaps be hard pressed to sustain and fund lengthy and expensive litigation, which in the final analysis it could not be assured of winning, given the uncertainties and risks inherent in the litigation system.   **21–120**

Similarly, a husband who is a businessman with a domineering manner may appear to have a clear power imbalance over a wife without remunerative employment and with a quiet manner. This may well be a true reflection of the power balance; but there may be other factors that would   **21–121**

---

[32] For a brief discussion of this concept, see Chap. 6 "Negotiation" under the sub-heading "Power".

make the situation more complicated. For example, the wife's quiet manner may conceal a determination and a strength which may have supported the family in stressful times, and on which the husband may have come to depend. Or alternatively, it may reflect unwillingness by the wife to participate in any process in a co-operative way, which can carry its own power.

21–122   The wife may have a more powerful position, actual or perceived, with regard to the children of the family. ("Do not use the children as pawns in your disagreement" is a very proper admonition to couples; but this may not recognise the complex and subtle nature of power relationships and family dynamics.) The husband's attitude may hide his own fears and concerns about the future: his bluster may conceal his anxieties about losing his spouse, his home, his children and financial security. There are likely to be other factors further affecting the power balance. This example again illustrates that power imbalances are not always what they seem. The wife in this example may have more power than may be apparent. This is not to suggest that subdued wives are necessarily powerful and that dominant husbands are necessarily vulnerable, which would be nonsense, but rather that power may be a more complicated notion than initially evident. Nor does this suggest any gender assumptions: an apparently powerful wife and subdued husband may equally have greater balance of power than may at first seem to be the case.

21–123   Practitioners need to be aware of the different forms of power and the way in which these manifest themselves. Power can be overt or covert. Maintaining silence and declining to co-operate effectively with the process can be very powerful. Practitioners cannot make premature assumptions about power because it can be more complex than may initially be appreciated.

Power imbalances: the mediator's role

21–124   Where two substantial corporations are in dispute with one another, engaging highly expert and experienced lawyers, there could well be a power balance between them. Even in that case, there could be a disparity because legal rights and prospects of success may vary, individual styles and skills of management and decision-making may be different, and other factors such as vulnerability to adverse publicity or shareholder criticism may apply differently to each.

21–125   A couple who are, for example, both articulate professionals earning similar amounts may seem to be balanced in their respective power. It cannot be assumed, however, that their power relationship is necessarily equal. They may however be able to achieve a broad form of equality, by one being stronger in some respects and the other being stronger in different ways. It is rare that power is identically based in such situations. Similarly, power may be balanced by one party having greater financial power where the other has greater power through children and family. This may not necessarily result in an equality of power: assessing the true balance may be a difficult task.

21–126   Where parties have equal power, they behave more co-operatively, function more effectively and behave in a less exploitative or manipulative manner than when the relationship is unequal.[33] In most cases, there is likely to be some power disparity between parties. This raises questions for practitioners who work in a facilitative mode, particularly mediators.

Should a mediator try to redress a power imbalance?

Employment mediators and conciliators who facilitate issues between employers and employees commonly take the view that it is not their function to redress power imbalances. The power balances, for example between large employers and trade unions representing employees, can be delicately poised. At times one side may have greater power, at times the other. Mostly, their joint interests are served by finding solutions that do not test their power balance. In this context, employment mediators and conciliators consider that the parties have to continue working with one another and that it would be inappropriate to contemplate trying to redress the power balance between them. **21–127**

Analogous points may arise in other kinds of mediation. If parties engage the mediator to help them resolve specific issues, does that entitle the mediator to assume the role of redressing their power balance (even if he or she could do so, which is seldom the case)? On the other hand, if power imbalances exist, can mediation, which depends on parties being able to negotiate with one another, work effectively and fairly? **21–128**

This issue has been debated among mediators. Christopher W. Moore outlines the arguments in his book, *The Mediation Process: Practical Strategies for Resolving Conflict.*[34] "One argument states that a mediator has an obligation to create just settlements and must therefore help empower the underdog to reach equitable and fair agreements. Another school argues that mediators should do little, if anything, to influence the power relations of disputing parties because it taints the intervenor's impartiality".[35] **21–129**

The following thoughts may be useful in this regard: **21–130**

- Mediators cannot assume that in the ordinary course they can or should automatically try to address issues of power balancing that arise in the mediation. They should consider whether this is part of the brief required by the parties, and whether it would be proper and possible for them to do so.

- The mediator's responsibility is not to seek to change the power relationship between the parties, but rather to ensure that any power disparity that exists does not impact on the process in such a way as to make it unworkable or unfair. This approach accepts the existence of power disparities and places some responsibility on the mediator to deal with these, but only insofar as may be necessary to render the process fair and effective.

- The mediator should appreciate that power imbalances are complex and that superficial appearances of imbalance may not give the whole

---

[33]Christopher W. Moore, *The Mediation Process: Practical Strategies for Resolving Conflict* at p. 334 (see n. 34).

[34]Jossey-Bass (1996) at pp. 68, 69 and 333–337.

[35]At p. 69.

picture. However, mediators can initially take power imbalances at their face value and need not delay in dealing with those that present themselves. If other facets of the imbalance manifest themselves, the mediator can then consider whether and how to address those.

- Where imbalances are observed, the mediator should always be vigilant in guarding against any abuse of the process. He or she will be likely to observe as the process unfolds whether the parties can use the process effectively, perhaps testing the position from time to time with appropriate questions, and assessing whether there are any indications that the power imbalance is affecting the negotiations.

- If power imbalances are severe, affect the process and cannot be redressed, they will almost certainly prevent one of the parties from being able to negotiate with the other effectively in the mediation forum. This may for example occur where one party consistently dominates, harasses, threatens or abuses the other. In such event, the mediation is unlikely to be able to continue and the mediator would have a responsibility to end it. However, power imbalances that do not affect the process, such as financial power, would not necessarily be a reason to end the process.

21–131   A well and sensitively managed mediation can be effective in redressing some of the power imbalances that may be brought into the process, and many people have found that mediation can be empowering. However, it cannot and does not undertake to rearrange the reality of the power relationships between parties. What it can aspire to do is to ensure that mediators are sensitive to such imbalances and able to suggest procedures or use strategies which help to exclude these imbalances from the communications and negotiations between the parties so far as this is realistic and practicable. Parties need to be able to move to terms mutually acceptable for the resolution of their differences without the imbalances prejudicing this outcome.

21–132   The *transformative model of mediation*[36] does not directly address the issue of power imbalances. Instead, it does so indirectly through its twin approach of empowerment and recognition. Instead of viewing disputes as problems, it sees a conflict as "first and foremost a potential occasion for growth in two critical and interrelated dimensions of human morality. The first dimension involves strengthening the self. This occurs through realizing and strengthening one's inherent human capacity for dealing with difficulties of all kinds by engaging in conscious and deliberate reflection, choice and action. The second dimension involves reaching beyond the self to relate to others. This occurs through realizing and strengthening one's inherent human capacity for experiencing and expressing concern and consideration for others, especially others whose situation is 'different' from one's own."[37]

21–133   Transformative mediators would therefore not approach the issue of power from the perspective of seeking ways to balance power. Their approach

---

[36]See para. 1–040.
[37]Bush & Folger *The Promise of Mediation* (1994) at p. 81.

would be to see the conflict as an opportunity for parties to discover and strengthen their resources for dealing both with the substantive issues and the relationship questions, to develop their inherent capacities for strength of self and relating to others. Power would arise in a very different way from the concept of a mediator helping to redress imbalances. Rather, it would arise through the concept of empowerment, which, in general terms, is said to be "achieved when disputing parties experience a strengthened awareness of their own self-worth and their own ability to deal with whatever difficulties they face, regardless of external constraints".[38] All people engaged in conflict (even "powerful" executives) are said to feel unsettled, fearful and vulnerable, and can be empowered as to goals, options, skills, resources and decision-making, irrespective of outcome. By empowerment and by giving recognition (by voluntarily becoming more open, attentive, sympathetic and responsive) based on this empowerment, it is said that parties will experience the "strengthening of self and greater actualization of their capacity for relating to others, and they will advance in both critical dimensions of moral development".[39]

Bush and Folger say "As we are using the term, empowerment does not   **21–134** mean 'power balancing' or redistribution of power within the mediation process itself in order to protect weaker parties. Indeed, empowerment is always practised with both parties. Of course, empowering *both* parties, in our sense, may indeed change the balance of power, if one party starts off with greater self-confidence and self-determinative ability. That, however, is a side effect of empowerment and not a conscious objective."[40]

What steps could a mediator take to redress power imbalances?
A mediator may consider it necessary to act to try to redress power   **21–135** imbalances where these are adversely affecting the fairness and efficacy of the process.[41] If the weaker party is unable to function effectively in the mediation forum, the mediator may wish to intervene to make it more possible for him or her to be more effective. The problem about this is that it could become or be perceived as partial and lacking the even-handedness that should characterise proper mediation practice.

Moore distinguishes between "the situation in which a mediator assists in   **21–136** recognizing, organizing, and marshaling the existing power of a disputant and that in which a mediator becomes an advocate and assists in generating new power and influence. The latter strategy clearly shifts the mediator out of his or her impartial position, whereas the former keeps the mediator within the power boundaries established by the parties".[42] Moore acknowledges that "there is no easy answer to this strategic and ethical problem....".

The mediator might use any of the following strategies for addressing   **21–137** unequal power positions between parties that affect the process:

---

[38]Bush & Folger at p. 84.
[39]*op. cit.* at p. 95.
[40]*op. cit.* at pp 95, 96.
[41]The mediator may be obliged by the Code of Practice to do so. See for example s. 6 of the Law Society's Family Mediation Code, reproduced in Appendix II.
[42]*op. cit.* at p.69.

- Trying to ensure that proper information is brought into the process to redress any imbalance in the possession of data (because having and controlling information is a form of power).

- Assisting parties in considering any such information.

- Providing legal or other information on an even-handed basis, without purporting to advise the parties as to their respective rights.

- Allowing both or all parties a proper opportunity to express their views and to be heard.

- Preventing abusive, threatening or harassing behaviour including sarcasm or other forms of belittling or ridicule.

- Helping a party to articulate their views and proposals (always ensuring that they remain the party's views and proposals, and not becoming the party's spokesperson).

- Agreeing rules with the parties to make communications and negotiations more effective.

- Helping the parties to deal with their concerns and interests in a way that is constructive and not unduly threatening to them.

- Discussing and agreeing rules that prevent a party from exercising undue power or influence that could improperly affect the outcome of the mediation, either inside the process or, as far as practicable, outside it.

- If the parties are not legally represented, suggesting that they take independent legal advice, or suggesting that legal advisers join them in the process, where appropriate.

21–138   A practitioner who remains concerned about the issue of power imbalance, either initially or perhaps after having worked with the parties for a while, could discuss this issue with the parties in some appropriate manner, to establish their views about it. While eventually having to make his or her own decision, the practitioner may be guided by the parties' views and preferences, in particular the genuine preference of the party perceived as having less power, so far as these can be effectively established.

21–139   If a practitioner believes that a party is participating unwillingly in the process or is in any respect not acting in a voluntary way, or if despite all reasonable steps, the issue of power imbalance remains an obstacle to proper and effective negotiation, that would need to be dealt with, and if necessary, the process should be terminated. In this regard, a Code of Practice would help to inform the mediator's actions.

21–140   As mediation and other ADR processes are voluntary and consensual, a party who feels that a power imbalance or any other consideration is leading to an unacceptable or unfair result can refuse to continue with the process or to enter into an agreement.

21–141   If the existence of power imbalances between parties meant that they could not negotiate settlements of their disputes with one another, but would have to get those resolved by the courts, no cases would ever be settled unless parties had equal power. That, of course, is not the reality of the position. In fact, parties are constantly settling their cases, many of them finding that the litigation system does not in practice offer them power equalisation any more than any other process could do so.

Nevertheless, litigation does offer those who can afford it or who are **21–142** funded by legal aid the opportunity to come to court with their more powerful opponents on relatively even terms. Where the disparities in power are so great that no agreement could realistically be negotiated, either between parties and their lawyers bilaterally or in an ADR process, litigation may well be the way to proceed. Most cases are, however, amenable to ADR processes despite the fact that power disparities may exist, as long as these are not so great as to exclude effective negotiation and agreement.

8. CONCLUSION

The issues addressed in this chapter are important in private and public sector **21–143** mediation of all kinds. They are particularly important in court-annexed mediation especially if there is an element of compulsion as where, for example, judges exercise their powers under the new Rule 26.4. If public confidence in ADR is to develop, clear and generally acceptable standards of ethics for mediators will be necessary. Sanctions for breach will be required, initially imposed by the professional or other bodies to which the mediators may belong, but alternatively, in the case of court-annexed mediation, by the judges. For example, judges may perhaps disbar a mediator from acting in any further court-annexed mediation or, in extreme cases of misconduct, even make a wasted costs order against a mediator who has breached the trust of the parties. Similar principles should apply to practitioners using all other kinds of ADR processes.

CHAPTER 22

CONFIDENTIALITY AND PRIVILEGE

22–001   In this Chapter, the legal issues of confidentiality and privilege are considered. For a discussion of moral and ethical aspects of confidentiality see Chapter 21. These issues of confidentiality and privilege are of considerable importance to mediation and other ADR processes. Parties using these processes will usually do so on the basis that they can discuss matters freely in the expectation that they will be disclosed neither publicly nor to a court in the event of the process not resulting in an agreed outcome.

22–002   Confidentiality and privilege are different concepts and either one can exist in relation to material without the other being present. However, because they may overlap in respect of the same material, they are sometimes blurred.

22–003   Whereas English law relating to confidentiality is relatively straightforward, the position concerning privilege in relation to mediation and other ADR processes is less clear, and remains unresolved. This situation is not peculiar to England and Wales, but has been and continues to be a subject grappled with in most jurisdictions throughout the world where ADR is used. Some examples of the debate and discussion taking place in this connection may usefully be mentioned. In Scotland, the Scottish Law Commission published a Discussion Paper in 1991 on the subject of "Confidentiality in Family Mediation"[1] which contains a very useful summary of the law on this subject in Scotland, England and Wales and other jurisdictions. It outlines those areas where reservations or uncertainties exist and presents the issues and the options for reform. A paper published in 1992 entitled "Evidence in Family Mediation" followed this.[2] In Victoria, Australia, the Attorney General's Working Party on ADR submitted a report in 1990, addressing the issues of confidentiality and privilege. It indicated some of the gaps in the law so far as ADR was concerned, and suggested the desirability of considering the enactment of legislation to meet the situation. In the United States, a symposium of jurists, scholars and mediators met under the auspices of the Center for Public Dispute Resolution and discussed critical issues in ADR including the subject of mediator confidentiality. They considered the inconsistencies of the statutes and judicial decisions applicable

---

[1] Discussion Paper No. 92, published by the Scottish Law Commission of 140 Causewayside, Edinburgh EH9 1PR.

[2] SLC–136. It was also followed by the Civil Evidence (Family Mediation) (Scotland) Act 1995, which provides for a family mediation privilege.

in this field, and expressed differences of view as to how this might be remedied.[3]

These subjects will be considered separately, but their overlap has been observed. **22–004**

Confidentiality has been the subject of some debate in the context of arbitration. In 1995 the High Court of Australia rejected the view that a general duty of confidence does exist, a decision later described as "nuclear" by Lord Neill Q.C. (commenting in the 1995 Bernstein lecture[4] on *Esso Australia Resources Limited & Others v. Ploughman (Minister for Energy and Minerals) & Others*.[5] The shock waves of the *Esso Australia* decision were felt outside Australia. The New Zealand Arbitration Act 1996, which came into force on July 1, 1997, included provisions in section 14 creating a general rule of confidentiality but allowing the parties to agree otherwise. **22–005**

In England, the Court of Appeal considered the issue in *Ali Shipping Corp. v. Shipyard Trogir*.[6] Citing the *Esso Australia* case, the Court of Appeal held that the English law position was that the arbitration agreements in that case included terms implied as a matter of law which obliged the parties to maintain confidentiality in the proceedings. The Admiralty Court has since followed the *Ali Shipping* case, although the judge found that confidentiality in the relevant arbitration agreements was qualified by the custom and practice in that trade of making awards available to arbitrators and counsel in other cases concerning the standard form of agreement. **22–006**

The *Esso Australia* decision came as the Departmental Advisory Committee (advising the Secretary of State on the new arbitration legislation) was in the first steps of its work on a new arbitration statute. The Committee was emphatically of the view that confidentiality was fundamental to the conduct of arbitration as traditionally presented in England. However, it was felt that to attempt a comprehensive statutory definition of confidentiality in English arbitration was fraught with difficulty and that it was best left to the courts to develop a pragmatic theory in the light of actual cases. Consequently, there is no provision for confidentiality in the new arbitration legislation. **22–007**

1. CONFIDENTIALITY

General principles

If someone communicates information not generally available to the public to another person in confidence on the basis, either explicit or implicit, that it will not be disclosed to anyone else or used for an unauthorised purpose, any unauthorised use or disclosure can lead to an action under English law for breach of confidence. **22–008**

---

[3] See the report on this symposium in 12(1) Seton Hall Legis J. (1988) and the articles contained in it "Toward Candor or Chaos: The Case of Confidentiality in Mediation" by Michael L. Prigoff and "The Model Mediator Confidentiality Rule: A Commentary" by Jonathan M. Hyman, the latter with attached useful annotated bibliography.

[4] "Confidentiality in Arbitration" published in *Arbitration* August 1996.

[5] (1995) 128 A.L.R. 391.

[6] [1998] 1 Lloyd's Rep. 643.

22–009   The plaintiff can establish a cause of action by showing:

- that he communicated information of a confidential nature to the defendant;

- that the circumstances under which it was communicated imposed an obligation on the defendant to maintain confidentiality;

- and that the defendant used or disclosed the confidential information in a way which was not intended and without authority.[7]

- For a private individual to bring such an action, it is also necessary to show that he has suffered some actual or potential detriment.[8]

22–010   Where information is widely known then it will not ordinarily acquire confidential status sufficient to found a cause of action merely by the person disclosing it adding a stipulation for confidentiality. Similarly, information which was confidential but which has been made public cannot be protected by an injunction.[9]

22–011   There are also separate considerations as to the professional implications of an unauthorised breach of confidence, whether or not a legal action can be founded. For example, a solicitor who breaches this trust may be reported to the Law Society for unprofessional conduct; and such a breach could infringe the Code of Practice of some mediation organisations.

22–012   The duty to keep information confidential may arise explicitly or by implication. To make it explicit, the person communicating the information specifies in terms before giving it that it will be furnished on a confidential basis. This may be oral or contained in a written communication, such as a letter or agreement. Alternatively, it may be implied by the circumstances surrounding the communication. For example, an employee who receives secret information in the course of his employment will ordinarily be expected to maintain it confidentially and a duty of trust and confidence would be implied, as well as "an obligation binding his conscience" quite apart from contract.[10] The courts are likely to restrain the disclosure of confidential information passing between husband and wife.[11]

Confidentiality in ADR[12]

22–013   One of the features of ADR is that, unlike most litigation, it is usually confidential. An ADR practitioner will invariably have some duty of confidentiality towards the parties, which may arise by explicit agreement or by implication. Some forms of ADR are not confidential in nature, for

---

[7]See *Halsbury's Law of England* (4th ed.) para. 1455; *Coco v A. N. Clark (Engineers)* [1969] R.P.C. 41; *Fraser v Evans* [1969] 1 Q.B. 349, [1969] 1 All E.R. 8.

[8]See *Attorney-General v. Guardian Newspapers Ltd (No. 2)* [1988] 3 All E.R. 545 (the "Spycatcher" case).

[9]*O. Mustad & Son v. S Allcock & Co. Ltd* [1963] 3 All E.R. 416, *sub nom. Mustad & Son v. Dosen* [1964] 1 W.L.R. 109.

[10]See *Halsbury's Laws of England* (4th ed.) para. 1455; and *Saltman Engineering Co. Ltd v. Campbell Engineering Co. Ltd* [1963] 3 All E.R. 413.

[11]*Argyll v. Argyll* [1967] Ch. 302

[12]This chapter deals with the legal aspects of confidentiality; but see also the section on the ethics of confidentiality in Chap. 21.

example, the mediation of public policy issues which may positively require public exposure; or there may be some private processes which, because of the nature of the issues or other particular reasons, the parties may agree necessitate disclosure. In most cases, however, the parties will expect, and the ADR practitioner will offer, privacy and confidentiality.

Confidentiality may relate to different aspects of the process: **22–014**

Process confidentiality

There is the duty that the neutral may owe to the parties to treat as **22–015** confidential all matters dealt with in the process. The practitioner's duty of confidentiality may arise from the agreement to enter into the process, from the code of practice regulating it, and/or from representations made when the ADR service was offered to the parties. If none of these apply, then the question may arise as to whether there is any such duty on the part of the practitioner. In the absence of any special features militating against confidentiality, it is likely that the maintenance of confidentiality by the neutral practitioner will be understood to be an implicit feature of the ADR process.[13]

Confidentiality of separate meetings or caucuses

In those models where the neutral practitioner meets the parties separately by **22–016** way of caucusing, there may be a further duty to each party to maintain confidentiality in relation to the separate matters confided to the practitioner by the separate parties. The practitioner may have agreed not to disclose without authority. The caucusing procedure involves the practitioner, usually a mediator, meeting each party separately and engaging in a form of shuttle diplomacy, carrying messages back and forth and assisting them with their negotiations. While it may be agreed that any matters discussed separately will be disclosed to the joint meeting, it will more usually involve the practitioner asking each party to confide in him or her. The usual promise is that such confidences will be respected, and that nothing will be said to the other party without specific authority. The practitioner uses the information gained in this way to facilitate a resolution. The risk, however, of inadvertently breaching the duty of confidentiality owed to each party could be considerable, and practitioners must act with the greatest of care to avoid any such lapse. In practice, they should check the limits of their authority to disclose information at the end of each separate meeting.

Some mediators are understood to reverse the onus of disclosure, by **22–017** arranging with the parties that, unless specifically asked not to do so, they will assume that they are authorised to disclose what has been discussed. This, however, creates a different dynamic in the process and is not commonly used.

In the United States, most statutes and court rules establishing court- **22–018** annexed mediation programmes include confidentiality provisions, for example, in Arizona, Florida and Texas. Some states, for example, California

---

[13]Though the *Esso Australia* case mentioned above might raise doubts about this. The *Ali Shipping* case did not establish an automatic principle of confidentiality for arbitration, but linked it to implied contract terms.

and Massachusetts, have mediator confidentiality provisions as part of their rules of evidence, or otherwise independent of a court-annexed programme (though in some cases written agreement between parties is also required).

22–019   Many confidentiality provisions incorporate exceptions to the general rule of confidentiality. Several provide that information disclosed in mediation may be subject to discovery if there is an independent ground for discovery.[14] A few of the statutes have an exception for discovery in actions between the mediator and a party to the mediation for damages arising out of the mediation.[15] In others, confidentiality may be subject to policy-based exceptions, such as where child abuse (Washington D.C., Texas and Colorado) or abuse of the elderly (Texas) is disclosed, where any statute requires disclosure (Arizona), where violence occurs or is threatened (Arizona), where the information reveals an intent to commit a felony (Colorado), or a criminal or illegal act likely to result in death or serious bodily harm (New Jersey), or where public interest requires disclosure (New Jersey).[16]

When confidentiality is not applicable

22–020   Where a process is based on express or implied confidentiality, how far is a neutral practitioner bound to maintain that confidentiality in the event of receiving information that he or she considers it necessary to disclose? This could, for example, relate in a family mediation to an allegation or admission of child abuse. In a commercial mediation it could relate to information that a state of affairs exists which constitutes a danger to third parties' safety or health such as a public structure which has serious flaws and is in danger of collapse.[17]

22–021   The answer to this may be found either in the terms of the contract providing for the process or in the general law.

Confidentiality excluded or limited by agreement

22–022   Parties may contract to have confidentiality or to exclude it; or they may agree to confidentiality with specified exceptions.

22–023   The first question therefore is to establish in each individual situation the actual terms of the duty of confidentiality. This can, of course, be regulated by the mediator or by the organisation providing the process, by providing carefully considered provisions in its rules, agreement or code of practice.

22–024   There seems to be an increasing tendency to provide exceptions to confidentiality in organisational rules, codes and agreement terms. For examples, see Chapter 21. These provisions generally provide that if a mediator believes from information received in the process that some specified harm might arise, the mediator is freed from the duty of confidentiality.

22–025   In order for such provisions to be legally effective, they must be

---

[14]See *e.g.* Colo. Rev. Stat. ss. 13–22–307 (4); N.J. Sup. Ct. R. 1:40–4(b); Tex. Civ. Prac. & Rem. Code 154.073(c); Va. Code. Ann. ss. 8.01–581.22.

[15]See, *e.g.* Ariz. Rev. Stat. Ann ss. 12–134(B)(2); Colo. Rev. Stat. ss. 13–22–307 (2)(d); Va. Code. Ann. ss. 8.01–581.22.

[16]See Chap. 21 for further details of exceptions and for the ethical implications.

[17]See Chap. 21 at paras 21–093 *et seq.*

incorporated into the terms of the agreement with the parties for the conduct of the process. It is little use a mediator being bound by the terms of a Code of Practice regulating confidentiality if those terms are not known and accepted by the parties.

This may be done in specific terms, or by reference to those terms, or by incorporating the Code into the agreement. If disclosure took place properly within the terms of an incorporated exception, a party would not have cause for complaint or action.

22–026

Confidentiality excluded or limited by legal principles

The further question arises as to whether a mediator may under any circumstances be freed from the duty of confidentiality, even if this has not been excluded by agreement. If a mediator who is contractually bound by confidentiality, without any exclusionary provisions, obtains information as to child abuse or a dangerous public structure, are there circumstances under which the duty of confidentiality will not be applicable?

22–027

The test must be whether the public interest justifies the disclosure notwithstanding what would otherwise be a duty of confidence.[18] It has been said that the confidential information will not be restrained from being disclosed where there is a just cause for such disclosure[19]: "The true doctrine is that there is no equity in the disclosure of iniquity".[20] It may be more difficult to decide what constitutes iniquity, and whether its nature is such that it overrides the duty of confidence. If so, is it of such a nature as to be reported to some appropriate authority, or indeed released to the public through the mass media?[21]

22–028

ADR does not constitute an exception to the general law of confidentiality, nor does it provide a cloak to protect a party from an iniquity disclosed during its course.

22–029

Summary of principles guiding decisions on confidentiality

A mediator or other neutral practitioner has a legal duty in the first instance to maintain the confidentiality contractually promised to the parties, explicitly or implicitly. Consequently, the practitioner must be alive to those obligations and must carry them out, subject to contractual or legal exceptions.

22–030

The contractual exceptions may allow a practitioner to be released from confidentiality in certain specified circumstances. The practitioner needs to be aware of these and their implications.

22–031

A practitioner contractually bound to maintain confidence without contractual exclusions faced with having to choose between the conflicting duties of confidence and public interest may need to ask the following questions: first, is there iniquity? Secondly, is there a public interest to disclose it? Thirdly, does the public interest override the duty of confidentiality? The general law will guide the mediator in considering these questions. Great care will be needed, because of the inherent responsibilities

22–032

---

[18]See *W. v. Egdell* [1990] Ch. 359.
[19]*Fraser v. Evans* [1969] 1 Q.B. 349.
[20]*Gartside v. Outram* (1857) 26 L.J. Ch. 113.
[21]*Initial Services Ltd v. Putterill* [1968] 1 Q.B. 396. There is a question of balancing interests involved here: see also *Lion Laboratories Ltd v. Evans* [1985] Q.B. 526.

to the parties and to the process, balanced against public duty and conscience; also because of the risk of personal liability in the event of a disclosure that is considered to be wrongful and actionable.

2. PRIVILEGE[22]

22–033   The general rule of evidence is that all persons are both competent (legally qualified) to give evidence and compellable (obliged by law) to answer all questions put to them which are competent (do not contravene any rule of law) and relevant (sufficiently related to the matter under investigation).

22–034   There is a small category of witnesses who are deemed not to be competent such as those who through youth or mental or physical incapacity are unable to understand questions or answer them intelligently. In addition, certain persons are not competent witnesses in certain matters; for instance judges in proceedings before them, jurors as to their deliberations and arbitrators as to their awards.

22–035   In criminal proceedings section 80 of the Police and Criminal Evidence Act 1984 (PACE) governs the competence and compellability of the spouse of an accused. Broadly, a spouse is competent to give evidence for the prosecution against the accused if not also charged, but only compellable in respect of certain offences of violence and sexual abuse. For the defence, a spouse is competent and compellable unless jointly charged.

22–036   Two categories of witnesses are deemed competent but are able to choose whether to testify. First, there are those who are not compellable such as the sovereign, foreign heads of state and holders of diplomatic immunity. Secondly, there are those who are privileged.

22–037   Privilege may be defined as follows: "Privilege in the law of evidence is the right of a person to insist on there being withheld from a judicial tribunal information which might assist it to ascertain certain facts relevant to an issue upon which it is adjudicating".[23]

22–038   The ground for allowing the information to be withheld is that to answer the question or to supply the documents would infringe some interest, the protection of which is more important in the eyes of the law than the ascertainment of the truth and administration of justice in the particular case.[24] There is an important distinction between the privilege attaching to disclosure of documents and admissibility. Thus a note of a without prejudice discussion which may be inadmissible if privilege is claimed cannot be privileged from disclosure.[25]

22–039   The law of England and Wales traditionally recognises three classes of privilege:

---

[22] A useful summary in relation to privilege in family disputes is provided in the report of the Scottish Law Commission Discussion Paper No. 92 published in March 1991, see n. 1 above.
[23] Law Reform Committee, 16th report (Privilege in Civil proceedings), Cmnd. 3472 (1967), para. 1.
[24] C. Tapper, *Cross and Tapper on Evidence,* 8th ed., 1995.
[25] *Parry v. News Group Newspapers Ltd,* (1990) 140 New L.J. 1719.

- First, the exclusion of evidence on the grounds of public policy, known as public interest immunity.

- Secondly, the exclusion of certain information, principally communications in relation to litigation, on the grounds of confidentiality.

- Thirdly, a party will not be compelled to give disclosure of documents or answer questions that tend to incriminate or expose the party to proceedings for a penalty.

The House of Lords has emphasised that this area of the law has developed over the years and the categories are not closed and are at times interlinked.[26]   **22–040**

To establish public interest immunity the claimant needs to be able to show that the public interest requires that the information shall not be disclosed and that the public interest is so strong as to override the ordinary right and interest of the litigant that he should be able to lay before the Court of Justice all the relevant evidence.[27] Such claims are not restricted to departments or organs of central government.[28]   **22–041**

The third head of privilege, the "privilege against self-incrimination", protects an accused from the need to give evidence which may incriminate and was authoritatively formulated by Goddard L.J. in *Blunt v. Park Lane Hotel.*[29] It is, however, not an absolute rule. It is subject to certain statutory exceptions such as those of the Criminal Evidence Act 1898 (no privilege in respect of the offence for which the accused is being tried) and section 14 of the Civil Evidence Act 1968, (no privilege in respect of liability for penal proceedings abroad).   **22–042**

Confidentiality creating privilege

The mere fact that information may be regarded as confidential by reason of a contractual, professional or moral obligation does not of itself create a right or privilege to withhold it in legal proceedings.[30] The primary heads of privilege that arise from the concept of confidentiality are: **22–043**

Professional privilege

The first head is that communications between a professional legal adviser and his client are privileged although they may not relate to any suit pending or one which is contemplated or apprehended.[31]   **22–044**

The reason for this privilege is that it is believed that it promotes the public interest because it assists and enhances the administration of justice by facilitating the representation of clients by legal advisers.[32]   **22–045**

It should be noted that communications must be made for professional   **22–046**

---

[26]*D. v. NSPCC* [1977] 2 W.L.R. 201.
[27]*R v. Lewes JJ., ex p. Home Secretary* [1973] A.C. 388.
[28]*D. v. NSPCC*, n. 26 above.
[29][1942] 2 K.B. 253 at 257.
[30]*Santa Fe International Corp. v. Napier Shipping S.A.* 1985 L.T. 430. This distinction between confidentiality and privilege is a significant one.
[31]*McCowan v. Wright* (1852) 15 D. 229.
[32]*Grant v. Downs* (1976) 135 C.L.R. 674, (High Court of Australia).

purposes (with a lawyer whom the client has engaged in a professional relationship) to be broadly construed.[33] The privilege lies with the client and if waived the lawyer must testify and produce any documents sought. Communications made to or by a litigant or his legal adviser to a third party about a matter relevant to litigation at hand is privileged only if made in contemplation of the litigation.[34] If privilege is waived for one particular transaction, it is waived for all relevant documents.[35]

22–047 Once the privilege has been validly claimed, it ordinarily continues to have permanent effect, irrespective of, for example, a change of solicitors. It has been upheld in relation to a new claim by a different plaintiff, even if the subject-matter differs. So, in *The Aegis Blaze* a survey report prepared on behalf of the defendant for one claim remained privileged when a different Plaintiff sued the defendant.[36]

22–048 The privilege may be waived expressly or by implication or it may be lost. If part of a document is disclosed, privilege will be waived for the whole unless the remaining part deals with a different subject-matter.[37]

22–049 Privilege may be lost by inadvertent disclosure of documents which would otherwise have been privileged. The applicable rules were summarised by Slade L.J. in *Guiness Peat Properties Ltd v. Fitzroy Robinson Partnership (a firm).*[38]

Without prejudice

22–050 Admissions made by a party in a course of abortive negotiations for settlement of a dispute may not be admitted as evidence in future proceedings. This is normally referred to as the "without prejudice" rule.

22–051 In *Cutts v. Head* Oliver L.J. noted that the without prejudice rule rests on:

"... [the public policy] ... that parties should be encouraged so far as is possible to settle their disputes without resort to litigation and should not be discouraged by the knowledge that anything that is said in a course of such negotiations (and that includes, of course, as much the failure to reply to an offer as an actual reply) may be used to their prejudice in the course of the proceedings. They should ... be encouraged freely and frankly to put their cards on the table."[39]

22–052 The use of the term "without prejudice" is commonly misunderstood and it is applied in inappropriate circumstances. For example, where parties are communicating about a matter which does not involve settlement negotiations in any way, they wrongly use the term, perhaps intending to import confidentiality or perhaps just misperceiving the function of the privilege. In fact, however, communications will not be privileged simply because they are

---

[33] *Balabel v. Air India* [1988] 1 Ch. 317.
[34] *Crompton (Alfred) Amusement Machines Ltd v. Customs & Excise Commissioners* [1972] 2 Q.B. 102.
[35] *Great Atlantic Insurance Co. v. Home Insurance Co.* [1981] 1 W.L.R. 529.
[36] [1986] 1 Lloyd's Rep. 203, CA.
[37] *Great Atlantic Insurance Co. v. Home Insurance Co.* [1981] 1 W.L.R. 529 and *Pozzi v. Eli Lilly & Co., The Times,* December 3, 1986.
[38] [1987] 2 All E.R. 716 at 729.
[39] [1984] Ch. 290 at 306; also [1984] All E.R. 597 and [1984] 2 W.L.R. 349.

marked "without prejudice". The test is not the description used by the parties, but whether or not the communications are actually directed towards reaching a settlement.

Only such communications will be protected, whether or not they are stated to be "without prejudice". Such communications may, however, be admissible where the issue is whether or not there was a settlement. **22-053**

In the case of *Rush & Tomkins Ltd v. Greater London Council and Another,*[40] the Court of Appeal cited with approval the principle expressed in *Tomlin v. Standard Telephones*[41] which was originally propounded in *Walker v. Wilsher*[42] that: **22-054**

> " . . . I think they mean without prejudice to the position of the writer of the letter if the terms he proposes are not accepted. If the terms proposed are accepted a complete contract is established, and the letter, although written without prejudice, operates to alter the old states of things and to establish a new one."[43]

This quotation was approved as an accurate statement of the meaning of "without prejudice" with the qualification "if that phrase be used without more."[44] Parties could give the phrase a somewhat different meaning, for example where they reserved the right to bring a without prejudice offer to the attention of the court on the question of costs if the offer should not be accepted. Subject to any such modification, the court held that "the parties must be taken to have intended and agreed that the privilege will cease if and when the negotiations 'without prejudice' come to fruition in a concluded agreement." **22-055**

The Court of Appeal in *Rush & Tomkins* went on to lay down a number of principles as to the nature of the without prejudice privilege. These are in outline as follows: **22-056**

(1) Its purpose is to enable parties to negotiate freely without the risk that their proposals could be used against them if the negotiations failed; but that once a settlement is concluded, the privilege goes, having served its purpose.[45]

(2) Parties could use a form of words enabling without prejudice correspondence to be referred to, even if a settlement was not concluded, for example, on the question of costs.[46]

(3) On the other hand, parties could use a form of words to preclude

---

[40] [1988] 1 All E.R. 549.
[41] [1969] 1 W.L.R. 1378.
[42] (1889) 23 Q.B. 335.
[43] *per* Lindley L.J. at 337.
[44] *per* Balcolmbe L.J. at 1297.
[45] But this principle was varied on appeal, as amplified in the text.
[46] The principle was established in *Calderbank v. Calderbank* [1975] 3 All E.R. 333 that an offer (a *Calderbank* offer) could be made on a without prejudice basis, while expressly reserving the right to produce the letter to the court on the issue of costs. Without fettering the court's discretion, if the offer is rejected and the court order is for no more than the *Calderbank* offer, the court would be invited to order costs from the time of the offer against the party rejecting the offer.

reference to any such correspondence even after a settlement had been reached.

(4) The privilege does not depend on the existence of proceedings.

(5) Even before any settlement, and while the privilege continued to subsist, there are a number of real or apparent exceptions to it.

(6) The privilege extends to the solicitors of the parties to such negotiations.

22–057   The *Rush & Tomkins* case was taken on further appeal to the House of Lords,[47] on the question as to whether the without prejudice privilege did indeed end once a settlement was achieved, as decided by the Court of Appeal. Lord Griffiths, expressing the unanimous view of the House of Lords, disagreed with the proposition that if the negotiations succeed and a settlement is concluded, the privilege goes, having served its purpose. The cases considering the without prejudice rule showed that "the rule is not absolute". "Resort may be had to the 'without prejudice' material for a variety of reasons when the justice of the case requires it."[48] He held that as a general rule the without prejudice rule "renders inadmissible in any subsequent litigation connected with the same subject-matter proof of any admissions made in a genuine attempt to reach a settlement." This applies to the same parties to the negotiations and settlement. "Admissions made to reach settlement with a different party within the same litigation are also inadmissible whether or not settlement was reached with that party."[49] He concluded that (subject to his earlier comments about having recourse to the without prejudice material when the justice of the case required it) without prejudice communications between parties to litigation needed to be protected from production to other parties in the same litigation.

22–058   In *Parry v. News Group Newspapers Ltd*[50] it was held that a note made by a plaintiff's solicitor of a telephone conversation with the defendant's solicitor was not privileged, even though the conversation itself was without prejudice. The reason given was that as the note was merely a record of the substance of the conversation, it could not be a communication and therefore did not fall to be classed as without prejudice.

22–059   In *Unilever Plc v. Procter & Gamble Company*,[51] Laddie J. considered the scope of information arising in the course of without prejudice discussions which were protected from subsequent disclosure by the without prejudice rule. In line with what may be seen as a tentative but developing support for party-based resolution of disputes, the court held the without prejudice rule to be of wide application. Citing *Walker v. Wilsher, Cutts v. Head* and *Rush & Tomkins Limited v. Greater London Council*,[52] the court concurred with the view that parties should he encouraged as far as possible to settle their disputes without resort to litigation and should not be discouraged by the

---

[47][1989] A.C. 1280.
[48]*ibid.* at 1300.
[49]*ibid.* at 1301.
[50]See n. 25 above.
[51][1999] 2 All E.R.
[52]Cited at nn. 39, 42 and 47 above.

knowledge that anything that is said in a course of such negotiations maybe used to their prejudice in the course of the proceedings. "They should... be encouraged fully and frankly to put their cards on the table". Laddie J. noted that the Civil Procedure Rules, though not in force at the date of his judgment, represented "the current policy aimed at making litigation a last resort... the policy in favour of encouraging pre-litigation settlement is now much stronger than it has been".

The without prejudice rule is very important in the ADR context, because **22–060** it is one of the bases on which privilege is commonly claimed for communications made in ADR processes. At the commencement of commercial or civil mediation, for example, and similarly in divorce mediation, it is usual for the mediator to explain that the communications aimed at the settlement of the dispute will be conducted on a without prejudice basis. Parties will usually be required to agree to this. Many written agreements between the parties and the mediator regulating the terms of the mediation stipulate specifically to this effect. The without prejudice basis is as effective in ADR as it would be in analogous bilateral negotiations. In addition to and apart from the without prejudice rule, however, a public policy privilege could also be sought for mediation.[53] Consequently, both bases for claiming privilege may be maintained.

ADR practitioners should not assume that the without prejudice rule on its **22–061** own would necessarily protect every communication made in the course of mediation or any other ADR process from being admissible in evidence. Foskett outlines a number of circumstances in which the without prejudice veil would be lifted or disregarded.[54] These include communications involving threat, abuse of the rule and lack of good faith; the admission of a fact independent of, or collateral to the subject-matter of the dispute; the situation where the without prejudice document would prejudice the recipient, also where there is no dispute between the parties.

In the family setting, it seems that communications concerning the welfare **22–062** of children, made in the context of without prejudice discussions, may not necessarily be privileged as a result of the without prejudice rule. Depending upon their context and content, they are likely though to be protected by virtue of Practice Directions or under a public policy privilege.[55]

It should be noted that the without prejudice rule is intended to provide a **22–063** privilege to the parties themselves, rather than to any third party through whom they may conduct their negotiations or communications. Consequently the parties may agree to waive or lift the without prejudice aspect and treat any such communications as open, without requiring any consent from any third party intermediary. If therefore a mediator relies exclusively on the without prejudice aspect to prevent anything said in the mediation from being disclosed to the court, or from being called to give evidence in any case, the agreement of the parties may override this. However, there may be alternative provisions which could affect the mediator's personal position, including for example a contractual provision regulating the mediation

---

[53] As to the question of a public policy privilege for mediation, see paras 22–041, 22–051 and 22–079 *et seq.*
[54] *The Law and Practice of Compromise* (4th ed., 1996).
[55] See below for "Mediation about children".

whereby the parties agree not to call the mediator to testify,[56] or perhaps a mediator's privilege in those jurisdictions where this exists.

Reconciliation

22–064 Another limb of privilege has arisen out of the concept of confidentiality, which as Lord Hailsham of St. Marylebone observed "has now developed into a new category of a public interest exception based on the public interest in the stability of marriage".[57] This privilege relates to the intervention of a third party who acts as an intermediary with the object of bringing about a reconciliation between the parties to a marriage and reflects the fact that "in matrimonial disputes the state is an interested party. It is more interested in reconciliation than divorce".[58] It seeks to overcome the established principle that communications between parties in dispute are not privileged unless they are without prejudice.[59]

22–065 There has been a series of decisions in which the courts have supported the notion of privilege for communications between spouses made with a view to establishing a reconciliation, including those made through a third party acting in a mediatory capacity. In one of the earliest of these,[60] Denning L.J. took the view, in relation to spouses' discussions with a probation officer, that even if nothing specific was said in this regard, the parties must be taken to have held their discussions on the basis that what they said would not be disclosed. He extended this in *Mole v. Mole*[61] to cover not only probation officers, but also other persons such as clergy, doctors or marriage guidance counsellors to whom either or both parties may go with a view to effecting a reconciliation. This principle has been applied to communications made through a vicar[62]; a priest acting as marriage guidance counsellor,[63] and even to a private individual who tried to assist spouses to move towards reconciliation.[64] It applies also to letters and to third party witnesses of such efforts.[65]

Mediation about children

22–066 In a significant decision for mediation, *Re D. (minors)*,[66] the Court of Appeal acknowledged the growth and evolution of conciliation concerning children, in court and out of court. Sir Thomas Bingham, M.R., (as he then was) stated "In our judgment the law is that evidence may not be given in proceedings under the Children Act 1989 of statements made by one or other of the parties in the course of meetings held or communications made for the purpose of conciliation save in the very unusual case where a statement is

---

[56] But would this be enforceable? In the interests of the integrity of the mediation process, it is to be hoped that the courts will respect such a provision.
[57] *D. v. NSPCC*, n. 26 above.
[58] *Mole v. Mole* [1950] 2 All E.R. 328 *per* Bucknall L.J.
[59] *Grant v. South Western Properties Ltd* [1974] 2 All E.R. 465.
[60] *McTaggart v. McTaggart* [1948] 2 All E.R. 754.
[61] See n. 58 above, at 329.
[62] *Henley v. Henley* [1955] 2 W.L.R 851.
[63] *Pais v. Pais* [1970] 3 W.L.R 830; [1970] 3 All E.R. 491.
[64] *Theodoropoulas v. Theodoropoulas* [1963] W.L.R 354; [1963] 2 All E.R. 772.
[65] *Slade-Powell v. Slade-Powell* (1964) 108 S.J. 1033.
[66] *Re D. and anor (minors) (conciliation: disclosure of information)* [1993] 2 All E.R. 695; [1993] Fam. 231.

made clearly indicating that the maker has in the past caused or is likely in the future to cause serious harm to the well-being of a child.''

The case of *Re D. (minors)* relates only to children and not to financial and **22–067** other issues arising on divorce. As contended below, this may help in the development of a more general mediation privilege that the courts might in time establish. However, until that has been done, parties in mediation will have to rely on the without prejudice principles to provide evidential privilege for their communications in mediation concerning matters other than children and reconciliation.

A further development in confidentiality in proceedings concerning **22–068** children was made in *Re E.C. (Disclosure of Material)*.[67] A parent was persuaded to admit to causing the death of a child in care proceedings concerning her sister, with the assurance of protection from admissibility of that evidence in criminal proceedings. It was a matter for the court's discretion whether material covered by the protection (under section 98(2) of the Children Act 1989) should be released to the police. In the case, the public interest in promoting frankness, which was in the interests of the child, predominated and material covered by section 98(2) would not be released to the police.

Part 36 of the Civil Procedure Rules
Part 36 of the Civil Procedure Rules introduced a court-sponsored regime for **22–069** the settlement of disputes, adding to the old concept of a payment into court a new concept of an offer to settle. If an offer to settle or payment into court is made in accordance with the provisions of Part 36, cost consequences follow.

The regime extends to offers to settle before proceedings are begun and **22–070** provides that the court will take any such offer into account when making any order as to costs. Part 36 includes restrictions on disclosure of an offer or payment made under that Part, providing in the case of an offer that it will he treated as "without prejudice except as to costs". In the case of a payment into court, that fact is not to be communicated to the trial judge until all questions of liability and the amount of money to be awarded have been decided.

Nothing in Part 36 prevents the parties from pursuing settlement strategies **22–071** outside of the civil procedure rules, in the normal way.

Pre-action offers may be made by a prospective claimant or defendant **22–072** (Rule 36.10). The offer must be open for at least 21 days. If made by the defendant, the offer must include an offer to pay the claimant's costs up to the date 21 days after the offer is made. If served with a claim form, the defendant has to follow up the offer with a payment into court of at least the value of the pre-action offer. Once an action is commenced, a defendant's offer to settle a money claim takes the form of a payment into court.

Financial Dispute Resolution (FDR)
A pilot scheme, the Ancillary Relief Pilot Scheme, was tested in a number of **22–073** courts throughout England and Wales and is now being extended (from June

---

[67] [1996] 2 F.L.R. 123.

2000) to the whole country. Its objective is to provide stricter court control and improved procedures to reduce delay, limit costs and facilitate settlements of family disputes.

22–074   One of the procedures introduced by this scheme is the Financial Dispute Resolution procedure (FDR) in which a District Judge meets the parties and their lawyers with a view to helping move them towards the settlement of financial issues arising on divorce.[68] This FDR hearing is evidentially privileged, to allow the parties and their lawyers freedom to discuss the matter freely and to negotiate settlement terms.[69] The judge dealing with the FDR does not hear the case if the parties do not settle: it is appointed to another judge. In this evidentially privileged environment, the judge can comment on the proposed terms and can, if appropriate, indicate his or her views on the issues.

Estoppel

22–075   Estoppel is a rule that in certain circumstances a person cannot deny the truth of something that he or she has previously asserted. This would, for example, apply where the other person has acted on that assertion and would be prejudiced by the denial, or where the assertion was made in a deed.

22–076   Where parties contract to enter into mediation, the question might arise whether by agreeing to the process or to certain classes of information being treated as privileged, a party may be estopped from introducing in evidence anything arising in the process or any such information obtained. There do not appear to be any reported cases in which such a line has been adopted or rejected; and it is unclear whether or not such an argument would be upheld.

22–077   However, mediation agreements commonly address this possibility. CEDR for example provides as follows in its Model Mediation Procedure:

> "**17.** All documents (which includes anything upon which evidence is recorded including tapes and computer discs) or other information produced for, or arising in relation to, the Mediation will be privileged and not be admissible as evidence or discoverable in any litigation or arbitration connected with the Dispute except any documents or other information which would in any event have been admissible or discoverable in any such litigation or arbitration."

Statutory privilege

22–078   In addition to the general head of confidence, statute has ascribed privilege to certain specific classes of conciliation. Sections 133 and 134 of the Employment Protection (Consolidation) Act 1978 provide that any evidence given to a conciliation officer in the performance of his duties shall not be admissible in evidence. Section 10 of the Contempt of Court Act 1981

---

[68] The FDR is considered in Chaps 3, 10 and 16.

[69] The Family Proceedings (Amendment No. 2) Rules 1997 inserted Rules 2.71 to 2.77 into the Family Proceedings Rules 1991 to cover this scheme. Rule 2.75 deals with the FDR. A Family Division Practice Direction of June 16, 1997, at [1997] 3 All E.R. 768, stipulates that "the FDR appointment is part of the conciliation process and should be so regarded by the courts and the parties". It refers to Rule 2.75(1) and to *Re D. (minors)* and concludes that, with specified exceptions, "evidence of anything said or of any admissions made in the course of an FDR appointment will not be admissible in evidence".

provides protection for journalists and publishers unless it can be shown that disclosure is necessary in the interest of justice, national security or for the prevention of disorder or crime. The Copyright, Designs and Patent Act 1988 provides other specific protection in relation to information passing between agent and client. Practice Directions in the Family Division set out conciliation schemes for disputes over custody and access in which "these discussions will be privileged and will not be disclosed in any subsequent application. Anything said before a district judge on such appointments will also remain privileged".[70]

A mediation privilege?

It remains to be resolved definitively by the English courts (if not by the legislature) whether there is a privilege attaching to the whole mediation process, including all communications passing within that process, whether the mediation relates to family matters, civil or commercial disputes or any other kind of issue.

22–079

As indicated above, the courts from *McTaggart* onwards have supported the existence of a privilege where parties are negotiating towards achieving a reconciliation, on the broad principle that as a matter of public policy this is a desirable end and that the state is more interested in reconciliation than divorce.

22–080

Re D. (minors) was a major step forward towards the development of a general mediation privilege. There is a clear public policy consideration that settlement is a desirable end to disputes and that settlements are preferred to litigation, as appears from *Cutts v. Head*.[71] Given this, it would not be a very substantial step for the courts to extend the privilege established in *Re D. (minors)* to cover also financial, property and other aspects discussed in family mediation and settlement negotiations taking place in civil or commercial negotiations.

22–081

The principles upon which *Re D. (minors)* was based suggest that the courts might well decide in the future that a privilege should attach to other aspects of the mediation process that should be similarly protected on the grounds of public policy. In it, the Court of Appeal said that "in this field as in others it is undesirable that the law should drift very far away from the best professional practice" and that a practice existed which followed the law "in recognising the general inviolability of the privilege protecting statements made in the course of conciliation."

22–082

The courts may take the view that the principle established in *McTaggart* and others related to something in which the State had a public interest, namely the preservation of marriage, whereas it might be said that the State has no such view in relation to the desirability of settlements generally. However, the present indications from the authorities and from public statements by members of the judiciary are that the State does indeed support the principle of consensual dispute resolution. The courts might therefore

22–083

---

[70]Practice Direction (Family Division: Conciliation Procedure) (Nos. 1 & 2) [1982] 1 W.L.R. 1420; [1984] 1 W.L.R. 1326; and particularly [1992] 1 W.L.R. 147 recording the Practice Direction of October 18, 1991. See also the Practice Direction of June 16, 1997, n. 69 above.

[71]See n. 39 above and Oliver L.J.'s words, quoted at para. 22–051 above.

well be expected to support the existence of a privilege for mediation generally.

22–084   It has been submitted that privilege, whether it extends from public interest or from the without prejudice rule, extends to all third parties who act as mediators with a view to enabling the parties to reach a settlement or compromise, whether or not that party is a legal representative.[72] Such was the concern about the uncertainty in this regard that the Booth Committee[73] called for an absolute privilege attaching to conciliation and others have called for the privilege attaching to reconciliation to be extended specifically to statements made in the course of conciliation.[74]

22–085   The Law Commission inquiry into grounds for divorce[75] stated that it now appeared well settled that privilege attached to communications between spouses with a view to reconciliation. It referred to the principle that it was in the public interest for disputes to be settled and litigation avoided.[76] It expressed the view that there should not be doubt about this question of privilege, and recommended that a statutory privilege should be conferred on statements made during the course of conciliation or mediation processes. Its reference was to processes connected with separation or divorce, but it saw no reason in principle why the privilege should not be extended to all disputes which are or may become the subject of family proceedings.[77]

22–086   The Law Commission's view that doubt needs to be resolved and replaced with certainty seems to be beyond question. Equally, there seems to be no logical reason why their proposal for the provision of a statutory privilege should not be extended to all mediation, and not just in relation to family proceedings (of course, the Law Commission was limited by its terms of reference). If the principle is accepted that it is in the public interest for disputes to be settled and litigation avoided, then support is needed for those processes that promote the resolution of disputes in a non-adversarial way.

22–087   It should be said that while there is considerable support for statutory privilege among ADR practitioners, this is not universal. There are those in the United States whose views are widely respected who question whether it is advisable to seek legislation on confidentiality.[78] They query whether blanket legislation could properly cover all forms of ADR and believe that there is adequate protection under existing law. They also express concern about the rights of third parties unless the terms of the privilege were most carefully expressed and delimited. Certainly, if any privilege were to be formulated, it would need to have regard to these concerns.

A privilege or immunity for mediators?

A mediator's privilege

22–088   As the law presently stands, any privilege that might exist attaches to the parties and not to the mediator. Consequently, the parties may agree to waive

---

[72]*Phipson on Evidence,* 14th ed., 1990.
[73]The Report of the Matrimonial Causes Procedure Committee (1955).
[74]For example, Bromley's *Family Law* (7th ed., 1987) at p. 215. See also the 8th ed., 1998.
[75]Law Com. No. 192: October 1990.
[76]Para. 5.40.
[77]Para. 5.44.
[78]*e.g.* Prof. Eric Green, who has written an article "A Heretical View of the Mediation Privilege" at (1986) 2 Ohio St. L.J. 1 and who participated in the symposium, see n. 3 above.

that privilege and allow the mediator to provide the court with any information that arose in the mediation process. There is an issue, however, as to whether privilege should be attached to the mediator as well as the parties involved in the process.

Strong views exist that privilege should extend to the mediator(s) as well **22–089** as the parties. For example, Professor John P. McCrory, Director of the Dispute Resolution Project at Vermont Law School has argued that "if mediators can be compelled to testify, it is likely to influence the way they function".[79] He regards immunity from disclosure as essential to the proper functioning of matrimonial mediation. Others have taken a similar view.[80]

The CPR Institute for Dispute Resolution reports that in the U.S. **22–090** "Increasingly, federal and state court ADR programs have promulgated rules that protect confidentiality and the court-appointed mediator from having to testify, produce documents or otherwise breach the confidentiality of the court ADR process."[81]

Views to the contrary have also been expressed. The Scottish Law **22–091** Commission refers, for example, to the 1967 Law Reform Committee's views that the "without prejudice" rule adequately covered the position.[82] A similar view was expressed by the English Law Commission in their 1990 Report "Family Law: The Ground for Divorce".[83]

A mediator's immunity

A separate question may arise with regard to the appropriateness or otherwise **22–092** of a possible immunity for mediators in relation to the risks to which they may be exposed as a consequence of an actual or alleged breach of confidence, or other matters such as defamation or negligence.

Some contracts for mediation specifically seek to exempt mediators from **22–093** liability for breaches of contract, negligence or other tortuous conduct.[84] Where this is not the case, should there be a statutory immunity for mediators, or should the nature and limit of any immunity be a matter for the common law? A similar debate took place in the preparatory work for the Arbitration Act 1996. Initially, the Departmental Advisory Committee advising the Secretary of State for Trade and Industry, in its second report of

---

[79]"Confidentiality in Mediation of Matrimonial Disputes" (1988) 51 M.L.R. 442 at pp. 454–455, quoted in Scottish Law Commission Discussion Paper No. 92 of March 1991 at para. 5.50.

[80]Diana Parker and Lisa Parkinson express the view that privilege in family mediation should attach to the mediator(s) as well as the parties, to avoid inappropriate potential credibility conflicts between mediators and parties. See "Solicitors and Family Conciliation Services: A Basis for Professional Co-operation" in (1985) 15 Fam. Law 273.

[81]See Kathleen M. Scanlon's *Mediator's Deskbook* (CPR Institute for Dispute Resolution, 1999) at p. 100. This in turn refers to other supporting works including Elizabeth Plapinger and Donna Stienstra's *ADR and Settlement in the Federal District Courts: A Sourcebook for Judges and Lawyers* (Federal Judicial Center & CPR, 1996).

[82]At para. 5.53 of the Discussion Paper, see n. 79 above.

[83]Law. Com. No. 192 at paras. 5.45 and 5.46. It should be noted, however, that para. 5.45 indicates that this recommendation would accommodate "some types of mediation, in which there is both an 'open' and a 'closed' statement...". This refers to having financial information open and settlement proposals privileged. Presumably, however, any mediator's privilege in family mediation could be stated as excluding information specifically provided on an open basis. This would meet this aspect of the Law Commission's concerns.

[84]See, *e.g.* CEDR's Model Mediation Procedure at para. 21, which contains a waiver of liability for any act or omission in connection with the services provided in, or in relation to, the mediation, unless the act or omission is fraudulent or involves wilful misconduct.

May 1991 considered that no statutory immunity should be given to arbitrators. However, such a provision was enacted together with the complementary provision for arbitral institutions. As discussed in Chapter 4, this was for policy reasons given the vulnerability of arbitrators and institutions to personal challenge by parties seeking to derail or delay the process.

22–094   There is a strong arguable case for mediators to be immune from liability for mediation undertaken by them other than for fraud or gross abuse of their position and trust. There is in principle no difference between the protection of a mediator and an arbitrator in this respect and the policy reasons that led to statutory immunity being given to arbitrators apply with equal force to mediators. Some statutory protection is desirable, especially if mediation develops as part of, or as an adjunct to, court procedures.

Clarification and reform

22–095   It is clear that there is still scope and need for clarification and reform of the law relating to privilege in mediation. A statutory privilege for mediation in all fields of activity would achieve this, and would enhance the process. Undoubtedly much care would have to go into both the questions of principle and the pragmatic formulation of the terms and effect of the privilege, as well as any mediator immunity which may, as a separate issue, be considered.

22–096   As previously mentioned, the Scottish Law Commission addressed the whole question of confidentiality and privilege in relation to mediation. Although limited to family matters, their discussion document and the subsequent papers nevertheless covered many of the issues that are relevant to matters other than family. They posed the general question as to whether, in principle, some kind of privilege should attach to information acquired in the course of family mediation; and their provisional conclusion was in the affirmative.[85] They examined whether the scope of the privilege should be left to be developed by judicial decision or defined by statute; and in the latter event, to what extent and with what implications. They suggested for consideration that "the scope of the privilege should be defined by legislation in conventional terms."[86] Their further consideration of the various issues relevant to the subject was comprehensive and thorough, and well worth attention by anyone concerned with the reform of the privilege applicable to any form of mediation.

22–097   The issues outlined in this chapter were raised in the first edition of this work and still remain equally relevant. The trend has, however, developed towards protecting mediators from having to give evidence in court[87] and towards providing immunity for arbitrators.[88] The use and understanding of mediation have developed over the years. To some extent, practice is likely to lead the law; but the issues do need to be addressed thoughtfully and carefully and initiatives in this regard would be welcomed.

---

[85] At para. 5.1.
[86] At para. 5.16. This led to the 1995 Act, see n. 2 above.
[87] See para. 22–090 above and n. 81.
[88] See para. 22–093 above.

CHAPTER 23

ENFORCEMENT OF ADR OUTCOMES

1. DISTINGUISHING ADJUDICATORY AND CONSENSUAL CONTEXTS

Litigation has its own court machinery to enforce its judgments and orders. **23–001**
ADR processes do not, but depend on a number of factors for the
enforcement of the decisions made in them. These factors include the kind of
process used, whether court or other adjudicatory proceedings are pending,
the nature of the resolution arrived at and the intention of the parties.

The primary question will be whether an adjudicatory or non-adjudicatory **23–002**
(consensual) process was used. If adjudicatory, the process is likely to have
its own machinery for enforcement. This chapter will outline the ways in
which adjudicatory determinations are enforced.

If a non-adjudicatory, consensual process was used, the next question will **23–003**
usually be whether it was used in the context of a pending adjudication (for
example, mediation might have been used to settle a case pending in the
court or in arbitration). If so, the settlement agreement might well be
converted into a consent judgment, order or award in the pending
adjudicatory proceedings. In such event, the adjudicatory machinery would be
available for enforcing the consensual outcome as if it was a determination in
the adjudication.

If a consensual process was used in its own right, unconnected to any **23–004**
adjudication, the next question will be whether or not the parties intended
their resolution to constitute a legally binding agreement. In most cases, the
parties are likely to want their settlement terms to be recorded in a legally
binding and enforceable way. In such event, the ADR practitioner will wish
to ensure that this is achieved. Such settlement terms would usually be
legally enforceable as binding contracts between the parties. This Chapter
will consider this further in the consensual context.

Some parties, however, may not want the terms of their resolution to be **23–005**
concluded in a legal context, but would rather have a non-binding, personal
agreement honoured through the commitment of the parties and not
enforceable in law. This kind of outcome is more likely to arise in inter-
personal disputes, including for example disagreements between neighbours,
or involving local children or other issues arising in a community context. In
this event, the practitioner needs to find a form of recording that satisfies the
parties and meets their requirements. If agreements of this nature were
breached, they would not be enforceable through the legal process.

23–006   The enforcement of terms arrived at in an ADR context, whether adjudicatory or consensual, is a matter for the party to undertake personally or through his or her lawyer. It is obviously not a matter for the ADR practitioner concerned with the original process.

2. ADJUDICATORY PROCESSES

23–007 Determinations made in adjudicatory processes must be enforceable to be of value. As a general rule, enforcement is achieved by converting the determination into the form of a court order and then using the resources of the court to enforce the decision. This is not, however, invariably the case as the following analysis will indicate:

Litigation: enforcement of judgments/court orders
23–008 Since April 26, 1999 when the Woolf reforms came into effect, CPR Schedule 1 of the Rules of the Supreme Court, Order 45, covers the enforcement of judgments and orders. The way in which these are enforced will depend on their nature and terms and whether or not any time limit has been imposed for compliance; but there has been no fundamental change from the position prior to April 26, 1999.

23–009   CPR Schedule 1 RSC, Ord. 45, r. 1 deals with the enforcement of a judgment or order for the payment of money, by one or more of the following means, namely:

- Writ of *fieri facias* (*fi. fa.*), under which the debtor's goods are seized and sold as far as necessary to meet the debt.

- Garnishee proceedings, under which money owed by a third party to the debtor is payable directly to the creditor.

- A charging order, which may be placed on the debtor's land or property with an eventual sale if the debt is not paid.

- The appointment of a receiver, who will receive and manage the debtor's property.

- Where Rule 5 applies (see below), an order of committal, under which the debtor may be sent to prison.

- In the latter case, a writ of sequestration, under which the debtor's assets can be seized and dealt with under the authority of and for the benefit of the court.

23–010   In addition to these means, a money judgment or order may be enforced under the Debtors Acts 1869 and 1878, by bankruptcy or winding-up procedures, or under section 105(1) of the County Courts Act 1984 (High Court judgment enforceable by the county court on application).[1]

23–011   The enforcement of a judgment for the possession of land is covered by

---

[1] For further information see The Civil Procedure Rules 1998, Sched. 1, RSC 45.

CPR Schedule 1, Ord.45, r. 3, which provides for a writ of possession in addition to an order of committal and a writ of sequestration where applicable. Where delivery of goods is concerned, a writ of delivery may be issued, the type of writ depending on the nature of the order.

Enforcement of judgments and orders of the court to do or abstain from doing any act are governed by CPR Schedule 1, R.S.C., Order 45, rule 5. Where a judgment or order is not complied with, it may be enforced by: **23–012**

   (i) a writ of sequestration against the property of the defaulter;

   (ii) where the defaulter is a body corporate, a writ of sequestration against the property of any director or other officer of the body;

   (iii) an order of committal.

There is, of course, also machinery for the enforcement of county court judgments and orders,[2] and for the enforcement of other forms of orders, for example, in family proceedings.[3] **23–013**

Enforcement of arbitration awards[4]

Since the first edition of this work, the statutory regime for the conduct of arbitration in England and Wales has been substantially changed by the enactment of the Arbitration Act 1996, which came into force on January 31, 1997. The regime of the new Act has been extensively discussed in Chapter 4. The Arbitration Act 1996 made provision for the recognition and enforcement of arbitral awards whether given under Part 1 of the Act or made outside the jurisdiction of England and Wales. **23–014**

As regards awards made in England and Wales, section 66 of the Arbitration Act 1996 provides that **23–015**

> "**66(1)** An award made by the Tribunal pursuant to an arbitration agreement may, by leave of the Court, be enforced in the same manner as a judgment or order of the court to the same effect.
>
> (2) Where leave is so given, the judgment may be entered in terms of the award."

It is only then that the arbitrator's award can be enforced against the assets of the party against whom the award is made, but it should be noted that leave to enforce an award "shall not be given where, or to the extent that, the person against whom it is sought to be enforced shows that the Tribunal lacks substantive jurisdiction to make the award" (section 63(3)). Where the monetary amount of the award falls within the county court jurisdiction there is power to enforce in the same way as a county court judgment or order. **23–016**

The Arbitration Act 1996 establishes a regime for challenging an award in a number of ways. One is pursuant to section 67 with respect to a challenge **23–017**

---

[2] See County Courts Act 1984, Courts and Legal Services Act 1990, s. 2.

[3] See, *e.g.* s. 29 of the Family Law Act 1986.

[4] See Mustill & Boyd (1989) at pp. 416–419 and 424–426; and *Handbook of Arbitration Practice* by Ronald Bernstein Q.C., John A. Tackaberry Q.C. and Arthur L. Marriott Q.C. (eds.) (1997).

to the substantive jurisdiction of the arbitral tribunal, though the right to do so may be lost pursuant to section 73 of the Act (the waiver section). By section 68 of the Act there is a new regime for challenge on grounds of serious irregularity which has replaced the old regime of misconduct. By section 68(2) serious irregularity means

"an irregularity of one or more of the following kinds which the court considers has caused or will cause substantial injustice to the applicant:

(a) failure by the tribunal to comply with section 33 (general duty of tribunal);

(b) the tribunal exceeding its powers (otherwise than by exceeding its substantive jurisdiction: see section 67);

(c) failure by the tribunal to conduct the proceedings in accordance with the procedure agreed by the parties;

(d) failure by the tribunal to deal with all the issues that were put to it;

(e) any arbitral or other institution or person vested by the parties with powers in relation to the proceedings or the award exceeding its powers;

(f) uncertainty or ambiguity as to the effect of the award;

(g) the award being obtained by fraud or the award or the way in which it was procured being contrary to public policy;

(h) failure to comply with the requirements as to the form of the award; or

(i) any irregularity in the conduct of the proceedings or in the award which is admitted by the tribunal or by any arbitral or other institution or person vested by the parties with powers in relation to the proceedings or the award."

23–018   If serious irregularity is established the court then has to decide whether to remit the award to the tribunal in whole or in part for reconsideration or to set it aside or to declare the award to be of no effect in whole or in part. But the court shall not exercise its power for setting aside or declaration "unless it is satisfied that it would be inappropriate to remit the matters in question to the tribunal for reconsideration" (section 68 (3)).

23–019   There is also a provision under section 69 for appeal on a point of law unless the parties have otherwise agreed. This section in essence re-enacts some of the provisions on appeal which appeared first in the Act of 1979 and gives statutory form to the NEMA guidelines.[5]

23–020   It is also possible to bring an action on the award which will take the form of a full trial, but this is more expensive and more cumbersome than the procedure under section 66 of the Arbitration Act 1996.

23–021   The Arbitration Act 1996 enacts provisions for the enforcement of awards which are made outside the jurisdiction of England and Wales. The provisions for enforcement of such awards is found in Part 3 of the Act which makes provision firstly for the enforcement of awards under the Geneva Convention and secondly, and far more importantly, for the

---

[5] These were formulated by the House of Lords in *BTP Tioxide v. Pioneer Shipping Ltd and Armada* Marine S.A. (The Nema) [1982] A.C. 724.

recognition and enforcement of awards made under the New York Convention. By section 103(1) recognition or enforcement of a New York Convention award shall not be refused except in the cases set out in section 103(2) which reflect in essence the provisions of Article 5 of the New York Convention. Rights of challenge to the enforcement of a Convention award are therefore limited.

The policy of the Arbitration Act 1996 regarding the recognition and **23–022** enforcement of arbitral awards is very clear. The courts will only interfere in the specific instances provided by the Act. These have now been carefully defined as, for example, the power to intervene on the grounds of serious irregularity now contained in section 68.

Enforcement of expert determination

As with an agreement to refer a dispute to arbitration, an agreement to **23–023** resolve a dispute by means of expert determination is a contractual term.[6] The outcome of the expert determination is a decision that the parties to the contract containing the relevant provision have agreed to accept and to implement, either expressly or by implication. Consequently, such agreement provides the basis for the enforcement of the determination, in that any failure to accept and implement the determination constitutes a breach of the contract. Enforcement is accomplished by way of an action on the contract: the determination does not have the authority or effect of an arbitration award. If the expert has properly carried out his remit, his determination cannot be challenged in the courts.[7]

3. NON-ADJUDICATORY PROCESSES

Because by definition non-adjudicatory processes do not involve a third party **23–024** determination of the issues but rather a consensual resolution between the parties, it follows that any such resolution will necessarily be in such terms and recorded in such form as the parties may agree. It further follows that the method of enforcement will be one that is appropriate to such terms and form.

The following factors will affect the enforcement of settlements arrived at **23–025** in mediation or any other non-adjudicatory ADR forum.

Do the parties intend their settlement to become enforceable as a matter of law?

While in the vast majority of cases the answer will be affirmative, this cannot **23–026** always be taken for granted. In some situations the parties may not envisage enforceability; for example, where personal or family relationships are concerned and the parties merely wish to resolve matters as between themselves and not in law, or where parties wish to establish a principle and not create enforceable rights or obligations.

---

[6]See *Campbell v. Edwards* [1976] 1 W.L.R. 403 and the passage by Lord Denning M.R. at 407.
[7]See *Jones v. Sherwood* [1992] 1 W.L.R. 277, and the discussion under "Expert Determination" in Chap. 4.

23–027   There is a school of thought in the United States that, as mediation is a voluntary process, any settlements arrived at by parties using it should similarly be voluntary and that coercion of any sort should not be a part of the process. That is the view of a tiny minority. Practitioners overwhelmingly subscribe to the view that although parties may enter mediation voluntarily, and although agreements must be reached without coercion, agreements must if the parties require be able to be converted into a binding form and become enforceable at law to make the process effective.

23–028   The enforceability of court-annexed ADR processes is generally regulated by the relevant statute or rules under which these are established. Under some, the court must enter a judgment based on the mediation agreement[8]; under others, the agreement is binding as a contract.[9]

At what stage will a settlement arrived at in an ADR process become enforceable?

23–029   This will depend on the parties' intention, which may be gleaned from their original contract to enter into the process and from the document recording their settlement.

23–030   The parties' contract may well provide that no agreement arrived at by them is to be binding or enforceable unless and until reduced to writing and signed by the parties or their authorised representatives.[10] Or a contract to mediate may provide that no such resolution is to be binding unless and until the parties have had an opportunity to obtain advice from their individual solicitors or other professional advisers, and have thereafter agreed to be bound.[11]

23–031   Practitioners preparing or supervising the preparation of the memorandum of any settlement arrived at in mediation or any other ADR form should always have regard to the initial contract, to ensure that the form of the memorandum properly reflects the original intention, to avoid any misunderstanding or ambiguity.

23–032   The settlement memorandum should itself state clearly whether it is binding on the parties, or if not, when and how it becomes binding and enforceable. So, for example, if the memorandum is merely a non-binding note of the settlement terms, which only become binding at some later stage, say, when the parties' respective lawyers have prepared a formal document and it has been duly executed, this should be explicitly stated in the memorandum. Or if the memorandum is binding, but conditional upon the

---

[8] See, *e.g.* E.D. Mich. R. 53. 1(i).

[9] See, *e.g.* Tex. Civ. Prac. & Rem. Code 154.071 (also authorises the court to incorporate terms into order disposing of the case); S.D. Calif. R. 600–7(d); S.D. Calif. Bankr. R. 7016–3(e) (6) (parties may also submit an agreed judgment under R. 7016–3(f)(1)).

[10] *e.g.* one of the terms in the Model Procedure of CEDR, the Centre for Dispute Resolution, reads "Any settlement reached in the Mediation will not be legally binding until it has been reduced to writing and signed by, or on behalf of, the Parties." See Para. 13 of the Model Procedure in Appendix II.

[11] *e.g.* the Code of Practice of the Law Society of England and Wales provides: "The parties must be offered the opportunity to obtain legal advice before any decision can be turned into a binding agreement on any issue which appears to the mediator or to either party to be of significance to the position of one or both parties". See Para. 5.4 of the Code in Appendix II.

happening of a specified event, this should be absolutely clear and unambiguous.[12]

In the absence of any qualification or reservation in the contract or in the **23–033** memorandum recording settlement terms, an unconditional written agreement signed by or on behalf of the parties may be assumed to be binding on the parties and enforceable in law. Indeed, a question may well arise as to whether such an unqualified and unconditional agreement may not be binding as soon as it is orally agreed between the parties, irrespective as to whether or not a memorandum is entered into. That would be on the assumption that the agreement was not one which as a matter of substantive law required a memorandum or some other formality such as being entered into under seal as a deed.[13]

An oral agreement reached in ADR may well be binding without a written **23–034** memorandum. This may be the wish and intention of both or all parties; but there is a risk that one party may perhaps believe that the privileged nature of the process results in agreements not being binding until formally confirmed or recorded. In fact, once an agreement is reached, even on a "without prejudice" basis, it will be binding on the parties subject obviously to the actual terms of settlement.[14]

Because of this risk of misunderstanding as to when an oral agreement **23–035** becomes binding, it is a sensible precaution to stipulate in the initial agreement establishing the process when and under what circumstances an agreement becomes binding. In any event, oral agreements sometimes need to be amplified in further discussion.

In addition to these general principles, there may also be specific **23–036** provisions applicable to particular fields of activity, which need to be borne in mind. For example, some agreements in divorce proceedings may not necessarily finally bind a couple until endorsed by an appropriate order of the court. The principle behind this is that the parties cannot by agreement oust the power of the court to make a determination about the resolution of their finances on divorce. Of course, any agreement the parties may reach will influence the court. If arrived at in the context of a proper exchange of information and especially if the parties were each legally represented, the court will generally confirm the agreement, and any party wishing to vary those terms could have difficulty doing so. This different procedure and culture will affect the recording and binding effect of agreements in matrimonial disputes.[15]

Enforcement as a matter of contract
Where parties to an ADR process have arrived at a settlement, it will usually **23–037**

---

[12]As to drafting settlement agreements and summaries, see Appendix II.
[13]Foskett, *The Law and Practice of Compromise* (1996) at p. 259 sets out the formalities required by different kinds of agreements, *e.g.* those relating to interests in land, and those involving employment relationships. As to the latter, see also Chap. 11 above.
[14]See *Rush & Tomkins v. Greater London Council and Another* [1988] 1 All E.R. 549; and on appeal [1989] 1 A.C. 1280.
[15]The risk of an "agreement" between a couple, even provisional or conditional, allowing a divorce court to consider the terms of settlement has led some family mediators to avoid the notion of "agreements" until each party has had the opportunity to consider the proposed terms with their respective legal advisers.

be recorded in writing, by the practitioner or by the parties' professional representatives, if any, and at some stage signed by the parties themselves or their authorised representatives. In the ordinary course, such an agreement will have the legal force of a binding contract, and will be enforceable as such.[16]

23–038 Enforcement of a settlement contract will ordinarily be for the party to take action on it in the appropriate courts of the country having jurisdiction. As with the enforcement of all contracts, the remedy may be damages or, where appropriate, specific performance or an injunction.[17] The parties can in their settlement contract, specify which courts are to have such jurisdiction; and especially where the parties reside or carry on business in different jurisdictions, or there is any other international aspect, it is sensible for such a jurisdictional provision to be recorded. In the absence of any such provision, the ordinary rules of jurisdiction will apply.

23–039 Any party wishing to escape the obligations of the settlement agreement may try to do so in the context of these court proceedings, on the same grounds as might be used in relation to any other form of contract, such as fraud or duress. Obviously, however, the onus of establishing any such defence would be on the party asserting it, as any such agreement would ordinarily be upheld and enforced by a court in the absence of a good reason not to do so.

Enforcement as an arbitration award or order of the court

23–040 Where adjudicatory proceedings are pending parallel to mediation or any other non-adjudicatory process, the parties may record any settlement agreement reached by ADR as an award or order in those formal proceedings. So, if an arbitration is pending, the agreement may be recorded as a consent award (depending on the rules and procedures of the arbitration process); or in the case of pending litigation through the courts, the settlement could be recorded by consent as an order of the court.[18]

23–041 Where the settlement has been recorded as an arbitration award, it can be enforced as outlined above. Where it has been recorded as a court order, it can ordinarily be enforced using the machinery of the court. Obviously, the advantage of a court order is that parties do not have the same opportunity to challenge the agreement as they would where a contract is sought to be enforced. The court will not as readily reopen a consent order as they will entertain defences about a contract which is sought to be enforced.[19]

23–042 Even if no proceedings are pending, it may in some circumstances perhaps be possible for parties, in the context of their settlement negotiations, to initiate proceedings so that their agreement can be made an order of court by

---

[16]The legal requirements for a binding contract will be needed. If in any particular settlement there is any doubt as to whether any or adequate consideration is being given to render the settlement effective and enforceable, this should be addressed by the parties; and either consideration given or the settlement recorded in a deed.

[17]See Foskett, *The Law and Practice of Compromise* (1996).

[18]In England and Wales, the Tomlin Order procedure could be used, under which the parties record the terms of their agreement and have it made an order, staying proceedings and reserving the right to revert to the court in relation to any questions arising in the course of implementation.

[19]See *Stalco v. Mercer Alloys & Rolls Royce* (1971) CA. (unreported).

consent. This might, for example, occur where a claimant who is about to institute court proceedings defers doing so pending mediation, and in the context of the mediation is only willing to consider settlement terms if his intended action is prosecuted and the defendant will agree to any settlement terms being recorded as a consent order. The lawyers acting in any such circumstances would need to ensure that this did not constitute an abuse of the court process. If an agreement was concluded, the cause of action might no longer exist and the proceedings could constitute an abuse; whereas if there was no settlement but merely a willingness to review and finalise the settlement terms after the launch of proceedings then that might be proper.[20]

In the absence of a statute or rule, a mediated settlement agreement **23–043** entered as a judgment is likely to be treated as a consent judgment.

Option to be released from settlement
In some cases, either the contract initiating the ADR process or the terms of **23–044** settlement themselves may contain a provision that if a party fails to give effect to the settlement terms in the specified manner, the other party may, at their discretion, be released from the terms of settlement. In such event, that would constitute an option to a party, in the event of non-performance by the other, either to seek enforcement as a contract or to be released from the settlement terms.

Such a provision needs to be carefully framed, to make it clear what the **23–045** consequences are of an exercise of the option to be released from the settlement terms. Presumably the intention would be to revert to the original dispute, and to treat the position as if no settlement agreement had been entered into. This should be explicit and unambiguous; or if any other consequence is intended, this should be stated.

ADR enforcement parallels bilateral settlement
It will thus be seen that the enforcement of a settlement agreement reached **23–046** in ADR is substantially similar to the enforcement of any settlement agreement arrived at in the course of bi-partite negotiations. The added factor is the intercession of a neutral facilitator; the consequences as to enforcement do not significantly differ.

---

[20] See also the *Law Society's Report on ADR* prepared by Henry Brown (1991) at para. 14.10, raising for discussion the question "as to whether agreements reached in mediation might in some cases be able to be made into consent orders, even where no court proceedings are pending. Rules would need to regulate the circumstances under which this could be done: for example, the parties might be required through their solicitors to lodge with the court a statement of the issues in lieu of pleadings, and a draft order... Being able to have an order made in this way would be like obtaining a consent order under existing rules, and would enhance the mediation process in cases where enforceable orders are needed."

CHAPTER 24

REGULATION, FUNDING AND INSURANCE

1. REGULATION

The debate about regulation?

24–001   The first edition of this work reiterated the questions raised in the report by Henry Brown for the Law Society's Courts and Legal Services Committee in 1991, as to whether and to what extent it was appropriate to accredit and regulate ADR practitioners. It was thought that this question might engender debate in the United Kingdom as it has done in the United States, with some voices raised against a move towards yet further "professionalisation".

24–002   In the event, no debate has taken place in the United Kingdom about the principle of regulation, but only as to what it should cover and how and by whom it should be done. A trend has continued to develop, towards individual mediation and ADR organisations establishing their own criteria for accreditation and regulation and joining together with others on matters of common concern.

24–003   A number of factors have tended to guide the issue of accreditation and regulation:

- The common, and almost certainly correct, perception is that the public expect mediators and other practitioners to be appropriately skilled and qualified. Some benchmark to satisfy the public is needed.

- With ADR increasingly being used or considered under court rules and directions, and judges adjourning proceedings for mediation or other dispute resolution processes, the need to have qualified mediators and consistent and reliable standards of practice is compelling.

- Most ADR and mediation organisations have established and published criteria for practice and in some instances training. This helps to ensure that practitioners work effectively, and that the public can feel secure in engaging them.

- The U.K. College of Family Mediators, comprising seven organisations providing family mediation, has adopted the function of co-ordinating and setting standards for its members and promoting mediation to the public.

- The Law Society has taken a lead among professional bodies in setting training criteria for its members engaged in mediation by publishing a Mediation Code of Practice to which members are required to conform, and in establishing a distinct mediator role for lawyers. It is establishing a panel of family mediators and is committed to regulating solicitors who mediate as part of their practices. It sets standards for mediation training and practice by its members.

- The Legal Aid Board has devised a competence test for family mediators, and has imposed requirements for supervision/consultancy and other criteria on mediators entering pilot schemes. It may well formulate criteria for civil mediators whom it funds though it has given no indication that it intends to do so.

- Mediation bodies operating in different areas, including civil and commercial, family and neighbourhood fields, have been liaising under the ambit of the Joint Mediation Forum. This umbrella group is examining standards common to all kinds of mediation and is establishing an executive arm, or "over-arching body" to take forward its objectives.

Elements of regulation
Aspects that can be regulated include the following: 24–004

Code of Practice[1]
Some regulatory bodies stipulate for their Code of Practice or Model   24–005
Procedure to be adopted by practitioners, or may provide a draft code by way
of guideline.
   The code in turn substantially regulates mediation or other ADR practice,   24–006
and provides the vehicle through which the rules for individual practice can
be implemented. It generally deals with practice rules and guidelines, ethical
considerations and practical and administrative matters.

Lawyers as mediators
Both in the United States and the United Kingdom, discussions have taken   24–007
place as to whether mediation undertaken by lawyers is regulated as a
separate and autonomous profession or whether it is part of the practice of
law.
   In the U.S., the American Bar Association (ABA) has not yet adopted   24–008
rules to regulate its lawyer members in their practice of mediation or other
ADR processes. However, a Commission appointed by the prestigious CPR
Institute for Dispute Resolution and by the Georgetown University Law
School has in 1999 produced a paper embodying a Model Rule for lawyers
who act in their law practices as mediators or other kinds of third party
neutrals. The Commission recommended that lawyers who undertook ADR
activities including mediation as part of their legal practice should be

---

[1] For examples of Codes and a Model Procedure see Appendix II.

required to do so under a different set of rules from their traditional law practices in which they represented and advised parties.[2]

24–009   In England and Wales, the Law Society has been proactive in requiring its solicitor and legal executive members who mediate within solicitors' practice to do so in a way that distinguishes their mediatory role from their traditional advisory or representative role. Indeed, it has provided a mediation Code of Practice for its lawyer members, training criteria and rules of practice.

24–010   While the Law Society's Code, training standards and rules apply to its members mediating within practice, it cannot regulate members who mediate outside practice. However, members who mediate outside their law practice cannot refer to themselves as solicitors in the context of their mediation practice, and will not be covered by their practices' professional indemnity insurance. The Law Society, however, retains overriding power over solicitors who commit fundamental breaches of their professional duties, even if done outside practice, such as committing criminal offences.[3]

Selection of practitioners

24–011   Mediation and other ADR organisations vary in their policies for the selection of practitioners for training and practice. So, for example, some groups such as LawWise, the ADR Group, the SFLA (Solicitors' Family Law Association) and PDT (Professional Development and Training) only or primarily select lawyers for training.[4]

24–012   Some organisations, such as the FMA (Family Mediators Association) select primarily from applicants who may either be family lawyers, or mental health or other relevant professionals. The FMA also has a pre-selection meeting with applicants and checks aptitude. NFM (National Family Mediation) selects from applicants who may or may not have relevant professional qualifications, based on aptitude, references and an interview.

24–013   CEDR (the Centre for Dispute Resolution), now one of the largest ADR organisations in England and Europe, does not have qualifying criteria for prospective mediators. Its members tend to be drawn from professional, management or business backgrounds.

24–014   Mediators working in the field of neighbourhood and community disputes and criminal reparation are largely drawn from a community and non-professional background. Mediation U.K., the umbrella organisation for mediators working in these and other fields, does not impose selection criteria on its members.

24–015   With such a wide disparity in selection processes and criteria, individual organisations may be able to regulate selection, but any attempt to centralise such a policy would be likely to be ill-fated.

Training

24–016   At least two regulatory bodies, the Law Society and the U.K. College of Family Mediators, have published training standards that they require their

---

[2] The CPR-Georgetown Commission's Model Rule is more fully dealt with in paras 21–025 *et seq.*

[3] See also Chap. 19 on the professional ethics of legal practice.

[4] Some might have further criteria for selection, *e.g.* SFLA require commitment to their Code of Practice for traditional legal practice, substantial family law practice, at least 3 years family law experience and a current practising certificate. LawWise also considers aptitude.

members to follow. Both these organisations presently or prospectively approve mediation bodies that comply with the required standards.

Components of training regulation for foundation training courses may for example, include: **24–017**

- Length of training required. This varies considerably, but minimum periods tend to range between 40 and 60 hours of face to face instruction.

- Required mix of training methods such as lectures, group discussions, videos, demonstrations, role-play and other exercises. Mediation and skills training courses usually tend to involve a combination of teaching methods. The emphasis is often on participation and involvement rather than passive note-taking. The object of the training is to provide the trainee with process expertise and skills, entailing a theoretical appreciation of the process and its implications, ethical awareness and a practical ability to work competently as a neutral.

- Acceptable extent of off-course reading and distance learning.

- Course contents (in outline rather than detail).

- Requirements and qualifications, if any, of trainers.

- Optimum sizes for courses or desired trainer/participant ratio.

There is a consensus among practitioners that those working as neutrals in the field of dispute resolution need proper training in order to undertake their duties and responsibilities. This applies even to people with a natural facility for conciliating. Most ADR training is for mediators, but similar principles apply to practitioners in other dispute resolution processes. **24–018**

The Law Society of England and Wales, in its Codes of Practice relating both to family mediation and to civil and commercial mediation, require solicitors who mediate within their practices to comply with the training and other requirements and criteria set out by it. Those criteria have been subject to a consultative process involving mediation organisations and relevant training bodies. **24–019**

All mediation bodies in the United Kingdom have stipulated training requirements for those who wish to practise as mediators. Increasingly, there is a view that basic or foundation training is a prerequisite to mediation practice, and that this should be followed up with a programme of continuing education. **24–020**

Basic training courses may be supplemented in a number of ways: advanced courses, seminars and conferences help to provide more specialist ADR expertise, and publications, journals and articles are published which constantly develop the theoretical base of ADR and the quality of practice. **24–021**

Mediators are drawn from many walks of life, and most, if not all, seem to benefit from ADR training irrespective of their occupational background. However, where they bring into ADR processes set attitudes or rigid professional methods that are not compatible with the mediation mode, that will make them ineffective and ultimately unsatisfactory as mediators. **24–022**

Mediation training usually involves a transition from a background profession into a new way of neutral working. On the other hand, being able to draw sensitively and appropriately on the experience of a background profession can often enhance practitioners' skills as mediators.

Accreditation

24–023 This is of course a critical element for regulation, covering in effect the practitioner's qualification to practise.

24–024 The factors that are commonly comprised in the regulation of accreditation are, or may include, some or all of the following:

- Attendance on and satisfactory completion of a training course of prescribed length and quality.

- Prescribed reading and theoretical knowledge.

- Skills competence.

- Ethical awareness and compliance with an acceptable Code of Practice or Model Procedure.

- A period between training and accreditation during which the practitioner may be required to comply with pre-accreditation criteria such as a period of pupillage (working with an experienced practitioner) or co-mediation, and/or undertaking a stipulated level of additional training, education, supervision/consultancy and practice.

- A report from the practitioner's consultant/supervisor confirming suitability for accreditation or from an experienced practitioner(s) or co-mediator(s) with whom the practitioner has worked.

- Commitment to further education and professional development.

- A self-analytical practice appraisal.

- An interview with an accreditation panel.

- In some cases, where regulation is governed by a professional body such as the Law Society, continued compliance with practice criteria and the holding of a practising certificate.

- Payment of an accreditation fee.

24–025 Accreditation criteria vary between different areas of activity, and even between different bodies within similar areas. However, reputable ADR and mediation organisations in all fields share a commitment to training, mediator skills, ethical propriety and a high standard of process; so although details may differ, it is to be hoped that broad principles are held in common.

Competence testing

24–026 The testing of mediator competence as an element of regulation is a difficult issue that has engaged regulatory bodies in many dilemmas, and continues to do so.

24–027 In the United States, there are no national standards for competence testing. Some individual states prescribe requirements for the licensing of mediators, but there is no consistency of practice. In the family field, after more than a decade of consideration of the issue, the main mediation body, the Academy of Family Mediators (AFM) has embarked on an exploration of the possible introduction of a voluntary certification programme for its members, based on competence testing. In collaboration with the Mediator Skills Project at the University of Georgia, the AFM is creating a written examination that mediators and mediation organisations nationally might take voluntarily to confirm competency. This is being funded by a grant from the William and Flora Hewlett Foundation and is supported by an advisory committee with representatives from six major dispute resolution bodies including the Section of Dispute Resolution of the American Bar Association. The examination is to be based on the core knowledge, skills and competencies of mediation, which the project is in the process of identifying and will include theory, ethics, skills and processes. At this stage, a performance-based test is not being introduced, but it is envisaged as a possibility after the written examination has been devised and implemented. The process is being slowly developed, in an effort to be inclusive rather than exclusive, and with a view to making appropriate allowances for diversity of culture and of practice. The AFM has not yet committed itself to implementation of the testing, but at this stage merely to its exploration.

In Canada, a certification project has for some years been developing a   **24–028** process of consensus-building towards a skills-based assessment of mediator competence. This has been funded by a grant from the Federal Department of Justice. The proposed test comprises a video recorded assessment, with an observer noting the level of skills of mediation practice observed, using a checklist that grades behaviour along a continuum from "no skills demonstrated", through "inadequate skills demonstrated", "satisfactory skills demonstrated", "strong skills demonstrated" to "outstanding skills demonstrated". In addition, there is to be a written examination. In Australia, skills testing in some areas include a more rigorous practical assessment of over two hours, recorded on video.

In England, the issue of competence testing has been led by the need of   **24–029** the Legal Aid Board (LAB) for standards of competence ("quality assured standards") that applied nationally to all mediators who were to be funded by it. Historically the LAB has funded legal services provided by lawyers, including ancillary disbursements incurred for necessary aspects such as medical reports. It had practice criteria, particularly for its franchise holders, but did not need to undertake competence assessment of practitioners because admission by the Law Society as a solicitor or by the Bar Council as a barrister constituted an acceptable qualification to practise.

The LAB was faced with funding family mediation by a range of   **24–030** practitioners, some of whom were solicitors but most of whom did not have legal backgrounds, and many of whom did not have any relevant professional occupations of origin. Standards of mediation practice varied. This created a problem as to how to ensure an acceptable level of competence in family mediation practice.

The LAB explored the possibility of contracting out the responsibility for   **24–031** competence testing but decided against doing so during the pilot phase of the

Family Law Act 1996. Instead, in consultation with various bodies (and accepting some of the thoughts offered by them but rejecting others), the LAB established its own requirements and criteria for family mediators seeking funding by it. These included requiring mediators to provide a portfolio outlining their experience and their understanding of the mediation process[5] and undergoing an interview with an assessment panel.

24–032 The LAB's requirements and criteria have been through various stages of development. Some of these are useful and relevant, others seem to be inappropriate. The competence testing is a bold initiative that must eliminate some incompetence, but it needs further refining.

24–033 The U.K. College of Family Mediators has taken the LAB's lead in seeking to assess mediator competency. Most of its members have been assessed as competent using the LAB's test. The U.K. College is devising a test, based loosely on the LAB's model, for assessing the competence of those of its members who do not work within a legally-aided practice or service and who consequently do not wish or need to undertake the LAB's test. The Law Society is similarly formulating compliance assessment tests and criteria, which will apply to its family mediation panel. Both the UK College and the Law Society are committed to seeking harmonisation on these.

24–034 Apart from these competence-testing assessments, most mediators in the United Kingdom are assessed by their trainers during training, based on the skills demonstrated by them during the course including during individual role-play. This is rather different from the position in the U.S., where trainers do not generally regard it as part of their function to assess competence.

Practice/Complaints

24–035 Following the satisfactory completion of training and any other formalities that may be stipulated, mediators and other practitioners can commence substantive practice. For some this may be after they have been accredited. For others, it may be part of the process leading to formal accreditation.

24–036 It is, of course, difficult to regulate individual practice because by its nature it takes place in a confidential context. That indeed is a reservation that has been expressed about ADR: that unlike the traditional court process (which is largely open and subject to an appeal procedure), what happens in the mediation room is private and not subject to any appeal.[6]

24–037 Nevertheless, it is possible to maintain regulatory control over practice, as follows:

- By accrediting practitioners for a limited period, requiring periodical re-accreditation, rather than for their lifetime.

- By fixing criteria that must be met if re-accreditation is to be sought, such as minimum levels of further education, supervision/consultancy and peer group consultation.

---

[5] The LAB used the NVQ (National Vocational Qualifications) format, which seeks to reduce all activities in all fields of work to a standard layout approach and language.

[6] See, *e.g.* the views of Prof. Lon Fuller and Prof. Owen Fiss, as outlined in Chap. 18 at paras 18–101–102. But these are to ignore the other shortcomings of the court system and the fact that over 90% of cases are in any event settled out of court in a private context.

- By stipulating that practitioners must work to a specific Code of Practice or Model Procedure.

- By making continued membership of the ADR body or the regulatory organisation subject to compliance with the Code and with any other policy guidelines or requirements that may be stipulated, for example, as to the way in which records are to be made and maintained and any equal opportunities or non-discriminatory practice policies they may have.

- By requiring the practitioner to work to a complaints procedure known to the parties, so that complaints about practice can be dealt with by the ADR body or regulatory organisation, leading if appropriate, to the termination of membership.

A complaints mechanism is needed by mediation organisations, and is usually incorporated into the organisation's practice documents. This may be informal, requiring parties to express views to the organisation, or formal. In either event, principles of natural justice will require there to be a mechanism for notifying the practitioner of the complaint and providing an opportunity for him or her to respond, and for the complaint to be fairly determined. This is particularly important if the outcome of the complaint could lead to termination of membership or removal from a panel.   **24–038**

Compliance with practice criteria can be more onerous for some practitioners, if they have to comply also with the practice requirements of their underlying professions. So, for example, solicitors must comply not only with requirements as to their mediation practice, but also to the ethical standards of their legal practice.   **24–039**

Continuing Professional Development (further education)
Most mediation and other ADR organisations stipulate that their members should give a commitment to a programme of further education and training after having completed their foundation training.   **24–040**

The concept of continuing professional development (CPD) is one that has been embraced by a number of professions, and some bodies regulating mediation have similarly adopted it. They include CEDR, the Law Society, the U.K. College of Family Mediators, the SFLA, FMA, NFM, LawWise and PDT.   **24–041**

Regulation takes the form of stipulating the minimum number of hours per year that mediators are required to undertake CPD, and the kind of further education that is considered appropriate. Some regulators accredit training organisations to provide authorised education, allowing members to accumulate authorised CPD hours.   **24–042**

Supervision/consultancy
If regulatory bodies wish to regulate the supervision or consultancy arrangements for mediators or other ADR practitioners, they may want to address the following: **24–043**

- What is the role of the supervisor/consultant?

- Who may be appointed as supervisors/consultants and what qualifications, if any, are required?

- What level of supervision/consultancy should a practitioner have? Is there a minimum time requirement or a per case requirement? Or should this be the responsibility of the professional practitioner to decide?

- How is supervision/consultancy to be delivered? In person, by telephone, written or electronic communication or some permutation?

- Is supervision/consultancy only required for a pre-accreditation period, or also post-accreditation? It the latter, how should it change post-accreditation?

24–044   Practice concerning supervision/consultancy is varied. Family mediation in England, drawing on the tradition of counselling and social work, has imported the concept of supervision/consultancy into its practice. Most family mediators find it helpful to their professional development, providing both practice support and an enhancement of their standards.

24–045   Questions arise, however, as to what "supervision" implies, both to the mediator and the public. There are different kinds of supervision, one being the concept of professional role support and the other being a more limited concept of file management. The term "supervision" may also imply (certainly to the public) a closer control over the mediator's process than the occasional meeting and discussion commonly involves. Mediators employed by mediation services may have supervision within this meaning of the word, but independent mediators may only have "supervision" on an occasional basis. This is not just an issue of terminology. "Supervision" could be argued to imply a legal accountability by the supervisor for the mediator's practice. While that may be neither intended nor correct, it is an interpretation that seems to have been placed on the process by the U.K. College of Family Mediators, but which may be under review.

24–046   For these and other reasons, some bodies such as the Law Society and the SFLA prefer the concept of "consultancy". This is very similar to "supervision" but places a greater obligation on the mediator to seek support (though consultants will work proactively in certain circumstances, and minimum required levels of consultancy are stipulated). Also, it does not imply the degree of control over process that "supervision" might, nor should it import any issue about accountability. An alternative term gaining currency is "mentoring" which also conveys the sense of supported development inherent in "supervision" and "consultancy".

24–047   In mediation outside of family issues, the concept of supervision/counselling seems to be more limited, even non-existent in some areas. Perhaps this reflects the fact that there is no tradition of it in law, accounting, business and other occupations from which civil and commercial mediators are drawn (though family lawyer mediators have learned to adopt it).

24–048   Whether supervision/consultancy constitutes a form of mentoring, a professional support system, or a management tool, it does seem to have value in an enormously demanding and often isolating activity.[7]

Peer Groups

Practitioners can gain value from working with their peers to discuss issues and examine practice. This can be regulated in any of the following ways: **24–049**

- Whether any minimum requirement is stipulated for peer group discussions to gain accreditation or maintain membership.

- What constitutes a peer group for regulatory purposes.

- What topics meet regulatory requirements.

Re-accreditation

A primary issue for regulators is whether a mediator or other ADR practitioner having qualified to practise as such, should be accredited for life (as most professions do) or for a limited period, subject to periodical renewal. In the latter event, what conditions should apply to re-accreditation? **24–050**

Requirements for re-accreditation might include a continuing level of relevant practice, maintenance of continuing education (which many professions are increasingly requiring), and minimum levels of supervision/ consultancy and/or peer group consultation. Professionally-based organisations might also require continuation of the underlying practice. For example, solicitor mediators are required by the Law Society and the SFLA to continue to be in family law practice and to hold a practising certificate on an application for re-accreditation as a family mediator. **24–051**

Who regulates whom and by what authority?

At present, ADR is regulated in the United Kingdom in the following ways: **24–052**

Voluntary membership regulation

Practitioners may choose to join a mediation or other ADR organisation, which is commonly but by no means invariably one with which they may have trained. They may do so in order to obtain the support of that organisation in their mediation or other ADR practice, to facilitate their marketing, to obtain referrals or for other professional or personal reasons. In order to remain on its panel of practitioners if it has one, they must comply with the rules and criteria of that organisation. **24–053**

Membership of all such organisations is voluntary. A practitioner may choose to remain a member of CEDR, the ADR Group, the SFLA, FMA, NFM, PDT, the UK College of Family Mediators, Mediation U.K., or any other such body if he or she chooses, or may decide not to do so. The **24–054**

---

[7] Referring to supervision, the authors of *Supervision in the Helping Professions,* Peter Hawkins and Robin Shohet say (at p.4) that it "can be very important. It can give us a chance to stand back and reflect; a chance to avoid the easy ways out of blaming others—clients, peers, the organisation, 'society', or even oneself, and it can give us a chance to engage in the search for new options, to discover the learning that often emerges from the most difficult situations, and to get support".

organisation can only regulate people who choose to be members as long as they remain members.

Professional practice regulation

24–055 Mediators who belong to professional bodies with regulatory powers are likely to find that those bodies regulate their mediation activities. For example, the Law Society of England and Wales will regulate its members who mediate. If they do so within their practice as solicitors, the Law Society will expect them to have undertaken training that accords with its criteria and to comply with its recommended Family Mediation Code of Practice. If they do not mediate within their practice as solicitors,[8] the Law Society still has a regulatory function, insofar as if any solicitor breaches fundamental ethical rules, he or she may face disciplinary proceedings. This would not however apply to breaches of specific mediation criteria that do not fundamentally affect the solicitor's capacity to practise as such.

24–056 Other professional bodies may have or may develop similar rules, for example the Bar Council in relation to barristers mediating.

Indirect regulation by the Legal Aid Board (LAB)

24–057 The LAB insofar as it funds family mediation in England and Wales, has created a regulatory regime for mediators funded by it.

24–058 The provision of state funding for mediation is a very positive step, and the LAB needs to be supported in its efforts to provide this in a fair and effective way through competent practitioners. Its competence testing procedures may not be ideal, but at least it constitutes a thoughtful and constructive attempt to address this difficult issue. Apart from the testing of competence, the LAB has set out quite detailed rules and guidelines for the conduct of mediation funded by it. These rules included aspirational elements, not easily realisable, that are being pressed into practice.

24–059 Unfortunately, the LAB's good intentions in some respects have had the effect of distorting the mediation process that it seeks to promote. For example, note-taking and record-keeping, to be audited, have assumed a substantial role, changing the process from a sensitive, client-centred one into a rather burdensome, administrative one. Inevitably, changes such as these may adversely affect the quality of the process. Much of the value of mediation lies in the creativity and flexibility that its practitioners can bring to situations of impasse. The LAB approach tends towards rigidity of process rather than to creativity.

24–060 It is interesting to note that a trend is emerging among many family mediators in North America towards a model of mediation that is moving away from the problem-solving structure that dominated the initial decades of family mediation practice. Proponents of this model, the transformative model,[9] are widespread and include, for example, the currently outgoing and the previous Presidents of the U.S.'s main family mediation organisation, the Academy of Family Mediators. In transformative mediation, the

---

[8] See paras 21–010 and 21–014 *et seq.* for the meaning and effect of this.
[9] For further information about this model, see paras 1–040–041 and 21–132 *et seq.*

empowerment of the parties is one of the central themes, and parties control both process and substance. Mediators do not bring fixed positions or procedures into the mediation, but "follow the parties". Not every mediator supports the transformative approach, but it undoubtedly brings some fresh perspectives to the process. The LAB's procedures, in their detail, are difficult for many traditional mediators to accept and would very likely be anathema to the philosophy of transformative mediation.[10]

Yet the LAB cannot be faulted for seeking a demonstrable consistency of high standards, and should be supported in that objective. Clearly, more discussion is needed. Meanwhile, the LAB calls the regulatory tune for those mediators who are state-funded.

24–061

Unregulated practice and possible options

Aside from these limited forms of regulation, there is no compulsory regulation of ADR in the United Kingdom. This means that anyone without any training or qualification could offer mediation services to the public. Is this acceptable, or should there be some attempt to control and regulate the practice of mediation? If so, who would be responsible for defining the regulatory components and criteria, for undertaking the massive job of regulation and for paying for it?

24–062

These questions do not have easy answers, but perhaps the following thoughts may contribute to them:

24–063

- Mediation and other ADR organisations should take responsibility for establishing and maintaining panels of their practitioner members competent to mediate or undertake other ADR processes.

- Certain bodies will have regulatory functions in respect of their members, such as the Law Society for solicitor mediators, the Bar Council for barrister mediators, or the UK College for its family mediator members.

- A body such as the Joint Mediation Forum, comprising practitioners from different backgrounds, could co-ordinate the setting of standards for those organisations or individuals who choose to allow it do so, but not for organisations or individuals who do not give it that authority. Nor should it have regulatory functions competing with those of its component organisations. No individual mediation or other ADR organisation or grouping of these should be allowed power to regulate anyone other than its own members.

- The courts and the LAB should establish panels of acceptable mediators or other ADR practitioners. They could be "passported" by virtue of their membership of organisations approved by the courts and the LAB or because of their inclusion on the Law Society's family mediators' panel or the U.K. College of Family Mediators' list of mediators. Individuals should be acceptable to court or LAB

---

[10]Similarly, other organisations such as the U.K. College of Family Mediators would be likely to find their attempts to impose detailed control of the mediation process unacceptable to the transformative philosophy.

panels, even if not "passported", if they can evidence their mediation qualifications.

- The public should be educated to appoint mediators who are on the panels of reputable mediation or other ADR organisations, on court or LAB panels (as far as these are published), on the Law Society panel, or who are demonstrably qualified as individual practitioners. "Kite marks" of quality standards should be encouraged for bodies and for individuals.

- Systems of voluntary certification may be undertaken by organisations in the United Kingdom and elsewhere. In England, there is already a head start by virtue of the voluntary, professional and LAB schemes outlined above. There are similarly voluntary and professional bodies regulating mediation in Scotland.

- Whatever voluntary or professional certification schemes might be developed, people must have the right to appoint anyone they choose to act as a mediator, whether or not he or she has trained or is regulated as such, as they have to appoint an untrained and unregulated arbitrator.

- Given the diversity of activities, models, cultures and practitioners covered by ADR, it would be very difficult, if not impossible, to reach a consensus about regulation across all fields of dispute resolution activity or even just mediation. Standardised regulation, in the unlikely event that it could be achieved, would probably create as many problems and anomalies as solutions, and would be unlikely to distinguish between good and poor mediators.

- Perhaps, in time, mediation may have a statutory base as arbitration does. That might bring advantages, but would need to be done with great care and wide consultation to ensure that it does not have as its purpose or effect any limitation of the range of ways in which disputes can be addressed. Creativity and flexibility are an essential part of the process and of its growth, and attempts to control it in any inappropriate ways could have a stifling effect.

Self-assessment

24–064 Finally, in addition to all the options for regulation that have been discussed, the concept of self-assessment should not be omitted. While this is obviously not regulation, it is a form of personal discipline and self-regulation, and can supplement formal regulatory measures. Self-assessment can be conducted on an individual basis, or with the support of a peer group, or under the guidance of a supervisor/consultant. It usually involves a reflective consideration of aspects of practice, and can be combined with the submission of case reports or summaries to supervisors/consultants.[11]

---

[11] The SFLA, *e.g.* requires unaccredited mediators to submit memoranda of a number of cases to their consultants, accompanied in each case by a report form containing a reflective assessment of the case. For further ideas about this, see *Self-Assessment Tool for Mediators* (1998) published by the Wisconsin Association of Mediators (e-mail: cow@mailbag.com).

2. FUNDING OF ADR

The following are the principal sources of existing and potential funding for **24–065**
mediation and other ADR procedures:

Civil and commercial disputes

Initially, civil and commercial ADR in the United Kingdom comprised only **24–066**
mediation, which was entirely privately funded. Two changes have since
arisen. Firstly, legal aid is now available for civil and commercial mediation
in addition to family mediation. Secondly, evaluation is developing as a
credible ADR process in the private sector.

Private funding

Civil and commercial ADR not qualifying for legal aid will generally have to **24–067**
be privately funded. In this regard:

- Disputants may engage a mediator or other ADR practitioner through
  an ADR organisation. In such event, the organisation may set up the
  arrangements for the process, including preliminary discussions with
  the parties, recommending or appointing a practitioner from its panel,
  organising the documentation, and fixing the venue, timetable and
  practical arrangements. The parties will commonly pay the ADR
  organisation an agreed fee, shared equally between them. There are
  different bases for calculating the fee. The main factors will usually
  be the length of time required for the process, the value and
  complexity of the dispute and sometimes the seniority of the
  practitioner. The ADR organisation will collect the costs from the
  parties and out of this will pay the practitioner.

- Some mediation organisations will act as referral agencies, and will
  put the parties in touch with mediators on their panels, without taking
  any responsibility for administration or receiving any administration
  fee.

- Parties may engage the practitioner direct, saving the administration
  costs but placing the burden of arranging the venue, timetable and
  other practical administrative matters on the practitioner or assuming
  it themselves.

- Although costs will in the first instance ordinarily be equally shared,
  parties may sometimes agree to assume the whole or a substantial part
  of these costs as part of a settlement agreement. There is no reason
  why the issue of an adjustment of the costs of the mediation may not
  be on the agenda for discussion.

- It is common but not invariable practice for the costs to be paid in
  advance of the process being undertaken.

Public funding

24-068 In a landmark decision,[12] the Legal Aid Board Appeals Committee decided that legal aid should be granted to cover the costs of mediating a civil dispute. This establishes the principle that funding should be made available for the mediation of all civil or commercial cases that qualify for legal aid.

24-069 Apart from legal aid, public funding for civil and commercial disputes may take the form of provision through the court system. In the Central London County Court, for example, a pilot mediation scheme[13] has been extended and is being converted into a permanent resource. Referral is to mediators appointed from outside the court.

24-070 The Small Claims Court is a possible forum for the development and use of ADR in cases falling within its jurisdiction, offering a low-cost form of resolution for such cases, especially if a form of court-annexed arbitration were to be introduced.

Insurance funded

24-071 In certain kinds of disputes, such as professional negligence claims, the defendant is likely to be covered by insurance. In such cases, the insurers commonly take responsibility for the funding and conduct of the case, but do not necessarily wish to have their interest openly known, although this may be a matter of general but tacit knowledge. Insurers, including professional indemnity providers such as the Solicitors' Indemnity Fund, are increasingly using mediation for the resolution of such cases.

24-072 In the United States, many insurance companies use mediation for the settlement of pending claims. According to Gerald S. Clay, an American lawyer, the Travelers Insurance Co. is one such company; and another on the West Coast that insures design professionals offers cost-free mediation to all plaintiffs when one of their insured is sued.[14] The Travelers has been involved in ADR since 1983, and appointed a National Director of ADR, whose article "ADR in the Insurance Industry" is of interest in this respect.[15] She writes that after introducing ADR, Travelers "saw good results immediately and rapidly expanded our ADR program across the country". Finding the civil justice system as "too costly, too time-consuming and too unpredictable". the Travelers "expanded their strategic thinking to include ADR". Within a few years, many of the 61 insurance companies participating in the American Arbitration Association's ADR programme had developed formal ADR procedures similar to those initiated by the Travelers.

24-073 Where disputes relate to claims covered by insurance, the insurers can authorise their insured to use mediation or any other ADR process. It may be advantageous for the insurers to take part, in order to be involved in the negotiations and the rationale for settlement, and to provide the necessary authority. They can, however, leave it to the parties and their lawyers to participate in the process, provided that they give them the requisite authority within which to conclude a settlement. In this respect, the position is not

---

[12] The case of *Wilkinson*, decided in October 1998.
[13] See paras 3–060 *et seq.*
[14] See "Counseling Clients on Mediation" in Wilkinson, *ADR Practice Book* (1990) at p. 162.
[15] Kathleen M. Cullen, in the 1986 Proceedings of the 14th International Conference of SPIDR, the Society of Professionals in Dispute Resolution, at p. 84.

very different from traditional bi-partite settlement negotiations undertaken by the solicitors for the insured, save only as to the timing and procedure for giving settlement authorisation.

Family issues

Mediation is the main ADR process currently available in the family field in the UK. Mediation's background has two strands, each with different funding implications. The one is the voluntary sector, which initially focused on parenting issues and which operated with state or other public funding, offering a free or low-cost service. The other is the private or independent sector, which developed the concept of all-issues (comprehensive) mediation, and which, following an initial low-cost pilot scheme, moved towards charging private sector rates for its mediation.   **24–074**

Other family ADR includes court conciliation and evaluative judicial settlement conferences, called FDR (Financial Dispute Resolution).   **24–075**

Private funding

The private or independent sector is largely comprised of family lawyers (solicitors, barristers and legal executives), counsellors, psychotherapists, social workers and others involved in a private capacity with couples, families and marital breakdown. Typically, United Kingdom organisations working largely in the independent sector, include the FMA (Family Mediators Association), SFLA (Solicitors' Family Law Association), CALM (Comprehensive Accredited Lawyer Mediators), PDT (Professional Development & Training), LawWise and the Academy of Experts.[16]   **24–076**

Charging rates for privately funded mediation vary according to a number of factors. These may include location (Central London tending to be significantly costlier, than, say, the North East of England), background professional practice (lawyers charging at or tending towards their traditional charging rates), and the seniority of the practitioners. Some mediators from some organisations have standard charging rates in local areas.   **24–077**

Mediation by two people working in the co-mediation mode will invariably be more costly than sole mediation by one of them. It would not, however, ordinarily be double the cost, but would rather be incremental, with the mediators re-arranging the division of the fee, bearing in mind their sharing of the responsibilities for the mediation. Those who favour the co-mediation model consider that there is added value for the extra cost: that may commonly but not invariably be the case.   **24–078**

The cost of family mediation is usually shared equally between the couple, but they may agree that it is to be paid in any other proportion, or one may pay it entirely. There was at one time a view that each should make some payment, albeit unequally, so that both could feel that they were "the clients". While some mediators may still want to do this, it is now accepted practice for parties to agree that one of them will pay the mediation costs.   **24–079**

---

[16]However, many members of these organisations also work extensively within the public sector, undertaking legally-aided mediation.

Public funding

24–080 The ill-fated Family Law Act 1996 introduced the concept of legally aided family mediation and counselling into the mainstream of the English legal system. This was contained in Part III of the four-part statute. Under the provisions for introducing mediation and providing information to the public, pilot schemes were set up and the LAB stipulated for the testing of mediator competence.

24–081 When, however, the Lord Chancellor decided in June 1999 to abandon Part II of the Act, which contained the substantive provisions for a new no-fault divorce law on which the mediation and counselling provisions were hung, that left the legal aid funding of mediation somewhat in the air.

24–082 The Lord Chancellor's Department and the LAB hastened to issue reassurances that the legal aid funding of divorce, as contained in Part III, would not be abandoned. Pilot legal aid and related schemes that had been established throughout the country would continue as planned. They would simply apply to the existing law rather than the proposed new law.

24–083 Part III would, it later transpired, need to be abandoned and the provisions for the legal aid funding of family mediation transferred to the LAB's Funding Code. That removed the statutory obligation and left the LAB with an obligation that could be varied with any subsequent changes to the Funding Code.

24–084 The LAB published a report in January 1999, under the heading *Modernising Justice* as "The Funding Code: a new approach to funding civil cases". The Code is designed to operate under the provisions of the Access to Justice Bill, which when brought into force, is intended to repeal the Legal Aid Act and establish a new approach to the funding of civil cases.

24–085 The LAB's Funding Code report sets out the criteria that will be applied to individual civil cases to decide whether they justify public funding, subject to financial eligibility. It emphasises some of the fundamental features of the Code. Funding will no longer be available as a universal entitlement. The Code's criteria, although flexible, are intended to be "tough and rigorous so that weaker claims can be excluded from the scheme far more effectively" and public funding may, as suggested by the Bar Council, "be the hallmark of a strong case".[17] Percentage prospects of success and thresholds for damages and costs will be applied. An important new principle, described elsewhere as proportionality, will guide decisions on applications for legal aid. Funding will usually only be available for cases in which "a prudent private paying client would be prepared to litigate using his or her own resources." However, funding might be granted where there is a genuine public interest.

24–086 The January 1999 version of the Code serves as a consultation paper. Consultation is still under way as this book goes to press but there is a commitment to provide in it for the mediation of family issues.

Community and neighbour disputes

24–087 Many of the community and neighbour schemes operating throughout the United Kingdom have faced financial constraints and have had to find ways

---

[17] Report summary at p. 2.

to raise funds in order to survive. Some have been able to do so, some have not and no longer operate.[18]

Some local authorities have established and fund community mediation schemes, enabling them to function in the local community without necessarily having to charge parties for dealing with their disputes. **24–088**

Even the umbrella organisation, Mediation U.K., has itself faced financial crisis with the potential withdrawal of state funding. Its funding has been temporarily secured, but its future remains uncertain and vulnerable. **24–089**

Employment disputes

As outlined in Chapter 11, the Advisory, Conciliation and Arbitration Service, ACAS, has a significant role in dealing with employment disputes through a range of processes including individual conciliation, collective conciliation, dispute mediation, advisory mediation, joint working parties, workshops and arbitration. Although operating independently, it is state funded and is accordingly able to provide a free service to disputants. **24–090**

3. PROFESSIONAL INDEMNITY INSURANCE

Although claims against mediators and other ADR practitioners are hardly known, if there is an error by the practitioner which results in loss or damage, a claim in negligence could arise. **24–091**

This might happen in a number of possible ways. For example, a mediator may go beyond his or her proper role and may give advice which proves to be wrong and results in a loss. A mediator may disclose confidential information contrary to an undertaking not to do so, or may draft an agreement that does not give proper effect to the intentions of the parties. **24–092**

Parties may have expectations of mediators that may or may not be justified. If mediators were to act contrary to those expectations, and loss resulted, claims might result. For example, if one party in a family mediation were to charge or dispose of the family home in his or her sole name, the other might complain that the mediator ought to have drawn attention to this possibility and to the available steps to protect against it. Mediators might well contend that this is not part of their function; but in such situations, if the mediator's role is unclear, there could be a dispute. **24–093**

Not all of these examples necessarily involve negligence. They do, however, illustrate that mediators and other ADR practitioners could find themselves facing negligence actions if they err in the course of their activities. **24–094**

In some parts of the United States, a further source of possible claims arises from the argument that the mediator owes a positive duty to the participating parties to ensure that the process is fair. This argument would seek to hold the mediator personally liable if this duty is not maintained; indeed, perhaps even if the mediator has not uncovered certain facts that ought to have been exposed.[19] **24–095**

---

[18]For further information about this, see chap. 12.

[19]See the article by Gracine Hufnagel, "Mediator Malpractice Liability" in (1989) 23 M.Q. 33–

24–096   Clearly these risks should serve as an additional incentive, if any were needed, to ensure that ADR processes are conducted with scrupulous care and integrity. In addition, a practitioner could protect himself or herself against possible claims in two ways. First, the contract with the practitioner or the ADR organisation under which the process is undertaken could provide a disclaimer or indemnity against any acts or omissions by the practitioner.[20] This is not uncommon in such agreements, especially in relation to commercial and civil mediation. Secondly, professional indemnity insurance cover could be obtained against such risks.

24–097   For many mediators, obtaining professional indemnity insurance is not an option but an obligation. Various mediation organisations or regulatory bodies stipulate this as a requirement, such as the Law Society in its Family Mediation Code of Practice and the U.K. College of Family Mediators. The Law Society's draft Civil and Commercial Mediation Code of Practice contains a similar stipulation.

24–098   The following considerations will be relevant to this:

- A practitioner covered by a professional indemnity insurance policy in his or her traditional professional role should check whether that policy covers working in an ADR capacity; and if not, what needs to be done to extend the policy or to get additional cover. So, for example, a solicitor acting as a mediator may, under the Law Society's current rules, do so in either of two alternative capacities, which must be clearly identified. He or she may do so within practice as a solicitor (in which event the solicitor's professional indemnity policy should apply); or outside practice as a solicitor (in which event, the solicitor's professional indemnity policy would not apply, as the work is not being done *qua* solicitor). In the latter event, separate cover may need to be arranged.

- Some organisations, for example the Family Mediators Association, arrange to provide professional indemnity cover for their members. CEDR offers a similar facility as an option for its mediators. In some cases, individual mediators may be able to arrange their own top-up cover to supplement the cover provided by organisations.

- Where professional indemnity cover is sought, the terms on which the practitioner contracts with the parties to undertake the process may be relevant in affecting the premium level. Those practitioners or organisations that use contract terms and procedures that have the effect of minimising the risk of claims are likely to face lower premiums than those who do not.

- Co-mediators should check that they are both covered by insurance for that joint activity. If two solicitors co-mediate within their

---

36. The arguments that the mediator may have a duty to ensure fairness of process had not been supported by case law at the time of the article nor is there yet any authority for that proposition. Certainly, there is a consensus that the mediator cannot be responsible for fairness of outcome. See also paras. 21–055 *et seq.*

[20] However, the efficacy of such a disclaimer or indemnity has not yet been tested in the English courts.

respective practices, they should be covered by their professional indemnity policies.

Mediation is a relatively low risk activity, and anecdotal evidence suggests 24–099 that no (or very few) claims have been made and pursued against any English mediators. That is not a cause for complacency, but rather for continued care.

CHAPTER 25

FUTURE DIRECTIONS

25–001 Since the first edition of this work there have been very substantial changes in the approach to civil dispute resolution in England. The new Arbitration Act of 1996, which came into effect after much travail, has provided arbitrators and parties with almost unfettered autonomy in seeking effective means of resolving their differences. The Act rests on the fundamental principle, which is radically innovative, that in return for recognition and enforcement of arbitration agreements and awards and limited interference by the courts, the State imposes on arbitrators and parties an obligation to seek to achieve the fair, economic and expeditious resolution of their disputes and to collaborate to that end.

25–002 Lord Woolf's reforms of civil litigation are based on collaborative case management with a view to streamlining procedures and facilitating settlement before litigation begins and if it starts, at the earliest possible stage thereafter. Legal aid, the basis of access to justice in the civil courts for 50 years, is being abolished in the form in which it has previously operated and a new system of funding and administration is being put in place. The object is to cap expenditure, to ensure better value for public money and a more efficient allocation of resources between different forms of civil dispute resolution. The first steps have been taken towards the creation of the Community Legal Service which will, when taken in conjunction with other changes, such as to funding, to rights of audience and the removal of other restraints, have a profound effect on the structure and practice of the legal profession.

25–003 The reforms of the last few years have been provoked by a growing concern at the costs and delays of civil dispute resolution, particularly in the courts, though arbitration has not been free of criticism. It is no exaggeration to say that civil dispute resolution in the courts is in a state of crisis and change is essential. It is recognised that access to the civil courts is denied to all but the very rich or the poor (the latter financed hitherto by the State) and that this is unacceptable in a democratic society.

25–004 There has also been a growing realisation that there is a range of procedures which can be used to resolve civil disputes. The idea that such disputes could only, or principally, be resolved in the courts has been replaced by the belief that arbitration, mediation and ombudsmen all have a role to play. Furthermore, various techniques are available to be applied to a broader range of disputes than considered hitherto. We see this reflected in the use of community mediation and the tentative steps being taken towards mediation between victims and offenders in criminal cases. Probably, the most significant change has been in the recognition of the central role of mediation in family law. The very significant increase in the breakdown of marriage and co-habitation has had very serious economic and social effects. Parliament has decided that couples require mediation to be available to help them manage the transition from a unified family structure to separate family units on divorce, particularly where there are children. Mediation is at the root of the reform of family law, as the adjudicatory role of the courts needs to be underpinned by mediation in helping couples to find their own solutions by agreement. Such solutions are likely to be more durable than those imposed by the court.

Indeed, the effective reform of civil dispute resolution in the future may lie **25–005** in appreciating that the resolution of civil disputes is largely concerned with managing the transition from one legal status to another. This is comparatively straightforward in, for example, a breach of contract case where damages or specific performance may be an immediate, practical and sufficient remedy. But it is far from straightforward in other cases. Thus, long-term joint ventures and partnerships may require adaptation to enable them to continue, or constructive negotiation with the aid of a third party to dissolve them in an amicable and effective way. Relationships in the work place may be similarly complicated and require long-term and collaborative solutions.

In deciding how to reform civil dispute resolution, it is essential that we **25–006** adopt this basic approach of trying to manage efficiently and fairly the transition from one relationship to another. For it is then that we can properly deploy the various methods which may produce the best results. Also, this will lead us to consider the application in a principled way of combining different methods within essentially the same process. For example, a combination of adjudicatory decisions by arbitrators or judges and the mediation of damages or other issues could help to resolve a relationship between parties.

ADR as an instrument of reform
A recurring theme of this second edition has been the use of ADR as part of **25–007** litigation reform to improve access to justice. It is in this respect that ADR faces its greatest challenge. If experience elsewhere, particularly in the United States, is anything to go by, private sector ADR will develop in response to the demands of the marketplace. However, the stimulus to private sector ADR produced by court-annexed systems should not be underestimated. It appears to have been the case in the United States that private sector ADR, in the civil and commercial fields at least, grew out of dissatisfaction with the delay and cost of the court system. There is a correlation in the United States between the increasing use of ADR in the court system and the acceptance of ADR by commercial parties for the resolution of their disputes which have not yet reached litigation or arbitration.

Growth of ADR in the private sector in England has been slow; in certain **25–008** areas virtually non-existent. Thus, ADR has made no significant impression

535

upon the resolution of personal injury or clinical negligence disputes which continue to be resolved by litigation. It is to be hoped that the new requirements of pre-action protocols will encourage the use of ADR in these cases before litigation starts. There has also been a reluctance to use ADR to any substantial extent within the financial services community, though the work of the City Disputes Panel and CEDR in certain prominent cases should encourage those who provide financial services to believe that there are other, faster and more efficient ways of resolving disputes than going to court. The preference for the courts to resolve such disputes does not only exclude consensual forms of ADR. Arbitration has long been regarded with suspicion by banks, insurance companies and other financial institutions as a means of resolving disputes between them or with their customers.

25–009   The movement to reform litigation has been driven by concern at the ever rising cost of funding the legal aid system for civil disputes and by the realisation that access to justice is denied to the vast majority of citizens. Initially, ADR was not regarded as an integral part of litigation reform, the emphasis being on case management and cost control. It would be unfair to say that mere lip service was paid to the benefits of ADR in litigation reform, but until Lord Woolf's Final Report it was undoubtedly regarded as an optional process for which no specific provision needed to be made in any new rules of court.

25–010   However, it has become increasingly clear, particularly from experience in the United States, that despite all the difficulties of cost benefit analysis as revealed by RAND and the 1997 report of the Federal Judicial Centre, the advantages and necessity for ADR allied to effective case management as part of litigation reform, has been recognised and has found mandatory expression. In the United States the debate has clearly been won by the advocates of ADR as the provisions of the 1998 Act make abundantly clear.[1]

25–011   But is this confidence in ADR well founded? As court-annexed ADR develops are there likely to be substantial benefits in terms of cost control and improving access to justice? It is important to recognise the limits of ADR. As has been pointed out ADR is not a panacea. It is not suitable for every case which will come before the courts. Obvious examples are disputes between the citizen and the State, though as the Americans have demonstrated ADR has a role to play in administrative procedures. ADR is not suitable where binding decisions of principle are required for the operation of a market or of standard forms of contract, though once such decisions are made, ADR may well be suitable for solving many of the resulting problems.

25–012   It must also be recognised, that the scope for significant cost savings in civil litigation is limited even if ADR systems are employed. It is a fundamental misconception to approach litigation reform principally by trying to save costs. The reality is that in any democratic and pluralist society access to the courts is and must remain a fundamental constitutional right. Provision of that right is inevitably expensive, and will remain so. But the price must be paid. The State cannot privatise to any significant degree by sub-contracting out its dispute resolution systems to the private sector. The

---

[1] For reference to these reports and developments, see Chap 5.

State has a fundamental obligation to provide efficient and fair court systems for the resolution of many types of dispute, some of a private law nature and others involving fundamental questions of public law. The State has, for example, an obligation to ensure through the courts the proper enforcement of laws enacted in the public interest which cover economic issues such as antitrust and prevention of abuse of economic power, the protection of consumers, of those in rented housing and in making proper provision for the compensation of citizens injured in the workplace or by clinical negligence.

We must therefore be careful not to diminish the role of the courts. Procedural reform and ADR can buttress and facilitate the work of the courts as well as functioning in their own right. ADR and the courts can clearly co-exist.

25–013

Role of the private sector

There will need to be safeguards against the charlatan and abuse of the system by the incompetent and the powerful, particularly if as we believe likely, mandatory court-annexed ADR will become more and more used. It is here that the private sector has a vital role. The courts cannot introduce and administer systems of court-annexed ADR without radical changes in their organisation and approach to dispute resolution. Of course, court officials and administrators can be trained in ADR systems and judges could be both adjudicators and mediators. But the reality is that the resources are not there and the existing demands upon the courts are so great (and will increase under the new regime) that any radical expansion of the courts' activities to practise ADR is highly improbable. It is therefore for the private sector to assist by developing the use of court-annexed ADR.

25–014

It is, for example, the private sector that must take the primary responsibility for the training, education and supervision of those who would mediate in a court-annexed system. Training in mediation must become part of the education of lawyers and other professions such as accountants, engineers, architects and surveyors who may expect to mediate disputes as part of their normal professional career. For those already in practice, specialist training should be provided by the professional institutions and by others suitably qualified and experienced. It would be regrettable if the provision of training was left solely to commercial organisations. They clearly have a major role to play, but we must be careful about commercial institutions becoming the only source of well-trained and qualified mediators.

25–015

The professions must regulate those who mediate in the same way as they regulate other professional activity. There is no reason why the solicitor who mediates should be subject to any different ethical standards than the solicitor who conducts litigation or who conveys houses. Mediators must also owe a duty to the court akin to that of the advocate in the sense of performing their duties in good faith and to the highest standards.

25–016

It would be unfortunate if mediators were drawn exclusively from the ranks of the professions. The necessary qualities of common sense, judgment, fairness and persuasion are not confined to the professions. There are many with specialist knowledge of different trades and industries who could offer mediation services, particularly in consumer and contractual disputes by way, for example, of an extension of the highly successful small claims arbitration

25–017

system in the county courts. It should not be difficult for a system of civil magistracy to be established which with appropriate procedures for vetting and approval could enable people from all classes of society to perform an important public service.

25–018   It is vitally important that ADR methods, either alone or in combination with adjudicatory procedures in arbitration and in the courts, do not become rigid and inflexible. We have suggested in this work, for example, that the old distinctions between facilitative and evaluative mediation are largely sterile and misguided. New techniques will undoubtedly emerge, particularly as practitioners gain greater experience of existing processes and as advances are made in technology, and party autonomy is essential to the healthy development of ADR just as it has been to arbitration. If over-zealous attempts are made to place ADR in a conceptual and regulatory strait-jacket, then it will not realise its potential and will handicap effective resolution of civil disputes. Therefore, it is of vital importance that those who train and accredit mediators do so with imagination. It is also essential that regulation be imposed with a light, though effective, touch.

Developing court-annexed schemes

25–019   A fundamental question which confronts those who would reform civil procedure by means of court-annexed ADR is: whether schemes should be mandatory or voluntary? This is, as has been indicated in Chapter 5, a highly controversial topic, though it is likely that if court attached ADR develops to any significant extent, it will be because of orders made by judges which border on compulsion. Old habits are too deeply ingrained to imagine that practitioners will voluntarily and suddenly embrace ADR and abandon litigation.

25–020   A second question of great importance is: how should court-annexed schemes be developed? One view is to introduce on a national basis in every Civil Trial Centre and High Court, a mediation scheme along the lines of the pilot scheme at the Central London County Court. This would require the collaboration of the private sector and a system of funding not only for the court administration, but also for the mediators. In many cases mediators can be expected to work *pro bono*, or for nominal reward, in cases which cannot bear commercial rates of charging; and it is perhaps there that the civil magistracy could work to greatest effect. But it is unrealistic to expect that any national system of court-annexed ADR could work without a proper scale of remuneration for mediators; and insofar as this could not be covered by court fees then Government funding would need to be made available.

25–021   The alternative approach is to encourage local initiatives by providing private sector assistance to individual courts which wish to set up schemes along the lines of the Central London County Court. But whichever system is adopted the same issues of accreditation and monitoring arise.

25–022   There are other ways in which the use of ADR in the public sector could be encouraged. There are, so it appears, no obstacles of policy or principle to the use of ADR in Government contracts of construction and procurement. However, in practice ADR is not used in Government contracts and in Government administrative procedures. Experience elsewhere shows that ADR can be helpful. In Hong Kong it was the decision of the Government in the mid-1980s to establish a pilot scheme for the mediation of disputes arising in Government civil engineering contracts which led to mediation becoming the primary means of dispute resolution in both the public and the private sector. It is clear from statutes and regulations in the United States, Canada, Australia and New Zealand that the legislature in those countries considers that ADR is of value in a diverse range of Government activity. There is obviously scope for such systems being introduced in the United Kingdom. There is every reason to do so. If Government is serious about encouraging the use of ADR it can begin in its own backyard.

Changes in substantive law

There need to be not only changes in practice, but also in the law. There **25–023** must be a clear recognition and enforcement of contractual obligations to negotiate in good faith. Lord Ackner's opinion in *Walford v. Miles*[2] that good faith is inherently repugnant to adversarial negotiation is an obstacle to enforcing agreements to mediate as can, for example, be seen from McKinnon J.'s judgment in the *Halifax* case.[3]

In the meantime, Lord Ackner has himself offered a possible solution **25–024** whereby parties may undertake to use their best endeavours in negotiating and implementing contracts. Careful drafting of dispute resolution provisions based on the use of best endeavours, may well provide a way round the problems created by *Walford v. Miles*. Hopefully, a case will reach the House of Lords which would allow *Walford v. Miles* to be interpreted in such a way as not to prevent or impede the implementation of dispute resolution methods involving ADR which the parties have agreed upon.

However, it would be better if English law, which is clearly out of step **25–025** with other developed jurisdictions, could develop a clear and comprehensive duty of good faith and fair dealing in the negotiation and implementation of commercial contracts. Fortunately, there has been a substantial affirmation in recent years of the need for constructive interpretation of what parties have agreed. Judges are increasingly concerned now to avoid interpretation of a contract by (as it were) mere reference to a dictionary. Contractual interpretation is also more and more influenced by what is fair and reasonable. Distinguished judges such as Lord Bingham have already indicated, as, for example, in the *BSkyB* case, that were it material to do so, an obligation of good faith would be implied. But it is about time that in this country the nettle of good faith in negotiation was grasped.

One way of grasping the nettle would be to consider whether we need a **25–026** statute which can legislate for the most important aspects of ADR, whether used independently or court-annexed. Much of this book has been devoted to a discussion of standards, accreditation, confidentiality, ethics, immunity and other aspects considered important to the proper functioning of ADR processes. There is something to be said for ad hoc pragmatic development of such issues, leaving it to the common sense of practitioners and occasional intervention by the courts to develop solutions to problems as they appear. A

---

[2] [1992] 2 A.C. 128, HL.
[3] *Halifax Financial Services Ltd v. Intuitive Systems Ltd* [1999] 1 All E.R. 303.

precedent is the approach of the Departmental Advisory Committee[4] and of the courts towards the issue of confidentiality in arbitration. But, there are those who believe that some form of statutory enactment is desirable if we are to establish a framework within which ADR processes can flourish rapidly, particularly if we have within a short time a widespread system of court-annexed ADR. If such matters as standards, immunity, court control and ethics are to be addressed in a statute, then the opportunity could be taken to lay down principles of good faith and fair dealing in negotiation which are at the root of ADR processes.

Conclusion

25–027   In the first edition of this work we were far from certain that ADR would be recognised in England as having a fundamental role to play in the resolution of civil, commercial and community disputes. Six years later we are far from a position where ADR is the order of the day. But it is clear, that in all fields of civil dispute resolution ADR is now playing a role which it did not play before. ADR is more important in some kinds of dispute resolution than in others. It is for example very important in family law matters. Its role in the courts has just begun with the two pilot schemes at Central London County Court and in the Court of Appeal. Public funding of ADR processes has barely begun with the first few tentative steps being taken in the context of family law and the court-annexed pilot schemes. So there is much, much more to be done. But we believe that in 1999 we can be more optimistic and affirmative in our view of the future of ADR than we were in 1993. We believe firmly that the proper use of ADR will come to be seen as essential if the Woolf reforms and the Community Legal Service are to realise their undoubted potential. We consider also that individuals and companies in the private sector will increasingly realise the advantages of ADR in the resolution of their disputes.

25–028   However, much will depend on the quality of those who practise ADR. If, as has been the case in arbitration, the practice of ADR loses its essential flexibility and becomes too controlled by vested interests, then that could have a damaging effect. But we expect if and when the third edition of this work appears, to be able then to describe a civil justice system in which ADR plays a central and rather important role. The opportunity to improve access to justice is clearly there. It must not be missed.

---

[4]Advising the Secretary of State on arbitration reforms: See Chap. 4.

APPENDIX I

DISPUTE RESOLUTION ORGANISATIONS

This does not purport to be a comprehensive list of all dispute resolution   **A1–001**
organisations and their regulatory bodies. It indicates some of the principal
ADR organisations and regulatory bodies in the United Kingdom as at the
summer of 1999, and a small section of those operating outside the United
Kingdom. The categories listed below are not rigid: some organisations
overlap areas of activity. For those more specifically operating in cyberspace,
see Chapter 17.

1. UNITED KINGDOM AND IRELAND

Civil and Commercial

ADR Net/ADR Group   **A1–002**
Grove House
Grove Road
Bristol BS6 6UN
Tel: 0117 946 7180
Fax: 0117 946 7181
E-mail: *info@adrgroup.co.uk*
Web site: *www.adrgroup.co.uk*
A national network of lawyer/mediators.

Centre for Dispute Resolution (CEDR)
Princes House
95 Gresham Street
London EC2V 7NA
Tel: 0207 600 0500
Fax: 0207 600 0501
E-mail: *mediate@cedr.co.uk*
Web site: *http://www.cedr.co.uk*
An independent dispute resolution organisation supported by industry and
professional advisers encouraging more effective commercial resolution of
disputes. Arranges mediation and other ADR processes for civil and
commercial disputes.

City Disputes Panel (CDP)
Fifth floor
3 London Wall Buildings
London EC2M 5PD
Tel: 0207 638 4775
Fax: 0207 638 4776
e-mail: *CDPLondon@aol.com*
Internet: *http://members.aol.com/cdplondon/cdp.html*
A dispute resolution service for the wholesale financial services industry providing conciliation, mediation, arbitration, evaluation, expert determination and review.

The Academy of Experts
2 South Square
Gray's Inn
London WC1R 5HP
Tel: 0207 637 0333
Fax: 0207 637 1893
E-mail: *admin@academy-experts.org*
Internet: *http://www.academy-experts.org/*
An organisation of experts in all fields, undertaking expert reports, mediation (commercial and family) and other expert services.

The Chartered Institute of Arbitrators
International Arbitration Centre
24 Angel Gate, City Road
London EC1V 2RS
Tel: 0207 837 4483
Fax: 0207 837 4185
E-mail: *info@arbitrators.org*
Internet: *http://www.arbitrators.org/ContactDet.htm*
Professional body with multi-disciplinary membership promoting alternative means of dispute resolution to litigation, especially arbitration.

The Law Society of England & Wales
113 Chancery Lane
London WC2A 1PL
Tel: 0207 242 1222
Fax: 0207 831 0344
Internet: *http://www.lawsociety.org.uk*
Professional solicitors' organisation that regulates solicitors who mediate, establishes and maintains standards and is developing specialist panels of solicitor-mediators.

London Court of International Arbitration (LCIA)
Hulton House
161–166 Fleet Street
London EC4A 2DY
Tel: 0207 936 3530
Fax: 0207 936 3533
E-mail: *lcia@lcia-arbitration.com*
Internet:
http://www.lcia-arbitration.com/town/square/xvc24/intouch/intouch.htm
Arbitration organisation that also has provision for mediation.

The Centre for Dispute Resolution Limited
79, Merrion Square
Dublin 2
Ireland
Tel: (3531) 661 3929
Fax: (3531) 661 8706
E-mail: *cdr@indigo.ie*
Mediation organisation dealing with business partnership and other disputes.

Family

Comprehensive Accredited Lawyer Mediators (CALM)
c/o S. J. Brand, Thorntons W. S.,   **A1–003**
50 Castle Street
Dundee DD1 3RU
Scotland
Tel: 01382 229111
Fax: 01382 202288
E-mail: *sbrand@thorntonsws.co.uk*
Scottish family mediators' organisation comprising lawyer mediators.

Family Mediators Association (FMA)
46 Grosvenor Gardens
London SW1W 0EB
Tel: 0207 881 9400
Fax: 0207 881 9401
E-mail: *hmcc@globalnet.co.uk*
Internet: *www.familymediators.co.uk*
Family mediation organisation operating nationally with members from legal,
counselling, therapy and related backgrounds.

Family Mediation Scotland (FMS)
127 Rose Street
South Lane
Edinburgh EH2 4BB
Scotland
Tel: 0131 220 1610
Fax: 0131 220 6895
Co-ordinating body for those Scottish mediation services affiliated to it, some
of whom also provide counselling services for children of separating parents.

Irish Family Mediation Service
Block 1, Room 5, Irish Life Centre
Lower Abbey Street
Dublin 1
Ireland
Tel: 00 3531 872 8277
Mediation organisation specifically dealing with family issues.

LawWise/British Association of Lawyer Mediators (BALM)
The Shooting Lodge
Guildford Road
Sutton Green
Guildford
Surrey GU4 7PZ
Tel: 01483 235000
Fax: 01483 237004
E-mail: *info@balm.org.uk* or *info@lawwise.com*
Internet (BALM): *www.balm.org.uk*
Internet (LawWise): *www.lawwise.com*
BALM is an association of lawyers who also mediate, in some cases in fields
other than family law. LawWise is the training arm of BALM.

NCH Action for Children
85 Highbury Park
London N5 1UD
Tel: 0207 226 2033
Fax: 0207 226 2537
E-mail: *kathyh@high.nchasc.org.uk*
Internet: *www.nchasc.org.uk* and jointly with the SFLA: *http://
www.carelaw.org.uk*
Organisation concerned about children in separation and divorce. With its
Scottish body and NFM it manages several family mediation services in
England, Scotland and Wales, which are also likely to manage counselling
services for children.

NCH Action for Children Scotland
17 Newton Place
Glasgow G3 7PY
Scotland
Tel: 0141 332 4041
See under NCH Action for Children.

National Family Meditation (NFM)
9 Tavistock Place
London WC1H 9SN
Tel: 0207 383 5993
Fax: 0207 383 5994

E-mail: *general@nfm.org.uk*
Internet: *www.nfm.u-net.com*
National service-based family mediation organisation comprising some 70 dedicated family mediation services, some of whom provide a counselling or listening service for children of separated or divorced parents.

Professional Development and Training (PDT)
17 Whitefriars
Sevenoaks
Kent TN13 1QG
Tel: 01732 453227
Fax: 01732 464133
e-mail: *s.madge@prof-dev-train.freeserve.co.uk*
Family mediation body with primarily but not exclusively lawyer mediators. Took over the family mediation programme of LawGroup.

Solicitors' Family Law Association (SFLA)
PO Box 302
Orpington
Kent BR6 8QX
Tel: 01689 850227
Fax: 01689 855833
E-mail: *sfla@btinternet.com*
Internet: *http://www.sfla.co.uk*
And jointly with NCH Action for Children: *http://www.carelaw.org.uk* National association of over 4,000 family solicitors and legal executives who subscribe to a code to work in a fair and conciliatory way. Provides mediation training with members around the country who undertake family mediation.

The Academy of Experts
(See under civil and commercial)

The Law Society of England & Wales
(See under civil and commercial)

The Law Society of Scotland
26 Drumsheugh Gardens
Edinburgh EH3 7YR
Scotland
Tel: 0131 226 7411
Fax: 0131 225 2934
Governs standards of Scottish solicitors and can provide details of solicitors who provide family law and mediation.

U.K. College of Family Mediators
24–32 Stephenson Way
London NW1 2HX
Tel: 0207 391 9162
Fax: 0207 391 9165

E-mail: *info@ukcfm.co.uk*
Internet: *www.ukcfm.co.uk*
Family mediation organisation regulating its members who are drawn from individual family mediation bodies approved by it. Has a register of members, promotes mediation and sets standards.

Employment

A1–004 ***Advisory, Conciliation and Arbitration Service (ACAS)***
27 Wilton Street
London SW1X 7AZ
Tel: 0207 210 3613
Fax: 0297 210 3708
Web site: *http://www.acas.org.uk*
Independent and impartial statutory employment service providing assistance in the resolution of employment conflicts, collective and individual, and the encouragement of positive employment policies and practices.

Environmental issues

A1–005 ***Environmental Resolve***
The Environment Council
212 High Holborn
London WC1V 7VW
Tel: 0207 836 2626
Fax: 0207 242 1180
E-mail: *stakeholder.dialogue@envcouncil.org.uk*
Internet: *http://www.greenchannel.com/tec/er.htm*
An undertaking of the Environment Council, this is a mediation service helping to prevent and resolve environmental disputes using consensus-building processes.

Community/Neighbourhood and General

A1–006 ***Mediation U.K.***
Alexander House
Telephone Avenue
Bristol BS1 4BS
Tel: 0117 904 6661
Fax: 0117 904 3331
E-mail: *mediationuk@cix.compulink.co.uk*
Web site: *http://www.cix.co.uk/~mediationuk/*
An umbrella organisation of networks, projects, organisations and individuals interested in mediation and other forms of constructive conflict resolution. See its directory of mediation services and resources in the United Kingdom and Ireland.

2. NORTH AMERICA (US & CANADA)

Academy of Family Mediators (AFM)   A1–007
5 Militia Drive
Lexington MA 02421
USA
Tel: (781) 674–2663
Fax: (781) 674–2690
E-mail: *afmoffice@mediators.org*
Internet: *http://www.igc.org/afm/*

Association of Attorney Mediators (AAM)
One Galleria Tower
13355 Noel Road, Suite 500
Dallas, TX 75240
USA
Tel: (972) 869–1183 or (800) 280–1368
Fax: (214) 739–2056
E-mail: *aam@counsel.com*
Web site: *http://www.attorney-mediators.org*

Association of Family and Conciliation Courts (AFCC)
329 W. Wilson Street
Madison
WI 53703
USA
Tel: (608) 251–4001
Fax: (608) 251–2231
E-mail: *afcc@afccnet.org*
Internet: *http://www.afccnet.org/*

American Arbitration Association (AAA)
335 Madison Avenue, 10th Floor
New York NY 10017–4605
USA
Tel: (212) 716–5800
Fax: (212) 716–5901
E-mail: *usadrsrv@arb.com*
Internet: *http://www.adr.org*

American Bar Association Section of Dispute Resolution
740 15th Street NW
Washington DC 20005–1009
USA
Tel: (202) 662–1680
Fax: (202) 662–1683
E-mail: *dispute@abanet.org*
Internet: *http://www.abanet.org/dispute/*

Arbitration and Mediation Institute of Canada Inc. (AMIC)
Institut d'Arbitrage et de Médiation du Canada Inc.
329 March Road, Box 11
Kanata
Ontario K2K 2E1
Canada
Tel: (613) 599–0878
Fax: (613) 599–7027
E-mail: *amic@igs.net*
Web site: *http://www.amic.org*

CPR Institute for Dispute Resolution
366 Madison Avenue
New York NY 10017–3122
USA
Tel: (212) 949–6490
Fax: (212) 949–8859
E-mail: *info@cpradr.org*
Web site: *http://www.cpradr.org*

Family Mediation Canada
528 Victoria St. North
Kitchener
Ontario N2H 5G1
Canada
Tel: (519) 585–3118
Fax: (519) 585–3121
E-mail: *fmc@fmc.ca* or *fmc@web.net*
Internet: *http://www.fmc.ca/*

International Academy of Mediators (IAM)
1807 Jancey Street
Pittsburgh
Pennsylvania 15206–1065
USA
Tel: (412) 362–3470
Fax: (412) 363–7913
E-mail: *iam@mediate.com*
Internet: *http://www.iamed.org/right.html*

Mennonite Central Committee (MCC)
21 South 12th St., P.O. Box 500
Akron
PA 17501–0500
USA
Tel: (717) 859–1151
E-mail: *mailbox@mcc.org*
Internet: *http://www.mcc.org/info/contact.html*

National Association for Community Mediation (NAFCM)
1726 M Street NW, Suite 500
Washington DC 20036
USA
Tel: (202) 467–6226
Fax: (202) 466–4769
E-mail: *nafcm@nafcm.org*
Web site: *http://www.nafcm.org*

National Institute for Dispute Resolution (NIDR)
1726 M Street NW, Suite 500
Washington DC 20036
USA
Tel: (202) 466–4764
Fax: (202) 466–4764
E-mail: *nidr@nidr.org*
Web site: *http://www.nidr.org*

Society of Professionals in Dispute Resolution (SPIDR)
International Office
1527 New Hampshire Avenue NW, Third Floor
Washington DC 20036
USA
Tel: (202) 667–9700
Fax: (202) 265–1968
E-mail: *spidr@spidr.org*
Internet: *http://www.spidr.org*

3. EUROPE

ADR centrum voor het Bedrijfsleven   A1–008
Bezuidenhoutseweg 12
Postbus 93002, 2509 AA
Den Haag
The Netherlands
Tel: (31) 70–3490 493
Fax: (31) 70–3490 295
E-mail: *ACB@vno-ncw.nl*

Arbitration and Dispute Resolution Institute of the Oslo Chamber of Commerce
P.O. Box 2874 Solli
N - 0230 Oslo
Norway
Tel: (47 22) 55 74 00
Fax: (47 22) 55 89 53
E-mail: *chamber@online.no*
Web site: *www.chamber.no*

Association pour la Promotion de la Médiation Familiale (APMF)
325, rue de Vaugirard
75015-Paris
France

Dansk Forening for Mediation
(Dansk Forligsnaevn)
c/o Jakob Arrevad
Ved Stranden 18
1012 Copenhagen K
Denmark

European Forum on Family Mediation Training and Research
c/o M. C. Talin
Val d'Azur C3
19 Chemin de Chateau-Gombert
13013 Marseille
France

Foreningen af Famileretsadvokater (FAF)
(Family Lawyers of Denmark)
c/o Advokat Annelise Lemche
Niels Hemmingsens Gade, 10, 5
Postboks 15
DK-1001 København K
Denmark
Tel: (45) 33–93 03 30
Fax: (45) 33–93 03 10
E-mail: *al@nhglaw.dk*

International Chamber of Commerce (ICC)
38 Cours Albert ler
75008 Paris
France
Tel: (33) (1) 49 53 28 28
Fax: (33) (1) 49 53 29 42
E-mail: *ARB@ICCWBO.ORG*
Internet: *http://www.iccwbo.org/what/what0.htm*

Mouvement International de Réconciliation (MIR)
68 rue de Babylone
75007-Paris
France
Tel./fax: (33) (1) 47 53 84 05

Netherlands Arbitration Institute
Schevengseweg 58
2517 KW The Hague
The Netherlands
Tel: (31) 70–525 456
Fax: (31) 70–540 483

Stichting Nederlands Mediation Instituut
Beursplein 37, Kamer 1559,
Postbus 30137
3001 DC Rotterdam
The Netherlands
Tel: (31) 10–405 6989
Fax: (31) 10–405 5452
E-mail: *info@nmi-mediation.nl*
Web site: *http://www.nmi-mediation.nl*

Université de Paix
4, bld du Nord
B-5000, Namur
Belgium
Tel: (32) 81 22 61 02
Fax: (32) 81 23 18 82
E-mail: *universite.de.paix@skynet.be*

World Intellectual Property Association (WIPO)
34 Chemin des Colombettes
P.O. Box 18
1211 Geneva 20
Switzerland
Tel: (41) 22–338 9111
Fax: (41) 22–740 3700
E-mail: *arbiter.mail@wipo.int*
Internet: *http://www.arbiter.wipo.int/center/contact/index.html*
Webmaster: *webmaster.arbiter@wipo.int*

Zurich Chamber of Commerce
Bleicherweg 5
Postfach 4031
8022 Zurich
Switzerland
Tel: (41) 1–211 0742
Fax: (41–1) 211 7615
E-mail: *direktion@zurichcci.ch*

4. AUSTRALIA & NEW ZEALAND

A1–009   ***Australian Commercial Dispute Centre (ACDC)***
Level 4, 50 Park Street
Sydney NSW 2000
Australia
Tel: (61) 2–9267 1000
Fax: (61) 2–9267 3125
E-mail: *acdcltd@msn.com*
Web site: *http://www.austlii.edu.au/au/other/acdc/*

LEADR
Head Office:
Level 4, 233 Macquarie Street
Sydney NSW 2000
Australia
Tel: (61) 2–9233 2255
Fax: (61) 2–9232 3024
E-mail: *leadr@leadr.com.au*
Web site: *http://www.leadr.com.au_www*
New Zealand Branch:
Hesketh Henry Building
Level 4, 2 Kitchener Street
Auckland
New Zealand
Tel: (64) 9–373 5020
Fax: (64) 9–373 5087
E-mail: *leadrnz@xtra.co.nz*

New Zealand Institute for Dispute Resolution
Victoria University of Wellington
Law Faculty
P.O. Box 600
Wellington 6001
New Zealand
Tel: (64) 4–463 6327
Fax: (64) 4–463 5184
Internet: *http://www.vuw.ac.nz/nzidr/Cont.htm*

The Institute of Arbitrators & Mediators Australia
Level 1, 22 William Street
Melbourne
Victoria 3000
Australia
Tel: (61) 3–9629 6799
Fax: (61) 3–9629 5250
E-mail: *instarb@werple.net.au*
Internet: *http://www.instarb.com.au/index.html*

5. AFRICA, ASIA AND OTHER TERRITORIES

Alternative Dispute Resolution Association of South Africa (ADRASA)   A1–010
PO Box 4284
Johannesburg 2000
South Africa
Tel: (27) 11–838 8830
Fax: (27) 11–838 5088

Asociacion Respuesta (Family Mediation)
Salguero 2142 piso 8
1425 Buenos Aires
Argentine
Tel/Fax: (54) 11–4826–1208
e-mail: *horowi@einstein.com.ar*

Cairo Regional Centre for International Commercial Arbitration
Al-Saleh Ayoub St.
Zamalek, Cairo
Egypt
Tel: (20) 2–340–1333 and (20) 2–041–335/6/7
Fax: (20) 2–340–1336
E-mail: *crcica@idscl.gov.eg*

Commission for Conciliation, Mediation and Arbitration (CCMA)
Private Bag X94
Marshalltown 2107
South Africa
Tel: (27) 11–377–6650
Fax: (27) 11–834–7351
E-mail: *infoservices@CCMA.org.za*
Internet: *http://www.ccma.org.za/*

Commonwealth Mediation Association
Secretary: Jide Olagunju
234 Murtale
Muhammed Way
Lagos
Nigeria
Tel: (234) 186 7967
Fax: (234) 186 0806

Dispute Resolution Centre
PO Box 57792
Nairobi
Kenya
Tel: (254) 2–570 600
Fax: (254) 2–573 071
E-mail: *mediate@africaonline.co.ke*

Hong Kong International Arbitration Centre (HKIAC)
38th Floor, Two Exchange Square
8 Connaught Place
Hong Kong S.A.R
China
Tel: (852) 2525 2381
Fax: (852) 2524 2171
E-mail: *adr@hkiac.org*
Internet: *http://www.hkiac.org/*

Kuala Lumpur Regional Centre for Arbitration
No. 12, Jalan Conlay
50450 Kuala Lumpur
Malaysia
Tel: (60) 3–242 0103
Fax: (60) 3–242 4513
E-mail: *klrca@putra.net.my*
Internet: *http://www.klrca.org/intro/index.html*

Independent Mediation Service of South Africa (IMSSA)
1 Park Road
Richmond 2092
Johannesburg
P.O. Box 91082, Auckland Park 2006
South Africa
Tel: (27) 11–482 2390/1
Fax: (27) 11–726 2540

The NCMG Centre for Dispute Resolution
8 Boyle Street
Onikan
P.O. Box 72001 Victoria Island
Lagos
Nigeria
Tel: 264 7421 and 264 7426
Fax: 264 7149
E-mail: *mediate@NCMG.org*

Singapore International Arbitration Centre (SIAC)
1 Coleman Street #05–08
The Adelphi
Singapore 179803
Tel: (65) 334 1277
Fax: (65) 334 2942
E-mail: *sinarb@singnet.com.sg*

MEDIATION DRAFTING: DOCUMENTS AND PRECEDENTS

1. CONTENTS

The following documents and precedents are contained in this appendix. **A2–001**
Documents provided by third parties are individually acknowledged, and the
authors thank them all for giving the necessary permission for inclusion in
this book. Each document will be accompanied by a brief commentary:

Mediation codes of practice and model procedures: **A2–002**

Contract clauses - civil/commercial dispute resolution: **A2–003**

Agreement to mediate: **A2–004**

Precedent agreements and summaries recording settlement terms: **A2–005**

2. DRAFTING MEDIATION DOCUMENTS

A2–007   Mediators need to be able to draft documents effectively. Their appointment and contract to mediate has to be recorded. Various documents may have to be prepared during the course of the mediation. After the conclusion of the mediation, the outcome has to be effectively and appropriately recorded. This may have to comprise a binding agreement (for example, in recording most civil and commercial settlements) or a non-binding memorandum or summary that can be used as a basis for the subsequent drafting of binding terms (as commonly required in family mediation).

A2–008   Mediation organisations also need carefully to consider drafting. They will usually need to have a Code of Practice and to provide precedent documents for their members, such as standard contract terms to include provision for mediation and other dispute resolution processes, Agreements to Mediate, practice forms, draft summaries of outcome and forms of agreement, and checklists.

A2–009   This appendix outlines some of the principles of mediation drafting, and contains precedents of many different kinds of documents that are likely to be relevant to mediators and mediation organisations. It should be emphasised that these are not meant to be comprehensive or definitive. They will generally need to be adapted with judgment for individual use.

Codes of practice and model procedures and standards

A2–010   Codes differ according to the field of activity of the mediation. In the civil and commercial field, there is no standard Code in the United Kingdom, but separate Codes for each organisation.

A2–011   The Centre for Dispute Resolution (CEDR) has published a Model Mediation Procedure applicable to civil and commercial disputes, which is ordinarily attached to the Agreement to Mediate and which, therefore, constitutes part of the agreement between CEDR, the parties and the mediator. A copy of this is included in this appendix, together with its guidance notes.

A2–012   In the family field, different organisations have their own Codes. However, two forms of Code have predominated in the United Kingdom. The U.K. College of Family Mediators has created and published a Code that it recommends as a standard for family mediation: a copy is included in the appendix. For solicitors who mediate as part of their practice, the Law

Society has published a family mediation Code of Practice: a copy is also included in the appendix. These two Codes have been largely harmonised in the course of discussions between the two organisations, but some differences remain, largely relating to the Law Society's Code being geared specifically for solicitors who have other ethical and practical considerations to take into account.

Neighbourhood and community mediators may also use different Codes, but a standard form has been recommended by Mediation U.K.: a copy is contained in the appendix.   A2–013

The agreement to mediate
The mediator should enter into an agreement with the disputants setting out the terms and basis on which the mediation is undertaken. This should be done before the substantive mediation process is started.   A2–014

The agreement ought to cover confidentiality, privilege and other process matters. It should also deal with practical matters such as fees. If the mediator is working to a Code of Practice that needs to be incorporated into the Agreement, this can be done directly by inserting the terms or indirectly by reference to the Code.   A2–015

The Agreement can be formal, which is more common for civil and commercial work. Alternatively, it can be relatively informal, which family mediators tend to prefer.   A2–016

Examples are given of an agreement that can be adapted for any civil/ commercial use; also specimens used by the Centre for Dispute Resolution, the Solicitors' Family Law Association and the Family Mediators Association.   A2–017

Contract clauses
Contracts, particularly those of a commercial nature, commonly contain clauses regulating which country's law is to apply to their terms and how disputes are to be dealt with. Dispute resolution clauses sometimes merely state which courts are to have jurisdiction; but frequently they set out the machinery for addressing disputes without using the courts. So, for example, provision is often made for arbitration; and increasingly, provision is made for negotiation and mediation or other ADR processes to be undertaken before adjudication, whether by way of arbitration or litigation.   A2–018

Dispute resolution clauses allow parties to choose in advance how they want any disputes to be dealt with. That avoids the tendency for parties to become polarised if they try to work out this machinery only after a dispute has arisen. Some parties simply use this to record an alternative form of adjudication, to avoid the courts. Others go further and outline a sequential procedure, starting with negotiation, moving on to mediation or other consensual processes if necessary, and then to adjudication if the matter remains unresolved.   A2–019

Examples of contract clauses are set out in this appendix. Those drafting the clauses should adapt these as required to the needs and circumstances of their individual contracts.   A2–020

Settlement agreements
Who drafts?

A2–021 This is likely to depend on the practice within the field of activity being mediated. In civil and commercial mediation, where agreements are almost always required to be signed before the parties leave the process, the agreement has to be drafted "on the spot".

A2–022 Where lawyers have represented the parties in the mediation, the mediator may liaise with them on the drafting of the settlement document, or the lawyers may agree between themselves as to the procedure and responsibility for such drafting. In the latter event, the mediator may still wish to review the document before signature, in case there are any points which the draftsmen may have misunderstood or inadvertently overlooked. The mediator's role in this event will usually be minimal, with the responsibility for drafting resting with the parties' lawyers.

A2–023 Where the parties are not represented in the mediation, or where for any other reason the mediator needs to be more closely involved in drafting—for example, where the mediator has kept notes which will facilitate drafting— the mediator may be primarily responsible for preparing the agreement. In such event, the mediator will need to take care to ensure that the document correctly reflects the agreed resolution and that all relevant details and conditions are incorporated.[1] It must be binding and enforceable if this is what is required, or non-binding if this is the requirement.

A2–024 It is helpful for civil/commercial mediators to have a template or precedent settlement agreement with them when they mediate, to facilitate drafting if the matter is settled. This might be general or it might be specific to the case being mediated. Some mediators have a laptop computer and portable printer with them to enable them to produce documents even when regular secretarial facilities are unavailable.

A2–025 In family mediation, there is a different culture and expectation concerning the recording of settlement terms. First, parties would not ordinarily sign an agreement in the mediation meeting, but would expect the necessary documentation to be sent to them afterwards. Secondly, and related to the first point, the record of the settlement terms would not be immediately binding, but would specifically be non-binding, to allow each party to take the document to his or her respective lawyers for individual advice.

A2–026 Consequently, it is usual for family mediators to undertake the drafting of the proposed terms. Most do this some time after the end of the meeting, although some may engage the couple in drafting in the meeting. If the respective lawyers approve the terms, they will arrange between themselves for those terms to be incorporated into a binding document, either a formal agreement or deed or a court order. The mediator would not ordinarily be involved in that aspect of the recording.

A2–027 In some kinds of inter-personal or community mediation, oral agreements binding in honour only may sometimes suffice or be preferred. Others may wish to have the terms of their agreements recorded, albeit usually

---

[1] Gracine Hufnagel, an American professional liability insurance manager, writes in "Mediator malpractice liability" M.Q. No. 23 (1989), that claims have been seen in the mediator's drafting of the settlement agreement. See Chap. 24 for mediation insurance.

informally. Even if a mediation is informal, and the parties do not want their proposed agreement to be binding, it may be helpful to have a written record of their understandings for the avoidance of possible future good faith misunderstandings.

Format

Formats for the recording of settlement terms vary according to the field of ADR in which one is working. Even within the same field, differences of approach and style exist.   A2–028

In the civil and commercial field, agreements tend to follow the form, layout and content of traditional commercial contracts. Practitioners may vary in style, but broadly speaking, the recording of settlement terms arrived at in civil or commercial mediation would look very familiar to a commercial lawyer.   A2–029

In the family field, a very different format is used. As indicated above, parties are not ordinarily bound by the settlement terms that they may have approved until they have had the opportunity to take independent legal advice on them. It is not, therefore, policy to record the proposed terms in the form of an "agreement". The usual practice instead is for the mediator to prepare a document, known either as the Summary of Proposals, or more commonly now, the Memorandum of Understanding, which contains a brief outline of the issues and the proposals. The Memorandum of Understanding is generally written as an evidentially privileged document, and is accompanied by an open (not privileged) Financial Disclosure Summary, setting out the financial circumstances of the parties. Some organisations also have a covering summary, explaining the distinction between the two kinds of summaries that follow.   A2–030

The summary can incorporate any matters that the mediator or the parties may consider appropriate. The mediator may for example wish to reflect some cautionary matter in the summary, such as a note of having recommended that the parties seek legal advice on certain issues.   A2–031

In community and neighbourhood mediation, settlement terms may remain oral. If recorded, the memorandum recording them would usually be brief and informal.   A2–032

3. SOME PRINCIPLES OF MEDIATION DRAFTING

Binding or non-binding

The drafter must be clear whether the terms being recorded are to be immediately binding. If not, will they become binding when some further stage has been reached or condition met? This must be clearly stated. If parties do not wish to have a binding agreement, whatever they sign must be sufficiently clear in its terms and effect not to constitute a binding agreement.   A2–033

The agreement under which the parties entered into the mediation may make provision whether or not and in what circumstances the agreement reached in the mediation will be binding on the parties.[2]   A2–034

---

[2] See, *e.g.* the Centre for Dispute Resolution Model Mediation Procedure at para. A2–110 below.

A2–035   A potential pitfall may arise where the agreement provides for the matters contained in it to be embodied in a more formal and detailed contract, to be drafted outside the mediation at a later date, for example by the parties' lawyers. Pending such formal documentation, the memorandum signed in the mediation records the main points that the subsequent document will contain. However, that earlier memorandum may well constitute a binding agreement having full force and effect although a later document is not signed. If that is not the intention of the parties, it should be explicit in the initial memorandum that it is not binding unless and until such a formal contract is executed, and that it is subject to contract. A practical problem may well be the ambivalence of the parties. They may want on the one hand to defer commitment until a formal document has been prepared, while on the other, they may be anxious that the settlement arrived at in the mediation should not be lost by a change of mind in the meantime. Mediators should be alive to the inconsistency inherent in these conflicting requirements, which must be resolved in discussion with the parties.

Conditional or unconditional

A2–036   This is not the same issue as whether an agreement is binding or non-binding. A conditional agreement is one which may or may not come into effect contingently upon whether or not a specified condition or conditions are met; or particular terms of a binding agreement may come into effect in the event of certain conditions being fulfilled. For example, it is possible for parties to agree on a binding basis that X will pay Y a specified sum of money if some specified event occurs, say, if the profits of a company exceed a defined level within a prescribed period. In that event, the test is an objective one which may be outside the control or will of the parties. If the condition is met, the relevant term of the agreement will come into effect.

A2–037   Similarly, parties can firmly agree that their terms of agreement will come into effect on condition that specified insurers agree to contribute, say, £100,000 to the settlement. In that event, the test for the effectiveness of the agreement will be whether or not the insurers so agree. Again, the agreement is binding, but whether or not it comes into effect depends on whether the condition is met. This may be outside the control of the parties.

A2–038   That is different from parties reaching a provisional non-binding "agreement" on terms which will not come into effect at all until some act is done by the parties which brings it into binding effect, for example, that it is subject to contract and only becomes binding when a formal contract has been prepared and executed by the parties. In this case, the parties can decide whether or not they wish to make the contract binding.

Principle or detail

A2–039   The document signed by the parties at the conclusion of the mediation may either record the principles of their agreement and/or the key points, perhaps in the form of Heads of Agreement, or it may deal in depth with all the

---

See also the Solicitors' Family Law Association and the Family Mediators Association agreements to mediate. Both of these provide that no resolution arrived at in the mediation will be binding until the parties have each had an opportunity to consult their individual solicitors and have thereafter agreed to be bound.

relevant provisions. The drafter needs to establish what degree of detail the parties require. As a rule, it is usually appropriate and important for the document to be as detailed and precise as reasonably possible, for the avoidance of subsequent misunderstanding and disagreement. Furthermore, unless all the material terms are agreed, clearly and unambiguously, there is a risk that the court could subsequently find that no agreement exists.

However, there may be cases where the parties prefer to have their understandings recorded in principle, without particularisation. In other instances, different factors may necessitate a briefer form of outline agreement, for example, time constraints may inhibit the preparation of a fully detailed document. Despite such constraints, every effort should be made to draft and execute a comprehensive agreement before the parties go their separate ways following the conclusion of a mediation. Serious problems could arise if parties, having put their energy and commitment into resolving a dispute through mediation, find that it has been inadequately recorded or executed.   **A2–040**

Formality and style

The degree of formality in the drafting of a settlement agreement or any summary will depend on the style and preference of those drafting it, the requirements of the parties and the conventions of the field within which they are operating. However, whether the document tends towards formality or informality, the terms must be clear and precise, and all necessary provisions must be included and unambiguous, to enable it to be implemented without misunderstanding or further dispute. Informality of style should not be confused with imprecision or sloppiness.   **A2–041**

In some cases the parties may want or need the agreement to be recorded as a deed, for example, if there is a doubt about the adequacy of the consideration.[3] The agreement may need to be made into an order of the court, in which event the drafting of the documentation may be in the form of a Tomlin Order or other form of consent order.[4] Alternatively, in some circumstances an agreement may be filed and made a rule of court. Settlement terms that have to be made into court orders are likely to require legal expertise. In such event, the parties will probably be legally represented in the pending or anticipated litigation, if not also in the mediation, and their lawyers can deal with the drafting and formalisation of the order.[5] It may well be sufficient for the mediator to record the terms and fact that a court order is required and will be arranged by consent.   **A2–042**

Inasmuch as ADR processes tend to be less formal than court processes, there is greater scope to avoid a legalistic approach to drafting and to make documents more understandable. It is worth mentioning the organisation   **A2–043**

---

[3] A deed must comply with the Law of Property (Miscellaneous Provisions) Act 1989.

[4] A Tomlin Order provides for a stay of proceedings on agreed terms, save to carry such terms into effect, with liberty being reserved to revert to the court in relation to such terms.

[5] With regard to the drafting of Tomlin Orders and other consent orders, see *The Law and Practice of Compromise* by David Foskett Q.C. (4th ed., 1996) which contains precedents and samples of agreements and orders. See also paras 23–040 *et seq.* above.

"Clarity", which is committed to simplifying legal language, and which provides helpful guidelines.[6]

Authority to sign

A2–044 Those who sign the agreement must have the necessary authority to do so if attending in a representative capacity. This ought to have been established by the mediator at an early stage of the process.

3. CHECKLISTS

A2–045 Checklists can be helpful to mediators, both in their substantive practice and in relation to their drafting of settlement terms. This appendix contains both kinds of checklists, substantive and drafting, separately dealing with family mediation and civil/commercial mediation.

---

[6]Clarity is contactable at c/o Mark Adler, 74 South Street, Dorking, Surrey RH4 2HD, England.

5. DOCUMENTS AND PRECEDENTS

Precedent 1. Law Society Code (family mediation) (2nd edition, April 1999)

The Law Society of England and Wales has published two Codes of Practice   **A2–046**
(including commentary on each section) for solicitors who mediate as part of their practice, one for family mediation and the other for civil and commercial mediation. The Law Society family mediation Code is published below. The authors of this work wish to acknowledge the Law Society for permitting the reproduction of this Code.

The Introduction to the Family Mediation Code refers to Principle 22.04 of the Guide to the Professional Conduct of Solicitors, Seventh Edition, which recommends that solicitors who offer ADR services comply with a code of practice. The Family Law Committee of the Law Society recommends that all solicitors offering family mediation within their practices comply with this code. It is designed to deal with the fundamentals of family mediation and is not intended to cover every situation that may arise. The concept of not giving advice when acting as a mediator permeates the entire Code.

SECTION 1—OBJECTIVES OF FAMILY MEDIATION

Family mediation is a process in which: **A2–047**

1.1 a couple or any other family members

1.2 whether or not they are legally represented

1.3 and at any time, whether or not there are or have been legal proceedings,

1.4 agree to the appointment of a neutral third party (the mediator)

1.5 who is impartial

1.6 who has no authority to make any decisions with regard to their issues

1.7 which may relate to separation, divorce, children's issues, property and financial questions or any other issues they may raise.

1.8 but who helps them reach their own informed decisions

1.9 by negotiation

1.10 without adjudication.

Commentary
From time to time the dispute between a couple may involve a wider group   **A2–048**
of family members than just the couple. Family members may include step-parents, grandparents, aunts, uncles, children and even potential family members. Any of these may participate in the mediation with the agreement

of the couple and the mediator, but with regard to involving children in the process, see the commentary to section 8.

A2–049 The code is aimed at those undertaking family mediations on a commercial basis, although it may be observed equally by those undertaking family mediations on a pro bono basis.

A2–050 Whilst the mediation may deal, typically, with the whole of any dispute, the parties may, should they so choose, deal with only one aspect of a dispute, for example, liability or quantum.

A2–051 In one model of family mediation, two or more mediators co-mediate the dispute. In those circumstances, the solicitor-mediator should be aware that the co-mediator may need to comply with his or her own ethical rules and will need to obtain his or her own insurance cover.

A2–052 The mediator must not give legal advice to the parties individually or collectively. The mediator may however provide legal information to the parties to assist them in understanding the principles of law applicable to their circumstances and the way in which those principles are generally applied.

A2–053 In the context of this Code, adjudication means the formal determination by a third party.

SECTION 2—QUALIFICATIONS AND APPOINTMENT OF MEDIATOR

A2–054 2.1 Every mediator must comply with the criteria and requirements for mediators stipulated from time to time by the Law Society, including those relating to training, consultancy, accreditation and regulation.

2.2 Save where appointed by or through the court, a mediator may only accept appointment if both or all parties to the mediation so request, or agree.

2.3 Whether a mediator is appointed by the parties or through the court or any other agency, he or she may only continue to act as such so long as both or all parties to the mediation wish him or her to do so. If any party does not wish to continue with the mediation, the mediator must discontinue the process. Also, if the mediator considers that it would be inappropriate to continue the mediation, the mediator shall bring it to an end, and may decline to give reasons.

Commentary

A2–055 This section should be read in conjunction with paragraph 4.1.

SECTION 3—CONFLICTS OF INTEREST AND IMPARTIALITY OF MEDIATOR

A2–056 3.1 The impartiality of the mediator is a fundamental principle of mediation.

3.2 Impartiality means that:

3.2.1 the mediator does not have any significant personal interest in the outcome of the mediation;

3.2.2 a mediator with any personal interest in the outcome of the mediation may act if, and only if, full disclosure is made to all of the parties as soon as it is known and they consent;

3.2.3 the mediator will conduct the process fairly and even-handedly, and will not favour any party over another.

3.3 The mediator must not act, or, having started to do so, continue to act:

3.3.1 in relation to issues on which he or she or a member of his or her firm has at any time acted for any party;

3.3.2 if any circumstances exist which may constitute an actual or potential conflict of interest;

3.3.3 if the mediator or a member of his or her firm has acted for any of the parties in issues not relating to the mediation, unless that has been disclosed to the parties as soon as it is known and they consent.

3.4 Where a mediator has acted as such in relation to a dispute, neither he or she nor any member of his or her firm may act for any party in relation to the subject matter of the mediation.

Commentary

Whilst impartiality is fundamental to the role of the mediator, this does not mean that a mediator may never express a comment or view that one party may find more acceptable than another. However, the mediator must not allow his or her personal view of the fairness or otherwise of the substance of the negotiations between the parties to damage or impair his or her impartiality.   **A2–057**

The mediator must appreciate that his or her involvement in the process is inevitably likely to affect the course of the negotiations between the parties. This will apply whether the mediator intervenes directly or whether he or she deals with issues indirectly, for example, through questions. Consequently all mediator intervention needs to be conducted with sensitivity and care in order to maintain impartiality.   **A2–058**

There may be circumstances where the mediator may have some personal interest in the outcome of the mediation (for example, he or she has a very small shareholding in a company which is a party to the mediation). In those circumstances and where the mediator feels able to act impartially, he or she must disclose full details of his or her interest to the parties immediately, inviting them to decide whether or not the mediator should continue to act.   **A2–059**

The mediator should decline to act if he or she feels he or she will be prejudiced (for example, he or she knows one of the parties socially), or in circumstances where either party may perceive there to be a prejudice.   **A2–060**

It is important that, not only must the mediator be neutral, he or she must be perceived by the parties to be so. The mediator must therefore take particular care to avoid conflicts of interest, whether actual or potential.   **A2–061**

Whilst a mediator may not undertake cases in respect of which his or her   **A2–062** firm has already provided legal advice to one of the parties, the mediator would not be precluded from acting as such in respect of unrelated issues involving a party for whom his or her firm has previously acted, provided that, before undertaking the mediation, the mediator discloses this fact to the parties and the parties consent to the mediation.

A2–063 It is usual in mediation for the parties to agree that the mediator should treat as confidential, information which he or she acquires during the course of private meetings; almost inevitably such information will be relevant to the dispute but will not give rise to a conflict situation as described in Principles 15.02 and 15.03 of *The Guide to the Professional Conduct of Solicitors*. However those principles will apply where the mediator has acquired confidential information relevant to the dispute or to any of the parties involved in the mediation from another source (for example, another client or firm). Similarly, during the course of mediation, the mediator may acquire confidential information relevant to another client of his or her firm. Both of those situations would give rise to a conflict of interest as defined in Chapter 15, necessitating that the mediator withdraw from the mediation.

A2–064 If the mediator is in any doubt on any possible conflict of interest point, the mediator should contact the Professional Ethics Division of the Law Society for further advice.

SECTION 4—MEDIATION PROCEDURES

A2–065 4.1 The mediator must ensure that the parties agree the terms and conditions regulating the mediation before dealing with the substantive issues. This should ordinarily be in a written agreement which should reflect the main principles of this Code. Such agreement should also contain the terms of remuneration of the mediator.

4.2 The procedure for the conduct of the mediation is a matter for the decision of the mediator. Insofar as the mediator establishes an agenda of matters to be covered in the mediation, the mediator should be guided by the needs, wishes and priorities of the parties in doing so.

4.3 In establishing any procedures for the conduct of the mediation, the mediator must be guided by a commitment to procedural fairness, the fostering of mutual respect between the parties and a high quality of process.

Commentary

A2–066 This section should be read with section 5 and its commentary. The mediator is the manager of the process and should manage the mediation at his or her discretion, with the object of meeting as best as possible the wishes of the parties.

SECTION 5—THE DECISION-MAKING PROCESS

A2–067 5.1 The primary aim of family mediation is to help the parties to arrive at their own decisions regarding their issues, on an informed basis with an understanding, so far as reasonably practicable, of the implications and consequences of such decisions for themselves and any children concerned.

5.2 The parties may reach decisions on any issue at any stage of the mediation.

5.3 Subject to paragraph 5.4, decisions arrived at in family mediation should not be binding on the parties until they have had the opportunity to seek advice on those decisions from their own legal representatives.

5.4 The parties must be offered the opportunity to obtain legal advice before any decision can be turned into a binding agreement on any issue which appears to the mediator or to either party to be of significance to the position of one or both parties.

5.5 The mediator must not seek to impose his or her preferred outcome on the parties and should try to avoid becoming personally identified with any particular outcome.

5.6 The mediator shall, however, be free to make management decisions with regard to the conduct of the mediation process, and may suggest possible solutions and help the parties to explore these, where he or she thinks that this would be helpful to them.

5.7 The mediator should assist the parties, so far as appropriate and practicable, to identify what information and documents would help the resolution of any issue(s), and how best such information and documents may be obtained. However, the mediator has no obligation to make independent enquiries or undertake verification in relation to any information or documents sought or provided in the mediation. If necessary, consideration may be given in the mediation to the ways in which the parties may make such enquiries or obtain such verification.

5.8 Family mediation does not provide for the disclosure and discovery of documents in the same way or to the same extent as required by Court Rules. The mediator may indicate any particular documents that he or she considers each party should furnish.

5.9 Parties should be helped to reach such resolution of such issues which they feel are appropriate to their particular circumstances. Such resolutions may not necessarily be the same as those which may be arrived at in the event of an adjudication by the Court.

5.10 The mediator should, if practicable, inform the parties if he or she considers that the resolutions which they are considering are likely to fall outside the parameters which a court might approve or order. In such circumstances the mediator should re-affirm the advisability of the parties each obtaining independent legal advice. If they nevertheless wish to proceed with such resolutions, they may do so. In these circumstances the mediation summary may identify any specific questions on which the mediator has indicated a need for independent legal advice. If, however, the parties are proposing a resolution which appears to the mediator to be unconscionable or fundamentally inappropriate, then the mediator should inform the parties accordingly and may terminate the mediation, and/or refer the parties to their legal advisers.

5.11 Parties may consult with their own solicitors as the mediation progresses, and shall be given the opportunity to do so before reaching any binding agreement on their substantive issues. Where appropriate, the mediator may assist the parties to consider the desirability of their jointly or individually seeking further assistance during the course of the mediation process from professional advisers such as lawyers, accountants, expert valuers or others, or from counsellors or therapists. The mediator may also assist the parties by providing relevant lists of names.

5.12 Mediation meetings are commonly conducted without lawyers present. However, solicitors or counsel acting for the individual parties may be invited to participate in the mediation process, and in any communications, in such manner as the mediator may consider useful and appropriate, and as the parties may agree.

Commentary

A2–068 The mediator is the manager of the process. The mediator should consult the parties on management decisions such as the ordering of issues and the agenda for each mediation session. The mediator must not relinquish control of the *process* to the parties.

A2–069 Family mediation does not provide for disclosure and discovery of documents and information in the same way, or to the same extent as is possible under existing court rules. However, mediators should explain to the parties why full and frank disclosure is essential to the mediation process, and at all stages should encourage the provision of full information and documentation. The mediator may indicate any particular documents or information that he or she considers each party should have. If either party declines to furnish any information and the mediator considers that the mediation cannot properly continue without it, the mediator must discuss this with the parties and may bring the mediation to an end.

A2–070 Mediators cannot be responsible for issues of justice and fairness; the parties must define their own "fairness" and criteria for agreeing terms and the mediator must not try to influence them with his or her own ideas of fairness. However, the mediator must be able to dissociate him or herself from the proposed resolutions in certain extreme circumstances.

A2–071 The decision to include solicitors for the individual parties should be taken by the parties with the help of the mediator, and not by the solicitors.

A2–072 Mediators are likely to find that decisions can be made at any stage of the mediation. Early decisions may include, for example, interim arrangements for contact, the sale of items to raise cash, or holiday arrangements for children. The mediator should ensure that the parties do not arrive at decisions on some issues prematurely, if those decisions might prejudice either party in relation to an overall resolution.

A2–073 Some decisions reached in mediation are unlikely to affect the long term rights and responsibilities of the parties, for example, decisions might be reached on interim contact arrangements, contact over an approaching holiday period, the sale of a non-material item or division of contents of the formal matrimonial home with no real monetary value. In those circumstances, whilst parties should not be discouraged from seeking independent legal advice should they so choose, it would not be necessary for the mediator to offer them the opportunity to obtain such advice before these decisions are turned into binding agreements on those limited issues.

SECTION 6—DEALING WITH POWER IMBALANCES

6.1 The mediator should be alive to the likelihood of power imbalances existing between the parties. These may relate to various different aspects including for example, behaviour which is controlling, abusive or manipulative; finance; children and family; status; communication and other skills; possession of information; the withholding of co-operation; and many other kinds of power.   **A2–074**

6.2 If power imbalances seem likely to cause the mediation process to become unfair or ineffective, the mediator must take appropriate steps to try to prevent this.

6.3 The mediator must ensure that the parties take part in mediation willingly and without fear of violence or harm. Additionally, the mediator must seek to prevent manipulative, threatening or intimidating behaviour by either party.

6.4 If the mediator believes that power imbalances cannot be redressed adequately and that in consequence the mediation will not be able to be fairly and effectively conducted, he or she may discuss this with the parties, but in any event must bring the mediation to an end as soon as practicable.

Commentary

Where power imbalances involve potential violence or harm, mediators must take particular care to establish whether mediation can take place at all, and if it can, under what circumstances and conditions.   **A2–075**

Cases of potential violence and harm should be identified as soon as possible. The Family Law Act 1996 requires that this is undertaken in legally-aided cases (see section 11 below); but it is to be regarded as good and required practice in all mediation matters, whether or not legally aided.   **A2–076**

If mediation is to take place where a party is thought to be at any risk of harm by the other party, the mediator must take steps to try to ensure that both parties and the mediator are safe in the mediation. This should, for example, be addressed by appropriate arrangements for reception on arrival and for departure after the mediation, and by any other arrangements or conditions the mediator may consider suitable.   **A2–077**

SECTION 7—CONFIDENTIALITY AND PRIVILEGE

A2–078

7.1 The mediator must maintain confidentiality in relation to all matters dealt with in the mediation. The mediator may disclose:

7.1.1 matters which the parties and the mediator agree may be disclosed;

7.1.2 matters which the mediator considers appropriate where he or she believes that any child or any other person affected by the mediation is suffering or likely to suffer significant harm (and in such case, the mediator should so far as practicable and appropriate discuss with the parties the way in which such disclosure is to take place); or

7.1.3 matters where the law imposes an overriding obligation of disclosure on the mediator.

7.2 Any information or correspondence provided by any party should be shared openly with both and not withheld, except any address or telephone number and except as the parties may otherwise agree.

7.3 All information material to financial issues must be provided on an open basis, so that it can be referred to in court, either in support of an application made with the consent of the parties or in contested proceedings.

7.4 However, discussions about possible terms of settlement should be conducted on the "without prejudice" basis; and in any event a mediation privilege should ordinarily be claimed for them, so that parties may explore their options freely.

7.5 The mediator must discuss arrangements about confidentiality with the parties before holding separate meetings or caucuses. It may be agreed that the mediator will either:

7.5.1 report back to the parties as to the substance of the separate meetings; or

7.5.2 maintain separate confidences: provided that if separate confidences are to be maintained, they must not include any material fact which would be open if discussed in a joint meeting.

7.6 The mediation privilege will not ordinarily apply in relation to communications indicating that a child or other person affected by the mediation is suffering or likely to suffer significant harm, or where other public policy considerations prevail, or where for any other reason the rules of evidence render privilege inapplicable.

Commentary

A2–079 Before the mediation commences the parties should agree in writing as to the provisions concerning confidentiality and privilege that will apply to the mediation. The principles are outlined in section 7, which the following commentary will amplify.

Confidentiality

The couple may expect a mediator to keep confidential all matters they have **A2–080** discussed in mediation. However, there are some circumstances when a mediator has a duty of disclosure which is greater than the duty to maintain confidentiality. Even without a Code of Practice or Agreement between the parties, confidentiality might have to be broken where this is justified, as where public policy considerations prevail. Paragraph 7.1 of the Code specifies circumstances in which a mediator would be expected to disclose matters arising in mediation; but this would not be a breach of confidentiality, nor would it be unexpected, since the parties would have been aware from their agreement to mediate of the mediator's duty in this regard.

In essence there are two main circumstances in which disclosure may take **A2–081** place:

1. Those involving children: the Code and corresponding agreement to mediate make it clear that there may be disclosure where the mediator believes that any child is suffering or likely to suffer significant harm. This should be read with paragraph 8.3, which outlines the obligations of the mediator where he or she has this belief.

   In some cases, the mediator will have the difficult task of assessing whether or not a party's right to confidentiality should prevail over the possible risk of harm to a child or other person. Solicitor mediators faced with this difficulty may wish to contact the Professional Ethics Division of the Law Society for further advice.

2. Other issues of public policy: these may involve similar principles to those outlined above, but relate to adults suffering or likely to suffer significant harm, or they may involve any other issues of public policy where public disclosure outweighs any duty of confidentiality to the parties.

Privilege

Here again, two situations may be distinguished: **A2–082**

1. Where communications in mediation relate to children, there are two principles affecting the issue of privilege. On the one hand, a mediation privilege has been established by a line of cases relating to children's issues. On the other hand, that privilege will not ordinarily apply in relation to communications indicating that a child is suffering or likely to suffer significant harm.

2. The mediation privilege afforded by the courts to children's issues has not yet been extended by the courts to other matters covered in the mediation. A general mediation privilege may exist or may become established, but this has not yet occurred in any reported case.

Information furnished in mediation material to financial issues is treated as **A2–083** open, whereas information and communications relating to negotiations and attempts to reach a settlement are treated as privileged. This privilege should be asserted by requiring parties to deal with these matters on a "without prejudice" basis; and it is also hoped that the mediation privilege established in children's cases will be confirmed by the courts as having been extended to other issues in mediation.

A2–084   Even if privilege is established, there are some exceptions to the privileged nature of communications, as outlined in paragraph 7.6.

SECTION 8—FAMILIES AND CHILDREN

A2–085   8.1 Mediators shall have regard at all times to the provisions of Part I of the Family Law Act 1996.

8.2 In working with the parties, the mediator should also have regard to the needs and interests of the children of the family.

8.2.1 When it appears to the mediator that a child is suffering, or is likely to suffer significant harm, the mediator should consider with the parties what steps should be taken outside mediation to remedy the situation. But in exceptional circumstances where there is serious risk of harm to any person the mediator may decide not to inform the parties.

8.2.2 Where it is necessary to protect the child from significant harm, the mediator must in any event contact an appropriate agency or take such steps outside the mediation as may be appropriate.

8.3 Occasionally children might be directly involved in mediation. The mediator should consider whether and when children may be directly involved in mediation. The mediator should not ordinarily invite children to be directly involved in the mediation unless specifically trained to do so, and alive to the issues such as confidentiality, and the dynamics inherent in doing so.

Commentary

A2–086   Section 27 (8) of the Family Law Act 1996 requires the mediator to have arrangements designed to ensure that the parties are encouraged to consider "whether and to what extent each child could be given the opportunity to express his or her wishes and feelings in the mediation".

A2–087   The value of involving children directly in mediation has been widely discussed and debated, and this continues. Meanwhile the involvement of children directly in the mediation should only be undertaken with extreme caution and after careful consideration with parties as to the objectives of such involvement and the rules concerning confidentiality and other aspects. The needs, wishes and interests of children should generally be introduced and dealt with in the mediation through their parents.

A2–088   It is important that any mediator considering involving children directly in mediation should undertake specific training covering these issues. Even then, the question remains as to the value of bringing children into the mediation room, and what children's perceptions and expectations might be of that. In consultation with mediation training providers, the Law Society's ADR Working Party is considering what constitutes appropriate training and what further guidance might be issued to assist mediators in this complex area. Such guidance will be published as soon as possible.

SECTION 9—PROFESSIONAL INDEMNITY COVER

9.1 All solicitor mediators must carry professional indemnity cover in respect of their acting as mediators.   **A2–089**

9.1.1 Solicitors who practise as mediators will be covered by the Solicitors' Indemnity Fund in respect of their acting as a mediator, provided they are doing so in their capacity as a member of their firm.

9.1.2 If a solicitor is acting as a mediator as a separate activity outside his or her legal practice, separate indemnity insurance must be obtained.

Commentary

Solicitors who mediate outside their practices as members of mediation organisations may be covered by block insurance provided by those organisations. If not, they must make their own arrangements for appropriate cover.   **A2–090**

A solicitor practising as a mediator outside of his or her legal practice must have regard to rule 5 of the Solicitors' Practice Rules 1990 and to the Solicitors' Separate Business Code 1994, set out in *The Guide to the Professional Conduct of Solicitors* (7th edition). Further guidance can be obtained by contacting the Professional Ethics Division of the Law Society.   **A2–091**

SECTION 10—PROMOTION OF MEDIATION

10.1 Solicitor mediators may promote their practice as such, but must always do so in a professional, truthful and dignified way. They may reflect their qualification as a mediator and their membership of any other relevant mediation organisation.   **A2–092**

10.2 Solicitor mediators must comply with the Law Society's Publicity Code, set out in *The Guide to the Professional Conduct of Solicitors* (7th edition).

SECTION 11—SECTION 27 FAMILY LAW ACT 1996, (SECTION 13B LEGAL AID ACT 1988)

Every mediator must have arrangements designed to ensure: **A2–093**

11.1 that parties participate in mediation only if willing and not influenced by fear of violence or other harm;

11.2 that cases where either party may be influenced by fear of violence or other harm are identified as soon as possible;

11.3 that the possibility of reconciliation is kept under review throughout mediation; and

11.4 that each party is informed about the availability of independent legal advice.

Commentary

A2–094 This section should be read with section 6 and its commentary. As to keeping reconciliation under review, this may be inappropriate in many cases, but even in such cases, mediators should not ignore the possibility of reconciliation if it becomes appropriate.

Precedent 2. U.K. College of Family Mediators Code of Practice (family mediation)

A2–095 *The authors wish to acknowledge the U.K. College of Family Mediators for permitting the reproduction of this Code.*

U.K. COLLEGE OF FAMILY MEDIATORS

CODE OF PRACTICE

1 DEFINITIONS

A2–096 1.1 This Code of Practice applies to all family mediation conducted or offered by mediators registered by the U.K. College of Family Mediators.

1.2 Family mediation is a process in which an impartial third person assists those involved in family breakdown, and in particular separating or divorcing couples, to communicate better with one another and reach their own agreed and informed decisions concerning some or all of the issues relating to the separation, divorce, children, finance or property.

1.3 This Code applies whether or not there are or have been legal proceedings between any of the participants and whether or not any or all of them are legally represented.

1.4 In this Code, "mediation" means the family mediation to which this Code applies, "mediation" means any person offering such mediation, and "participant" means any family member taking part in it. The "College" means the "U.K. College of Family Mediators".

2 AIMS AND OBJECTIVES

A2–097 2.1 Mediation aims to assist participants to reach the decisions which they consider appropriate to their own particular circumstances.

2.2 Mediation also aims to assist participants to communicate with one another now and in the future and to reduce the scope or intensity of dispute and conflict within the family.

2.3 Mediation should have regard to the principles that where a marriage or relationship has irretrievably broken down and is being brought of an end it should be brought to an end in a way which minimises distress to the participants and any children, promotes as good a relationship between the participants and any children as possible, removes or diminishes any risk of violence to any of the participants or children from the other participants, and avoids unnecessary cost to the participants.

2.4 By virtue of the Children (Scotland) Act 1995, mediators in Scotland are required to have regard to the principles contained in Part 1 of that Act on Parental Rights and Responsibilities.

2.5 By virtue of the Family Law Act 1996, mediators in England and Wales are required to have regard to the general principles set out in section 1 of that Act when exercising functions under or in consequence of it.

3 SCOPE OF MEDIATION

3.1 Mediation may cover all or any of the following matters: **A2–098**

i options for maintaining the relationship between the adult participants and the consequences of doing so;

ii with whom the children are to live; what contact they are to have with each parent and any other person such as grandparents; and any other aspect of parental responsibility, such as schooling and holidays;

iii what is to happen to the family home and any other property of the adult participants and whether any maintenance is to be paid by one to the other either for that adult or for the children;

iv how any adjustments to these arrangements are to be decided upon in the future.

3.2 Participants and the mediator may agree that mediation will cover any other matters which it would be helpful to resolve in connection with any breakdown in relationships between the participants and which the mediator considers suitable for mediation.

4 GENERAL PRINCIPLES

Voluntary participation

4.1 Participation in mediation is always voluntary. Any participant or   **A2–099**
mediator is free to withdraw at any time. If a mediator believes that any participant is unable or unwilling to participate freely and fully in the process, the mediator may raise the issue with the participants and

may suspend or terminate mediation. The mediator may suggest hat the participants obtain such other professional services as are appropriate

Neutrality

4.2 Mediators must at all times remain neutral as to the outcome of mediation. They must not seek to move the participants towards an outcome which the mediator prefers, whether by attempting to predict the outcome of court proceedings or otherwise. They may, however, inform participants of possible solutions, their legal and other implications, and help participants to explore these.

Impartiality

4.3 Mediators must at all times remain impartial as between the participants. They must conduct the process in a fair and even-handed way.

4.4 Mediators must seek to prevent manipulative, threatening or intimidating behaviour by any participant. Mediators must conduct the process in such a way as to redress, as far as possible, any imbalance in power between the participants. If such behaviour or any other imbalance seems likely to render mediation unfair or ineffective, the mediator must take appropriate steps to try to prevent this, terminating mediation as necessary.

Independence and conflicts of interest

4.5 Mediators must not have any personal interest in the outcome of the mediation.

4.6 Mediators must not mediate in any case in which they have acquired or may acquire relevant information in any private or other professional capacity.

4.7 Mediators who have acquired information in the capacity of mediator in any particular case must not act for any participant in any other professional capacity in relation to the subject matter of the mediation.

4.8 Mediation must be conducted as an independent professional activity and must be distinguished from any other professional role in which the mediator may practise.

Confidentiality

4.9 Subject to paragraphs 4.11 and 4.14 below, mediators must not disclose any information about, or obtained in the course of, a mediation to anyone, including a court welfare officer or a court, without the express consent of each participant or an order of the court.

4.10 Mediators must not discuss or correspond with any participant's legal adviser without the express consent of each participant. Nothing must be said or written to the legal adviser of one, which is not also said or written to the legal adviser of the other(s).

4.11 Where a mediator suspects that a child is in danger of significant harm, or it appears necessary so that a specific allegation that a child has suffered significant harm may be properly investigated, mediators must ensure that the local Social Services (England and Wales) or Social Work Department (Scotland) is notified.

Privilege and legal proceedings

4.12 Subject to paragraph 4.14 below, all discussions and negotiations in mediation must be conducted on a legally privileged basis. Participants must agree that discussions and negotiations in mediation are not to be referred to in any legal proceedings, and that the mediator cannot be required to give evidence or produce any notes or recordings made in the course of the mediation, unless all participants agree to waive the privilege or the law imposes an overriding obligation upon the mediator.

4.13 Participants must, however, agree that any factual disclosure made with a view to resolving any issue relating to their property or finances may be disclosed in legal proceedings.

4.14 In Scotland, admissibility as to what occurred during family mediation is protected by the Civil Evidence (Family Mediation) (Scotland) Act 1995 in any subsequent civil proceedings. Mediators must be aware of the exceptions to the general rules of inadmissibility, including where there are civil or criminal proceedings related to the care or protection of a child.

Welfare of children

4.15 Mediators have a special concern for the welfare of all children of the family. They must encourage participants to focus upon the needs of the children as well as upon their own and must explore the situation from the child's point of view.

4.16 Mediators must encourage the participants to consider their children's own wishes and feelings. Where appropriate, they may discuss with the participants whether and to what extent it is proper to involve the children themselves in the mediation process in order to consult them about their wishes and feelings.

4.17 If, in a particular case, the mediator and participants agree that it is appropriate to consult any child directly in mediation, the mediator should be trained for that purpose, must obtain the child's consent and must provide appropriate facilities.

4.18 Where it appears to a mediator that any child is suffering or likely to suffer significant harm, the mediator must advise participants to seek help from the appropriate agency. The mediator must also advise participants that whether or not they seek that help, the mediator will be obliged to report the matter in accordance with paragraph 4.11.

4.19 Where it appears to a mediator that the participants are acting or proposing to act in a manner likely to be seriously detrimental to the welfare of any child of the family, the mediator may withdraw from mediation. The reason for doing so must be outlined in any summary which may be sent to the participants' legal advisers, who may be recommended that it would be appropriate for a court welfare officer's (or other independent) report to be obtained.

Violence within the family

4.20 In all cases, mediators must discover through a screening procedure whether or not there is fear of violence or any other harm and whether or not it is alleged that any participant has been or is likely to be violent towards another. Where violence is alleged or suspected mediators must discuss whether any participant wishes to take part in mediation and information about available support services should be provided.

4.21 Where mediation does take place, mediators must uphold throughout the principles of voluntariness of participation, fairness and safety and must conduct the process in accordance with paragraph 4.4 above. In addition, steps must be taken to ensure the safety of all participants on arrival and departure.

5 QUALIFICATIONS AND TRAINING

A2–100

5.1 Mediators must have successfully completed such training as is approved by the College to qualify them to mediate upon those matters upon which they offer mediation.

5.2 Mediators must be an Associate or Member of the College. They must therefore have successfully demonstrated personal aptitude for mediation (Associate and Member) and competence to mediate (Member).

5.3 Mediators must satisfy the College that they have made satisfactory arrangements for regular supervision/consultancy in relation to their professional practice with a supervision or consultant who is a Member of or approved by the College.

5.4 Mediators must agree to maintain and improve their skills through continuing professional development courses approved by the College.

5.5 Mediators must not mediate upon any case unless they are covered by professional indemnity insurance.

5.6 Mediators must abide by the complaints and disciplinary procedures and the ethical and equality requirements as laid down by the College.

5.7 Mediators registered by the College must adhere to this Code of Practice.

6 CONDUCT OF MEDIATION

6.1 Participants must be clearly advised at the outset of the nature and **A2–101** purpose of mediation and of how it differs from other services, such as marriage counselling, therapy or legal representation. In particular, they must be informed of the general principles above, of the extent of the disclosure which will be required particularly in cases relating to their property and finances, of the nature and limits of the principles of confidentiality and privilege and of the mediators' special concern for the welfare of the children of the family. Each participant must be supplied with written information covering the main points in this Code and given an opportunity to ask questions about it.

6.2 Mediators must keep the possibility of reconciliation under review throughout the mediation.

6.3 The terms upon which mediation is to be undertaken should be agreed in advance. Such agreement should preferably be in writing and must be in writing where finance and property issues are involved. Such agreement must include the basis upon which any fees are to be charged and should if practicable indicate the anticipated length of the mediation. Participants must be advised to notify any legal advisers acting for them of the appointment of a mediator.

6.4 Mediators must assist participants to define the issues, identify areas of agreement, clarify areas of disagreement, explore the options and seek to reach agreement upon them.

6.5 Mediators must ensure that participants make their decisions upon sufficient information and knowledge. They must inform participants of the need to give full and frank disclosure of all material which is relevant to the issues being mediated and assist them where necessary in identifying the relevant information and any supporting documentation.

6.6 Mediators must not guarantee that any communication from one participant will be kept secret from the other(s), except that they may always agree not to disclose one participant's address or telephone number to the other(s). They may see participants separately if both agree, but if any relevant information emerges which one participant is not willing to have disclosed to the other(s), mediators must consider whether or not it is appropriate to continue with mediation.

Precedent 3. Centre for Dispute Resolution: Model Mediation Procedure

A2–102 *The authors wish to acknowledge the Centre for Dispute Resolution (CEDR) for permitting the reproduction of this Model Mediation Procedure.*

CENTRE FOR DISPUTE RESOLUTION

Model Mediation Procedure including guidance notes

Mediation procedure
A2–103 1. The Parties to the Dispute or negotiation in question will attempt to settle it by mediation. Representatives of the Parties [and their Advisers] and the Mediator[s] will attend [a] Mediation meeting[s]. All communications relating to, and at, the Mediation will be without prejudice.

2. The Representatives must have the necessary authority to settle the Dispute. The procedure at the Mediation will be determined by the Mediator, after consultation with the Representatives.

Mediation agreement
A2–104 3. The Parties, the Mediator and CEDR will enter into an agreement ("Mediation Agreement") based on the CEDR Model Mediation Agreement ("the Model Agreement") in relation to the conduct of the Mediation.

The mediator
A2–105 4. The Mediator will:

☐ attend any meetings with any or all of the Parties preceding the Mediation, if requested or if the Mediator decides this is appropriate;

☐ read before the Mediation each Summary and all the Documents sent to him/her in accordance with paragraph 9;

☐ determine the procedure (see paragraph 2 above);

☐ assist the parties in drawing up any written settlement agreement;

☐ abide by the terms of the Model Procedure, the Mediation Agreement and CEDR's Code of Conduct.

5. The Mediator [and any member of the Mediator's firm or company] will not act for any of the Parties individually in connection with the Dispute in any capacity either during the currency of this agreement or at any time thereafter. The Parties accept that in relation to the Dispute neither the Mediator nor CEDR is an agent of, or acting in any capacity for, any of the Parties. The Parties and the Mediator accept that the Mediator (unless an employee of CEDR) is acting as an independent contractor and not as agent or employee of CEDR.

CEDR

6. CEDR, in conjunction with the Mediator, will make the necessary   **A2–106**
arrangements for the Mediation including, as necessary:

☐ assisting the Parties in appointing the Mediator and in drawing up the
Mediation Agreement;

☐ organising a suitable venue and dates;

☐ organising exchange of the Summaries and Documents;

☐ meeting with any or all of the Representatives (and the Mediator if
he/she has been appointed) either together or separately, to discuss
any matters or concerns relating to the Mediation;

☐ general administration in relation to the Mediation.

7. If a dispute is referred to CEDR as a result of a mediation (or other ADR)
clause in a contract, and if there is any issue with regard to the conduct of
the Mediation (including as to the appointment of the Mediator) upon which
the Parties cannot agree within a reasonable time from the date of the notice
initiating the Mediation ("the ADR notice") CEDR will, at the request of
any Party, decide the issue for the Parties, having consulted with them.

Other participants

8. Each Party will notify the other party[ies], through CEDR, of the names of   **A2–107**
those people (the Adviser[s], witnesses etc—in addition to the
Representatives) that it intends will be present on its behalf at the Mediation.
Each Party, in signing the Mediation Agreement, will be deemed to be
agreeing on behalf of both itself and all such persons to be bound by the
confidentiality provisions of this Model Procedure.

Exchange of information

9. Each Party will, simultaneously through CEDR, exchange with the other   **A2–108**
and send to the Mediator at least two weeks before the Mediation or such
other date as may be agreed between the Parties.

☐ a concise summary ("the Summary") stating its case in the Dispute;

☐ copies of all the documents to which it refers in the Summary and to
which it may want to refer in the Mediation ("the Documents").

In addition, each Party may send to the Mediator (through CEDR) and/or
bring to the Mediation further documentation which it wishes to disclose in
confidence to the Mediator but not to any other Party, clearly stating in
writing that such documentation is confidential to the Mediator and CEDR.
10. The Parties will, through CEDR, agree the maximum number of pages of
each Summary and of the Documents and try to agree a joint set of
documents from their respective Documents.

The mediation

A2–109 11. No formal record or transcript of the Mediation will be made.

12. If the Parties are unable to reach a settlement in the negotiations at the Mediation and only if all the Representatives so request and the Mediator agrees, the Mediator will produce for the Parties a non-binding written recommendation on terms of settlement. This will not attempt to anticipate what a court might order but will set out what the Mediator suggests are appropriate settlement terms in all of the circumstances.

Settlement agreement

A2–110 13. Any settlement reached in the Mediation will not be legally binding until it has been reduced to writing and signed by, or on behalf of, the Parties.

Termination

A2–111 14. Any of the Parties may withdraw from the Mediation at any time and shall immediately inform the Mediator and the other Representatives in writing. The Mediation will terminate when:

☐ a Party withdraws from the Mediation; or

☐ a written settlement agreement is concluded; or

☐ the Mediator decides that continuing the Mediation is unlikely to result in a settlement; or

☐ the Mediator decides he should retire for any of the reasons in the Code of Conduct.

Stay of proceedings

A2–112 15. Any litigation or arbitration in relation to the Dispute may be commenced or continued notwithstanding the Mediation unless the Parties agree otherwise.

Confidentiality etc

A2–113 16. Every person involved in the Mediation will keep confidential and not use for any collateral or ulterior purpose:

☐ the fact that the Mediation is to take place or has taken place; and

☐ all information, (whether given orally, in writing or otherwise), produced for, or arising in relation to, the Mediation including the settlement agreement (if any) arising out of it

except insofar as is necessary to implement and enforce any such settlement agreement.

17. All documents (which includes anything upon which evidence is recorded including tapes and computer discs) or other information produced for, or arising in relation to, the Mediation will be privileged and not be admissible as evidence or discoverable in any litigation or arbitration connected with the Dispute except any documents or other information which would in any

event have been admissible or discoverable in any such litigation or arbitration.

18. None of the parties to the Mediation Agreement will call the Mediator or CEDR (or any employee, consultant, officer or representative of CEDR) as a witness, consultant, arbitrator or expert in any litigation or arbitration in relation to the Dispute and the Mediator and CEDR will not voluntarily act in any such capacity without the written agreement of all the Parties.

Fees, expenses and costs

19. CEDR's fees (which include the Mediator's fees) and the other expenses of the Mediation will be borne equally by the Parties. Payment of these fees and expenses will be made to CEDR in accordance with its fee schedule and terms and conditions of business.   **A2–114**

20. Each Party will bear its own costs and expenses of its participation in the Mediation.

Waiver of liability

21. Neither the Mediator nor CEDR shall be liable to the Parties for any act or omission in connection with the services provided by them in, or in relation to, the Mediation, unless the act or omission is fraudulent or involves wilful misconduct.   **A2–115**

GUIDANCE NOTES

The paragraph numbers and headings in these notes refer to the paragraphs and headings in the Model Procedure.   **A2–116**

Text in the Model Procedure in square brackets may be inappropriate and therefore inapplicable in some cases.

Introduction

The essence of mediation (and many other ADR procedures) is that: **A2–117**

- ☐ it involves a neutral third party to facilitate negotiations;

- ☐ it is quick, inexpensive and confidential;

- ☐ it enables the parties to reach results which are not possible in an adjudicative process such as litigation or arbitration and may be to the benefit of *both* parties, particularly if there is a continuing business relationship;

- ☐ it involves representatives of the parties who have sufficient authority to settle. In some cases, there may be an advantage in the representatives being people who have not been directly involved in the events leading up to the dispute and in the subsequent dispute.

The procedure for the mediation is flexible and this model procedure can be adapted (with or without the assistance of CEDR) to suit the parties. A mediation can be used:

☐ in both domestic and international disputes;

☐ whether or not litigation or arbitration has been commenced; and

☐ in two party and multi-party disputes.

Rules or rigid procedures in the context of a consensual and adaptable process which is the essence of ADR are generally inappropriate. The Model Procedure and the Model Agreement and this guidance note should be sufficient to enable parties to conduct a mediation.

In some cases the agreement to conduct a mediation will be as a result of an "ADR clause" (such as one of the CEDR Model ADR clauses) to that effect in an underlying commercial agreement between the Parties. Where that is the case the Model Procedure and Mediation Agreement may need to be adapted accordingly.

The Model Agreement, which has been kept as short and simple as possible, incorporates the Model Procedure (see para. 3). The Mediation Agreement can include amendments to the Model Procedure; the amendments can be set out in the body of the Mediation Agreement or the Mediation Agreement can state that amendments made in manuscript (or otherwise) to the Model Procedure and initialled by the Parties are to be incorporated into the Mediation Agreement.

Mediation procedure—paras 1 and 2

A2–118   The Advisers, normally lawyers, can and usually do attend the Mediation. Although a lead role in the Mediation is often taken by the Representatives, the Advisers can play an important role in the exchange of information, in advising their clients on the legal implications of a settlement and in drawing up the settlement agreement. However, the commercial interests of the Parties will normally take the negotiations beyond strict legal issues, hence the importance of the role of the Representatives.

It is essential that the Representatives are sufficiently senior and have the authority of their respective Parties to settle the Dispute.

Mediation agreement—para 3

A2–119   If CEDR is asked to do so by a party wishing to initiate a mediation, it will approach the other party(ies) to a dispute to seek to persuade it/them to participate.

Ideally the Representatives, the Advisers (and the Mediator if he/she has been identified) and CEDR (or whatever other ADR body is involved, if any) should meet to discuss and finalise the terms of the Mediation Agreement.

Alternatively, the party who has taken the initiative in proposing the Mediation may wish to send a draft agreement based on the CEDR Model Mediation Agreement to the other party(ies).

The mediator—paras 4–5

A2–120   The success of the Mediation will, to a large extent, depend on the skill of the Mediator. CEDR believes it is very important for the Mediator to have had specific training and experience. CEDR has its own body of trained and experienced mediators and can assist the Parties in identifying a suitable mediator.

In some cases it may be useful to have more than one Mediator, or to have an independent expert who can advise the Mediator on technical issues ("the Mediator's Adviser"). All should sign the Mediation Agreement which should be amended as appropriate.

It is CEDR's practice, as part of its mediator training programme, to have a pupil mediator ("the Pupil Mediator") attend most mediations. The Pupil Mediator signs the Mediation Agreement and falls within the definition "the Mediator" in the Model Procedure and the Mediation Agreement.

It is advisable, but not essential, to involve the Mediator in any preliminary meeting between the Parties.

CEDR—paras 6–7

The Code of Conduct covers such points as the Mediator's duty of confidentiality, impartiality and avoiding conflicts of interest. **A2–121**

The Model Procedure envisages the involvement of CEDR because in most cases this is likely to benefit the Parties and generally to facilitate the setting up and conduct of the Mediation. Its involvement, however, is not essential and this Model Procedure can be amended if CEDR is not to be involved.

Exchange of information—paras 9–10

Documentation which a Party wants the Mediator to keep confidential from the other party(ies) (e.g. a counsel's opinion, an expert report not yet exchanged) must be clearly marked as such. It can be disclosed by the Party before or during the Mediation. It will not be disclosed by the Mediator or CEDR without the express consent of the Party. **A2–122**

One of the advantages of ADR is that it can avoid the excessive discovery process (including witness statements) which often blights litigation and arbitration. The Documents should be kept to the minimum necessary to give the Mediator a good grasp of the issues. The Summaries should be similarly brief.

The mediation—paras 11–12

The intention of paragraph 12 is that the Mediator will cease to play an entirely facilitative role only if the negotiations in the Mediation are deadlocked. Giving a settlement recommendation may be perceived by a Party as undermining the Mediator's neutrality and for this reason the Mediator may not agree to this course of action. Any recommendation will be without prejudice and will not be binding. **A2–123**

Settlement agreement—para 13

If no agreement is reached, it is nonetheless open to the Parties to adjourn the Mediation to another time and place. Experience shows that even where no agreement is reached during mediation itself, the Parties will often reach a settlement shortly after, as a result of the progress made during that mediation. **A2–124**

Stay of proceedings—para 15

A2–125   Although a stay may engender a better climate for settlement, it is not however essential that any proceedings relating to the Dispute should be stayed. If they are stayed, the effect on limitation periods needs to be agreed. Although under English law the parties can agree to limitation periods not running the position may differ in other jurisdictions and the position on this should be checked.

Confidentiality—paras 16–18

A2–126   The CEDR Code of Conduct provides that the Mediator is not to disclose to any other Party any information given to him by a Party in confidence without the express consent of that Party.

In any related litigation in England and Wales such documents (see paragraph 16) should in any event be inadmissible and privileged as "without prejudice" documents since they will have been produced in relation to negotiations to settle the dispute. Documents which pre-existed the Mediation and would in any event have been discoverable will, however, not become privileged by reason of having been referred to in the Mediation and will therefore still be discoverable. The position may differ in other jurisdictions and should be checked.

Fees, expenses and costs—paras 19–20

A2–127   The usual arrangement is for the Parties to share equally the fees and expenses of the procedure, but other arrangements are possible. A party to a dispute which is reluctant to participate in a mediation may be persuaded to participate if the other party(ies) agree to bear that party's share of the mediation fees.

International disputes—Language and governing law/jurisdiction

A2–128   The Model Agreement is designed for domestic disputes but can be easily adapted for international cross-border disputes by the addition of the following paragraphs:

"Language
The language of the Mediation will be … Any Party producing documents or participating in the Mediation in any other language will provide the necessary translations and interpretation facilities."

"Governing Law and Jurisdiction
The Mediation Agreement shall be governed by, construed and take effect in accordance with [English] law.

The courts of [England] shall have exclusive jurisdiction to settle any claim, dispute or matter of difference which may arise out of or in connection with the Mediation."

Where the law is not English or the jurisdiction not England the Mediation Agreement may need to be amended to ensure the structure, rights and obligations necessary for a mediation are applicable.

Precedent 4. Mediation U.K. Standards for Mediators (general mediation)

The authors wish to acknowledge Mediation U.K. for permitting the reproduction of this Code. **A2–129**

STANDARDS FOR MEDIATORS

ETHICAL VALUES:

These values underpin all that mediation do when working with parties **A2–130**
and in their relationships with other mediators, the mediation service, and other agencies. Reference is made to them in the National Vocational Qualification (NVQ) in Mediation (Community Mediation Evidence Route).

This ethical framework is based on ideals of: fairness, impartiality, justice, integrity, empowerment, trust, peace, excellence, growth and healing.

- People should always be treated with respect and without unfair discrimination.

- People should not be coerced into taking part or staying in the mediation process.

- The anonymity of all parties should be fully protected and confidentiality preserved within the service's published guidelines.

- Mediators should declare any conflict of interest which may put their neutrality into question.

- Mediators should maintain clear boundaries between mediation and other forms of intervention such as advice, counselling and advocacy.

- Mediators should seek to enhance the autonomy of parties and remain impartial regarding the objectives and outcomes of mediation.

- Mediators should treat each party fairly and endeavour to serve the best interests of all parties in conflict.

- Mediators should be aware of their own values and prejudices, and work to challenge discrimination in their own and others' behaviour.

- Mediators should recognise their own limitations regarding competence, values and experience and acknowledge that these could adversely affect their capacity to mediate in some circumstances.

- Mediators should evaluate their own practice regularly and be open to feedback from others.

PRINCIPLES OF MEDIATION

The Mediation Process: **A2–131**

- Encourages and maintains the voluntary participation of all parties.

- Encourages the participation and self determination of all the parties involved so that they retain responsibility for both the content of the conflict and the outcome of the mediation.

- Encourages collaboration and working with people (rather than against them).

- Seeks creative and flexible approaches and solutions, within an ethical framework.

- Encourages parties to recognise their abilities to work towards mutually acceptable and viable outcomes.

- Offer a structured and challenging approach to conflict resolution.

- Values the resources and skills of the participants and where possible uses and develops them.

- Creates the conditions for openness, participation, collaboration, flexibility, tolerance, respect and non-violence.

- Acknowledges the value of 'telling the story' (the past) first but encourages movement to focus on a positive outcome for the future.

- Seeks to help parties identify their own and others' feelings and interests, rather than defend positions.

GUIDELINES FOR PUTTING PRINCIPLES INTO PRACTICE

(These practice standards are reflected in the Mediation NVQ)

A2–132   All Mediators must:

- Know and understand the ethical values, principles and practice standards for mediation.

- Know and implement equal opportunity legislation and service policies and know how it relates to mediation.

- Possess the required skills and qualities and maintain them through regular mediation practice.

- Be committed to extending their knowledge of the community context within which they mediate.

- Be willing to take part in regular support and supervision sessions.

- Evaluate their own practice; seeking to up-date their knowledge and understanding; and be willing to develop their skills through further training.

WHEN PREPARING FOR A MEDIATION mediators should:

- Check that all relevant and appropriate information relating to the   **A2–133**
proposed mediation has been received.

- Establish a working relationship with their co-mediator.

- Make all appropriate preparation and plans for their first contacts,
taking account of access, equal opportunities and safety.

- Make contact with the party(ies) to establish communication, to create
the right environment, ensure their understanding of the process and
the potential of the mediation service.

- Listen actively and make an initial assessment of the appropriateness
of mediation and other possible options for a way forward.

- Agree with parties the conditions and boundaries of mediation,
including confidentiality and ways of working.

- Keep the co-ordinator/manager fully informed of progress (or lack of
it).

- Plan each subsequent stage with minimum delay.

DURING THE MEDIATION mediators should:

- Develop interaction with the party(ies), encouraging voluntary   **A2–134**
participation in the process.

- Establish all the major issues with each party, promoting shared
responsibility for the content of the mediation.

- Explore issues with each party, enabling them to express concerns and
feelings.

- Facilitate exchanges between parties (face to face or indirectly) -
fairly and without personal bias.

- Manage conflict and address power imbalances, recognising cultural
differences which may influence the process.

- Help parties to clarify for themselves where their best interests lie.

- Help parties to identify and evaluate potential options for the future.

- Help parties move towards building and agreeing outcomes for
themselves which are workable and can be reviewed as appropriate.

- Be confident to bring a session to a close if the above is not achieved.

- Aim to bring a session to a close to the satisfaction of all involved

- Aim for written agreements on outcomes, involving statements which
incorporate some element of self-help and co-operation.

- Agree arrangements with parties for follow-up support to be offered
by the mediation service.

AFTER THE MEDIATION mediators should:

A2–135

- Complete all records to the standard required by the service.

- Review and evaluate the mediation independently, and then with the co-mediator and/or supervisor as appropriate.

- Seek to learn from each experience and plan to improve their practice.

- Maintain complete confidentiality regarding the parties involved in each mediation.

Precedent 5. Expert Determination Guidelines: City Disputes Panel

A2–136 *The authors wish to acknowledge the City Disputes Panel for permitting the reproduction of these guidelines.*

1. The timetable commences on the date the expert's instructions and timetable are agreed.

2. Within a specified timescale the parties and their advisers shall provide the expert with at least two copies of their written submissions stating their case and shall provide or make available to the expert such documents as they consider relevant to the issues in dispute. The submissions should clearly cross refer to the relevant documents. The expert will then immediately provide one copy of each party's submission to the other party.

3. Within a specified timescale each party will provide the expert with two copies of a written response to the other party's written submission. These will similarly be made available to the respective parties.

4. Within a prescribed period of the receipt of the response submissions the expert will seek any clarification required from the parties in writing, within a specified time limit. The expert will retain the right to question parties separately or together, and to request any further written information.

5. Upon receipt of all information the expert will proceed to produce the determination promptly.

6. Both parties shall be jointly and severally responsible for the payment of the fees of the CDP and the expert, together will all reasonable out of pocket disbursements which will be allocated between the parties by the expert. The determination will be made and issued to each party simultaneously upon settlement of the CDP's and the expert's fees and expenses in full.

Precedent 6. Mediation clause (short form)

Two alternative short forms follow. The first is for general civil/commercial   **A2–137**
*use. The second is the core wording suggested by the Centre for Dispute
Resolution for appointing its mediators (and amplified wording is available
from them).*

If any dispute arises out of this agreement, the parties shall in the first
instance attempt to resolve it by mediation. In such event, the mediator shall
be [name] [nominated by (mediation organisation)] and shall mediate in
accordance with the [rules][mediation Code of Practice] of [the Law Society
or other organisation, as the case may be].

If any dispute arises out of this agreement, the parties will attempt to settle
it by mediation in accordance with the Centre for Dispute Resolution (CEDR)
Model Mediation Procedure.

Precedent 7. Arbitration clause (short form)

The following is a specimen short form for domestic arbitration: **A2–138**

If any dispute arises out of this agreement, including any dispute about its
performance, construction or interpretation, it shall be referred to arbitration
in accordance with the provisions of the Arbitration Act 1996. A single
arbitrator [name] [nominated by . . . . . .] shall conduct the arbitration, whose
decision in relation to any such dispute shall be final and binding.

Precedent 8. Combined negotiation, mediation and arbitration clause

Parties may wish to stipulate in a contract that they will try to resolve   **A2–139**
*differences by negotiation in the first instance. If that fails, it is to be
followed by mediation if necessary. That would be followed by arbitration if
the mediation were not to produce an agreed outcome. The following is a
specimen of this:*

If any dispute arises out of this agreement, including any dispute about its
performance, construction or interpretation, the parties shall in the first
instance endeavour to resolve it by agreement through negotiations
[conducted in good faith].[7] If they are unable to agree, the dispute shall be

---

[7] As to the questionable effect of contracting to negotiate "in good faith", see Chap. 6 under the
sub-heading "Good faith in negotiation".

referred to mediation by [name] [nominated by (mediation organisation)] who shall mediate in accordance with the [rules][mediation Code of Practice] of [the Law Society or other organisation, as the case may be].

The parties reserve all their rights in the event that no agreed resolution is reached in the mediation. Neither party shall be precluded from [taking interim formal steps as may be considered necessary to protect such party's position] [commencing or continuing litigation, arbitration or other adjudication] while the mediation is pending.

If the dispute is not resolved by mediation within [28][42][60] days of its initiation, or such extended period as the parties may agree, the dispute shall be referred to arbitration in accordance with the provisions of the Arbitration Act 1996. A single arbitrator [name] [nominated by (relevant arbitral or other body)] shall conduct the arbitration, whose decision in relation to any such dispute shall be final and binding. In such event, the rules of the [relevant arbitral body] shall apply in relation to such arbitration.

The law of [England] shall apply to this agreement, which shall be interpreted and construed in accordance with such law.

Precedent 9. Dispute resolution clause (City Disputes Panel)

A2–140 *The authors wish to acknowledge the City Disputes Panel for permitting the reproduction of this clause. It provides for the non-binding use of ADR, followed by arbitration if the matter is not resolved.*

> (x) The parties will consider using alternative dispute resolution ('ADR') techniques for any dispute or difference arising out of or in connection with this [Contract]. The parties may consult the City Disputes Panel Limited (CDP) for assistance in selecting the most appropriate technique. If [either/any] party does not wish to use, or continue to use, ADR techniques, or such techniques do not resolve the dispute, the parties shall refer the dispute to arbitration under the Arbitration Rules of CDP in force at the date the dispute or difference arises.
>
> (y) The agreement contained in clause [x] above is governed by English law.

Precedent 10. Civil/commercial mediation agreement

A2–141 *The variations here provide for mediators who work alone and those who work through their firms. For example, it is drafted for solicitors who will mediate as part of their practice. For other mediators and solicitors who mediate outside their practice, it will have to be adapted. Provision must be* *inserted as to the relevant complaints procedure. It also contains provision for an evaluative element to be introduced, if required.*

MEDIATION AGREEMENT

This records the terms on which I will act as a mediator in relation to the issues between X and Y relating to *[summarise briefly]*. These terms will constitute the ground rules for the mediation: **A2–142**

1. You both agree that you will try to settle the dispute between you by mediation. You further agree to appoint me as mediator, and I accept that appointment on the terms of this Agreement.

2. I confirm that I have not acted and will not act for either of you individually in any capacity in connection with the dispute. I have no personal interest in the outcome of this dispute and am not aware of any conflict of interest that would preclude me from acting as mediator.

3. Although I am a solicitor, and I act in the mediation as part of my legal practice at [firm], I do not advise or represent either or both of you or take sides between you. I act specifically as an independent, neutral and impartial mediator, to facilitate the resolution of the differences between you. This does not mean trying to anticipate what the outcome would be if the issues were adjudicated upon. Rather, I will help you to reach an agreement on terms that both of you find acceptable. You may each be separately advised and represented by your own independent legal representative.

4. The mediation process is confidential and I undertake to maintain confidentiality. Both of you undertake to one another and to me that you will similarly maintain confidentiality in respect of all statements and matters arising in or from the mediation. The only exceptions to these confidentiality provisions are:

   4.1 Confidentiality does not apply insofar as either or both of you need to disclose any such statements and matters in order to [comply with any statutory obligation], obtain professional advice and to enforce any settlement agreement.

   4.2 Confidentiality also does not apply if I believe that any person mentioned in the mediation is at risk of suffering significant harm, or if the court or any public policy requirement exceptionally overrides the duty of confidentiality.

5. You both confirm that you come to the mediation with the necessary authority to settle the dispute so that, if terms are agreed either at the mediation or afterwards, you will be able to sign an agreement which gives effect to those terms.

6. I will determine the procedure at the mediation, after consultation with you and your legal representatives. You both agree to treat the mediation as privileged and that it will be conducted on the same

basis as without prejudice negotiations in an action in the Court. All documents and statements whether written or oral produced for the purpose of the mediation will not be admissible or subject to disclosure in any Court or arbitration proceedings which may subsequently take place. However, any evidence that is otherwise admissible or disclosable will not be rendered inadmissible or non-disclosable because of its use in this mediation. Neither of you may have access to any of my notes or call me as witness in any proceedings relating to any of the issues between you.

7. I may meet with you together or separately. I will treat any separate meetings as confidential to the party with whom I am meeting and will not disclose anything to the other without specific authority. My efforts will be geared to helping you to find a mutually acceptable resolution of your issues.

8. Both of you reserve your respective rights should the mediation not result in a settlement of the issues under discussion; and neither of you shall be precluded from taking any Court action as may be necessary to protect your rights or position while the mediation is pending.

9. If you agree on terms that you both find acceptable, they will not be legally binding unless and until reduced to writing and signed by both of you. [You will each have an opportunity to take legal advice from your independent solicitors before entering into any such agreement, should you both so agree. However,] once such a settlement agreement has been entered into and duly recorded and signed by you both, then it will be fully binding in law and you both undertake to give effect to such settlement within such period as may be agreed in the terms of settlement.

10. I will act in good faith as a neutral throughout the process. I will not be liable to either of you for any act or omission in respect of my services under this Agreement. The responsibility for any resolution of the matter rests with both of you, and not with me as a mediator.

11. [If you both require, I may if I consider it helpful furnish an informal and non-binding view on the issues and/or recommendations as to terms of settlement. In doing so I will not necessarily attempt to anticipate what a court might order but will suggest what I think are appropriate settlement terms in all the circumstances.]

12. Either of you, or I, may terminate the mediation at any time. However, as long as it is pending, you both agree to co-operate with the process, to furnish documents and information as may be necessary and to work in good faith towards seeking an acceptable outcome.

13. My firm's charges for my services as a mediator in relation to this matter are £ per hour plus VAT, which applies to meetings and to all other time required to be spent by me in working on the matter

including considering documents and drafting. These charges will be shared between you equally, i.e. at the rate of £ per hour plus VAT each and will be payable [in advance of the mediation taking place, based on my estimate of the likely time involved. If the preparation or the mediation itself take longer than estimated you will remain responsible for the balance of my firm's charges—or *as the case may be*].

14. In addition to my firm's charges you are each responsible for your own costs and expenses of taking part in the mediation.

Dated etc.

Precedent 11. CEDR's Model Mediation Agreement

The authors wish to acknowledge the Centre for Dispute Resolution for agreeing to allow their Model Mediation Agreement to be reproduced here. **A2–143**

CENTRE FOR DISPUTE RESOLUTION

MODEL MEDIATION AGREEMENT

Date **A2–144**
Parties
1:                                    ("Party A")
2:                                    ("Party B")
[3:   ("Party C") etc]
    (jointly "the Parties")   *Add full names and addresses*
[4:]   ("the Mediator")
[5:   ("the Pupil Mediator") ("the Mediator's Adviser")]
    (jointly and individually "the Mediator")
[6]   Centre for Dispute Resolution, Princes House, 95 Gresham Street, London EC2V 7NA ("CEDR")

Dispute ("the Dispute")
Brief description of the dispute. **A2–145**

Participation in a mediation

1. The Parties will attempt to settle the Dispute by mediation ("the **A2–146** Mediation"). The provisions of the CEDR Model Mediation Procedure ("the Model Procedure") (a copy of which is attached) as supplemented and/or varied by this agreement will apply to the Mediation and are incorporated in, and form part of, this agreement. The definitions in the Model Procedure are used in this agreement.

The mediator

A2–147   2.   The Mediator[s] will be   [The Pupil Mediator will be]

[The Mediator's Adviser will be   ]

The representatives

A2–148   3.   The Representatives for the Parties at the Mediation will be: *Add full names and corporate titles*

Party A:

Party B:

[Party C etc:]

(jointly "the Representatives")

A Party will immediately notify the other Party[ies] and the Mediator of any change to the above.

Other participants

A2–149   4.   The following, in addition to the Representatives, will be present on behalf of the Parties at the Mediation

Party A:

Party B:

[Party C:]

A Party will immediately notify the other Party(ies) and the Mediator of any change to the above.

Place and time

A2–150   5.   The Mediation will take place

at:

on:

starting at: o'clock

Confidentiality

A2–151   6.   Each Representative in signing this agreement is deemed to be agreeing to the confidentiality provisions of the Model Procedure (paras 16–17) on behalf of the Party he/she represents and all other persons present on behalf of that Party at the Mediation.

Litigation/arbitration

A2–152   7.   No litigation or arbitration in relation to the Dispute is to be commenced [Any existing litigation or arbitration in relation to the

Dispute is to be stayed] from the date of this agreement until the termination of the Mediation.

This paragraph is only necessary if there is to be a restriction on litigation/arbitration - see para 15 of Model Procedure.

Model procedure amendments

8. *Set out amendments (if any) to the Model Procedure—see introduction to Model Procedure guidance notes.* **A2–153**

Law and jurisdiction

9. *For wording see Model Procedure guidance notes. This paragraph only necessary if the Dispute involves parties from different jurisdictions.*

Signed:

Precedent 12. Family mediation Agreement to Mediate (Solicitors' Family Law Association)

The authors wish to acknowledge the Solicitors' Family Law Association for permitting the reproduction of their standard form of Agreement to Mediate. **A2–154**

Mediation terms and conditions

Parties are asked to agree to the following terms and conditions for mediation to be undertaken by me (and by any co-mediator where applicable). These are based on the Family Mediation Code of Practice of the Solicitors' Family Law Association (SFLA).

Contract to mediate

1. I agree to act as an impartial mediator and confirm that I do not have any conflict of interest in doing so. I will try to help you both to agree on the decisions that you need to make. You agree in good faith to use the mediation process to try to reach decisions acceptable to you both. **A2–155**

Functions of mediator

2. As a mediator, I do not advise or represent parties, but rather function as a mediator who is neutral and impartial. I do not give legal advice to you, jointly or individually. I may, however, provide legal or other information on an even-handed basis, to assist you in understanding **A2–156**

the principles of law applicable to you, and the way those principles are generally applied.

3. Notwithstanding the distinction in the way I function, as outlined above, I undertake this mediation as part of my practice as a solicitor, and subject to the Law Society's rules and guidelines.

4. I will help you both to explore the options available to you, with a view to your reaching a resolution appropriate to your circumstances. That may not necessarily be the same conclusion that might be arrived at by the court. If practicable, I will tell you if I consider that your proposed terms are likely to fall outside of the parameters that a court might approve.

Confidentiality and privilege

A2–157

5. I will treat all matters in the mediation as confidential, except as otherwise agreed, and subject to Paragraph 9. I ask you to agree that the mediation and any summaries may be reviewed on a strictly confidential basis by an SFLA mediation consultant or other appointee.

6. Information, written or oral, which either of you may provide to me will not ordinarily be maintained confidentially as between yourselves, except any address or telephone number, and except as you may both otherwise agree.

7. All financial information is provided on an open basis, which means that it can be used in court. This may be in support of a consent application made by either of you or in contested proceedings.

8. However, communications about possible terms of financial settlement are conducted on a "without prejudice" basis. In any event, a mediation privilege will ordinarily be claimed for all attempts to resolve matters in the mediation.

9. The provisions concerning confidentiality and privilege will not apply if it appears that any child or other person is suffering or likely to suffer significant harm. In this event, I would normally, so far as practicable and appropriate, consider with you how disclosure should take place and what steps should be taken to remedy the situation. These provisions are also subject to any overriding obligations of disclosure imposed by law and by the SFLA Family Mediation Code of Practice.

10. You both agree not to call me (or any co-mediator if applicable) to give evidence in court, nor will you seek to have any of my or our notes brought into evidence.

Financial and other information

A2–158

11. You both undertake to provide a complete and accurate statement of

your financial circumstances, and to furnish any supporting documents reasonably required. I will try to help you to identify what information and documents would help the resolution of any issues, and to consider how best these may be obtained. You should note that mediation does not provide for the disclosure and discovery of documents in the same way or to the same extent as required by Court Rules.

12. I cannot make independent enquiries or undertake verification in relation to any information or documents sought or provided. If required, we can consider the ways in which you may make such enquiries or obtain such verification.

13. Any material non-disclosure or inaccuracy could in some cases result in the outcome, whether agreed or adjudicated, subsequently being set aside by the court.

Professional advice and qualified nature of agreements

14. Any decisions arrived at in mediation which appear to be significant   **A2–159**
to either or both of your positions (including any settlement proposals) will not be turned into a binding agreement until you have each had the opportunity to seek advice on them from your legal advisers.

15. However, decisions on matters that are not significant to your respective positions or to the substantive outcome, may be entered into as binding agreements without legal advice.

16. Mediation meetings are commonly conducted without lawyers present. However, your legal advisers may by agreement between you both and myself participate in the mediation process in any useful and appropriate way.

17. You may each consult with your individual solicitors as the mediation progresses. I may also help you to consider the desirability of seeking assistance from other professional advisers such as accountants, expert valuers or others, or from counsellors or therapists.

Summaries and recording of agreements

18. I will ordinarily provide summaries of the financial position and   **A2–160**
settlement proposals, to help you to obtain independent legal advice. If after consulting your advisers either of you should have any queries, I would if required meet you again (with your advisers if necessary) to try to resolve these.

19. Your solicitors will usually undertake the formal recording of any agreements that may be reached after you have each been able to seek their advice.

Mediation fees

A2–161   20. My fees, payable at the end of each session or as otherwise arranged, are £...plus VAT per hour (i.e. £...plus VAT for a 1½ hour session, totalling £...). These will be shared between you as to £...each per session or in any other way you may agree. The hourly rate also applies for any work that may be required between sessions for example in drafting documents.

Termination of mediation

A2–162   21. Either of you may terminate the mediation at any stage. If I think that the continuation of the mediation is no longer helpful, or that it is inappropriate, I will discuss this with you and I may in that event end the mediation.

SFLA regulation

A2–163   22. Mediation under these rules is subject to regulation by the SFLA, to whom any professional issue should be addressed (so far as you feel that it cannot be resolved directly with me). Details of the SFLA's written Complaints and Grievance Procedure will be provided on request.

Precedent 13. Family mediation Agreement to Mediate (Family Mediators Association)

A2–164   *The authors wish to acknowledge the Family Mediators Association for permitting the reproduction of their standard form of Agreement to Mediate.*

Agreement to Mediate

BASIC PRINCIPLES AND TERMS OF MEDIATION

A2–165   *The following terms are the basis for mediation conducted by mediators governed by Family Mediators Association. Please would you read each point carefully, noting any questions you may have to bring to the first meeting with the mediator/s. You will be asked to sign this document as an indication of your commitment to the process and the terms listed. Thank you.*

     1. As *mediators/a mediator we/I* act in an impartial way. *We/I* therefore seek to help both participants equally. *We/I* do not express opinions or make judgements about your individual or joint situation. *Our/my* role is to assist you both to explore possible ways of resolving disputes or

making arrangements on any range of matters related to your separation or future separate living or in any matters relating to family issues.

2. Mediation cannot take place if *we/I/the mediators/mediator have/has* prior knowledge of the situation through a previous involvement as a solicitor, counsellor or in any other professional role.

3. *We/I* may only provide legal and/or financial or other information in a neutral way in order to help you understand the options available to you. *We/I* may not, do not and cannot provide any advice (of any nature) on a 'best interests' or personalised basis. The choices and decisions remain yours to make. It is possible and often very helpful for you to have advice from your solicitor during the mediation process in order to make informed decisions and allowing your respective advisers to remain informed as to progress.

4. *We/I* act in *our/my* professional role as *mediators/a mediator*. *Our/my* practice is governed by Family Mediators Association. Although *we/I* may have other qualifications *we/I* act only as *mediators/a mediator* and *only [insert mediation practice name] is involved OR no other firm/organisation is involved in the mediation.* Any concern you may have as to *our/my* practice should be referred to *us/me* in the first instance but if unresolved or otherwise, in writing to: Family Mediators Association, 46 Grosvenor Gardens, London. SW1 OEB.

5. Mediation is an open process between us. All information or correspondence from either of you will be shared openly with you both. The only exception to this is an address or telephone number which either one of you wishes to keep confidential.

6. *We/I will* ask both of you to provide complete and accurate disclosure of all your financial circumstances, with supporting documents where necessary. *We/I* do not verify the completeness and accuracy of the information you provide but *we/I will* ask you to sign and date a statement confirming that you have made a full disclosure. If it should emerge that full disclosure has not been made, any agreements flowing from the proposals reached in mediation based on incomplete information can be set aside and the issue re-opened.

7. Information about your finances and other relevant facts related to personal finance is provided on an open basis. This means that the information is available to your individual legal or financial advisers and can be referred to in Court, either in support of an application made with your joint consent or in contested proceedings. This would be the case in any situation relating to financial disclosure on separation or divorce. It will assist your individual legal adviser and avoids information having to be provided twice over or duplicated. (However, it does reinforce the importance of full and accurate disclosure as your individual legal or financial adviser is required to check with you as to the completeness and accuracy of all information received.)

8. The discussion you have with *us/me* with regard to possible terms of settlement or proposals for the future are understood to be **legally privileged**. This means that your discussion about the matters you need to settle and the proposals for settlement cannot be referred to in Court unless you both agree to waive your privilege. *We/I* also ask that you each and both agree not to call *us/me* to give evidence in Court.

9. At the completion or closing of the mediation process, *we/I will* draw up:

   - **A privileged summary** (the memorandum of understanding) of your proposals for settlement which will include your proposals on all matters discussed in the mediation, arrangements for any and each child, property, finance, maintenance, child support and any other matters discussed and as appropriate to each of you.
   - **An open summary** of your financial circumstances.

   These documents are provided to help you obtain separate and independent legal and/or other advice before entering into a legally binding agreement. It is also to safeguard you from making a legally binding agreement without fully understanding how it may affect your own individual position. *The charge for the preparation of the documents is inclusive of the hourly rate quoted by us/me OR The charge for the preparation of the documents is generally £ . If your issues are particularly complicated or you require interim documentation for consultation with your personal adviser/s, the cost will be negotiated separately and in consultation with you both. We/I also undertake to provide you with cost estimates wherever possible and practicable in order to assist your planning of likely costs. [See also point 14]*

10. Mediation is a confidential process. *We/I* will not give information to your legal or other advisers or to any other third parties without obtaining your joint permission. The only exception to this confidentiality would be where you or any other person (most particularly a child) is at risk of serious harm. In these exceptional circumstances, *we/I* would normally seek to discuss the action to be taken with both of you before taking any action to contact the appropriate authority/ies in line with the FMA Code of Practice.

11. *We/I* work to our governing association's Code of Practice at all times and will be concerned to ensure that each of you enter into the mediation process able to negotiate freely together and without risk of threat or harm. *We/I* ask that you inform *us/me* if there are concerns for you with regard to your ability to negotiate freely.

12. Either of you may terminate the mediation at any stage. *We/I* may also terminate the process if we do not think it appropriate or helpful to continue. If such a termination should occur on either basis, *we/I* shall endeavour to provide information as to other appropriate options for progressing your issues/situation.

13. *Our/my* practice is monitored by our governing association, Family Mediators Association and *we/I* are required to have professional supervision/consultancy of *our/my* practice. From time to time, therefore, *we/I* discuss professional practice with *our/my* supervisor/ consultant. Such discussions are treated on a confidential basis and no identifying details regarding individuals will be available or required by my supervisor other than matters raised as in item 10 above.

14. *We/I* charge at the rate of £   per hour for each of you. (The total charge for each 90-minute session will therefore be £   for each person). *We/I* shall ask you to pay at the end of each session (ways to pay are set out in *my/our* accompanying letter). *We/I* will issue receipts for payments received. *The hourly rate is inclusive of all work undertaken on your behalf including the preparation of memorandum of understanding and open financial summary. OR The charge for the preparation of documents is generally £ .*

If your issues are particularly complicated or you require interim documentation for consultation with your personal adviser/s the cost will be negotiated separately and in consultation with you both. We/I also undertake to provide you with cost estimates wherever possible and practicable in order to assist your planning of likely costs.

15. *We/I* shall do our best to help you both. *We/I* ask you to show your integrity and commitment to the mediation process and to co-operate as fully as possible in looking for workable solutions.

I have read and understood the above:

Signed . . . . Signed . . . .

Date: Date:

Precedent 14. Civil/commercial terms of settlement (framework)

Because of the range of possible agreements and the diversity of styles and requirements, the precedent will merely outline a possible template. The substantive terms would be attached as a schedule.   **A2–166**

The format and content of the agreement will vary, depending on whether a draft consent order is required, a deed, a complete formal agreement, heads or points of agreement, an exchange of letters or an even more informal record. Style will vary from one drafter to another.

AGREEMENT made this   day of   between:

(1) ABC   (Mr. C)

(1) XYZ Investments Limited   ("XYZ")

A2–168   **PREAMBLE:**

    A. Mr C and XYZ have been in dispute with one another about various issues as outlined in the respective case summaries prepared by their legal representatives for the pending mediation, as particularised in the bundle of documents.

    B. There are two sets of court proceedings pending as set out in those summaries and as identified below.

    C. The parties agreed to deal with their disputes in mediation with DEF as mediator. The mediation took place on [date]. Mr C was represented by [solicitor/counsel]. XYZ was represented by [solicitor/counsel].

    D. In the mediation the parties settled their differences in relation to all pending disputes, and they wish to record the terms of such settlement on a binding basis in this Agreement.

IT IS AGREED:

A2–169   1. A more formal document may be prepared to incorporate any more detailed provisions that may be agreed between respective solicitors and/or counsel in the future. Meanwhile, this Agreement shall be fully and effectively binding on both parties by way of a complete and final settlement of all pending disputes. Tomlin Orders and/or any other court orders as provided for below shall be obtained by consent to give effect to these terms.

    2. The following definitions shall apply in this Agreement:

"the Company"	XYZ Superior Holdings Limited
"the 1995 Proceedings"	The action, as amended, brought by Mr C against XYZ in the Chancery Division of the High Court, No.
"the Section 459 Petition"	The Petition under Section 459 of the Companies Act 1985 filed in the Chancery Division of the High Court, No.
"all Proceedings"	Collectively, the 1995 Proceedings and the Section 459 Petition

    3. The terms of settlement agreed between the parties are set out in the

schedule to this Agreement. They are in full and final settlement of all disputes, differences and claims:

3.1 which Mr C has or may have against XYZ and its shareholders; and

3.2 which XYZ and its shareholders has or may have against Mr C.

4. This Agreement shall be immediately binding upon signature by the parties. The signatories to this Agreement on behalf of XYZ jointly and severally warrant that they are duly authorised to enter into this Agreement on its behalf.

5. In the event of any dispute or difference arising in relation to the obtaining of the necessary court orders required as a consequence of this settlement, or the implementation or performance of its terms, the parties reserve their rights to have those resolved by the Court. However, they agree that before doing so they will first attempt to resolve such dispute or difference by negotiation, and failing that, to refer it to further mediation by DEF (subject to his availability, otherwise by a mediator appointed by [mediation organisation]). If it remains unresolved within 4 weeks of such referral to mediation, either party shall be free to take such action as he or they may see fit. These provisions shall not, however, preclude either party from taking any injunctive or other interim legal proceedings considered necessary for the urgent protection of such party's rights.

6. Each party will pay their own legal costs in relation to the mediation, and will share equally the costs of the mediation including the mediator's fees.

Precedent 15. Family: Memorandum of Understanding

The authors acknowledge the Solicitors' Family Law Association for permitting the reproduction of their draft summaries, used in mediation conducted under the SFLA's rules and Code of Practice. The names, details and circumstances used in the following summary are fictitious and are merely illustrative. Each summary will have to be adapted to its individual needs. **A2–170**

Without prejudice

Miles Flurry and Katherine (Kate) Jane Flurry have been in mediation with [Name] regarding various matrimonial issues. They have had six mediation meetings, during which they have examined their respective financial and personal circumstances, and have been looking at proposals for their financial **A2–171** settlement. They have also had regard to the position as it affects their children, Oliver (aged 8) and Tamsin (aged 5).

This memorandum is furnished on an evidentially privileged and "without prejudice" basis. It is intended to help Miles and Kate to consider and obtain advice on the current proposals and does not record or create a binding agreement. An agreement will only come into being should they both decide to commit themselves to it, and they execute an appropriate formal document, after having each had an opportunity to take independent legal advice.

Background circumstances

A2–172   Miles is a director and shareholder in the company Manifest Occult Publications Limited which publishes fantasy and occult books. He has expressed concern about the future of this specialist field of publishing, but accepts that for the foreseeable future, the company is likely to continue to be profitable. Kate is a full-time primary school teacher. She is currently being considered as deputy head of her school.

Miles and Kate are both living at 33 Aspinall Road, London N3, but are conducting their lives separately. They wished to separate and used the mediation to discuss how they could do so in an orderly way and on terms that they could both accept.

Kate and Miles had a number of factors in mind in formulating their proposals. They were concerned to ensure that any arrangements they might reach in the mediation would be best for Oliver and Tamsin and would provide them with the necessary security. They wanted to achieve a "clean break" settlement but recognised the difficulties in doing this. They wanted the settlement terms to feel fair to themselves and to one another.

Settlement discussions and proposals

A2–173   The following are the matters discussed in the mediation, including the proposals which Kate and Miles find mutually acceptable:

Future of the relationship

1. Miles and Kate have resolved to separate. This will be achieved in practice when they sell their property at 33 Aspinall Road, London N3, and can buy separate homes.

2. They have accepted that their marriage has broken down and that a divorce is now inevitable. They do not regard this as urgent, though both wish to have this properly formalised in the ordinary course.

3. Miles and Kate discussed the possible changes to the divorce laws that have been published. If the new law becomes effective, they will discuss the position further with one another and with their respective solicitors to decide how to proceed so as to formalise the divorce. Otherwise they will proceed under the existing law.

Recording the proposed terms

4. Meanwhile, they will record their settlement terms in a Deed of Separation, or in whatever way they may be advised by their solicitors; and they will implement such terms. They realise that until a court order is obtained, there is a possibility that either of them might seek to vary any such terms and that the court retains the power (if it considers it appropriate) to re-open matters. However, neither of them has any present intention to seek to vary the terms, and barring anything wholly unforeseen that might materially change the position, neither would expect or wish to do so in the future.

Arrangements for Oliver and Tamsin

5. Both Kate and Miles have expressed their concerns for the needs and interests of Oliver and Tamsin. They wish to maintain a good relationship with one another in the children's interests, and propose to arrange their separation, housing and future contact and communications generally in such a way that this is achieved.

6. Detailed practical arrangements concerning Oliver and Tamsin, including decision making, communications and other matters still need to be discussed and agreed. Kate and Miles have, however, arrived at a broad understanding as to how they will approach these aspects:

   6.1 Oliver and Tamsin will continue to reside with Kate when she moves into her new home.

   6.2 Kate and Miles will establish a framework for Oliver and Tamsin to spend time with Miles.

   6.3 The kind of pattern that Miles and Kate have in mind will be something like Miles spending time with Oliver and Tamsin for a weekend every fortnight. Provisionally, the idea is that he will fetch them on Friday evening and bring them back on Sunday evening; but the details remain to be discussed. Miles will also speak to them freely on the phone between weekend visits, and may visit them if he is in the area. However, he will always check in advance whether interim visits will be convenient for them and for Kate. He will also arrange to have them with him for part of the holiday periods.

   Kate and Miles both recognise that Oliver and Tamsin need a good relationship with them both. They want to support one another in achieving this.

   6.3 Once the pattern is in place, both Kate and Miles accept that there will need to be flexibility. They will try to establish a mechanism for making changes without unduly inconveniencing the children or one another.

   6.4 They have in mind to liaise with one another about Oliver and Tamsin as necessary, and where practicable to deal jointly with matters such as schooling, health needs and the like. They will try to devise a way to ensure that these communications take place, and how each will deal with emergencies in case they cannot contact the other.

6.5 The detailed arrangements concerning these matters have been deferred, partly because of time constraints and partly because both Miles and Kate will find it easier to discuss these matters more usefully when they have actually separated and have established themselves in their separate homes. Meanwhile they are satisfied that these broad principles will be able to guide them in their discussions. If necessary, they will arrange further mediation to deal with any difficulties, should they arise.

Sale of 33 Aspinall Road and division of proceeds

7. The house at 33 Aspinall Road is to be marketed immediately at an asking price of £300,000. Any genuine offer of £300,000 or more will be acceptable. (A tentative offer of that sum has already been received.) If that level cannot be achieved within three months, Kate and Miles will consider accepting less, as advised by their agents, Creative Sales (who are being given an initial three months sole agency).

   Contracts will not, however, be exchanged on any sale or separate purchases until agreement between Kate and Miles has been reached and formalised.

8. The mortgage redemption, costs of sale and provision for both parties to move to their new homes are set out in the schedule provided by Miles and Kate. Provisionally, this is expected to total approximately £60,000. It is proposed that the net proceeds of sale will be paid to Kate absolutely, in settlement of all her capital claims against Miles. Assuming a price of £300,000, such net proceeds will be about £240,000. If there is any surplus over £240,000 this will be shared as to 67%(Kate): 33%(Miles).

9. Kate intends to use the proceeds of sale of 33 Aspinall Road to buy a house for herself and the children for about £220,000. She will pay all costs of purchase and any other expenses out of her capital. It is not her intention to have a mortgage. She has seen a house in the nearby area, which will enable her to remain in the same catchment area for the school. The asking price is £210,000, but it requires £10–15,000 of work to be done to it. She believes that it (or something similar) will be suitable.

10. Miles has made an offer of £165,000 on a flat for himself, which has been accepted, subject to contract. He will be using his capital towards this, and intends to borrow about £75,000 by way of mortgage.

11. If Kate and Miles wish to proceed with the sale of 33 Aspinall Road and the purchase of new homes for themselves, then they are aware

that certain steps will be necessary before any binding legal commitments are made on the sale and purchases.

11.1 Both Miles and Kate intend to obtain specific advice from their respective solicitors on the agreement they are proposing to enter into between themselves, to satisfy themselves about doing so.

11.2 They propose to sign a written agreement on an open basis, in terms approved by their respective solicitors.

11.3 If a comprehensive settlement is not yet reached, they know that an interim agreement should be entered into on an open basis. It will be expressed to be without prejudice to any further adjustment that might need to be made in the context of any overall resolution of the financial issues and to both of their rights generally. It will also be without prejudice to any argument that either of them may wish to pursue in any subsequent proceedings if matters are not settled by agreement. Its intention would be expressed as being to facilitate their separation, to be taken into account in any final resolution of the matter. The terms of the interim agreement would need to be agreed between the solicitors.

12. If final terms of settlement are now reached and approved by Miles and Kate after having been advised by their respective solicitors, then an interim agreement would not be necessary. In that event, all terms can be incorporated into a final agreement as advised by the respective solicitors (for example, in a Deed of Separation or in minutes of order if proceedings are envisaged).

Maintenance for Oliver and Tamsin

13. Miles proposes to pay Kate the sum of £450 per month as maintenance for each of Oliver and Tamsin, with effect from the first day of the month following completion of the sale of 33 Aspinall Road. That would be acceptable to Kate. This will continue until each child attains the age of 18 years or completes fulltime schooling, whichever is the later, or further agreement or order. This offer is being considered within the context of Kate's income needs generally. It is not being considered within the provisions of the Child Support Act. Kate and Miles have declined to have CSA calculations informally made, but may revert to this if they wish.

Maintenance considerations for Kate

14. In consideration of the imbalance of payment of the proceeds of sale of 33 Aspinall Road in favour of Kate, Miles wished to be relieved of any further maintenance obligation towards Kate personally. He accordingly proposed that the settlement terms should constitute a "clean break", with Kate having no claims at all against him. The implications and effect of a "clean break" were considered and discussed.

Having regard to her other financial resources, Kate was willing to consider these proposals, and to accept the capital imbalance and the maintenance figure of £900 per month for the children, in return for receiving no personal maintenance. However, she did not feel able to agree to waive her right to maintenance permanently, in case anything should arise while the children were still young, which might preclude her from working. She therefore proposed that Miles's offer would be acceptable if instead of a clean break, he was willing to pay her a nominal sum of £1 per year in order to reserve her rights.

Considerable time was spent in trying to find a solution to this issue. Ultimately, both agreed to consider the following formula:

14.1 The above terms would be acceptable, with a nominal maintenance payment of £1 per annum to Kate, on the basis of the further matters set out below.

14.2 It would be recorded that a substantial capital imbalance had been paid in consideration of Kate's personal maintenance being waived, and that although she was reserving her rights, that would only be against an unforeseen and serious problem arising, which could not be met in any other way. Maintenance would not be sought to meet any day-to-day difficulties that Kate might experience in managing on her income. (Both parties acknowledged that it would be difficult to know which way the court would exercise its discretion if the issue ever had to be dealt with by the court.)

14.3 If and to the extent that Kate sought any future maintenance, either directly for herself or attributable to her within a Child Support Agency context, she would agree to credit Miles with a corresponding capital sum by way of an interest in her property subject to a maximum of £25,000. She would hold that by way of a Declaration of Trust. (It was understood that this provision might not necessarily be legally enforceable.)

14.4 Attempts would be made to cover Kate by way of sickness and, if possible, redundancy insurance for a period of 10 years. By that time, Oliver would attain his majority and Tamsin would be 15 years of age. Miles would contribute 50% of the premiums for the duration of this period (subject to these not being "loaded" in any way, otherwise 50% of the unloaded level).

14.5 Kate's claims for personal maintenance would be dismissed 10 years from the date of an Agreement being formalised on this settlement. She would not be entitled to apply for this term to be extended.

Division of assets

15. Miles and Kate will each retain their own motor car and other personal possessions. They will share the contents of 33 Aspinall Road, according to their respective needs, which they expect to be able to resolve without assistance. Broadly, they envisage that Kate will have all bedroom furniture for herself, Oliver and Tamsin, and

that the remaining furniture will be divided approximately 3:1 in Kate's favour. If they have any difficulty in resolving this, they will arrange a further mediation meeting.

16. Miles will pay Kate's Visa and personal debts in full as listed in her financial statement.

17. Subject to the above, Kate and Miles will each retain as their sole property all assets respectively in their own name or under their individual control.

Full settlement of all capital claims

18. Subject to the above terms, Kate makes no further claim on Miles's assets, nor Miles on Kate's. This is a full and final settlement of all capital claims that either of them may have against the other, however arising. All capital claims are to be reciprocally dismissed in any court proceedings to be brought in due course. All claims under the Inheritance (Provision for Family and Dependants) Act 1975 are similarly to be dismissed as and when Kate's maintenance claims are extinguished: meanwhile will be reserved. The implications of that Act were briefly discussed, but Kate and Miles will discuss and consider these further with their solicitors.

Dealing with future issues

19. Miles and Kate have resolved to try to deal in a reasonable way with any issues that may arise in the future, whether to do with Oliver and Tamsin, or of a financial nature, so far as the latter aspect has been reserved. If they have any problems about doing so personally, they intend to revert to mediation.

Miles and Kate will now wish to consult their respective solicitors for advice on these proposals. If, having received advice, they wish to enter into an agreement to settle all issues, the solicitors will prepare the necessary documents. Alternatively, the solicitors may assist with the preparation of interim documents (in discussion with me if so agreed) to enable the house sale and purchases to proceed in the meanwhile.

If after seeing solicitors Miles and Kate wish to discuss matters further, then further mediation meeting(s) can be arranged for that purpose (attended by the solicitors as well, if that is considered helpful and necessary).

Precedent 16. Family: Financial summary

The authors acknowledge the Solicitors' Family Law Association for permitting the reproduction of their draft summaries, used in mediation conducted under the SFLA's rules and Code of Practice. The names used are fictitious.   **A2–174**

Miles Flurry and Katherine (Kate) Jane Flurry have been in mediation with [Name] with regard to various matrimonial issues.

As outlined in the covering explanatory document, this summary and its enclosures are furnished on a formal and open basis. They reflect the financial information disclosed by each of the parties as being a complete statement of their financial circumstances. They include amplifying information provided by Kate and Miles during the course of the mediation.

Copies of the following are attached to this summary:

- Schedule to this summary containing the amplifying information provided during the mediation.

- Financial disclosure statement of each party [with attachments]. This has already been copied to both parties.

- Summary of the flipchart outlining the parties' capital position in tabular form, as reflected at the meeting of [Date].

- Documents relevant to finance furnished by the parties during the course of the mediation, comprising [list].

Supporting documents have not been required, other than those attached, nor has independent verification taken place as to accuracy or completeness of the information generally.

Kate and Miles have confirmed that the attached documents, read with the supplementary information outlined above, reflect a complete statement of their financial circumstances.

Precedent 17. Family: Covering summary

A2–175　*The authors acknowledge the Solicitors' Family Law Association for permitting the reproduction of their draft summaries, used in mediation conducted under the SFLA's rules and Code of Practice. The names used are fictitious.*

Introduction
A2–176　Miles Flurry and Katherine (Kate) Jane Flurry have been in mediation with [Name] with regard to various matrimonial issues. This document explains the summaries that have been prepared in relation to this mediation, and the basis on which they have been written.

Mediation Rules
A2–177　The mediation has been conducted in accordance with the family mediation Code of Practice of the Solicitors' Family Law Association.

Under these rules, information furnished by either party relevant to their respective financial circumstances will be open and may be used in court proceedings. However, evidential privilege will be claimed for communications and negotiations that have taken place in the mediation. These are without prejudice and may not be referred to in any court proceedings.

The agreed rules also provide that (save for certain exceptions regarding interim matters) no binding agreements are made in the mediation. Parties are given the opportunity to obtain independent legal advice before entering into any legally binding agreement, and will only be legally bound after having had that opportunity and having then decided to bind themselves. Summaries provided in the mediation facilitate obtaining independent advice and do not record or create binding agreements.

Summaries now furnished

The Summary of Financial Information and any documents attached to it are **A2–178** furnished on an open basis.

The Memorandum of Understanding (incorporating summary of proposals) is furnished on a privileged, without prejudice basis.

Precedent 18. Civil/commercial mediation checklist

Mediators may find it helpful to have a checklist, by way of an informal **A2–179** *guide. Subject to the caution at the end, the following checklist could serve in relation to commercial and civil mediation, adapted as necessary to suit individual requirements:*

MEDIATION CHECKLIST

A. Before meeting **A2–180**

1. Have both/all parties agreed to the mediation? If not, is any assistance required in getting all parties to agree? Any documents to be sent?

2. Has a formal agreement been signed with the parties regulating the terms on which the mediation is to be undertaken, including mediation fees?

3. Preliminary communications with each party to arrange initial procedure: getting written summary of case and copy of relevant documents, arranging for exchange between parties. Fix timetable.

4. Advise parties to prepare properly for the meeting, indicating that presentations will be required if this is the case (specify approximate length).

5. Check authority of representatives of parties. Will they be able to conclude an agreement or will they need to seek further authority?

Will lawyers attend? Will all necessary parties be present or contactable, e.g. insurers, sub-contractors? If not, do parties all agree to proceed in any event, and will this be viable?

6. Check summary and documents when received. Any supplementary documents or information necessarily required before meeting?

7. Are date and venue of initial meeting agreed? Is length of meeting likely to be sufficient? If mediation may need more time, do parties prefer to set aside one block of time, continuing day after day, or is it preferable to meet periodically over a length of time?

8. Are ground rules understood by parties, at least in principle? Any clarification needed? Is a preliminary meeting needed to discuss procedure and ground rules before commencing substantive mediation?

9. Ensure adequate accommodation is available. Is a room needed for each party? Are the rooms apart from one another, and, if adjoining, are they soundproof? Are special reception arrangements needed? Practical arrangements to be set up in advance for working lunches, refreshments, etc.

10. Any special circumstances requiring special preparation? Flip-chart, video, overhead projector, photocopying facilities or any other devices or facilities needed and available?

B. At initial meeting

1. Mediator's introduction, welcome, acknowledging summaries and documents, outlining procedure (including in particular confidentiality aspect and without prejudice basis for discussions) and dealing with any queries.

2. Where mediator considers appropriate, each party, personally and/or through their lawyer, to make a brief case presentation.

3. Check whether there are any deadlines, e.g. limitation period shortly to expire, court hearing date or the like. If so, ensure that they are noted and built into timetable or that there is a binding agreement for limitation period to be suspended or otherwise covered.

4. If any additional factual information is still needed, consider whether this should be sought from the parties together, or whether considerations of confidentiality indicate that these should be obtained privately in caucus.

5. Consider (i) how long to continue with all parties together; (ii) when to caucus, for how long, and whether and when to meet together

again; (iii) whether and how best to work with legal representatives; (iv) whether to seek expert input or other third party involvement and how to do so.

6. When any party is not with the mediator, is there any useful task that can be done while waiting, e.g. getting supplementary information or considering options?

7. Maintain notes sufficient to ensure that all aspects covered, confidentiality between parties preserved, tasks of parties noted, and terms recorded to enable mediator to prepare heads of agreement when this stage is reached.

8. Consider how to obtain any missing expertise, whether technical, legal or other. Consult with parties' advisers (with the necessary agreement in this regard)? Engage an independent expert? Will parties pay the cost of this? Status of advice received?

9. If caucusing with one party takes longer than expected, check out periodically with other parties if necessary. If other parties are waiting together while caucus takes place with one party, are they comfortable being together? Is there any risk in this?

10. If issues unresolved at end of initial meeting:

   10.1 Consider procedure for future: Fix new appointment? Meet parties separately by appointment? Any other procedure or specific matter for agenda?

   10.2 Any practical tasks which the parties and/or the mediators need to undertake before next stage? Additional information or documents? Third-party inquiries? Legal or other professional advice? Specify, with timetable if appropriate.

   10.3 Any settlement-geared steps parties can take in the meanwhile, e.g. formulating proposals, considering existing options, looking at new settlement permutations?

   10.4 Check whether any interim matters need to be urgently resolved before next step in mediation, e.g. decisions which need to be taken in the meanwhile and which parties cannot resolve themselves?

   10.5 Consider and check whether an interim summary would be helpful, covering the matters partially resolved and indicating outstanding issues. This could be prepared and sent after the meeting.

   10.6 Any other matters which need to be discussed with the parties or arrangements made?

C. In the event of impasse

1. Can the issue in deadlock be deferred or dealt with on a temporary basis? Alternatively, is there a short-term basis for dealing with it for a trial period?

2. Have the parties examined their best and worst alternatives to a negotiated resolution?

3. If the deadlock issue arises in relation to a symbol or form of words, have the underlying needs and concerns been examined?

4. Do the parties have different perceptions of fairness in relation to the outcome? Has this been examined?

5. Will a non-binding evaluation of the sticking issue help the parties to budge? Or might this just entrench positions further? Who should provide this? The mediator or a third party? Or perhaps a binding adjudication, limited to the sticking issue?

6. If strong emotional responses are creating a block, can it help for these to be expressed or for some other person to be asked to take over representing a corporate party or to join an adjourned meeting?

7. Will it help the parties if the mediator provides a written summary of the position setting out the aspects resolved and those awaiting resolution, with the alternative proposals and settlement parameters? Can and should the mediator suggest some possible permutations of existing proposals which may take matters forward?

8. Will it help and would it be appropriate for the mediator to make recommendations for the settlement of the issues?

9. Are there any other impasse strategies that may be used? Consider the specific sticking issue, and examine the possibilities. Go back to basics: examine why the parties came to mediation, what they hope to achieve, what other advantages there are in continuing, can the proposals be reconstructed more acceptably? Can the parties themselves suggest any basis for breaking the deadlock or re-establishing the negotiations?

10. If the deadlock cannot be resolved and the mediation must come to an end, do the parties realise this and have they considered what the implications would be?

D. When issues resolved

1. Prepare or arrange for the parties' lawyers to draft a careful note of matters resolved, e.g. Heads of Agreement, for parties' immediate signature or draft terms of consent order if court proceedings are

pending. Be clear as to what is required: do parties want to be immediately and unconditionally bound on signature? Or is the agreement conditional upon the fulfilment of any stated contingency, and if so, exactly what? Or is there to be no binding agreement, but merely a note of acceptable proposals which the parties will finalise through their legal advisers? Or some other reservation or nuance?

2. Are there any provisions in the agreement to mediate or in the ground rules which may affect the terms of settlement? Check this. If, for example, there is a provision that if a party does not give effect to a settlement, the other may be released from the settlement terms on written notice, check if this is required; if so, strict time scales should be specified; if not required, alternative provisions should be specified.

3. If legal representatives have not attended the mediation, do the parties want the mediator to communicate with those advisers? Clarify requirements.

4. Check with parties if anything else required from the mediator or the ADR organisation: for example (i) mediator or ADR organisation to act as stakeholder, with specific directions; (ii) mediator to be supervisor of settlement terms, with specific instructions and authority; (iii) mediator being available if any issue arises during implementation of settlement; (iv) mediator to act as expert or adjudicator in relation to implementation.

E. If mediation ends with issues unresolved

1. Do not close the door on any particular options. Leave as much scope as possible for parties to continue their own discussions.

2. Check if the parties want a without prejudice summary of the position to facilitate any continuing discussions, or anything else from the mediator.

3. Do the parties want an evaluation and is it appropriate to furnish one? Or perhaps the mediator's recommendations for settlement? Have appropriate explanations been given about these options and their implications?

4. Offer the parties the opportunity to return to mediation if required.

5. Check whether the parties would find it helpful to use the mediation to narrow and define the issues for adjudication.

Checklist caution

A caution along the following lines should be issued with any checklist given to mediators, to ensure that mediators exercise proper individual judgement and discretion and do not rely exclusively on such a checklist:

"This checklist is for guidance only, and cannot be comprehensive or definitive. It must obviously be used with discretion and personal judgment. It remains the responsibility of individual mediators to ensure that all relevant matters are covered and properly dealt with, whether or not included in this checklist."

Precedent 19. Family mediation checklist

A2–181   *This checklist is based on a model of mediation structured into stages as envisaged by this book (with acknowledgements to the Solicitors' Family Law Association, for whom the authors prepared the checklist on which the following one is based). It is, however, obviously adaptable to any other way of working. It assumes that the couple are not legally-aided and that they have a range of issues and that they have not expressed any preference for prioritising. As in all mediation, checklists are for guidance only and do not prevail over parties' wishes and preferences. It cannot be comprehensive or definitive and mediators must use their discretion and judgment in amplifying and adapting it appropriately.*

Dealing with initial phone enquiry

A2–182

- Check if the call is individual or on behalf of both parties. Make it clear that both parties will need to agree to mediate.

- Do not accept information about the merits of the matter. Avoid this by saying that you prefer to find out more about the merits when both are together.

- Deal with any procedural inquiries, and give a brief outline of how mediation works. Indicate costs and estimate number of sessions.

- Check whether the other party will be contacting you. Explain that this will be needed before mediation can commence.

- Establish the name, address and telephone number of the inquirer, and check whether explanatory written material is required, and if so, whether a duplicate set is needed for the inquirer to provide to the other party.

- Check urgency and timetable if a meeting is requested in the telephone call.

- Sole mediators may want to mention whether and under what circumstances co-mediation might be considered.

- Co-mediators need to discuss any special arrangements necessary for the appointment of a co-mediator.

- Check discreetly on the phone that each party is not under improper pressure to mediate.
  Preliminary screening for domestic abuse or threat.

- Write to the inquirer enclosing information material. If an appointment is fixed, confirm details of place, date and time with both parties. Enclose the Agreement to Mediate and the preliminary information form.

Arrangements for initial meeting

- Ensure that both parties are aware of the arrangements and send a confirmatory letter.   **A2–183**

- Check that both parties have returned the preliminary information form. If not, consider phoning the party whose form is missing to check that it is being sent. Familiarise yourself with the information furnished.

- In co-mediation, ensure that the co-mediator is briefed with a copy of the preliminary information forms.

- Have the following documents available for the meeting, namely a spare copy of the Agreement to Mediate, for signature, two sets of financial disclosure documentation to hand to the parties and the preliminary information forms, as completed by the parties.

- Have the following available namely, flip-chart and marking pens, tissues, diary, calculator and any relevant tax, financial, welfare benefits or other tables.

- Set up the room for the meeting. Clear files and papers, establish a professional but informal ambience. Arrange the chairs at suitable positions. Ensure privacy, non-disturbance and diversion of calls.

- Establish reception arrangements. Ensure that you are immediately notified as each party arrives so that they are not left together for any length of time (and not at all if there is any hostility). If the parties are thought to be hostile, arrange separate reception areas or place the first arriving in the mediation room.

- Arrange for the availability of tea/coffee/water.

Initial meeting

- Put the couple at ease, offer tea/coffee.   **A2–184**

- Check permission to use first names all round (unless inappropriate).

- Check that both have read the Agreement to Mediate. Outline its key elements. These may be restating the mediator's impartial role. (If you are a solicitor acting outside your practice as such, this must be stated and it must be clear that your firm is not involved.) Parties' decisions will not generally be binding until they have each had the opportunity to check them with their independent lawyers. They will be required to provide financial disclosure for informed decision-making. All financial disclosure is open whereas all discussions and attempts to resolve matters are privileged/without prejudice. Explain confidentiality rules including position if any child or person is at risk of harm. Any other key terms should be explained.

- Check if they have any queries, and deal with them. Subject to this, sign the Agreement, ask them each to sign, and retain it on your file.

- Consider whether the preliminary information form raises anything needing to be addressed at the outset.

- Ensure that there is a screening mechanism for possible problems of abuse, violence or threat. These must be addressed. Ensure that mediation can properly and effectively take place. Consider seeing each party separately if this may allow freer discussion about abuse.

- Check parties' agenda and priorities. Avoid contention in establishing the agenda.

- Check if there are any urgent issues requiring attention in the first session. If so, address them, checking if there are competing priorities. If so, discuss how to allocate the time.

- Check the framework within which decisions are to be taken: exploratory, separation, divorce? Discuss and clarify options if required.

- Sole mediators who may co-mediate in some circumstances should consider whether the dynamics or issues indicate that co-mediation might be appropriate. If so, discuss it with the couple and make any necessary arrangements for the future.

- Acquaint yourself with facts of situation especially regarding children, housing and general circumstances. Consider and discuss how best to establish the needs, wishes and feelings of any children involved.

- Hand the parties financial disclosure documentation to be completed by each of them and explain how these are to be dealt with. Arrange how and when these should be returned to the mediator.

- If either party is legally represented, seek permission to write to their solicitor(s), and clarify what may be said to them.

- Deal with concluding practicalities such as summarising matters to be dealt with by each, fixing date of next meeting, obtaining payment, and any other matters.

After initial meeting

- If financial disclosure documents have not arrived by the agreed date, contact the defaulting party and check the position. **A2–185**

- When the financial disclosure documents are received, make copies for the parties.

- Prepare the flip-chart by writing up any outline, agreed information, but not data that needs to be checked.

- Consider information given by the parties and reflect on any further information likely to be needed.

Second meeting

- Acknowledge the financial disclosure documents. Check if anything material has happened since the last meeting and review agenda. **A2–186**

- Unless other issues are to be dealt with, continue with information disclosure. Take couple through documents, page by page. Start with capital position. Complete flip-chart as you progress with this. Check for completeness. Indicate what further information is needed for the next session.

- Move from disclosure and recording into checking needs and wants against available resources. In the absence of specific stipulations, start with respective housing needs. This may interrelate with children's accommodation needs and whom they will be primarily living with. Have preliminary discussion about the children (if any) and their needs and wishes.

- Start helping the couple to generate options, including housing and finance.

- Consider what action parties can each take pending the next session, for example, checking house value, exploring prices and availability of alternative housing, etc.

- Deal with concluding practicalities such as summarising matters to be dealt with by each, fixing date of next meeting, obtaining payment, and any other matters.

Further meetings

- Each meeting will have to be conducted according to the needs of the situation as it develops. No standard format can be given. **A2–187**

- Financial issues will be dealt with by generating, developing and exploring options and by assisting the parties with their negotiations.

- On children issues, establish a picture of the children and their circumstances, wishes, interests and needs. Consider how to bring those factors into the process. These issues can be dealt with through exploring alternative options. Mediators who have specifically trained to work with children in mediation may consider whether it would be appropriate and helpful to see the children.

- Consider whether any third party assistance is needed, *e.g.* counselling, legal, financial or any other input, valuations or tax assistance.

- Consider possibilities of reconciliation throughout.

- Consider impasse strategies if necessary.

- Consider providing a written summary of partly resolved issues.

When issues are resolved

A2–188
- Check with the parties that the terms are understood and that they are acceptable.

- Ensure as far as possible that you have all necessary information on hand to enable the summaries to be prepared in sufficient detail to make it unnecessary for any further negotiations to take place.

- Arrange for summaries to be prepared by you. Estimate time-scale and cost, and practical arrangements for furnishing and checking the summaries, correcting any errors on the draft.

- Recommend the couple to see their respective solicitors with the summaries when finalised. Check if you are required to communicate the outcome to the solicitors.

- Remind the couple that the resolution is provisional and not binding until both parties confirm acceptance after having had legal advice (or declining to obtain such advice having had the opportunity to do so).

- Suggest that a further mediation meeting be held if there are any issues raised by solicitors that cannot be readily resolved between the parties or their solicitors. The solicitors can also be invited to attend that meeting if necessary.

Precedent 20. Civil/commercial mediation drafting checklist

A2–189
The following brief checklist may be helpful in drafting settlement terms (subject to the same cautions set out in para. A2–190):

- Check with all parties and/or their lawyers that the terms of settlement are understood and agreed.

- Are the terms to be binding immediately? If not, when and under what circumstances do they become binding?

- Are the terms unconditional? If not, what are the conditions applicable to them? These need to be clear, specific and unambiguous.

- Are all dates, periods, amounts, methods of calculation and other directions and formulae clear, specific and unambiguous?

- What are the consequences of non-compliance with the settlement agreement? Does this need to be specified?

- Check the terms on which the ADR process was established, such as the Agreement to Mediate. Does this specify any terms that may be relevant to the settlement agreement?

- What format is appropriate for the settlement agreement? A formal document, heads of agreement, a letter of agreement, a deed or some other?

- Do the parties envisage that a further and more comprehensive document will be entered into later? In such event, what is the status of the settlement terms in the meanwhile? Is it clear what the effect of the settlement agreement will be if no such further document is executed?

- In some cases the mediator's professional indemnity insurance cover may be based on the use of a certain format or form of introduction for the settlement agreement. Does this apply?

- Is a court order required? If so, are its terms to be agreed immediately or will this be done later, and with what consequences if there is a later problem in relation to the drafting and finalising? Who will deal with the formalities of getting the order made?

- If proceedings are pending in court, what is to happen with such proceedings? Are they to be discontinued? Is there any agreement as to costs?

- If an existing relationship is to continue, is this on the same terms as at present, or are these to be varied, and if so, are the new terms clear and explicit?

- Does confidentiality need to be confirmed or is this already explicitly covered? Are there any special requirements as to confidentiality of the settlement terms?

- Do any aspects involve a neutral third party role after execution of the agreement, such as acting as a stakeholder? Are documents to be held in escrow or items to be retained pending completion? Is there to be any supervision by the neutral? Do these need to be provided for in the agreement?

- Does the agreement need to specify which country's laws are to apply to the construction and implementation of the settlement agreement or to any aspect arising from it? Do the parties wish to submit to the exclusive or non-exclusive jurisdiction of any court? Or provide for arbitration or any other form of adjudication if any further disagreement arises? Or for further mediation?

- Will the parties execute the agreement in personal or representative capacities? In the latter event, do the signatories have the necessary authority?

- Check the draft agreement with parties and lawyers before finalising.

Precedent 21. Family mediation drafting checklist

A2–190 *The authors wish to acknowledge the Solicitors Family Law Association for permitting the reproduction of this checklist, which outlines matters to be dealt with in drafting mediation summaries following the SFLA model. It is of course effectively a checklist of matters to be covered in the substantive mediation as well as in the drafting. It cannot be comprehensive or definitive and it remains the responsibility of individual mediators to ensure that all relevant matters are covered, whether or not included here.*

Summary of financial information:

A2–191
1. Attach photocopies of the financial disclosure statements furnished by each party. (Consider making and retaining two spare copies for this purpose when copying the form for use at the session when working on financial disclosure.)

2. Consider attaching a transcript of the flipchart setting out the capital position of the parties. (This is optional, but recommended as generally helpful.)

3. As far as practicable, list and attach copies of any other material documents relevant to finance that have been furnished.

4. Any financial documents obtained in the mediation where copies are not attached to the summary should be listed as having been furnished, but as not being attached.

5. If any information is furnished in the mediation that does not appear from the financial statements and the other documents, this should be set out in a schedule to the summary of financial information. Most mediations are likely to have such schedules, which are in any event helpful to provide an outline summary of the position.

6. Any other open information can be recorded that does not fit under any other heading, but which it is necessary to record. This may, for example, include any continuing reservation about disclosure that the

mediator feels particularly necessary to mention e.g. "W questioned whether the disclosure was complete and H confirmed that it was. Various documents, as listed, were furnished. The mediator cannot investigate this question, and H&W should discuss this with their respective solicitors if they have any queries".

7. Ensure that lawyers for the parties who receive this summary with schedule will have a full picture of the financial position to enable them to advise their clients effectively without necessarily having to raise any further enquiry.

Memorandum of Understanding (Summary of proposals)

1. Mark this summary "Without prejudice."   **A2–192**

2. Ensure that the legal status of the document is clear. Its non-binding nature must be maintained, unless there are specific reasons to the contrary. There should be no reference or implication that it is an "agreement," even conditional or provisional. Rather, the summary contains proposals that both parties would find acceptable, but which are subject to legal advice.

3. Give a brief outline of the relevant facts, to help explain the arrangements that follow. For example, it can assist to set out any background to the couple's thinking and approach. Perhaps also set out their respective occupations, or whether either is not working; and any other basic non-contentious information.

4. Introduce the proposals, either indicating whether the couple find them all mutually acceptable or whether there are any aspects that are still outstanding, and if so how they will be dealt with in the summary (*e.g.* any unresolved issues will be mentioned in italics and/or within square brackets).

5. Set out the proposals in a clear way and orderly sequence. Imagine that you are the lawyer having to advise either party: do you have complete information sufficient to enable you to draft a comprehensive deed or order without further enquiry?

6. The items that follow are merely examples of matters to be considered.

7. *Future of the relationship:* If the couple are intending to divorce, either now or after a period of time, this should be stated. Alternatively, if they are proposing to separate, or have done so, this may be stated. It will provide the framework for the documentation to follow any agreement.

8. *Children:*

    8.1 If there are any children, it would ordinarily be best to record the position that relates to them at an early stage of the drafting and under a separate heading. Where will they live, and what arrangements are proposed for them with regard to contact? This does not necessarily have to be expressed as "residence" and "contact." While it is fine to do so, the language of a parent "spending time with" the children may be less legalistic. Also, try to use their names rather than always referring to "the children" where practicable. Any language that explains the arrangements that the couple have in mind will be in order.

8.2 Try to individualise the children. Mention them individually by name, and provide separately for each as appropriate.

8.3 If the arrangements are intended to be short-term or provisional in any way, for what period do they apply and how and when will they be reviewed?

8.4 If there are any particular aspects to note, this can be done in a neutral way. For example, the couple may wish to provide how a child's education is to be dealt with, school reports copied to one another, school visits handled, etc. Or how to liaise about holidays, or half-term arrangements, or any other matters.

9. *Accommodation:*

9.1 Proposals concerning the family home should be covered. If it is owned, what is to happen to it and to each party's interest in it? Are principles, amounts, dates and details all clear? If it is to be sold, when and how is it to be marketed? Who will be responsible for appointing and dealing with agents and seeing prospective purchasers? Who will be the agents and on what terms? Is a minimum figure agreed, and a machinery for dealing with offers? Is an acceptable time frame agreed? Which solicitors will act on the sale? Are there any other practicalities to be dealt with?

9.2 If the home is owned, and it is to be retained by either, on what terms? If permanently, what adjustments (if any) are to be made, and when? If for a temporary period, what events trigger disposal and how are the proceeds to be divided? How will other arrangements as outlined in 9.1 be handled? Will there need to be any registration of either party's interest, *e.g.* by way of charge? Does the mortgagee need to be contacted, and if so, how will this be dealt with?

9.3 If the home is rented, who will remain in it? Is it necessary to contact the landlord and if so how will this be done? Do any other practicalities have to be dealt with? If the tenancy is to be given up, when, how and by whom will this be handled?

9.4 Check that the proposed arrangements are workable, *e.g.* that there is sufficient capital and mortgage facility to enable intended purchases to be achieved.

10. *Capital:*

Apart from the matrimonial home, is there any other capital to be dealt with? If so, how is this to be divided? Is the apportionment clear and complete? Are all jointly owned assets fully covered? How and when will they be separated?

11. **Debts:**

Have the couple agreed who will pay any outstanding debts including liability for unpaid taxes, if any? At what date are the debts fixed? Are there any further debts accruing and how will they be paid?

12. **Spouse maintenance:**

12.1 If this is applicable, have all necessary particulars been discussed, including amount, date of commencement (and is this to be linked to a sale of property, if so, how?). How long is it to continue, and when and how is it reviewable? If it is index-linked, with what index (the index of retail prices maintained by the Department of Employment?) and taking what date as the base date?

12.2 If maintenance is for a fixed term, what term? Can this term be extended or will that be specifically precluded? Do the couple envisage that reviews will be able to take place during the term? Any other details they want or need to record?

13. **Child maintenance:**

13.1 Fix all necessary particulars, including commencement date, to whom payable, how long to continue and when and how reviewable. See 12.1 about index linking. Has the Child Support Act been discussed? Has a calculation been discussed, or perhaps made? Mention this as appropriate in the summary.

13.2 Check if all other arrangements for children's finance are covered. Are special school fee arrangements needed? Pocket money provision? Extras?

14. **Tax:**

14.1 Have all relevant tax considerations been considered in the mediation and recorded in the summary? Tax reliefs? Potential Capital Gains Tax (CGT) liabilities on sale of any assets, and if so, whether these can and need to be further addressed (for example by an accountant)? Are there any CGT liabilities that may arise on any deferred sale of the property (especially if for example one retains an interest without living there)? Possible Inheritance Tax implications?

14.2 If any arrangements are envisaged that have particular tax implications, *e.g.* wife to receive "golden handshake" if giving up employment with husband, or any other unusual provision, have these been checked with a tax adviser?

15. **Pension, insurance and other security:**

15.1 Has this been addressed and recorded? Has the pension been valued and taken into account and dealt with? Are any insurance policies to continue in force by either party for the benefit of the other? If so, who will pay the premiums, will this need to be checked, and how will the beneficial interests be recorded?

15.2 If appropriate, is there sufficient security in the event of the death of the paying party? Does this need to be further discussed? Do the couple need to consider any other form of security, *e.g.* insurance against illness or redundancy?

16. *Household contents:*

If the couple feel able to deal with this themselves, this should be mentioned. If not, what provision exists for dealing with this? A formula needs to be specified.

17. *Dismissal of claims:*

17.1 If this is proposed, are the details clear. Is a court order needed, now or later? What are the terms, and will each party's lawyer be able to understand from the summaries why this is proposed? If not, amplify as necessary.

17.2 Do the couple fully appreciate the implications of dismissal? Have these been dealt with by way of reality testing as to what will happen in the future? This may need to be addressed and confirmed in the summary.

17.3 Is a dismissal of Inheritance Act claims appropriate? Has this been discussed?

18. *Costs:*

If legal costs have been incurred, how and by whom are they to be paid? If they are to be incurred in the future, for example in any divorce proceedings and in getting any ancillary relief consent order, who will pay the costs? With regard to the mediation costs, is there to be any adjustment of these, for example by either meeting more than half of these?

19. *Contingencies:*

19.1 Various aspects of the proposals might potentially depend on certain contingencies. For example, future housing arrangements may depend on a certain price being obtained for the matrimonial home, or a mortgage being procured. What happens if these contingencies are not met? If it is practicable to have alternative proposals, have these been discussed? If it is not practicable, does there need to be a formula for review so that the whole arrangement does not break down if an individual component is not met?

19.2 If any aspect of the proposal is subject to review at a later date (for example, spouse or child maintenance), is there a machinery for dealing with this, or do the couple prefer to leave this open? Might further mediation be reflected as an option in the event that their review machinery does not produce an agreement?

20. *Reservations and cautions:*

20.1 The summary may need to reflect any reservations or cautions noted by the mediator. For example, if a party is proposing to agree to something that the mediator feels is outside of what a court may approve, and this has been discussed in the mediation, the mediator should generally note this. The mediator may indicate that this was discussed but that both parties nevertheless wish to go ahead. There may be many other such examples. A couple might specifically wish to agree on something without exploring its implications because of time pressures. The mediator may wish to record something like "H & W briefly considered this aspect, but owing to time constraints decided that it was not necessary to do so in any greater detail in making their decision. The mediator remains willing to spend more time on looking further into this if required."

20.2 If there are any other aspects that the mediator considers should be drawn to the attention of the couple and their solicitors in the summary, these should also be included. For example, any applicable time limits or deadlines should be mentioned. Or if the couple considered registering a notice or a land charge to protect a right of occupation, this should be mentioned (whether or not action was actually taken). Anything that the parties should check with their solicitors should certainly be specifically mentioned in the summary.

21. *Further mediator functions:*

Is there any other aspect with which the mediator might be able to assist? Invite the couple (and their solicitors if appropriate) to a further meeting? Any appropriate neutral role on implementation aspects?

Appendix III

PRACTICE DIRECTIONS, STATEMENTS AND NOTES

Contents

A3–001   The following documents are contained in this section: *Page*

ADR Guidelines (Paragraph 11) for the Court of Appeal ADR Scheme

A3–002   11. ALTERNATIVE DISPUTE RESOLUTION (ADR)

11.1.1. A *pro bono* scheme commenced in 1997. The scheme has to take into account the fact that cases which have already been tried at first instance raise different issues, so far as ADR is concerned, to cases which have yet to be tried.

11.1.2. The scheme has recently been refined. Now in appropriate cases, as soon as an appeal set down with the Civil Appeals Office, a letter of invitation to consider ADR, signed by the Master of the Rolls, is sent to the parties' solicitors. The letter encloses an explanatory leaflet and a response form. A member of staff is available to answer queries, provide general information and help with specific cases.

11.1.3. The supervising Lords Justices responsible for particular categories of work are vigilant in their case management for those cases that appear suitable for referral to ADR. Recently a very substantial commercial appeal was compromised as result of a referral by the supervising Lord Justice. Equally, presiding Lords Justices are able to propose a referral to ADR at the determination of appeals which otherwise will lead to a re-hearing or the issue of further proceedings.

11.1.4. Legal aid covers the costs of ADR for an assisted party.

11.1.5. Further information is available from the Civil Appeals Office, Royal Courts of Justice, Strand, London, WC2A 2LL (tel. 0207 936 6486)].

ADR: Section 14 of the Chancery Guide, April 1995

Alternative dispute resolution (ADR)

14.3 Parties are reminded that there exist alternative methods of dispute resolution which do not involve the court but which may provide a more suitable or cheaper or quicker method of resolving matters in a particular case. The clerk to the Commercial Court maintains a list of the individuals and bodies that offer ADR services. The list is for information and not by way of recommendation of any particular person.   **A3–003**

Appendices 2 and 3 of the Second Report of the Commercial Court Committee Working Party On ADR (ADR Orders in the Commercial Court.)

Appendix 2   **A3–004**

ADR Orders in the Commercial Court
Guidance Notes for Litigants and their Lawyers

Introduction

1. This guidance refers only to mediation (the most common method of ADR) and to Early Neutral Evaluation, but not to Adjudication or Arbitration).

2. This guidance is intended as an outline only. Parties or their lawyers

should take expert ADR advice if they are unclear about the process in any way.

Mediation Essentials

3. Mediation is a well-tried, robust and powerful process. It is safe because no ultimate outcome can be imposed on any party except by agreement and because what is said or done during a mediation should be confidential and covered by 'without prejudice' privilege up to the point when agreement is reached.

The neutral Mediator, chosen by the parties direct or through one of the ADR institutions, will direct procedure but it is for the parties to choose their own outcomes in negotiation with the other parties assisted by the neutral Mediator.

The power of the process comes from the mixture of direct negotiation and private meetings helped by the experience of the Mediator, and the skill and experience of the parties and their lawyers. It can provide considerably more than direct negotiation. For that reason, even where direct negotiations have failed and where the parties are instinctively hostile to further attempts to settle, mediation often achieves a settlement. The range of possible solutions can be much wider than is possible in Court.

The ultimate aim of a mediation is a binding agreement.

Time

4. Normally, the Court will wish the parties to proceed to mediation swiftly, so that Court time is not wasted with procedural or other steps which become unnecessary - and so that trial dates are not affected.

The most effective and speedy mediations are usually those in which the parties appoint a Mediator very quickly and then make use of the Mediator's experience and skills to help construct the procedure.

A mediation could take place in a matter of days. Even the most complex mediation should be capable of being arranged and dealt with in a few weeks at most.

Appointment of Mediators

5. This is usually done by the parties, sometimes direct or perhaps after consulting one of the mediation institutions, who will put forward names on request. In choosing a Mediator, parties should look for experience of mediation, after formal ADR training if possible. If subject matter expertise is thought necessary (but it is usually unnecessary, the parties and their advisers know much more about the technicalities than anyone) an expert in the field can be appointed. However, experience as a Mediator is much more important and a suitably qualified co-Mediator or Pupil Mediator can supply any specialist knowledge which might be thought necessary. Fees may be prescribed by the mediation institution or negotiated on a daily rate with the Mediator.

Mediation Agreements

6. These are usually short and uncomplicated. Some mediation institutions supply standard model agreements. A Mediator chosen in principle can help

in framing the agreement. It will usually be a mistake to negotiate a complex mediation agreement without first choosing a Mediator or consulting a mediation institution for help.

Steps in a typical Mediation

Day 1   Commercial Court ADR Order

Days 1–5 Discussion between the parties and their lawyers and consultation with a mediation institute produces a short-list of three suitable Mediators

Day 6   Parties agree on one of the three.

Day 10   Preliminary meeting of the parties, their lawyers and the Mediator when the Mediator suggests a timetable for subsequent meetings, a form of mediation agreement, an exchange of background information and a short summary of each side's case. The procedure is agreed.

Day 15   Parties exchange a 10 page summary of each other's position with copies of a core bundle including pleadings in the action.

Day 20   Mediation, Day 1. Mediation commences, lasts all day and part of the evening. Parties attend with their lawyers.

Day 21   Mediation, Day 2. Settlement reached, documented by the parties and their lawyers.

Day 22   The Court is informed of the settlement with a draft Tomlin Order putting the settlement into place and a request to vacate the trial date.

Early Neutral Evaluation

The function of this procedure is to provide the parties to a dispute with a non-binding assessment by a neutral of their respective chances of success were the litigation to be pursued.

The procedure normally involves the selection of a neutral, who may be a Commercial Judge, and the concise presentation to the neutral of the nature of the dispute and the parties' respective contentions. The neutral will then give the parties his evaluation of the issues, indicating the strength and weaknesses of the claim and defences.

There will usually first be a preliminary meeting at which the neutral meets the parties and their representatives and agrees the future procedure.

Normally, the neutral will initially be provided with a limited amount of pre-reading, such as skeleton arguments, pleadings, witness statements and the key documents. There may then be a short hearing, not normally exceeding one or two days, in the course of which each party orally presents its case. That may in appropriate cases involve key witnesses and/or experts giving evidence. Such a hearing should always be attended by a board member or other representative of the parties with authority to settle the case.

In simpler cases or where the parties wish to save costs there is no reason why the entire procedure should not be in writing without the need for an oral hearing.

The neutral will not normally act as a mediator and when the evaluation is to hand it will be up to the parties to take whatever further course they consider best towards settlement. Or they may prefer to let some or all of the issues go to trial. If they do so, what passed in the course of the early neutral evaluation is entirely privileged.

Where a Commercial Judge is appointed as early neutral evaluator, he will taken no further part in the litigation unless the parties wish that he should do so. Application for the appointment of a Commercial Judge should normally be made to the Listing Office.

A3–005   Appendix 3

Form of ADR Order

1. The parties shall within 5 days exchange lists of 3 neutrals each who are available to conduct ADR procedures in this matter prior to (date).

2. Within 2 days thereafter the parties shall in good faith endeavour to agree a neutral from the lists so exchanged.

3. Failing such agreement by (date) this summons will be restored to enable the court to facilitate agreement on a neutral.

4. The parties shall take such serious steps as they may be advised to resolve their disputes by ADR before the neutral so chosen by no latter than (date).

5. If the matters in issue are not finally settled, the parties shall inform the court by letter prior to (exchange of list of documents or of witness statements or exchange of experts' reports or setting down for trial) what steps towards ADR have been taken and (without prejudice to matters of privilege) why such steps have failed. If the parties have failed to initiate ADR procedures they are to appear before Mr Justice . . . for further consideration of the Order.

6. Costs in the ultimate cause.

A3–006   PRACTICE DIRECTION (FAMILY DIVISION: CONCILIATION PROCEDURE)

Husband and Wife—Divorce—Children—Conciliation procedure—Contested applications for custody and access—Conciliation appointment before registrar and welfare officer

As from January 1, 1983, the Principal Registry of the Family Division will operate a pilot scheme of conciliation in contested applications in matrimonial proceedings for custody, access and variation thereof. The object of the scheme is to give an opportunity for agreement to be reached without the bitterness and exchange of recriminations which often develops between the parties when these issues remain in dispute. It may sometimes also result in considerable saving of time and expense both to the parties and the court.

General experience has shown that the earlier a conciliation effort is deployed the more likely is the prospect of success. It is emphasised that it is extremely important that no affidavit should be filed or exchanged until after an unsuccessful conciliation appointment or until the registrar has so directed.

When such an application is lodged, the return date which is given will be that on which the conciliation appointment will take place before a registrar. It is intended that two registrars will be available on each of two days each week. Each registrar will be attended by a court welfares officer. It is essential that both the parties and any legal advisers having conduct of the case attend. The nature of the application and the matters in dispute will be outlined to the registrar and the welfare officer. If the dispute continues, the parties and their advisers will be given the opportunity of retiring to a private room together with the welfare officer to attempt to reach agreement. These discussions will be privileged and will not be disclosed on any subsequent application. Anything which is said before the registrar on such appointments will also remain privileged.

Any application to vacate a conciliation appointment must be made in writing to the registrar at least seven days before the return date.

If the conciliation appointment is successful, the registrar will make such orders as are agreed between the parties. If the appointment does not result in agreement being reached, any other subsequent application to a registrar will normally be dealt with by a different registrar and any further inquiry by a court welfare officer will be made by a different officer. Conciliation appointments which have been adjourned will be brought back before the same registrar whenever possible. Applications for variation of custody or access orders made as a result of conciliation will generally be dealt with by the same registrar who dealt with the initial conciliation appointment.

If the conciliation appointment is unsuccessful the registrar will give such directions as he considers appropriate as to the obtaining of welfare officer's reports and the filing of affidavits.

The party who has living with him or her any child aged 11 years or over, in respect of whom the dispute exists, should bring that child to the conciliation appointment, because it will sometimes be appropriate for the child to be seen by the registrar or the welfare officer.

Any party upon whom a summons is served and who wishes to apply for legal aid should do so immediately. The Law Society will consider applications for emergency certificates in appropriate circumstances.

Urgent applications made by summons will be referred to the registrar for the day to determine whether they are outside the scope of the conciliation scheme.

B. P. TICKLE
Senior Registrar.

November 2, 1982.

A3–007   PRACTICE DIRECTION (Family Division: Conciliation)

Children—Family   Division—Conciliation   procedure—Referrals   for conciliation before district judge and welfare officer—Matrimonial Causes Act 1973 (c. 18), s. 41—Children Act 1989 (c. 41). s. 8

The conciliation scheme which has been operating in the Principal Registry of the Family Division since 1 January 1983 has been modified from 14 October 1991 to reflect the changes brought about by the Children Act 1989.

1. *Referrals*

(1) The district judge may, at any time whilst considering arrangements for children under section 41 of the Matrimonial Causes Act 1973, direct a conciliation appointment.

(2) When an application is made for an order under section 8 of the Children Act 1989, it shall: (a) if it is an application for a residence or contact order, be referred for conciliation; (b) if it is an application for a prohibited steps or specific issue order, be referred only if the applicant so requests.

(3) The district judge may refer a summons for wardship to conciliation where orders under section 8 of the Act of 1989 are sought. This would normally be done at the first appointment.

2. *Procedure*

There will be one conciliation list on four days—Monday to Thursday—of each week. The district judge will be attended by a court welfare officer.

It is essential that both the parties and any legal advisers having conduct of the case attend the appointment. The nature of the application and matters in dispute will be outlined to the district judge and the welfare officer. If the dispute continues, the parties will be given the opportunity of retiring to a private room, together with the welfare officer, to attempt to reach agreement. These discussions will be privileged and will not be disclosed on any subsequent application. Anything which is said before the district judge on such appointments will also remain privileged.

The party who has living with him or her any child aged nine years or over, in respect of whom the matter concerns, should bring that child to the conciliation appointment. If only one of two or more children concerned is aged nine, the younger child or children may attend.

Any application to adjourn a conciliation appointment must be made to a district judge.

If the conciliation is successful the district judge will make such orders, if any, as may be appropriate.

If the conciliation proves unsuccessful the district judge will give directions (including timetabling) with a view to the early hearing and disposal of the application. In such cases that district judge and court welfare officer will not be further involved in that application.

Where in a matter referred by a district judge under paragraph 1(1) the conciliation appointment is concluded, a certificate shall be issued by the district judge dealing with the conciliation, that the court has complied with the requirements of section 41 of the Matrimonial Causes Act 1973.

Urgent applications made by summons will be referred to the district judge of the day to determine whether they are to be referred to conciliation.

The Practice Directions of 2 November 1982 (*Practice Direction (Family Division: Conciliation Procedure)* [1982] 1 W.L.R. 1420), 23 September 1983 and 31 October 1984 (*Practice Direction (Family Division: Conciliation Procedure) (No. 2)* [1984] 1 W.L.R. 1326) are cancelled, save in so far as they affect pending proceedings.

GERALD ANGEL
Senior District Judge

18 October 1991

PRACTICE STATEMENT (COMMERCIAL CASES: ALTERNATIVE   A3–008
DISPUTE RESOLUTION) (PRACTICE NOTE 1994)

Commercial Court - Practice - Alternative dispute resolution - Parties to be informed of most cost effective means of dispute resolution - Guide to Commercial Court Practice, Apps. IV, VI

While emphasising the primary role of the Commercial Court as a forum for deciding commercial cases the judges of the court wish to encourage parties to consider the use of alternative dispute resolution ("A.D.R.") (such as mediation and conciliation) as a possible additional means of resolving particular issues or disputes. The judges will not act as mediators or be involved in any A.D.R. process but will in appropriate cases invite parties to consider whether their case, or certain issues in their case, could be resolved by means of A.D.R. By way of example only, A.D.R. might be tried where the costs of litigation are likely to be wholly disproportionate to the amount at stake.

The Clerk to the Commercial Court will keep a list of individuals and bodies that offer mediation, conciliation and other A.D.R. services. It would be inappropriate for the Commercial Court to recommend any individual or organisation for this purpose. The list will also include individuals and bodies that offer arbitration services.

This practice statement will be drawn to the attention of all persons commencing proceedings in the Commercial List.

Appendix IV (Information for the Summons for Directions) and Appendix VI (Pre-Trial Check List) to the Guide to Commercial Court Practice (see *The Supreme Court Practice 1993*, vol. 1. paras. 72/A29, 72/A31) will be amended to include additional questions to ensure that legal advisers in all cases consider with their clients and the other parties concerned the possibility of attempting to resolve the particular dispute or particular issues by mediation, conciliation or otherwise.

While the Commercial Court will remain the appropriate forum for deciding most disputes in its list, legal advisers should ensure that parties are fully informed as to the most cost effective means of resolving the particular dispute.

CRESSWELL J.
Judge in charge of the Commercial List

10 December 1993

A3–009 Practice Direction (Civil Litigation: Case Management)

Practice - Civil litigation - Case management - Importance of reducing costs and delay of civil litigation - Moves to speed up civil litigation.

1. The paramount importance of reducing the cost and delay of civil litigation makes it necessary for judges sitting at first instance to assert greater control over the preparation for and conduct of hearings than has hitherto been customary. Failure by practitioners to conduct cases economically will be visited by appropriate orders for costs, including wasted costs orders.

2. The court will accordingly exercise its discretion to limit: (a) discovery; (b) the length of oral submissions; (c) the time allowed for the examination and cross-examination of witnesses; (d) the issues on which it wishes to be addressed; and (e) reading aloud from documents and authorities.

3. Unless otherwise ordered, every witness statement shall stand as the evidence-in-chief of the witness concerned.

4. RSC Ord 18, r 7 (facts, not evidence, to be pleaded) will be strictly enforced. In advance of trial parties should use their best endeavours to agree which are the issues or the main issues, and it is their duty so far as possible to reduce or eliminate the expert issues.

5. RSC Ord 34, r 10(2)(a) to (c) (the court bundle) will also be strictly enforced. Documents for use in court should be in A4 format where possible, contained in suitably secured bundles, and lodged with the court at least two clear days before the hearing of an application or a trial. Each bundle should be paginated, indexed, wholly legible, and arranged chronologically and contained in a ring binder or a lever-arch file. Where documents are copied unnecessarily or bundled incompetently the cost will be disallowed.

6. In cases estimated to last for more than ten days a pre-trial review should be applied for or in default may be appointed by the court. It should when practicable be conducted by the trial judge between eight and four weeks before the date of trial and should be attended by the advocates who are to represent the parties at trial.

7. Unless the court otherwise orders, there must be lodged with the listing officer (or equivalent) on behalf of each party no later than two months before the date of trial a completed pre-trial check-list in the form annexed to this practice direction.

8. Not less than three clear days before the hearing of an action or application each party should lodge with the court (with copies to other parties) a skeleton argument concisely summarising that party's submissions in relation to each of the issues, and citing the main authorities relied upon,

which may be attached. Skeleton arguments should be as brief as the nature of the issues allows, and should not without leave of the court exceed 20 pages of double-spaced A4 paper.

9. The opening speech should be succinct. At its conclusion other parties may be invited briefly to amplify their skeleton arguments. In a heavy case the court may in conjunction with final speeches require written submissions, including the findings of fact for which each party contends.

10. This direction applies to all lists in the Queen's Bench and Chancery Divisions, except where other directions specifically apply.

PRE-TRIAL CHECK-LIST
[Short title of action]
[Folio number]
[Trial date]
[Party lodging check-list]
[Name of solicitor]
[Name(s) of counsel for trial (if known)]

Setting down
1. Has the action been set down?

Pleadings
2. (a) Do you intend to make any amendment to your pleading?
(b) If so, when?

Interrogatories
3. (a) Are any interrogatories outstanding?
(b) If so, when served and upon whom?

Evidence
4. (a) Have all orders in relation to expert, factual and hearsay evidence been complied with? If not, specify what remains outstanding.
(b) Do you intend to serve/seek leave to serve/any further report or statement? If so, when and what report or statement?
(c) Have all other orders in relation to oral evidence been complied with?
(d) Do you require any further leave or orders in relation to evidence? If so, please specify and say when will you apply.
5. (a) What witnesses of fact do you intend to call? [Name]
(b) What expert witnesses do you intend to call? [Name]
(c) Will any witness require an interpreter? If so, which?

Documents
6. (a) Have all orders in relation to discovery been complied with?
(b) If not, what orders are outstanding?
(c) Do you intend to apply for any further orders relating to discovery?
(d) If so, what and when?
7. Will you not later than seven days before trial have prepared agreed paginated bundles of fully legible documents for the use of counsel and the court?

Pre-trial review

8. (a) Has a pre-trial review been ordered?

(b) If so, when is it to take place?

(c) If not, would it be useful to have one?

Length of trial

9. What are counsels' estimates of the minimum and maximum lengths of the trial? [The answer to question 9 should ordinarily be supported by an estimate of length signed by the counsel to be instructed.]

Alternative dispute resolution (See *Practice Note* [1994] 1 All ER 34, [1994] 1 WLR 14)

10. Have you or counsel discussed with your client(s) the possibility of attempting to resolve this dispute (or particular issues) by alternative dispute resolution (ADR)?

11. Might some form of ADR procedure assist to resolve or narrow the issues in this case?

12. Have you or your client(s) explored with the other parties the possibility of resolving this dispute (or particular issues) by ADR?

[Signature of the solicitor, date]

Note This check-list must be lodged not later than two months before the date of hearing with copies to the other parties.

Lord Taylor of Gosforth Q.C.

January 24, 1995

Practice Statement (Court of Appeal: Procedural Changes)

A3–010 *Court of Appeal (Civil Division) - Limiting oral arguments in certain applications - Skeleton arguments - Documentation - Core bundles - Mediation.*

1. As reported in successive Reviews of the Legal Year, there has been an alarming increase in the backlog of unheard appeals in the Court of Appeal and a corresponding increase in the delay before most appeals can be heard. These results have occurred despite increases in the judicial strength and the professional and administrative support of the court and despite measures introduced to weed out appeals with no prospect of success.

2. It is now generally accepted that steps must be taken to improve existing procedures and (in particular) shorten the time currently spent on oral argument of cases in court. With the help of the Court of Appeal Users' Committee (representing judges, barristers, solicitors and the Citizens' Advice Bureaux) the judges of the Court of Appeal have considered, at some length, how to achieve these ends without undermining the quality or fairness of the court's decisions.

3. The accompanying practice direction (see [1995] 1 W.L.R. 1191) (which comes into force on 4 September 1995) aims to ensure that applications and appeals are handled and decided as efficiently and expeditiously as is

practicable in current circumstances consistently with fairness and sound decision-making.

4. It is plain that paper applications for leave to appeal can be more expeditiously and efficiently considered if the documents submitted are limited to those truly necessary to enable a Lord Justice to decide whether the prospective appellant has an arguable ground of appeal. The same is true of applications for leave which proceed to an oral hearing. At present it is frequently the practice to burden the court with much irrelevant documentation. This practice must cease. The Lord Justice's decision will also be facilitated by a clear summary of the argument which the prospective appellant wishes to pursue. Where a Lord Justice has familiarised himself with the issues and has granted leave to appeal or ordered a hearing of the application for leave inter partes, it will often be convenient and possible for directions to be given for the lodging of sequential (and therefore responsive) skeleton arguments and for a maximum period to be allotted to each party for oral presentation of its case in court.

5. In the absence of specific directions, the court will expect oral argument in support of applications for leave to appeal to be confined to a maximum of 20 minutes and oral argument in support of renewed applications for leave to move for judicial review to be confined to a maximum of 30 minutes. It is hoped that it may prove possible, in the light of experience, to shorten these periods without detriment to the fairness of the outcome. In either of these cases short skeleton arguments will be required.

6. The consultations the court has conducted, and its own experience, suggest that pre-hearing procedures should in many cases differ, depending on the expected length of the hearing.

7. For shorter appeals the existing procedures on the whole operate satisfactorily, *provided* the time limit for delivery of skeleton arguments is observed (as it too frequently is not). The court hopes that it may increasingly be able to read the judgment appealed from, the notice of appeal, the skeleton arguments and the key documents sufficiently far in advance of the hearing to enable it to judge, and inform the parties, of the time which will be allowed to each party for oral argument.

8. For longer appeals it will often be desirable that skeleton arguments should be prepared and lodged with the court at an earlier stage. The advantages are: (1) skeleton arguments can then be exchanged sequentially, which has the benefit that they are responsive to each other; (2) it may in some cases be advantageous to invite the parties to attend a directions hearing, probably conducted by a single Lord Justice, in advance of the main hearing, with a view to simplifying and streamlining the conduct of the hearing; (3) consideration can be given to allotting periods of time for the presentation of oral argument, with knowledge of what is to be argued.

9. The court is reluctant, unless obliged, to lay down rules governing the length, format and layout of skeleton arguments. It is, however, concerned at the observable tendency of some counsel to settle skeleton arguments which exceed all reasonable bounds. It considers that in a one to two day appeal on a point of law against a final order, the skeleton argument should not ordinarily exceed a maximum of ten pages. If the appeal is on fact, a maximum of 15 pages will ordinarily suffice. In longer appeals it may, but

need not, be necessary to submit a somewhat longer skeleton. These specified maxima should not be treated as establishing a norm. A sound argument can usually be briefly summarised, and such a summary is ordinarily the more effective for being more readily assimilated.

10. A large percentage of skeleton arguments are currently lodged late, often very late. This has the result that much administrative time in the Civil Appeals Office is devoted to pursuing overdue skeleton arguments, and also that the court is denied the opportunity of considering the argument when pre-reading the case. The reason for lateness sometimes is that solicitors fail to provide the papers and instructions to counsel in time for counsel to draft the skeleton argument, and sometimes that counsel fail to set aside time to undertake this task, in good time before the deadline for lodging it. Timely delivery of skeleton arguments calls for realistic co-operation between solicitors and counsel. The court would remind solicitors of their duty to give counsel all necessary papers and instructions in good time: while some cases will require more time, it is suggested that counsel should be provided with all necessary papers and instructions to draft the skeleton argument at least two to three weeks before the deadline for lodging it. The court would also remind counsel and their clerks of their duty to ensure that enough time is set aside for the task to be completed in time.

11. In the light of the experience of the court and technical changes in recent years, the current practice directions governing the documentation in appeals and applications call for revision. Revised directions are given in the accompanying practice direction.

12. By the time cases come before the Court of Appeal, whether on applications or appeals, the issues have usually narrowed and much of the documentation placed before the court below, if ever relevant, is no longer so. Parties must take care to ensure that the materials placed before the Court of Appeal are those reasonably thought to be necessary for decision of the issues before the court. If anything of relevance is omitted, it can be called for. There is no justification for the cost and labour involved in the preparation of bundles which are never read or referred to. Attention is drawn to the court's powers under RSC Ord 62, r 11, and to its power to invite the taxing master to consider the cost of unnecessary copying.

13. Particular attention must be paid to the preparation and provision of core bundles, which are in cases other than the shortest an indispensable aid to effective pre-reading. A core bundle is required in any case where the appeal bundle (excluding the judgment appealed against) would comprise more than 100 pages. The provision of core bundles is frequently overlooked. There are also a number of misconceptions about them: it is supposed by some that the core bundle itself should not exceed a set number of pages, and that the core bundle need only contain documents which were not in the trial bundles in the court below (such as the notice of appeal and the order appealed against). The court will expect the rules on core bundles to be strictly observed.

14. The practice hitherto has been that appellants are not required to provide respondents with copies of appeal bundles, but merely a copy of the index. The court has decided to change that practice, to avoid the time and expense (which can be considerable) of the respondent's solicitors having to

prepare bundles for themselves and their advocate from an index, and to reduce the number of occasions on which the parties' advocates find themselves working with different bundles.

15. Since the issue of the practice direction on 22 October 1986 (see [1986] 3 All ER 630, [1986] 1 WLR 1318) recording facilities have been introduced for hearings before Queen's Bench judges in chambers and in certain county courts, and the practice of judges handing down judgments has become much more widespread. To take account of these and other changes, that practice direction has been amended and appears in its revised form as Part II of the accompanying practice direction.

16. The court hopes that it may be possible to identify cases which might be susceptible to settlement by mediation. Such resort to mediation cannot, in the absence of rule changes, be other than voluntary, and it is not thought likely that mediation will be fruitful in a majority of appeals. It is, however, thought that some appeals may be found to be capable of resolution by mediation and it is hoped to introduce a trial scheme. If any party to an appeal (appellant or respondent) considers that the appeal might be resolved by mediation, an indication to that effect may be given in confidence to the Registrar of Civil Appeals.

Sir Thomas Bingham M. R.

July 26, 1995

Practice Statement (Commercial Cases: Alternative Dispute Resolution) (No. 2)

A3–011

Commercial Court - Practice - Alternative dispute resolution - Early neutral evaluation - Role of judge.

On 10 December 1993 Cresswell J issued a practice statement ([1994] 1 WLR 14) on the subject of alternative dispute resolution (ADR) indicating that the judges of the Commercial Court wished to encourage parties to consider the use of ADR. In consequence of that practice statement, amendments were made to the standard questions to be answered by the parties in preparation for the summons for directions and to the standard questions to be answered as part of the pre-trial check list. Additional questions were inserted in order to direct the attention of the parties and their legal advisers to ADR as a means of settling their disputes. By that practice direction, legal advisers were urged to ensure that parties were fully informed as to the most cost effective means of resolving the particular dispute.

The judges of the Commercial Court in conjunction with the Commercial Court Committee have recently considered whether it is now desirable that any further steps should be taken to encourage the wider use of ADR as a means of settling disputes pending before the court. In the belief that, whereas the Commercial Court will remain an entirely appropriate forum for resolving most of the disputes which are commenced before it, the settlement of actions by means of ADR (i) significantly helps to save litigants the ever-mounting cost of bringing their cases to trial; (ii) saves them the delay of litigation in reaching finality in their disputes; (iii) enables them to achieve settlement of their disputes while preserving their existing commercial relationships and market reputation; (iv) provides them with a wider range of settlement solutions than those offered by litigation; and (v) is likely to make a substantial contribution to the more efficient use of judicial resources, the judges will henceforth adopt the following practice on the hearing of the first inter partes summons at which directions for the interlocutory progress of the action are given or at subsequent inter partes hearings at which such directions are sought.

If it should appear to the judge that the action before him or any of the issues arising in it are particularly appropriate for an attempt at settlement by ADR techniques but that the parties have not previously attempted settlement by such means, he may invite the parties to take positive steps to set in motion ADR procedures. The judge may, if he considers it appropriate, adjourn the proceedings then before him for a specified period of time to encourage and enable the parties to take such steps. He may for this purpose extend the time for compliance by the parties or either of them with any requirement under the rules or previous interlocutory orders in the proceedings.

If, after discussion with those representing the parties, it appears to the judge that an early neutral evaluation is likely to assist in the resolution of the matters in dispute, he may offer to provide that evaluation himself or to arrange for another judge to do so. If that course is accepted by the parties, the judge may thereupon give directions as to such preparatory steps for that evaluation and the form which it is to take as he considers appropriate. The parties will in that event be required to arrange with the Commercial Court Listing Office the time for the evaluation hearing, having regard to the availability of the judge concerned.

Where early neutral evaluation is provided by a judge, that judge will, unless the parties otherwise agree, take no further part in the proceedings either for the purpose of the hearing of summonses or as trial judge.

Except where an early neutral evaluation is to be provided by a judge, the parties will be responsible for agreeing upon a neutral for the purposes of ADR and will be responsible for his fees and expenses. As indicated in the practice statement on ADR made by Cresswell J on 10 December 1993, the Clerk to the Commercial Court keeps a list of individuals and bodies that offer mediation, conciliation and other ADR services. If, after ADR has been recommended to them by the judge, the parties are unable to agree upon a neutral for ADR, they may by consent refer to the judge for assistance in reaching such agreement.

On the hearing of any summons in the course of which the judge invites the parties to take steps to resolve their differences by ADR, he may on that occasion make such order as to the costs that the parties may incur by reason of their using or attempting to use ADR as may in all the circumstances seem appropriate.

Should the parties be unable to resolve their differences by ADR or otherwise within the period of any such adjournment as may be ordered, they may restore the summons for directions or other summons for the purpose of reporting back to the judge what progress has been made by way of ADR (such report to cover only the process adopted and its outcome, not the substantive contact between the parties and their advisers) and whether further time is required for the purposes of ADR and, where efforts towards settlement by means of ADR have proved fruitless, for the purpose of obtaining further interlocutory directions in the proceedings.

Parties to pending proceedings who consider that ADR might be an appropriate form of dispute resolution for those proceedings or who wish to discuss the applicability of ADR with a commercial judge will be strongly encouraged to bring on the summons for directions at an earlier stage in the proceedings than would otherwise be justifiable. The fact that in such a case pleadings have not yet closed or that discovery has not yet been completed will not be regarded by the court as a reason for declining to consider the applicability of ADR in that case.

Waller J.

June 7, 1996

Practice Note (Arbitration: New Procedures) A3–012

Arbitration - Practice - Arbitration applications - New procedures - R.S.C. Ord. 73.

Although it will be widely known that the Arbitration Act 1996 comes into effect on 31 January 1997, it may well not yet be appreciated by the profession that, in order to give effect to the new Act, an entirely new Ord 73 of the Rules of the Supreme Court is to come into force on the same day (see the Rules of the Supreme Court (Amendment) 1996, SI 1996/3219, r 5).

There will apply to arbitrations governed by the new Act substantially different procedures to those which now apply. In general, the new Act will apply to all arbitrations commenced on or after 31 January 1997. Part I of the new Ord 73 sets out the new procedures which are to apply to those arbitrations. The new Act and Pt I of the order will also apply to applications to the court made on or after 31 January in respect of arbitrations yet to be commenced at the time of the application.

For arbitrations commenced before 31 January 1997 the new Act will not apply and for applications to the court in respect of such arbitrations and for applications made before that date in respect of arbitrations yet to be commenced and also in respect of arbitrations commenced on or after 31 January, the applicable procedure will be almost identical to that now in force but will be subject to very minor alterations. That procedure is set out in Pt II of the new order.

Part III of the new order relates to enforcement of arbitration awards and introduces a procedural regime of universal application regardless of the date when the arbitration was commenced.

Amongst the most important procedural changes introduced by the new Ord 73 is that providing for a new multi-purpose form of originating process and of subsidiary process in existing proceedings to be known as an 'arbitration application'.

The form is to be used for all applications in respect of arbitrations to which the 1996 Act applies except enforcement and including applications to stay judicial proceedings, to determine issues as to jurisdiction, to enforce peremptory orders, to make orders in support of arbitral proceedings, to challenge awards on the grounds of want of jurisdiction or serious irregularity and to appeals on a question of law arising out of an award.

In conjunction with the introduction of the new uniform process for arbitration applications Ord 73, r 13 introduces a comprehensive series of directions relating to such applications which will apply automatically unless the court otherwise orders. The judges of the Commercial Court will require strict compliance with these directions except with leave of the court. Parties who do not comply will be at risk as to the dates of their hearings being vacated and/or as to adverse costs orders.

Applications for leave to appeal on a question of law arising out of an award will be determined without a hearing unless the court considers that one is required as provided by s 69(5) of the 1996 Act. Apart from the substantive hearing of appeals and of preliminary points of law, all arbitration applications will be heard in chambers unless the court orders that the hearing be in open court.

The time limit for applications challenging an award is extended from 21 to 28 days. The court may without a hearing extend that time limit upon application.

An important change in service of arbitration applications on overseas parties to arbitrations is introduced by Ord 73, r 7(2). Where an overseas party has been represented by an English solicitor who was authorised to accept service of notices or documents in the arbitration and has not determined that solicitor's authority to act in the arbitration, the arbitration application can be served on that solicitor and it will be unnecessary to obtain leave to serve the party outside the jurisdiction.

The Commercial Court will continue to have primary responsibility for the administration and monitoring of the supervisory jurisdiction over arbitrations and awards under the 1996 Act. Although such applications can be made not only in the Commercial Court but also in the mercantile courts and the Central London Country Court Business List, the decision whether to retain the application or to transfer it to the Commercial Court or to some other court is to be taken by the mercantile or business list judge, as the case may be, but in consultation with the judge in charge of the Commercial List.

In giving effect to the 1996 Act and to the new Ord 73, the judges of the Commercial Court will endeavour as far as possible to achieve consistency in matters of construction both of the Act and of the new Ord 73. In order to facilitate consistency of approach, arrangements have been made for decisions on matters of construction and application to be circulated between the judges immediately they are given. Investigations are in progress as to the feasibility of the wider circulation of these decisions to the rest of the profession without the delay ordinarily entailed in awaiting published reports. Since most of the judgments on arbitration applications are likely to be given in chambers, it is hoped that all parties will co-operate in facilitating publication of those judgments which are concerned with matters of construction or application of the 1996 Act and the new Ord 73.

It is impossible to envisage in advance every problem that may arise in relation to the operation of the new Act by the new Ord 73. In the course of the next few months there will be developing experience of the working of the new regime. Members of the profession who identify particular problems in the working of the new Ord 73 are strongly encouraged to bring them to the attention of the judge in charge of the Commercial Court List to enable the judges to carry out their function of monitoring the effective working of the Act and the new Ord 73.

Colman J.

January 13, 1997

Practice Direction (Family Division: Family Proceedings: Financial Dispute Resolution)

A3–011

Practice - Family proceedings - Ancillary relief - Concilation - Financial dispute resolution appointment - Admissibility in evidence of things said during appointment - Court's expectations of parties and legal representatives

1. This direction applies to all ancillary relief applications under rr 2.70 to 2.77 of the Family Proceedings Rules 1991, SI 1991/1247.

2. The Family Proceedings (Amendment No 2) Rules 1997, SI 1997/1056, which came into force on 21 April 1997, incorporate into the Family Proceedings Rules 1991 the new ancillary relief procedure which was initially introduced by the direction of 25 July 1996. The new procedure is intended to reduce delay, facilitate settlements, limit costs incurred by parties and provide the court with more effective control over the conduct of the proceedings than exists at present.

3. A key element in the procedure is the financial dispute resolution (FDR) appointment. Rule 2.75(1) provides that the FDR appointment is to be treated as a meeting held for the purposes of conciliation. Conciliation has been developed as a means of reducing the tension which inevitably arises in matrimonial and family disputes. In order for it to be effective, parties must be able to approach conciliation openly and without reserve. Non-disclosure of the content of conciliation meetings is accordingly vital. The FDR appointment is part of the conciliation process and should be so regarded by the courts and the parties. As a consequence of *Re D and anor (minors) (conciliation: disclosure of information)* [1993] 2 All E.R. 693, [1993] Fam. 231, evidence of anything said or of any admission made in the course of an FDR appointment will not be admissible in evidence, except at the trial of a person for an offence committed at the appointment or in the very exceptional circumstances indicated in *Re D*.

4. Courts will therefore expect:
- parties to make offers and proposals
- recipients of offers and proposals to given them proper consideration

- that parties, whether separately or together, will not seek to exclude from consideration at the appointment any such offer or proposal.

5. In order to make the most effective use of the first appointment and the FDR appointment, the legal representatives attending those appointments will be expected to have full knowledge of the case.

6. The direction of 25 July 1996 is withdrawn.

7. Issued with the concurrence of the Lord Chancellor.

SIR STEPHEN BROWN P.

June 16, 1997

GLOSSARY

TERMS AND ABBREVIATIONS

AAA: American Arbitration Association.

ACAS: A statutory body, the Advisory, Conciliation and Arbitration Service, which is designed to provide an independent industrial relations service to industry.

Adjudication: Generically, a dispute resolution process in which a neutral third party hears each party's case and makes a decision which is binding on them. There are various forms of adjudication, for example litigation and arbitration; also in some jurisdictions, private judging. There is also a more specific meaning in some industries, particularly the construction industry, of a procedure by which a neutral adjudicator is empowered and required by contract to make summary binding decisions about disputes arising under that contract without following litigation or arbitration procedures. This specialised meaning, also called "fast track adjudication" and "interim adjudication", generally provides for the determination to be binding only until the parties have reached some further agreement on the issue or have taken it to litigation or arbitration.

ADR: See Alternative Dispute Resolution.

Adversarial process: A process in which each party to a dispute presents his case to the other(s) and to a neutral adjudicator, seeking to demonstrate the correctness of his own case and the wrongness of the other(s). It may be distinguished from consensual ADR processes, which may be more problem-solving, or from an inquisitorial approach, in which a neutral investigator seeks to establish the truth by making inquiries of the parties and others, as used in certain countries in Europe.

Advisory mediation: This term is used by ACAS (the Advisory, Conciliation and Arbitration Service) to refer to the facilitation of joint discussions and procedures between employers, employees and employee representatives and by the use of joint working parties and workshops.

Alternative Dispute Resolution (ADR): This term covers an agglomeration of dispute resolution procedures which are alternatives to litigation. They usually entail helping the parties to arrive at a negotiated agreement, often but not necessarily using a third party neutral. Arbitration is sometimes included in the term ADR; but as it is now in the mainstream of adjudicatory processes and as it is adversarial rather than consensual, the term ADR often excludes arbitration, sometimes but not invariably being used to refer only to consensual processes. Some practitioners do not consider that the term "alternative" should apply to mediation and other processes that should be viewed as primary dispute resolution methods. See also "Dispute resolution" and "Dispute management".

Amiable composition: The power which may be given to arbitrators in certain civil law jurisdictions to render an award according to what they believe to be just and fair, so as to be able to introduce principles of equity to the applicable substantive law.

Arbitration: A dispute resolution process in which the issues are adjudicated upon by a neutral third party who is either selected privately by them or under some agreement for his or her private selection and/or who acts under the rules of arbitration, and whose decision is binding on them.

BALM: British Association of Lawyer Mediators.

Baseball arbitration: See "Final offer arbitration".

BATNA: "The Best Alternative to a Negotiated Agreement" or the best outcome which a party can achieve if the matter is not settled by negotiation. A concept introduced by Fisher & Ury in *Getting to Yes* as the standard against which a proposed settlement can be measured. See also WATNA.

Brainstorming: Putting forward as many ideas and options as possible as they come to mind without at that stage inhibiting their flow by examining them individually.

CALM: Comprehensive Accredited Lawyer Mediators (Scotland).

Case evaluation: See "evaluation".

Caucusing: One of the procedures used in mediation in which the mediator meets the parties to a dispute separately, as part of a strategy to assist in the resolution of the dispute. This is often part of a process of shuttle diplomacy in which the mediator moves backwards and forwards between the parties, caucusing each in turn, in order to try to narrow the issues between them with a view to eventual resolution. In the field of industrial relations, the term "caucus" has a different meaning, being used to relate to a private meeting that a conciliator has with negotiators from both sides.

CEDR: Centre for Dispute Resolution.

Co-mediation: Mediation by two or more mediators who may be from the same or different disciplines and who may work in tandem or share different tasks within the mediation, or both.

Complementary Dispute Resolution: A form of ADR used as an adjunct to the litigation system, such as court-annexed arbitration, court-annexed mediation or private judging.

Conciliation: This term is often used interchangeably with mediation though conciliation is often viewed as being more facilitative and non-interventionist, whereas mediation is seen as allowing for more mediator pro-activity. Sometimes however the reverse usage is employed: there is no consistency. It is sometimes used as a generic term to cover third-party facilitation generally. The Finer Committee (1974) called it "a process of engendering common sense, reasonableness and agreement". Conciliation in the family context should not be confused with "reconciliation", nor is this generally the objective, though it may sometimes be a consequence.

Concilio-arbitration: Could refer to med–arb or to a process for a "concilio-arbitrator" to consider the case informally and make a non-binding award along the lines of an arbitrator in the court-annexed arbitration model.

Conflict: A state of incompatibility of interests, objectives or positions between people or groups. It may include a dispute, which is a form of conflict that is justiciable.

Consensual processes: Processes of dispute resolution based on the parties having to reach agreement in order for the issues to be resolved, such as negotiation and mediation. They are distinct from adjudicatory processes, in which a third party can impose a binding decision upon them, such as litigation and arbitration.

Consensus-building: Used particularly, but not exclusively, in public policy, environmental and employment mediation, this involves engaging all stakeholders in a process of participative and collaborative problem-solving, so that they can be effectively heard and their views taken into account.

Court-annexed (or court-ordered) arbitration: A form of arbitration by a court-approved neutral. In various models of this, the neutral's finding is initially non-binding, but it will become binding if neither party seeks a rehearing by a judge. Sanctions, such as a costs award, may be applied to an applicant for a rehearing who does not materially improve his position at a trial.

Court-annexed (or court-ordered) mediation: Mediation ordered by or arranged through a court, and undertaken by a judicial officer or a court welfare officer, or by an outside third party approved by the court.

CPR: CPR Institute for Dispute Resolution (United States).

Culpa in contrahendo: A doctrine developed by courts and commentators in some civil law systems under which the mere initiation of negotiation creates a pre-contractual relationship as a matter of law which, *inter alia,* imposes on the negotiating parties a reciprocal duty of care.

Dispute: A dispute is a disagreement about an issue or issues which are capable of being decided upon by a third party, that is to say, they are justiciable.

Dispute management: Some practitioners consider that "dispute resolution" is a less accurate term for what they provide than "dispute management", in which they help disputing parties to manage, rather than necessarily resolve, their disputes. There are similar distinctions between "conflict resolution" and "conflict management".

Dispute resolution: The determination of a dispute, which is generally achieved by adjudication or by an agreed settlement between the parties. A distinction is sometimes drawn between a "settlement" which merely indicates that terms have been agreed to end the dispute though the underlying issues may not have been disposed of, and a "resolution" which infers that all issues have been satisfactorily resolved and determined. However, settlement is generally equated with resolution. The term "dispute resolution" is also sometimes used instead of "alternative dispute resolution", indicating that ADR processes should not be regarded as "alternative". See also "Dispute management".

Dispute review board: Also called a "dispute resolution committee", this is a board set up at the commencement of a contract, particularly in the construction industry, to consider and try to deal with disputes as they arise, through informal meetings and discussions, and perhaps also by interim adjudication.

Early neutral evaluation (ENE): A process developed in the Northern District of California for a neutral evaluator to meet parties at an early stage of a case in order to make a confidential assessment of the dispute. Partly this procedure helps them to narrow and define the issues, and partly it promotes efforts to arrive at a settlement.

Evaluation: This term has two usages. Generically, it is a non-binding expression of opinion about the merits of issues between parties. It is sometimes also used to refer to assessing the merits of proposed settlement terms. More specifically, as a process in its own right, evaluation (or "case evaluation") is used as a non-binding ADR process. Under it, a case may be submitted to an evaluator or an expert panel, who can consider submissions and if necessary hear witnesses. The evaluator or panel then makes a reasoned, non-binding evaluation of the case that can be used in attempts to facilitate settlement. See also "Early neutral evaluation".

Ex aequo et bono: Principle of dealing fairly and in good faith.

Executive Tribunal: Term used by CEDR to describe the mini-trial.

Expert determination or appraisal: A procedure whereby a dispute, perhaps of a technical nature, is to be resolved by an expert, nominated or identifiable, whose decision is to be final and binding on the parties, and who need not follow the rules of arbitration or litigation.

Facilitation: The assistance provided to the parties to a dispute by a third party, usually neutral, to help them to deal constructively with the issues between them.

Fact-finding expert: See "Neutral fact-finding expert".

Fast track adjudication: See "Adjudication".

Final offer arbitration: Also known as "pendulum arbitration", "flip flop arbitration" and as "baseball arbitration" because of its usage in relation to the resolution of disagreements concerning the salaries of baseball players in the United States. Each party makes a final settlement offer and the arbitrator chooses the one considered more reasonable. This puts both sides under pressure to submit a reasonable offer.

Flip flop arbitration: See "Final offer arbitration".

FMA: Family Mediators Association.

FMS: Family Mediation Scotland.

High-low contract: Used in the United States to refer to a procedure in which parties agree to adjudication, but limit the parameters of the financial award. For example, a personal injury claim may be referred to court on the issue of liability only on the terms that if the finding is for the plaintiff, an agreed sum will be payable which will be less than the plaintiff was hoping for. If the finding is in favour of the defendant, there will nevertheless be a payment of an agreed smaller sum to the plaintiff. This allows each party to hedge against an adverse award.

Hybrid processes: Dispute resolution processes created by drawing on the primary processes and using them in different ways or permutations; such as mini-trial, med–arb or moderated settlement conference.

ICC: International Chamber of Commerce.

Impasse strategies: Strategies and tactics employed by a neutral to try to overcome a deadlock in negotiations.

Interim adjudication: See "Adjudication".

653

Intermediate dispute resolution: A procedure, especially in the construction industry, by which contracting parties provide in their contract for the appointment of a neutral third party or board to deal with or advise on the resolution of disputes progressively as they arise. This may be through mediation or informal adjudication.

Judicial settlement conference: An ADR procedure used in United States state and federal courts in which the judge convenes a meeting in his or her chambers to see whether the parties can find a basis for settlement by agreement without a trial.

Kompetenz–Kompetenz: The extent of the arbitrator's power to decide upon his own jurisdiction, when the validity of an arbitration agreement is in question and the clause providing for arbitration is contained in that agreement.

LCIA: London Court of International Arbitration.

Litigation: A dispute resolution process in which the issues are argued before and adjudicated upon by a judge or other State-appointed official, whose decision is binding on them.

Med–arb: Med–arb refers to "mediation–arbitration" and is a composite of these two procedures. A neutral is required to mediate, and if this fails, to go on to make a binding decision by way of arbitration. In some versions the parties are given the option to decide whether or not to proceed to arbitration before its commencement; in others the arbitration is non-binding, for guidance of the parties only.

Mediation: A facilitative process in which disputing parties engage the assistance of an impartial mediator, who has no authority to make any decisions for them, but who uses certain procedures, techniques and skills to help them to resolve their dispute by negotiated agreement without adjudication. Mediation is invariably interest-based (parties are helped to explore and enhance their mutual interests). In some models where rights are relevant, the mediator may, with the parties' agreement, in some way evaluate the merits. This can help parties to have regard to such rights if that is what they wish. The term "mediation" is sometimes used interchangeably with "conciliation". Sometimes mediation is understood to be more pro-active and evaluative than conciliation, which is more facilitative; and sometimes the reverse usage is used. There is no national or international consistency of usage.

Michigan mediation (Michigan evaluation): A form of case evaluation developed in Michigan, USA in which a panel meets the parties' lawyers separately to seek an agreed settlement. Failing agreement, the panel makes its own settlement proposals, which become binding if not objected to within a specified period. The use of the term "mediation" is now said by its proponents to be misleading and is being dropped in favour of "evaluation".

Mini-trial: (Called an "executive tribunal" by CEDR.) A procedure in which the parties (or in the case of corporations, their senior executives), with the help of a neutral, observe an abbreviated form of non-binding trial, presented by their respective lawyers so that they may assess relative strengths and weaknesses, and then enter into settlement negotiations. The neutral helps clarify the issues, assess the presentations, and evaluate the case; and may assist the parties with their negotiations and/or provide a non-binding opinion. Thus the mini-trial may be a form of evaluative mediation.

Moderated settlement conference: This is a modification of court-annexed arbitration but instead of an arbitrator, there is a panel of impartial third parties.

Multi-door courthouse: The concept of a court official making a preliminary case analysis and then providing or referring disputants to a wide range of dispute resolution facilities and processes and not merely litigation. A number of American cities or counties offer multi-door programmes.

NFM: National Family Mediation.

Negotiation: Discussions or dealings about a matter, with a view to reconciling differences and establishing areas of agreement, settlement or compromise.

Neutral: A third party who is independent of the parties in dispute and neutral in relation to their issues, and who assists them in the resolution of their dispute by acting as a mediator or conciliator or other ADR practitioner. Neutrality may be thought to imply that personal values will not be brought into the process. Some only use the adjective "neutral" in relation to outcome rather than process. Generally, the concept of neutrality is given its Oxford dictionary usage as "not helping or supporting either of two opposing sides, especially states at war or in dispute".

Neutral fact-finding expert: A neutral expert appointed by parties to investigate facts and to form a legal or technical view either about certain specified issues, or on all issues generally, and to make a non-binding report to the parties. The neutral may facilitate subsequent settlement discussions. The neutral's report may by agreement be open to the court in any subsequent proceedings, without precluding any party from submitting further evidence and expert reports.

Ombudsman: An independent person who deals with complaints by the public against administrative and organisational injustice and maladministration in certain specified areas, with the power to investigate, criticise, make issues public and sometimes with limited powers to award compensation.

Partisan: A third party who supports one of the parties to a dispute, whether personally or professionally, and who does not have or profess neutrality.

Partnering: A voluntary, non-binding collaborative process used mainly in the construction industry that focuses on solving common problems between different groups, such as owners, designers and builders, working on the same project. It is primarily a means of dispute prevention.

Pendulum arbitration: See "Final offer arbitration".

Primary processes: The primary procedures used for dispute resolution, namely negotiation, mediation and adjudication. (Adjudication is sometimes divided further into sub-categories including litigation, arbitration and statutory and administrative determination). When elements are drawn from the primary processes and rearranged into new permutations these are known as hybrid processes.

Private judging: A process introduced by law into certain jurisdictions in which the court refers the case to a referee chosen by the parties to decide some or all of the issues, or to establish any specific facts. The referee is given most of the powers of a judge, and the referee's report to the court stands as an enforceable, binding and appealable judgment.

Privilege: The right in the law of evidence of a person to insist on there being withheld from a judicial tribunal information which might assist it to ascertain certain facts relevant to an issue upon which it is adjudicating.

Reconciliation: Literally the restoration of friendly relations after an estrangement. In divorce terms, it is the decision by a couple to try to re-establish their marriage relationship after a separation or other differences. It is sometimes confused with the similar-sounding word "conciliation" which has a different meaning.

Reframing: This refers to a communication technique which changes the frame of reference against which an event is viewed by a person, so that the judgment placed on that event takes a different meaning or perspective and it can be seen in a different light. More loosely, it is a redefining of issues or of views in a more constructive way.

"Rent-a-Judge": See "Private judging".

Reparation: A process in the criminal justice system in which an offender makes voluntary restitution to the victim by paying compensation, performing a service or apologising, which may be accomplished through mediation.

Settlement: Conclusion of a dispute by agreement, generally implying some compromise between the parties.

SFLA: Solicitors' Family Law Association.

Shuttle diplomacy (or shuttle mediation): A term used where a mediator caucuses with each party in turn as part of a strategy to narrow and help resolve the issues between them. It is based on the activities of diplomats who go back and forth between the representatives of countries or groups in dispute, to try to resolve their differences by agreement.

SPIDR: Society of Professionals in Dispute Resolution.

Stakeholders: This term is used to refer to the parties to a public issue or environmental mediation. Stakeholders may not necessarily be easily identified and there may be a large number of them. Some may share common interests, others may have opposing interests, and others may have varying or overlapping interests.

Summary jury trial: A U.S. adaptation of the mini-trial in which cases are presented to mock juries, who make findings which indicate to the parties the likely reaction of a real jury to the issues, and which help them to engage realistically in settlement negotiations.

Transformative mediation: This term has developed from the transformative approach to mediation suggested by Robert A. Baruch Bush and Joseph P. Folger in their 1994 book, *The Promise of Mediation.* Instead of basing mediation on a problem-solving approach, it suggests a theoretical framework for understanding conflict and mediation based on mediation's potential for growth in strengthening both the self and the capacity for experiencing and expressing concern and consideration for others. These potential outcomes are achieved through "empowerment" and "recognition".

UNCITRAL: The United Nations Commission on International Trade Laws, which has developed a set of uniform arbitral rules, the UNCITRAL rules, for world-wide use. Although these rules have been adopted in Scotland, they have not been adopted in England.

WATNA: "The Worst Alternative to a Negotiated Agreement". A development introduced by John Haynes of Fisher & Ury's BATNA, being the worst anticipated outcome if a dispute is not settled by negotiation.

Win–win: The concept that parties can arrive at settlements (often arrived at through using problem-solving techniques) in which each gains some advantage, rather than an adjudicated resolution in which generally one party will win and the other will lose. The opposite of a zero-sum game.

Zero-sum game: A situation in which there is no room for a win–win resolution, because every penny gained by one party must necessarily involve a loss of that amount by the other without room for any advantage to accrue to the latter.

Zone of agreement: The parameters of the range of possible terms of settlement within which a particular dispute may be resolved.

BIBLIOGRAPHY

The following authorities have been cited in this book or are considered to be of possible interest to readers:

BOOKS, DIRECTORIES, JOURNALS (MARKED*) AND REPORTS

Abel, Richard L. (ed.), *The Politics of Informal Justice* (New York: Academic Press, 1982).

ACAS, Annual Reports 1988–1998.

Acland, Andrew Floyer, *A Sudden Outbreak of Common Sense: Managing Conflict through Mediation* (London: Hutchinson Business Books, 1990).

———, *Resolving Disputes Without Going to Court* (London: Century Books, 1995).

Alternatives, Center for Public Resources, New York.

Arbitration, Chartered Institute of Arbitrators.

Arbitration and Dispute Resolution Law Journal The,– Lloyd's of London Press, London.

Attorney General's Working Party Report on Alternative Dispute Resolution (Victoria (Aus.), 1990).

A-Z of Ombudsmen: A Guide to Ombudsman schemes in Britain and Ireland (London: National Consumer Council, 1997).

Bar Council Report, Committee on ADR chaired by Rt. Hon. Lord Justice Beldam (1991).

Bartels, M. *Contractual Adaptation and Conflict Resolution* (1985).

———, *Commercial Arbitration for the 1990's* (Deventer: Kluwer, 1985).

Beer, Jennifer E. (ed.), *Peacemaking in Your Neighbourhood: Mediator's Handbook* (Philadelphia: Friends Conflict Resolution Programs, 1990).

——— & Eileen Stief, *Mediator's Handbook* (New Society Press, 1997).

Belshaw, Chris & Mike Strutt, *Couples in Crisis: Does Your Relationship Have a Future?* (Revised ed.) (London: Ward Lock, 1996).

Berne, Eric, *Games People Play: The Psychology of Human Relationships* (New York: Penguin Books Limited, 1964).

Bernstein, Ronald Q.C., John A. Tackaberry Q.C., Derek Wood Q.C. and Arthur L. Marriott Q.C. (eds.), *Handbook of Arbitration Practice* (London: Sweet & Maxwell/Chartered Institute of Arbitrators, 3rd edition 1997).

Bevan, Alexander H., *Alternative Dispute Resolution* (London: Waterlow Publishers, 1992).

Bingham, Gail, *Resolving Environmental Disputes: A Decade of Experience* (The Conservation Foundation, 1986).

Bishop, Gillian, David Hodson, Dominic Raeside, Sara Robinson and Ruth Smallacombe, *Divorce Reform: A Guide for Lawyers and Mediators* (London: FT Law & Tax, 1996).

Blades, Joan, *Mediate your Divorce* (New Jersey: Prentice-Hall Inc., 1985).

Brams, Steven J. and Alan D. Taylor, *Fair Division: From cake-cutting to dispute resolution* (Cambridge: Cambridge University Press, 1996).

Breidenbach, Prof. Dr. Stephan, *Mediation* (Köln: Verlag Dr. Otto Schmidt, 1995).

Bridges, William, *Transitions: Making Sense of Life's Changes* (London: Nicholas Brearley Publishing, 1996).

British Academy of Experts, Report of the Committee on the Language of ADR (1992).

Bush, Robert A. Baruch and Joseph P. Folger, *The Promise of Mediation* (San Francisco: Jossey-Bass, 1994).

Campbell, Dennis (General editor) and Susan Cotter (ed.) *Dispute Resolution Methods: The Comparative Law Yearbook of International Business* (Salzburg: Center for International Legal Studies and Graham & Trotman/Martinus Nijhoff, 1995).

Carter, Jimmy *Keeping Faith: Memoirs of a President* (1982).

Chornenki, Genevieve A. and Christine E. Hart *Bypass Court: A Dispute Resolution Handbook* (Butterworths, 1996).

Colman, Sir Anthony D., *The Practice and Procedure of the Commercial Court* (London: Lloyd's of London Press, 1995).

Consensus, Public Disputes Network, Harvard Law School Program on Negotiation.

Conway, Helen L., *Domestic Violence: Picking up the Pieces* (Oxford: Lion Publishing plc, 1997).

Cooper, Christopher, *Mediation & Arbitration by Patrol Police Officers* (Lanham, Maryland, New York, Oxford: University Press of America, 1999).

Council of Europe, "Text of Recommendation No. R (98) 1 of the Committee of Ministers to Member States on Family Mediation and its Explanatory Memorandum" (1998).

CPR and Georgetown University Law Center, Commission's draft "Proposed Model Rule of Professional Conduct for the Lawyer as Third Party Neutral" (1999).

Craig, W. Laurence, William W. Park and Jan Paulsson, *International Chamber of Commerce Arbitration* (New York, London, Rome: Oceana Publications Inc.; Paris: ICC Publishing S.A., 1990).

Crawley, John, *Constructive Conflict Management: Managing to Make a Difference* (London: Nicholas Brearley Publishing, 1992, 1995).

Crum, Thomas F., *The Magic of Conflict* (New York: Touchstone/Simon & Schuster, 1987).

——— *Journey to Center* (New York: Fireside/Simon & Schuster, 1997).

D'Ambrumenil, Peter, *Mediation and Arbitration* (London: Cavendish Publishing Limited, 1997).

Davis, Gwynn, *Partisans and Mediators: The Resolution of Divorce Disputes* (Oxford: Clarendon Press, 1988).

——— & Marian Roberts, *Access to Agreement* (Milton Keynes/Philadelphia: Open University Press, 1988).

——— with Heinz Messmer, Mark Umbreit & Robert Coates, *Making Amends: Mediation and Reparation in Criminal Justice* (London: Routledge, 1992).

Debell, Bob, *Conciliation and Mediation in the NHS* (Radcliffe Medical Press, 1997).

De Board, Robert, *The Psychoanalysis of Organisations* (London: Tavistock Publications, 1978).

——— *Counselling for Toads: A Psychological Adventure* (London: Routledge 1998)

de Boisséson, Matthieau, *Le droit française de l'arbitrage interne et internationale* (Paris: GLN-éditions, 1990).

de Bono, Edward, *Lateral Thinking: A Textbook of Creativity* (Penguin Books Limited, 1970).

——— *Conflicts: A Better Way to Resolve Them* (Penguin Books Limited, 1985).

Dingwall, Robert & John Eekelaar, *Divorce Mediation and the Legal Process* (Oxford: Clarendon Press, 1988).

*Dispute Resolution, Information Update of the Standing Committee on Dispute Resolution of the American Bar Association.

"Dispute Resolution Forum" Court-Ordered Arbitration issue. National Institute for Dispute Resolution (Washington D.C.: August 1985).

Domke, M., *The Law and Practice of Commercial Arbitration* (Deerfield, New York, Rochester: Clark Boardman Callaghan, 1984).

Donohue, William A. & Robert Kolt, *Managing Interpersonal Conflict* (Sage Publications, 1992).

Doyle, Brian J, *Employment Tribunals: the New Law* (Bristol: Jordans, 1998).

Dryden, Windy (ed.), *Marital Therapy in Britain* (London: Harper & Row, 1985).

——— (ed.), *Individual Therapy* (Milton Keynes & Philadelphia: Open University Press, 1990).

Egan, Gerard, *The Skilled Helper: A Systematic Approach to Effective Helping* (California: Brooks/Cole Publishing Co., 1986).

———, *The Skilled Helper: A Problem-Management Approach to Helping* (6th ed., 1997)

Ellis, Desmond & Noreen Stuckless, *Mediating and Negotiating Marital Conflicts* (California, London & New Delhi: Sage Publications, Inc., 1996)

Emery, Robert E., *Renegotiating Family Relationships: Divorce, Child Custody & Mediation* (New York: The Guilford Press, 1994)

*Family Law, Jordan & Sons Ltd.

Fisher, Roger, *International Mediation: A Working Guide* (Harvard Negotiation Project, 1978).

—— & William Ury (1981) *Getting to Yes: Negotiating Agreement Without Giving In* (Boston: Houghton Mifflin; Penguin, 1981).

—— & Scott Brown *Getting Together: Building a Relationship that Gets to Yes* (London: Business Books, 1989).

——, & Elizabeth Kopelman & Andrea Kupfer Schneider, *Beyond Machiavelli: Tools for Coping with Conflict* Cambridge, Massachusetts and London, England: Harvard University Press, 1994).

Folberg, Jay & Alison Taylor, *Mediation: A Comprehensive Guide to Resolving Conflicts Without Litigation.* (San Francisco: Jossey-Bass, 1984).

—— & Ann Milne (ed.), *Divorce Mediation* (New York/London: The Guildford Press, 1988).

Folger, Joseph P. and Tricia S. Jones (eds.), *New Directions in Mediation: Communication Research and Perspectives* (Sage Publications, 1994).

Foskett, David Q.C., *The Law and Practice of Compromise* (4th ed.) (London: Sweet & Maxwell, 1996).

Freund, James C., *Smart Negotiating: How to make good deals in the real world* (New York: Fireside/Simon & Schuster, 1993).

Friedman, Gary J., *A Guide to Divorce Mediation* (New York: Workman Publishing Co., 1993).

Genn, Professor Hazel, *Evaluation Report of the Central London County Court Pilot Mediation Scheme No. 5/98* (London: Lord Chancellor's Department, July 1998).

—— *Mediation in Action: Resolving Court Disputes without Trial* (London: Calouste Gulbenkian Foundation, 1999).

Goldberg, Stephen, Eric Green & Frank Sander, *Dispute Resolution* (Boston/Toronto: Little Brown & Company, 1985).

——, *Dispute Resolution: Supplement* (1987).

——, Frank Sander & Nancy Rogers, (2nd ed.) (1992).

Goldmann, Robert (ed.), *Roundtable Justice* (Boulder, Colorado: Westview Press, 1980).

Goldman, *La lex mercatoria dans le contrat et l'arbitrage internationaux, réalité et perspective* (Clunet, 1979).

Grainger, Ian & Michael Fealy, *An Introduction to the New Civil Procedure Rules* (London: Cavendish Publishing Limited, 1999).

Gray, John, *Men are from Mars, Women are from Venus* (London: Thorsons, 1993).

Green, Eric, "The CPR Mini-trial Handbook" in *Corporate Dispute Management* (New York: Matthew Bender & Co., 1982).

——, *The Complete Courthouse (Dispute Resolution Devices in a Democratic Society)* (Washington DC: Roscoe Pound Foundation–ATLA, 1985).

Gulliver, P.H., *Disputes and Negotiations: a Cross-Cultural Perspective* (New York: Academic Press, 1979).

Gurman, Alan S. and David P. Kniskern (eds.), *Handbook of Family Therapy* (New York: Brunner/Mazel, 1981/1991).

Hackney, H. and L. S. Cormier, *Counseling Strategies and Objectives* (New Jersey: Prentice-Hall, 1979).

Hall, Lavinia (ed.), *Negotiation: Strategies for Mutual Gain* (Sage Publications, 1993).

Hawkins, Peter and Robin Shohet, *Supervision in the Helping Professions* (Buckingham: Open University Press, 1989).

Haynes, John M., *Divorce Mediation* (New York: Springer Publishing Co., 1981).

—— & Gretchen L. Haynes *Mediating Divorce* (San Francisco and London: Jossey Bass, 1989).

——, with Thelma Fisher and Dick Greenslade (eds.), *Alternative Dispute Resolution: The Fundamentals of Family Mediation* (Old Bailey Press Limited, 1993).

Hibberd, Peter and Paul Newman *ADR and Adjudication in Construction Disputes* (Oxford: Blackwell Science, 1999).

Holtzmann and Neuhaus, *A Guide to the UNCITRAL Model Law on International Commercial Arbitration* (Deventer: Kluwer, 1989).

Hough, Alison and Kala Nathan, *Employment Law: Recent Developments* (London: Old Bailey Press, 1998).

Hunter, Martin, Jan Paulsson, Nigel Rawding and Alan Redfern, *The Freshfield's Guide to Arbitration and ADR: Clauses in International Contracts Arbitration* (Deventer, Boston: Kluwer, 1993).

Institute of International Business Law and Practice, *Multi-party Arbitration: Views from international arbitration specialists* (Paris: International Chamber of Commerce, 1992).

Jamaica/Capital Project for Dispute Resolution, *The Mediator Handbook* (Columbus Ohio: Jamaican Bar Association/Capital University Law & Graduate Center, 1990).

*Journal of Dispute Resolution, University of Missouri-Columbia.

Karrass, Chester L., *The Negotiating Game: How to Get What You Want* (HarperCollins, 1994).

Kendall, John, *Expert Determination* (2nd ed.) (London: Sweet & Maxwell, 1996)

Kennedy, Gavin, *Everything is Negotiable* (London: Arrow Books, 1997).

—— *The New Negotiating Edge: The Behavioral Approach for Results and Relationships* (London: Nicholas Brearley Publishing: 1998).

Kessler, Ian and John Purcell, *Joint problem-solving* (ACAS, undated).

Kolb, Deborah M. and Jean M. Bartunek (eds.), *Hidden Conflicts in Organisations: Uncovering Behind-the-Scenes Disputes* (Sage Publications, 1992).

—— and Associates, *When Talk Works* (San Francisco: Jossey-Bass Inc., 1994, 1997)

Kovel, Joel, *A Complete Guide to Therapy* (Pantheon Books, 1976; Penguin Books, 1991).

Landau, Barbara, Mario Bartoletti & Ruth Mesbur, *Family Mediation Handbook* (Toronto: Butterworths, 1987).

*Law Institute of Victoria Journal (Jan/Feb 1991). "Seminar in Print: Alternative Dispute Resolution".

*Law Society's Gazette, The Law Society of England & Wales.

Law Society *Guide to the Professional Conduct of Solicitors* and Professional Standards Bulletins (London).

Law Society Report on ADR by Henry Brown for the Courts and Legal Services Committee (London, 1991).

————— "Alternative Dispute Resolution" (2nd Report, June 1992).

Lax, David A. & James K. Sebenius, *The Manager as Negotiator: Bargaining for Co-operation and Competitive Gain* (New York: Free Press (Macmillan Inc.) 1986).

Lewis, Jane and Robin Legard, *ACAS individual conciliation* (ACAS, undated circa 1998).

Liebmann, Marian, *Community & Neighbour Mediation* (London: Cavendish Publishing Limited 1998)

Lindstein, Thomas with Barry Meteyard, *What works in family mediation: mediating residence and contact disputes* (Lyme Regis: Russell House Publishing, 1996).

Locke, Don C., *Increasing Multicultural Understanding: A Comprehensive Model* (Sage Publications, 1992).

Loquin, M, *L'amiable composition en droit comparé et international* (Paris: Libraries Techniques, 1980).

Lord Chancellor's Department *Resolving Disputes Without Going to Court* (London: Lord Chancellor's Department, December 1995).

Lovenheim, Peter, *Mediate, Don't Litigate* (New York: McGraw-Hill, 1989).

—————, *How to Mediate your Dispute* (Nolo Press, 1996).

MacFarlane, Julie (ed.), *Rethinking Disputes: the Mediation Alternative* (London: Cavendish Publishing, 1997).

Mackie, Karl J. (ed.) *A Handbook of Dispute Resolution: ADR in Action* (London and New York: Routledge and Sweet & Maxwell, 1991).

—————, *ADR Route Map* (London: Centre for Dispute Resolution, 1991).

—————, David Miles and William Marsh, *Commercial Dispute Resolution: An ADR Practice Guide* (London, Dublin, Edinburgh: Butterworths, 1995).

Maddux, Robert B., *Successful Negotiation* (London: Kogan Page, 1998).

Markham, Ursula, *Managing Conflict: Strategies to help you make and keep the peace* (London: Thorsons, 1996).

Marks, Jonathan B., Earl Johnson Jr. and Peter L. Szanton, *Dispute Resolution in America: Processes in Evolution* (Washington D.C.: National Institute for Dispute Resolution, 1984).

Marshall, Tony, *Reparation, Conciliation and Mediation* (London: Home Office Research & Planning Unit, Paper 27, 1984).

————— & Martin Walpole, *Bringing people together: Mediation & Reparation Projects in Great Britain* (London: Home Office Research & Planning Unit, Paper 33, 1985).

————— & S. Merry, *Crime and Accountability* (London: HMSO, 1990).

MEDIATION and MEDNews, Mediation U.K., Bristol.

Mediation U.K., *Training Manual in Community Mediation Skills* (Bristol, 1995).

————— *Guide to Starting a Community Mediation Service* (Bristol, 2nd edition 1996).

————— *Development of Mediation Networks* (Bristol, June 1997).

Mediation News, The journal of the Academy of Family Mediators (USA).

Mediation Quarterly, Jossey-Bass Inc., San Francisco.

Middlesex Multi-Door Courthouse Evaluation Project (U.S.), *Final Report* (National Center for State Courts, 1991).

Mitchell, Christopher and Michael Banks, *Handbook of conflict resolution: the analytical problem-solving approach* (London & New York: Pinter, 1996).

Moore, Christopher W., *The Mediation Process* (San Francisco: Jossey-Bass Inc., 1986).

Morris, Desmond, *The Naked Ape* (London: Cape, 1967).

————, *Intimate Behaviour* (London: Cape, 1971).

————, *Manwatching* (London: Cape, 1977).

Mosten, Forrest S., *The Complete Guide to Mediation: The Cutting Edge Approach to Family Law Practice* (American Bar Association, 1997).

Mowbray, Richard, *The Case Against Psychotherapy Registration: A Conservation Issue for the Human Potential Movement* (London: Trans Marginal Press, 1995).

Munro, Anne, Bob Manthei & John Small, *Counselling: The Skills of Problem-solving* (London: Routledge, 1989).

Murray, John S., Alan Scott Rau & Edward F. Sherman, *Processes of Dispute Resolution: The Role of Lawyers.* (New York: Foundation Press, 2nd edition, 1996).

Mustill, Sir Michael J. and Stewart C. Boyd, *The Law and Practice of Commercial Arbitration in England* (London: Butterworths, 1989).

Newcastle Report "Report to the Lord Chancellor on the Costs and Effectiveness of Conciliation in England and Wales" (University of Newcastle upon Tyne, Conciliation Project Unit, 1989).

Noone, Michael, *Mediation* (London: Cavendish Publishing Limited, 1996).

Palenski, Joseph E. & Harold M. Launer (eds.), *Mediation Conflicts and Challenges* (Charles C. Thomas, 1986).

Palmer, Michael & Simon Roberts, *Dispute Processes: ADR and the Primary Forms of Decision Making* (London, Edinburgh, Dublin: Butterworths, 1998).

Parkinson, Lisa, *Conciliation in Separation and Divorce: Finding Common Ground* (London, Sydney: Croom Helm, 1986)

————, *Family Mediation* (London: Sweet & Maxwell, 1997)

Pease, Allan *Body Language: How to read others' thoughts by their gestures* (London: Sheldon Press, 1981, 1997).

———— & Barbara Pease, *Why men don't listen and Women can't read maps* (Mona Vale, NSW: Pease Training International, 1998, 1999).

Pembridge, Eileen (ed.), *Legal Aid Practice Manual* (Sweet & Maxwell) Updated twice annually).

Plapinger, Elizabeth & Donna Stienstra, *ADR and Settlement in the Federal District Courts: A Sourcebook for Judges and Lawyers* (Federal Judicial Center & CPR, 1996).

Prevezer, Sidney (ed.) *Alternative Dispute Resolution* (London: Euro Conferences Limited, 1991).

Pruitt, D.G., *Negotiation Behavior* (New York: Academic Press, 1981).

Quill, Deidre & Jean Wynne, *Victim & Offender: Mediation Handbook* (Save the Children and West Yorkshire Probation Service, 1993).

Raiffa, Howard, *The Art and Science of Negotiation* (Cambridge, USA: Harvard University Press, 1982).

Ray, Larry and Prue Kestner, (eds) *The Multi-door Experience: Dispute Resolution and the Courthouse of the Future* (Washington D.C.: American Bar Association, 1988).

Redfern, Alan & Martin Hunter, *International Commercial Arbitration* (3rd ed.) (London: Sweet & Maxwell, 1999).

Relate Centre for Family Studies, (Janet Walker, Peter McCarthy & Noel Timms) *Mediation: the Making and Remarking of Co-operative Relationships* (University of Newcastle upon Tyne, 1994).

————, *Evaluating the Longer Term Impact of Family Mediation* (Newcastle: 1996).

Resolution, Australian Commercial Disputes Centre, Sydney.

Resolutions, Centre for Dispute Resolution, U.K.

Roberts, Marian, *Mediation in Family Disputes: Principles of Practice* (2nd ed.) (Aldershot: Arena–Ashgate Publishing Limited, 1997).

Roberts, Simon, *Order and Dispute: An Introduction to Legal Anthropology* (Penguin Books Limited, 1979).

Robinson, Gwen, *Victim-Offender Mediation: Limitations and Potential* (Oxford: Centre for Criminological Research, University of Oxford, 1996).

Robinson, Margaret, *Family Transformation through divorce and remarriage* (London: Routledge, 1991; and with postscript, 1993).

Rogers, Nancy H. & Richard Salem, *A Student's Guide to Mediation and Law* (New York: Matthew Bender, 1987).

———— and Craig McEwen, *Mediation: Law, Policy and Practice* (New York: Lawyers Cooperative, 1989).

Rubino-Sammartano, *International Arbitration Law* (Deventer, Boston: Kluwer, 1990).

SACRO, *Young Offenders Mediation Project: Annual Report 1997/1998* (Edinburgh: SACRO, 1998).

Scanlon, Kathleen M., *Mediator's Deskbook* (New York: CPR Institute for Dispute Resolution, 1999).

Schlosser, P., *Das Recht der internationalen privaten Schiedsgerichtsbarkeit* (Tübingen: Mohrverlag, 1975).

Schwab, K.H., *Schiedsgerichtsbarkeit* (München, Beck Verlag, 1979).

Schornstein, Sherri L., *Domestic Violence and Health Care: What Every Professional Needs to Know* (California, London and New Delhi: Sage Publications, 1997).

Scottish Law Commission, *Confidentiality in Family Mediation* (Discussion Paper No. 92, 1991).

Skynner, Robin and John Cleese, *Families and how to survive them* (London: Methuen, 1983).

————, *Family Matters* (London, Methuen Limited, 1995 & Cedar, 1996)

Smit & Pechota, *World Arbitration Reporter* (Parker School of Foreign & Comparative Law, 1992).

Smith, Roger (ed.), *Shaping the Future: New Directions in Legal Services* (London: Legal Action Group, 1995).

SPIDR News and Annual Conference Proceedings (1986–95) (Washington D.C.: Society of Professionals in Dispute Resolution).

Stewart, Susan, *Conflict Resolution: A Foundation Guide* (Winchester: Waterside Press, 1998).

Supreme Court Practice 1999 *(The White Book),* Sir Richard Scott V.C. (ed.) (London: Sweet & Maxwell, 1998).

Susskind, L.E. and J. Cruikshank *Breaking the Impasse: Consensual Approaches to Resolving Public Disputes* (New York: Basic Books, 1987).

The Alternative Newsletter, Resource Newsletter on ADR: James B. Boskey (ed.)

Thrier, Adam, *Judgement Day: The Case for Alternative Dispute Resolution* (London: Adam Smith Institute/ASI (Research) Limited, 1992).

U.K. College of Family Mediators: *Mediators Directory & Handbook* (London: FT Law & Tax, 1997/98, 1998/99 and 1999/2000).

UNCITRAL Arbitration Rules.

Ury, William *Getting Past No: Negotiating with Difficult People* (London: Business Books Limited, 1991).

———, J. M. Brett and S. B. Goldberg, *Getting Disputes Resolved: Designing Systems to Cut the Costs of Conflict* (San Francisco: Jossey Bass, 1989).

Walsh, Elizabeth, *Working in the Family Justice System: A Guide for Professionals* (Bristol: Jordan Publishing, 1998).

Walton, Richard E., *Managing Conflict: Interpersonal Dialogue and Third Party Roles* (Reading, Mass.: Addison-Wesley, 1987).

West Yorkshire Probation Service/Care & Justice Yorkshire *Victim/Offender Mediation Handbook* (Leeds: Care & Justice Yorkshire, 1991).

Whetten, David, Kim Cameron & Mike Woods, *Effective Conflict Management* (London: HarperCollins, 1996).

Wilkinson, John H., (ed.), *Donovan Leisure Newton & Irvine: ADR Practice Book* (New York, Chichester, Brisbane, Toronto, Singapore: Wiley Law Publications, 1990 and Cumulative Supplements 1992–1998).

Williams, Michael, *Mediation: Why people fight and how to help them to stop* (Dublin: Poolbeg Press, 1998).

Williams, Rowland, *Saving Litigation* (1999).

*World Arbitration & Mediation Report (Washington D.C.: BNA Inc.).

Wright, Martin and Burt Galaway (eds.), *Mediation and Criminal Justice: Victims, Offenders and Community* (London: Sage Publications Limited, 1989).

——— *Justice for Victims and Offenders: a restorative response to crime* (Milton Keynes: Open University Press, 1991).

York, Stephen, *Practical ADR Handbook* (2nd ed.) (London: Sweet & Maxwell, 1999).

ARTICLES, PAPERS AND TRANSCRIPTS

Abbreviations:

A.B.A.J.	American Bar Association Journal
A.B.S.	American Behavioral Scientist
A.D.R.L.J.	The Arbitration and Dispute Resolution Law Journal
Arb.J.	Arbitration Journal
Arb.Intl.	Arbitration International
A.Rev.Intl.Arb.	American Review of International Arbitration
Cath.U.L.Rev.	Catholic University Law Review
C.C.R.	Conciliation Courts Review
C.L.J.	Construction Law Journal
CEDR	Centre for Dispute Resolution
Disp.Resol.J	Dispute Resolution Journal
E.C.L.	Euro Conferences Limited
E.G.	Estates Gazette
Fam.Law	Family Law
Harv.Bus.Rev.	Harvard Business Review
Harv.L.Rev.	Harvard Law Review
HDR	Handbook of Dispute Resolution
IBA	International Bar Association
IFLR	International Financial Law Review
ILP	International Law Practicum (N.Y. State Bar Assoc.)
JCI Arb.I	Arbitration (Ch. Inst. of Arbitrators)
J.D.R.	Journal of Dispute Resolution
J.Intl.Arb.	Journal of International Arbitration
J.L.E.	Journal of Legal Education
JMDU	Journal of the Medical Defence Union
J.S.W.L.	Journal of Social Welfare Law
L.S.Gaz.	Law Society's Gazette
Med	Mediation (Mediation UK)
Med.News	Mediation News, Academy of Family Mediators (U.S.)
M.L.R.	Modern Law Review
M.Q.	Mediation Quarterly
Negot.J.	Negotiation Journal
New L.J.	New Law Journal
N.S.W.L.S.J.	New South Wales Law Society Journal
Ohio S.L.J	Ohio State Law Journal on Dispute Resolution
SetonHall Legis. J.	Seton Hall Legislative Journal
S.J.	Solicitors' Journal
SPIDR	Society of Professionals in Dispute Resolution
U.Chi.L.Rev.	University of Chicago Law Review
Yale L.J.	Yale Law Journal

Abrams, Jeff & Sam Imperati, "Successful Skills & Strategies for Partnering in a Diverse and Demanding Work Environment" SPIDR 23 November 1997

Allen, Elizabeth J.D., Robert Kory J.D. and Donald Mohr M.A., "Team Mediation: Are Two Heads Better than One?" Med. News 11(3) (1992)

Angyal, Robert S., "Alternative dispute resolution clauses: are they enforceable?" (1991) N.S.W.L.S.J. 62

Antes, James R, Donna Turner Hudson, Erling O. Jorgensen and Janet Kelly Moen "Is a Stage Model of Mediation Necessary?" 1999 M.Q. 16(3)

Assefa, Hizkias "Conflict Resolution Perspectives on civil wars in the Horn of Africa" (1990) 6 Negot. J 173

Barrett, Jerome T. "The Psychology of a Mediator" SPIDR Occasional Paper No. 83–1 March 1983

Benjamin, Robert, "The Mediator as Trickster: The Folkloric Figure as Professional Role Model" 1995 M.Q. 13(2) 131

———, "The Use of Mediative Strategies in Traditional Legal Practice" Journal of the American Academy of Matrimonial Lawyers, (1997) Vol. 14, No. 2, 203

———, "Negotiation and Evil: The Sources of Religious and Moral Resistance to the Settlement of Conflicts" 1998 M.Q. 15(3) 245

Bentley, Marigold "Rising Tide of School Exclusions" *Mediation* Vol. 14, No. 4, Autumn 1998

Bickerman, John "Evaluative mediator responds" in *Alternatives* Vol. 14, No. 6, June 1996

Billings, Annie "The mini-trial: misunderstanding and miscommunication may short-circuit its effective use in settlements" J.D.R. Vol. 1990 No. 2

Black, the Hon. M.E.J. "The Courts, Tribunals and ADR", Australian Disp. Resol. J., May 1996.

Brazil, Kahn, Newman & Gold "Early Neutral Evaluation: An Experimental Effort to Expedite Dispute Resolution" 69 *Judicature* 279 (Feb–March 1986).

Brett, Jeanne and Stephen Goldberg "Grievance Mediation in the Coal Industry: A Field Experiment" 37(1) Indus. & Lab Rel Rev. 49 (1983)

——— "Mediator–Advisers: A New Third Party Role" in "Negotiating in Organisations" (M. Bazerman & R. Lewicki, eds) (1983)

Brown, Henry "NHS indemnity, no-fault compensation and ADR" J.M.D.U. Vol. 8 No. 1 1992

——— "Dispute Resolution Methods: England" in *The Comparative Law Yearbook of International Business* (Center for International Legal Studies and Graham & Trotman/Martinus Nijhoff) (1995)

——— & Arnold Simanowitz, "Alternative dispute resolution and mediation" in *Clinical Risk Management* (Charles Vincent ed., BMJ Publishing) (1995)

Burch, Karen A "ADR in the Law Firm: A Practical Viewpoint" J.D.R. (Missouri) Vol. 1987 149

Campbell, Alan, "Mediation of Children Issues When One Parent is Gay" 1996 M.Q. 14(1)

Carne, Simon "An easier life for the expert" N.L.J. 7/6/1991

Carroll, Eileen "The American Experience: What is ADR?" Paper in *Alternative Dispute Resolution* E.C.L. 1991

Chornenki, Genevieve "Mediating Commercial Disputes: Exchanging 'Power over' for 'Power with'" in Macfarlane (ed.), *Rethinking Disputes: the Mediation Alternative* (1997)

Chupp, Mark "Reconciliation Procedures and Rationale" in *Mediation and Criminal Justice: Victims, Offenders and Community* Wright and Galaway (eds.) (1989)

Coates, R and J Gehm "Victim meets offender: an evaluation of victim offender reconciliation programs" (1985) in "Mediation of Victim Offender Conflict" Umbreit J.D.R. 1988

Cohen, Avern, "The Summary Jury Trial—A Caution" J.D.R. Vol. 1995, No. 2, 299

Cohen, Lester "Mandatory Mediation: A Rose by Any Other Name" 1991 M.Q. 9(1)

Dembart and Kwartler "The Snoqualmie River Conflict: Bringing Mediation into Environmental Disputes" in *Roundtable Justice* (1980) by Robert Goldmann (ed.)

Denson, Alexander B., "The Summary Jury Trial: A Proposal From The Bench" J.D.R. Vol. 1995, No. 2, 303.

Dick, S. Gale, "ADR at the Crossroads" Disp. Resol. J., March 1994

Dingwall, Robert, David Greatbatch & Lucia Ruggerone "Gender and Interaction in Divorce Mediation" 1998 M.Q. 15(4) 277

Dominguez-Urban, Ileana, "The Messenger as the Medium of Communication: the Use of Interpreters in Mediation" Vol. 1997 No. 1 J.D.R. 1

Ehrmann, John R. & Michael T. Lesnick "The Policy Dialogue: Applying Mediation to the Policy-Making Process" 1988 M.Q. 20

Feinberg, Kenneth R. "A Procedure for the Voluntary Mediation of Disputes" Paper to IBA Business Law Section Hong Kong Sep/Oct 1991

Fisher, R. "Negotiating Power: Getting and Using Influence" 27 A.B.S. 149 (Nov.–Dec. 1983)

Fiss, Owen "Against Settlement" 93 Yale L.J. 1073

Flake, Richard P., "Nuances of Med–Arb: A Neutral's Perspective" *ADR Currents* June 1998

Forster, Stephen and Thomas Lee (Winter 1991/2) "Hong Kong: Are ADR Clauses Enforceable?" McKenna Law Letter

Frankel, Emil H, "Public outcry prompts collaboration at New Haven's 'Q' Bridge" *Consensus* No. 28 of October 1995

Frenkel, District Judge, "On experts and protocols" L.S. Gaz. 6 January 1999.

Fuller, Lon "Collective Bargaining and the Arbitrator" Proceedings, Fifteenth Annual Meeting, National Academy of Arbitrators 8, 29–33, 36–48 (1962).

——— "Mediation—Its Forms and Functions" (1971) 44 S. Cal Law Review

——— "The Forms and Limits of Adjudication" (1978) 92 H.L.R. 353 *et seq.*

Galanter, Marc "The Day After the Litigation Explosion" 46 Maryland L. Rev 3, 32–37 (1986) in Murray, Rau and Sherman's "Processes of Dispute Resolution" (1989)

——— "The Quality of Settlements" J.D.R. Vol. 1988

Gentry, Christine, Eleanor Ingham and Louise Spitz "Ancillary Relief Pilot Scheme seminar" SFLA Review, Issue 76 December 1998

Gilkey, Roderick W and Leonard Greenhalgh "The Role of Personality in Successful Negotiating" N.J. 1986 2/3

Gray, Ericka B. "What is 'Real' Mediation?" *AFM Mediation News* Vol. 15, No. 2, 1996

Green, Eric "Growth of the Mini-trial" 9 *Litigation* 12 (1982)

―――― "The Complete Courthouse" (1985) in "Dispute Resolution Devices in a Democratic Society" Roscoe Pound Foundation―American Trial Lawyers Association

Gunning, Isabelle R., "Mediation as an Alternative to Court for Lesbian and Gay Families: Some Thoughts on Douglas McIntyre's Article" 1995 M.Q. 13(1)

Harrell, Susan W., "Why Attorneys Attend Mediation Sessions" 1995 M.Q. 12(4) 369

Harrison, John, "Dialogue of the deaf: English land-use planning often ignores public input" *Consensus* No. 31, July 1996

Harter, Philip J. "Negotiating Regulations: A Cure for Malaise" 71 Georgetown L.J. 1 (1982)

―――― "Regulatory Negotiation: the Experience So Far" Resolve Winter 1984 in Goldberg Green & Sander *Dispute Resolution* (1985)

―――― "Government ADR Policies and Practices" in "Report of the Administrative Conference of the United States" Washington D.C. Government Printing Office (1987)

Haygood, Leah V. "Negotiated Rule Making: Challenges for Mediators and Participants" 1988 M.Q. 20

Haynes, John "Power Balancing" in *Divorce Mediation: Theory & Practice* (ed.) Folberg & Milne (1988)

Hellmuth, Theodore H. "Using ENE as a Gatekeeper to Dispute Resolution Process" *Alternatives* Vol. 13, No. 8, August 1995 at p. 99.

Henderson, D., "Mediation Success: An Empirical Analysis" 11 Ohio S.L.J. No. 1 (1996)

Hensler, Deborah R. "Court-Annexed ADR" in the Donovan Leisure Newton & Irvine *ADR Practice Book* (1990)

Hill, Richard, "Dispute avoidance and resolution mechanisms" [1996] A.D.R.L.J. 287

Hufnagel, Gracine "Mediator Malpractice Liability" 1989 M.Q. 23

Hyman, Jonathan M. "The Model Mediator Confidentiality Rule: A Commentary" S.H.L.J. Vol. 12 No. 1 1988

Jansenson, Dina R., "Representing Your Clients Successfully in Mediation: Guidelines for Litigators" in *The NY Litigator,* Vol. 1. No. 2 (November 1995)

Joyce, Daniel P., "The Roles of the Intervenor: A Client-Centred Approach" 1995 M.Q. 12(4)

Katsh, Ethan, "The Online Ombuds Office: Adapting Dispute Resolution to Cyberspace" at *http://www.law.vill.edu/ncair/disres/katsh.htm*

Katzeff, Paul, "Governors electing more mediation" *Consensus* No. 38, April 1998

Kellett, Ann J R.N. "Healing Angry Wounds: The Roles of Apology and Mediation in Disputes between Physicians and Patients" J.D.R. (Missouri) Vol. 1987, 111

Kelly, Joan B. "Mediated and Adversarial Divorce Resolution Processes: A Comparison of Post-divorce Outcomes" [1991] F.L. 382 (Vol 21)

King, Andy "No Legal Aid Without Mediation—Section 29" [1998] Fam. Law 28 p. 331.

Kolb, Deborah M "How existing procedures shape alternatives: the case of grievance mediation" J.D.R. Vol 1989

Krivis, Jeffrey "Mediating in Cyberspace" [1998] A.D.R.L.J. 19 (and *Alternatives* Vol. 14 No. 10 November 1996)

Lemley, Jack K. "Dispute Resolution Provisions in International Construction" Paper in *Alternative Dispute Resolution* E.C.L. 1991

Lesnick, Michael T. and John R. Ehrmann "Selected Strategies for Managing Multiparty Disputes" M.Q. No. 16 Summer 1987

Levine, David I. "Early neutral evaluation: a follow-up report" *Judicature* Vol. 70 No. 4 Dec–Jan 1987

——— "Early Neutral Evaluation: The Second Phase" J.D.R. 1989

Lide, E. Casey "The role of alternative dispute resolution in online commerce, intellectual property and defamation" [1998] A.D.R.L.J. 31 (and Ohio S.L.J. 1996)

Lindsay, Paul "Conflict Resolution and Peer Mediation in Public Schools: What Works?" 1998 M.Q. 16(1) 85

Ludlow, Michael "Resolving Disputes under United Kingdom construction contracts through alternatives to litigation: controlling the cost" [1996] A.D.R.L.J. 3

Lurie, Paul M., "The Importance of Process Design to a Successful Mediation" *Punch List* Vol. 19, No. 4, Winter 1996/97

Mackie, Karl "The Development of ADR in the UK" Paper in *Alternative Dispute Resolution* E.C.L. 1991

——— "Negotiation and mediation: from inelegant haggling to sleeping giant" in H.D.R. (1991)

Marks, Jonathan "Evaluative Mediation—Oxymoron or Essential Tool" Internet article (Ref: *http://jams-endispute.com/articles/evalmed.html*) December 1998

Marriott, Arthur, Q.C., "Freshfields Lecture 1995", Arb. Intl. Vol. 12, No. 1, 1996

Marshall, Tony F "The power of mediation" 1990 M.Q. 8(2)

——— "Mandatory Mediation" Med 7/2 (1991)

——— "Neighbour disputes: community mediation schemes as an alternative to litigation" in H.D.R. (1991)

——— "Criminal Justice Conferencing: Calls for Caution" in *Mediation* Vol. 13 No. 1 (Winter 1997) and Vol. 13 No. 2 (Spring 1997)

Marshall, Valerie "Big Wayne and the White Gang" Med 9/2 (1992)

Mathis, Richard D., "Couples from Hell: Undifferentiated Spouses in Divorce Mediation" 1998 M.Q. 16(1)

Maute, Judith L. "Mediator Accountability: Responding to Fairness Concerns" J.D.R. Vol. 1990 No. 2

Mawrey, Richard B., Q.C. "Good Faith" *The Commercial Lawyer* July/ August 1995

McGaw, Mark C., "Adjudicators, Experts and Keeping Out of Court" Paper to Centre of Construction Law and Management, September 1991

McIntyre, Douglas H., "Gay Parents and Child Custody: A Struggle Under the Legal System" 1994 M.Q. 12(2)

McIsaac, Hugh "Court-connected mediation" C.C.R. 21/2 Dec 1983

——— "Family Mediation and Conciliation Service: Standards and Procedures" Los Angeles County Superior Court. (1984)

Merry, Sally Engle "Myth and practice in the mediation process" in *Mediation and Criminal Justice: Victims, Offenders and Community* Wright and Galaway (eds.) (1989)

Mnookin, Robert and Lewis Kornhauser "Bargaining in the Shadow of the Law, The Case of Divorce" 88 Y.L.J. 950 (1979)

Moore, Christopher W. "The Caucus: Private Meetings That Promote Settlement" 1987 M.Q. 16

Murray, John "Understanding Competing Theories of Negotiation" 2 N.J. 179 (1986).

Naughton, Philip Q.C. "Alternative Forms of Dispute Resolution—Their Strengths and Weaknesses" C.L.J. 1990 Vol.6 No. 3

——— Transcript of address for the Chartered Institute of Arbitrators, the Inns of Court and the Bar Council on "Conciliation, Mini-trials and other alternative forms of dispute resolution" on December 5, 1988.

——— "Mega mediation—a case history" [1996] A.D.R.L.J. 215

Neslund, Nancy "Dispute Resolution: A Matrix of Mechanisms" J.D.R. 1990 Vol. 2

Olson, R. "An Alternative for Large Case Dispute Resolution" (US) 6 *Litigation* 22 (Winter 1980)

Patterson, Roger J. "Dispute Resolution in a World of Alternatives" Catholic Univ. Law Review Vol. 37 1988 No. 3

Peachey, Dean E., "The Kitchener Experiment" in *Mediation and Criminal Justice: Victims, Offenders and Community* Wright and Galaway (eds.) (1989)

Pearson, Jessica "Mediating When Domestic Violence Is a Factor: Policies and Practices in Court-Based Divorce Mediation Programs" 1997 M.Q. 14(4) 319

Plesent, Emanual "Mediation for Reconciliation" 1988 M.Q. 21

Podgers, James, "Maine Route: Multi-Door proposal reflects growing role of ADR" 79 A.B.A.J. 118 (September 1993).

Prigoff Michael L. "Toward Candor or Chaos: The Case of Confidentiality in Mediation" S.H.L.J. Vol. 12 No. 1 1988

Pruitt, Dean G. "Trends in the Scientific Study of Negotiation and Mediation" 2 N.J. 237 (1986)

Reeves, Helen "The Victim Support Perspective" in *Mediation and Criminal Justice: Victims, Offenders and Community* Wright and Galaway (eds.) (1989)

Rehm, Peter H. and Denise R. Beatty, "Legal Consequences of Apologising" J.D.R Vol. 1996, No. 1, 115

Riskin, Leonard L. "Understanding Mediator's Orientations, Strategies and Techniques: A Grid for the Perplexed" 1 Harvard Negotiation L.R. 7 (1996)

Roberts, Marian "Systems or Selves? Some Ethical Issues in Family Mediation" J.S.W.L. January 1990

Roberts, Simon "Mediation in Family Disputes" M.L.R. Vol. 46 No. 5 September 1983

———— "Toward a Minimal Form of Alternative Intervention" 1986 M.Q. 11

———— "Three models of family mediation" in *Divorce Mediation & The Legal Process* (1988) Clarendon Press

Rowe, Mary P. "The Ombudsman as Part of a Dispute Resolution System" SPIDR 1990 Proceedings

Salata, Anthony "New lease of life for ADR" in The Lawyer, 23 June 1998.

Sander, Frank E. A. "Varieties of Dispute Processing" Address to The Pound Conference (1976) 70 F.R.D. 79

Saposnek, Donald T. "Aikido: A Systems Model for Maneuvering in Mediation" 1986/1987 M.Q. 14/15

———— "The Value of Children in Mediation: A Cross-Cultural Perspective" 1991 M.Q. 8(4)

Scarlett, Sarah "Use of ADR in Lloyd's R&R plan" in *Insurance Day,* February 25, 1997

Schuck, Peter H. "The Role of Judges in Settling Complex Cases: The Agent Orange Example" U.C.L.R. 1986 53:337

Schwebel, Andrew I., David W. Gately, Maureena A. Renner and Thomas W. Milburn "Divorce Mediation: Four Models and Their Assumptions about Change in Parties' Positions" M.Q. 11/3, Spring 1994

Severn, Kenneth "Progressive Mediation in the Construction Industry" in *Alternative Dispute Resolution* E.C.L. 1991

Susskind, Lawrence "Multi-Party Public Policy Mediation: A Separate Breed" in *Dispute.*

Singer, Linda R. "The Quiet Revolution in Dispute Settlement" 1989 M.Q. 7(2)

Smart, Louise "Mediator Strategies for Dealing with Dirty Tricks" 1987 M.Q. 16

Street, The Hon. Sir Laurence, "Mediation and the judicial institution" [1997] A.D.R.L.J. 88

Stulberg, Joseph B. "A Mediator's Responsibility for Fairness" Selected SPIDR Proceedings 1987–1988

Susskind, Lawrence "Multi-Party Public Policy Mediation: A Separate Breed" in *Dispute Resolution Magazine,* Fall 1997

Swaine, Kate "IP and IT—the way forward" in "In Focus Intellectual Property Newsletter" No. 46 June 1998

Tomm, Karl "Interventive Interviewing: Intending to Ask Lineal, Circular, Strategic, or Reflexive Questions" "Family Process" (1988) 27(1)

Uff, John Q.C., and Joanna Higgins "The structured avoidance of disputes" [1995] A.D.R.L.J. 179

Umbreit, Mark S. "Mediation of Victim Offender Conflict" J.D.R. Vol. 1988

———— "Humanistic Mediation: A Transformative Journey of Peacemaking" 1997 M.Q. 14(3) 201

———— and Jean Greenwood "National Survey of Victim–Offender Mediation Programs in the United States" 1999 M.Q. 16(3) 235

Wade, John "Current Trends and Models in Dispute Resolution" Australian Disp. Resol. J., February 1998.

Volpe, Maria R. and Charles Lindner "Mediation and Probation: The Presentence Investigation" 1991 M.Q. 9(1)

Walker, Janet "Family Mediation in England: Strategies for Gaining Acceptance" M.Q. 1991 8/4

———— "Family conciliation: from research to practice" in H.D.R. (1991)

———— "Family Mediation" in *Rethinking Disputes: the Mediation Alternative* ed. Dr Julie Macfarlane (1997).

———— "Introduction to family mediation in Europe" Report to the Fourth European Conference on Family Law (1998)

White, James J, Essay Review: "The Pros and Cons of Getting to Yes" 34 J.L.E. 115–117 (1984)

Wilkinson, John H., "A Primer on Mini-trials" in the Donovan Leisure Newton & Irvine *ADR Practice Book* (1990)

Williams, Rowland "Concilio-Arbitration: A New Proposal for the Quick and Inexpensive Resolution of Disputes" L.S. Gaz November 23, 1983

———— "Concilio-Arbitration: The Service Commences" L.S.Gaz May 28, 1986.

———— "Slaying the Litigation Monster" L.S.Gaz July 11, 1990

———— "The Case for Further Change" L.S.Gaz June 15, 1994

Woodley, Ann. E, "Saving the Summary Jury Trial: A Proposal to Halt the Flow of Litigation and End the Uncertainties", J.D.R. Vol. 1995, No. 2, 213

Wright, Martin "Designing the future of criminal justice" *Mediation,* Vol. 13 No. 3, Summer 1997

———— "Implications of the Crime and Disorder Act 1998 for mediation" *Mediation* Vol. 15 No. 2, Spring 1999

Wulff, Randall W and Alan E. Harris "Tips for a successful construction mediation" *Punch List* Vol. 18, No. 1, Spring 1995

Wyrick, Phela A. and Mark A. Constanzo "Predictors of Client Participation in Victim–Offender Mediation" 1999 M.Q. 16(3) 253

INDEX

All references are to paragraph numbers